Inequality in Canada

MCGILL-QUEEN'S STUDIES IN THE HISTORY OF IDEAS
Series Editor: Philip J. Cercone

Inequality in Canada

THE HISTORY AND POLITICS OF AN IDEA

Eric W. Sager

McGill-Queen's University Press
Montreal & Kingston • London • Chicago

© McGill-Queen's University Press 2020

ISBN 978-0-2280-0579-7 (cloth)
ISBN 978-0-2280-0580-3 (paper)
ISBN 978-0-2280-0595-7 (ePDF)
ISBN 978-0-2280-0596-4 (ePUB)

Legal deposit fourth quarter 2020
Bibliothèque nationale du Québec

Printed in Canada on acid-free paper that is 100% ancient forest free
(100% post-consumer recycled), processed chlorine free

This book has been published with the help of a grant from the Canadian Federation
for the Humanities and Social Sciences, through the Awards to Scholarly Publications
Program, using funds provided by the Social Sciences and Humanities Research
Council of Canada.

Funded by the   Financé par le
Government   gouvernement      Canada Council   Conseil des arts
of Canada   du Canada   for the Arts   du Canada

We acknowledge the support of the Canada Council for the Arts.
Nous remercions le Conseil des arts du Canada de son soutien.

Library and Archives Canada Cataloguing in Publication

Title: Inequality in Canada : the history and politics of an idea / Eric W. Sager.
Names: Sager, Eric W., 1946– author.
Series: McGill-Queen's studies in the history of ideas ; 81.
Description: Series statement: McGill-Queen's studies in the history of ideas ;
    81 | Includes bibliographical references and index.
Identifiers: Canadiana (print) 20200328514 | Canadiana (ebook) 20200328603
    | ISBN 9780228005797 (cloth) | ISBN 9780228005803 (paper) | ISBN
    9780228005957 (ePDF) | ISBN 9780228005964 (ePUB)
Subjects: LCSH: Equality—Canada—History. | LCSH: Equality—
    Political aspects—Canada—History.
Classification: LCC JC575 .S24 2021 | DDC 320.01/1—dc23

This book was typeset in 10.5/13 Sabon.

Contents

Table and Figures

Acknowledgments

I begin by expressing deep gratitude to Dr Michael Perchinsky, Dr Anthony Della Siega, Dr Larry Sterns, and many others who work in cardiac care at the Royal Jubilee Hospital in Victoria, British Columbia. To all of them I owe the years of good health that allowed me to complete this book.

I am indebted to the Social Sciences and Humanities Research Council of Canada for a grant in support of the research in its early stages. A dedicated group of research assistants made an indispensable contribution: Erin Cotton, Julien Dicaire, Josephine Gray, Tiffany Gunton, Darrell Harvey, Derek Murray, Katharine Rollwagen, and Rosaline Trigger. Luis Meneses, a fellow at the Electronic Textual Cultures Lab at the University of Victoria, offered valuable technical assistance, and so did Patrick Szpak in the Humanities Computing and Media Centre at UVic. I join with the entire community of historians in Canada in giving thanks to Library and Archives Canada and the many professionals who work in that great institution. My work was also assisted by the MacPherson Library at the University of Victoria, the University of British Columbia Library Special Collections, and the United Church Archives in Toronto.

It has been an honour and a joy to live and work within an extraordinary community of historians at the University of Victoria. That group includes many hundreds of students since 1983, who have taught me more than they ever realized. I am especially grateful to the students in our graduate Historiography seminar, History 500, who pushed me to read and to think as never before. Colleagues in History and other departments patiently listened to my efforts to explain what I was doing, and offered many helpful suggestions.

Peter Baskerville, Greg Blue, Mitch Lewis-Hammond, and Lynne Marks offered valuable comments on specific chapters. Many others at UVic gave me ideas and suggestions, including Andrew Buck, Peter Cook, John Lutz, Colin MacLeod, Rick Rajala, Veronica Strong-Boag, and Paul Wood.

For four decades I have found challenge and inspiration in the work of Ian McKay, and he has helped me again by reading a draft of the entire manuscript and offering cogent critique and warm encouragement. I am sincerely grateful to two anonymous readers for the press: thank you for persuading me to think again and for helping me to improve the book. I am also indebted to several generous scholars for comments on one or more chapters: Jonathan Fournier, Peter Gossage, Malcolm Rutherford, Shirley Tillotson, and Michael Veall. I was so bold as to give a very preliminary conference paper on the early nineteenth century to Michel Ducharme, Elsbeth Heaman, Jack Little, and Jeff McNairn, and they responded generously, patiently, and very helpfully. I am also indebted to Lars Osberg and Michel Ducharme for specific suggestions and to Christopher Brooke for sharing with me his deep reflections on distributive justice. To all of these scholars I offer sincere thanks, and a note of regret that I have not met adequately the challenge that their insights offered.

My friend of over half a century, Robert H. Griffiths, professor emeritus of the Université Savoie-Mont Blanc (Chambéry), helped me in many ways, above all by translating the quotations from French-language sources in chapters 1 and 7.

It has been a genuine pleasure to work again with McGill-Queen's University Press. I thank especially Jonathan Crago for his strong support and his professional guidance during the publication process. For the fourth time in my career as a writer, I thank John Parry for his brilliant work as copy editor.

My project on inequality is borne upon rivers of thought, encouragement, and love that are wide and deep. Over many years, beginning long before this book was conceived, Brenda Clark and our daughters, Catherine and Zoë, sustained and supported my solitary hours. I hope that one day Christina and Kaity may read this book and learn what their grandfather was doing in his study downstairs. And through the long journey I have been borne aloft by the creative energy and boundless love of Jean Anne Wightman.

Inequality in Canada

The Inequality Problem

We shall not cease from exploration
And the end of all our exploring
Will be to arrive where we started
And know the place for the first time.

T.S. Eliot, *Little Gidding*

WHAT IS INEQUALITY?

Many voices speak of inequality in our time. A pope, an American president, a Canadian prime minister, and legions of scholars, religious leaders, and journalists – all have spoken, and so too have those who live with the material reality of inequality and its consequences.

But what are they talking about? What is inequality? In the first decades of the twenty-first century, the word often refers to specific economic conditions – the distribution of incomes or wealth in a nation-state or another large spatial or geopolitical unit.[1] Writers often represent the distribution with a numerical or statistical measure.[2] The word "inequality" refers to such measured distributions. Indeed, it has become virtually synonymous with them.

A decade ago, inequality had a remarkable political effect – it turned two percentages into slogans of protest, when the Occupy Wall Street movement declared that "we are the 99%" standing against the 1 per cent. A few years later Thomas Piketty's 577-page study of inequality, *Capital in the Twenty-first Century*, with lots of numbers and graphs, became a bestseller.[3] His recent *Capital and Ideology* is likely to fly off the racks.[4] No doubt many readers will expect my book to presume the reader's appetite, or at least tolerance, for lots of numbers, and to explore measured distributions for

Canada. I am about to disappoint them. For I assume such figures to exist already, and to be available. Instead I start, in this introduction, by sketching the recent trends that have brought the "problem" of inequality again to the fore.

In Canada during the Second World War, as in the United States and many other countries, the share of total income going to the few people with the highest incomes dropped steeply. In Canada the share of the top 1 per cent fell from about 18 per cent in the late 1930s to about 10 per cent in 1945. This lower level of inequality persisted for four decades, in an era known as the "great compression." In the late 1980s (slightly earlier in the United States) the shares held by the top percentiles began to rise. The upward trend continued into this century, though not reaching the level of the 1930s and earlier (as it did in the United States).

The causes of Canada's "great compression" (1940s–1980s) were complex.[5] Much of the explanation for the initial wartime change related to "fiscal shock in the corporate sector" because of the war's impact.[6] The share of income that came from capital (dividends, interest, other investment income) fell dramatically, and the economy's rewards migrated from capital towards labour. This shift played a huge role, but so did state intervention, and hence policy and the cultural-political context. Ottawa introduced extremely high marginal tax rates (90 per cent or more) on the highest incomes. The resulting four-decade compression flowed from a range of state actions and regulations, including legalized collective bargaining, income transfers by the state, and federal–provincial tax-sharing agreements. The crucial role of government becomes clear when we compare the varying experiences among industrialized countries, some of which retained relatively low levels of inequality much longer than Canada or the United States: for instance, France, Japan, and Sweden. For people who remain optimistic about solutions to inequality, the variation in distributions across countries is critical evidence that political and even cultural differences matter.[7]

So much for the worrying, even alarming changes, especially in North America. But should we equate "inequality" with measured distributions? A problem arises when we do so: "distribution" purports to be a value-neutral term; it carries no apparent ethical connotation. When we see distributions in numerical or statistical form, we do not detect any of the value-laden questions that initiated the display in this "neutral" presentation of material realities, or "fact." "Inequality," by contrast, is clearly a normative term – it implies a standard, a deviation from a standard, and the absence of something of value. The prefix "in-" connotes the lack or absence of "equality." And however loudly non-egalitarians seek to qualify or deny the moral worth of "equality," there is no escaping its positive moral connotation. Indeed, the anti-egalitarian protest merely confirms how highly our culture esteems equality.

This context suddenly makes the question "What is inequality?" very difficult. Inequality is the absence of, or even the opposite of equality, and to define it, we need to know what we mean by equality.

Equality and *égalité* are among the most complex words in the English and French languages. There is no absolute standard by which to assess one person or condition as "equal" to another, although we may refer to individuals as such – for example, before the law. Any assessed equality is necessarily conditional – it assumes some standard or measure. What do we mean when we say that ten Canadian dollars are equal to 6.69 euros? This is a meaningful statement only because we refer to a known exchange rate for currencies; it says nothing about any other comparability, such as that of purchasing power. Hence the question Amartya Sen asked many years ago: "Equality of what?"[8] Hence also the array of answers by philosophers and others, and the many dimensions of equality: equality of rights, of opportunity, of status, of religion, of gender, of race – of almost any condition that one can imagine.

Equality and inequality go hand in hand: each is an inverse correlate or reciprocal of the other (they may also co-exist in mutual embrace). To further complicate matters, neither equality nor inequality can be perfectly realized. There is no such thing as perfect equality of opportunity, for instance. Perfect economic inequality – one person owns everything, everyone else nothing – cannot exist, any more than perfect equality of income or property. Thus inequality exists only with respect to its referent (inequality of what?) and only in some approximate and inexact degree. We may assess inequality in terms of, for example, income or wealth, and measure these factors fairly reliably. This move, though attractive, is incomplete, because inequality remains a normative concept, even when we answer the "of what?" question in this way. The "in-" prefix remains, as does the question: absence of *what* exactly? What would a relative equality look like, such that an alleged inequality would no longer exist? Even if we posit a distribution that is, in some sense, more equal, we beg the question: by what standard of ethics or justice is this alternative distribution more equal?

Inequality is always a value-laden concept. Whenever one uses the word, it declares, or contains at some level, a set of values. However we employ it, the word assumes a condition of relative equality standing as its reciprocal. To make the point in another way: inequality is a value-laden concept in the domain of justice, specifically in distributive justice – the allocation of goods (broadly defined) among a society's members. Theories of distributive justice seek to specify the principles behind a just distribution.

Questions of justice are fundamental to this book – and, I would argue, to any discussion of inequality as a problem. Inequality is a subject for scholarly analysis by economists and other social scientists. Yet, since it relates to distributive justice, philosophers, particularly political philosophers and ethicists, are central intervenors in the field.[9] Theologians too wrestle with the ethics of the allocation of material goods among human beings. And it is a subject for historians. Since "*in*-equality" is about values and justice, its meaning depends on time and context. It is always a temporal and historical construct. If it constitutes a problem, then its existence as such, and any escape from it, are also historical – the outcome of processes of change and human agency in time and space.

This book is about the discovery of inequality as a problem in Canada, and about its long history. I refer to a specific form of inequality: that which may exist in the distribution of either wealth or income in the population. When, and in what contexts, did this form of inequality appear as a problem? The inequality problem is an idea, I assert, with an irreducible core, even as the words to discuss it change: material inequality is extensive; it is a social and economic problem, a defect of the social and economic order; and a society can reduce, even eliminate it. The emergence of this idea constituted a significant change in religious, social, and political thought in Canada, as it did elsewhere. Medieval and early modern Europeans had tended to view extreme differences in wealth, property, and income as intrinsic to the natural order, whether or not they attributed them to God. In specific times and places, that older assumption was qualified or rejected, as some people came to believe that differential distributions were a human-created problem that could be cured or ameliorated.

THEORY AND METHOD

A half-century ago, at the beginning of my career as a historian, I was undertaking a lengthy search for the "origins" of a complex idea. I was trying to understand, in my callow but determined way, a pacifist conviction that attracted numerous followers in nineteenth-century England: the idea that all war was inconsistent with the teachings and spirit of Christianity. My youthful account of the idea as reflecting material interest and class position – as specific religious beliefs intersecting with the response of a commercial bourgeoisie to class conflict – would now invite critical responses from theoretical positions only beginning to emerge in the 1960s and 1970s.[10] Among other things, the notion that a core idea can exist and be the same idea in our own time as it was two centuries ago invites challenge. Is an idea, in the words of Quentin Skinner, "inescapably the embodiment of a particular intention, on a particular occasion, addressed to the solution of a particular problem, and thus specific to its situation in a way that it can only be naïve to try to transcend"?[11] A long conversation about ideas, meaning, and context flowed from that question, and even my extraction of Skinner's words from their original context does them injustice.[12]

Without entering deeply into that conversation, I offer a brief account of my stance. Surely we can answer the question affirmatively – yes, ideas are specific to their context – while also insisting that a mental representation or abstract concept may appear in more than one context. The similarity or likeness of the idea remains, even as the context shifts and the verbal expression of the idea changes. This observation is crucial for both the history and the politics of my subject: in different times and places, various people found their own ways of identifying, naming, and challenging inequality. Thus the inequality that some Lower-Canadian Patriotes identified in 1837 is not identical to the inequality that we may name today; but it is sufficiently similar that we can assign to both the same conceptual signifier – the word "inequality." More important, the historian's search for context is a critical inquiry in and of the present. Our history is, to borrow James Tully's words, "a reciprocal relation to the present ... a kind of permanent critique of the relations of meaning, power, and subjectivity in which we can think and act politically."[13] It is precisely because inequality appears in different contexts, and because it changes, that we can begin to perceive and to understand it in our own time. The past gives us alternative possibilities; it expands the horizon of what is thinkable, and shows us how narrow our own thinking is. This was true of my English pacifists: observe carefully what they were saying and doing, in the context of their time, and they will change what you think about peace and about anti-war protest. If we listen to what the Canadian discoverers of inequality said, as the problem arose and reappeared in changing contexts, we learn to think in new ways about inequality in our own time.

My attempt to define the problem of inequality does not entirely meet the problem of scope and selection. Inequality remains maddeningly elastic. E.A. Heaman's comprehensive study of taxation and tax revolts in Canada, with its clever and evocative title, *Tax, Order, and Good Government*, contains many references, implicit or explicit, to inequality and its close verbal homologues. The author relates taxation to imbalances or inequalities of power; shows tax sharing and federal subsidies to involve issues of equity and distributive justice; connects the terms of union in Confederation debates to distributions between rich and poor; and notes that tariffs and other taxes were inevitably about prices, living standards, and hence inequalities. Much of her book in effect examines debates over distributive justice. The same is true of *Give and Take*, Shirley Tillotson's invaluable analysis of twentieth-century taxation. [14]

I plead that scope is a tricky issue. I attempt to focus on the problem of inequality selectively, where it appears *in extenso* or as an initiating concept. To maintain the focus and to keep this book at a reasonable length, I cannot discuss all inequalities. Inequalities relating to gender and to race appear, albeit with regrettable brevity, where they connect to the inequality problem. Crucially, the problem of inequality, for most of its history, was a hermetic formulation – it excluded or evaded the intersections of economic inequality with inequalities rooted in gender and racialization. This book misses or under-emphasizes much else – it is not a history of equality, and it is not about poverty – and I leave many opportunities to others. [15]

Any search for an idea in its changing contexts raises serious questions about method, and the relation of method to theory. At one level, my project is a historian's version of salvage archaeology: are there hitherto-unseen discussions of inequality buried in our past?

Where can we find them? Do they fade at some point? The method follows from these questions: search in as many corners as time permits, and offer up a curated display of the texts that surface. In the act of searching, the analytical work has already begun. Who left these words, and in what place or context? The question of what historians are doing when they dig up ideas from the past has preoccupied historians and philosophers for a long time. If the task is to identify intentions, or context, what are these things, and how to find them? Context is forever elusive.

I set aside "intentions" as inherently problematic, in order to say something, very tentatively, about the inequality problem that presents itself as a "speech act." I wish to say something about context, reasoning inductively and abductively (the latter means observing cases and inferring a likely explanation or context). I also wish to say something about the ethical and political meaning of the speech act, as an act of dissent or contestation or opposition. Hence relevant "context" does not follow as an outcome of the evidence I have gathered – it is not something that is "found." Rather, context precedes the inquiry and works as a guiding hypothesis. As one instance, I am seeking inequality in the moral context of its utterances. Thus in the nineteenth century inequality appeared as an expression not simply of economic relationships of production and distribution, but of particular Protestant moral principles.[16]

I stick closely to my texts; I offer many direct quotations. There are two reasons for doing so. First, my history is a salvage operation: I need to convince the reader that many British North Americans and Canadians in the past really did address the problem of inequality, and that they did so in many ways. Second, my history is present-directed and even political. Such history risks a tendentious selection of evidence and a neglect of context; it risks forgetting that the past really was a foreign country. I meet this risk, in part, by presenting past words in their context and doing so fulsomely. This textuality actually serves my purpose in writing history in and for the present: sustained immersion in past words and ideas makes the present unfamiliar and even uncomfortable. Many received economic nostrums and assumptions become alien. Fernand Braudel made the point in a perfect analogy: spend a year in a foreign country and you learn a little about that country, but when you return to your own country you understand better some of its deep-seated characteristics. "With regard to the present, the past too is a way of distancing yourself."[17]

In our time, changes in the technology and techniques available to historians complicate the challenges of method. The present study would have been impossible three decades ago, before archives and libraries could digitize massive collections of primary and secondary sources. Search tools allow one to uncover references to inequality and its verbal homologues ("distribution," "rich and poor") in many sources across long spans of time.

As a result, I expanded my time frame from fifty years (my original intention) to more than a century and a half. Search technology has assisted my move away from micro-history, though certainly not to a study of *longue durée*. The technology has permitted me, as all historians, to vastly expand both gaze and temporal scope.[18] Difficult issues of method arise, and these have spawned a growing literature. Selection and digitization introduce bias into the sources made available. Keyword searches can predetermine results and context. The big toolbox available to the digital humanities broadens horizons but introduces technical challenges that historians have only begun to meet.[19] How does a historian relate to theory and evidence when a topic-modelling algorithm generates a "topic" of study?

In this project I largely avoid confrontation with such issues. I search keywords, using the same few keywords in all contexts, but acknowledge that no search is complete. I can explore all issues of the *Globe and Mail* over four decades and can note the shifting frequencies of a particular word, but I cannot quantify any such change.[20] No search can be complete, and the historian will miss much. Even a tentative entry into this world of digitized sources shatters any lingering illusion of a pure inductive method – the idea that we enter the archive while suspending our preconceived assumptions and values, unearthing evidence that yields forth its patterns and conclusions.

This project's large temporal scope and reliance on digitized sources may obscure biases source compilers have introduced. In searching Canadian newspapers, for instance, I am aware that I have largely ignored Quebec and the Maritime provinces: Peel's Prairie Provinces and the UBC [University of British Columbia] Digitized Collections have led the way by making newspapers west of Ontario available and searchable. I have done my best to compensate for selection bias in the wonderful Canadiana corpus, but the central-Canadian bias in my use of pamphlets, magazines, and books remains evident. Of more concern, this study under-represents sources by women authors and treats gender inadequately. Inequality, in both ethics and political economy, was a masculinist conception emerging from male-dominated professions. And, of course, women reformers and politicians focused on the rights of women and specific social questions. I have found few parallels in Canada to the American writer and lecturer Charlotte Perkins Gilman (1860–1935), who grasped the connection between the status of women and society-wide distributions of wealth and material advantage.[21] The English economist Hugh Dalton (1887–1962), a Labour economist and politician, in 1920 connected women's under-representation in the workforce to the overall distributions of income – but attracted little interest in Canada.[22]

The digital expansion of scope pushes the historian into new fields of knowledge and subject areas. A great historian may spend decades thinking and writing about the history of an idea, and then produce a study that covers centuries.[23] My spatial and temporal scope is much smaller, and the idea I seek to trace is more circumscribed. Nevertheless, with scant prior knowledge of most of the specific periods and people, I tread onto other experts' territory and draw heavily on their work. In doing so, I skirt or over-simplify important matters of interpretation, and no doubt I will offend some more experienced scholars. I hope that this book will invite corrections and revisions that advance our knowledge, both of Canada and of the problem of inequality. I hope also that the results will do more to inspire than to discourage others. The expanded time frame, the audacious exploration beyond one's own horizon, should not be the preserve of the few great historians among us. Above all, humanity faces problems of great urgency; inequality, along with global climate change, is among the most pressing (and the two are related). The history and politics of these problems demand action, in advance of predictably certain success. So it is for historians: we must offer what we have rather than await perfection or completeness.

DISTINCTIVE CANADIAN RECKONINGS

The expansion of temporal gaze makes it difficult to know where to begin. No Canadian discovered the idea of inequality for the first time. When the idea surfaced, it did so above small currents in wide rivers originating well beyond Canada. Modern understandings of inequality and distributive justice emerged within the intellectual heritage of the Enlightenment.[24] That heritage taught that even if divine order or natural law ruled humanity, society had institutions and laws that humans could adjust, reform, even create anew. Jean-Jacques Rousseau could write his *Discourse on the Origin and Foundations of Inequality among Men* (1755) to distinguish between natural and moral inequality and to put inequalities of status and wealth in the latter category. He located the origin of moral inequality in human convention, particularly in private property, but his argument is not mono-causal. While inequality began with property, its enduring foundations lay in law, in the relationship between the desire for power and that for wealth, and in *amour propre* (the esteem that comes from the opinion of others). Human institutions and induced psychological conditions sustain this inequality. Rousseau denaturalized inequality and put it within history and social relations. He also opened the door to political solutions, even if he remained pessimistic.[25] If evil is a social thing, then society should be able to cure it.

The eighteenth century saw the first expressions of ideas that resurfaced in the next. In Rousseau, readers could find brilliant rhetorical tirades on the privileges of the rich and the corruption of politics by wealth. Kant proffered the potentially subversive idea that material provision was a matter of right, not of need, and that every human being "has an equal *right* to the good things which nature has provided."[26] Condorcet offered a prescription for breaking down inequalities of condition; his methods included cooperative banks to extend credit to small producers, contributory insurance for old-age pensions, and universal access to schooling through a state education system.[27] In Gracchus Babeuf, one could read about schemes for redistribution through progressive taxation on land and incomes, and even ideas about minimal subsistence and a national health service.[28] Adam Smith rejected the idea that greater wealth always represented a just reward to ability or moral worth: "The opulence of the merchant is greater than that of all his clerks, though he works less; and they again have six times more than an equal number of artisans, who are more employed."[29] One could go on to cite many other original ideas that would resurface after 1800. The eighteenth century also illustrated the connection of theory to practice, in the levelling and welfare provisions of the Jacobins in revolutionary France.[30]

These various eighteenth-century ideas appeared within wide-ranging and complex philosophical explorations of justice, rights, and property, which none the less tended to explain, even justify inequalities of property and wealth. Locke removed natural-law limitations on the private holding of property, and so contributed a moral legitimacy to accumulations of property. He was not alone in seeing that "different degrees of Industry were apt to give Men Possessions in different proportions," and even more so after the invention of money.[31] Just over sixty years later David Hume offered a case for the transfer of resources that many others would adopt: the marginal benefit of a transfer to the poor is of greater value than the same transfer to the rich; and wherever we depart from an equality in which all have at least the "necessaries" and most of the "comforts" of life, "we rob the poor of more satisfaction than we add to the rich."[32] At the same time Hume offered justifications of inequality that would reappear later. Attempts at near-equality of distribution, he argued, would merely spread poverty, restrict liberty, and undermine the political order necessary to ensure justice.[33] Adam Smith's legacy was enormous, of course, but it was complicated. He made valuable contributions to distributive justice, and he re-imagined poverty and the poor in ways that have been described as "genuinely revolutionary."[34] Yet his way of reconciling moral sentiments with self-interest, virtue with commerce, would allow later generations to justify inequality as necessary to a flourishing and productive economy.

These few observations do not indicate direct origins or progenitors of nineteenth-century British North American and Canadian thought, but indicate merely that nothing in that era was *de novo*. No discovery of the problem of inequality was entirely original; every surfacing of the idea occurred within an intellectual milieu that was already contesting understandings of social order, property, and wealth. In the British North American colonies, the disruption of older ways of thinking, especially by the intrusions of secular philosophy, were later and gradual, but no less unsettling.

We must try to imagine an intellectual and cultural world in which many of the new ideas about equality, liberty, and social order were alien and scarcely thinkable. There are useful analogies in the history of music, when our imagination is challenged to comprehend the responses of people in the past. To many mid-eighteenth-century listeners, for instance, the sound of the glass harp was so strange and even frightening that many thought it could cause madness. Such reactions make sense only if we can imagine a sonic universe totally different from our own, absent of amplification, car horns, electronic sounds, and the other dissonant noises that surround us. In Lower Canada in the early nineteenth century, unsettling Enlightenment ideas percolated slowly and met the formidable powers of priests and bishops seeking to suppress and repel alien notions. "*Égalité*" was, in the literate Catholic communities of the colony, a glass harp – a new and terrifying idea connected to revolution, regicide, and the destruction of holy places. In this world the notions that wealth was *not* the just reward for merit, and that material provision was a *right* rather than a need that charity could answer, were almost beyond comprehension. "Levellers" who spoke of redistribution from rich to poor were known to exist, but as alien beings infesting dark hollows in France. It would require major political disruptions, and a delayed manifestation of the Atlantic revolutions, before a version of the idea of inequality could surface in British North America.

Inequality – the idea, that is – did not follow anything like a linear trajectory. With certain economic concepts, such as wage theory or comparative advantage, one might be able to discern a development, in which each generation responds to and departs from previous iterations of the idea. In British North America and Canada we can observe some words surviving over time, acquiring new connotations and different political targets in new contexts: "privilege," "monopoly," and "aristocracy" are obvious examples. But rarely do we see one generation elaborating on its predecessor's theories of inequality. While remaining attentive to intellectual borrowings, this book's salvage excavation is episodic. There is a historical point here: the idea of inequality surfaces in many very different and often unconnected contexts. It is no more a Protestant ideation than it is a Catholic one. Even so simple an observation may carry political weight: an idea of such dispersed instantiation may defy all attempts at coherence in political action or movement. Yet, as we see below, an idea of such enduring resilience has the potential to sustain more insurgency than we may have realized.

I wish to claim that the problem of inequality we examine here was distinctively colonial and Canadian in its appearance. It is not enough merely to make this assertion: I must confirm it. I must also show that what followed, from the mid-nineteenth century into the twentieth, was *Canadian*. If there were silences in Canada, we can detect these only comparatively, as the absence of what people said and heard elsewhere. It is essential therefore for me to provide context – to show what was happening to the problem of inequality in the North Atlantic world of which Canada was a part. Chapter 1 provides the indispensable template for grasping the distinctiveness of Canadian reckonings with inequality. The survey there, while integral to the structure of the whole, can also introduce the first great era of inequality in British and U.S. thought (I believe firmly that thinking about inequality today requires awareness of that era's seminal ideas).[35] This book is, I hope, a modest foray into transatlantic history, a huge field to which Canadian scholarship has much to contribute.[36]

The problem of inequality appeared in political discourse in Lower and Upper Canada in the 1830s (chapter 2), and reappeared gradually (1830s–1880s) in Protestant critiques of wealth (chapter 3). The idea arose, contested but potent, among a few generations of labour leaders and worker intellectuals (chapter 4). It was proclaimed by rural romantics, agrarian populists, and social gospellers (chapter 5); perceived but often ignored by English-Canadian political economists (chapter 6); propelled with sudden force into political economy in Quebec in the 1930s (chapter 7); and submerged within the buoyant egalitarianism of the 1930s and 1940s, as Canada moved cautiously towards a version of social security (chapter 8). The idea resurfaced, muted and fragile, within the political ethos of the post-1945 welfare state (chapter 9).

The history of the distribution of wealth, says Thomas Piketty, "cannot be reduced to purely economic mechanisms." The history of inequality – as an idea and as a material condition – is always "shaped by the way economic, social and political actors view what is just and what is not, as well as by the relative power of those actors and the collective choices that result."[37] "What is just" puts the subject firmly within the domain of ethics, and there is no separating ethics from political economy.[38] The relationship between ethics and the scholarly discipline of economics goes back a long way, of course. In the last half of the twentieth century the two fields of knowledge were virtually distinct, with economics a rigorous and quantitative science analyzing what happens in the world under particular assumptions. "Morality ... represents the way that people would like the world to work – whereas economics represents how it actually *does* work."[39] I cite the simple, positivist assumption of separation merely to point out that the history of inequality denies it; the only question of interest is how the assumption of distinctive fields arose and endured. Furthermore, in seeking the early appearances of the idea of inequality, we enter a world in which the assumption did not exist. Few people in the early twentieth century considered political economy an empirical science distinct from ethical knowledge. My university-educated grandparents, devout Protestants raised in the social-gospel era, would have considered the idea incomprehensible, for the self-evident reason that in human thought and action morality has no borders or limits.

Every significant question about inequality is moral in nature, and also political. What level of inequality meets the test of social justice? Can we choose between alleviating poverty and reducing inequality? Is there a point at which redistribution infringes unjustly on liberty?[40] Is an extreme disparity between rich and poor intrinsically wrong, or wrong only in so far as it has harmful effects?[41] And critically, once we accept that the problem is real and very serious, is there a politics that offers hope of deliverance?

SIX PROPOSITIONS

Our ancestors asked, and answered, these and many other questions about inequality. Today we can understand things that they could not; in particular, we can measure, and hence know, inequalities of income and wealth over space and time that they could not. But we may learn from their ways of knowing. What follows in this book is an effort at deconstruction and reconstruction; I am tempted to call it a heuristic experiment. I invite readers to consider the following six propositions, extracted perhaps unfairly from contexts that I urge readers to explore (please refer to the notes). I could have chosen others, but these are certainly among the prominent ethical-political stances relevant to inequality in our time.

"It seems to me, however, that our most fundamental challenge is not the fact that the incomes of Americans are widely *unequal*. It is, rather, the fact that too many of our people are *poor*." (Harry G. Frankfurt, 2015).[42]

"It does matter that some people can buy tickets for space travel when others are queuing for food banks." (Anthony Atkinson, 2015).[43]

"A deep and important contribution of the discipline of economics is that greed is neither good nor bad in the abstract." (Daron Acemoglu, 2009).[44]

"We need inequality ... Without inequality you lack incentives to do practically anything – to work, to invent new things or to invest. Nobody is going to do things for nothing and we know that monetary rewards are really crucial, so this is the good part of inequality. We should not forget that inequality is indispensable for the development of a society." (Branko Milanovic, 2015).[45]

"Across recorded history, the periodic compressions of inequality brought about by mass mobilization warfare, transformative revolution, state failure, and pandemics have invariably dwarfed any known instances of equalization by entirely peaceful means." (Walter Scheidel, 2017).[46]

"Social and economic inequalities are to satisfy two conditions: (a) They are to be attached to positions and offices open to all under conditions of fair equality of opportunity; and (b). They are to be to the greatest benefit of the least-advantaged members of society (the difference principle)." (John Rawls, 2001).[47]

I invite readers to follow me through my history, to see whether you arrive, in the Conclusion, at the same location as I do. Whether or not you are with me at the end, if my history has succeeded, your reactions to these six propositions will have changed or, at the very least, will rest on firmer ground. And so let us examine the idea of inequality in our past, in order to see more clearly the inequality of today and tomorrow.

CHAPTER ONE

North Atlantic Thinkers on the Problem of Inequality (1770s–1920s)

The British North American colonies were small communities within the wider North Atlantic world, and they reacted slowly to the intellectual and political changes occurring in Europe in the century after Rousseau wrote his *Discours* on inequality in the 1750s. The efforts of Lower Canada's Catholic church to insulate the faithful from secular evils were only one barrier deflecting the complex Enlightenment heritage. The vitality of Protestant religion in Upper Canada meant that it resisted the "radical Enlightenment" (Jonathan Israel's term) or absorbed it incompletely. In so far as that new worldview meant "the philosophical rejection of revealed religion, miracles, and divine Providence" – "replacing the idea of salvation in the hereafter with the highest good in the here and now" – only a weak strain reached the colonies.[1] Thus a secular political economy was slow to appear. Even more than in England, we may speak, as does Boyd Hilton, of "Christian economics."[2]

Should we set aside the problem of inequality as it evolved in that wider world, especially in Britain and the United States, and consider Canadian borrowings only where they become apparent? To do so would be expedient but severely limiting. There was a distinct Canadian articulation of inequality, which becomes visible only within the larger transatlantic frame. American and British writers created a large public repository of sources and ideas from which Canadians could draw. Any effort at summary will be selective and brief, oversimplifying and leaving much out.[3] But a survey is necessary. If we can observe selections in use – what Canadians did and did not borrow – we may begin to perceive the distinctive Canadian reckoning on inequality as it emerged between roughly 1830 and

1920. The international literature also gives us benchmarks for the arrival of new ideas as a complex political economy of wealth distribution evolved. Here we may find the outer limits of what was conceivable, the horizons of the problem of inequality and its ethical correlate, distributive justice, as they developed in the nineteenth and early twentieth centuries.

This chapter looks at the long but urgent search for a stable foundation for virtue and justice, when God was no longer the centre of all moral argument and when Christian teachings were losing their exclusive primacy as a source of ethics. As David Wootton says, thinkers such as David Hume, who did not argue from deistic beginnings, had to find another way of linking virtue and interest, benevolence and self-interest.[4] That search would prove long and arduous, and it would lead directly to the problem of the distribution of wealth and to a series of secular principles of distributive justice. This chapter traces that quest from classical political economy to Britain's new liberalism in the decades around 1900, and from republican theory and critics of inequality in the United States – and contributions from Europe – to theories of distributive justice and the discovery of their limits by the 1920s.

CLASSICAL POLITICAL ECONOMY

In classical political economy, distribution referred to the functional distribution of income and wealth among workers, capitalists, and landlords. Inequality was mainly its by-product.[5] This simple summary risks masking the complexity of thinking about distribution in classical economics. To take only the most obvious example, Adam Smith (1723–1790) – quite apart from his original views on poverty – presented a complicated problematization of distribution and "inequality" (the word appears more than twenty times in *The Wealth of Nations* [1776]). He knew that inequality was the inevitable accompaniment of growth in a commercial society, and he saw it as necessary to an appropriate distinction of ranks and status.[6] Yet his sympathetic view of the poor enabled specific, if limited, distributive recommendations.[7] And, as Dennis Rasmussen has pointed out, Smith was deeply concerned that extreme inequality distorted moral standards and sympathies. The wealthy too often abandoned the path of virtue, Smith said; their vices became fashionable; and an inordinate desire for wealth became a source of envy, avarice, and ambition.[8] At a deeper level, Smith's political economy was a challenge to any notion of Christian economics. His political economy set aside any idea of a just price: the market determined prices. "As soon as you make this move," observes David Wootton, "you inevitably create a tension between the amoral world of market forces and the moral world of human interactions."[9] Canadians would eventually confront this profound tension, and seek to resolve or evade it.

Long before many Canadians reckoned with Adam Smith, another challenge emerged: the promise and peril of utilitarianism. The utilitarian emphasis on the happiness of as many people as possible readily supported a simple form of distributive justice: shifting resources away from the rich and towards the poor increased the sum of happiness. The utilitarian principle could be used to reject the idea that individuals have absolute rights: Jeremy Bentham (1748–1832) could see no reason why the good of any one individual should take priority over the greater good of many others.[10] The egalitarian promise of utilitarianism was realized by the Irish radical and philosopher William Thompson (1775–1833), whose use of the labour theory of value in a theory of exploitation would impress Marx.[11] But Thompson was an exception, both in his "social science" (his term) and in his politics. Others perceived a great peril in the utilitarian reduction of ethics to summary calculation and what Coleridge called "the general contagion of its mechanic philosophy."[12] Utilitarianism would find only limited space in Canadian "critical inquiry," although it eventually resurfaced in Canadian political economy.[13] More remarkable, perhaps, early-nineteenth-century Canada lacked critics of wealth in the tradition of secular political economy. Thompson was virtually unknown, and so also was the Swiss economist J.C.L. Sismondi (1773–1842), whose critique of wealth accumulation and the problem of inequality were available in French and, by the 1840s, in English.[14]

More likely to attract notice in English Canada was John Stuart Mill (1806–1873), especially after his *Principles of Political Economy* appeared in 1848. Mill sought to revise classical political economy and the understanding of distribution. He stated an idea that found a following among many who never read his *Principles*. This idea endorsed an assumption fundamental to liberal thought on the problem of inequality, in Canada and elsewhere:

The laws and conditions of the Production of wealth partake of the character of physical truths. There is nothing optional or arbitrary in them. Whatever mankind produce, must be produced in the modes, and under the conditions, imposed by the constitution of external things, and by the inherent properties of their own bodily and mental structure. Whether they like it or not, their productions will be limited by the amount of their previous accumulation, and, that being given, it will be proportional to their energy, their skill, the perfection of their machinery, and their judicious use of the advantages of combined labour. Whether they like it or not, a double quantity of labour will not raise, on the same land, a double quantity of food, unless some improvement takes place in the processes of cultivation ...

It is not so with the Distribution of wealth. That is a matter of human institution solely. The things once there, mankind, individually or collectively, can do with them as they like. They can place them at the disposal of whomsoever they please, and on whatever terms. Further, in the social state, in every state except total solitude, any disposal whatever of them can only take place by the consent of society, or rather of those who dispose of its active force.[15]

Mill separated distribution from production and placed both distribution and inequality within the domain of human institutions. His distinction contained unresolved problems, of course. He failed to keep "physical truths" and "human institution" apart; the qualification "unless some improvement" immediately begged the question as to why some change in human institution might not double the quantity of food. Yet he made distribution subject to different rules and conditions than production. His argument was consistent with the series of harmful inequalities in his *Principles*: unequal remuneration, taxation, opportunities, and legal rights. His reasoning supported a progressive vision of remedy by such institutional means as cooperatives and education for the working class, and his political economy has been interpreted as "an early form of institutionalist social economics."[16] The distinction between production and distribution grounded later statements of principles of distributive justice[17] in Canada and elsewhere.

In Mill's time there were clear alternatives to his liberal conception of distribution. One forceful alternative rejected any separation of distribution from production. "Any distribution whatever of the means of consumption is only a consequence of the distribution of the conditions of production themselves. The latter distribution, however, is a feature of the mode of production itself."[18] The author, of course, was Karl Marx (1818–1883), writing in 1875. At mid-century other sources located inequality and its cure in the exploitation inherent in capitalist production. Even Louis Blanc (1811–1882), for all his emphasis on the evil of competition, saw "a more equitable distribution" as dependent on a prior application of "the associative principle" in the process of production.[19] At the centre of the problem of inequality and its subsequent history would lie this opposition between its liberal articulations and the socialist alternative. In Canada the opposition was not always clear, but it was fundamental.

Political economy in Mill's time and thereafter offered a sustained response to the challenge of socialism. It was also, and increasingly, a reckoning with what the British economic historian Arnold Toynbee called the "industrial revolution."[20] Economics, as it embraced marginalist theory in the 1870s and 1880s and moved into its neo-classical formation, sought to submit vast economic changes to human understanding and control, by discovering laws to explain the movement of forces that seemed at times to threaten society, social order, and even the spiritual foundations of order. The problem of inequality – the apparent chasm, both material and spiritual, between rich and poor – offered a simplifying ontology that seemed to capture the essence of social disorder and its underlying discontents.[21] The "distribution" problem now took centre stage in the evolving drama of economics and moral philosophy, bearing forth its mix of certitude, confusion, and ambiguity.

The United Kingdom's much earlier encounter with industrial capitalism was merely one key difference between it and Canada. In Britain, wealth evoked landed wealth and the great estates. The influence of landowning aristocracy meant that inheritance laws would remain central to the discussion of inequality. As for labour, British economists knew that labour was distinct from other factors of production because it was human rather than material, but the imprecisions of the labour theory of value were very apparent, so it did not retain a following as long in Britain as it did in the United States and Canada. In contrast, population growth remained an issue for the British. For Mill, it impeded equitable distribution.[22] In both Canada and the United States (at least until the closing of the American frontier late in the century), the relative abundance of land appeared to allow more people landed independence, easing fear of a Malthusian population crisis.

Several factors affected discussion of wealth distribution. Britain adopted income tax as early as 1842 (there were precedents), while the United States did so much later (1913), followed by Canada. Not unrelated, in the United Kingdom the state's administrative capacity expanded rapidly between the 1830s and the 1870s. In 1830 local administration of the poor laws was the chief means of social improvement; by the 1870s a central administrative structure could initiate (if not always implement) national-level programs, most notably in education, with Whitehall's direction often challenging local control.[23] The expansion of male suffrage in 1867 promised to empower the lower orders of society, who would proceed, many observers assumed, to make increasing demands of the state. Redistribution became conceivable, and the state's possible role in distributive justice came to the forefront of politics and political economy. Arnold Toynbee reflected this shift in thinking. We do not abandon our old belief in liberty, he said in his lectures on the industrial revolution, if "we say that under certain conditions the people cannot help themselves, and that then they should be helped by the State representing directly the whole people." The state could help remove great social evils without weakening "habits of individual self-reliance and voluntary association."[24]

We can see how much the threat of socialism inspired and inflected the discussion of inequality in the work of Henry Sidgwick (1838–1900). In his *Principles of Political Economy* (1883) socialism and communism were recurring themes. He rejected "laisser faire" and followed a utilitarian path when he argued that the marginal utility of income for individuals was related to income level. An addition of one unit to the income of the poor yielded greater value than the same addition to the income of the rich. Therefore "the more any society approximates to equality in the distribution of wealth among its members, the greater on the whole is the aggregate of satisfactions which the society in question derives from the wealth that it possesses."[25] This utilitarian calculus implied support for redistributive policies by government. But Sidgwick applied firm conditions: for example, any redistribution must not affect total economic output, thereby avoiding one peril of a communist system.[26] He also analysed taxation, but did not see it as a route to redistribution. [27] His effort to balance equitable distribution with maintenance of incentives and just rewards led him to a cautious secular principle of distributive justice. "So far as we aim at realising Justice or Equity ... the proportionment of the individual's share of produce to his Deserts is the primary end to be sought, and the removal of inequalities only as a means to this; that is, only so far as these inequalities are due to other causes than the different worth of the exertions unequally remunerated."[28] Much could be said about this principle; it is enough to note that, though not radical, it refused to leave the determination of just reward to market forces alone.

THE NEW LIBERALISM

The liberal conception of the state and its role shifted in the late nineteenth century, as did the understanding of inequality. The "new liberalism" involved changing understandings of the individual, liberty, and community. The seminal figure in the Oxford tradition was T.H. Green (1836–1882), the idealist philosopher whom some historians believe shaped an intellectual template for liberal interventionism and even social democracy.[29] Green and his followers rejected hedonistic utilitarianism, which saw the rightness of an action in terms of the amount of pleasure that it tended to produce and the amount of pain that it tended to prevent. Green instead sought to reconcile self-interest and benevolence through a concept of "common good."[30] As Yuichi Shionoya puts it: "The common good does not refer to particular entities which individuals commonly desire ... but rather to the common pursuit of self-realization by the members of a given society."[31] Green turned Hegelian idealism in a radical direction with implications for the state's role: criteria of common good and positive freedom could justify its intervention.[32]

Among Green's "new liberal" disciples, many accepted an expansive role for the state. David Ritchie (1853–1903) stated: "If we hold that the liberty of individuals in any real and positive sense is one of the principal objects which the State ought to secure, then it is indispensable that the State should claim the right of interfering, where necessary, with the actions of voluntary associations" (these included family, church, joint-stock company, and trade union). Ritchie added: "The State can only secure the real well-being of its citizens, by taking over the functions of which it deprives the family and performing them in a higher or better way." It was true, he admitted, that no state might yet be ready for such intervention. "Yet all modern States are consciously or unconsciously moving in that direction."[33] The liberal conceptions of common good and community could even lead to the discovery of common ground with socialism (a discovery that occurred less often among Canadian liberals in the new-liberal era). Edward Caird (1835–1908) saw individualism and community being reconciled; it is a mistake, he said, to assume that individualists and socialists are "absolutely opposed sects."[34]

By the early 1910s L.T. Hobhouse (1864–1929) was reconstructing Mill and Green's liberalism, preserving individualism and property rights while moving towards what his volume *Liberalism* (1911) called "Liberal Socialism."[35] As for economic inequality, Hobhouse offered a simple law of distributive justice based in "common" or social utility. "If it is really just that A should be superior to B in wealth or power or position, it is only because when the good of all concerned is considered, among whom B is one, it turns out that there is a net gain in the arrangement as compared with any alternative that we can devise."[36] The principle placed a moral boundary on accumulation of wealth, by requiring that any such superior accumulation be justified in terms of "net gain" and common good. The principle gave the state a duty of intervention; for Hobhouse, it also served to justify a "super-tax" on very large incomes.[37] Yet its outcome depended very much on what was invested in "net gain." And the passive "is considered" begged the obvious question: what agency had the power to evaluate alternatives in terms of "the good of all"?

For Hobhouse, the principle justified national insurance, a social minimum, a "living wage," and certain kinds of state regulation of private enterprise. It did not imply either state socialism or a strongly *dirigiste* state.[38] Reduction of inequality did not mean equality of condition, of "treatment," or of power. The principle set the conditions in which "the existence of millionaires on the one hand and of paupers on the other" could be considered consistent with the common good.[39] In short, it justified inequality *and* a state-sponsored social minimum.

New-liberal thinkers were beginning to open the door to redistributive action by the state. In 1902 an English economist used wealth distribution to open it much wider.[40] J.A. Hobson (1858–1940) was a central figure in the history of studies of wealth and inequality.[41] A student at Oxford in the 1870s, moving into the political ferment of London in the 1880s, he absorbed Mill, T.H. Green, British idealist philosophy, John Ruskin, and contemporary studies of social problems and poverty, including those by Charles Booth. One starting point for Hobson was Mill's association of economic rent with monopoly in *The Principles of Political Economy* (book II, chap. 16).[42] Hobson was among those radicals who located the source of rent not only in land but also in large corporations (and eventually in finance capital as well as industrial capital).[43] Though working at first with marginal theory, he was moving in a direction that would bypass and then transcend it. He was thinking outside key neoclassical assumptions, rejecting those about equilibrium and the absence of friction in markets. Hobson put disequilibrium and friction at the centre of political economy.[44]

By the late 1890s Hobson's theory of distribution embraced monopoly, rent, and historically generated accretions of power in markets, which last, he argued, made pure competition impossible. The historical application of machinery and new sources of energy to production had substituted capital for labour and transformed "the balance of power in bargaining among the different classes of owners of capital and labour-power." We can see the unequal distribution of power in "forced gains," "unearned income," and "surplus value."[45] Hobson had arrived at a non-Marxist identification of surplus value.[46] In his *Economics of Distribution* (1900) he used "inequality" to refer to both material inequalities in society and the absence of anything like equality in "all departments of economic activity."[47]

Hobson did not stop there. "Mal-distribution" (his word) had profound and extensive structural dimensions. The rapid concentration of power and wealth in the late nineteenth century created enormous incomes for a "class" of "financial and industrial capitalists." These plutocrats could not spend their whole incomes on luxuries, so they saved or invested the rest. Even if workers spent all of their income on consumption, and if all the ultra-wealthy spent massively on luxuries, the latter could not usefully invest the rest in expanding production, because output would then exceed consumer demand.[48] Everywhere excess capital was searching for investment: "It is this condition of affairs that forms the taproot of Imperialism."[49] Hobson had expanded enormously the scope of inequitable distribution. Its pathologies now included the business cycles of capitalism ("gluts and depressions") and imperialism.

Hobson's problematizing of maldistribution did not stop there. By 1909 he was looking at the "moral economy" of industry and what we would call social psychology ("a psychological interpretation").[50] Here and elsewhere Hobson owed much to John Ruskin's rejection of the equation of human welfare with money, or wealth with true value.[51] Hobson expanded wealth's meaning to embrace "human welfare or well-being."[52] He stretched the frame of distribution beyond income and material wealth to the work process in industry. Surplus value and "inequality of bargain" caused vast income inequality and "unequal distribution of work." Industrial labour, he said, necessarily involved "continuous monotony of narrow manual toil" as well as muscular strain and an "atrophying" of "productive energy." He turned these conditions into a distributional problem with a distributive solution. They formed part of "the natural history of parasitism." The solution was "a proportionate distribution of work" so that manual labour included both "manual and mental skill" and the "intellectual work of planning." In a tentative but provocative way Hobson again expanded the scope of inequality. He challenged directly the foundations of scientific management in industry and, however implausibly, turned the psychic "disutility" of industrial labour into a problem of maldistribution.[53]

Much of what Hobson wrote could have served socialists (and, of course, it influenced Lenin).[54] Nevertheless, Hobson remained securely within a liberal framework. He was trying to reconcile individuals' rights and self-realization with an organic view of society. His solutions to maldistribution and parasitism focused on redistributing opportunity. He referred frequently to equality of opportunity, to be secured not only by education but also by equalizing opportunity within the industrial workplace.[55] Above all, he offered a rationale for progressive taxation, whereby, he argued, the state could appropriate surplus value without reducing reinvestment and productive capacity. It would thereby suffocate the "taproot" of imperialism, balance production and consumption, and reconcile capitalism and social welfare.[56]

What might a Canadian reader interested in social questions have learned from Hobson? Hobson visited Canada in the winter of 1905–06 and wrote newspaper articles and a book about his impressions.[57]

He had published articles in American journals. He was certainly read by leading U.S. economists and was respected by many (certainly not all) who worked on the economics of welfare.[58] English Canadians might have rejected Hobson's anti-imperialism, but those who read *The Social Problem* (1901) or *Work and Wealth* (1914) could easily miss the anti-imperialism and respond instead to the ethical humanism.[59] Even casual readers might have learned from Hobson that wealth was not the same thing as an accumulation of material goods. Hobson encouraged the belief that the old laissez-faire ideas were dead, giving way to new ideals of common good. Economics, as a study of the real world, did not part company with ethics. Utilitarianism did not need to be an individualistic or hedonistic calculus; it could be about a broad social utility, the maximizing of well-being or welfare. Economic policies on specific issues, from free trade to taxation to labour legislation, should not be about narrowly defined economic effects alone: they were about "total effects," including health and culture and morality, as these existed "in organic relation to the direct gains of increased industrial wealth."[60] Above all, the state could intervene in the economy in ways that, far from hindering private enterprise or economic growth, fostered these while increasing the well-being of the whole, or "organic welfare."[61] Finally, if one selected only a few of these lines of argument and applied them to poverty, then it was no longer possible to explain poverty, or the gaps between rich and poor, by reference to the personal failings of the poor.[62]

The attentive reader could also find in Hobson an explicit principle of distributive justice, more radical than that of his friend L.T. Hobhouse. This principle illustrated the use of the organic metaphor, and it indicated the extent of new liberalism's rhetorical accommodation with socialism: "A sound human economy conforms to the organic law of distribution, 'from each according to his power, to each according to his needs,' and that precisely so far as the current processes of economic distribution of work and of its product contravene this organic law, waste accrues and illfare displaces welfare ... The Human Law of Distribution ... aims ... to distribute Wealth in relation to its production on one hand and its consumption on the other, so as to secure the minimum of Human Costs and the maximum of Human Utility."[63]

In Hobson's formulation "needs" were not merely material, and utility was not that of marginal utility theory, which he was at pains to reject.[64] His principle justified redistributive action by the state and limited accumulation by the criteria of "need." Although the needs of capital or of the wealthy might differ from those of the poor, in Hobson's formulation "functionless wealth," "unearned increment," and a host of market failures drastically reduced the entitlement of capitalists. As a redistributive principle, however, Hobson's "organic law" was fully consistent with a rejection of socialism. He was justifying equality of opportunity, not of outcomes, and offering principled cover for state regulation of industry and the use of tax revenues to improve the living standards of the poor. Another obvious limit to the principle was that "from each" could be read as a condition of "to each": the right to welfare or well-being rested not on one's existence as citizen or even as human being, but on one's status as producer.

The new liberalism was not a homogeneous or internally consistent ideology. In the work of Hobson it was moving in the direction of what we now call welfare economics, which may be defined as the analysis of social goods as distinct from total production or material wealth, and the development of principles to guide government actions in realizing social goods or collective well-being. Welfare economics was directly related to the inequality problem: it grew out of previous thought on the distribution of wealth, from Alfred Marshall (1842–1924), Sidgwick, Hobson, and others to its pre-eminent English co-founder, Arthur Pigou. Another precursor to welfare economics in Britain was the Italian-born economist and politician Leo Chiozza Money (1870–1944).[65] His widely read *Riches and Poverty* (1905) was a unique contribution to the empirical analysis of distributions of both income and wealth. Money estimated that a mere 2.9 per cent of the population took 34 per cent of total income.[66] Containing much more than statistical display, his book reached to the limits of new-liberal thinking on "the terrible error in the distribution of the nation's income."[67] Money was seeking to balance economic growth with "national welfare" or "public welfare."[68] He proposed doing so through steeply graduated income taxes and inheritance taxes. He also endorsed public ownership of "common services" or "natural monopolies" and foresaw gradual expansion of public ownership.[69] Here was a liberal accommodation to socialism that would find no parallel in Canada.

The year 1912 was a critical moment in the development of liberal thought on distribution. In that year the Cambridge economist Arthur Pigou (1877–1959) published *Wealth and Welfare*.[70]

For anybody interested in inequality or social problems in general, Pigou's books were essential reading. *Wealth and Welfare* was explicitly about inequality – Pigou used the word throughout.[71] The volume was a catalogue of market failures, leading to a prescription for remedial government policies.[72] Pigou (quoting his contemporary Edwin Cannan) challenged Adam Smith: "The working of self-interest is generally beneficent, not because of some natural coincidence between the self-interest of each and the good of all, but because human institutions are arranged so as to compel self-interest to work in directions in which it will be beneficent."[73] Working within the economics of marginal utility, Pigou isolated not a surplus available to consumers but what he called "national dividend" – the social product or total value of output, measurable in money terms. Market failures reduced the national dividend and impeded its distribution. Private net products diverged from social net products.[74] A classic instance occurred with an externality (Pigou's concept), where production and exchange resulted in a social disservice, such as pollution, that is not factored as a cost in the private exchange.[75] Part III of *Wealth and Welfare* explored the distribution of the national dividend and the conditions for "transferences" from the "relatively rich to the relatively poor," whether through private or state action, that maximized the national dividend and total welfare.

Pigou's conclusion was that "artificial wage rates" for the very poor and a national minimum met the tests in certain conditions. For all its qualifications, and despite Pigou's suspicion of the general public and his strict limits on the hand of government, his work offered the backing of economic science for redistribution, including through state action. His book gave its readers a new sense of the pervasive extent of market failures, and an arsenal of economic arguments for redistribution within a renovated capitalism.[76] It also proposed that specific state welfare expenditures could be self-financing.[77]

Whatever else Canadian readers might have learned from Pigou, they might have taken the idea that transfers could be benevolent and efficient, individually and collectively. Here, in a single sentence, lay the thought: "If we assume all members of the community to be of similar temperament, and if these members are only two in number, it is easily shown that any transference from the richer to the poorer of the two, since it enables more intense wants to be satisfied at the expense of less intense wants, must increase the aggregate sum of satisfaction."[78] Eight years later Hugh Dalton took up this idea and turned it into what became[79] the Pigou–Dalton principle: a transfer of income from a richer household to a poorer one decreased inequality (or increased social welfare) if it did not reverse the ranking of the two households in the income distribution or alter total income. The principle had serious limits, which generated a vast literature.[80] In our context, the inequality problem had generated a historical climacteric, when the decades-old problem of wealth distribution generated a seminal principle of distributive justice.

There was another original contribution in this moment: the idea of inequality and the "theory of distribution" found its first historian. In 1920 there appeared Labour economist and politician Hugh Dalton's (1887–1962) history of the idea of inequality from the eighteenth century to the present, and he included British and continental sources.[81] His historical analysis led him to suggest the redistributive potential of trade unions, an improved education system, and a welfare state. He saw education as the key to "vertical mobility" – an early statement of a reformist response to inequality still common today, despite the inequitable distributions and structures blocking upward mobility.[82] Dalton did not realize the potential of the connection he noted between "inequalities due to sex" and income inequality. He did not fully elaborate it but listed "the extension of the field of employment to women" among the "practical policies" to reduce total inequality. He discussed women in the context of trade unions and equality of opportunity. However tentatively, he was relating one systemic inequality to another, and he offered liberal, reformist remedies: opening paid employment to women; removing customary and legal restrictions to their entering the professions; making them equal in trade unions; and mandating equal pay for equal work.[83]

The history of inequality since 1920 may well be little more than a series of footnotes to the new liberalism of the early twentieth century. By 1920 the discourse had changed substantially in less than fifty years, yielding a language and a politics that we can recognize, for all the differences that remain between us and them. The influence of both Herbert Spencer and Thomas Malthus had waned: there was no future either in the natural progress of evolutionary laws or in the inexorable workings of population balanced against resources. There was no future to be sought in a Christian millennium, although Christian ethics had often initiated the search for equity in an era of class conflict. Instead there were new secular principles of distributive justice emerging from a secular science of society. These ideals sought in science the security and stability of religious faith. At times they echoed the discursive forms of Christian ethical axioms. Marginal utility, and differing needs of rich and poor at the margin, were Christian ideas, after all: "When you reap the harvest of your land, you shall not reap your field right up to its edge, neither shall you gather the gleanings after your harvest ... You shall leave them for the poor and for the sojourner" (Leviticus 19:9–10). But these were echoes and no more; inequality had entered a secular and positivist epistemology.

REPUBLICAN THEORY AND CRITICS OF INEQUALITY

To cross the Atlantic in the second half of the nineteenth century was to enter a very different context. In the United States a republican theory of wealth distribution still endured. That theory, according to its historian James L. Huston, had rested on four pillars. The first was the labour theory of value, which held that justice was achieved when each man (not yet woman) received the just fruit of his labour. The second was the idea that equality and justice required land, which the political system of aristocracy had denied in the old world. The third was that aristocratic control of land through inheritance laws, particularly primogeniture, skewed wealth distribution. The fourth was that population growth was a cause of inequality and pauperism, especially in Europe. The vast American frontier made landowning independence possible for most people, if not all, thereby reducing inequities.[84] Between about 1880 and 1910 the republican theory faced new challenges from industrialization and its violent conflicts. A "new aristocratic enemy" appeared in the form of monopoly capital. The old labour theory of value collapsed. "The demise of the labor theory of property/value in the twentieth century has been one of the most monumental changes in popular and intellectual thought in American history."[85]

It is easy to see how parts of the republican theory could work against the idea that inequality was a social problem. Until the American frontier was clearly no longer capable of absorbing population – and awareness of its "closing" dawned slowly – virtually free access to land easily camouflaged or denied inequality. The absence of a European-style landed aristocracy sustained the republican ethos of egalitarian opportunity, and so did the celebrated abolition of primogeniture in most states in the Revolutionary period. It was possible to believe that the new wealth, stunningly apparent in the 1870s and 1880s, was a product of republican virtues and new-world opportunities. Wealth could be celebrated, as it was by the Baptist minister Russell Conwell in his famous lecture "Acres of Diamonds," precisely because opportunity was so abundant.[86] While Conwell urged sympathy for the poor, he qualified his compassion: "There is not a poor person in the United States who was not made poor by his own shortcomings, or by the shortcomings of some one else."[87] A more subtle celebration of "the land of millionaires" was Andrew Carnegie's popular essay on "the Gospel of Wealth" (1889).[88]

Any notion that inequality was a social problem in urgent need of remedy would struggle against the myth of egalitarian opportunity. When the celebration of wealth was combined with an evolutionary teleology, it could neutralize and even justify the new aristocratic threat – oligopoly and monopoly. An example is the work of the labour autodidact George Gunton, whose *Wealth and Progress* (1890) began by acknowledging that poverty was a serious problem and that "a greater diffusion of wealth among the masses" was highly desirable. The source of the problem, however, was not wealth. Wealth was the solution: its better distribution required "a larger aggregate production." The solution therefore was to increase wealth per capita.[89] This in turn required concentration of production, even in the form of trusts, to render both production and distribution more efficient. "All statistics show that where productive wealth is most concentrated the products are cheapest and most abundant."[90]

In the 1880s and 1890s critics of inequality challenged apologists. The idea that inequality was a primary source of social evils and conflict had a distinctly American provenance in social-gospel Protestantism, which held that social regeneration led directly to distributive justice.[91] But Christian teaching also raised questions about commutative justice. The economy presented itself to social gospellers as a vast collection of exchanges between individuals, and also between individuals and corporations with the legal status of persons. It was not clear that these exchanges conformed to Christian principles. The ideal of "just reward" thus had a longer life than did the labour theory of value. The apparent departure of the wealth-creating economy from deeply held principles of justice demanded explanation and, if possible, correction. The matter was all the more urgent because the alternative social justice promised by socialism was gathering support, not least through its claims about systemic exploitation. Were American workers being cheated and robbed of their just reward?

For social gospellers who were also economists, the question took a specific form: was the creation of industrial wealth benefitting some people while leaving others in poverty? There were two questions here, as economists well knew. First, had industrialization allowed an increase in material living standards over time for everyone, including workers? And however one replied, second: had the gaps between rich and poor been growing? Answers to these questions were an ethical imperative. Virtually all of the American economists who produced books on the subject in this period came from social-gospel backgrounds: these included Charles B. Spahr, John Bates Clark, Richard Ely, John R. Commons, and Thomas Carver.

The ethical imperative led directly to secular social science. The questions social gospellers asked required empirical answers. The limits to the available data were painfully obvious; they inspired determined, even heroic, research. As he prepared his 1896 *Essay*, Charles Spahr (1860–1904) was determined to refute optimistic interpretations of industrialization, such as that in the Englishman Robert Giffen's *The Progress of the Working Classes* (1884).[92] Spahr used a range of American and European sources to confirm the presence of inequality of both wealth and income; he also cited tax data to argue that labour bore an increasing burden of the costs of government in the United States. Like many Americans interested in the distribution question, he owed much to the great statistician Carroll D. Wright and his work for the Massachusetts Bureau of Labor Statistics.[93]

Spahr's evidence seemed to support a pessimistic interpretation. In the United States, "seven-eighths of the families hold but one-eighth of the national wealth, while one percent of the families hold more than the remaining ninety-nine." The "one percent" had entered American discourse – in 1896! As for income, "one-eighth of the families in America receive more than half of the aggregate income, and the richest one per cent receives a larger income than the poorest fifty per cent."[94] Furthermore, Spahr concluded, inequality had increased in recent decades. Here was a work that Progressives and socialists could use to good effect. Scholars pointed to data problems and Spahr's tendentious reasoning, and most economists ignored him.[95]

The American preoccupation with wealth distribution continued through the Progressive era. The economists were one set of voices within a much wider conversation. For what it is worth as an indicator of discursive trends, Google NGrams shows a steep rise in the appearance of "distribution of wealth" in American English in the early 1900s.[96] By this measure the 1900s and 1910s continued the first great age of inequality in American literary culture, as the discussion of wealth begun in the 1880s and 1890s continued through the era of trusts and monopoly.

In the transnational world of political and ethical economy, the intellectual ground was shifting in ways that few thinkers in Canada noticed at the time. The work of the American John Bates Clark (1847–1938) linked the ethical imperative and empirical research in a new theoretical framework.[97] Though assiduous borrowers from U.S. authors, few Canadians looked to Clark. He was not easy to understand, and he did not seem an apologist for laissez-faire capitalism: his positions on trusts, trade unions, and property allowed for different readings in his own time and ever since.[98] Like other progenitors of the marginalist revolution in economics, he did not shed his Christian faith in favour of a secular political economy. On the contrary: he set out to render Christian ethics compatible with a rigorous theoretical and empirical framework. In Clark's work homo economicus was not a purely self-interested maximizer of material utilities; he was also homo moralis, whose moral impulses shaped his utility calculations (this homo was gender-specific, a reminder that the entire framework assumed, and further entrenched, masculine factors of production).[99]

By 1899 Clark was offering a well-developed theory of distribution – marginal productivity.[100] Behind its emergence lay Clark's search for a natural law that reconciled the economy's evolution with moral laws. His driving impulse was a moral question: "Is present society rooted in iniquity, and does it give to a few men the earnings of many?"[101] Underneath this imperative lay his desire to counter the threat of socialism. Here, as elsewhere, the roots of neoclassical economics linked with the perceived socialist threat.

Clark applied a theory of marginal utility in use since the 1870s. In a condition of competition, capital and labour came together to convert resources into products; the return to labour, and hence the division of returns, reflected the productivity of the last unit of labour. Thus each factor of production received in proportion to what it contributed. Rewards to capitalists followed the same principle, being proportional to what they created. "This law, if it worked without friction, would give to every agent of production the amount of wealth which that agent creates."[102] The production process, assuming the presence of competitive markets for goods and labour, thus met two standards: efficiency and justice. Therefore there was no surplus or exploitation, at either micro or macro levels.[103] Clark's natural law of distribution asserted a natural harmony of interests in capitalist society, even when competition led to the rise of oligopoly.[104]

In their context Clark's ideas were deeply subversive and offered a potent challenge to contemporary labourite and socialist understandings of the distribution of wealth. Less clearly, they departed from social-gospel strictures about wealth, because they assumed that production and distribution were propelled by economic laws that functioned independently of the human conscience.[105] With perhaps less inconsistency, Clark was rejecting the old labour theory of value, while retaining the idea that labour deserved a just reward.[106] The labour theory said that values flowed from inputs of labour and that the amount of labour in commodities determined their values. Marginal utility held that value came from exchanges in markets and so varied according to consumers' utilities.[107]

Clark was also rejecting Mill's separation of distribution from production. Marginalist economics integrally connected production with distribution, which was a function of marginal productivity – the relative incomes or returns to each factor of production depended on its marginal productivity. At a level that might have been clearer to his contemporaries, Clark's departures from Mill questioned beliefs dear to labour advocates. For Clark, machinery had not reaped an unfair share of the returns to productivity, thereby generating massive inequality.

For Mill's famous statement "It is questionable if all the mechanical inventions yet made have lightened the day's toil of any human being," we may, Clark said, safely substitute, "It is the natural tendency of useful inventions to lighten the toil of workers and give them, withal, a greater reward for their work."[108] Inventions, he noted, caused "disturbances," but over time they brought rewards "in greater and greater measure as the years go by." It mattered not that such statements referred to changes in absolute material rewards rather than the distribution of either incomes or wealth. Clark was rejecting deeply held claims about historical increases in exploitation and immiseration. He was also offering a sophisticated argument to the effect that distributive justice did not require any collective redistributive action outside the natural evolution of the capitalist economy.

As John F. Henry has pointed out, Clark saw economic laws operating regularly over time and space. These laws were "natural," not historically contingent, and thus beyond contravention. Society could attempt to modify these laws according to ethical or social principles but could not defeat them.[109] Clark claimed to be uncovering the "natural law of distribution." This does not mean that morality was irrelevant, because specific individual or group behaviour could be dishonest or selfish or criminal. And at a macro-economic level, a natural law was guiding society away from the corruption of greed and wealth. In this secular economic science, natural law was a new divine law. Clark had fulfilled his youthful goal "to discover the laws of nature that reveal the divine intellect that created them."[110] The apparent consistency of his mature economics with his youthful Christian reformism cannot, however, conceal a deep ambiguity. While proclaiming the union of his ethics and his economics, he was separating empirical "fact" and ethics: "Our study may lead to a moral verdict without being itself an ethical study; we limit the inquiry to questions of fact."[111] The result was an unreconciled ambiguity between the positive and the normative: Clark suffused his empirical accounts of what happened in the economy with norms, accounts of what ought to be.[112]

In the United States scholarly reactions to Clark's early neoclassical position on distribution varied.[113] Outside academe, his challenge attracted little notice, sacrificing the opportunity and need to expose its flaws and inconsistencies.[114] In his statistical study *Poverty* (1904), Robert Hunter, a socialist and Progressive reformer with distribution central to his analysis, did not mention Clark at all. Non-academics may have neglected Clark simply because readers had more congenial scholarly alternatives. John R. Commons (1862–1945), for instance, in *The Distribution of Wealth* (1893, 1905), accepted marginal-utility theory, but his emphasis on monopoly's disruptive effects on markets and competition would have resonated with critics of inequality. "The prime importance of monopoly privileges in the distribution of wealth" had been confirmed empirically, Commons argued.[115] Capital deserved its reward, he said, but "profits may often be higher than a just distribution may warrant." Moreover, "when temporary profits have been transformed into permanent monopolies" an unjust distribution necessarily followed.[116]

Profits, and especially very large profits, were due not to any natural law – so went the argument – but to social relations and to historically contingent rights granted by society. If Canadians had sought intellectual backing for this idea, they could have found it in another founder of institutional economics – Thorstein Veblen. Veblen did not offer a specific theory of the functional distribution of income; he is remembered as a social theorist, as a theorist of institutions, and for the phrases "conspicuous consumption" and "conspicuous leisure." Yet he pushed the idea of inequality in new directions, famously rejecting the neoclassical theory of distribution. Where Clark posited a form of justice emerging within the competitive workings of the capitalist economy, Veblen saw the competitive system and its enabling rights as merely contingent outcomes of culture and institutions.[117]

Thorstein Veblen (1857–1929) offered original ideas about inequality's effects. In the *Theory of the Leisure Class* (1899) he showed how the effects of "the unequal distribution of wealth,"[118] through the historical creation of a leisure class, had effects both direct and indirect on other classes. In the process of its emergence this class withdrew means of sustenance, means of consumption, and hence energy from "the lower class" taking away from that class the energy and opportunity to learn and improve its condition. "The accumulation of wealth at the upper end of the pecuniary scale implies privation at the lower end of the scale," and that privation was cultural and spiritual as well as material.[119] As well, it strengthened "the general conservative attitude of the community," because the leisure class might well want to leave things as they were, and because its "prescriptive example of conspicuous waste and conservatism" influenced the whole community.[120]

The originality of Veblen's approach lay not so much in his perception of effects, however, as in his understanding of the culture of materiality and the way in which inequities became constitutive of community. His major works offered a sociology of distributional hierarchies in capitalist society. Instead of theorizing the functional distribution of income, he offered a theory of dysfunctional distributions in capitalist society. "Conspicuous consumption" was not simply acquisition of luxury goods; it was use of such goods to display social status, so as to acquire esteem. "In order to gain and to hold the esteem of men it is not sufficient merely to possess wealth or power. The wealth or power must be put in evidence, for esteem is awarded only on evidence."[121] The impulse to acquire status and esteem spread through society; since "conspicuous consumption" was economically non-productive, "conspicuous waste" became endemic.

Veblen transformed late-nineteenth-century ideas about inequality. He described a past era of handicraft production that was relatively egalitarian, and in which some basic Christian principles, such as brotherhood, were often norms.[122] In the nineteenth century industrialists and financiers captured greater portions of income and wealth: a point that Veblen asserted rather than proved.[123] He started from this vision of inequality, a historical backdrop to a sociology of predatory power in the industrial era. *The Theory of the Leisure Class* did not mention "inequality" or "inequalities" but rather dealt with distribution, distinction, subservience, status, emulation, and, above all, predation. The author was describing a generalized condition of predation, quests for supremacy, and an "emulative contest for mastery."[124] This condition extended into the economy, politics, judicial contests, sports, and entertainment.[125]

Here was a compelling non-socialist and non-Marxist alternative to the neoclassical economic theory of distribution. Radical critics of capitalism found much to use in Veblen's accounts of the leisure class and conspicuous waste. But few noticed the disturbing implication of his sociology: despite Veblen's own gestures towards evolution, could a follower of his believe that society was evolving out of competitive capitalism and into some form of cooperative commonwealth? If predation, emulation, and contests for mastery were so deep and pervasive, how to transcend inequality? Veblen offered no political or ideological program for escape.[126] Nevertheless, his influence extended into Canada, making him a notable source on inequality and social justice.

In trying to understand how the problem of inequality evolved in Canada in the early twentieth century, we must focus not only on known borrowings from the United States, but also on available sources missed or forgone. It was easy to miss innovations occurring

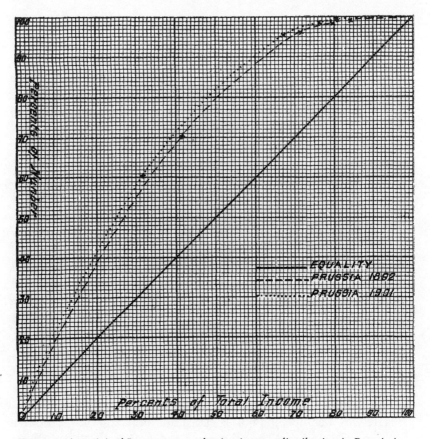

Figure 1 | An original Lorenz curve plotting income distribution in Prussia in 1892 and 1901.

in small corners of a large field. In one growing corner, statisticians led the empirical project of uncovering data on distributions. A 12-page 1905 article by a doctoral student at the University of Wisconsin may be the most influential single paper in the history of inequality studies. The student was Max O. Lorenz (1876–1959), and his graph became iconic as the Lorenz curve. Its original version plotted the percentage of the population of income earners on the vertical axis and the percentage of total income on the horizontal. If the poorest 1 per cent received 1 per cent of all income, and the poorest 2 per cent had 2 per cent of all income, and so on, the result was a straight line, indicating equality of distribution. "With an unequal distribution," Lorenz wrote, "the curves will always begin and end in the same points as with an equal distribution, but they will be bent in the middle; and the rule of interpretation will be, as the bow is bent, concentration increases."[127]

In a single representation, the graph gave the viewer the share of all income for all percentage points in the population. The graphic method allowed convenient comparisons across time and space; as Lorenz said, it "takes account of changes in wealth and population, thus putting upon a comparable basis any two communities of the most diverse conditions."[128] The temporal comparison was comprehensive, and it was immediately evident. As Lorenz said of his original graph, "a glance" showed greater concentration in 1901 than in 1892. The Lorenz curve compressed an enormous amount of information into an easily apprehended visual form. It allowed the viewer to *see* inequality and its extent. In 1912 another American statistician, Willford King, coined the term "Lorenz curve," and without explanation reversed the axes.[129] The "line of equal distribution" took the superior position; inequality was a condition of expanding inferiority below the line of perfect equality. Despite Lorenz's conscious intention to avoid normative content, the visual representation contained a standard, a baseline against which to perceive the extent of inequality. A straight line indicated perfect or universal equality. It mattered not that this condition was unattainable and undesirable, even in the view of many socialists. Lorenz's curve displayed inequality as a spatial or areal movement away from equality.

In Lorenz's work statistical rigour inextricably accompanied ethical reckonings. When he was thinking about measures of distribution, he was assisting Richard T. Ely (1854–1943), the eminent Progressive-era economist, social gospeller, and co-founder of the Christian Social Union.[130] In their *Outlines of Economics*, first written by Ely and then revised by Ely, Lorenz, and two others, the authors asked: "What is a just distribution of wealth?" Their answer merged economics with an ethics of distributive justice. The response to the conundrum "What is right living?" could be left to philosophers, they said. But not the question about distributive justice: that was one also for economists, they insisted. Their reply read like a moral corollary to Lorenz's graph. There was a standard, though probably unattainable, of universal equality of wealth (as so often in this period, the word referred probably to both income and wealth). Furthermore, an equal distribution would be "objectionable" because it would discourage "energetic members of the community."[131] The straight line of equality therefore was unattainable and objectionable; but the bulge of inequality – "the extreme inequality in wealth distribution that exists at the moment" – was a dangerous extreme, representing "swollen fortunes," "enormous fortunes," "odious" and "unregulated" monopolies.[132] Hence the ethical question: did the wealthy man have "the right to put down silk velvet on a muddy crossing to walk on it if he is rich enough to afford it"? The answer was an economist's negative, a moral censure of wasteful consumption: "When a man tramples in the mire the fruit of human industry, he tramples with it human rights and humanity."[133]

Ely and his authorial assistants struggled to find a coherent distributive justice, and they stopped well short of redistribution. They confronted Clark's marginal theory of distribution and, like others at the time, found a way to both accept and reject it. They did so by making a distinction between personal distribution and returns to factors of production. To say that the returns to land reflected the value of its marginal product did not mean that the landowner had earned those returns or should receive them.[134] This distinction allowed the Progressive theorist to separate the ethics of distribution from any "natural" workings of the economy and the market system. The authors also rejected a static-equilibrium model: income determination, they argued, was a function of a range of cultural, institutional, and historical conditions.[135]

Ely and his co-authors also confronted directly one of the most common objections, in their time and in ours, to limiting capitalists' accumulation of income or wealth – such limits would reduce incentives for and efforts by innovators, entrepreneurs, and investors. Their answer was clear and simple: incentives existed even in the absence of unearned incomes and bloated luxury. "There is little danger of discouraging industry and thrift. If the highest incomes were $100,000 per year, men would struggle just as hard as they do now to get into the highest class."[136] Furthermore, they argued, a re-direction of some inflated profits and rents away from luxury consumption and towards production would yield economic benefit.

Having dealt with objections to a program of distributive reform, the authors proposed "tests" for distributive justice. All human beings, even the lowliest, must be looked upon as ends, not as means to the happiness of others. The crucial test was "needs," difficult as these may be to measure: "not what the individual asks for, but what is required for a full development of his powers." The test of "needs" is met when the individual received everything necessary "for the full development of his [sic] powers" and to become "a good citizen."[137] In its context this was a bold move, risking a gesture in the direction of the socialist emphasis on needs. The gesture was quickly withdrawn. The pauperizing effect of charity remained a threat. Even if monopoly meant an odious distortion of just distribution, and even if the wealthy were prone to wasteful luxury, the rights of property must be preserved. Society had the right, even the duty, to modify methods of wealth accumulation, but only through "control of monopolistic privileges," the elimination of "fraud and favouritism," and taxation of inheritances.[138]

Several points can be made about this definition of distributive justice. First, it was hardly unique in its time: such formulations appeared in many other American authors, whether economists or not, who were sympathetic to reform politics in the Progressive era. Second, Ely and his co-authors showed early neoclassical economics' debt to the problem of the distribution of wealth. Their *Outlines of Economics* became a popular economics textbook, widely used and often revised and reprinted between the 1890s and the 1930s. The distribution question was not a series of afterthoughts, but a central issue in economics, conjoining ethics and scientific analysis. Third, the distributive justice formulated here was an updating of liberal and utilitarian ideals in the era of monopoly and oligopoly capital. "There is only one sense in which we must regard men as equal, and that is that the happiness of one is as important as the happiness of another."[139] This textbook's history of economic thought expressed no reservations about Bentham's "utilitarian philosophy, with its famous first principle or goal of social action – the greatest happiness of the greatest number."[140]

In the end, the program of Ely and his co-authors was not about redistribution. The authors were reducing the problem of inequality to the test of absolute standards of living. Their program, even if fulfilled, would not have shifted societal-level distribution or allocations of wealth. The space between perfect equality and actual distribution in Lorenz's graph would not shrink with anti-trust laws, elimination of fraud, or inheritance taxes. The writers never outlined "what is required for the full development of [individuals'] powers."

Ely and his co-writers may have sensed that their program was incomplete. Certainly their discussion was replete with conditional tenses and wishful thinking about modest reforms that "would be of some assistance." Certainly they feared, as did so many con-temporaries, that their answers might not adequately counter the appeal of socialism. "The right of private property, like other social institutions, is ever on trial."[141] They pushed themselves to find a way out of this dilemma: how do we rescue society from its vast inequalities while protecting the rights of private property? They found a way. Out of the yawning gulf between equality and reality in Lorenz's graph emerged a seemingly powerful answer: a perfect equality that would counter, if not eliminate, the reality of inequal-ity. The answer was equality – not of rights, not of condition – but of opportunity. This equality was known in the nineteenth century; formulations are present in J.S. Mill, T.H. Green, and other liberal philosophers.[142] Now, in the Progressive era, the principle would be proclaimed with greater intensity and frequency. As a reformist political ideal, equality of opportunity was probably a Progressive-era invention.[143] Here, it seemed, was what all citizens, including workers, really wanted and needed. "It is not so much high price that disturbs the modern man as it is inequality of opportunity."[144] Why were "unregulated monopolies" so "odious" and so "opposed to the principle of the laws of civilized nations"? Because "they are opposed to that endeavour to secure equality of opportunity which is fundamental in modern democracy."[145] Education was the path to equality of opportunity, and it became a recurring theme in Ely's textbook. One wonders whether any economics textbook ever paid such sustained attention to the subject. The education it touted was practical and utilitarian – an essential contributor to economic effi-ciency and growth. It was also a "factor in elevating the standard of life" and a key to upward social mobility.[146] Here was a real equality in the era of inequality.[147]

EUROPEAN CONTRIBUTIONS

Lorenz and Ely collaborated in one corner of a transnational colloquy on the distribution of wealth, wherein two decisive advances took place elsewhere. They were well aware of developments in Europe, and they certainly knew about the work of the Italian economist and sociologist Vilfredo Pareto (1848–1923).[148] Pareto pioneered, among other contributions, the comparative analysis of distributions of income and wealth across nations and developed a sophisticated mathematical argument for symmetry in distribution across societies. Pareto compared income levels (x) with the number of persons above each level (N) and found that for the societies he studied there was a logarithmic relationship between N and x. The implications of "Pareto's Law" were immediately evident, as American reviews of his *Cours d'économie politique* (1897) revealed.[149] If the distribution of income varied minimally across time and space, then egalitarian policies and institutional change could do little to alter this fact.[150] Pareto's findings offered powerful aid to critics of socialism and to those who rejected the idea that "the rich are getting richer and poor poorer."

Pareto made another seminal contribution, one that became central to welfare economics. Pareto efficiency, or Pareto optimality, was a general principle about efficiency in the allocation of resources or outcomes, applicable to a wide range of phenomena. Vis-à-vis materials, it indicated that, for a certain stock of goods, the distribution was Pareto optimal when there was no feasible alternative in which at least one person was better off and no one was worse off. One could apply it in social policy: an allocation of resources was non-optimal when it was still possible to make at least one individual better off, in his or her own estimation, while keeping others as well off as they felt before. The subsequent history of this concept is not relevant here.

The point is that this great era of inequality had produced yet another fundamental contribution to the economics and ethics of distribution – and we may compare Pareto efficiency to the others mentioned above in this chapter. It remained seminal, despite the connection it assumed between efficiency and ethics being problematic, and even though it might co-exist with extremely unequal wealth distribution. The ideological implications of Pareto's ideas, and their relationship to liberalism, remain the subjects of debate.[151] At the time, many observers, even among economists, missed their significance. Those familiar with them could not have missed their conservative political implications. Pareto optimality sealed welfare in a box, protecting it from any politics of redistribution. It was a severely limiting principle of justice: how could a society assist the oppressed or dispossessed, without worsening, in their own estimation, the situation of oppressors or those at the top of the income scale?[152]

Another statistical contribution of this generation would have far greater impact than observers realized in its time. Some challenged Pareto's comparative analyses and his proposed methods for measuring the concentration of wealth. In the early 1900s another Italian scholar was also finding weaknesses in the measures sustaining Pareto's claims to uniformity of wealth distribution across time and space.[153] Corrado Gini (1884–1965) worked for years on his refinements and in 1914 produced his final "index of concentration." The Gini coefficient has become the most common measure of inequality. Despite its weaknesses, it has framed all recent discussions of inequality as much as has the Lorenz curve, to which it bears a close relationship. It is used particularly in comparing income inequality among nations and across other geographical units. The Gini coefficient is the area between the line of perfect equality and the Lorenz curve, divided by the area of the triangle under the line of equality. Like the Lorenz curve, it is easy to comprehend: it produces a number that falls between 0 and 1, where a higher number indicates more intense concentration.[154] Calculation of the coefficient from a list of values does not require modern computers; the formulae were available at the time Gini developed it.

WRESTLING WITH DISTRIBUTIVE JUSTICE

The Progressive era had witnessed the emergence of a range of secular solutions to inequality, but would they work? Despite ongoing controversies and continuing data limitations, the empirical evidence for inequality had been established more securely than ever before. At the same time limits were being placed on the reform impulse. It was a great paradox of the era of inequality that even as evidence for inequality was expanding and as the tools for analysing it were becoming more sophisticated, new theoretical and ideological innovations were attempting to reduce the scope of distributive justice, although a practitioner in the new field of sociology and a Catholic theologian articulated decidedly more expansive visions.

A good example of narrowing scope was the comprehensive 1915 study of income and wealth by the American Willford King (1880–1962).[155] This work showed how far studies of wealth had moved in a few decades. King's book contained 58 tables and 29 figures, including several Lorenz curves. While noting the many problems with national-level data, the author concluded that 1.6 per cent of all U.S. families controlled about 19 per cent of all incomes, and that "since 1896, there has occurred a marked concentration of income in the hands of the very rich."[156]

Progressive critics of monopoly capitalism could find plenty of useful evidence in King's study, but its language and ethics downplayed the social gospel.[157] King favoured wider distribution of income and wealth, but for utilitarian reasons: to distribute "incentive" more broadly and so advance "economic progress."[158] King's empirical edifice offered elaborate reassurance, even absolution: the sum of individual utilities *was* being maximized, and per-capita income *had been* increasing rapidly.[159] In the concluding pages, King proposed his solution to the problem of inequality. The laws of supply and demand applied to labour as much as to goods. It followed that the lower classes should limit their population growth.[160] The state therefore did have a role to play in distributive justice: it must apply "proper educational and eugenic measures."[161] This major study of income and wealth distributions ended by arguing against redistributive measures, and blaming inequality on low-income families.

Between the 1880s and the 1910s American economists had accomplished a remarkable feat. Despite serious limitations in available data, and even before the existence of income taxes and national accounting systems, they had created an extensive empirical foundation for explaining distributions of both wealth and income. They differed over measurement of distributions, possible solutions (and even the need for them), and the role of the state. Nevertheless they had confirmed that inequalities were extreme and had been increasing since about 1880. Late-twentieth-century economic historians would confirm their broad conclusions about the so-called Gilded Age.

Society-wide distributions of income and wealth were a central focus of political economy from John Stuart Mill through the Progressive era. Distribution also appeared in the early development of sociology in the United States – and with it, a search for secular solutions very different from Willford King's. Lester Frank Ward (1841–1913), for example, rejected Herbert Spencer but saw inequality as endemic in natural laws of evolution.[162] Environment and evolution acted together to shape animals, said Ward; but "man" shaped environment and evolution and could plan this collective act of shaping according to shared ethical standards and "intelligence."[163] This evolutionary "sociogeny" left plenty of room for human agency. For Ward, the doctrine of laissez-faire was a dangerous superstition; the state was the greatest human invention for realizing human well-being. The present era suffered from "under-government" – the state had failed to keep pace, in its essential regulatory and protective functions, with the rapid changes occurring in modern industrial society.[164] Poverty and inequality were inseparably connected, Ward insisted. The poor tended to be enterprising and hard-working; inequalities of talent and brain-power were symptomatic of "inequality of *circumstances*" and, above all, of unequal access to knowledge (a major theme in Ward's sociology).[165] Ward also related social evils and inequities to the multiple inequalities of women. Social reform, in his view, was impossible without equality for women: equality of rights, of access to paid work, and of access to education. For those who had the stamina to wade through his books, Ward offered plenty of intellectual ammunition for a radical critique of inequality, and he offered preliminary justifications for a welfare state.

Generations of scholars who discovered the problem of inequality and its ethical correlate, distributive justice, were living in the long wake of an intellectual and cultural revolution: "the replacement of Aristotelian ethics and Christian morality by a new type of decision making which may be termed instrumental reasoning or cost-benefit analysis."[166] However they might finesse the instrumental and utilitarian paradigms, those who thought about distribution in the century and a half after Adam Smith were seeking explanations for inequality that lay outside older conceptions of honour, virtue, merit, and status. They sought rules or principles of justice that could justify some inequality while guiding a necessary triumph over inequality where their principles declared it to be a social evil. By the early twentieth century that long search had failed to produce stable verities around which any large community of believers might cohere. For all its sophistication and its empirical depth, social science had not produced answers to questions that began in ethics. The powerful challenge of socialists and communists – those who denied altogether the liberal conception of inequality – generated a range of ideological responses. An inclusive egalitarianism – a conception of equality that might extinguish material, racial, gender, and other inequalities – was yet to be imagined, at least by the liberal theorists of distribution. By the late nineteenth and early twentieth centuries, therefore, the problem of inequality was ubiquitous. There were many answers, but all were fragile and fugitive.

*

In the Progressive era there was one path to the problem of inequality – perhaps the most original of all – that took inspiration from sources before Adam Smith and prior to the Enlightenment. John A. Ryan (1865–1945) was a U.S. Catholic theologian, an economist, and a moral philosopher. Inequality was central to Ryan's books *A Living Wage* (1906) and *Distributive Justice* (1916). In Ryan's work current economic inequalities were epiphenomena, by-products of prior conditions. According to Ryan, ancient ideals such as just reward, just price, "*aequalitas rei ad rem*" (equivalence of exchange), and customary rights had lost force and credibility in the great historical disruptions of the previous century. New conceptions of justice had failed to cope with the new realities or to win widespread support.

Ryan dismissed "the greatest happiness of the greatest number": that notion was "equivalent in the concrete to the happiness of the majority," and so discounted the happiness of the minority. The hedonistic principle furthermore was not consistent with reason or "rational benevolence."[167] Laissez-faire was a pernicious variant of a liberalism whose contradictions Ryan perceived and exposed. Liberalism founded liberty on the individual right to property and on equality of rights; but the former right allowed inequalities of condition that compromised or negated the latter. The tradition of Hegelian idealism in which British new liberalism was rooted was a dangerous snare, because it saw rights based in a "Universal Reason" from which the individual derived all his worth and sacredness. To subordinate rights to a metaphysical entity risked moral relativism and the deification of the state: should any individual be seen as ceasing to embody Universal Reason, that individual may lawfully be put to death. The correlate of Universal Reason and liberal organicism was a new and pernicious inequality – "the lives of those who are less useful to society are essentially inferior to the lives of those who are more useful."[168]

Ryan's central moral principle derived from a theory of natural rights, and I summarize it as follows: The source of natural rights was the dignity of the human person, whose essential needs determined their scope. A man's natural rights were as many and as extensive as the liberties, opportunities, and possessions that would support the reasonable maintenance and development of his personality.[169] This principle meant that all workers, as individuals, had the right to a "Living Wage" or minimum income. They possessed this right not as members of society; not in proportion to a putative "product" of labour; and not as a positive right granted with reference to a wider social welfare or social utility. They had this right because they were human: it was "individual, natural, and absolute." Ryan's natural-rights principle may be compared with the distributive principles we looked at above (those of Hobhouse, Hobson, Pareto, and Pigou / Dalton). There is more than one obvious difference, but one stands out. The earlier principles were relativist and contingent: they involved net gains, increases and decreases, and gains under specific conditions. Ryan's principle was unconditional and absolute. The right to a material minimum was "natural" – it came from the natural, existential condition of being human.[170]

What then were essential needs? Ryan sought to invest his distributive justice with practicable meaning. A living wage did not mean an annual income for an individual, or an income sufficient to provide mere food, clothing, and shelter. It signified an income sufficient to support a family (he assumed a male breadwinner family as the norm) and allow modest savings, access to cultural goods, and savings for the education of children. The standard was high (over $600 per year for a family of six in 1906) and, if realized, would by itself have substantially narrowed income inequalities.[171] How to achieve the universal minimum? Ryan's principle of natural right granted to the state a duty of extensive intervention in the economy. Statute would enforce the universal living wage, and such intervention was not a violation of rights of property. To compel a person to work for less than a living wage was a form of theft. "In a wide sense it is also an attack upon his life."[172] A statutory minimum therefore would fulfil the state's duty to protect life and property.[173]

Ryan's work was a particular American variant of social Catholicism. His intellectual roots and stated debts included Aristotle, Aquinas, nineteenth-century Catholic thinkers, and papal encyclicals.[174] A later communitarian perspective inspired by the Second Vatican Council, or Vatican II (1962–65), gave Catholics different grounds for arguing for redistribution and for both minimum incomes and income ceilings.[175] Until then, Ryan's natural-law justice was not superseded.[176] What is remarkable, in the context of 1916, is how far his natural-law approach enabled – perhaps even required – consideration of the moral limits to income and wealth. Look again at his natural-rights principle: the right to a material minimum. It also implied upper limits: one's rights extended to nothing more than what one needed for maintenance and the development of personality. Virtually alone among economists of his time, Ryan contemplated not only the "duty of distributing superfluous wealth" but also the "legal limitation of fortunes."[177] He discussed even the specific levels beyond which incomes and inherited wealth were "superfluous" and subject to redistribution. He proposed two means of redistribution: voluntary giving enforced by church sanction (one would expect this from a Catholic thinker); and graduated income and inheritance taxes. He endorsed top marginal tax rates that were extraordinarily high by the standards of his time: they could not be confiscatory, but could be as much as 100 per cent on the greatest incomes.[178] Despite these rigorous applications of his natural-rights principle, he rejected the idea of legal limits on total wealth as "socially inexpedient."[179]

Here we have arrived at a fragile moment, a revealing compromise. This pragmatic concession allowed conditional acceptance of standard capitalist practices.[180] Ryan had reached the limit of non-socialist argument for redistribution in the Progressive era. As much as any American, he created intellectual justifications for the welfare state, and he later became a prominent supporter of Franklin Roosevelt's New Deal legislation.

THE LIMITS OF LIBERAL DISTRIBUTIVE JUSTICE

Ryan was exposing, and trying to avoid, inconsistences in the liberal understanding of inequality. New liberals and Progressives had themselves made those inconsistencies glaringly apparent. Unearned income, capitalist parasitism, conspicuous waste, costly externalities: did not economic efficiency and justice require that the state intervene to appropriate or eliminate these systemic products of industrial capitalism?[181] The question exposed the contradiction in liberal thought on inequality in the Progressive era. The state had the duty to protect the right of private property, including property in its corporate forms; why did it not have to recover, appropriate if necessary, wealth or income that had been unearned, stolen, wasted, or even destroyed? And when the economy created wealth in the form of a national dividend belonging to the citizens who created it, should not the duty to protect property require the state to preserve and use such wealth? Such were the unanswered questions in the liberal politics of inequality and distributive justice in the Progressive era.

Liberal distributive justice reflected unresolved tensions within the heritage of Enlightenment rationalism and instrumentalism. Perhaps also it revealed the class position of the philosophers and economists who put inequality and distribution at the centre of their intellectual worlds. They were, after all, the sons of country parsons, farmers, lawyers, or small proprietors, and they had ascended to the common rooms of Oxford and Cambridge or the halls of venerable American colleges and universities. In the Gilded Age and the Progressive era, many had the ear of politicians and businessmen, and sat on boards and commissions with prominent men.

I conclude this long reflection with an anecdote. While not clearly an exemplar, the story serves to raise a question: was the problem of inequality somehow deflected or muted when its proponents visited Canada? In 1906 a leading English exponent of unearned income and capitalist parasitism crossed the Atlantic. It seems that John A. Hobson found no such evils in Canada. He detected instead "a spirit of boundless confidence and booming enterprise," especially in the big railway companies. In Montreal – a city notorious for its inequalities and its slums – he "could see no signs of a slum population, and beggars and loafers were not in evidence." In Ottawa he met Rodolphe Lemieux, Canada's Liberal minister of labour. Did he ask Lemieux whether the Dominion government was considering welfare legislation or graduated taxation of the kind the United Kingdom was then considering? Apparently not. Lemieux informed him that "we have no poor," and the English visitor recorded no personal doubt about the claim.[182] The polite conversation of these respectable gentlemen would not be disturbed by mention of such radical notions as graduated taxation, unearned increment, or surplus value.

CHAPTER TWO

First Sightings of Inequality in the Canadian Colonies (1790s–1830s)

Amury Girod was a farmer, author, and transatlantic migrant. In 1835 he wrote the following about property and its distribution: "Property is one of the main causes of all good and all evil in society. If it is equally distributed, knowledge and power will be also ... A just proportion of these four things – property, knowledge, power and liberty – grant to men the capacity to enjoy the greatest possible happiness. But if, whether by force or by fraud, property passes into the hands of a few individuals, as is beginning to happen in Canada, then we see millions in poverty ... and society finds itself in such a sad state that it is forever enveloped by slavery, degradation, and crime."[1]

Girod was expressing a coherent idea about property and its accumulation. He was announcing the existence of a problem – the problem of inequality. Where property was more equally distributed, he insisted, so also was knowledge and power. A "just proportion" was basic to liberty. Where wealth fell into the hands of a few individuals, as he believed was happening in Lower Canada, one saw not only great poverty but also an increase in crime, social evils, and even a condition of slavery. In Lower Canada in the 1830s, Girod was not alone in expressing such alarm. An editorial in *La Minerve* put the matter clearly: "Of all aristocracies, the aristocracy of wealth is the worst, and certainly the most dangerous, because it can only come about through political upheavals . . . A spirit of intrigue and discord insinuates itself everywhere."[2]

The idea has a familiar ring, almost two centuries later. Replace aristocracy with plutocracy or the "1 per cent," and we feel at home. But let us pause: while recognizing the presence of a familiar idea, we should not hear only the echoes of our own preoccupations. These

words come from a particular time and place – Lower Canada in the
1830s – and take their meaning from a context different from our
own. Specific words alert us to differences that are not merely seman-
tic: *aristocratie*, *liberté*, *esclavage*, and even *propriété*. Our translation
must be historical, a journey into a distant political culture.

As we return to the 1830s, my intention is not to revise interpretations of the Rebellions of the 1830s or to enter into discussions
about the beginnings of liberalism in Canada. There is little in what
follows to reshape our understanding of the political thought of the
Patriotes or of their contemporaries in Upper Canada. My goal is to
observe an early identification of the problem of inequality – a distinctively Canadian articulation of inequality in its colonial context.
This chapter begins with a four-part survey of Lower Canada in
the early nineteenth century, looking at the influence of the Roman
Catholic church, the intrusion of money into rural communities,
constitutional problems, and the appearance of an egalitarian sensibility. These topics all connect to a theme: the problem of inequality
perceived, and bound within, a colonial commercial and agricultural
political economy.

We begin with the more populous colony, Lower Canada, and turn
mid-chapter to Upper Canada in the same era, before we examine
egalitarian reform in the 1830s in both Canadas. The two colonies
afford an opportunity to witness similar articulations of inequality
appearing in differing religious and ethno-linguistic contexts.

LOWER CANADA

The discovery of inequality in 1830s Lower Canada was the work
of radical reformers, some of whom were republicans, among that
diverse political miscellany known as Patriotes. The inequality they
perceived differed from later articulations of the problem, not least
because the word "*inégalité*" was absent from their discourse on
economic matters. How, then, can we say that they were discussing inequality at all? A concept of inequality was surely present in
their repeated condemnation of unjust divisions of material possession and advantage and in their assumption of a causal connection
between the advantages of a few and the disadvantages of many.
"The monopolizing of the best resources of the country ... the rise
and dominance of a small number," said Augustin-Norbert Morin,
related directly to "oppression and servitude for the mass of habi-

tants in the province regardless of class or origin."[3] This oppression of the many by the few, at once both political and economic, was not simply a matter of ethnicity. It was a societal corruption associated with *privilège*, which in this rhetorical frame no longer meant the just preferment owing to men of virtue. The word was bearing a new, pejorative weight.

How are we to make sense of this articulation of the problem of inequality? Where did it come from, and what if any conception of distributive justice did it express? To answer these questions we should begin before the 1830s, and catch glimpses of the world into which these political reformers were born. In so far as imagination allows, we may try to enter a culture of which the Catholic church of Lower Canada was a constituent element. Augustin-Norbert Morin, quoted above, was like many of his Patriote contemporaries: born to a large farming family and educated in Catholic schools and the Seminaire de Québec, he had to choose between a career in the church or a career in law. The Catholic church in Lower Canada saw and lamented the movement of young men like Morin into the secular professions. The church was disturbed by the impiety of the Patriotes and the high non-attendance rates in pro-Patriote communities.[4] The seminaries certainly contributed to the secular tendencies, not least through borrowings from Europe and an education in the classics of the ancient world; they sought, however, to contain the wisdom of pagan authors within the Catholic scholastic heritage.[5] These borrowings, and the secular language of Lower-Canadian politicians and journalists, should not obscure the extent to which Catholicism was a formative influence. The point needs underlining: in colonial Canada the problem of inequality had its roots in religious thought and in a religious containment of Enlightenment rationalism.

The Catholic church had a long history of response to the world of commerce and finance. Commerce was a material realm that appeared to lie beyond the control and discursive capacity of the clergy, or so it often feared. The long history of theological response to the sin of usury was part of the history of accommodation and resistance to the world of commerce. The Old Testament in particular contains many strict injunctions against lending money at interest or profiting from a loan. The injunctions remained intact in the thirteenth century of Thomas Aquinas: "It is by its very nature unlawful to take payment for the use of money lent."[6] In late medieval and early modern Europe there were ways of engaging in business and creating credit that did not violate the prohibition on usury. From the sixteenth century on it was clear that the prohibition applied only to acquiring gain or profit without any effort, expense, or risk. As for loans at interest, in 1745 the papal encyclical *Vix pervenit* specified the constraints more clearly and cited an ideal of "common good" as a criterion of justice. Contracts with interest made "in the spirit of upholding the common good" avoided the usury prohibition.[7]

Despite efforts at clarity and compromise, the prohibition on usury "stood astride the European credit markets" in unresolved tension with its exemptions.[8] The tension was fully evident in New France, where the church's strict ban on loans with interest coincided with commercial contracts for advances of merchandise that included high interest rates. After the Conquest of 1759, British law permitted loans at interest, although the permitted rates varied over time. The tension persisted, according to Christine Hudon, because the church in Lower Canada clung to the old position that to lend with interest was to commit the sin of usury and so denied the sacraments to a number of usurers. By the early nineteenth century a degree of flexibility had appeared, but Hudon maintains that priests in the confessional instructed parishioners to justify lending practices and to be sure that the recourse to loans with interest was a last resort. In some quarters, especially among teachers familiar with the theological debates, one might hear defences of interest, but it was not until the 1830s that a new and more flexible definition of usury began to emerge.[9]

Usury was at the tip of an iceberg. The Catholic encounter with the world of finance and commerce went much further than a series of changing teachings on lending. The encounter was rooted in Catholic understandings of property and wealth, which have attracted the attention of generations of scholars. At the risk of oversimplifying a complex set of principles, a brief summary is necessary, because the teachings helped shape how educated Lower Canadians reacted to the political economy of the 1820s and 1830s. The authority of Aquinas remained solid. Human actors, in this theology, exercised free will but were constrained within a hierarchical order ordained by God: "*Omnis potestas a Deo*" (All power comes from God). The moral necessity of attaining spiritual ends applied to all human action, in all spheres including the economic. "Human action should be a continual prayer," as the Italian scholar Amintore Fanfani put it; there was no rationalizing frame for human action other than the attainment of God's ends.[10] But how to reconcile these principles with the mundane necessity of business calculations relating to investment, credit, prices, and costs? The answer lay in understanding business necessities as means towards specific ends, and the final end must be spiritual. It followed that the Catholic business person might have to accept the more costly alternative, if the cheaper option violated spiritual ends.

In this conception of things material and spiritual, all earthly goods were means, not ends in themselves. As Aquinas said: "Temporal things are lawfully desired, not as our main and final goal, but as helps towards eternal happiness, since they may be used to support the life of the body and to serve as instruments in performing virtuous acts."[11] The principle applied both to wealth and to property; ultimately property belonged to God and was held in trust by legitimate owners for ends that were both spiritual and social. It followed that wealth itself was not condemnable because it was a gift of God. Nevertheless the possession of wealth was contingent on the means of its acquisition and use. Wealth might be acquired only by lawful means; its amount must be limited to what is necessary for corporeal sustenance and for the support of others. These constraints on the accumulation of wealth were severe. As Henry of Langenstein and other scholastics insisted, labour and investment and acquisitive effort were lawful and justifiable; but once a person sought to accumulate riches for goals such as higher social status, or greater power or wealth for his sons, then the seeking of wealth fell prey to the sins of avarice and pride.[12] Such constraints led R.H. Tawney to conclude that the Catholic theorist "condemned as a sin precisely that effort to achieve a continuous and unlimited increase in wealth which modern societies applaud as meritorious."[13]

The medieval suspicion of commerce waned, and in the centuries after Aquinas the justification of wealth widened. It was accepted that exceptional talents or qualities might justify status and wealth compatible with those talents or qualities. New conceptions of production allowed room for bankers and traders, who were no longer seen as parasites. To work, to save, and to expand a business in order to provide for future generations was no longer regarded as immoderate or avaricious. Quite the contrary: to expand a business was to serve God, because it enhanced one's capacity to serve others and to help others in acquiring corporeal sustenance. The biblical strictures on wealth were to be understood in this light. Luke 16:13 appeared to censure wealth: "Ye cannot serve God and mammon." But in the Catholic reading, well before the eighteenth century, such verses condemned sinful "man," not wealth, and the censure was read together with such verses as Luke 14:13–14: "But when thou makest a feast, call the poor, the maimed, the lame, and the blind: And thou shalt be blessed."

Despite these and other shifts in the early modern centuries, the church remained aware of the great perils facing investors, lenders, and traders. Tensions and ambiguities persisted. Where intention as much as action determined the line between justice and avarice, the world of traders lay beyond easy moral judgment and control. The uncertainty led to a long series of church ordinances relating to commutative justice: commands about the just price and the just wage, injunctions against adulteration and false measures, injunctions against working on holidays, and strictures on lending and interest. The eighteenth-century church was fully engaged in the subordination of economic activity to spiritual principles. In Lower Canada the church, preoccupied late in the century and afterwards with the evils of the French Revolution, was slow to respond to the challenge of capitalism. The challenge was on the horizon, however. New and powerful heresies were appearing – the idea of individual economic utility, for instance, and ideas about individual happiness. Pope Gregory XVI saw the threat when he attacked liberalism in his 1832 encyclical *Mirari vos*, widely circulated in Lower Canada.[14] Perhaps Leo XII had also seen it in 1825 when he declared that usury had "grown strong in present times" and called attention to "those who boasted to be liberators of human happiness."[15] *Mirari vos* was also about the spread of "indifferentism," and religious indifference was of great concern to priests and educators in Lower Canada. As one parish priest said in 1817, the "spirit of impiety" was spreading with the growth of prosperity through trade and industry.[16]

As Peter Moogk and Frank Abbott have argued, the dualities of flesh and spirit, body and soul, material and spiritual were deep-rooted in the Christianity of New France, and succeeding generations inherited these distinctions. "The Church warned that the temptations of the physical world came in many forms and had various guises," and they spawned greed, lust, envy, and gluttony.[17] In its *mandements*, catechisms, rituals, and schools, the church had a vast array of mechanisms whereby it could inculcate and enforce its moral censure of material and bodily sins. Historians have taught us that the relationship between church and parishioners was complex, that behaviour often defied clerical teaching, and that habitants lived in a culture that contained mixes of popular belief, non-Christian customs, and "peasant pragmatism."[18] We cannot assume that parishioners, whether habitant farmers or seigneurs or urban professionals, took the church's prohibitions literally and acted on them. Nevertheless, we can say that the material–spiritual duality penetrated a culture in which secular and spiritual cannot be separated and nourished a moral sensibility highly attuned to the presence of greed.

It is in this context that we must understand the changing meanings of "privilege." Privilege, like its material manifestations, was part of the natural order. It meant not only material entitlement but also status and many signs of preferment. To live in a Catholic parish was to witness at many levels the connection between affluence and social hierarchy. The church itself was a place where one saw the material contained by the spiritual, where the sacred was manifest in the ornate tapestry of altar, candles, cross, and priestly vestments. The church was also a spiritual and social hierarchy where one paid honour to virtue and merit, where families sat in pews according to their rank. One participated not as an individual, but as a member of one's family and also as a member of a community, which included even the men smoking their pipes outside the church. The church was a site for the public enactment of community, family, and patriarchy. The parish had its own means of influence over the priest and the church, including gossip, letters of denunciation, non-compliance, and the giving and withholding of tithes and other support. The curé could not afford to ignore the opinion of his parishioners, and it was even possible for the community to petition for the removal of a priest who was believed to have committed the sin of usury.[19]

Church rituals were a realization, even a performance of community. As Ollivier Hubert says, "For a rite to exist, a social consensus must be established, and everybody must act as though they accept it."[20] The sacred space of the church was a site of power, where the institution asserted its hegemony through the performance of an array of rituals. At the same time as the choreography of word, gesture, and sacred objects established a distance between priest and communicant, and even as social divisions were enacted in the spatial distribution of worshippers, there was also a process of

integration. In the ritual of the Mass, both priests and communicants were helping to create the sacred. Their attitudes, movements,
postures, and words drew communicants into the collective ritual.
Even the disobedient could participate, for they provoked corrective
mandements and renewed their efforts to normalize behaviour.[21]

This hierarchical but integrative community experienced new disruptions in the last half of the eighteenth and the early nineteenth
centuries.[22] As markets, commercial capital, and systems of debt and
credit penetrated further into rural communities, they introduced
alien forces seemingly beyond the control of community. Wealth,
hitherto either the just reward for effort or merit or the sign of the
benevolent hand of God, now arose in a domain outside the moral
parameters of community and church. To people for whom power
and authority were visible and inclusive, embracing the communicant in enclosed spaces – to those for whom the holders of material
wealth were identifiable persons – capital, prices, and credit must
have seemed alien and capricious forces. They were governed neither
by community nor by any discernible laws or rules – mysterious
forces operating in an unseen world.

The mental and moral response to commerce must remain difficult
terrain for the historian. At a more mundane and less conjectural
level, we can discern responses. The visible sign of family status in
the community was the pew, which required a level of prosperity
to obtain. In many places the cost of a pew was rising in the late
eighteenth and early nineteenth centuries, and the necessary prosperity was no longer so tightly linked to inherited land. The rural
parish was becoming a more fluid social space, especially where a
rural bourgeoisie appeared and competed with small proprietors for
pews.[23] The sale of pews to the highest bidder detached the pew, and
hence the status of one's family, from its connection to the inherited,
long-established patrimony. Losers in the bidding for a pew were
receiving a sharp lesson in the power of money. In the Richelieu
valley, Allan Greer tells us, habitants responded by demanding a
hereditary system for transmitting the entitlement to one's pew.[24]

The problem with commerce was that it detached virtue, merit,
and honour from their locus in the community. A parish might petition for the removal of a priest who had committed usury. How
could one remove a usurious merchant or banker? What if any control did the small proprietor have over the terms of credit? What

limits on usury or greed constrained the lenders and price fixers who were outside the community and not even visible? The questions were urgent for habitants who sought credit. They were also pressing for the professionals – notaries and *avocats* – who were involved directly in the negotiation of debt and credit. And among the notaries and *avocats* and other literate Catholics who read newspapers in the early nineteenth century, it was clear that the usurers were defying both community and church. "Certain it is," said the money-lenders and their apologists, "that private interest is public good."[25] The liberal calculus was an explicit rejection of the Catholic notion of common good.

Catholic teaching was surely one ingredient in the moral assault of Louis-Joseph Papineau on the political schemer and commercial *"parvenu"* who stood outside the bonds of community. He was, said Papineau, a *"Thersite de sentiment de nos Conseils,"* referring to Thersites, the greedy and evil-tongued man slain by Achilles. "The spirit of Thersites in our Councils has begun by sweeping everything under the carpet. Fortune and success in commercial speculations have brought him to the first rank of society, where they bestow on him the greatest honour, as if he had retained both modesty and moderation; but what renders his arrogance most unbearable, is that without losing the rusty coarseness of the streetsweeper, he has become intoxicated by his good fortune and is puffed up by the arrogance of a parvenu."[26]

What had given the elite its audacious superiority? According to another source in 1835, it was not only "the power of place" but also "the power of money, not of real money but of a fictional credit." This "system of paper money" infiltrated the countryside, because since the conquest "our habitants were so imprudent as to become used to cash, even though it was not hard currency that could be accepted by all people, and even though it had no value that would be accepted by people outside our walls."[27]

In a civilized society, claimed Amury Girod, all wealth was the product of labour. "Commerce belongs to the unproductive class in society; commerce alone profits, while agriculture, the linchpin of public happiness, languishes, together with industry."[28] When the Patriotes and Upper Canadian reformers adopted an anti-corporate, "hard money" response to the "market revolution," and struggled to create the alternative of democratic commerce and peoples' banks, they were offering a moral and egalitarian answer to "the concentration of wealth in a small number of hands."[29]

From *richesse* to *luxe, cupidité, corruption*: the shift in the language of reformers and eventually of republicans owed much to the Catholic teachings on wealth and commerce. The schools and colleges from which many of the *canadien* reformers graduated contributed another strand to the moral critique of mercantile wealth. As Louis-Georges Harvey has suggested, "The teachings of Roman history show that corruption begins in luxury and expands with the concentration of wealth in a few hands."[30] Lower Canadians were encountering the same dilemma that J.G.A Pocock found in the genesis of republican virtue in the eighteenth century. It was hard to see how the citizen "could become involved in exchange relationships, or in relationships governed by the media of exchange (especially when these took the form of paper tokens of public credit) without becoming involved in dependence and corruption."[31] The ideals of virtue and commerce were not easily reconciled, and this was especially true where Catholic teaching had already implanted principles of commutative justice that encouraged suspicion of commerce.

The best defence of virtue was the independence afforded by real property, especially property in land. The eighteenth-century republican equation of landed property with civic virtue was revived in Lower Canada, where defenders of the seigneurial system argued that it ensured access to land and the transmission of land across generations. Recoiling at a subdivision of patrimony among all descendants, a writer in *Le Canadien* in 1807 applauded ancient Athens and Sparta: "The legislators of the ancient world, having understood that landed property was the basis of all social order, brought about laws to preserve landholding within the family and to prevent its division."[32] The writer was expressing a widely accepted connection between landed property and political virtue. The poor and dispossessed risked becoming "slaves to the great capitalists who are already taking over all the land in the townships." The landholder was attached to the land that he cultivated, whereas the landless farmer "is becoming a machine that adapts to anything. In a state so constituted one can expect to see the disappearance of political virtue."[33]

A week earlier *Le Canadien* published a diatribe against the "odious traffic" of the "Bourgeois." "It is true that this noble commerce enriches a few individuals, who have much less need of talent than of boldness to succeed, but its fatal consequence is to ruin industry and the morals of the country, which should be the true sources of our wealth."[34] The moral tirade continued: commerce was tearing off the arms of agriculture, paralyzing the physical and moral force of those it left behind, and sowing "the contagion of immorality, the furies of licentiousness and debauchery, and the habit of unquenchable thirst for strong drink." The writer went on to condemn the fur trade, an "apparatus of cupidity" that corrupted both the "*sauvages*" and all levels of Europeans who engaged in it. The fur trade took men from the land and thereby disconnected landed property and virtue. "For if landed property is the basis of civilization, a people, even an ancient one, becoming vagabond and savage, losing by commerce or otherwise their moral ideas and disregarding the laws of a good order, abandons the culture of the country to become coureur de bois."[35] The villain was not the English bourgeois; it was commerce. In 1808 it was even possible to deny that Canada would ever be a commercial country.[36]

Here was a moral assault on commercial wealth that was not driven by ethnic resentments, although the presence of English bourgeois in the fur trade must have sharpened the vitriol. Such moral attacks on commerce – and there were many others in *Le Canadien* and elsewhere in the early nineteenth century – were in part a response to the *Quebec Mercury*, a paper founded in 1805 to represent the views of English merchants. The *Mercury* went after the seigneurial system, promoted commerce, and pushed for a property tax rather than taxes on imports and exports.[37] The critique of commercial wealth in *Le Canadien* coincided with its continuing expressions of loyalty to the British constitution and the monarchy. Indeed, it saw the constitution as a necessary defence against the tyranny of the merchant class and against those who would create "a merchant aristocracy."[38]

When objections to the workings of the constitution emerged in the pages of *Le Canadien* and in the *Parti canadien*, they focused on a specific inequality. The colony's Legislative Council, said one writer in *Le Canadien*, consisted of "the richest merchants and landowners" who sought only to preserve their immense properties. The Legislative Assembly, in contrast, represented "the less rich people or class." Political and economic inequalities reinforced each other and affected the political economy of taxation. People of lesser wealth wanted the burden of taxation to fall on "luxury goods" rather than on land. A simple principle of just or equitable taxation was at work here. Taxes should be paid in proportion to the advantage or benefit one received from the maintenance of government. The main benefit was the protection of person and property. Thus if taxes were levied on a per-capita basis, the poor would be paying more than their fair share, and the wealthy too little. Another principle, not necessarily consistent with the first, was also at work: sparing the economy's most productive sectors. If taxes fell on property, and if the burden fell on all property, then this would penalize agriculture, which "is the principal source of wealth; and it will happen that the most laborious class, those who work to feed others, will also bear the burden of taxation, which would obviously be unjust." The political logic followed: the Legislative Council must not have too much influence over the Assembly, because, if it did, there would be no limit on the self-aggrandizing projects of the "rich landowners." [39]

Twenty-five years after these commentaries on commerce and wealth, Patriote politicians and journalists were still talking about inequality without using the word. By the 1830s the political ground had shifted, the Parti patriote had supplanted the Parti canadien, and a republican orientation had gained strength in Patriote circles.[40] By the 1830s the working (or failure) of the constitution, especially the relationship between the Legislative Council, the Assembly, and the electorate, was firmly in the foreground of political debate. In this context the distribution of political influence had priority; the language was that of interest, influence, and just desert. Furthermore, debates rarely led to discussion of principles or abstract ideals. Despite the existence of the specifically Canadian political egalitarianism that Michel Ducharme outlines, Louis-Georges Harvey and Mark Olsen find that the word "*égalité*" appeared rarely in the leading French-Canadian publications.[41] Also relatively rare was *liberté*, and when these terms surfaced in the French-Canadian texts, they did so not as abstract principles, indicating universal rights or existential truths ("All men are created equal"), but as specific rights such as *liberté de la presse* or the liberties of British subjects.[42] Where theoretical or philosophical discussion of liberty and equality was rare, so too was explicit reference to inequality and to principles of distributive justice.

The subject was present none the less. It surfaced most clearly in comparisons between Europe and the Americas, and in idealized images of the United States that appeared in the pages of *Le Canadien* and *La Minerve*. The new world, it was argued, gave birth to a natural equality of condition that rendered old-world social formations not only redundant, but potentially dangerous sources of corruption. As in Upper Canada, the subject of primogeniture (despite its absence in French-origin civil law) occasionally prompted the contrast with Europe. As Papineau put it in 1833, in condemning a hereditary nobility as inappropriate to the colonies: "Canada, a country made poor by the harshness of its climate, and where laws and morals have always favoured an equal division of property, turns down substitutions, condemns the privileges of primogeniture, and must hence be the last place where one would attempt a measure so inept and unenforcable."[43]

Papineau also saw equality of condition in the colonies as a source of civic morality. "We live in a condition of society favourable to the nourishment of morality, peace, and the unity of citizens. We do not see those colossal fortunes that generate ambition and vices disruptive of social order; we do not see extreme poverty holding a large class in servile dependence. The distribution of property is so equal and so general, in fact, that we have the same agrarian laws that the Romans demanded, without having acquired them through rivers of blood."[44] As Louis-Georges Harvey concludes, this valorization of the distinctive egalitarian nature and the associated virtue of American societies sustained the political assault on corruption and despotism.[45]

On 17 February 1834 Elzéar Bédard presented the Ninety-two Resolutions to the Legislative Assembly of Lower Canada. The document can be read in many ways, but certainly it was a defiant protest against specific forms of inequality and advanced a claim to equality of political and legal rights. Just as American leaders fifty-eight years earlier had trumpeted fundamental differences between Europe and America, Papineau and his colleagues declared a similar departure from the old world's inherited inequalities. In Europe, "custom and law have given so many artificial privileges and advantages to birth and rank and fortune." This House, said Resolution 13, had sought "to consult the opinions generally received in America, where the influence of birth is nothing, and where, notwithstanding the importance which fortune must always naturally confer, the artificial introduction of great political privileges in favour of the possessors of large property, could not long resist the preference given at free elections to virtue, talents, and information, which fortune does not exclude but can never purchase, and which may be the portion of honest, contented and devoted men."[46]

The choice of words was important. This articulation of equality was cautious, qualified, and bound within a specific political frame. Fortunes differed in size, and "importance" might be conferred "naturally." Virtue and talent were the characteristics of "honest, contented and devoted men," and the entire discourse was gender-specific.[47] Virtue and talent were rewarded in "free elections." But note the repetition of "artificial" and the qualifiers "great" and "large." The inequality identified here was the "artificial" introduction of "great" privileges granted to owners of "large" property.

The moral economy of the Catholic community remained intact in the secular language. An artificial privilege had intruded on the natural order of the new world and interrupted the recognition of true virtue and talent – and these could not be purchased. If we move ahead a few years, to the crisis in the autumn of 1837, the moral assault on privilege was even more explicit. God has created no artificial distinctions between man and man (a repetition of the U.S. Declaration of Independence); yet the greed of a rapacious political-economic faction has robbed the people of their liberty and their prosperity. "Finally the day came when we no longer seem attached to the British Empire for our happiness and our prosperity, our liberties and the honour of the people and that of the Crown, but only for the sake of fattening a horde of useless officials, who, not unhappy to enjoy salaries enormously disproportionate to the responsibilities of their assignments and the resources of the country, have combined in a faction solely motivated by the private interest to oppose all reforms, and to defend all the iniquities of a government hostile to the rights and liberties of this colony."[48]

Specific words in the Patriote vocabulary expressed the fusion of economic with political inequity. Monopoly was one such word, and it did not refer to the presence of a single seller in a market. It meant the capture of both power and wealth, usually by office-holders but also by corporate entities such as the British American Land Company. The 36th of the Ninety-two Resolutions made the connection between monopoly and the political system: "The extension of the elective system" would prevent "a monopoly of power and profit in favour of the minority."[49] The word "corruption" embraced many evils, but referred especially to the overlap of political or judicial office with personal or sectional interest. As the Address of the Confederation of the Six Counties that November explained: "The men in office in this province devour our revenues in salaries so extravagant that they deprive us of the funds necessary for the general betterment of the country."[50] The corruption was systemic, in this perspective, and it had distributional consequences for society as a whole. The opposite of corruption, in this view, was virtue, which included disinterest, a vision of communal good free of personal interest. Such disinterest the republicans claimed for themselves: "We humbly beg for blessings on our disinterested efforts."[51]

Was there a connection between the republican concept of liberty and the problem of distributive inequity? The Patriote equation of power and profit clearly made such a link. A more subtle but instructive connection between liberty and distributive justice may be present in the thought of Étienne Parent, the Patriote intellectual. The origins of liberalism in Canadian political thought lie beyond our scope, but with Parent we have the sense of being present at the genesis of an identifiable liberalism. It was in man's nature to be free – "absolutely free" – he stated in 1834. This liberty meant answering for one's actions only to one's creator, and "to enjoy the entire fruits of one's labour." In the realization of this liberty, a simple principle of commutative justice governed relations between citizen and state: "To ensure enjoyment of the fruits of labour more fully, he consents to give up a portion; to enjoy in peace his natural liberty, he willingly sacrifices a portion; if, in a word, he consents to live in society in order to enjoy its advantages, it is clear that he intends to have these advantages in the best conditions possible, that is to say by sacrificing the least possible amounts of liberty and of goods."[52]

The citizen gave his minimum, and received in return the protection of his liberty. It followed also that the state gave and the citizen received the minimum necessary for the liberty and independence of each citizen. The United States, according to Parent, had a model of government that worked towards these principles. What prevented their realization in the colonies? "The love of the people's money is the dominant passion of all administrations."[53] The colonial state required that the citizen give more than was necessary for his liberty and transferred that "more" to a "dominant caste," which obtained far more than its members required or deserved. Not only that – this tiny caste decided for itself what sufficiency it deserved. "What a constitutional anomaly!"[54] The absence of the word "inequality" was moot: Parent's conception of liberty led him to perceive a profound distributive injustice. A small elite of monopolists and acquisitive speculators was transferring national wealth to itself. "It is really only a question of an Oligarchy, composed of public employees, monopolists and speculators who are protected in their speculations by the Legislative and Executive Councils."[55]

There were egalitarian claims here – focusing on an equality of political rights and equality before the law. And in these egalitarian claims Patriotes were seeking reductions in inequality. These included a specific lessening of economic inequality: a transfer of economic rights and wealth from commercial, financial, and landed elites, and especially from corporations, to middle and small landowners. The Patriotes introduced key elements of distributive justice, though not a fully developed theory: the ideas that possession of large amounts of property was not a priori a sign of status and privilege, that wider ownership of property was a desirable social goal, and that political reform could equip the state to effect a degree of redistribution. These changes were not steps towards some "modern" theory of justice; they were bound within their own time and place. Nevertheless, the reformers of the 1830s introduced ideas and language that would endure into the era of industrial capitalism: a language of equality, of rights, and of their opposites – corruption, monopoly, slavery, privilege.

A historically specific language of equality: we are referring to something that was both cultural and political, and there is no escaping the nexus, even if it leads the historian to uncomfortable speculative leaps. Equality went hand in hand with liberty, as Michel Ducharme says; equality also stood opposed to hierarchy, and hence inequality. So what were the reformers of the 1830s saying? They did not give us, and we should not expect, a formal definition of either equality or inequality. Certainly they were echoing ideas that had percolated from Enlightenment thinkers into a wider discourse in the era of the Atlantic revolutions. At another, cultural level, we may speculate that they were reflecting a change in sensibility that was broader than any specific politics, and that owed little or nothing, directly or indirectly, to readings of Enlightenment authors.

No less elusive than *mentalité*, sensibility is a concept with a lineage in literary and cultural studies and occasional uses in historical analysis. Sensibility refers, according to Daniel Wickberg, to "modes of perception and feeling, the terms and forms in which objects were conceived, experienced and represented in the past."[56] In the history of egalitarianism, an oft-cited example signalling a new egalitarian sensibility was Pierre Beaumarchais's 1778 play, which Mozart and Lorenzo de Ponte turned into the opera *The Marriage of Figaro*. In it, disparities of status dissolved as servants appeared on the same moral and emotional plane as master and mistress: both music and drama conveyed Enlightenment thought into a mode of perception and feeling.[57] "*Se vuol ballare, signor contino*" (You, the Count, will dance to my tune). We are at the beginning of a change in the common sense of what is possible in the social order. More immediately relevant is Pierre Rosanvallon's discussion of "the spirit of equality" and his reference to equality as "mental representation."[58] In crucial respects, notes Samuel Fleischacker, it was a change in sensibilities that led to a modern conception of distributive justice – a change in perceptions of the poor and conceptions of social order.[59]

To conceive of equality in this way – not merely as legal status but as sensibility or moral common sense – one must be able to see others as occupying a status or position comparable to one's own, or at least within the same moral plane – one must be willing to make a comparison. Rosanvallon refers to "imaginary equality," wherein "similarity is established by psychological comparison with other individuals." One can grasp "the possibility of a change of situation ... can imagine himself [or herself] in the condition of every other individual."[60] One must be able to say: there are advantages others in my social sphere possess that I do not; were circumstances to change, I too might possess these advantages.

Such an imaginary capacity may emerge within an agricultural and even a feudal society, but it is rare. The comparative disposition is more likely to appear within a political economy in which accumulation occurs via mechanisms open to a widening share of the population. Commerce and markets provided those mechanisms. Their intrusion into agrarian or feudal societies was one solvent of the hierarchical common sense. "The hierarchical and/or organic view of society prevailed wherever the market was weakly developed," claims Patricia Crone.[61] British North America had at the same time market economies and landholding economies, which included a larger proportion of rural smallholders than Britain. Moving into this economy and onto the land induced in settlers a constantly renewed comparative vision. They compared their current condition with past expectations and future goals, their means of accumulation with their neighbours'. Where the means of occupying land were varied, the opportunities for comparison multiplied.

UPPER CANADA

There was greater variation in landholding in Upper Canada than there was in Lower Canada, which rendered a comparative impulse among residents more readily observable (which is not to say that it was absent in Lower Canada), and it proved a powerful impulse to egalitarian ideas. So too did the variety of Protestant denominations – our second topic, below – in a colony where the majority was non-Anglican, and both impulses challenged the Tory defence of order – our third topic.

Catharine Wilson has documented the wide range of means by which settlers acquired access to land, and the fluid meanings of ownership. One might occupy land as a free grant, or as a lessee, or by purchase, or in freehold after a period of lease, or as a squatter, and even these came in different types.[62] One's neighbour likely acquired land by different means and at a different time: a comparison is made, and with it, a sensitivity to advantage or disadvantage. The perception may evolve as the occupant works and expands the holding, or works it and sells or abandons it.

We can observe the settler engaging in the act of comparison. According to Catherine Parr Traill, "the blessings and evils of this life owe their chief effect to the force of contrast, and are to be estimated by that principally."[63] Peter Russell quotes another settler: "When he [a newcomer] goes ... to his next neighbour's house, and sees him, if he has been ten years on his farm, with plenty of everything he needs, his farm well cultivated, and no debt, knowing that he [the ten-year settler] was in the same position formerly that he [the pioneer] is now, this cheers him up."[64] John Strachan, Church of England bishop of Toronto, was aware of the habit of comparison, and delivered sermons warning that it was a cause of envy and unhappiness. "You compare your situation with that of your superiors. This will turn your attention to advantages you want rather than to those you possess ... But compare it to the inferior stations of life, and the effect will be more favourable to your comfort."[65]

The inveterate act of comparison nourished perceptions of inequality in land markets. One's neighbour was very often not another farm family but might, as John Clarke, Catharine Wilson, and others have pointed out, be a speculator, or a clergy reserve. The economy operated within a system of debt and credit; the larger the landholding, the greater the credit that was available. As Clarke has argued, where the private or corporate sector or clergy reserves held much of the land, the new settler had a limited choice and had to deal with the corporation and often with a speculator.[66] Everyone was equal in the need for and right to land; all settlers could convert their labour into property. Yet individuals' access to land and to the markets for land differed. And the returns on speculation were different from the returns to mere labour. In Clarke's study, speculators paid less for land than did the general population, at least until 1841.[67] Their profits were substantial, better than returns on mortgages. The Canada Company's rates of return on investment in Essex County averaged 12 per cent per year on a resource it obtained for very little.[68] Such were the conditions in which inequality became an injustice, and in which claims to "equal rights" and "equal justice" acquired force and meaning. Money, it has often been said, was a great leveller; but the market economy was also a great unleveller.

Settlers from Britain arrived with their own expectations – not of any idealized equality in the distribution of property, but of a land free of aristocrats, free of inherited landed estates, and full of (as one settler put it) "the blessings of a country where there are no taxes, tithes, nor poor-rates."[69] The colonies were a good "poor man's country," and in these expectations of independence lay the seeds of an egalitarian ideal and a powerful myth – of the independent yeoman whose land provided for family and inheritance. "The sturdy yeomanry of the Canadas," asserted a pamphlet on religious equality, "soon imbibe a consciousness of their own independence, of their own importance in this Hemisphere, where equality of rights seems a principle, an element of the very air we breathe, of the very soil we tread."[70] The apparent abundance of land, the strong demand for labour, and immigrants' expectations of a better life combined to undermine traditional notions of status so that some contemporary observers would see a widespread assumption of equality. Susanna Moodie detected an "ultra-republican spirit" among Yankees in Upper Canada, which she attributed to "a sudden emancipation from a state of utter dependence into one of unrestrained liberty." She made the same point about domestic servants: because there were few of them in Upper Canada and because they could leave one employer for another, they lost the old-world habit of "servile obedience" and assumed egalitarian airs: "They tell you, with a high hand, that 'they are as good as you.'"[71] Status, rank, and class did not dissolve; nevertheless, the signs of status and rank were fluid and uncertain. Colonial conditions encouraged a perception of social levelling, and among many a fear of it.

Other specifically Canadian sources of egalitarianism existed, and these could nourish the idea that inequality was a form of injustice. Protestant religion offered its own multiple paths towards a new egalitarian consciousness. J.R. Pole writes: "In safeguarding the free exercise of religion, the government treats all individuals as equals; in avoiding establishment, it makes the irreligious conscience equal to the devout."[72] While the irreligious conscience was very rare, on both sides of the Atlantic there was a tension between the implied equality of religious freedom and the official preference accorded to some churches. In British America the peculiar relations between church and the colonial state exacerbated the tension.[73] While not "established" in the same ways that they were in Britain, the Church of England and the Church of Scotland were granted specific legal advantages and prerogatives, either by the Constitutional Act of 1791 or by subsequent colonial legislation. The religious clauses of the 1791 act fell within the responsibility of colonial legislatures and created fertile soil for the perception of favouritism. But the grounds for egalitarian complaint went further. Where (in the early years at least) members of dissenting churches were denied places in the parish cemetery, where dissenting ministers could not perform marriage ceremonies, and where some denominations could not engage in the corporate ownership of property, the claim to "equal rights" acquired a powerful following.[74]

Religion and land markets cannot be separated in the gestation of reformers' understanding of equality. The Church of England, a minority group in Upper Canada, had a legislated access to land, and its schools had an economic base denied to others. Yet the labour of the entire population had increased the value of the clergy reserves, as some reform petitioners understood.[75] As one of them put it, grants of money to the Church of England were "powerful weapons, unjustly put into the hands of one class of persons, to carry on proselyting [sic] warfare against the conscientious opinions and civil liberties of other numerous and equally loyal and deserving" people.[76] The ongoing efforts to settle the clergy-reserve question and to allow access by Methodists and others to such reserves rested on claims to equal treatment and equal rights. "Whatever theories of church and state might be proposed," writes John Webster Grant, "it was becoming evident that most Upper Canadians thought of their churches as having equal rights to existence and support."[77]

Beyond the tensions at the official level of church and state, there existed deeper spiritual and even theological sources of an egalitarian sensibility. Within the walls of the many new church buildings, often erected by the labour of their members, Protestant denominations embraced egalitarian practices of worship and education that changed the relationship between the individual believer and authority. The tension in Christianity between an egalitarian moral intuition and church authority goes back a long way, and even precedes the Reformation, or so Larry Siedentop has argued.[78] That tension took new forms in the changing religious practices of the late eighteenth and early nineteenth centuries. Less often did Sunday worship mean merely listening to lengthy sermons, frequent as those undoubtedly remained. The congregation consisted of "members" and participants, who responded to sermons and gave voice to their faith. Choirs, increasing in number in Upper Canada in the early nineteenth century, meant that all voices were equally heard.[79] All believers were equal in their possession of a Christian conscience that could be shaped and tutored: Sunday schools, Sunday school libraries, and the new religious periodicals all reinforced the message.[80]

The evangelical movement, affecting as it did all Protestant denominations in different ways, bore with it a potentially subversive egalitarianism. Revivals and camp meetings emphasized the individual's spiritual and even emotional meeting with God, an encounter that involved passion as much as reason. The religion of experience "allowed many individuals and groups to follow the light of their own feelings to a wide range of religious and social destinations," William Westfall tells us.[81] At its extremes, evangelicalism turned the new convert into his or her own master, whose experience of being saved brought an unassailable power to judge the world. There was no ordained perfection, no immutable order, and no singular righteousness. Even time itself would yield to the transformative power of the community of the saved. And so we hear the following, from the defenders of religious equality: "It is a law of God, and nature, that diversity of time and space shall create a diversity in the civil and ecclesiastical state. No human laws are, in their nature, perfect, or incapable of amelioration. To none, hath God given a charter of immutability. Change of time and place, and circumstance, generally implies a change, in the same degree, of law and order, in every social constitution."[82] The boundaries between sacred and secular dissolved in this vision, in which the recognition of diversity is also a claim to equality.

Among the Protestant opponents of church establishment, the rhetoric of equality presented itself as a direct translation into politics of the freedom of the self-directed conscience. The theoretical basis of the campaign for denominational rights was the "*perfect and universal liberty of the conscience and of the mind – religious and intellectual.*"[83] Liberty and equality were conjoined in a rehearsal of a liberal principle of positive liberty. "All true liberty is based upon, and draws its vital spirit and power from that primary and essential liberty, mental and moral, which secures to us the fullest exercise of the right of thinking, judging and acting, according to our own views of propriety, duty or interest, so long and so far as we do not thereby infringe any of the just and equal rights of our fellow-men."[84]

The "equal rights" attack on church establishment was at once religious and secular, accusing Anglican elites of trying to establish an aristocracy and to form "an oligarchy of placemen, place-hunters, pensioners and parsons."[85] The egalitarian insurgence often took the form of a fiery sermon on the sinfulness of such Tory defenders of church privilege as Christopher Hagerman. With the "unreserved freedom ... of a drunk man" Hagerman "throws open his whole soul, and exposes to the public eye, the unbounded selfishness, the coarse and vulgar insolence of a monopolizing faction, which is chargeable with the whole original sin of the past mismanagement and present unhappy distractions of the Colony."[86] Such radical egalitarianism echoed the sermon of the revivalist preacher wrestling with the devil before his congregation of sinners.

Echoes of Protestant homily resounded through the reform discourse of Upper Canada. As radical protest evolved into republican and rebel insurgence, the echoes became more frequent. William Lyon Mackenzie's "call to arms" of 1 December 1837 invoked previous North American "strikes for independence" from European tyranny, but his egalitarian manifesto referred more often to God and the Bible than to the U.S. Declaration of Independence. Slavery and the priests of Baal would be put down in the name of God, who "sees with an equal eye." It was "God's law" that would bring down the tyrants, the wicked, and the "reverend sinners."[87] Mackenzie's diatribe against the priests of Baal was an Upper Canadian derivation of an older Calvinist teaching on secular "callings." A few centuries earlier, the Protestant dethroning of priests and religious orders affirmed the value and equality of all vocations, so long as they served God. Here was a spiritual egalitarianism that could provide moral fuel for the critique of hierarchy. The Puritan stricture and the Canadian reform message sounded very similar: "They profane their lives and callings that imploy them to get honours, pleasures, profites, worldly commodities etc. for thus we live to another end then [sic] God hath appointed."[88]

As Albert Schrauwers has commented, there were other connections between religious egalitarianism and the colonial economy. One of many outcomes of the smallholder quest for independent subsistence was the moral economy of the Children of Peace, a sect that broke from the Quakers in 1812. That group's economy "was predicated on smallholder subsistence production, an economic regime that fit the radical egalitarianism they inherited from the Society of Friends."[89] Schrauwers has shown how an egalitarianism rooted in religious faith and practice shaded into political critique. David Willson, the sect's leader, linked economic egalitarianism and Christian neighbourly love to a critique of British rule: "If a man has two coats, and gives one to his naked brother, the two extremes have met – the mountains and the valley has become equal; and he that hath most, says John, 'let him do likewise,' loving our neighbours as ourselves, equalizes the world; and this is the prince that is wanting in England."[90]

The egalitarianism of the Children of Peace emanated from the conjunction of a particular Protestant spirituality and colonial commercial economies. Networks of debt and credit facilitated commercial markets and the market for land. Almost everyone had debt, which constrained the quest for independence by Upper Canadian farmers, fishing families in Nova Scotia and Newfoundland, and many other small producers. The transactions between creditors and debtors, between lenders and borrowers, could easily appear as an inequality – a manifestation of unequal power. The search for freedom from that inequality led to a range of experiments. To the smallholder, chartered corporations, especially banks, were monopolies. Voluntary associations, cooperatives, and the Bank of the People, by contrast, were "mini-republics" whose members had equal standing.[91] The small joint-stock company could practise a type of egalitarianism in its decision-making, especially when stockholders knew each other. Utopian communities appeared in both the United States and British North America, seeking to undercut or avoid unequal exchanges through an egalitarian moral economy. Cooperatives and Owenite communities, spreading in both lands in the 1820s and 1830s, were among the "experiments in democratic sociability," as McNairn calls them.

In the face of these cultural underpinnings of equality, we can see older assumptions about inequality becoming fragile and contestable. Consider the older common sense that "high birth or great fortune indicates merit and makes it rather noticeable."[92] Consider also the following common sense: "It follows, as a necessary consequence of . . . [the] determination of nature, that order and subordination must be introduced, by which the different members of the community may have their proper tasks allotted to them, the talents of each be directed to their proper objects, injustice and violence be restrained, and as great a sum of common felicity be produced, as the condition of man will permit."[93]

In this mental world virtue and privilege coincided. Privilege was phylogenetic and hence permanent. Merit was in the blood. The distribution of rewards was ordained, subject only to minor adjustments within the inherited structure. Such assumptions did not disappear, of course. The point is that they were no longer a ubiquitous common sense.

The Tory belief in order made sense in the context of an idealized English landscape, where order was manifest in great landed estates, tidy villages, parish churches, hedgerows, and drystone walls. As William Westfall has shown us, the environment of Upper Canada did little to sustain this conservative vision. The colonial landscape was largely devoid of the familiar markers of order and hierarchy. "It took considerable imagination to proclaim the inherent harmony and order of nature and society at a time when the colony was still a wilderness devoid of hedgerows and well-kept fields."[94] It would prove difficult to defend an order that had yet to be established. The Tories who erected barriers against republicanism had to defend an imagined order – what ought to be, not what already existed. Any appeal to the model of England's rural order would find more derision than support among the mass of the population who sought freedom and independence by escaping that old order.

Tory supporters of the older common sense began to sound defensive. They even borrowed and used the word "equality." They construed society's distinct orders as embracing a form of equality:

"A diversity and an equality of orders are not contrary to the will of God, but agreeable to his own government; and until there is some express command to the contrary ... it is better to endeavour to imitate the divine conduct than to adopt the inconsistent and unprofitable inventions of man."[95] As Michel Ducharme has revealed with great clarity, the Tory defenders of the constitution of 1791 embraced equality within their understanding of British Liberty. That founding document, said John Strachan, was based on "the most equitable, rational and excellent principles"; it was a "constitution of free and equal laws."[96]

In response to the egalitarian argument that equal merit deserved equal reward, Tories deployed merit in the defence of hierarchy. There was, they said, a differential distribution of ability, energy, and character in human populations, which made hierarchy, or a "pyramid," inevitable. In former lieutenant-governor Francis Bond Head's formulation: "The '*family compact*' of Upper Canada is composed of those members of its society who, either by their abilities or character have been honoured by the confidence of the executive government, or who, by their industry and intelligence, have amassed wealth. The party, I own, is a comparatively small one; but to put the multitude at the top and the few at the bottom is a radical reversion of the pyramid of society which every reflecting man must foresee can only end by its downfall."[97]

Whether the word used was "class" or "order," the assumption that merit, quality, and hierarchy went hand in hand found currency well beyond the Tory elite. "We want Colleges for the learned professions, Grammar Schools for the middle class, and Common Schools ... for the great body of the people. In all civilised countries there have been, and no doubt always will be, three classes, or ranks in Society – all attempts of the levelling system to the contrary notwithstanding."[98] Such precise enumeration of ranks or classes was uncommon; more often hierarchy was perceived as an upward slope, or "one unbroken chain" (as Colonial Secretary Lord Glenelg put it), from dependence to independence and from the condition of those without property to the condition of those with property, wealth, and privilege.[99]

SEEDS OF EGALITARIAN DISRUPTION

The founders of Lower and Upper Canada in the 1790s erected barriers against the republican rhetoric on equality. The problem they saw with the American idea of "equality" was that it rejected both divine intention and the reality of different natural endowments among human beings. "Such an equality is impossible," argued Thomas Dalton, who was no friend of American "democracy." "If men were made equal today, they would be unequal tomorrow, owing to the difference of their understandings, their diligence and self-denial ... It is clearly the will of the Almighty that such distinctions of rank and circumstances should prevail."[100] The barriers constructed against republicanism were formidable, and went beyond the constitution, clergy reserves, and preferential land grants. In Lower Canada they included the Catholic church, whose defence of hierarchy was also a command to submission: "Submit to all those who are above you, whether to the king as head of state or to governors or those who command you on his behalf."[101] In both colonies an embryonic egalitarian sensibility confronted defences of hierarchy that were both political and cultural.

This section explores five themes in the shaping of egalitarianism and its framework in the 1830s: the rhetoric of British liberty, the influence of Jacksonian democracy, the emergence of a defensive egalitarianism that emphasized political redistribution, the role of the rural smallholding ideal, and the influence of a then-common assumption that individuals had differing capacities for improvement. Within each of these themes we discern emergent and contested disruptions to elite defences of hierarchy.

The barriers against republican equality, formidable as they were, contained the seeds of conflict. For one thing, the colonial elites brought with them a vocabulary of rights and British Liberty that proved useful in unintended ways to many who found cause for grievance in the colonial experience. And defences of the 1791 constitution contained ambiguities that fed discontent. Its advocates maintained that, as Lieutenant-Governor John Graves Simcoe said, it was "the very image and transcript of that of Great Britain."[102] Reformers and Tories agreed that colonial subjects inherited British liberties. "The inhabitants of the Province, as British subjects, have an inherent right, co-existent with birth, to the rights and liberties of their fellow subjects in England."[103] The absence of the word "equality" in this and so many other similar statements is moot: this was a claim to equal constitutional status. Even in Lower Canada, the resulting "British liberty" found a following, and loyalty to the British constitution could qualify enthusiasm for American principles, especially in the early years of the century.[104]

Of course a colony could not be in the same position as its imperial creator. It was the tension between this reality and the rhetoric of symmetry that fuelled endless discussion and debate. For many colonists, "image and transcript" seemed to imply an identity of constitutional condition; identity or sameness, a type of equality. British intrusions and an unelected Legislative Council denied such identity. The arguments for responsible government grew directly from the tensions set up by the constitution. Responsible government, for reformers such as Robert Baldwin, was not an innovation but a belated implementation of the constitutional symmetry promised in 1791.[105]

The rhetoric of British liberty was injected into a colony where many men had political rights. Where the franchise was based on a property qualification, and many people owned land, a sizable number could vote. The result was a social and public mixing of people who would not otherwise have met and mingled. And politics meant much more than brief appearances at voting stations – public meetings, petitions, and debates in town squares and inns. Knowledge of the art of government was no longer the preserve of a narrow educated elite. When Robert Gourlay called on every man to organize and attend township meetings, he was practising and reflecting a nascent egalitarianism of political action that prompted his enemies to accuse him of promoting republican "*Égalité.*"[106] When Lower Canadian reformers began to challenge political privilege, they voiced a new egalitarian consciousness: where political argument seemed the purview of a privileged few, "the voice of reply is open to all," insisted a writer in *Le Canadien* in 1806. "Are not all habitants in the province British subjects?"[107]

Colonial governors and their political allies were determined to erect social order through landholding. The American republic contained no aristocracy where title and status passed on across many generations, and neither did the Canadas. To compensate for this absence, colonial governors sought to establish a governing elite whose status and stability were based on accumulations of property. The result appeared to many outside the elite as an attempt to create an English-style aristocracy, or a class of "mimic Peers."[108] Equality therefore was proclaimed as a way to prevent emergence of such a group, with its association of political power and wealth. In 1837 the freeholders of Terrebonne voiced an opinion heard in both colonies: "We ought to employ all means in our power to equalize the social conditions, to deprive the Government of all hope of establishing in this country the germs of aristocracy however weak it might be."[109]

The legal conditions of property-holding were different in Lower Canada than in Upper Canada. However, the former's seigneurial system did not prevent the rise of a myth of the independent *culti-vateur* and, with that myth, of another specifically colonial variant of egalitarianism. Habitants accepted their subordination and the necessity of rents and other dues. But they used the ambiguities in seigneurial tenure to their advantage, as Allan Greer has argued; they allowed "no recognition that seigneurs had a legitimate claim to the title of proprietor."[110] The campaign for freedom from feudal exactions peaked in the Rebellions and embraced a conception of the independent habitant who owned the land he farmed and held legitimate claim to the seigneury's forest tracts. In this context egalitarian rhetoric sustained the assault on seigneurial exactions.

How much did American republicanism influence the egalitarian reform impulse in the Canadas? According to Louis-Georges Harvey, the United States served as the platform for much of the discourse on anti-colonialism and republicanism.[111] By 1837 public meetings in Lower Canada echoed the U.S. Declaration of Independence and its promise of equality: "We hold these truths to be sacred and self-evident, that God has created no artificial distinctions among men."[112] There was also an affinity with, and often a borrowing from, a contemporary American source: the egalitarianism of Andrew Jackson (president 1829–37), who, according to James L. Huston, "encapsulated perhaps as well as any American between 1776 and 1890 the republican theory of the distribution of wealth."[113] That chief executive's best-known pronouncement on wealth came in 1832, when he vetoed the re-charter of the National Bank. His statement left little if any room for redistribution: "Distinctions in society will always exist under every just government. Equality of talents, of education, or of wealth can not be produced by human institutions." Yet parts of his message fed into colonial egalitarianism. "It is to be regretted that the rich and powerful too often bend the acts of government to their selfish purposes. When the laws undertake to add to these natural and just advantages artificial distinctions, to grant titles, gratuities, and exclusive privileges, to make the rich richer and the potent more powerful, the humble members of society ... have a right to complain of the injustice of their Government." And then the president stated a specific egalitarian doctrine for government – the idea of equality of protection against abuse. "In the full enjoyment of the gifts of Heaven and the fruits of superior industry, economy, and virtue, every man is equally entitled to protection by laws ... There are no necessary evils in government. Its evils exist only in its abuses. If it would confine itself to equal protection, and, as Heaven does its rains, shower its favors alike on the high and the low, the rich and the poor, it would be an unqualified blessing."[114]

There was perhaps an echo of these sentiments in Resolution 28's references to "equal ... protection" and "distinction": "The extension of the elective principle is the only measure which appears to this House to afford any prospect of equal and sufficient protection in future to all the inhabitants of the province, without distinction." This was a defensive egalitarianism of protection against abuses and privilege. The end was "that all may enjoy freely and equally the rights and advantages of British subjects, and of the institutions which have been guaranteed to and are dear to the country" (Resolution 51). The accumulation to assail was not merely that of wealth, but rather that of offices and the "artificial" accumulation of wealth that led the few to appropriate offices and power.[115]

There were specifically Lower Canadian dimensions to this limited, protective egalitarianism. Most obviously, it was an English minority that was particularly guilty of accumulating offices. Resolution 75 reported the population estimates for those of French and of British origin, and the number of government office-holders in 1832: 157 of "British or foreign origin" and only 47 "who are apparently natives of the country, of French origin." The problem was "the partial and abusive practice of bestowing the great majority of official places in the province on those only who are least connected with its permanent interests, and with the mass of its inhabitants" (Resolution 76). The solution was a redistribution of offices by extension of the elective principle.

The same "equal protection" claims surfaced a few years later during the Rebellions in Lower Canada. At the meeting at St-Denis on 26 December 1837, one of the resolutions stated that under the present constitution "all the Subjects of His Majesty in the Province have an equal right to the protection of the law." The next resolution affirmed equality as a protection against abuse: "That if according to this order of things ... a certain number of subjects between them are able to injure all the others, in violation of the constitution of government, then in this case the law resulting from this social order ceases to be equal for all, a part of the subjects of His Majesty oppresses the other; the equality and protection of the constitution is destroyed."[116]

In Upper Canada, the proliferous ferocity of Mackenzie's rhetoric embraced a wide range of elitist targets, and – against the avaricious "few" – he claimed to be protecting "the natural aristocracy of Canada, the hardy yeomanry who own the soil."[117] The rich "have pawned the industry of the poor" and sacrificed the interests of producers to "the profit, pleasure and immediate advantage of the few." Here too this protective egalitarianism was focused and limited. It was a way of heaping moral censure on specific political targets labelled as "rich." The solution was a degree of political redistribution that would also involve a limited economic redistribution. In 1837 Charles Duncombe wrote that "our oppressors have shown us more clearly than ever before, that their great object is to make the rich richer and the poor poorer."[118] Such ideas were commonplace, often accompanied by a simple labour theory, that wealth was ultimately the product of labour. But we should not read too much into the rhetoric of rich and poor.

Despite notable differences between the egalitarian discourses of Upper and Lower Canada, both were similarly defensive and focused on political redistribution as a means to rebalance society. As soon as Duncombe inveighed against the growing gap between rich and poor, he made clear that his concern was its political effect. Narrowing the gap was to be welcomed: "If the people should become wealthy they would become intelligent and unwilling slaves." Duncombe's remedy was not so much redistribution as it was the education of the people, literacy, political unions, and more reform newspapers.

Ferocious as was Mackenzie's rhetoric, his approach entailed a limited and defensive distributive justice. His and fellow reformers' 500-page Seventh Report on Grievances of 1835 was a detailed attack on specific inequalities: patronage, offices, salaries, pensions, and the "Executive usurpation of popular rights." Inequality of wealth was not a concern "because population and capital spreading constantly in the wilderness, there is no great accumulation of capital in a few hands."[119]

The same priority re-emerged in Mackenzie's call to arms of 1 December 1837. The tyrants "will continue to roll their splendid carriages, and riot in their palaces, at our expense." But the real problem was the effect of wealth on political consciousness and political power. "There are some rich men now, as there were in

Christ's time, who would go with us in prosperity, but who will skulk in the rear, because of their large possessions." On the eve of rebellion, Mackenzie argued for confiscation and redistribution of Canada Company lands and clergy reserves. His purpose was motivational: every volunteer who joined the "friends of liberty" would be rewarded with land. His conception of equality and inequality remained civil and legal. His target was the "aristocracy of wealth": his solution was "a government of equal laws."[120]

The protests of 1837, with their repeated invocations of the American precedents of 1776, voiced an opportunistic egalitarianism that ran in many reform currents. Neither reformers nor republicans produced a coherent statement on equality or inequality. In Upper Canada the clearest statements emerged on inheritance of land, specifically from reformers' repeated efforts to abolish primogeniture.[121] Jeffrey McNairn has carefully linked the reform position on this issue to the idea that Upper Canada was a "truncated society," lacking the inherited hierarchy of England and hence extremes of wealth and poverty.[122]

It was Marshall Spring Bidwell, the American-origin lawyer and reformer who articulated most succinctly the reform position on inequality. Primogeniture, which he opposed, appeared to him a mainstay of aristocracy, an affliction of English society from which the colonies were so far free. "The immense accumulation of property in the hands of a few persons" in England did not make that country more happy or prosperous and led to "extreme want" and the "wretchedness of dependence" of many thousands. The problem, for Bidwell, was not poverty in itself, but rather the fact that inequality reduced loyalty and community among the population. "If only one out of six (or any number of) children inherited the whole of their father's land, the others would feel less interest to prevent and suppress intestine convulsions, or to repel an enemy, than if they had succeeded to a share of the patrimonial property. What interest, indeed, could they have in maintaining a system of law, that was unjust in principle and injurious in its operation?" The reformer was accepting the relationship between possession of land and social order.

The idea of inequality was clearly bounded, for Bidwell, within the ideal of property holding for the mass of the population. "Instead of a peasantry, let us have a yeomanry; and the country, on the one hand, would be more free, and all its liberal and popular institutions be supported with more spirit; and, on the other, the Government, within the just limits of its constitutional power and influence, would be vastly stronger." Bidwell's conclusion was a Canadian version of the Jacksonian position on inequality. "An equal division of property in a country was most favourable to its morality and happiness." But this was still a limited egalitarianism, because Bidwell did not endorse legislated limits on the accumulation of property. "He would not, to be sure, interfere with a man's right to dispose of his property; nor would he limit the extent of wealth, which a man might possess. So far, he would not legislate against the accumulation of property." Yet he would oppose legislation that would "increase and promote a disparity of property in the country." This was a protective and preventive egalitarianism – the wished-for equality of a moderate reformer. "He wished there might be none very wealthy, and none very poor."[123]

The image of freedom and equality here was that of the rural smallholder, free in his possession of self and of land. The image of the independent yeoman was crystallized by repeated reference to its opposite – the slave. Slavery was bondage of the person, denying all rights to independence of person and property. But reformers and rebels' references to slavery confirmed the limits of their attack on inequality, which was defensive: person and property must have legal and political independence. An existing economy of egalitarian promise must be defended against arbitrary authority and monopoly. Wealth redistribution, in so far as it was envisaged here, would follow from political emancipation for a wider set of property holders.[124]

The egalitarianism of the 1830s existed in a distant political economy, in a political culture that is difficult for those of us living in the early twenty-first century to penetrate. We are accustomed to seeing political positions and interests as reflections of economic interests or class position. In American political culture in this period, argues James L. Huston, "politics caused economic relationships."[125] It followed that "equal rights" in law and politics, for all property owners, was a sufficient guarantee of an appropriate equality of condition (which did not mean a perfect equality of wealth and income for everyone). The same conclusion did not apply without qualification to Upper and Lower Canada, where so many radicals and republicans saw economic relationships, and in particular economic privilege, as conditions of political corruption and oppression. Nevertheless, the solution to the interconnectedness of economic and political corruption lay in the ethical politics of the rural smallholding ideal: dismantling the artificial supports for privilege within the political system would dismantle monopoly and illegitimate accumulations of wealth.

Where in our time we might see laissez-faire leading to vast gaps between rich and poor, radical reformers of the 1830s associated it with reduction of inequality. We can perhaps grasp this logic in the radical U.S. Democrat group known as Locofocos.[126] Canadian reformers knew about them, and articles on them appeared in colonial newspapers. By "equal rights" the Locofocos did not mean "an equal division of property" – that was an "absurd impossibility." They insisted that the labourer had a right to the fruits of his labour, but not that the state should intervene in labour markets or compel employers to pay certain wages. Quite the opposite: everyone had an equal right to acquire property and to dispose of it freely. "They mean an equal participation in all those privileges which now enable the rich to become richer, and cause the poor to become poorer, and which are now enjoyed by monopolies."

Most radical reformers in Upper Canada would have agreed with the Locofocos that "property and privileges are altogether different things." The problem, in their view, was privilege, which led to monopoly. Privilege meant exclusive rights "conferred by legislative favour, folly or corruption." Eliminating it would restore the "natural order of society," assuring labour its just material reward. [127] As the example of the Locofocos suggests, we must read the meaning of equality and inequality in the setting of its time. Inequality, in the 1830s, meant privilege and monopoly; equality meant the wider distribution of specific rights, which would enable any redistribution of existing accumulations of wealth.

The critique of monopoly in the 1830s did not lead to a critique of capital, nor apparently any sustained concern over the relations between capitalist employers and waged workers, hardly at issue in a pre-industrial society. Gaps between rich and poor existed, but reformers and republicans said little about the causes or amelioration of poverty. When English civil law entered the colonies it left behind the laws relating to maintenance of the poor. An act providing for houses of industry was passed in Upper Canada in 1837, but was never implemented.[128] The 1830s saw the arrival of thousands of pauper emigrants, the solidification of the "less eligibility" principle, and an increasingly frequent distinction between deserving and undeserving poor.[129] Despite the growing awareness of poverty, no connection was made between the increasing numbers of poor and the problem of inequality. As for capitalists, the problem was that there were not enough of them. Under a "frugal Administration," Mackenzie argued in 1833, "the settlement of the country [would be] much facilitated by a numerous and intelligent class of capitalists," who might be discouraged from emigrating to Canada in the absence of "civil and religious freedom."[130]

When radical reformers said that labour was the source of all wealth, they did not draw the conclusion that employers were exploiting workers. They were attributing wealth to the labour of farmers – the majority of the population.[131] To the extent that they were articulating a simple "labour theory," their claim was egalitarian: each producer was an equal of every other producer, because each contributed to humanity's stock of material goods. Everyone was equal because each was entitled to a share of what they contributed, even if the shares were not equal in size. This formulation contained a subversive challenge to older defences of inequality that assumed an inherent inequality prior to any economic output. It proved to be a powerful basis for the critique of aristocracy and monopoly, and of any accumulation or advantage won by political connection.

At the same time, and often in the same breath, the labour theory could endorse an existing inequality of distribution. First, if wealth was the creation of labour, then existing accumulations must be the just reward for labour, whether manual or mental, including the labour of one's ancestors. Second, and more seriously, the labour theory was a form of nominalism: "producer" was a signifier used to label and exclude those deemed non-productive. Aristocrats, monopolists, corporate bankers were parasites in the labour theory as it was applied in the 1830s, but other viewers might name different groups. The theory erected a new hierarchy of the deserving and undeserving – a new inequality.

These understandings of equality and inequality could efface inequalities that seem obvious to us. In Lower Canada, said one reform advocate, "all great inequality of condition" was "obliterated" after the conquest. "Lower Canada at this moment possesses a population exhibiting less of inequality than perhaps any other country in the world."[132] According to another reformer, speaking in 1845, "It was the absence of this [landowning] inequality which constituted the happiness of the habitants in Lower Canada, who were the happiest and most contented people in the world."[133] So much for the inequalities of the seigneurial system and the growing numbers of rural and urban poor. Mackenzie, referring to the United States, wrote: "They speak of equality in this country, but it is in Upper Canada that it can be seen in all its glory."[134] His evidence was a "respectable" black family in York who employed white servants.

Equality and inequality co-existed within the limits of a discursive frame specific to the colonies in the 1820s and 1830s. That frame gave the words a meaning and a politics that we may not clearly perceive, if only because we place our own, different boundaries around the same words. The Freemasons and other fraternal associations that expanded rapidly in the first half of the nineteenth century provided one example. These communities proclaimed and practised equality and discarded or set aside old inequalities of status. Artisans, mechanics, and merchants mingled as brothers and equals and deployed a republican language of equality. Yet their fraternal equality contained exclusions, perhaps essential to it, that we would perceive as inequalities. For equality of rights and condition belonged only to those within the polity; outside it were the unqualified and unfit, including women, slaves, the property-less poor, Aboriginals, and the morally impure.[135] Thus did fraternal equality exhibit its hermetic quality. Equality was proclaimed, as it had been in the American colonies in the 1770s, within national, masculinist, and racialized frames.

There was another boundary around equality in the early nineteenth century, attenuated though never entirely dismantled in the twentieth. Where we may assume that everyone is equal in the possession of a capacity for moral and educational improvement, even the reformers and republicans of the 1830s were likely to assume limits to any such capacity. The presence of an innate endowment or a birthright precluded equality of condition and even of right. Jeffrey McNairn makes the point: "an honest, upright and just man" was not created by correct parenting, good schooling, and a benign environment; such a man was God's creation, and God did not bestow virtue and talent either similarly or equally among men, or between women and men.[136]

Today our understandings of inequality fit within economic frames in which ethical criteria are more often implicit than explicit; theirs

functioned in a moral frame that foregrounded the polarity of virtue
and corruption. Inequality meant the privilege accorded to corruption; equality meant the award of political and legal rights to men
of virtue. "Are wealthy, greedy, avaricious, worldly minded men the
only wise men? And if so, how different the road to honour on earth
and the road to honour in heaven must be!"[137] Within this moral
frame, the problem of inequality demanded not a moral economy of
provision or distribution, but recognition of the association of virtue – in particular, "manly virtue" – with political merit. This manly
virtue, as Michel Ducharme has detailed, consisted of ethical deriva-
tions from the world of rural smallholders: independence, simplicity,
frugality, honesty, diligence, and the ability to distinguish public
from private interest.[138] Writing in the decade after the Rebellions,
Clément Dumesnil, an immigrant from France, offered a republican
association of virtue and equality that would surely have met with
wide acceptance in both Upper and Lower Canada: "A good villager
is better than a high-placed tyrant. It is not in the power of all men
to be raised in dignity; but all have the power to be good citizens and
to be virtuous; in this they are all on an equal footing."[139]

Under the banner of equal rights, radical reformers and republicans fought for political inclusion and for protection against
privilege. They lost many battles, but bequeathed to reformers of the
1840s a rhetoric of equality that informed the political slogans of
that decade, and that even conservatives would occasionally borrow.
This Canadian-born egalitarianism would be invoked in support
of many causes, including responsible government, representation
by population, the end of the seigneurial system, the rise of state
schooling, separate schools, and much more. But it did not move
far beyond its roots in the political economy of the commercial and
agricultural societies of the early nineteenth century.

PLACING 1830S INEQUALITY IN CONTEXT

We may now understand a little better what would be required to
take this early egalitarianism and guide it towards the problem of
inequality in the Canadian liberal order. There were specific absences
in the 1830s that we may see as barriers to this process. A few are
obvious. Later ideals of redistribution would assume the presence
of a financial and administrative apparatus – a state system – that
did not exist in the 1830s. They would look to a very different tax

regime, capable of influencing society-wide allocations of income and wealth. The *idea* of such a regime was crucial, though not necessarily the reality. Absent also was the idea of systemic, economy-wide exploitation: not merely the appropriation of power and wealth by a privileged elite, but the structural capture of economic surplus by an entire stratum of the socio-economic system. Missing too, despite early manifestations, was the concept of a systemic regime of subordination and superordination by gender.

Less obvious are cultural conditions, absent in the 1830s, that evolved along many paths in Europe and North America in the nineteenth century. As Pierre Rosanvallan has argued, the idea of redistribution emerged through an "intellectual and moral revolution" that made societal inequality and redistribution thinkable.[140] The reformers of the 1830s could distinguish between public interest and private interests, and public opinion existed as a signifier of shared values. But their moral universe of virtue and corruption still rested securely on a conception of society as an aggregate of individuals possessing differing moral endowments. Probably they would have agreed with Archdeacon William Paley, that influential common-sense synthesizer of Enlightenment moral philosophy: "Although we speak of *communities* as sentient beings, nothing really exists or feels, but *individuals*. The happiness of a people is made up of the happiness of single persons, and the quantity of happiness can be augmented only by increasing the number of individuals, or the pleasure of their perceptions."[141] Happiness (one of Mackenzie's favourite words) was a social good, and maximizing public goods was measurable as the optimal aggregate of individual happinesses.

While this way of thinking did allow for notions of common interest (as, most obviously, among Patriotes in Lower Canada), it did not envisage society as an organism that evolved according to laws beyond the volition of individuals or groups of individuals. Gradually through the nineteenth century there emerged varying conceptions of societies as living and evolving organisms, and individuals as constituted by the contexts that created their identities. The "self" was no longer a being whom God created and endowed with capacities for sin and goodness. Instead the individual was dependent on the culture in which he or she was situated; the individual self was therefore not an independent but an interdependent being. Furthermore, the society of interdependent beings was an evolving organism, and since (especially after Darwin) institutions and even the state could be adaptive, then the laws governing societal evolution could and must be brought within the realm of human reason and science. The emerging sociology of the nineteenth century, from Comte to Marx and Herbert Spencer, reflected and propelled the shift.

These and other changes would not suddenly liberate equality and inequality from the older world of republican liberty and its moral universe of manly virtue and corruption. Still less would they secularize equality and inequality, shedding the Christian sources of egalitarianism. Much that was present in the older understandings of equality and inequality would survive and become elements in new ways of thinking about social evils and social change, and in new imaginings of the future. The distinctive political economy of Victorian Canada would reimagine and reignite equality and inequality.

CHAPTER THREE

Emerging Protestant Critiques of Wealth
(1830s–1880s)

One day in 1889 the president of the Board of Trade in Belleville, Ontario, gave a lecture – later printed – to the local assembly of the Knights of Labor. His subject was "the unequal distribution of wealth." Thomas Ritchie was a Presbyterian, a former student at the University of Toronto, and a partner in a merchant business in Belleville. He began his speech by asserting that among the pressing public questions of the day the unequal distribution of wealth was "without exception the most important." "There is something fundamentally wrong in our social system," he insisted. Despite the increase in wealth during the previous century, "the rich are only becoming richer and the poor poorer, and more dependent on the wealthy few." The result had been "the enslavement of the people as thoroughly and as truly as if they were the personal property of their wealthy masters." There were those among us, said Ritchie, who proposed that the order of things in society was inevitable, the result of a sort of divine providence. Their theories, he said, were "little short of blasphemy."[1]

Ritchie's words revealed the distance between our world and his. What is the likelihood, in our own time, that the president of the Chamber of Commerce in Belleville, or any other Canadian town, would appear before a labour organization to speak about the lamentable inequalities of income and wealth in Canada? How likely is it that such a representative of business interests would claim that inequality was threatening modern civilization? In the political culture of Canada in 1889 Ritchie's lecture would have prompted disagreement among many listeners; yet the giving of such a talk, even by a person outside the working class, was not an act of radical eccentricity. Ritchie was repeating claims and arguments that had percolated widely, both within and beyond the working class.

How are we to understand his address and its sweeping moral attack on inequality? It is a question about his world and also about ours. In Canada in the early twenty-first century we may occasionally hear such moral outrage over the evil of inequality, but hardly ever from the mouths of business leaders. Today we might refer to the force of neoliberalism and its secular faith in markets to explain why anything like Ritchie's critique was unlikely in our chambers of commerce. Yet neoliberalism at best partially accounts for the distance between these two Canadas. For a more complete understanding, we should explore the political culture of the last three decades of the nineteenth century, when specific social and economic disruptions interacted with powerful moral impulses to propel the search for an "ethical economy."[2]

We should begin by taking Thomas Ritchie at his word: the question of wealth distribution "is pre-eminently a moral one"; it also related to "natural rights" and to principles of justice as they applied to the "social compact."[3] Echoes of the Enlightenment amid the blast of Protestant ethics: Ritchie's words put his thought in the later throes of the long evangelical revival of the eighteenth and nineteenth centuries and its interaction with Enlightenment concepts in the schools and colleges of the British North American colonies. The writer's mix of ethics and economics grew in the heritage of Protestant piety that shaped his moral universe.[4]

Ritchie was discussing "the distribution of wealth" – a subject that by his time had a substantial lineage in political economy. But his balance of Christian and secular was weighed towards the former. He mentioned Adam Smith, but only to endorse the importance of property ownership. He declared that Malthus's doctrine on population was "a calumny on the goodness of the Almighty." He made no mention of John Stuart Mill, and he needed no distinction between production and distribution to know that "there is something fundamentally wrong in our social system." Instead an evangelical moral imperative told him that personal relationship was becoming "impersonal thing" and the economy "inanimate machine."[5] To understand how a businessman in the 1880s could arrive at such a position, we must revisit the history of Christian evangelicalism in the colonies. We see how the evangelical moral imperative led to reconsiderations of property and wealth, to attempts to reconcile wealth with Christian ethics and justice, and to complex responses to socialism and to the ideas of Henry George.

AN EVANGELICAL MORAL IMPERATIVE

Michael Gauvreau has told us about the colonial climate in which the evangelical awakening arose and evolved. Anglo-Scottish Enlightenment thought found a foothold in the United States in that nation's early decades; in the British colonies the priority of divine revelation meant stronger resistance to Enlightenment rationalism.[6]

By the time of Reverend Samuel Nelles, who became principal of the Methodist Victoria College in Cobourg, Canada West, in 1851, and of his student, the young Methodist Nathanael Burwash, older oppositions to Enlightenment rationalism had weakened or dissolved. Between rationalism and empiricism on the one hand, and the evangelical insistence on faith as a spiritual awakening on the other, there was a cautious alliance of mental forces.[7] It was not always a comfortable alliance, and, according to Gauvreau, this generation of evangelicals saw its faith "embattled" as it confronted the attractions of philosophical speculation and of science.[8] At what point did rationalism spill over into scepticism? Was there a risk that reason, in arguing this-worldly consequences of action, took priority over scripture as the ultimate guide to life and thought?

The young Nathanael Burwash (1839–1918) was not alone among his devout contemporaries in seeing scoffers and blasphemers everywhere in the world beyond the walls of his college.[9] The expanding encounter of the college's devout with the heady mix of rationalism and the Scottish philosophers demanded reinforcement of their commitment to revelation and the authority of scripture. Certainly the latter faith must triumph. Reason might be a valuable servant, but it risked being the unwitting slave of the passions and the conduit of unholy secular forces.

Mid-century evangelicals engaged with the religious experience differently from the revivalists of previous generations. Few ministers and college students experienced anything like the intense emotionalism of revival meetings in the first "great awakening" of the 1730s and 1740s, nor any of the pessimism that historians have detected in the Adventist movements of the 1830s and 1840s.[10] The religious experience was still very personal and even emotional for them, and sin must be defeated, but this was an engaged and even

optimistic generation, seeing sin as existing in the real world, a force
to confront and overcome. Its members directed the inward wrestling of the soul, the spiritual quest for salvation, outward, towards
the sins of this world and the earthly redemption that faith made
possible. Sin, says William Westfall, was beginning to acquire a more
social meaning.[11] Methodists and Presbyterians found many social
sins in the mid-century colonies – intemperance, tobacco-smoking,
greed, idleness, profligacy. It was possible, they said, to establish the
kingdom of God on earth: "The old revivalist had become an evangelical romantic," concludes Westfall.[12] As one of them put it: "The
churches are centres of sacred influence, as a city set on a hill which
cannot be hid. Their commission is to the world, proclaiming to its
people salvation through Jesus Christ. They are the salt of the earth.
The lights of the world."[13]

Consider the social vision, the "commission to the world," of the
Baptist immigrant Rev. Newton Bosworth. We know what he saw
in his city of Montreal, because he has told us in great detail. Taking
time from his ministerial duties, he wrote a history and description
of the place (1839). He found improvement, progress, and, in the
benevolent institutions, "common ground, on which all Christians
may unite to promote the honour of God."[14] He saw banks, the
customs house, ships in the harbour, many businesses large and
small, and the mansions of the wealthy – all in all "an increasingly
prosperous and flourishing city."[15] He also noted many evils, from
poor roads to the drunkenness that the Temperance Society sought
to eliminate.

Bosworth was not an economic neophyte. In the 1830s he had
acquired personal experience of the world of rent, taxes, loans,
and markets, because he had tried farming in Upper Canada. He
stood at the intersection of independent small landholding and the
expanding world of debt and credit. He knew that newcomers who
purchased land were often "taken in."[16] Moving between preaching, farming, and business, he learned something that did not sit
easily beside the benign view of commercial prosperity in his book
on Montreal. He knew about the "crooked policy which vitiates the
purity of commercial intercourse, and introduces interminable jeal-
ousies, suspicions and discords among men." He saw that commerce
was a world in which reason, calculation, and worldly interest took
priority over all rules derived from divine revelation. "The rapacious

spirit of modern commerce" had "thrown off all moral restraint." The only question commerce asks "is whether the gain which is sought, be it just or unjust, is likely to be obtained. All other considerations are thrown to the winds." By engaging in "the careless exposure of borrowed capital" the seeker of wealth risked not only his own savings in "hazardous speculations" but drew others into temptation and possible ruin.[17] In commerce and finance Bosworth found a model of impurity that served, by contrast, to define the Christian virtues of integrity, "do unto others," purity of motive, fairness, and "universal equity."

We have arrived at the birth of inequality – a vision of material distress in the midst of material plenty: "Commodities of every kind are every where to be found; the only difficulty is to obtain and pay for them. Providence has been very bountiful to us; but in the midst of our sufficiency we are in straits. How is this to be accounted for? Evidently by a derangement of that artificial and delusive system which a morbid craving of accumulation, and a neglect of moral considerations, have introduced into the commercial world."[18] Bosworth went no further with this thought. But he had hit on a key element in the modern conception of inequality: a "derangement" in the system (we would call it a structural problem), and it could be fixed!

Bosworth's vision of inequality was tentative and not supported with evidence, and in the decades that followed it found scant echoes. Few Protestant writers followed Bosworth's move from a moral censure of wealth to the idea that growing wealth came with expanding misery. The moral reservations about wealth and materialism endured, often it seems as a kind of instinctual reflex, a comforting iteration of the theme that "my kingdom is not of this world." Engrossed in a course on mental philosophy, determined to sustain a nexus of human reason and divine revelation, the young Nathanael Burwash wrote in his diary in 1859: "O how fatal a spirit of speculation and a desire for riches are to true piety."[19] Towards the end of a sixty-four-page (!) sermon in 1855 on the history of the Methodist church and its educational and missionary work in the colonies, William Case offered what might seem a non sequitur – the familiar nostrum about "the prevailing sin of the age, – the *love of gain*."[20]

Protestant commentary on wealth was not consistent.[21] Moral reservations stood uneasily beside a sometimes-complacent acceptance of commercial and financial wealth as signs of progress.[22] The mid-century intellectual context, however, was yielding up the elements of a more sweeping and strident condemnation. The "moral science" taught in the Protestant colleges contained the seeds of subversive ideas that could be turned into a powerful critique of capital. Parts of the *Elements of Moral Science* (1835) by the American Francis Wayland, widely used in U.S. and Canadian colleges for decades, tentatively explored emergent liberal principles in a mix of religious and secular language. Men, said Wayland, stand to each other in a relation of equality – not of condition, but of right. God bestows advantages differently among individuals, giving some wealth, others intellect, others physical strength. At the same time, he noted, all exist in circumstances of "perfect equality" in one key respect: "Each separate individual is created with precisely the same right to use the advantages with which God has endowed him as every other individual."[23] It made no sense, he argued, to say that superiority of condition conferred superior rights. Grant more rights to some people because of their wealth, and you must with equal logic ascribe the same to those who were physically stronger, and the result was "that the right of every one absolutely annihilates that of every other."[24] The principle of equality was respected only when each individual pursued his own happiness to the extent that he did not disturb others doing the same and exercising the common rights bestowed on everyone. The egalitarian message was clear: wealth had no rights and no freedom in the pursuit of happiness that labour did not also possess.

Wayland was joining equality to a negative idea of liberty, creating complex issues that his thoughtful Canadian students may well have struggled to resolve. One issue is worth considering, in the context of Jonathan Israel's view of modern egalitarianism, which locates its genesis in the radical Enlightenment.[25] Israel's interpretation raises the question of whether, and how far, modern egalitarianism can have roots in a Christian worldview that tends to divide humanity into saved and sinners, superiors and inferiors. Among Canadian Protestants equality was not a carefully developed concept, and the word appeared rarely. It was common sense that even if all human beings were capable of receiving the word of God and of exercising the faculty of reason, not all were equally able to do so. It seems unlikely that a Protestant egalitarianism could have offered much to the discovery of economic inequality. Yet there was the wisdom of Egerton Ryerson: he saw a "grand truth of creation" – which Greek and Roman philosophy lacked – in "the glorious doctrines of the universal fatherhood of God"; this truth was "the universal equality of all mankind," in the presence of which "all earthly distinctions of title, of rank, of attainments, of age, of nations, disappear."[26] In such thinking lay a potent source for a critique of inequality, but the potential was as yet unrealized.

RETHINKING PROPERTY AND WEALTH

One barrier to egalitarianism lay in the Protestant acceptance of the right of private property. To declare that right universal in no way implied a right to equal amounts. Once again Francis Wayland had his finger on the pulse. From him the college student learned that the right to property derived from the will of God. But humans may exercise God's will in many ways, and may acquire property by gift of God, by "the labor of our hands," or indirectly by gift, exchange, or inheritance. There is no labour theory of value here, and no assumption of equal distribution. Qualifications, however, feed directly into the critique of wealth. Morality restricted the legitimate means of accumulation: a man had no right "to anything more than to the *results of his labor*. He has no right ... to the results of the *labor of another*."[27]

This principle opened a door to inferences that Wayland did not state and likely did not foresee: one could as easily infer that the stockholder had no right to a share in the labour of others. In an even more potent qualification to property rights, Wayland stated a Protestant version of the idea of property as trust. "Everything which we behold is essentially the property of the Creator; and he has the right to confer the use of it upon whomsoever, and under what restrictions soever, he pleases."[28] The restrictions God imposes were those of moral science and divine revelation. The door was wide open to a radical claim: the capitalist could not do as he pleased with his property; he was bound to respect the common rights of his employees and their freedom to pursue happiness.

Of course few Protestant preachers would draw such inferences. The point is that the moral ground was shifting, and in much of evangelical thought the right to property rested on ambiguous foundations. An extreme case, however untypical, serves to suggest how unstable these foundations could be. In 1863 an evangelical Anglican in Saint John, New Brunswick, published two essays on "the tenure of property" and "the nature and quality of evil."[29] R.B.

Wiggins subordinated property rights to a principle of commutative justice (justice in exchanges between individuals or groups): title to property was acquired only by rendering a "full equivalent in the honest exercise of my faculties." His logic was that title to property rested only with God; thus "men" held it only "under tenure from the Lord of the Universe," by means of a transactional right: "That only is *yours* which you are willing to use for the benefit of the neighbour."[30] You could do so either by directly relieving others' wants or by managing property for society's benefit. In the absence of such clearly demonstrated use, your title was void. Because use was so commonly for personal gain or self-indulgence, it followed that "vast numbers of the human race have no legal title whatever to their own possessions."[31] Wealth, in this radical anti-materialist critique, was not a sign of virtue, hard work, or creative freedom in the use of private property but a "shield" that protected evil from "the righteous indignation of the injured and the oppressed."[32]

Wiggins's essays radically formulated a complex Protestant response to the world of commerce and finance. The response emerged prior to, and without direct reference to, the conflict of capital and labour that intensified in the third quarter of the century. When their relations acquired new political intensity in the 1870s and 1880s, a political ethics was already in place that allowed no easy defence of the interests of either side. The Presbyterian James Bennet neatly summarized that political ethic in 1861: the principle of supply and demand cannot ground relations between employers and employees. Material progress, he proposed, had been achieved through the squalor and ruin of large classes of humanity. Supply and demand, he argued, led inexorably to a kind of wage "slavery" – a concept voiced not only by workers but also by Protestant ministers. According to Bennet, neither supply and demand nor the need for economic growth, but rather the "scriptural principle" of "justice and equality," must govern relations between capital and labour.[33]

We should not dismiss this ethical political economy as pious and ineffectual homily, begging more questions than it answered. For this ethical economics reverberated far beyond the walls of the churches on Sunday morning, and it penetrated deeply the more secular domains of Canada's labour movement and its nascent socialism.[34]

The Protestant strictures on wealth offered a clear answer to a question about luxury that has surfaced in our own time. When a wealthy person obtains a luxury good, for his or her own personal satisfaction alone, is the acquisition justifiable? Does one have the right to amass vast wealth, and then to spend it on anything, merely because one is free to do so? One type of answer, consistent with the Protestant critique of wealth, was a resounding negative: in the absence of any demonstrable good or benefit, No. These responses were powerful: they morally condemned two sides of wealth: its acquisition and its use. On the acquisition of wealth: "What shall it profit a man if he gain the whole world and lose his soul?"[35] "How to purge trade of corruption is perhaps the greatest moral question before the world at this time."[36] "Wealth is seldom gained in absolute consistency with justice and mercy."[37] On the use of wealth: "The commonest vice of the time is extravagant living."[38]

Reiterated and sustained into the 1880s and 1890s, the critique of wealth was not always consistent or coherent, and it never crystallized into a political or ethical economic theory. The targets shifted: extravagance, luxury, wealth, profit, or even capital. At the core of this diffuse critique was fear of an alien power, a living entity with its own insatiable "nature," spreading its tentacles everywhere:

> The last thing that learns wisdom is money; the last power that surrenders to the Divine Maker is capital. By nature it is hard, mercenary, and cunning; ambitious to rule, and controlled by an insatiable greed. By nature it has neither morals nor religion, neither culture nor charity, neither benevolence nor mercy. Its sole desire is to increase its possessions and subject all things to its sway. It oppresses the poor; it overburdens production; it levies excessive charges on commerce; it exacts extravagant prices from purchasers, and delivers deficient quantities and fraudulent qualities, and at the same time withholds a just return to those whose needs compel them to sell.[39]

Here Canada's Methodist *Christian Guardian* was quoting, as it often did, an American source, and apparently agreeing. This quotation, from Charles C. Bonney's 1886 article, was unusual, in the pages of the Methodist weekly, only in its reference to taxation: "Unconsecrated capital evades just taxes for the public welfare."

Every condemnation contains a solution, either explicit or implicit; every sin offers the opportunity for redemption in this world, especially in nineteenth-century Ontario Protestantism. What then was the answer to the moral problems of wealth and profligacy, especially when these problems were clearly social or collective sins? How to enforce the moral proscription against greed? What did the moral conquest of excessive materialism look like?

CHRISTIAN DOCTRINE AND JUSTICE

To answer these questions we need to look more closely at the Protestant critique. At its core lay Christian principles of commutative justice – the justice that applies to the relationships or exchanges between individuals.[40] The golden rule "Do unto others" was its most obvious principle. Much of what Protestant writers saw in the economic world, especially in trade, contravened commutative justice. "A large portion of the wealth of the world is obtained, in violation of these laws [of God]."[41] The man of commerce bought cheap and sold dear: the inevitable consequence was the purchase of labour at less than its real worth, the sale of products for more than their true worth, and other nefarious marketing practices, including price-fixing and the creation of "an artificial demand for goods."[42] Charles Bonney's list of the evils of capital, quoted above, enumerated commutative evils – of exchange, return, and exaction.

What of profligacy and indulgence in luxury? Were these violations of commutative justice? Profoundly so: they amounted to denials of benevolence – the spiritual duty to think first of one's neighbour in all of one's doings. This obligation applied to all Christians, but especially the wealthy, who had a peculiar need to quench pride and covetousness. "As our privileges increase, so does our obligation; for unto whomsoever much is given, of him shall be much required."[43] Wealth entailed a duty of "proportionate giving,"[44] which usually meant simply giving at a constant percentage as one's wealth grew, rather than increasing the proportion. If a man did not allow his charities to keep up with his income, he was "robbing God" and damaging his own soul.[45]

The Protestant critique of wealth related to the doctrine of atonement, which was fundamental to evangelical religion. At its simplest, it refers to the propitiatory sacrifice by which Christ took upon himself the sins of humankind. In the evangelical world it meant not simply acceptance of Christ's redeeming sacrifice, but an active making of amends, a personal enactment in this world of being "at one" with

Christ: "Our relations to God are such as to require, on our part, some tangible acknowledgment of His sovereignty, and of our obligation to Him, and confidence in Him, as the God of providence and of grace. The divine law of beneficence is founded on these relations."[46]

Such active atonement was incumbent on everyone, but especially on the wealthy. Sacrifices were "an acknowledgment of the need of an atonement," and the wealthy were most in need, because they were most deeply immersed in the material world and had most to give. As one Presbyterian minister put it: "The atonement which the Saviour offered for your sins was a perfect one," freely offered to those "eagerly immersing themselves in business, or piling up gold and property."[47]

In 1880s Canada the Protestant critique of wealth confronted more directly than ever before the complex relations of capital and labour, which deeply troubled the Methodist *Christian Guardian*. In the previous decade the paper had given attention to labour issues – the Nine Hours' movement, labour reform, socialism, trade unions. The 1880s saw a much more sustained response to social questions, prompted by the rise of the Knights of Labor, major strikes in Canada and the United States, the increasing popularity of Henry George, and newspapers and governments' focus on the relations of capital and labour. The Protestant heritage allowed no easy or predictable answers to the new era of class conflict. A belief in spiritual progress and the optimism that accompanied the growth of Protestant churches in the third quarter of the century could lead to a confident faith that benevolence was advancing and would inevitably permeate the world of capital and labour. But the Christian vision of justice and equity, combined with the moral denunciations of wealth, could become, as William Westfall puts it, "a fulcrum for overturning capitalism itself."[48]

Inequality entered the frame, and so did distribution, but both usually in reference to the division of returns between capital and labour. The big issue of the day was "the relations and rights of labor and capital," or "the more equitable division of the profits of business between employer and employee."[49] Responses were varied, even incoherent, and certainly under-theorized – we would not expect a coherent theory of distributive justice. Nevertheless, they are worthy of attention, for this was one of the first concentrated engagements with the problem of inequality in Canada's era of industrial capitalism. However uncertain, the responses were seminal: they evolved and endured into the twentieth century, where many became cultural bedrock.

Atonement and commutative justice were keys to the response to inequality. Atonement set action within the frame of personal or individual responsibility; it stood firmly within the Christian onto-logical foundations of the individual.[50] Believers could not easily transfer it into collective action, other than by joining with others in charitable giving. "Substitution," or Christ's vicarious atonement, took human action beyond the level of secular law: "The substitu-tion of the Lord Jesus Christ is indeed contrary to *our processes of law*, but not because it contravenes them; it rises above and passes beyond their finite limitations."[51]

The reduction of "justice and equality" to commutative principles meant that distributive justice was rarely broached. Some writers did endorse a curtailment of profits and higher pay for employees.[52] The churches did encourage material transfers from rich to poor and urged a new distribution among the faithful, especially through greater transfers from wealthy members to the church itself. Had more members undertaken proportionate giving, or donated a tenth of their income to charity, wealth would have been redistributed, and not merely within the church community.[53] There occasionally sur-faced a more radical principle – that no members, however wealthy, should retain for personal or family use more than they needed for a modest standard of living.[54] Application of this principle would have more thoroughly redistributed income or wealth.

Nevertheless, the emphasis on exchange relationships and the benev-olence of "Do unto others" rendered distributive justice individual-istic. The answer to the problem of wealth lay in applying specific moral values in personal exchanges with others – honesty, fair dealing, benevolence – but there was no manual of ethical business practices to guide such application, and the individual conscience remained the agent of justice. So long as one did not knowingly cheat or falsely represent, one could claim to be just and equita-ble. If one did not advertise fraudulently, took reasonable returns on investments and non-usurious interest on loans, and was able to sell one's products, it was easy to assume one was giving value for the value received. The Protestant critique had erected no precise stan-dards of ethical practice to judge exchanges and to translate scrip-tural injunctions into business practice.

The Protestant emphases on the individual conquest of sin and on the spiritual transformation of the heart and soul were formidable barriers to collective redistribution. The individualist impulse was more than doctrine; it was a mental framework that subordinated collective action by secular authority. Although redistribution through state action was now thinkable, it might be a dangerous denial of individual responsibility. "Too Much and Not Enough" (1887) in the *Christian Guardian* in 1887 revealed this train of thought, mentioning "inequality" and addressing redistribution by the state. It began by terming "inequality of human conditions" an old evil that had become much greater in modern times. To solve the problem, and "if the relief of distress is to be conducted on principles of equity," then "every one who has more than is required for his absolute necessities must share in the work." There were, the article noted, two ways of "equalizing conditions of wealth": by taking from those who had and giving to those who had not, and by limiting the ability of any man to gain more than others. Neither method was acceptable; together they would "put an end to human progress." The flaw in collective redistribution: it denied individual responsibility. "All experience shows the acceptance of money from the State by people who have not earned it, to be destructive of independence and self-respect. In other words, pauperism is as great an evil as poverty."[55]

The "legislation habit" had already gone too far, said an 1887 editorial in the *Christian Guardian*; it was "an artificial stimulus" that removed "the discipline of Nature."[56] The same ethics that informed the Protestant critique of wealth inhibited secular distributive justice. In the generation that followed, Protestants associated with the social gospel would revise the relationship between spiritual and secular, but they would not overthrow the emphasis on individual responsibility.

The ethic of individual responsibility and personal redemption was a greater barrier to distributive justice than was the Protestant devotion to private property. The latter was flexible; the former was not. As Samuel Fleischacker has postulated, the main obstacle to rethinking distributive justice was not absolutism on property rights, but rather "a belief in the value of keeping the poor in poverty."[57] Poverty reminded believers of the consequences of specific sins, and was thus an incentive to virtue. The idea of poverty as a virtue in itself was unusual in Protestant discourse but, as Jean-Marie Fecteau points out, an occasional corollary of wealth's moral taint. As one Quebec writer put it: "Poverty of spirit, genuine detachment from riches, is a grace, a precious, a necessary virtue."[58] More often poverty was understood as an opportunity for redemption, for both the poor and those who gave them succour.

It is better to see the two concepts – the ethic of responsibility and the commitment to property rights – as intertwined and mutually reinforcing. Property was the product of and reward for labour, intelligence, and frugality; owning it became a sign of individual responsibility. The result was an unresolved tension, especially vis-à-vis property in the form of trusts and large corporations. These aggregations of property could reflect unadulterated selfishness but were also signs of self-discipline and even of benevolence – the desire to produce goods of benefit to others.[59] The much-maligned devotion to self-interest suddenly became a positive social value: "It cannot be denied that self-interest has promoted industry, intelligence, and improvement."[60]

SOCIALISM AND INDIVIDUAL RESPONSIBILITY

In the 1880s Protestant writers responded to socialism and to the ideas of Henry George, and in doing so they reinforced the association of property and individual responsibility. They easily turned the labour theory of value against a socialist reading. Accumulated property in land or capital "is generally the result of previous thrift and toil" – thus the owner had a just claim to that property.[61] Socialism had to be confronted and repelled, because it could confuse people by proclaiming the same values that Protestants accepted: equity, equality, benevolence. A common Protestant refrain was that socialism universalized selfishness and materialism. But the response was often more subtle. In rejecting socialism, Protestants discovered an argument about inequality that has remained with us ever since. Inequality was not the opposite of equality; it was the inevitable and acceptable result of an equality that already existed. "The equal right possessed by all to make the most of their natural endowments and advantages is itself productive of inequalities in the result."[62] At the same time the Protestant censure of luxury would not countenance anything like Bernard Mandeville's theory in the previous century that the luxuries of the rich set the nation to work and hence provided for the poor (the philosopher's main concern about inequality was that it would lead the poor to feel hard done by).[63] His idea that private self-interest was consistent with public good seemed a denial of morality.

The commutative duty of benevolence could absolve wealth in another way: to restrict the power to acquire wealth would limit "the duty of its charitable disposal." Making money, so long as it was "a means to an end," was wise, even noble.[64] One editorial in the *Christian Guardian* extended the exoneration to all acquisition of wealth: "The sayings of our Lord in regard to wealth had reference, not to the economic principles which govern its acquirement, nor the legal right by which it is held, but to its moral and religious uses."[65] The doctrine that property was never for personal use alone, that "wealth is a trust," could easily become an apologia: one need only cite the charitable works of the great capitalists, or their construction of housing for workers.[66] The critique of wealth was also undoubtedly muted in the last decades of the century by the desire to encourage wealthy members to donate to the churches, and to applaud their benefactions when they did so.[67]

Socialism, like the threat of materialism, hardened the Protestants' faith in the earthly power of benevolence. In the turbulent 1870s and 1880s a belief that benevolence was actually advancing became more urgent and necessary. Progress offered comfort: the direction of time was towards the fulfilment of the divine plan. Even the material world and its technological advances could be drawn into the reassuring teleology. Where many writers, including Protestant ministers, saw widening gaps between rich and poor, others saw material progress for all classes. Thus there emerged a classic reassurance, to be repeated in many forms over the next century: however deep the current gulf between rich and poor, progress meant that the poor today are better off than their predecessors. Even the impoverished handloom weavers of industrial England were wealthy compared to the poor of the medieval world or modern India.[68] The appeal to progress was a comforting answer to the very inequality that many Protestants perceived and feared.

At its extreme, the appeal became a form of millennialism, eloquently expressed by the popular American preacher Thomas Dewitt Talmage, whose column appeared regularly in the *Christian Guardian* in the 1870s and 1880s. His sermon on "Distribution of Rewards" contained a stark vision of inequality in the United States, where two million inhabitants "cannot get honest work" and five million "are on the verge of starvation." The sermon dissolved these present evils in a dream of the future, when "deserts will be irrigated" and "all the unproductive parts of all the continents will be turned into harvest fields and orchards." "Many of the millionaire estates will crack to pieces on the dissipations of grandchildren, and then dissolve into the possession of the masses, who now have an insufficiency." Talmage did not specify how this would occur; he did not need to, because God would provide. "God will not wait for the Day of Judgment. All these palaces of sin will become palaces of righteousness." "In some way there will be a new apportionment."[69] The faith in progress was a reassuring answer to the socialists, and a tranquillizer, suppressing the disturbing idea of distributive remedy.

HENRY GEORGE AND THE INDEPENDENT PRODUCER

Protestant writers struggled to contain social evils, and also to limit the force of their own critique of wealth. They would not entirely succeed, for they had let a big genie out of their bottle of ethics. The Protestant stance offered a rhetorical arsenal for the coming Progressive-era assault on monopoly capital. It did more: it rooted in Anglo-Canadian culture an egalitarian ethic of benevolence that guided the expanding conversation about exploitation and poverty, and helped locate the source of those evils in a societal condition – inequality.

We are closer to an understanding of Thomas Ritchie's lecture to the Knights of Labor in 1889, but the story is not quite complete. We need to remember something very important about Ritchie. He lived in a small town of about 10,000 people, which was thoroughly integrated with the surrounding rural economy. The products of farms and forest flowed through the town, by rail and by water, and the future appeared to lie in small-scale processing of agricultural products. Among male residents, the most common occupation in 1881 was farmer, and as always the official measurements underestimate farm labour by omitting women's unpaid work.[70] Ritchie's horizons were those of a retailer in a predominantly rural and agricultural economy. In his world self-employment was far more common than wage labour, and this was true not only of the small town but also of Canada as a whole.

In 1881 48.1 per cent of the Dominion's "gainfully occupied" were in agricultural pursuits – an underestimate, omitting women farmers.[71] Canada was a rural country with a scattering of large urban enclaves. The definitions are highly problematic, as Ruth Sandwell has pointed out, but whatever the definition of "rural," at least three of every four Canadians lived in such a place in 1881, and the rural population was growing.[72] As a result, manufacturing industry and even wage labour could be seen as recent arrivals and unfamiliar intruders, or at best promising extensions to the agricultural and resource-based economy. In this context, it was not difficult to believe that all wealth came from land and the labour applied to land.

The problem of inequality, as it surfaced in the 1880s, emerged in the confluence of two great cultural streams: the Protestant critique of wealth and the ideal of the independent yeoman, the small patriarchal landowner who supported his family from his labour and the soil. In the United States, the old republican ideal had evolved into a "free labor" ideology, emphasizing the vital economic contribution of the independent producer, the ownership of property as key to republican virtue, and wage earning as a stage in the quest for independence. Canadians, both workers and those in other classes, had their own version of the independent-producer ideology, usually shorn of republican overtones, but with the gender assumptions intact.

Another exemplary text, a speech published as a pamphlet in 1888, illustrated the merging of these two streams. Richard T. Lancefield was an evangelical Anglican.[73] He began by citing "the Gospel of Christ" and "reverence for the Christianity of the New Testament," which he thought to be spreading in Canadian society. His own faith resolved into "beautiful moral principles" and "danger signals" for the world around him. There followed a litany of familiar precepts from the critique of wealth. "And having food and raiment let us therewith be content." "The love of money is the root of all evil." "Lay not up for yourselves treasures upon earth."[74] Having learned these principles from childhood, said Lancefield, the young man of today ventured forth into the world of business, only to find them "totally impracticable" and "the sacred altars of God's temples ... profaned" by an "insensate race for wealth."[75]

Lancefield embarked on what he called "the new crusade" – like those in medieval times, to liberate sacred land. Infidels had captured the territory, alleged the speaker; the crusade would rescue "God's natural opportunities" from men who have seized and imprisoned them. Those dastardly few had seized land, separating the masses from it and leaving them in cities "packed close together – too close for religion, virtue or sobriety to flourish." When "poor people are herded together as though land was scarce," said Lancefield, at "that moment you lay the foundation for the superstructure of misery."[76] The "seeming scarcity" was a myth, however – and there followed a very Canadian vision of empty vistas waiting for occupation and use: "What folly to hear of wheat and potatoes being scarce, with millions of acres of virgin soil yet untouched by the plough, and only waiting to yield the harvest of to the husbandman!"[77]

The old ideal of the independent landholder, the manly independence of the patriarchal family farm, now inspired the Canadian followers of Henry George to argue for taxation and redistribution of land. "I have never yet met the man who could exist without access to land."[78]

The Protestant critique of wealth came together with the producerist vision of landed independence. The result was the problem of inequality – Lancefield's vision of "people half-starving in the midst of plenty." "While the rich are growing richer, the poor are growing poorer – the very thing that Christ warned us to guard against."[79] The problem could be solved, and the solution was consistent with the diagnosis. At the spiritual and material levels, the answer was individualist and egalitarian: owning and working land would liberate the individual conscience and secure universal benevolence.

Henry George and his followers produced the nineteenth century's most popular analysis of inequality. Their analysis and their proposed solution may seem naïve and utopian – certainly many contemporaries thought so. Nevertheless, the effect was immense and enduring. Inequality took its place in political discourse as never before. A new door had opened wide: the problem could be solved, through taxation. It was now possible to conceive of taxation as a society-wide mechanism of redistribution. The land-tax movement contributed something else: a non-socialist analysis of exploitation. The followers of Henry George had identified what in our own time we refer to as economic rent, and they had identified rent-seeking behaviour. Briefly, economic rent refers to any payment to a factor of production (land, labour, capital) above what would keep that factor in use or in production. Henry George saw in economic rent from land a systemic exploitation and the cause of inequality. Even where his specific diagnosis did not endure, two ideas had emerged: inequality was the symptom of a structural defect; and the defect could be repaired. The Protestant critique of wealth had already pre-pared the way with its version of the concept of economic rent, and to read Henry George is to hear powerful echoes of that critique: some people were taking from society's great productive capacities far more than they deserved, more than their inputs of virtue and knowledge warranted.

The land-tax movement reflected and reinforced another major change in the history of distributive justice. George's followers insisted on distinguishing symptoms from causes. Was intemperance the great social evil that reduced so many families to poverty? No: intemperance was a symptom of deeper evils. Was poverty the result of improvidence, laziness, and vice among the poor? No, said the tax reformer: the causation went in the other direction, and pov-erty was the cause of vice.[80] Did technological change, the use of more machinery in production, cause unemployment? No, said the single-taxer: loss of jobs was a symptom of a structural failure to secure to labour the right to earn wages.[81] Would either free trade or protection solve the problem of inequality? No, said the follower of George: wealth concentrated in the hands of the few under both types of regimes, and the debate over protection was a red herring.[82]

And so when Thomas Ritchie spoke to the Knights of Labor in Belleville, he trumpeted the problem of inequality and proclaimed a solution. Taxation of land and redistribution of the unearned incre-mental value in land would "secure to the individual the personal possession of what he rightfully owns."[83] This redistribution was a spiritual mission, in obedience to the "Almighty power above us who will have his Laws obeyed by moral agents ... on lines of jus-tice and righteousness."[84] The spiritual mission to cure inequality was a radical liberal affirmation of individual rights of property and conscience. The millennial dream of T. Dewitt Talmage was now a liberal teleology of progress, the proclamation of an immanent future of universal benevolence.

CHAPTER FOUR

Labour Voices, Worker Intellectuals, and the Politics of Immanence (1870–1920)

The discovery of inequality as a social problem takes place in disruption, in times when social forms are dissolving and reconstituting or when new economic practices are penetrating existing traditions. The intrusion of commerce and finance into the rural world of colonial agriculture was one such prolonged disruption (see chapter 2). Another occurred in Canada in the last half of the nineteenth century, when a working class confronted industrial capitalism and its constellation of wage labour, urban living, and insecure employment. The history of labour's struggles has been told in many ways, and a focus on the problem of inequality cannot revise what historians have given us; instead it may offer a slightly different angle of vision on older themes and understandings. This focus can tell us about a discovery of inequality that was different from, though owing much to, the discovery that stemmed from the Protestant critique of wealth (chapter 3). And the perception of inequality by workers and their intellectual advocates can perhaps illuminate labour's ambivalent and unresolved reckoning with the Canadian liberal order.

Among self-taught working-class thinkers and journalists sympathetic to labour, the distribution of wealth was not a discrete category of analysis or thought. What James Huston says about workers in the United States applied equally to those in Canada: their concepts about distribution, and especially their solutions, "remained fuzzy."[1] We should not expect to find a complete, Canadian-origin analysis of the distribution of income or wealth. Rarely will we uncover an explicit focus on inequality at the societal level. The word "inequality" did not surface much in working-class discourse and was rare in Canadian newspapers representing working-class interests. It did not occur once in the five volumes of testimony to the Dominion government's Royal Commission on the Relations of Capital and Labor (1889). "Distribution" in those volumes did not refer to income or wealth.[2]

Canadian workers, however, were discovering inequality in the decades after 1850, and they did so in their own way. We see this in scattered and diverse sources, in a vocabulary that they inherited from pre-industrial reform politics and cobbled together anew from their experience of wage labour and the transition to industrial-capitalist workplaces. The sources recorded the voices of workers themselves, and also those of journalists and others who claimed to speak in their interest. It follows that we cannot hear a single voice, and certainly no singular expression of working-class opinion. Nevertheless, we can say that Canadian workers and their advocates were heirs to and often used the language of radical reformers and republicans of the 1830s. While borrowing from American sources, they did so very selectively; their association of equality and liberty with landowning independence had its own Canadian roots. Their language on work and wealth owed much to Christian social ethics, and we hear many echoes of the Protestant critique of wealth. Their dominant source, however, was their experience of wage labour itself, which imparted a new and class-specific inflexion to the problem of inequality. We follow these inflexions from their first appearance, through labour's reckonings with Henry George and with socialism, through its conjoining of cooperation with commonwealth, to its reconstruction programs at the end of the First World War.

FIRST RECOGNITIONS OF INEQUALITY

If there was one principle on which most workers agreed, it was the idea that labour was the source of wealth. They inherited the labour theory of property or value from pre-industrial political economy, and it had a long life in Canada, where the industrial transition was slow and uneven.[3] Canadian republicans and others in the 1830s adapted the theory to their own political ends, especially in their attacks on banks, monopolists, and corrupt place-holders: "There shall never be created within this state any incorporated trading companies or incorporated companies with banking powers ... Labour is the only means of creating wealth."[4] This version of the theory made sense in an agricultural economy: products of value came out of the ground because the farm family applied its labour to the land. Equity and justice were realized when producers reaped the fruits of their labour, either by consuming the products they created or by exchanging them in markets for a fair return.

Wage labour presented a series of problems for those who accepted the labour theory, in whatever form. The theory seemed to offer a clear ethical standard for the distribution of returns from labour: one reaped in proportion to the labour that one invested; those such as the big landowners who received a benefit without investing labour committed a type of theft. But the standard was not always clear. Wage labour did not fit easily into existing value systems. In exchanging labour for a wage, the worker did not see the product of his and her labour flowing out of the ground. The wage system monetized the fruits of labour, and there was no obvious equation between the market value of goods workers produced and the wages they obtained. As David Montgomery says: "New forms of exploitation ... disguised the generation of wealth and the economy's creative and ruthless dynamism as market relations, in which everyone received some equivalent for what he or she had contributed."[5] The wage offered a specious precision to the exchange; in reality it merely invited debate over the level of a just and fair "equivalent."

Another question arose: what was labour, and who were the workers? Did labour consist only of manual effort and manually applied skill, or did it also include mental endeavours? If it did include the latter, what was the appropriate return for its fruits for merchants, as one example? Did the capitalist earn a reward for labour by virtue of his mental inputs of organization and administration, or even by his application of accumulated capital to the process of production? A related problem was one of measurement: since different quantities and qualities of labour went into production, what remuneration was appropriate to each? These questions would confound generations of Canadian workers and their advocates, who seemed unaware of British rejections of the labour theory.

A simple way to preserve the labour theory was to place capitalists in the same category as aristocrats, who used their ownership of land to remain idle while living from the surplus that dependent peasants and labourers created. If capitalists were doing something similar, then one could resolve any distributional inequity by eliminating their capital from the economy and them from the production process. In the first stage of industrialization, most Canadian workers did not choose this path, partly because of how they experienced the industrial transition. We have learned to see industrialization as an uneven evolution in which small units of production proliferated and preserved many craft traditions.

In the present context, we should recall something labour historians know well. In most industrial workplaces in the third quarter of the nineteenth century, employees knew their colleagues and their boss. The deep-sea sailing ship of the 1860s, with its crew of twenty-five or fewer, was a large workplace – much bigger than most textile "factories" (an average of twelve employees per establishment in Ontario in 1871).[6] The immediate employer was a master, often a former shop-floor worker, who could be seen contributing mental and even manual labour. If the master of the sailing ship received more than the Able Seaman, those extra earnings might seem an appropriate reward for quantities of skill, experience, and responsibility.

Paternalism was a way of dealing with distribution. It involved much more than occasional banquets and friendly courtesies. It was a basic strategy of employment, to recruit and discipline workers. It was a type of exchange, whereby workers offered labour and loyalty in return for wages and the promise of stable employment, or at least a stable income. Couched in a language of mutual benefit and reciprocity, paternalism embraced notions about sharing and distribution: masters and company servants accepted a hierarchy of rank and authority, but all were producers who shared the product of the collective enterprise. Often employers reinforced the message of sharing through material benefits other than the wage; railway-company benefit schemes and mutual-insurance plans are the most obvious examples. When workers toasted their employers at formal banquets, they were acting in accord with the labour theory of value by acknowledging the value of their masters' mental labour.

Historians have given us substantial studies of craft workers in this period, often differing on these employees' class position and the content of working-class consciousness by the early 1870s. Emphasizing the non-linear and overlapping industrial transition in Hamilton, Ontario, Robert Kristofferson labels craft workers' position as "trans-modal" – participating in capitalist institutions and markets while remaining independent producers by partly owning means of production, or expecting to.[7] While not all of Kristofferson's conclusions

convinced every historian, his and other accounts of craft consciousness help us to grasp when and why Canadian workers and their ideological supporters became aware of income and wealth inequality.

The craft workers' early trade unions were not conscious of a
society-wide inequality. Their multi-purpose associations protected
them while assuming a common interest with masters; all were producers seeking "a fair equivalent for our labour." Inequality required
a perception of distance and difference; it was not relevant for craft
mutualism, which assumed identity of interest among producers
and could even deny inequality: "When you speak of the working
man in Ontario, you include everybody. We all work. We all began
with nothing. We have all got by hard work all we own – and the
richest among us still work, and like to do it."[8] Such resilient egalitarianism prevented any admission of inferior status or position, and
hence of any inequality, whether moral or material. Craft workers
adopted their own version of a "self-made man" ideal, and wealthy
employers confirmed its feasibility: "By honesty and integrity he has
amassed for himself a considerable fortune."[9] Whether or not dispossession was still a "marginal experience" among these workers,
as Kristofferson suggests, the confident expectation of independence
and property – a family home, even small capital – had deep roots
in the craft aspiration of manly independence. To perceive one's
ensnarement in an unjust societal inequality would require a new
disruption and a failure of expectations.

Conditions for a discovery of inequality were emerging, however,
even within this craft world. In both the United States and Canada
trade unions were, among other things, a response to the problem of
distributing returns from the collective work of production. These
bodies were internally distributive, of course: many were provident societies, collecting dues and redistributing limited resources
among members. Even within the framework of mutualism and the
"producer ideology," a gap between rich and poor could open up.
For example: in Saint John, New Brunswick, in 1849, mill owners applied steam power and laid off some sawyers. The change
had "already disemployed a multitude of mechanics" and caused
"distress and misery amongst a class of men whose industry would
render them respectable[,] happy and independent." According to
the sawyers, the employers acted "for the purpose of Monopoly," in
the sense of dispossession – specifically, seizing a "monopoly of the
poor man's rights." No mention of inequality, but a moral principle

about the rich and the poor, "which inculcates upon the rich the propriety of respecting the interests and happiness of the poor."[10] The sawyers saw violation of a basic principle of paternalism and its mutual obligations. They were calling not for a redistribution, either of rights or of employment, but for recognition of a just distribution that, in their view, already existed.

When trade unions started presenting demands on wages, they were enacting a form of distributive justice, and by the 1860s and 1870s, if not before, the distributive intention was explicit. Discussions with masters were about "the right of the producer to an equitable share of that which he produces."[11] The present system, said the Saint John Crispins, "concedes to the labor [*sic*] only so much of his own production as shall make comfortable living a bare possibility, and places education and social position beyond his reach."[12] "To permit the lion's share of the profits to pass into the hands of capitalists, while the mechanics drag out a miserable existence, is to tolerate a condition of affairs which is inimical to the best interests of the country."[13] Workers might not be able to quantify an "equitable share," but they knew that it existed and was attainable.

Challenges to the workers' notions of distributive equity appeared, both intellectual and material. Employers' responses helped to focus local negotiations and conflicts on principles. In 1866 Quebec ship labourers heard: "Labour was simply a commodity, like everything else, and was regulated by the same laws."[14] In 1869 the Halifax painters and glaziers learned: "The law of supply and demand will always regulate the value of labour; and ... combination ... can never succeed in keeping up wages beyond their natural levels."[15] Such references to economic or "natural" laws prompted a variety of rejoinders deriving from a labour theory of value, or at least a defence of "the fruits of labour" ideal: "The line of the ruling class everywhere is – Property First, Man afterwards. We say: 'Man first, Property afterwards!'... The moneyocracy says: 'You shall not enjoy the fruits of your labour, only what we allow you. The balance of the value of your labour we will keep ourselves!' That's why we have trade unions and strikes."[16]

Another workers' rejoinder was to deny that laws of supply and demand determined the value of labour. Rather it was privilege, especially of the political type accruing to employers and their allies. This response was a crucial step towards a redistributive role for the state. If capitalists refused to respect the principle of just remuneration for labour, "What is the remedy for this state of things? There is only one, and that is for the Legislature to pass a law to give the workmen an equitable division in the profits of his own productions."[17] Securing a just and equitable division of the wealth being produced related integrally to the push for better political representation of workers.

The employers' appeal to supply and demand in this period was consistent with a simplified concept of a wage fund: a fixed amount or portion of capital available to pay wages at any given time.[18] It followed, in this view, that wage levels would vary only with the number of workers seeking work. An employer could not pay more than his or her available fund allowed, or the company would collapse. Even where employers might be flexible in determining wages, they still thought of wages as a share of revenues in a zero-sum game.[19] The more they gave to workers, the less they had for other remuneration, returns to shareholders, or reinvestment.

Workers began to respond to these assumptions. They might offer a historical perspective. There was no fixed wage fund, they said, because productivity changes over time made returns fluid, along with relative returns to capital and labour. The Toronto cooper John Hewitt made this point in 1872, in his preamble to a motion on the hours of work: "Whereas the progress of the present age has brought into existence many useful labour-saving devices, that have greatly increased the production of manual labour and whereas the producing classes have not received any benefit commensurate with the increase in production."[20]

The historical argument would recur frequently: machinery and the passage of time had yielded a vast outpouring of wealth. The thesis was redistributive. Redistribution upwards had already occurred: an increasing share of total incomes and wealth had accrued to a small number of people. By a range of means, including the work of trade unions, the working class would reverse the trend, reduce or eliminate the share going to machinery or its owners, and increase labour's share of both productivity gains and total wealth.

When workers in the third quarter of the century asserted that an increasing share of incomes and wealth was going to fewer people over time, they were substantially correct. Although data for nineteenth-century Canada are scarce, there are estimates for the U.S. pattern, and the trend for Canada was probably similar. The top 1 or 10 per cent's share of wealth increased in the first stage of industrialization (and in the United States it continued to rise into the 1910s).[21] Workers relied on what they observed around them. Everywhere they saw at first hand many changes of scale: larger urban property-holdings; bigger workplaces appearing beside small workshops; sizable churches being built for affluent worshippers; and larger mansions being erected in adjacent but still nearby neighbourhoods, or easily noticeable on the hill overlooking the town.[22] The signs of "bigness" were markers of an expanding wealth that was nearby but not shared.

This apprehension of material inequality was different from that of most commentators today. We observe such inequalities at the societal level, but usually at a distance. We may read about the lives and luxuries of the 0.1 per cent, but rarely do we witness them in person. For those of us in the middle-income quintiles, income differences may surface when we act as consumers, but usually lie within a fairly narrow range, except for those of us who work in food banks or shelters for the poor. The lowest income earners live and work apart from the highest, and those at the very top dwell in gated communities. Workers today may read about the differences between their annual pay and that of executives in their company, but rarely see those people or share a meal with them. Any connection between one's employment and societal inequality is distant from daily experience. It was not so for our Victorian working-class ancestors. They were reacting to direct impressions of material differences and changes in scale within the spaces where they walked to work and to leisure.

Impressions, however, were not enough for workers to confirm the historical thesis about inequitable distribution and the urgent need for redistribution. They needed empirical proof. And so we see them reaching for that proof. John Hewitt, writing in 1873, offered one example: "We increase our material wealth over and above our living requirements 3 per cent, while we pay for the medium of exchange at 7 to 12 per cent. Money is the power which swallows up and centralizes all, snatching from the labourer 4 to 9 per cent of his actual subsistence allowance. That is why wealth centralizes. Two per cent of our population possess half the wealth."[23]

We have arrived at a working-class discovery of inequality. It matters not that Hewitt's estimates may be rudimentary.[24] The path from the labour theory of wealth, through the experience of wage labour and capitalist markets, had led to a perception of inequality as a historical condition of emergent industrial capitalism – a perception, let it be noted, that was accurate in substance if not in detail.[25]

The strands of distributive thought came together in that most persistent of labour campaigns, the movement for shorter hours. The connection may seem counter-intuitive: after all, if workers spent fewer hours on the job, surely they would earn less, and capital's share would remain constant or even increase. In fact, as John Battye and other historians of the movement have shown, shorter hours was an egalitarian and redistributive project.[26] Where wages were at a daily rate, it was expected that they would remain constant; hourly or piece rates would go up to limit the net loss in income to workers. The effect would be an upward shift in the ratio of wages to total company revenues. Shorter hours would achieve another redistributive shift, by requiring employers to hire more workers to maintain production. The effect would be to reduce unemployment, shrink the pool of surplus labour, and strengthen the bargaining position of workers.

The Nine Hours "pioneers" of the early 1870s understood all this. They did not all agree that there was no basic conflict between the interests of capital and labour, but they appear to have been unanimous on the principle of equitable distribution. "The capitalist had profited by the labor and toil of his workmen, while the workmen themselves had not received a corresponding profit." Workers were urged to "claim your share in the prosperity you so greatly help to make."[27] Workers "did not receive a return for their labours equal to what the capitalist received for his capital."[28] The rhetoric of the movement is replete with the language of social elevation.[29] "The Equalization of all the Elements of Society in the Social Scale Should be the True Aim of Civilization," proclaimed the masthead of the *Ontario Workman*.[30] Opponents of the movement grasped the point when they denounced nine hours as a "communistic system of levelling."[31]

By the 1870s Canadian workers and their supporters had new sources of information and opinion, and wider channels of communication between towns and cities and across the border with the

United States. Newspapers such as the *Ontario Workman* sought to represent workers' interests; benefitting from John A. Macdonald's patronage, the paper was never non-partisan, but it did introduce readers to a range of social-reform topics, to American opinion on the relations of capital and labour, and to discussions of political economy. Founded in the campaign for Nine Hours, the *Workman* continued and widened the conversation about distributive justice.

The conversation contained something transparently obvious, but here as elsewhere the obvious is worthy of remark. Writers in the newspaper asserted not only that gaps between rich and poor were widening with economic growth; they insisted that there was a direct causal relationship between being rich and being poor. The argument was not new, because it appeared in the Protestant critique of wealth, but it stood at the forefront of labour's ethical economics. In its many forms of expression it combined moral outrage with a theory of economic surplus. It was "a glaring injustice" that "the money which enables the rich to wallow in the mire of enervated satiation, is distilled from the tears and sweat of the toiling, starving poor."[32] "Wealth breeds poverty, and poverty in turn breeds wealth."[33] Inequality, in this conception, was a consequence of exploitation within the system of production: "The annual increase of wealth, instead of going to increase the comforts of the workers, is wholly absorbed by the few in the shape of rent, usury, exorbitant profits, stock exchange winnings, or through some other form of legalized robbery. If some people are superfluously wealthy, others must be miserably poor. These social phenomena sustain the relation of cause and effect."[34]

The Protestant critique of wealth had developed no such theory of exploitation. Now workers and their supporters often connected inequality to exploitation to rebut the economics of "supply and demand" or Malthusian ideas that population was outgrowing available resources:

We are at present in such a stage of the development of the industry of all civilized nations that the increase in productive capacity far outstrips increase of population, so that the amount produced on an average by every person in the world far exceeds in quantity and value that which was ever before known ...
And who will deny that the value of the development of human society is not worth a great deal more than the value of the food

and other necessaries consumed by the human race? ... So the
workman who earns his wages gives the products of his labor
back to his employers, a value surpassing that of his earnings, if
this was not so, he would not have been employed.[35]

Again the question: does the possessor of great wealth have the
right to spend money on any luxury good?[36] The answer here was a
resounding "No," but the grounds were different. Now the basis of
the negative answer was simple: the money is not yours to spend –
you have stolen it from others.

It was this moral point, as much as anything, that propelled the search
for empirical proof of inequitable distribution. The *Palladium of
Labor* made the connection between statistics and social justice: "Statistics like those from which we have quoted, will do more to ripen
public opinion and convince the world of the justice of the demand
for Labor Reform than any amount of mere declamation and appeals
to emotions without the facts and figures to back them up."[37]

Historians have told us how statistics served the process of state
formation and the interest of elites. But statistics also aided working-class resistance. Workers demanded social statistics and saw it as
the state's duty to provide them. The first annual convention (1883)
of the Trades and Labor Congress of Canada asked for the creation
of Dominion and provincial bureaux of labour statistics, and later
meetings repeated the request.[38]

The search for quantitative confirmation of inequality accelerated
in the 1870s and 1880s. In the absence of Canadian data on wealth
and of national-income accounts, writers on labour issues looked to
the United Kingdom and the United States.[39] They plundered British
sources for data on landowning in England, whose aristocrats were
easy targets, offering prime examples of inherited and unearned
wealth. Thomas Galbraith of Port Hope, Ontario, used information
on taxation and on housing in Britain to compare the wealthy "one
and a half per cent" with those who lived in houses with annual
rental value of less than twenty pounds (sterling). He then offered
up the number of millionaires who died every year in Britain; estimates of the number of paupers and of vagrants in London; the
level of agricultural wages in England; the number of child labourers
in New York; and a flurry of other statistics. This rambling inven-
tory he linked explicitly to "the system by which the gross result

is appropriated by capital, and under which the self-indulgence of wealth soars to unimagined heights, whilst the area of misery, ignorance and exhaustion sinks even deeper."[40]

Progressive journalists were becoming data gatherers. They were seeking a quantitative basis for a moral principle – "just return" to labour. The assiduous amassing of statistics may reflect a naïve faith in the persuasive power of numbers, but it is consistent with the wider tendency to conscript science into politics.[41] The data-gathering in fact demonstrated ingenuity and occasional perspicacity. In 1886 Phillips Thompson (no habitual quantifier himself) used figures from reports of the Ontario Bureau of Industries to help dismantle the "self-made man" myth.[42] The bureau reported average wages by occupation, which Thompson applied to estimate the total potential savings of workers over time. Given the level of living costs, the savings over time were very small – a "mere flea bite" – and totally insufficient to allow anything that might be called wealth. "Rising through the ranks" was therefore possible for only a tiny minority, and, where it did occur, honest toil and thrift were not the cause. Wealth, therefore, was not *self*-made.

A humane ingenuity appeared in an article in the *Palladium of Labor* in 1885 – an early discovery, at least for Canadian newspapers, of the relevance of demographic data to inequality. "Rich and Poor" cited English evidence: "Turning to Chadwick's Sanitary Reports, where we have average durations of life of different classes of society, we find at page 155, the following with regard to Derby. Gentry and professional classes, 49 years, the middle classes, 38, and the working classes, 21 years."[43] The article presented as well life expectancies for Bolton, Liverpool, Leeds, Bethnal Green, and Manchester (in the last, average working-class life expectancy was 17). "Rich and Poor" concluded bluntly that "the working classes are murdered by wholesale."

Data on charity served to illustrate not the generosity of the rich but the increase in poverty alongside growing wealth. One analysis of charity in New York argued that while the city's population had grown by 134 per cent between 1850 and 1880, charitable transfers had risen by 539 per cent – a measure not of expanding generosity but of increasing need and exploitation. A tiny fraction of the riches of millionaires, "stolen from the earnings of the poor," was being returned to its rightful owners under the pretense of generosity.[44]

Labour supporters often cited data on wages and incomes from U.S. states' bureaux. While using statistics from government agencies and political economists, labour journalists could also be sceptical of their sources. In one article in 1885 we find a critique of a statistician's conclusions on the growth of wealth in specific European countries and in the United States. The estimates related to total and per-capita wealth, unadjusted for inflation but, as the writer pointed out, failed to decompose wealth by type and said nothing about its distribution.[45] The critique was perceptive but seems to have missed something obvious to us: statisticians and political economists' failure to consider *income* distributions. Why the focus on wealth, not on incomes? The absence of Canadian data on annual incomes certainly deflected attention towards wealth. But the lacuna was deeper. The prevailing assumption was that wealth came from specific forms of appropriation, mostly unearned – rents, usury, and the profits of corporate monopolies – not from income or earnings. Labour journalists and labour's autodidacts therefore rarely addressed the relationship between incomes and wealth accumulation.

INEQUALITY IN THE WAKE OF HENRY GEORGE

In the 1880s the scattered and inchoate theorizing about inequality began to coalesce around specific formulations of the problem. We see increasing use of the words "inequality" and "distribution," relating to wealth more often than to income. The change reflects the enormous influence of Henry George's *Progress and Poverty* (1879). Inequality was central to George's analysis, and his writings remain the most widely read American study of inequality.[46] His work resonated: it drew on past traditions in political thought and Christian idealism and spoke directly, in highly readable language, to workers' needs and fears as they confronted the material realities of late-nineteenth-century capitalism.[47] As Ian McKay says, those who believed that poverty and misery were not inevitable "found in George's work a systematic way of understanding what they felt to be true – that both wealth and poverty were increasing exponentially all around them."[48] As many people have noted, the book was timely, in Canada as in the United States. It appeared at a specific moment in the history of industrial capitalism. In Canada the 1880s saw the continuing expansion of capital investment, the growth of industrial employment, the rise of the Knights of Labor, the appearance of a national labour federation, well-publicized strikes, and increasing press attention to the "labour question."

This context blocked social elevation for an increasing number of craft workers. As Kristofferson argues, the "self-made man" ideal had become normative, and craft workers had begun to speak of propertied independence "as an inevitability, even a right."[49] Proponents gendered the ideal, investing the self-made man with specific masculine virtues, and feminizing the idle wealthy for their alleged frailty and enervation.[50] This conjuncture of the economic and the cultural yielded a powerful impulse to anger and a search for the obstacles to self-made status. Henry George located a set of obstacles not in the capital–wage labour relationship, but in a specific historical disruption – landowners' seizure of economic rent.[51] Inequality emerged here in a specific form, as a conflict between rentier and producer.

George's work deflected the Canadian perception of inequality in the direction of land and land taxation, but the conversation about inequality remained wide. For all the efforts of groups such as the Anti-Poverty Society, solutions never coalesced around George's "single tax." Although in many circles George helped to focus the discussion of taxation in Canada, debates over the subject were widening, as E.A. Heaman has shown.[52] The *Palladium of Labor* embraced a range of views on both taxation and inequality, often reprinting them from American or British sources. "Land monopolization – the private ownership of the soil – has been much discussed of late, while Labor monopolization, through the individual ownership of machinery, has received, as yet, little attention." The "Labor monopoly," argued this article, was much more pernicious than the land iteration. The "diffusion and distribution of wealth" therefore required much more than nationalizing or taxing land – nationalization of telegraphs and railways and a severely graduated income tax, exempting people earning less than $1,000 per year (i.e., virtually all wage-paid workers).[53]

The principle of taxing property, not labour or consumption, left the door open to many alternatives.[54] One was an inheritance tax, even confiscation of large properties according to "the principle that a man can do what he pleases with his own earnings and property so long as he lives, but that at his death that property should be equitably distributed by the State."[55] Such acquisition fitted the ideal that one should reap in proportion to what one sowed. Inherited

property was "income received without toil."⁵⁶ Of course the testa-
tor might provide for a widow and dependent children, but beyond
that was giving something for nothing.⁵⁷ An alternative to confiscation was a graduated tax on inherited property, exempting small
amounts going to relatives.⁵⁸ This was hardly a very radical proposal – in 1889 Andrew Carnegie also supported a graduated tax
on inheritances.⁵⁹

The wider conversation also embraced the cooperative ideal. Cooperatives were exemplars of distributive justice and a solution to the
problem of inequality. Their appeal to workers lay very much in
their promise of excluding the rentier and the finance capitalist; the
producer cooperative also promised to extend access to property
while eliminating any tendency to monopoly. For some advocates,
the principle meant the abolition of capital: when all workers held
shares, individual ownership evaporated, along with inequitable distribution. "The old worldwide difficulty disappears as to the relative
shares of labor and capital in the profits of industry."⁶⁰ The more
moderate claim was that cooperatives "equaliz[ed] profits between
capital and labor."⁶¹ In either case the effect was distributive justice
and "the emancipation of labor from the degrading thraldom of capital."⁶² Some writers noted that British precedents already offered
proof of the effect: "The work of redistribution has been settled in
a manner so accordant with equity that it is difficult to see how any
improvement can be made."⁶³

The cooperative ideal points to the deep and enduring ambiguity
in much of the late-nineteenth-century critique of capitalism, which
was often more radical than the solutions. Although cooperatives
might seem possible alternatives to capitalism and even to private
ownership, they merely offered a form of shared ownership and
did not do away with the market system. Even when exploitation
appeared endemic in economic relations, it was possible to blame
distributive inequity not on capitalism itself, but on anomalies or
egregious forces that interfered with the system.

The Canadian author who went furthest in confronting the ambiguity of inequality was Phillips Thompson. His book, *The Politics of
Labor* (1887), and his short-lived newspaper, the *Labor Advocate*,
offered Canadians the century's most comprehensive and original
analysis of inequality.⁶⁴ Thompson is worth revisiting, not because

he was influential or even representative, but rather because he stretched what was thinkable in his time, and because his questions and provocations stand in sharp contrast to so much of the political economy of his time and of ours. Thompson's political economy was remote from the institutionalized discipline emerging in Canadian universities. His intellectual world was distant from that of Adam Shortt and James Mavor. Any debts to the political-economy tradition in *The Politics of Labor* were few and indirect (he made one mention of Adam Smith, only to support the labour theory of value, and none of Malthus, Ricardo, or J.S. Mill).

His tome's first paragraph located it within a frame broader than "the rights of Labor." The book was not about employer–employee relations, which later became "industrial relations," but about the future and what values would govern social and economic relations. Would the dominant values be freedom, democracy, and equality of rights and opportunity? The question was urgent for Thompson because he perceived a profound threat to these values: "the power of wealth concentrated in the hands of a few."[65] Threatening equality of opportunity – which appeared here, in the forefront of social analysis, for perhaps the first time in Canada – was the widening "chasm between rich and poor."

Thompson understood the deeply entrenched barriers, or "stumbling blocks," preventing egalitarian or redistributive reforms. The apologists of wealth, he said, have corrupted literary and educational institutions and even the churches. He acknowledged the Protestant critique of wealth but saw how easily that turned against itself when the churches applauded the "liberality" and "beneficence" of millionaires. The stumbling blocks were "mental rather than physical," he said. Even the doctrine of evolution, which he saw at work in the inexorable movement away from individualism and towards collectivism, could become an obstacle: defenders of capitalism "eagerly seize upon it [evolution] to justify the existing inequality of conditions as a result of the natural superiority of the fortunate few."[66]

Where others might insist on human sinfulness and innate differences of character, Thompson hinted at a different social psychology. A cultural "virus" of envy induced workers to aspire to be millionaires, and modern education and popular journalism encouraged the dream of elevation and escape into the ranks of the wealthy. Where later rebuttals of the "self-made man" myth might emphasize low rates of social mobility, intergenerational rigidities, and the small numbers that make it from bottom to top, Thompson assailed the myth at its ideological core. Far from embodying an egalitarian ideal – anybody can rise through the ranks – the myth "embodies a radically false and un-Democratic notion." The very phraseology, he observed – "rising from the ranks" – degraded labour "as a condition to be endured only as long as it is inevitable."[67] The concept thereby sanctioned inequality and entrenched social envy; it bribed into acquiescence even the most intelligent workers. Thompson concluded with a satirical witticism. Talking about "the self-made man" was like saying that the prisoners in Sing Sing are starved and beaten, but they have nothing to complain about, because they all have an equal opportunity to scale the walls and run away.[68]

Inequality was basic to Thompson's conception of political and economic power. He described an erosion of democracy in the United States that was rooted not simply in the political influence and lobbying of "monopolists," but in a historical process in which corporate capital grew adjacent to government, appropriated public functions, and touched the lives of all citizens in ways that government did not. "The real government of our nineteenth century civilization is not the parliamentary or administrative bodies in the name of which laws are promulgated. It is the industrial and business and social organization which governs by its iron laws that need no popular assent."[69] Capitalism, warned Thompson, had the power to kill democracy, and the wealthy were moving in that direction (the attentive reader may think of movements by the super-rich in the early twenty-first century to suppress democracy).[70] The tactics, Thompson reported, included discouraging universal suffrage, manipulating voter-registration laws, introducing poll taxes as prerequisites to voting, and suppressing votes in other ways. He saw clearly the ways in which anti-democratic forces worked at cultural and intellectual levels.

In his insightful discussion of how political parties operated, Thompson prefigured a notion of hegemony when describing tactics of cooptation. To conciliate workers and to "head off any broad, comprehensive scheme of political action looking to a radical and organic change," political parties adopted "platforms embodying some of the demands made by organized labor." All too often the tactic worked, noted Thompson: the trivial concession functioned to "keep them [workers] in line" and to buy popular support.[71] Inequality, for him, involved differential distributions of material reward, and of much more – a veritable hydra of political and cultural power.

Thompson confronted the problem that would face all later advocates of redistributive justice. Given the formidable "stumbling blocks" that he had described, how would change come about? His "stepping stones" to a gradual and evolutionary movement away from "the system of capitalist rule and wage servitude" began with government, as he moved beyond Christian voluntarism, formal political economy, and other pro-labour answers such as the cooperative ideal. Without apparently having read Lester Frank Ward, he argued that modern corporations, having occupied so much of the state's domain, nevertheless remained its creatures. In this sense they were not merely "private," nor the outcome of the energies and talents of "self made men," nor the result of machines' vast wealth-generating capacities. "They are creations of the law" – they existed because of powers and privileges granted by the people's representatives.[72] To understand the corporation in this way was to see nationalization of railways, telegraphs, and other utilities as a small step, merely the people's re-acquisition of their own creations. Taking over utilities would prove exemplary and educative, launching an iterative and evolutionary process of public appropriation and control of labour-created wealth.

Moving beyond the old ideal of what he called the "independent self-owning citizen," Thompson saw the modern worker as a "proletarian, without local attachment and deep rootage in the soil which develops the virtues of citizenship."[73] Thus land reform could not undergird a reform program. Though indebted to Henry George, Thompson incorporated taxing and nationalizing land within a broader conception of evolutionary change. "The reform which more than any other would tend to redress social inequalities by lessening the stress of competition among workers would be the appropriation of all land values to public uses."[74] "Would tend" here was a key qualifier, for Thompson proposed that this goal was "too abstract and too distant" to gather sufficient popular support.[75] And he was trying to be realistic – there had been too much "utopianizing," he observed wryly.[76] Local land taxes, however, might demonstrate how to convert wealth to attainable public uses.

Thompson owed more to Herbert Spencer than to Henry George. Where later writers on inequality would conclude with a program of specific reforms, Thompson said that "the details of the mechanism of exchange and distribution, may well be left to solve themselves according to the law of evolution." What was first necessary was a cultural change – in "habits of thought" – and a "gradual breaking with bourgeois traditions."[77] How would this occur? Thompson envisaged a dialectical process whereby "law and public opinion act and react on each other," small reforms induced new demands for change, and failed reforms stimulated even stronger social movements. Such historical processes overthrew slavery and reformed the American constitution in the direction of political democracy. The dialectic was not that of class conflict leading to a crisis in capitalism but manifested itself as a regenerative educational process in which unearned wealth succumbed to "the regenerating influence of a great cause."[78]

The Politics of Labor was not Thompson's last word on inequality or on socialism. But his was the first lengthy discussion of inequality by a leading representative of "first formation" socialism in Canada. He offered a new, vastly expanded role for the state and a broader vision of taxation's role in distributive justice. His optimism derived from a new source of historical change – the collective pressure of organized labour. All of this stood in unresolved tension with the liberal project of rule: Thompson was ambitiously seeking to reconcile individualism, property rights, and political equality with collective and cooperative ideals, and the result was uncomfortable, ambiguous. His emphasis on the aristocracy of money and the labour theory of value put him securely in the first industrial revolution, prior to the era of monopoly capital that followed.

This context enabled for Thompson and others in this era a question too seldom posed in our own time. What is a just return to labour? What level of remuneration for each type of work would be socially just? Thompson quickly dismissed the "blind fatalism" of supply and demand or the iron law of wages. When human institutions and laws regulated other domains of life, it was mere "fanaticism" to argue that natural law beyond societal control determined wages.[79] The question was therefore urgent. Which principles did, and which should, govern the level of earnings for each occupation and profession? A possible answer was that a minimal standard of living was a right of citizenship, and a national minimum wage would serve that principle.

This was not the response of Thompson and many in that time. Their answer rested on another principle: all citizens did have a right to natural resources and economic opportunities, which they secured through labour, so that each received "an equivalent" for the labour that each contributed. Thompson believed that the principle would be very difficult to apply. Most obviously, how could one estimate the value of, and hence the commensurate return for, the brain work that many capitalists did contribute to the process of production? Thompson did not propose anything like a scale of remuneration. Instead, like many contemporaries, he proceeded by offering exclusions, listing examples of those who did no work, but lived as rentier investors. His operative concept here was "unearned increment" – usury, stock manipulation, and other forms of rentier accumulation – and he assumed that the "unearned wealth of the few" was very substantial.[80]

Thompson's position on Henry George and on distributive justice changed after he wrote *The Politics of Labor* in the winter of 1885–86. Breaking with George, he also moved further towards socialism, emphatically rejecting land reform, which, "though excellent as a beginning, as a finalty [sic] would be incomplete, partial & delusive. Like Free Trade in England, an essentially middle class reform, in which the proletariat indeed might incidentally share, but which would not solve the problem of unequal distribution."[81]

Thompson's split with Henry George seemed to dismiss mere reforms to capitalism and its markets, but he continued to wrestle with "unequal distribution," in effect hovering between reformist distributionism and Marxist materialism of class struggle. As Ian McKay suggests, he was closer to Edward Bellamy than to Marx.[82] On distribution of income and wealth, he did not reconcile the critical difference between Mill and Marx or come down clearly on one side. His social ethics sometimes derived from a simple utilitarian calculus. Class distinctions and inequitable privileges, he predicted, would disappear "when laws are made with the object of the greatest good to the greatest number."[83]

INEQUALITY AND SOCIALISM

However radically it condemned capitalism, the late-nineteenth-century discourse on inequality stood within an evolutionary paradigm. It was equally compatible with a labourite reform agenda and with much of the "first formation" socialism that was developing in the 1890s. At times it held the promise of mitigating, even transcending the exploitative features of capitalism without eliminating capitalism itself. At other times it proposed that inequality – the capture of more and more wealth production by a minority – preceded and even helped to propel the evolution from capitalism to a cooperative commonwealth. There was a deep ambiguity here that was rarely apparent to contemporaries. Was inequality rooted in capitalism itself, or in the political and distributive structures that had accompanied its development?

If we step outside the inequality discourse of the 1880s and 1890s, we can see more clearly the ambiguity, and the assumptions, behind inequality itself. By the end of the century Canadians could hear and read clear rejections of the inequality discourse. Among well-read socialists the dismissals may have owed much to Marx's *Critique of the Gotha Program* (1891), but the socialism of the period contained clear alternatives to inequality that had little to do with Marx.

A few exemplary texts allow us to step outside the distributionist ethical economy.[84] The American socialist John Spargo spoke to the founding meeting of the Canadian Socialist League in Toronto in November 1901 – "a superb introduction," says Ian McKay, "to the 'common sense' of much of the first formation."[85] In the published text "inequality" and its plural form did not appear at all; neither did "equality." "Distribution" was there twice, tightly linked to "production." Spargo rejected liberal individualism and its correlate, moral regeneration. Earnest men and women, he said, "seek to bring about a better social condition by and through the moral regeneration of the individual": "They ignore the all important fact that Society is not merely a large number of individuals; evolution has made it an organism, and each unit of the whole being interdependent upon all the other units; each life being affected by the lives of others, this individual appeal and effort must be, to a very large extent, abortive ... You might just as well argue that the pyramids of Egypt were built from the apex to the base, as contend that moral regeneration must precede economic change."[86]

Spargo repeated the commonplace maxim about wealth: "Those who possess the greatest share of the world's wealth are the idlers and those who produce the great bulk, nay, the whole of that wealth, are those who possess least." But this formulation of the "tragic paradox" led not towards but away from a distributionist agenda.[87] Where the whole of the economy is based on "production for profit" and the "exploitation of labor" it is pointless to "attempt the impossible," Spargo argued. Why concentrate efforts on getting old-age pensions for a few, or "municipalizing telephones," or asking "capitalist legislators for bread"? There was no justice short of "the social ownership and control of all the agencies of wealth production, distribution and exchange."[88]

Elsewhere in the penumbra of socialist writings surfaced similar departures from the inequality discourse. These appeared where specific end-of-century trends came together: rejection of liberal individualism in favour of conceptions of society as an organism; continuing emphasis on evolution; and increasing awareness of the durability of oligopoly and monopoly within capitalism. "We have been insisting that the wealth of such men [Rockefeller] would be distributed by natural laws in the course of time," said an article in *Wilshire's Magazine* in 1903.[89] So long as people believed this, they misunderstood evolution and put the cart before the horse: "They refuse to consider any change of society which would aim at preventing the concentration of wealth." This last, however, "gives no sign of being an ephemeral state of affairs, but has every indication of being a permanency," so prevention must take priority. "Under the existing social system there is no possible remedy for the inequality of wealth."[90]

Anti-trust laws, it followed, were mere palliatives. The *Wilshire's* piece saw them, however, within an evolutionary trend of gradual cultural learning and growing popular awareness of class oppositions; they indicated "the wish of the people to level wealth and to abolish conditions which make classes." "While we scoff at [these laws] as being ridiculous, yet we can see behind them the determination of the people to accomplish the establishment of an economic equality."[91]

In these socialist rejections we may hear echoes of Marx's critique of distributive ethics. Even at century's end, however, ideological diversity and ambiguity prevailed, within both the labour movement and the much smaller socialist communities. Radical orators delighted in offering parables to their audiences. Two serve to illustrate the ambiguity over distribution.

One is well known – Edward Bellamy's in his 1897 novel *Equality*.[92] The story, widely circulated in Canada, was certainly familiar to many Canadian workers. There was an economy with one industry: water collection. Workers earned a penny for every bucket they contributed; they paid two pennies for every bucket they bought. In this exchange of pay for labour, workers could not afford to buy all the water they put in the tank. The tank overflowed, workers were laid off, there was a growing gap between rich and poor, and depressions followed because workers were not paid enough to consume all that they produced. While this parable may be situated within a form of socialism, because the solution lay in workers' owning the tank, its model of capitalism had little to do with Marx. The story was about exchange relationships and distribution. It could easily support a distributive solution: the workers must be paid an equivalent to what they contributed. Phillips Thompson is often referred to as a Bellamyite, because of his praise of that author and his continuing emphasis on distributive ethics.

The second parable is, and was, much more obscure. John Spargo told it in his speech in Toronto in November 1901. Two men worked to get water from a pump on a farm. Their remuneration was water. But after much labour they had only two pints. They complained to the farmer: why are we getting so little for our efforts? The farmer explained that there was nothing wrong with the pump, but there was a secret pipe that sent the farmer a gallon of water for every pint the workers received. Spargo suggested "a very strong likeness between that ingenious pump and our present industrial system."[93] Oversimplified as the model certainly was – that's how parables work – it was very different from Bellamy's parable. In Spargo's story exploitation occurred in the process of production. There was no overproduction and no underconsumption. A post-production distributive remedy was not possible.

TOWARDS COOPERATION AND COMMONWEALTH

Unresolved and diffuse as it was, the labour discourse on inequality announced questions and solutions that would resurface in the twentieth century. The solutions included estate taxes as a means of redistribution; old-age pensions as part of "a fair system of distribution";[94] and a range of cooperative ownership alternatives that conjoined "cooperative" and "commonwealth." The labour discourse at times accepted tariff protection but eventually denied that either it or free trade guaranteed a more "equitable distribution of wealth."[95] As for inequality, labour journalists comprehensively rebutted the argument that it spurred thrift and hard work, were among the first to blame it for a range of social evils, including crime, ignorance, and social conflict,[96] and, above all, showed how taxation might solve it by dismantling extreme concentrations of wealth and preventing their creation.

Specific nineteenth-century parameters framed the labour discourse on inequality: the labour theory of value and its corollary, the "just reward"; the ideal of "manly independence"; and the preoccupation with landowning and landed wealth. This framework rendered taxes on incomes, which became a distributive mechanism in the next century, a minor theme in labour thought on inequality, less urgent than nationalizing banks, railways, or land.[97] There seemed much to fear in taxing incomes. It might further interfere with the "just reward." "The only taxation which has any approach to justice," said one writer, "is that which is direct, which is levied on property" – especially on large accumulations of property.[98]

When progressive income taxation did surface as a priority, it did so at a distance from organized labour and its leaders. Warren Franklin Hatheway was a businessman and Fabian socialist in Saint John, New Brunswick.[99] In 1900 he published a forty-six-page pamphlet. *Poorhouse and Palace: A Plea for a Better Distribution of Wealth* was a compendium of quantitative data on wealth and wages, culled from American state bureaux and two recent books: Thorold Rogers's 1884 *Six Centuries of Work and Wages* (an early contribution to the pessimistic interpretation of living standards in the English industrial revolution); and Charles Spahr's *Essay on the Present Distribution of Wealth in the United States* (1896).

Hatheway broadened the discussion beyond wealth. He compared the average family incomes of the "working classes" in the United Kingdom in 1883 to those of "gentry, middlemen, professions, etc."[100] For the United States, he cited evidence to the effect that in 1890 1 per cent of families owned 55 per cent of the nation's wealth. His attempt to include U.S. incomes ran into problems. The Massachusetts Labor Report for 1890, for instance, told him that average factory wages had declined between 1873 and 1891.[101] He knew also that increasing unemployment had hit yearly incomes in that period, and he noted that profits had risen or remained stable. From these observations he inferred that inequality was increasing and that Americans "have not received their full share."[102] Hatheway, however, could not estimate income distribution; he drew the inference on rising inequality by comparing wages and profits. As well, he had not adjusted average wages for price changes over time, and in the two decades after 1873 prices were declining.

Despite these limitations, Hatheway was moving the discussion of inequality beyond wealth concentration and the single-tax solution.

He argued that the incidence of municipal taxation furthered inequality. It often exempted millionaires altogether, but affected even low-income families.[103] His solutions included progressive provincial taxes on both wealth and incomes, but exempting all incomes below $800 a year. His proposed tax rates went up to 2.75 per cent at the top end (incomes above $5,000). These proposals tapped into the redistributive potential of progressive income taxes, which would allow investment in public infrastructure, "make the people prosper," and, for the poor, "give them back the bread that they had earned."[104] Hatheway placed progressive taxation within an original and broad program for "checks upon concentration of wealth." Other "checks" included profit sharing among employees; public ownership of railways, highways, and utilities; and a wider franchise (he did not mention women). Yet another "check": greater control over inventions, so that eventually "the government would have the right to buy the patent for the people," which, he suggested – rehearsing twentieth-century arguments about the relationship between intellectual property, monopoly pricing, and inequality – would "prevent the increase of monopolies" and limit price gouging.[105]

Hatheway bridged the two centuries. His statistical analysis of inequality and his defence of progressive taxation were rooted in a Protestant ethic of benevolence, a simple doctrine of just reward, and a Georgite critique of rentier appropriation. At the same time his historical account of progressive taxation announced its redistributive potential and the moral defence of tax rates that rose with income. In a series of quotations from a range of authorities, he explained why differential rates were socially just: "The adoption of a scale augmenting the rate of taxation upon incomes as they rise in amount, although unequal in one sense, cannot be considered oppressive or unjust, inasmuch as the ability to pay increases in much more than arithmetical proportion as the amount of income exceeds the limit of reasonable necessity."[106]

Hatheway also challenged the common objection that a progressive income tax would encourage tax evasion; the idea that it would drive away investment; and the notion that it was an attack on capital, when it was in fact a defence of the existing order: it is fair "that the rich contribute, not only in proportion to the wealth, but something in addition, in order to maintain this order which is so advantageous to them."[107] Hatheway's arguments also referred to a justification that acquired wide currency: the doctrine of equal or equitable sacrifice. The rich could afford a larger percentage than the poor, because the resulting hardship or loss would be easier to bear (he is quoting John Stuart Mill).[108] As his references to Mill indicated, Hatheway's inequality stood squarely in the camp of distributive reformism rather than that of Marxist-influenced socialism. Hatheway was that rare Canadian writer who borrowed extensively from both British and American political economy, in support of comprehensive reform.

How far did Hatheway's program anticipate developments in the 1900s and 1910s? Would other labourite reformers come to share his focus on graduated taxation? What would happen to the nineteenth-century producerist assumptions that framed the problem of inequality? There are no easy answers to these questions. The fate of inequality in these two decades is not easy to summarize. In many contexts the problem survived in a minor key – an occasional motif embellishing dominant themes. It also endured in an altered rhetorical garb: an egalitarian vocabulary secularized the force of Christian ethics. Where the problem of inequality endured, it did so in part because of specific continuities. The most obvious was the labour theory of value and its correlate, just reward. The labour theory in turn sustained the language of privilege, unearned increment, and parasitism. New or reinvigorated preoccupations – trust, monopoly, price-fixing, costs of living (what we call inflation) – easily fell within the frame of unearned increment and its violation of just reward. Another continuity was associating distribution of wealth with that of political power. During the 1910s blatant displays of this association, especially during the war, fuelled widespread moral revulsion and unprecedented levels of political activism within the labour movement.

Among the small but growing company of socialists, the problem of inequality surfaced occasionally as one of the evil offspring of capitalist exploitation. Socialist writers in Canada largely ignored the complexities of such core concepts as exploitation and surplus value. They seldom referred to falling average rates of profit or crises in capital accumulation. Instead they assumed that the rates of exploitation and of surplus value increased over time, exacerbating inequalities of income and wealth.[109] As capital expanded, "the division of social wealth between capital and labor" became "more disproportionate."[110] "The greater the accumulation of capital, the deeper the poverty of labor, the greater the inequality of wealth."[111]

The Platform of the Socialist Party of Canada offered a variation on the theme: "The capitalist system gives to the capitalist an ever-swelling stream of profits, and to the worker, an ever-increasing measure of misery and degradation."[112]

Even if inequality was an epiphenomenon, a by-product of exploitation in the production system, socialists believed that it could stimulate working-class consciousness. "The cleavage of society into a small, extremely rich class, and a great non-possessing class of wage-workers," would become increasingly apparent and help workers to perceive their economic and political disempowerment[113]: "Within the capitalist system the inequalities are of so glaring a character that even the veriest dub can observe them. Dull as are many workers, this glaring inequitableness is being brought to his notice more plainly as the system develops. But while it is easy to say 'it isn't fair; it's not right or just,' it takes a little study and mental exertion on the worker's part to know that he is the one who helps to produce the surplus wealth, evidence of which we see on every hand."[114] The socialist tendency to condescension towards workers was apparent. Awareness of growing inequalities could stimulate anger among them, but the worker was often "a queer, superstitious, chuckle-headed chump" who needed the guidance of scientific socialism in order to understand surplus value and exploitation in capitalism.[115]

Education of workers on the root causes of inequality was essential, the socialists argued, if only because they were vulnerable to an array of reformist and utopian palliatives. Where Marx and Engels became better known, and where the "impossibilist" orientation ruled out any reformist gradualism, the language of privilege and unearned increment was redundant, and inequality required no extended analysis. There was no point in discussing "the division and distribution of the spoils" between masters and slaves; so long as wage slavery existed, equality could not exist.[116] Publications of the Socialist Party of Canada insisted on separating production from distribution, or treating the latter as a product of the former. A "distribution of wealth" was "utterly impossible to slaves." It followed that arguments about prices and the rights of consumers were futile: "The producers of wealth are robbed as producers, not as consumers."[117] "If the working class desire to get what they produce they must abolish slavery. This they can only do by abolishing the class ownership of the means of production."[118] If we did not understand that "the cause of social inequality" lay in private ownership of "the social means of life," said the *Western Clarion*, then "we do but flounder in the quagmire of political reform."[119] In 1917 the Social Democratic Party of Canada's journal, *Canadian Forward*, reprinted Marx's *Critique of the Gotha Program*. The document skewered the reformist politics of inequality. Instead of the "vague phrase" about "the removing of all social and political inequality," the German Labor Party "should have said that with the abolition of class distinctions all social and political inequality springing from them will disappear of its own accord."[120]

Socialists did not explain what a just distribution would look like after the abolition of capitalism, but they did offer an ethical standard. The standard came directly from the labour theory of value, and it sustained a powerful moral condemnation of the existing distribution: "It must be granted that some individuals are stronger, wiser, more gifted and skilful than others. But what of that? Is there any moral ground for punishing the cripple, the invalid, the decrepit, the unfortunate step-children of nature, by reducing their rations of food and clothing? Is there any moral sanction for rewarding the man of physical strength or mental gifts from the storehouse of human society?"[121]

The socialist answer was that a just society could distribute differentially, so long as it followed a principle: "'From each according to his ability, to each according to his needs,' generally appears as the ideal rule of distribution in an enlightened human society."[122] The socialist nostrum neatly avoided problematic issues. Was "to each" conditional on "from each," or did each proposition stand alone? How and who to estimate needs?[123]

Among Canadian socialists some were sensitive to the accusation that socialism meant abrogation of freedom and a denial of individualism. Those who had read Herbert Spencer found the accusation in his *Man versus the State*.[124] Those who had applauded Edward Bellamy's utopian novel *Looking Backward* might well have been uncomfortable with the suppression of individualism in his collectivist utopia. A writer in the BC *Federationist* met the charge head on, equating inequality with cultural suffocation of freedom. Socialism, this writer argued, would not interfere with individual freedom because capitalism "knows no freedom." Freedom did not exist even for the very wealthy. Yes, they might appear to enjoy a "bed of roses," but they were "the slaves of wealth and fashion." Even art and science were unfree when subordinated to the quest for position and wealth. If freedom meant the ability to choose the colour of one's hats or the cut of one's suits, then it was a "fiction." Equality did not bring "uniformity of character or achievements." The opposite was true: "Uniformity is born of inequality" because inferior classes tended to imitate their superiors.[125] There was no evidence that this author had been reading Thorstein Veblen. Even so, he or she – identified only as "Socialist" – had hit on a simplified theory of inequality as cultural imprisonment.

The socialist position had the merit of clarity, but it sacrificed flexibility.[126] There was no point in discussing distributive reforms prior to the necessary abolition of class distinctions. In early-twentieth-century labourite reform politics flexibility ruled. The moral critique of capitalism sustained a political pragmatism that socialists often shared in opportunistic collaborations that seem to have increased in the First World War. As Craig Heron notes in his seminal 1984 article on "labourism and the Canadian working class," working-class reformers usually preferred to discuss issues of "practical and immediate importance" and "seldom presented lengthy or lofty statements of their perspective on the world."[127] They produced no "intellectualized doctrine," and so they would offer no deeply theorized positions on the related issues of equality, inequality, and distributive justice. They and their journalist spokespersons articulated, however, a robust egalitarianism rooted in workplace comradeship, fraternal organization, craft pride, and ideals of manly independence. Their fierce defence of equality was severely constrained by ideologies of gender and race that historians have carefully unravelled. This masculine egalitarianism produced a gender-specific rhetorical arsenal: equality, equal rights, equity, fairness, a square deal, cooperation. Against these words stood their opposites: privilege, unearned increment, special interests, landlordism, monopoly, millionaires, parasites. The "1 per cent" versus the "99 per cent" – the popular motif of a century later – also appeared at this time:

> There are ninety and nine that live and die
> In want and hunger and cold,
> That one may revel in luxury
> And be lapped in its silken fold;
> The ninety and nine in their hovels bare,
> The one in a place with riches rare.[128]

Working-class readers would have accepted without question the causal link between the wealth of the 1 per cent and the disadvantages of the rest.

INEQUALITY AND THE FIRST WORLD WAR

For Canadian workers, the First World War was an awesome display of those causal connections. Labour's response was a political program for the defeat of economic inequality. It is important that I state clearly the claim I am making here. The disruption of war accelerated trends already in progress; it did not create them. A robust labourite egalitarianism confronted the cataclysm of war and its blatant demonstrations of political and economic privilege and the repressive powers of the state. The effect of the war was to energize and refine the egalitarian impulse and to endow its moral underpinnings with a new collective anger. The result was a quest not for "reconstruction," which suggested a return to pre-war conditions, but for "construction" – the creation of a new society, a cooperative and egalitarian commonwealth that would displace the old world of privilege and systemic inequality.[129] The war was "capitalism's Waterloo."[130]

Wealth – already morally suspect – acquired a new pejorative cast in the campaigns for "conscription of wealth." We know about the responses of organized labour and organized farmers to conscription of personnel, introduced in 1917. It is worth remembering the extent and the depth of the moral outrage prompted by wartime profiteering, the profits of meat-packer "His Porkship Flavelle" (Sir Joseph Flavelle), the Dominion government's manipulation of the franchise for the 1917 election, and other demonstrations of political privilege.[131] Such scandals blew away any claim that profits or wealth were a fair reward for entrepreneurial risk-taking, investment acumen, talent, or ability. "I am not bound to keep my temper with an imposture so outrageous, so abjectly sycophantic, as the pretence [sic] that the existing inequalities of income correspond to and are produced by moral and physical inferiorities and superiorities."[132]

There was no more potent demonstration of inequality than the authorities' conscripting men but not wealth, in effect enslaving men, women, and children. "That the widow who has given her love and stay to the national cause should be splashed with mud by the luxurious car of a man who has coined drachmas from the life of her breadwinner – that is more than British flesh and blood will stand."[133] We are hearing not a critique but a rage that searched for words adequate to describe "ruling class bestiality, rapacity, and lust for blood and gore."[134] "If a young man who does not enlist is to be described as a 'shirker', what term is strong enough to describe the man who is taking advantage of this great calamity to pile up wealth for himself at the expense of his fellows?"[135] Tales of plutocratic privilege abounded. According to the *Industrial Banner* in June 1917, two rich women went into a Winnipeg café and bought a roast chicken to feed to their dogs. Their frivolous indulgence was "disgusting," an "outrage" committed by "callous and brainless creatures."[136] The nation was being "sapped by the profit-sucking proclivities of the useless scions of the House of Fat."[137]

Anecdotal evidence of inequitable distributions was not enough, and the war years saw an intensified search for hard data. As usual, solid Canadian statistics were unavailable. In his *Cotton's Compendium of Facts* the socialist publisher William Ulrich Cotton offered information on wealth distribution in France showing the number of deceased by category of holdings. For Canada he indicated the estimated wealth of the ten richest men in Toronto, the total net profits of corporations by economic sector, and the wealth of the "twenty-three men who control Canada," and he listed by name Montreal's hundred millionaires.[138] But for all his data-gathering, he found nothing on societal distributions of wealth or income.

Journalists continued to deploy evidence on U.S. and British wealth. Two per cent of Americans owned 60 per cent of the wealth, reported the BC *Federationist* in 1919, while 30 million lived in poverty and babies born to poor families were five times more likely to die than those born in rich families. "We are in the ditch – the ditch of economic inequality."[139] U.S. income-tax data became available. In April 1919 the *Industrial Banner* used U.S. Treasury Department statistics from 1916 to show the number of taxpayers in each of five categories of income above $10,000 a year. It framed its conclusion within the labour theory of "just reward": the majority of the population gained "a bare subsistence," claimed the *Banner*, whereas the incomes of the top percentiles came from rent, interest, dividends, and profits. Thus, "among the toilers, the whole family works and often starves. Among the wealthy owners frequently no one works, yet all live in abundance."[140]

*

In the context of heightened moral outrage, older hesitations over the role of the state and taxation began to give way. It may be true, as Craig Heron argued, that labourite reformers did not support the centralized planning dear to some Fabian intellectuals in Britain.[141] Nevertheless, the independent labour parties that grew rapidly in Canada during and after the war supported an expanded role for the state and borrowed directly from the British Labour Party's program for distributive reforms. Canada's labour newspapers quoted party sources, especially Labour's explicitly redistributive Reconstruction program of 1918, *Labour and the New Social Order*.[142] It foresaw "a death blow" to "the individualist system of capitalist production" and its "reckless profiteering" and "monstrous inequality of circumstances." The "four pillars" of Labour's program were minimum living standards (not by themselves redistributive) and – all redistributive – democratic control of industry, a revolution in national finance, and "appropriation of the Surplus, not to the enlargement of any individual fortune, but to the Common Good."

The Dominion Labor Party's reconstruction program was "a plan of attack on the plutocratic forces which now rule Canada." Its mission was "to secure to the producers ... the full fruits of their industry, and the most equitable distribution thereof." Even in local elections the general problem of inequality could appear: the Labor Party's platform in Toronto's municipal elections called for "the equitable distribution of wealth produced by labor." The British Labour Party's reference to "monstrous inequality of circumstances" was an oft-cited motto.

From the perspective of our dystopian era in the early twenty-first century, the labourite responses to inequality seem often unfamiliar and even surprising. Perhaps most remarkable: awareness of deeply embedded, structural inequities of power and wealth joined with expressions of hope and optimism. In April 1919, for instance, William Ivens delivered a wide-ranging indictment of capitalism, its inequities, and its stranglehold on governments, the press, and the people. Capitalism had corrupted and enslaved "the minds and souls of the people." Was this polemic a denial of agency and hope? Far from it: Ivens told his audience that they could "look with faces full of hope and expectancy towards a system which unites humanity. A system where each shall get the full product of his toil."[143] The refrain was commonplace. The people "have borne too long the inequalities and injustices inherent in an economic system based on competition instead of co-operation." They will put up with it no longer: "The politics of the future will be human politics, and the dominating party will be the party of the common people and of democracy. This is certain."[144]

The problem of inequality had become an inspirational cry of empowerment, not of pessimism. Such conjoining of sweeping indictment with seemingly naïve optimism was not mere utopian thinking. The link was not simply utopian, if by that we mean the imaginative construction of a future that did not exist.[145] Labourite optimisms allowed room for imagined futures, but related them to specific reforms, to political action, and to trends already in existence. The more apt descriptor is immanence – a presence that existed in an ongoing condition of self-realization. The descriptor embraced both religious and secular discourse, and labourite reformism was expressing Protestant ethics in largely secular language. A "divine discontent" was forging a new benevolence.[146] According to Thomas De Quincey: "The moral of an epos or drama should be *immanent*, not *transient*; ... it should be vitally distributed through the whole organization of the tree, not gathered or secreted into a sort of red berry or *racemus*, pendent at the end of its boughs."[147] Labour's reform politics was a politics of immanence. A new world was immanent in the presence of moral essences animating society.

Labourite reformers found evidence of moral transformation in current events. "No man dare say now 'This is my business, my private property, and I will run it as I please.'"[148] Why might no one say that? Because in war the state had shown that it would tax profits and even confiscate property when the common good required it: "The great war is shattering the sacred rights of property." The state created property rights and was modifying them in the public interest.[149] An even greater immanence lay in the collective power of the masses, visible in the extraordinary growth of trade unions during and just after the war. Never before had the masses' power been so great or so apparent to everyone. "A new flame is burning in the soul of the masses. They begin to see that it is they upon whom the destiny of the world depends ... It is they who work the mines and till the soil and run the factories and speed the shot and shell and pour the blood that will liberate the world." Britain's working class offered the clearest evidence of this expanding sense of empowerment. "The program of the British Labor party is the program of the new social order."[150]

*

The politics of immanence contained an economic logic. The great fiscal question was: how to pay off the huge war debts. Governments would have no choice but to draw on the profits and incomes that created millionaires. Canada's Income War Tax of 1917 seemed to confirm the trend, despite governments' refusal to consider the more radical idea of a levy on capital. Labourite thinkers reflected a distinctively Canadian obsession with land and resources. Paying down the war debts would require the state to appropriate the surplus from natural resources, even take them over. Government control of railways in Britain seemed to confirm the necessity and efficiency of state control; in Canada the failure of the new transcontinental railways and the imposition of Dominion control offered further evidence of the immanent realization of state action for common good.[151] War debts would result inevitably in a conscription of wealth, including through inheritance taxes.

And there was another fiscal logic: if income taxes were part of the solution, then the state had a vested interest in higher wages, which would cause more earners to rise above the threshold for tax liability. Furthermore, at a societal level, higher wages were immanent because consumer demand was driving economic growth. "The statisticians of the American Federation of Labor have been able to demonstrate that social prosperity follows from each increase of the wage scale."[152] Before such compelling logic, some people maintained, even capitalists would give way and allow better protection for trade unions and even for women workers. "The trend of law making is with us," and "the unequal distribution of wealth will be to some extent corrected."[153]

Such arguments certainly overestimated the extent of progressive trends. But we are observing not a simple utopian reflex, but serious attempts to interpret the war's impact and to re-imagine the role of the state and of taxation. Labour's older preoccupation with the difficult issue of tariffs was giving way to much wider conceptions. Many partisans still emphasized land taxation, and supporters of Henry George and a single tax could still be heard.[154] But the income tax changed and broadened the conversation: it was consistent with labour's desire to shift levies away from production; and it clearly had redistributive potential. "Of all the powers that we possess in our legislation, the most potent for good or evil is that of taxation." "By proper taxation we may distribute the burden with equity." Older suspicions of income tax were giving way, and some people saw it as "the agency through which permanent liberty can come."[155] The key issue was now the income level for exemption.[156]

The secular politics of immanence included a reform program – the first set of Canadian political platforms to pledge explicitly to reduce inequality and to realize a form of distributive justice in industrial-capitalist society. Labourite reformers accomplished something that eluded social gospellers. More remarkable, they produced a program that was beyond the capabilities or the interest of Canadian political economists, and of almost all intellectuals from outside the working class. The contrast with Britain was striking: there the Labour Party drew ideas and sometimes active participation from a legion of scholars and intellectuals. In all of the publications by and for the Canadian working class, Canadian intellectuals from outside the working class were conspicuous by their absence.

For all that Labour's political program was under-theorized and often internally inconsistent (it was, in fact, several platforms by different provincial and Dominion parties), it represented a serious, informed, and principled engagement with the world of wage labour and capitalist class relationships. Though borrowing from British and American sources, the program was a Canadian working-class conception. It emerged from, and gave voice to, the heritage of producerist egalitarianism, workplace collaboration, fraternal organization, and secularized Christian ethics.

The program addressed the maldistribution of wealth through a basic minimum standard of living and more clearly redistributive legislation. The former included pensions for the elderly and for disabled veterans and their dependants.[157] Later iterations added "national health and unemployment insurance" as well as "maternity benefits and free hospital service."

For Ontario labour, the attention to women evolved between 1917 and 1920. By 1920 "equal pay for equal work" was to go hand in hand with "equality of opportunity for men and women, politically, socially, and industrially." In addition: "every child to be guaranteed from its birth until it becomes a self supporting member of society, the material necessities of life, medical supervision, and unlimited education" (all state schools were to be free). Redistributive reforms clearly targeted excess profits and "unearned increment" and included public ownership of utilities and natural resources, "gradual elimination of unearned increment through increasing taxation," and nationalization of the banks and credit system.[158] J.S. Woodsworth's 1919 proposal for the Dominion Labor Party, for instance, would have guaranteed a "living wage" (unspecified amount) – clearly more than bare subsistence, and redistributive in effect.[159]

There was no single Labour platform. The 1919 "Reconstruction Program" of the Dominion Labor Party in Manitoba was relatively radical – proposing not "reconstruction" but "reorganization" of society, and explicitly attacking plutocracy and economic autocracy. It included government-subsidized housing projects, progressive taxation of land values, and a steeply graduated "levy on property" to deal with war debts. A clause was added on stock watering, calling for regulations to ensure that real assets backed stock issues.[160] Labour platforms stressed political inequities, most proposing to abolish property qualifications for election to municipal offices, for instance. Education and vocational training were also major themes, and at least one platform asked that "the teaching of patriotism" include attention to "the equitable distribution of the wealth produced by labor."[161]

Despite all its fluidity and lack of coherence, labourite reformism as it evolved between 1917 and 1920 may rightly be called a political program. Each element was in the process of immanent realization, or so the reformers believed, because for each they could find a real-world analogue or precedent. This resilient immanence held up even after the defeats of 1919: the crushing of the Winnipeg strike was "a splendid training in economics," merely delaying, not cancelling, the emerging "new world."[162] The program was not an exact blueprint for the welfare state that emerged a generation later, and it did not use such a term, but its vigorous endorsement of state action, minimum standards, and health and unemployment insurance contained elements of the later social-security system. It would be condescending to suggest that labourite optimism was a misreading by its authors of historical trends. A mere twenty-five years later Canada had a universal system of family allowances, and the marginal rate of tax on top incomes was over 80 per cent.[163]

LABOUR'S EGALITARIANISM

For all the intellectual and political effort that preceded the labourite program, there was a conspicuous absence: a coherent theory of egalitarian justice. The labour theory of value was an egalitarian claim, of course: all workers have an equal right to the product or value of what they produce. There was a specific doctrine of equal sacrifice: all must contribute equally, according to ability and means, even if there was no standard measure of equivalence. Nevertheless, while egalitarianism was becoming more inclusive, it remained hermetic (as we first noted in chapter 2). The claim to a universal equality – universal brotherhood – coincided with specific exclusions of gender and race (though in places these exclusions were being challenged). Equal pay for women and men was widely proclaimed but could mask an exclusionary intention or effect (employers would hire fewer women). The powerful egalitarianism of the suffrage movement related to political rights and contained its own exceptions (Indigenous people, Chinese Canadians). One begins to wonder: is equality always an endogamous value and a means to affirm in-group solidarity? However that may be, the various egalitarianisms of the early twentieth century did not come together in a coherent theory embracing economic and other equalities.

Despite all their limits and inconsistencies, working-class engagements with inequality offered hope and inspiration. In their determined efforts to discover and sustain an ethical foundation for social justice, in their traditions of solidarity and activism, in their principled defence of the ideal of common good – and, not least, in the optimism of their politics of immanence – our working-class ancestors have much to teach us.

CHAPTER FIVE

Spiritual Engineering from Rural Romantics to Social Gospellers (1900s–1930)

RURAL AND SMALL-TOWN CONTEXTS

Willie King, a member of the Berlin High School football team that won the Hough Cup in 1888, was born in the small town of Berlin, Ontario, in 1874. A keen footballer and cricketer, he was also a good student who would soon become president of the school's Literary Society. Later he would become a political economist, a labour-relations expert, and Canada's longest-serving prime minister. When he attended the high school his family lived a mile out of town, at Woodside, their "country home," where they kept chickens, pigs, a cow, and a horse.[1] In Berlin the young King would have his first sight of the world of industry and its workers, the world that he would soon study and then enter, not as a worker but as a mediator, legislator, and reformer.

When King was a child, Berlin was a town of fewer than four thousand people.[2] Here the new manufacturing businesses interacted in many ways with the adjacent farms, and not only as buyers and sellers. The merchants and factory owners knew many of the farmers and connected with them in the boards and societies and governing bodies of the town. Many of Berlin's residents were farmers; farmers and merchants depended on each other, and a series of poor crops would affect the merchants' account books. Country and city, urban and rural – such dichotomies are thoroughly blurred in this very Canadian configuration of place, people, and work. These images of the small town announce this chapter's theme – Canada's agrarian-inflected modernity and its reckonings with inequality.

In the 1870s the town of Berlin still revealed its recent incarnation as a village created by farming "pioneers."[3] The railway had arrived less than twenty years before King was born. Street lighting with coal-oil lamps appeared in the year of his birth. Between the flour mill on Queen Street and the homes on Schneider Avenue spread apple orchards and potato patches. Behind the frame houses with their pumps near the front door lay vegetable gardens; cows were "free commoners" of the town.[4] The brothers who owned the flour mill were noted fishermen and hunters. Children had their favourite fishing ponds; older boys took guns to the west of the town and shot squirrels or wild pigeons. Berliners and farmers met on Saturdays when the latters' families brought produce to the long market building at the rear of the town hall.[5]

In this expanding community there appeared artisan workshops and small family-owned factories. In King's infancy there were the tanneries, the button factories, the furniture makers, the paper-box factory, the rocking-horse maker, the planing mill, the flour mills, the carriage works, the knitting works, and the manufacturers of glue, felt, and cigars. The industrial firms of the 1870s employed about 700 people – a minority of the town's labour force, but a growing minority. Most workers knew who their employer was, and it was said that wage earners "preferred to discuss difficulties with their employer rather than with a foreman."[6]

"Where do your workers live?" asked a visitor. The answer was that we have no slums in Berlin and fully 80 per cent of the residents owned their own homes. The claim, exaggerated or not, reflected the aspiration of propertied independence. "For a man, the ownership of a home was an unwritten law and a yardstick of his worth as a citizen."[7] A worker could buy a small lot for one or two hundred dollars and, if necessary, use family labour to build an eight-room brick house; as well, daughters might earn money polishing buttons in a button factory or sewing in the shirt factory, and sons could enter many more of the workshops. To help pay off the money borrowed to buy or build a house, families saved cash by growing much of their own food. In a garden perhaps sixty by two hundred feet they grew vegetables, fruit, and flowers; many kept a cow, chickens, and a few pigs. Land and machinery were both working, it seemed, to provide an abundance or, if not that, the opportunity to acquire material independence. That freedom was both material and moral: the one was a reflection of the other.

From such spaces came the English Canadians who would define and respond to the problem of inequality in the 1900s and 1910s.

When Willie King was born, there were only seven Canadian towns with more than twenty thousand residents. There were even fewer places that might be called cities, and only one that had more than 100,000 people (and Montreal in 1874 was smaller than Kingston, Ontario, today). Canadians at the beginning of the twentieth century were a rural and small-town people, and many of those living in larger places had come from smaller ones. Most Canadians grew their own food; for their energy supply, the overwhelming majority depended on and used organic sources (animal power, human labour, wood burning, wind, flowing water).[8] At the end of the nineteenth century, no less than 72.5 per cent of Canada's working-age population were living in rural places or small towns of less than ten thousand people. Fewer than one in ten Canadians dwelled in larger urban centres, those of 100,000 or more.[9]

The small factories were not the only conspicuous new edifices in the Berlin of the 1870s. More prominent were the churches, if only because their Gothic spires reached above the skyline, proclaiming transcendence of all things mundane and material below.[10] There were at least fourteen churches in Berlin, including both Lutheran and Catholic churches established by the large German-origin population. The King family attended St Andrew's Presbyterian, where young Willie acquired his deep and abiding Christian faith and his sense of the church as both institution and community. A few decades later he would write a book in which he took great pride: its major themes were Humanity, Faith, and Community. To these words he applied capital letters.[11] His *Industry and Humanity* is a spiritual odyssey, romantic and even at times mystical. His "basis of reconstruction" is explicitly a rural idyll, a universalized projection of Kingsmere, his country home in the Laurentian hills, where a "perfect harmony" might be found amid "the chaos which envelopes human relations around the world today."[12]

The Canadian response to inequality in the late nineteenth and early twentieth centuries was that of a scattered settler population living in a political economy distinctively different from that of the United States and Britain. In this rural and small-town continental archipelago, four distinct cultural and political frames persisted and evolved, even as they waned or perished elsewhere: the labour theory of value, abundance of land, Christian commitment, and belief in progress. First, the labour theory of value survived well past 1900, and not only among labour reformers and socialists. The strength of agrarian ideals and farmer populism sustained it and a related, often overlapping proposition: the physiocratic idea that land is the source of all wealth.

Fuelling this claim too was a second frame, an English-Canadian variant of an older American foundation of the republican theory of wealth: the assumption that the nation possessed an abundance of land, an endless frontier of free land grants that gave to everyone, including immigrants, the opportunity to make a living. The small-town and rural origins of Canadians lent credibility to the promise of boundless opportunity: they had seen and they remembered available, abundant land.

A rural and small-town people that confronted the perils of modernity felt a strong attachment to Christian discourse and ethics, whether Protestant or Catholic. As we move from British and American discussions of wealth, inequality, and social conflict in the early 1900s to the Canadian conversations on the "social question" we cannot fail to notice the vitality of a renovated religious culture, which included but extended beyond the Protestant social gospellers and labour churches. In the United States and Britain we could see religious commitments energizing social action and then leading to secular and legislative solutions, most obviously among American social gospeller–economists. In Canada the boundary between religion and action was even less easily discernible. This is not to say that legislative solutions to social problems and inequality were not proposed and attempted. But in Canada the proposals and the political solutions emerged within social Protestantism and social Catholicism. This third frame embraced the other two.

These conditions probably contributed to a fourth striking characteristic of the Canadian conversations on both inequality and the wider social question: persisting optimism about evolution and progress. Herbert Spencer almost disappeared, along with analogies to Darwin and biology, but evolution survived in a Christian discursive garb, as an expression of faith in a divinely ordained future that combined benevolence with growth. The neo-Spencerian evolutionary teleology mutated into a prophetic and millennial vision shared by social gospellers and many others. By envisioning an ultimate triumph over the corruptions of wealth, this new evolutionary discourse survived as one answer to the problem of inequality.

*

Such is the larger comparative context. Let us return to the settings that formed Willie King and his generation. The small town is a Canadian motif, a setting for character and circumstance in the country's literary imagination. Stephen Leacock's Mariposa, Robertson Davies's Deptford, Alice Munro's southwestern Ontario – these are merely the best-known and most thoroughly scrutinized of such fictional spaces. More than a mere platform, such a setting was the crucible of character and relationships, the source of Leacock's relentless irony and Davies's darker imaginative play with the village mentality. Leacock achieved his ironic gaze only by an act of remembrance, a distancing that put that locale and its people into a dreamlike state of arrested development and innocent pretension.[13] His fictional setting was the construction of a viewer transplanted in time and space, from the village (Sutton, Ontario) of Leacock's youth to the big city of Montreal and his office at McGill University. Acts of distancing occurred in the literary imagination, and also in the collective memory of Leacock's generation, those who experienced or witnessed physical and social movements from rural or small-town childhoods to the urban spaces that they called "modern." From the streets and buildings and institutions and personal connections of their childhood many Canadians would construct the small town of memory, a place of ideals and of community, which rendered the urban, the industrial, and the "modern" an unfamiliar, even alien, new world. In Canada, the problem of "distribution of wealth" became part of these historical acts of transplanted remembrance and of imagination.

As Adam Crerar and others have argued, the rural idyll reached far into the culture of turn-of-the-century Ontario.[14] A genre of popular history arose that located the province's origins in the history of pioneers who received land from the hand of God and fought great battles against forests and wilderness. The United Empire Loyalists were "invented," argues Norman Knowles, in this myth-making construction of pioneers uniting in a common cause, a mythical communal bonding that erased the vast inequalities of early settlements in a romanticized dream of rural equality.[15] The myth-making had little to do with farming or the rural communities of the time; it was the work of urban dwellers. At times the political agenda of the popular historian was explicit. In 1915 Edith Marsh explained the contribution of county history to "social progress": "the spirit of the early days" helped to counter "the dangers of the present," which included political and economic conditions "that allow monopoly to dispossess the tiller of the soil."[16]

If Edith Marsh offered one example of the agrarian idealism and rural romanticism that were so powerful in Canada in the early twentieth century, another exemplar was Peter McArthur, a poet and journalist who was probably Canada's most widely read author on farming and rural life in the period. All of the larger themes appeared resolutely in his work: the belief in labour and land as the sources of wealth; the assumption that land bestowed endless opportunity; the inspiration of a deep Protestant commitment to benevolence and service; and a simple faith in evolution as progress. For those who like to play with such things, McArthur's message may be distilled from the word cloud (Figure 2) I take from his book *In Pastures Green* (1915): country, green, pastures, time, man, make, work. McArthur knew that inequality was an urban and industrial evil: "The increase of the well-being of the masses does not appear to be by any means proportionate to the general growth of wealth."[17] Inequality and "social cleavage" were products of the city; by contrast, "a good neighbourly spirit in pioneer days" meant that everyone was "on an equal footing."[18] On visiting a shoe factory he observed that "the workers in that factory were not simply slaves to their employer, but to merciless machines."[19] No such exploitation occurred in farming, the source of wealth and of satisfaction in work. "The work of the farmer is superior to that of any other man. The more wealth the farmer produces, the more mouths will be fed and the cheaper the cost of living will be."[20]

McArthur had a simple and optimistic answer to the associated problems of exploitation, urban misery, and inequality. Land was endless opportunity. Let us all go and get a farm, he said: "I do not hesitate to advise every one who can possibly go back to the land to go." "Men who are out of work" would find it "cheaper to spend the idle winter on a farm, and they could be ready by the spring to begin to make their living from the soil."[21] McArthur insisted that the single-tax followers of Henry George were wasting their time – they should "stop antagonising people."[22] More than that: serious discussions of social justice were also useless: "The time for dissertations on abstract justice is past."[23] Why were serious discussions of social justice of no use? Because evolution was taking care of the social problem: "The nationalisation of the land is nearer than any

Figure 2 | Word cloud of Peter McArthur, *In Pastures Green* (1915).

one supposes, and it will be brought about by the blundering logic of events." "Land hunger will force a solution of the land problem" – taxation and legislation were not necessary.[24] And if land hunger was too secular a motive force, McArthur reminded his readers that it was God who ordained a beneficent evolution. God's "benign control" led the early pioneers "by the hand" to "a land of homes where toil could make men free."[25] This was a Canadian version of Henry David Thoreau with a large dose of the social gospel.

Faith in a divinely ordained future benevolence did not, however, justify complacency. McArthur believed that individuals must struggle to realize the divine plan. He also selected from current trends those that he saw as confirming "the great law of brotherhood" and its power "to remove the evils of inequality."[26] One trend above all seemed to do that, and – strange as it may seem in a rural romantic – it came from the world of business. Its denizens had learned how to "tithe" their own incomes, by devoting "at least a tenth" of their earnings to life insurance – an effective method for McArthur of saving the family from death and hard times, and a fulfilment of the "law of brotherhood."

The businessmen who invented life insurance, McArthur asserted, "never dreamed that they were releasing a force that would in time take control of capital and Government out of the hands of capitalists, political parties and leaders and place it in the hands of the people."[27] Here then was a distinctively Canadian contribution to distributive justice. Was McArthur aware that he was reflecting a Canadian "mania" for that product and its remarkable growth after 1900, which Peter Baskerville has uncovered?[28] It took the solution away from national insurance, minimum wages, and taxation, as well as away from socialism, Henry George, Marx, or any need to consider the major contributions to distributive justice published in McArthur's time.

Optimism did not always prevail, however, even among the celebrators of agrarian and small-town life. The years after 1900 saw much hand-wringing over the fate of rural communities and the decline of rural populations. The "rural problem" received wide publicity, and there was even a Senate Committee on "The Unsatisfactory Character of the Movement of Population ... in the Older Provinces of the Dominion."[29] The chief source for the worriers was a remarkable compendium of statistics and possible remedies by John Mac-Dougall, published in 1913: *Rural Life in Canada: Its Trends and Tasks*. MacDougall was not a happy campaigner, and his vision of the contemporary rural world was very different from that of Peter McArthur. MacDougall used the 1911 Dominion census to claim that rural Ontario had lost 100,000 people in the previous decade, and that since 1871 prosperous agricultural districts in southern Ontario had lost between a quarter and a third of their populations.[30] He painted a bleak picture of abandoned farms and young people enticed to the city by false hopes of easy work and prosperity.

What has this angst to do with inequality? The two major connections were direct and profound. First, the movement of populations from country to city was a direct cause of inequality in the latter: "an almost inconceivably great increase in material production" was accompanied by widespread poverty and hardship. "Wealth has increased enormously, but an undue share of the reward has gone into the hands of the few."[31]

Second – and here was a distinctive Canadian contribution to the discussion of inequality – rural depopulation and agriculture's failure to expand at the same rate as industry meant insufficient farm products, whose rising prices exacerbated inequality. Inflation was eroding whatever gains in earnings the mass of the population achieved. "Amidst all the increase in the cost of living, that due to the enhanced prices of commodities from the farm stands easily first."[32] MacDougall's penchant for statistics served him well: he compared the index for all wholesale prices between 1897 and 1911 with the index for farm products and found that the latter had "soared" compared to the former.[33] He was drawing on and feeding a very Canadian concern with prices that arose in the 1900s, and he was linking the fate of agriculture directly to the problem of urban inequality.

Understood in this way, the rural crisis suggested its own solution. In the end, MacDougall's statistics offered a lesson not of despair but of optimism. Where prices were soaring, and where land was so obviously available, opportunity beckoned. Even abandoned farms were revivable through conservation of soil, scientific agriculture, and tax relief. In this way MacDougall offered a new lease on life to the ideal of taxation of rent and "unearned increment." "Men are today becoming millionaires through selfish exploitation of forest and stream and field and mine and ocean."[34] Taxation – "the whole complement of taxes" – should fall on the exploiters: not on land or labour, but on speculation in land and "unearned increment," which included "the interest of capital."[35] A further "requisite" was legislation to empower cooperatives and to safeguard their credit.[36]

To summarize MacDougall's solutions in this way could easily suggest that he was advocating a secular, legislative program for rural development and agricultural growth. But no: the heart of his book lay in its last four chapters: "The Function of the Church," "The Country Church Programme," "Students for the Ministry," and "Rural Uplift Elsewhere." Any program he had lay in the remedial ethics of a "Rural Life Movement." There was work to do in cities too: "The greatest ethical task for the church in the city is to place within the new corporate and commercial organizations the controlling motives of justice and brotherhood."[37] How to achieve all this? No need for legislation, because God was doing his evolutionary work, ensuring "a fresh stage in the divine education of mankind." Universal "Social Service" was "the trend of the age."[38] "Trend" – the word was in the book's title – was the new guarantee of progress, and only one term in MacDougall's litany of solace: "purifying, reconstructive power," "turning the world upside down," the "trend of modern science."[39] MacDougall's inexorable "trend" collapsed the distinction between normative and positive. He was, after all, both a compiler of statistics and a Presbyterian minister. He was bringing Christian economics into Canada's age of industry.

AGRARIAN IDEALISM AND SPIRITUAL ENGINEERING

Agrarian idealism was a politics of "spiritual engineering."[40] And it extended far beyond the works of writers such as McArthur and MacDougall. The farmer's movements of the early twentieth century absorbed the core ideas of the agrarian boosters and deployed them in a powerful political insurgency. They were about much more than tariffs and railways: they were a comprehensive defence of agriculture's place in politics and the social order. "Agriculture is the oldest of the arts and the most recent of the sciences."[41] It was of "vital importance to the welfare of the state."[42] The organized farmers proclaimed the doctrine that land was the source of all true wealth. They announced "a great awakening" with roots in the moral superiority of rural life.[43] They inherited and gave new force to an older rhetoric of common people versus privilege, aristocracy, monopoly, plutocracy, and the dichotomy of rich and poor.

The problem of inequality survived and evolved because a strong agricultural base generated an enormously powerful political movement. This agglomeration led to a political formation markedly different from those in Europe and elsewhere in North America. In 1919 the United Farmers became the government in Ontario; in 1921 the United Farmers of Alberta took office; and the 1921 Dominion election rendered the Progressives, the national voice of the united farmers, the second-largest political group in the House of Commons. It was, of course, a striking characteristic of Canadian political economy and class relations that major incursions into the political realm by organized farmers and organized labour occurred in the same decades. The result was a complex populism that challenged the established political parties at both national and provincial levels.[44]

The farmers' movement absorbed the idea of inequality and used it in an ideological struggle between "common people" and plutocracy. The farmers widened the focus beyond the maldistribution of income and wealth, embedding these economic inequities in wider conceptions of the inequitable distribution of power among classes and occupational strata. The idea of inequality was also helping shape a specifically Canadian regional politics: common people versus Big

Interests, each with their own spatial locations, the former widely scattered and especially strong in rural areas, the latter occupying the big cities, especially those in Ontario and Quebec. As the farmers' movements, and gradually the farmer–labour coalitions, absorbed the inequality problem, it weakened and attenuated – merely one element in the rhetorical arsenal and common sense of diverse populist movements that have absorbed generations of Canadian historians. The history of the idea of inequality in the agrarian populist insurgency is therefore the history of its rise and its gradual dissipation.

The problem of inequality found a place in farmer politics in part because the idea fitted easily in the agrarians' conception of conflict. The "rich and poor" dichotomy they inherited from nineteenth-century liberals and democratic socialists suited the simplified utopianism and egalitarian impulses of populism. While accepting the basic forms and institutions of parliamentary democracy, farmers and their representatives came to see state structures as captives of particular occupational interests, narrow elites, or a dominant class. The creation of "real democracy" required not revolution but corrective adjustments to the system of political representation. In the unsystematic mixing of utopian images and moral principles that David Laycock so clearly depicts, populism inherited the older vocabulary of privilege and enlarged it. The villains now were Big Business, Big Interests, Fifty Big Shots.

The result was a specifically Canadian inflexion in which the "rich and poor" dichotomy survived as a rhetorical gloss in the distributive justice of organized farmers. The well-known farmers' platforms illustrated the point. In the "Siege of Ottawa" on 15 December 1910, explicit references to inequality and "distribution of wealth" did not appear. These terms were entirely absent from E.C. Drury's opening address to the meeting of delegates. The problem of inequality surfaced, however, in the farmers' fusillades against the tariff, which, they claimed, had "take[n] a margin of millions out of the pockets of the great body of the people and place those millions in the hands of the few."[45] This formulation of inequality presented "the people" as both honest producers and innocent consumers. The product of their labour was being captured by a few, who were also extorting a surplus at the expense of consumers.

Roderick McKenzie, secretary of the Manitoba Grain Growers, used the 1906 Dominion census to document the claim. He took the average duty on dutiable imports (27.7 per cent), adjusted upwards by that percentage the total value of manufactured output in Canada, and thereby estimated the "tribute" consumers paid via "the excess prices they had paid due to the tariff." Here was an early instance of a populist economics of "special privilege" that evolved over the next three decades.[46] McKenzie's calculation fitted well with the physiocratic assumption stated in the Farmers' Platform of 1910, that the economy depended on agriculture's success and that Canada's greatest challenge lay in "retaining our people on the soil"[47]: "To have its people huddled together in great centres of population" was "the greatest misfortune which can befall any country."[48]

The new Farmers' Platform of 1916 was more explicit, both in its diagnoses of inequality and in its solutions. The protective tariff was part of the odious nexus of combines, trusts, "gentlemen's agreements," and "unjust privileges" that had built up "a privileged class at the expense of the masses, thus making the rich richer and the poor poorer."[49] The solutions now went way beyond reducing customs duties. They included a redistributive shift in taxes away from consumption and producer goods, and towards direct taxation: "a graduated income tax" on individuals and on corporations; a direct tax on unimproved land values; and a graduated inheritance tax on large estates.[50]

The problem of inequality was not always mere rhetorical gloss, however. A few of the more thoughtful farmer activists made the issue central. They grounded their conception of inequality in the nineteenth-century ideal of the independent producer, the values of equitable exchange, and the commutative justice of Christian benevolence.

This agrarian take on inequality was nowhere more apparent than in two books by men who were leaders in both the farmer's and the cooperative movements. Some observers might consider William Charles Good (1876–1967) and Edward Alexander Partridge (1861–1931) lightweight, even eccentric. Certainly their books lacked the intellectual heft of other post-1918 works on social questions. But their volumes deserve serious attention, because they represent major trends in Canadian political thought in that era. They presented the summative thoughts of two pre-eminent agrarian leaders and brain workers[51] – these inspirational and prophetic works were fully part of their authors' political praxis.

Good's *Production and Taxation in Canada* (1919) was about much more than that. The "nature of the problem," he wrote, "is essentially that of discovering the principle of the just distribution of wealth."[52] Understanding the problem required, he believed, a "clear definition of rich and poor."[53] Apparently unaware that economists and philosophers had been discussing these issues for at least a generation, he offered a definition that repeated a simple version of the labour theory of value. Wealth came from human effort, and wealth was therefore "service." The rich person was one who commanded more than he rendered; the poor person, less. It followed, "from the standpoint of ethics," that "the rich are the robbers and the poor are the robbed." Such was Good's "scientific precision."[54] His diagnoses lay within the Canadian physiocratic frame: agriculture determined "the fortunes of the nation and the opportunities and character of the population."[55] A "class of social parasites" had "capitalized" the rent of land.

Good's solution was "Socializing of the Ground Rent," taxing land values directly, and reducing tariffs.[56] These moves appeared to him sufficient, and they would require only a limited expansion of the state. "Freedom of Exchange" would inevitably end monopoly; he saw no need for laws to break up or prevent it, although he accepted state ownership of railways.[57] Good's focus on land and tariffs appeared profoundly self-limiting, when he started with the vast problem of wealth distribution. He failed, among other things, to resolve the problem of ownership. If, as he said, "exclusive ownership" of land "by any individual or class of individuals is not only ethically wrong, but fundamentally absurd," then what other form of possession was ethically acceptable? He had already ruled out the state.

To extract the secular argument in Good's writing, and to point out its limits, is to oversimplify and even to miss the direction of his thought. His book was essentially a work of Protestant ethics, an updating of the Protestant critique of wealth for agrarian politics in the 1910s. What was the point of his apparently crude definitions of rich and poor? The definitions in "popular usage" and secular social science would evade the ethical imperative. His definition, since he grounded it in an ethical principle, "would reconcile reason and conscience." It would also prevent *unjust* condemnation of the very wealthy; the assessment would rest on a principle of justice. Good insisted that by his definition the principle that it was easier for a camel to pass through the eye of a needle than for a rich man to enter the kingdom of heaven was "not figurative, but scientifically accurate."[58]

The same point applied to the just distribution of wealth among the deserving, which in Good's thinking did not require precise or "mathematical" calculation. He asked, what was the just reward to producers who exchanged their output? And what if one product had higher market value than another? The answer, he replied, was simple: divide the "purchase dividend on the basis of total purchases" and ignore the fact that purchases of one product might yield more to the seller than purchases of another. What more was there to say? Precisely because the ethical imperative solved the problem, "Each for All and All for Each" was the practical guide, he insisted.[59]

The conclusion to Good's book was clear and explicit. "The few have enriched themselves at the expense of the many." The solution was a matter of spiritual regeneration: "Seek ye first the Kingdom of God and his righteousness and all these things shall be added unto you."[60] Good found no assurances in evolution, but his work asserted the presence of redemptive powers. "*Better Business* begins at home, and has made progress everywhere." The war had dealt a great blow to injustice, and redemption was immanent: "Surely now ... surely now ... surely at last we can make an honest effort to establish in this, our native land, a Kingdom of Righteousness."[61]

In the work of Edward Partridge (1861–1931), the optimism of "surely now" became a fully developed utopian dream. Partridge's book *The War on Poverty: The One War That Can End War* (1925) was longer, more thoroughly researched, and much more radical than Good's. It was, according to Ian MacPherson, a "strange mixture," and, in Carl Berger's view, its nostrums "appear as quaint as the advertisements for magical liniments which were its accompanying period pieces."[62] There is more to say, however. If we treat the volume as a *sui generis* eccentricity, we miss its affinities with the reform thought of its time. It is rather a peculiarly Canadian variant of then-current intellectual trends in North America and also in Europe. Despite vast differences, there are interesting similarities to the early-twentieth-century romantic socialism and Jewish mysticism discussed by Michael Löwy and others.

Partridge's political imaginary was a Canadian instance of the long romantic protest against the utilitarian and materialist ethos of modern bourgeois, industrial civilization.[63] His many lengthy quotations from Tennyson, Wordsworth, and other poets were not rhetorical veneer: for Partridge, they contained knowledge that was vital to spiritual regeneration. "Come, shrewd speculator in real estate. Come, cunning cornerer of the means of life on this speck of dust, read these lines." Read these lines, he intoned: "Gaze into the depths of a star-spangled night sky," and never again will you be able to exploit "your co-heirs to this magnificent heritage of eternal and eternally changing life."[64] Partridge's use of poetry as a source of applied ethics and spiritual elevation was not a personal quirk; he was following in the path of many Christian socialists.[65]

Partridge's romantic imagination indulged in a nostalgic celebration of an idealized past. As in the romantic socialism of Gustav Landauer and Martin Buber a few decades earlier, he was dreaming not of a conservative restoration but of a new form of communitarian society.[66] In his cooperative commonwealth there would be no capital or private ownership; all production would be "for use instead of for profit,"[67] he hoped, evoking an idealized agrarian past in which families produced for their own consumption. Here, however, his atavism looked forward, part of a search for new ways to ground community. Production for use, Partridge suggested, "harmonizes the individual and the community interest."[68] His book seems an extended prayer for "complete community of interest" among citizens. "Within the old festering, disintegrating social organism, the elements of a wholesome, desirable community life are even now coming into being."[69]

In this context his speculation about reincarnation was not merely a quirky non sequitur. Partridge wanted there to be an "Immortal Ego," an "unconscious mind" that knew its affinity with all other beings. At the very least such a belief would sustain "the development of a sense of social solidarity, the organization of Society in the equal interest of all its members." Quotations from poets John Masefield and Edmund Spenser completed his thought on reincarnation.[70]

This romantic socialist was repelled by the rationalism and positivism of bourgeois culture.[71] Reacting against the positivist and materialist political economy of their time, romantic communitarians such as Buber and Landauer found a prophetic and mystical revolutionary language. In the case of Landauer, "a religious symbolic universe explicitly entered his revolutionary discourse and imbued it with a *sui generis* spirituality which seemed to escape the usual distinctions between faith and atheism."[72] Partridge was no atheist, but his thought made no distinctions between religious and secular. He was ready to use secular sources when they served his polemics and his prophetic vision, and the result was a mélange of political economy, romantic poetry, and populist diatribe. But he avoided the political economists of recent decades. He was aware of the writings of economists, and he quoted Richard Ely – the social gospeller–economist in whose work we might expect Partridge to find much support. But no: Ely, said Partridge, peddled "high brow stuff" that achieved nothing, and only "makes the preacher and the professor feel virtuous."[73]

Partridge was inspired instead by sources that served his romantic socialism. He was, he claimed, a disciple of John Ruskin, who offered to young men "a newer testament – the gospel according to Saint Ruskin."[74] The Englishman appealed to him because he mixed aesthetics and Christianity, condemned political economy, critiqued interest, rent, and luxury, grasped the corrupting power of wealth, and advocated fervently for education and moral regeneration. He also offered a moral critique of exchange relationships that echoed farmer populists' conviction that market exchanges had been corrupted by special interests and rentier appropriations at all levels of the commercial system.[75]

As Ian McKay has pointed out, Ruskin's uncompromising assault on mammonism appealed to the injured and those whose moral and aesthetic sensibilities were offended by capitalism. Canada's socialists and labour autodidacts immersed themselves in Ruskin and took him to be a prophet: "To those who could appreciate his often difficult prose, Ruskin seemed the prophet of a new, post-materialist age of co-operation, beauty, and unity with the cosmos."[76] He served to displace wealth from the conceptual universe of political economy to the terrain of aesthetics and ethics. Partridge, in his untutored way, was following him in linking aesthetics and ethics – "the religion of love and beauty, In field, or factory, mine, or mart."[77] The Canadian was not alone in invoking such an affinity; he was reflecting conjunctions and connections at play in the wider culture. Although he was probably not aware of it, philosophers such as John Dewey were exploring "aesthetic ethics" in his time.[78]

In this romantic socialism, the transcendent was immanent, echoing certain European advocates.[79] For Partridge, as for Landauer and Buber, the gradual progress of evolution – "Old Evolution," as he called it – was a barren conception of history. In Landauer and Buber a radical change or "great metamorphosis" would come as a "sudden irruption." Partridge said that change came as "a sudden and wide promulgation."[80] "Everybody knew things were wrong," and then "suddenly, quicker to sense the symptoms of social disintegration ... the efficients, after quick consultation, stepped into their rightful place."[81] The agents of change in this prophetic vision were not anonymous historical forces but specific enlightened persons, the "efficients," including "unmercenary-minded" scholars, scientists, and, of course, poets and philosophers. The elitism was reminiscent of the faith in experts that characterized much of the period's farmer-populist and social-democratic thought. Partridge's eclectic borrowings and his impetuous imagination had clear roots in farmer populism. But he had moved a considerable distance beyond the organized farmers' preoccupations with tariffs, taxation, and direct democracy. And his imagination had taken him into a utopian realm of thought that was distant from the political economy of wealth distribution in Britain and the United States.

Why devote so many paragraphs to a forgotten Canadian volume that won few followers when it appeared?[82] The first answer is that Partridge had produced one of the very few Canadian books in his generation that focused throughout on the problem of inequality. The study, nominally about a "war on poverty," said little about poverty – little or nothing about the living and working conditions of the poor, urban squalor, charity, unemployment, or any of the other subjects of then-current concern about poor people. From its first to its last pages, it was, obsessively, about "rich and poor," "wealth," and the mental, moral, and spiritual dimensions of unjust distributions.[83] It shifted discussion of economic injustice from farmers' specific grievances to the essence of capitalism, as Partridge understood it, which "sacrifices the interest of the 'many' to the interest of the 'few.'" "The rich not only refuse food to the poor: they refuse wisdom; they refuse virtue; they refuse salvation."[84]

The utopia that Partridge constructed resolved the problem of rich and poor by the simple expedient of eliminating these categories, and all the conditions of their existence.[85] There would be no markets, no businessmen, no lawyers, no landlords; there would be no debt and no credit, hence no financiers. The vision was not anarchist because it assumed a government. The ruling principles were few and simple, deriving from the cooperative tradition and the labour theory of value: production for use, and "Each for all and all for each." And another principle, deriving from the labour theory, severely limited Partridge's distributive justice and his humanitarianism: "If any man will not work neither shall he eat."[86] His radical vision was still rooted in nineteenth-century values.

A second reason for the attention here to Partridge: his study was a capsule of many recurring patterns of Canadian political thought in this era. For all his idiosyncrasies, Partridge was not alone. His fascination with Ruskin was merely one instance. The Victorian aesthete and moralist struck deep chords in the political consciousness of the rural and small-town literati of Canada. It is almost as though newspaper editors in western Canada kept his works on their desks and dipped into them whenever they needed to fill incomplete pages. "What Ruskin Said Sixty-Five Years Ago," announced the local newspaper in Wetaskiwin, Alberta: "The lawful basis of wealth is that a man who works should be paid the fair value of his work ... Therefore the first necessity of social life is the clearness of national conscience in enforcing the law – that he should keep who has justly earned."[87] Partridge took many cultural currencies – cooperation, community, the primacy of agriculture, the labour theory, Protestant ethics – and merged them into his utopia. He was echoing a common, romantic anti-materialism and a faith in immanent spiritual transformation. That faith was, we may reasonably speculate, a consoling transcendence of the mundane world of political parties and policies that had, by 1925, so obviously failed the farmers of Canada.

In Partridge's thought, inequality was not so much an economic condition as a form of spiritual entropy. He confronted but never resolved the problem inherent in all utopian visions. He wanted to be a "practical prophet" who offered a "practical religion"; but how to realize the utopia?[88] He offered no program of action to achieve any reform. His prophetic vision presumed no conception of historical change other than sudden, rootless spiritual metamorphosis.

SOCIAL-GOSPEL IMPERATIVES

Elevating inequality from material to spiritual planes occurred not only among specific farmer and cooperative thinkers. It was also the work of the social gospel. The social gospel, according to Richard Allen, "might well be termed the religion of the agrarian revolt," since the connections between the two movements were deep and extensive.[89] Both shared the Canadian physiocratic belief. Social-gospel leaders were born in the rural and small-town Canada of the nineteenth century.[90] When they turned to politics and social questions, they erased the distinction between sacred and secular. As Richard Allen reports, the social gospel contained a "theology of radical immanence" that was "the religious concomitant of populism and progressivism."[91] The theology was prophetic and post-millennialist, anticipating the establishment of the Kingdom on earth prior to Christ's return.[92]

The history of the social gospel has been well served by Canadian historians of religion. Incurring debts to their work throughout, and seeking to remain agnostic about debates that I am not qualified to enter, I focus here on a single theme: the fate of the problem of inequality.[93] From the late-nineteenth-century birth of the multifaceted transformations known as "social gospel," Protestants of many religious orientations reinvigorated the older Protestant critique of wealth and proclaimed their intellectual control of the problem of inequality.

A striking example was the remarkable essay on "The Gospel of Justice" by Albert R. Carman that the *Canadian Methodist Quarterly* published in 1891.[94] It delivered both a critique of the church and an ethical problematic. Carman grounded justice securely in a simple labour theory of value and a simple assumption about the universal necessity of landholding. "If I may not live upon land, I must die."[95] The churches, he charged, had been complicit in the rise of inequality. In a Christian land, he said, the devil's army, commanded by Mammon, had "taken the print of the golden age," subduing "nine-tenths of humanity" while "one-tenth are masters."[96] "The hackneyed truth is true – the rich are growing richer and the poor poorer."[97] The church stood with "closed lips" before "this giant system of robbery." Was it any wonder that the churches were losing members, when all they offered to the poor was charity and a "fairer distribution" only in "the future life"? Charity was not enough, and neither were "the senile methods of the old temperance societies." The remedy – following the labour theory – was not charity but "the simple, honest rule that every person shall have what he earns."[98]

But Carman was not merely reformulating conventional nostrums. He did something rare among Protestant critics of wealth: he attempted an empirical proof of his point about inequality. The average annual wage of workers in Ontario was $420.07; of this amount, $369.62 went for food, clothing, rent, and fuel (he did not cite his source). This left a mere $50.45 for taxes, books, furnishings, and the education of children – "all of life that lifts man above the animal." And this, he emphasized, was the condition of the average worker, not the poor! We do not have statistics on owners and employers' earnings, noted Carman – but we knew that they could afford education, "elegant homes," "costly equipages," tours, and whatever entertainment they wished.

From these observations Carman derived a fundamental question about the ethics of distribution. How should we value employers' labour? "Do they earn – i.e., do they contribute to the value of the products of the institution – ten, a hundred, five hundred times as much as the clear-headed foreman who is on duty from 7 a.m. until 6 p.m. every day?"[99] Carman was turning the Protestant critique of wealth into a challenge for the coming generation of Christian social activists.[100] It was no longer enough to preach about the sin of usury and the duty of benevolence. One now must specify the sins and justify the duties with evidence from the actual conditions of individuals and classes in the new world of wage labour. It was no longer enough to use the labour theory of value to proclaim that robbery was occurring. Prove the theft, and propose a non-theft alternative.

On the subject of land, Carman also posed a challenging question. The right to land was a natural right (either I have land or I die). It was also a divinely ordained right, proclaimed, said Carman, in Leviticus 25, with its vision of the sharing of land and its bounty. Carman wrote: "The land belongs not to the individual but to the community. God did not wait for Mr Henry George to discover that; He told it to Moses."[101] If the teaching of Leviticus "is not fatal to the private ownership of land, in the modern sense, then all laws of logic and exegesis fail."[102] Carman was certainly not endorsing public ownership; but he left the question of property rights open and unresolved. He concluded his essay with a series of questions, focusing on the rights to possess land and capital. What form of ownership was consistent with both natural and divine law? And what was right and what was wrong, "when honest industry appears to bring to one man bread and to another fabulous wealth?"[103]

Social gospellers clung to the problem of inequality, but failed to offer systematic and rigorous answers to Carman's questions. Tirelessly reiterated, the nostrum about the gap between rich and poor became a platitude. The social gospel was present at the birth of social science in Canada, yet failed to produce anything comparable to the empirical studies of wealth distribution by such American social gospellers as Richard Ely, Robert Hunter, and Charles Spahr.[104] Canadian adherents probably knew about British and U.S. economists and philosophers and their principles of distributive justice: as Nancy Christie and Michael Gauvreau point out, ministers were encouraged to read recent works in those countries' social science.[105]

They borrowed very selectively, however, mostly ignoring, for instance, the more radical arguments of J.A. Hobson and the work of Thorstein Veblen. As for the most original American contribution to the ethics of distribution in the first half of the twentieth century – the work of John A. Ryan – it gained only reviews in Catholic journals that evaded the radical challenges of Ryan's distributive justice.[106] Social gospellers occasionally struggled with property rights, but rarely went further than property-holding as a sacred trust.[107] This is not to say that they ignored the problem of inequality. Rather they turned the problem and its resolution in Canadian directions, which emphasized a social theology of radical immanence and reconciling individual and social salvation.

Few social gospellers persevered in a sustained encounter with philosophy, although a college education introduced many to the great works in "mental philosophy."[108] Historians have found in their thought an affinity with British idealism, as well as the influence of Canadian idealist philosophers John Clark Murray and John Watson. Consider, as one instance, James Shaver Woodsworth (1874–1942). Ordained a Methodist minister in Manitoba in 1896, before receiving his degree in divinity in 1900, Woodsworth wrestled with doctrines such as the Trinity, and his struggles with orthodoxy "seemed only to strengthen his acceptance of the spiritual revelation through Christ."[109] At the same time he was reading widely.[110]

In 1899–1900 he spent several months at Oxford, where he attended the lectures of the idealist philosopher Edward Caird.[111] We know what Caird was saying in his lectures. He was declaring a reconciliation of philosophy and religion, of science, ethics, and Christianity, at the moment when Woodsworth himself was seeking such a resolution. Caird found hope in the idea of "organic evolution."[112] "Ideas win their way by inches and very silently, but what ground they win is never lost."[113] Evolution was a "reconciling idea, which enables us to do justice to both the aspects of social life which have been opposed in the past, and to rise above their opposition." Thus individualism and community were coming together; it was a mistake to assume that individualists and socialists were "absolutely opposed sects."[114] "We are learning to look both upon nature and human nature with a new reverence," reported Caird.[115] Poetry affirmed this learning, he added (Edward Partridge would have loved this!). Caird was declaring a "salvation here and hereafter" that would echo through the speeches and sermons of Canadian social gospellers for years to come.[116]

Idealism sustained a powerful moral imperative, but the political outcomes in the early 1900s were varied and often incoherent. Woodsworth indicated one path from idealism to action. Inequality was present in his book *Strangers within Our Gates* (1909): people have been "sorted out by the money test," with the well-to-do idler on top and the poor tillers of soil on the bottom.[117] Thereafter the problem of inequality gave way to his book's focus on immigrants and the physiocratic preoccupation with land: land hunger was driving immigration, often attracting an inferior population of poor people to Canada. The social problem, in his view, ended up in a reckoning with "the competition of races" and the differing qualities of ethnic groups.[118]

Two years later *My Neighbor*, Woodsworth's study of "city conditions," presented inequality as a basic urban condition. "The incredible paradox of modern life," he said (quoting Walter Rauschenbusch), was that "when wealth was multiplying beyond all human precedent, an immense body of pauperism was growing up and becoming chronic."[119] But was this a Canadian paradox at all?[120] Instead of documenting the problem, Woodsworth gave pride of place to Hegelian idealism in the form of a mystical reverie about inequality, wherein high and low became palaces and putrefactions, vanity and misery, where a "proud Grandee still lingers in his perfumed saloons" and "wretchedness cowers into truckle beds." Woodsworth was quoting Thomas Carlyle's *Sartor Resartus* (1836), a work popular among American transcendentalists. Perhaps he was not aware that the novel was a deeply ironic and enigmatic play with language and also a parody of German idealism. He quotes at length Teufelsdrockh, which translates as "god-born devil-dung."[121]

My Neighbor dissolved the problem of inequality before the reader's eyes, turning Edward Caird's idealism into a dream. Communism and socialism, words of terror a few years ago, said Woodsworth, were now becoming real in the modern community and in the actions of government for collective benefit. Christian ethics was reconciling with common good; after all, "there is no secular." A "new spirit-movement," a "modern impulse," was "gradually per-meating and leavening our social life and is destined to transform our institutions. It is our zeitgeist, going forth conquering and to conquer."[122] This notion of an immanent transformation was not a simple updating of evolution (the word did not appear in the book) but assumed that crisis would precipitate a sudden change. "A crisis for the individual and society is created," but "heroism today meets not only the tests of courage, but of surprise." The Christian faith confronted industrial civilization and conquered it. The result was "a new civilization, new in its material basis, in its industry, in its social order, in its intellectual viewpoint, in its religious concepts."[123] This salvation could not be pre-ordained and independent of human will (the problem with Darwinian evolution was its apparent denial of human agency). Social salvation required its own enactment. The answer then to the problem of inequality was "social service." By this path the Methodist's idealism reduced the problem of inequality to the labour of urban social service and social work.[124]

In taking this path Woodsworth and others declined options that were consistent with a liberal reconciliation of individualism and community. If "there is no secular," then a range of political options became spiritual: minimum wages, national insurance, inheritance taxes, recognition of trade unions, collective bargaining. Of course many social gospellers eventually followed Woodsworth in these matters, and the labour churches were soon moving that way.[125] But most social gospellers gravitated instead towards non-state forms of social service and a theology of immanent social salvation. A similar bifurcation occurred in the United States, but in Canada the strong tendency was not towards but away from a legislative program of redistribution and distributive justice.

The process was complex, and, as we know, the social gospel was no procrustean bed. The Fourth Ecumenical Methodist Conference in Toronto in October 1911 can serve as an introduction. The 782-page proceedings showed that the moral problems of wealth and its distribution were recurring themes. The moral and social problems of the city also preoccupied the delegates, and at times the issues overlapped.

The system that produces abounding wealth for the few, that spells abject want for the many – that produces the millionaire on the one hand and the sweated workman on the other, cries for amendment.[126]

Abounding wealth and prodigal luxuriousness exist side by side with pinching poverty and semi-starvation. Some who produce much of the nation's wealth possess but little, and some who produce little possess much.[127]

I ask in anxiety and fear whether it be not true that this great trade system of our Christian civilization has been a constant menace and hurt to the personal Christian life? Whether the inequalities which the system fosters, the great poverty which it permits and promotes, the great wealth which it makes possible, the constant and growing contest between employer and employee ... whether such a system does not stand opposed to the law of Christ.[128]

The public conscience needs arousing. Never before were the extremes in the distribution of wealth so great as now. Wage earners are neither blind nor indifferent to this. Can we be surprised if they are dissatisfied with their housing, their life, and their conditions?[129]

The present city life divides men; it sifts them out according to their wealth or poverty into separate communities, and tends rapidly towards the creation of castes almost as self-contained and isolated as those of the Hindoos.[130]

The physiocratic assumption was also present in the obsession with land: "The ownership of the land is the fundamental economic fact in all communities. Unequal distribution of the land has always been accompanied by a hereditary landed aristocracy. Approximately equal distribution of the land is the necessary basis for a real and permanent democracy, both political and social."[131]

These quotations documented the troubled and uncertain reckoning of Methodist ministers with the world of wage labour, a realm still largely unfamiliar to them. Together with their American mentor, Walter Rauschenbusch, they saw and feared the appropriation of Christian ethics by atheistic socialists. Their moral assault on inequality was a means of recapturing the lost moral ground.

Among some this meant appropriating the language of socialism itself. Opposition to socialism, said one speaker in 1911, may have done good service by awakening Christians to social problems. "Happily, the atheistic type of socialism is fast passing away," and an unmistakably "Christian socialism" was taking its place.[132] Those who engaged in such rhetorical compromise did not go on to propose a program by which such socialism might reduce inequality or even alleviate its effects. None was necessary, since "the increasing application of Christian principles" to social problems was already occurring. [133]

The social gospellers' encounter with social problems entailed tensions, inconsistencies, and contradictions that grew partly from the class position of small-town and rural professionals. In their struggle to reconcile individual autonomy with community and private property with common good, their principles of social justice remained nebulous and even incoherent. Traditional evangelicals who insisted on the primacy of spiritual salvation remained largely outside the conversation on social problems. Many social gospellers within the discussion emphasized private property and rights of ownership. Jesus never taught socialism, they insisted, and no government or community had the right to take away a person's wealth.[134] This position led directly to a quagmire: if the answer to inequality was charitable relief for the poor and the duty of benevolence on the part of the rich, how was the giver to determine whether any destitute person was or was not deserving?

More radical social gospellers had answers to this question, when they did not evade it altogether. One response was that all were deserving and that providing equal opportunity, education, and technical education entailed no pauperizing effects. But even this reformist position barely concealed a recurring fear that workers were vulnerable to the same corrupting materialism that infected the rest of society. It was understandable that workers campaigned for a just reward, but they seemed highly suspect when they did so. The contradiction appeared in a story told to the 1911 Methodist Conference. A boy in a factory was asked to run and find a person whose presence was urgently needed. The lad went on the errand but walked slowly. When someone asked him why he did not run, he answered that he was not paid to run but would do so for a small increase in his wage. The story was offered as evidence of many "malingerers."[135] Such attitudes helped to prevent any extended discussion of whether a minimum living standard was a right or entitlement, let alone of what it might entail.

Those who agreed that workers and the poor deserved better living standards offered no common justification for action. Many would have concurred with the British MP Arthur Henderson, who told the Methodist Conference that the first principle of social justice must be "the value of every human life."[136] It followed that all persons were deserving of a minimal standard, by virtue of their humanity alone. But another popular axiom led to a very different outcome: the labourer was worthy of his hire, and his material reward must be in proportion to the labour he contributed. This updating of the labour theory of value served to justify old-age pensions and rhetorical support for trade unions, but little more. Squeezed between principles whose incompatibility they rarely perceived, social gospellers resolved all dilemmas by insisting on the inevitable immanence of social salvation and its attainment through social service.[137]

Social activism resolved the tension between a teleology of immanent salvation and the Christian emphasis on personal duty of conscience. If evolution was tending inexorably towards community and cooperation, then what was the role of free will? By acting in society, the believer enacted the prophetic vision. He or she resolved the dilemma of property, enacting social salvation without challenging property or its rights. Social service was spiritual engineering – the embodiment of conscience in property.[138]

Within a longer time frame, we may see the social gospel as a new manifestation of an old problem: how to hold together the discourse of Enlightenment rationalism with the spiritualism of evangelical religion? Historians have shown how the social gospel tempered and focused the latter, turning its motivational force into a movement of social regeneration. The social gospel in Canada also tempered and reduced the Enlightenment discourse, most notably in its adherents' indifference to theological scholasticism and secular philosophy.[139] At the 1911 Methodist Conference, for instance, it was American visitors who referred to such theologians as William Ellery Channing, William Newton Clarke, and Hans-Hinrich Wendt. It was the English theologian Henry Maldwyn Hughes who introduced Hegel and Bergson's ideas to the proceedings. It was the American theologian Francis J. McConnell who spoke about Kant's categorical imperative – a concept that clerical delegates would no doubt remember from their college days – but one wonders whether they were moved by McConnell's critique of philosophical pragmatism. Likely the delegates were more comfortable with Rev. George Elliott's rejection of "intellectual forms": John Wesley appeared "so utterly modern," the speaker suggested, because "he places the basis of religious life not in some intellectual forms of statement, but in that deeper realm of living experience."[140] In this context an extended discussion of the principles of distributive justice was extremely unlikely.

The submersion of inequality under the combined currents of social service and immanent salvation continued between 1914 and 1920 – but it did not disappear. The Moral and Social Reform Council, founded in 1907 and renamed the Social Service Council in 1913 with strong support from progressive Protestants, stood resolutely for "a more equitable distribution of wealth."[141] The large Social Service Congress gathering in Ottawa in March 1914 heard many iterations of the problem of inequality, including one in the welcoming address by former Liberal prime minister Sir Wilfrid Laurier.[142] The Congress passed several resolutions. None, however, mentioned inequality or a more equitable distribution of incomes or wealth. Why no resolution on this recurring theme? To ask the question is to miss an obvious point, shared undoubtedly by most if not all delegates: they considered the resolutions effective and sufficient responses to inequality. Labour organizations, unemployment bureaux, old-age pensions, temperance pledges, a Dominion department for child welfare, more social surveys and research – the widening panoply of "social service" *was* the solution to inequality.

The other answer to the problem of inequality was that its demise was immanent. The Presbyterian minister and novelist Charles W. Gordon offered the Congress his vision of the state as an "organism," a living entity with its own vital being. He then accused the modern state of "treachery," a failing of its vital functions, since "poverty and luxury exist in the same organism." His biological metaphors were unusual by this time; even more so, in the discourse of a Canadian social gospeller, were his statistics on wealth distribution (all U.S. data, of course, in the absence of solid Canadian figures). His brief flurry of empiricism, and hint of the need for state action, quickly evaporated. He apparently thought the treachery and corruption so obvious and so perilous that they could not endure – they were the seeds of an inevitable salvation. The greater the evil, the more certain its extinction. In Gordon's immanentalist vision there was a "New State," where "community interest" would be the prime consideration and "the thing of highest value will be man himself, not mere things that he can wear and eat." Such was Gordon's answer to the treachery of maldistribution: in his immanent Kingdom the common good magically transcended problems of food and clothing.[143]

Graham Taylor, the well-known Congregational minister and founder of the legendary Chicago Commons and a department of Christian sociology in that city, followed a well-worn path in his address, seeing evidence of "advances toward the Kingdom of God," not only in the expanding social-service movement, but also in collective behaviour in the world around him.[144] Taylor's vision was breathtaking in its optimism. Manufacturers, he said, "have forgotten the man behind the machine." "But they are waking up, thank God; they are getting human – they really are." His evidence for this awakening? The "marvellous marshalling of human forces," the "wonderful" organic perfection of the work process in the Ford Motor Company factory in Detroit![145]

The problem of inequality survived in the Canadian social-gospel world between 1914 and 1920, largely as a recurring motif or a simple moral axiom rather than as a guiding *problematique* of social justice.[146] The words "inequality" and "distribution of wealth" appeared in the major Protestant journals, and in *Social Welfare*, the journal of the Social Service Council, but by the late 1910s and early 1920s these words were rare. Elsewhere attention to the problem of inequality increased. "Inequality" and "distribution of wealth" grew in frequency in American English, in British English, and in British Columbia's newspapers during and just after the First World War.[147] To the extent that social gospellers had tried to claim the problem of inequality as their own moral turf, they were losing ground within the discursive domain in which literate Canadians lived.

The First World War helped in many ways to inspire social reformers, social-service advocates, and those who worked in urban missions and settlements. The war years also saw new affirmations of the theology of immanent transformation. There was more here than a simple search for hope in a time of horror and unprecedented loss. Canadian churches saw the moral foundations of civilization crumbling and sought to rebuild them through the leadership of their faith and their institutions. The war seemed to exacerbate social conflict; it also became the mirror image of its antithesis – a world of peace and social harmony. In this way social gospellers saw in war not a worsening of inequality, but its immanent extinction. "The new day has come ... There is a new social conscience, a new sense of social responsibility. The old social distinctions have been broken down. There were no lords and louts in the trenches ... All were brothers."[148]

The General Conference of the Methodist Church in 1918 rejoiced that "the war is the coronation of democracy." "The democratic control of industry is just and is inevitable ... Accepted commercial and industrial methods based on individualism and competition have gone down like mud walls in a flood."[149] The war put an end to production for profit: almost every industry in Britain "has been made to serve the national interest by the elimination of the element of private profit. That the present organization, based on production and service for profits, can be superceded [sic] by a system of production and service for human needs, is no longer a dream."[150]

We are coming to see, said an article in the Methodist *Christian Guardian*, that "society consists merely of two classes, workers and parasites." Nevertheless, in the spirit of the new day, "right has become might" and "unearned incomes" are no longer possible.[151] The war, in this vision of transformation, had completed the long-desired union of individual and community: "individual efficiency" had wed "social efficiency." Thus nothing could survive "that enables the privileged or the privilege seekers to skim the cream off the people's milk, to levy tribute upon the poor ... or otherwise to get fortunes for which they render in return no equivalent in value or in services."[152]

Specific economic conditions during and immediately after the war helped to advance a turn in Canadian conversations about inequality. A concern for price levels had arisen among those worrying about poverty, living standards, and labour relations (the pre-war preoccupation within the Dominion Department of Labour is well known). The war years saw rapid increases in prices of consumer goods; wages did not keep pace. Social-service advocates and others initiated social surveys in urban districts in an effort to apply scientific methods to social efficiency.[153] Social surveyors and social workers saw a direct connection between standards of living and costs of living, and hence to the maldistribution of incomes. The ·

Social Service Council urged collection of data on wages, prices, and rents, and also on "distribution of income by classes of work."[154]

Urban reformers and social-service workers were reducing the problem of inequality to one of prices. Frank N. Stapleford, a social-work advocate who was comfortable with economic questions, offers a good example of the underlying logic. The productivity gains of the last century, he said, had allowed higher pay together with shorter working hours. But rising costs of living often wiped out the "apparent" gains. "The real question is not how much a wage earner is receiving, but what he can secure with those wages." The political implications are clear: vis-à-vis industrial relations and social conflict, the state should focus on prices as much as or more than on wages.

Although the term "price spreads" had not yet entered political discourse, many (including H.H. Stevens, the "price spreads" commissioner of the 1930s) were already calling attention to middlemen and "food speculators." The long-standing Canadian preoccupation with price determination emerged partly from the fraught and erratic confrontation with the problem of inequality. "To secure an even distribution" required some as yet unspecified control of prices, in the interest of what Stapleford called "social efficiency."[155]

Some social gospellers saw much more radical answers to both social conflict and the more specific problem of inequality. In 1918 the radicals won important, if temporary victories within the Methodist and Presbyterian churches. The controversial and widely circulated report of the Methodists' Army and Navy Board declared for "giving the workers an equitable share in the wealth jointly produced" and offered support for industrial councils. The Presbyterians gave cautious endorsement for unemployment insurance, old-age pensions, pensions for widowed mothers, shorter hours of work, and the principle of collective bargaining.[156] The churches had taken major steps in the direction of the welfare state.

As historians have shown, however, these apparent radical victories spurred vigorous opposition. Especially difficult for conservative and pro-business Methodists: the report's statements about the "moral perils inherent in the system of production for profits" and about "the transference of the whole of economic life from a basis of competition and profits to one of co-operation and service."[157] The debate that followed revealed deep divisions within the church, and even among the social-gospel fraction, over collective bargaining, the role of the state, and property rights. The debate also revealed disagreement, even confusion, over the meaning of inequality and its antithesis, equality.

Did inequality end when the poor had attained a sustainable minimum standard? Or, asked the businessman S.R. Parsons, did "transference" mean a futile attempt "to create an equality between those who were naturally unequal"?[158] And what exactly did "transference" from a system of competition and profits mean? Salem Bland defended the radical position that he had helped to write. He did not mean "any violent overturning of the present system." The elimination of profit meant exactly that – "eventually," at some unspecified time in the future. And perhaps not quite that: rather, "profit should cease to be the incentive," Bland insisted.[159] So would it remain? If the motive or incentive was public benefit, consumer satisfaction, or quality of product, then profit could stay, because it was morally clean. S.R. Parsons may not have been reassured. But the question remained, both for contemporaries and for historians: what was Bland's meaning, and what, if anything, had the church said about the problem of inequality?

It is easy and even condescending to submit honest and deeply held convictions of a century ago to critiques emanating from very different assumptions and from the lofty perch of hindsight. We do better historical work if we can observe past beliefs and their limits from within their own ethical and political frames. On the problem of inequality, a trenchant and revealing critique of the social-gospel homilies appeared in a short article by J.H. Philp in the *Christian Guardian* in March 1919.

Philp seemed to grasp that there were "monstrous inequalities" in the present day; he certainly realized that some people grew rich by controlling markets and fixing prices, thereby acquiring wealth "by making society poorer." He proceeded to ask a series of questions. He began with the Methodist position of 1918 on "transference" from competition and profits to cooperation and service. What, he asked, did that actually mean? Will its "prophets" explain it? And what was competition? If producers and sellers competed under rules and standards their community accepted, was it not then a fair and productive rivalry? If monopoly and price-fixing were evils, then was not competition desirable? Was eliminating it really possible?

As for capital and profit, when were these not a just reward for skill, energy, or thrift? If the answer was that equal opportunity should apply to all who enter commerce and industry, then how to achieve this goal? Only "drastic" legislative changes could level the playing field, including perhaps steep death duties and state-owned enterprises. Was this what "transference" meant? Finally, in the social-gospel "Utopia," would all rewards be equal?

If there was to be some difference in reward, what standard – what "impartial arbiter" – would determine the distribution? Would the motion-picture star earn the same as the laundryman? Philp's questions came from within the church but outside the social gospel.[160] In the inchoate thinking of social gospellers on inequality, systematic answers did not exist. Yet these were basic questions of distributive justice and reform politics. Philp's critique cruelly exposed the fragility of the social-gospel iterations of inequality.

The clearest answer to such critiques came in those rare cases when the post-millennial vision of immanent transformation evolved into an uncompromising socialism.[161] Salem Bland had many opportunities to answer the critics of the Methodist radicalism of 1918. His most complete response came in *The New Christianity* of 1920. In this work he dispensed with any equivocation over profit. "A profit-seeking system ... cannot be cleansed or sweetened or ennobled." "There is only one way to Christianize [profit], and that is, to abolish it."[162] He did not shy away from state action: public ownership, he said, was "emancipating, educative, redemptive, regenerating." "To discredit and attack the principle of public ownership is to discredit and attack Christianity."[163] Industrial councils, as Britain's Whitley Commission recommended, were a mere beginning, not an end. The end was the "disappearance of the capitalistic control of industry" – where the community or workers owned and managed it.[164]

How to accomplish the "revolution"? Bland's prophetic optimism stemmed from his unorthodox (and non-Marxian) reading of history. The engine of change was "the mightiest organized force in the world" – "organized Labor."[165] Protestantism was not the source of the new historical transformation: deeply individualistic, shaping and shaped by capitalism since Luther's time, "Protestantism must pass away."[166] The new Christianity would be forged from the old in alliance with the egalitarian, democratic, and communitarian values of organized labour. Bland enriched his vision of inexorable change with rural metaphors: rivers, blossoms, soil, and "roots deep in common earth."[167]

Bland's theology of immanence may seem naïvely optimistic in the face of the deeply entrenched power of capitalism in his time. But was it really naïve to see capitalism, like feudalism, as a historically specific and temporally limited economic system? Humanity "is in the grasp of divine currents too strong to be resisted."[168] Such prophetic socialism left little room for the problem of inequality, which was a symptom, an epiphenomenon. Solving the problem was impossible inside the structures that created it. The word "inequality" appeared only five times in Bland's book; "distribution of wealth" not once.

IMMANENCE, UTOPIA, AND INEQUALITY

Within the emerging liberal order, the problem of inequality dotted many contexts in the 1920s,[169] but as a minor variation, subordinated to the louder melodic lines of other political themes. It was present in the thought of labourite reformers, the farmer's movement, and Progressive politicians. It appeared in academic sociology, as in the work of J.W. Macmillan, who supported minimum wages, old-age pensions, and health insurance to address inequitable distribution.[170] It emerged briefly, in a repetition of familiar incantations, in William Irvine's book *The Farmers in Politics* (1920), which boasted an introduction by Salem Bland.[171] Here as elsewhere inequality succumbed to the preoccupation with tariffs, democratic representation, and the party system. Inequality fell victim to the assurance and consolation of immanent salvation. A "new age" was not only necessary, insisted Irvine – it was coming about. Cooperation appeared everywhere, he commented, as proof of "the coming of the Kingdom of God on earth."[172] The "ought to happen" shaded into "is happening" when "the line between the sacred and secular is being rubbed out" and "everything is becoming sacred."[173] Principles of distributive justice received no further elaboration. The greater project was coming to be: Christian faith was securing its place in the unfamiliar and hostile world of industrial modernity.

The optimistic motif of immanence was not the same as utopianism – whether that of Edward Partridge or Edward Bellamy or Ernst Bloch – although the two shared similar modes of thought. A utopia, even when constructed on existing ideals, was distant and different from the present that it sought to transcend. By contrast, the immanent transformation so many Canadian social gospellers and others assumed was a future being born in the present; it was an evolution to which existing exemplars of cooperation, community, and benevolence bore witness. The motif of immanence, however, invited the same old question: how does the utopian relate to politics?[174] Utopias are deeply political; they present political answers to political problems, even when the worlds they create are imaginary. Yet utopian thought may transcend or even escape the political. Or, as Fredric Jameson put it, "Utopia emerges at the moment of the suspension of the political; I am almost tempted to say of its excision ... or even ... its 'encryptment.'"[175]

Applied to the motif of immanence, the question about politics allows us no simple answer, and the risk is a frustrating ambiguity of the kind only unrepentant postmodernists could love. Certainly the vision of a society in transformation offered hope, a sustaining inspiration, and real-world exemplars of progressive change. It was, after all, a Methodist idealist and former social-gospel minister – J.S. Woodsworth – who in 1935 became the first parliamentarian to read into the debates of the Canadian House of Commons estimates of economy-wide distributions of income, based on income-tax data.[176] Yet while he still believed in the earthly presence of divine providence, he no longer encrypted his politics within a doctrine of immanence. By 1935 he had moved well beyond that motif.

For much of social-gospel thought in the 1910s and 1920s, however, Jameson's answer applies: immanence entailed suspension or encryptment of both inequality and a politics of distributive justice. "By projecting my mind forward to that greater civilization I do succeed in throwing a veil of unreality over the solemn ineptitude of today" – and also over the politics of inequality.[177] When social gospellers made divine providence rather than the state the main agent for social salvation, they encrypted or, at best, severely constrained a politics of redistribution.[178] Their doctrine of immanence also worked against extended discussion of the empirical evidence for inequality and of principles of distributive justice. The insights of John A. Ryan, for instance – perhaps the era's most original contributions to the subject of inequality – could not open such a crypt. The problem of inequality was a presence resounding with absence.

As for the politics of utopianism, history offers the only answers. And so, for early-twentieth-century Canadian thought, the political debilitation of inequality occurred in a particular historical context. The problem of inequality lay, as we saw above, at the intersection of four themes: an enduring labour theory of value, physiocratic assumptions about land, the commonplace vision of a superabundance of vacant land, and a renovated, post-millennial Protestantism. Canada's political economy differed from that of the United States and Britain, and its people had mainly small-town or rural origins.

We can see the resulting confinement of inequality neatly through its fate in the world of social analysis. As Christie and Gauvreau have shown, the churches and the Social Service Council created social surveys and social data in Canada between the 1910s and the 1930s, and the problem of inequality was clearly present. Community surveys formed "a basis for social action" and were essential tools in applying scientific method to explore inequitable distribution.[179] They asked an astonishing range of questions and produced impressive volumes of data, including information on wage rates and prices. Despite the initial concern for society-wide inequity – and the array of American models and precedents – Christian social surveyors did not study vertical income distributions in Canada and missed the biggest data challenge of their time.

We cannot attribute the lacuna to an absence of evidence. National-level data on earnings existed; Americans had found ingenious, if often flawed, methods of solving the empirical problem.[180] Canada's social surveyors, however, saw social action in terms of alleviation and amelioration, not structural diagnosis. In 1923 Carl Dawson was explicit about how these pioneers approached their task: "We try to deal with the symptoms and not the disease in the body industrial."[181] That could have been their motto.

Another obstacle stemmed from conservative reactions to cautious reform ideas and to the churches' proposals for reconstruction in 1918. To ask businessmen to report their annual incomes was scarcely thinkable: the churches had already offended many of their more prosperous members. Social surveys, with their broad focus, remained within safer boundaries. And as Christie and Gauvreau have argued, "the central dynamic" of Protestant social investigations lay within rural Canada rather than in the city.[182]

In the wake of comprehensive rejections of laissez-faire liberalism in Britain, the United States, and Canada, the great question of the Progressive era was the articulation of individual and community.

How to balance individual rights and responsibilities with collective needs and community interests? The question prompted a bewildering range of answers within many communities of thought, from new liberalism to philosophical idealism to the social gospel. In Canada the pervasive surge of Christian religion set boundaries to political thought, especially on the state's role. For most social gospellers, government seemed a valuable, at times even indispensable ally, in the great project of spiritual-social engineering. Yet a resilient individualism set limits to its role, including its conceivably implementing distributive justice or any form of redistribution. A conclusion of Christie and Gauvreau is apt: "Social Christianity in Canada was upheld by a powerful strand of individualism which preserved a large degree of independence for private culture within a broad ideal of community citizenship, in contrast to the United States where the social gospel and progressivism more directly privileged the communal above the individual, so that the notion of the private and the public were almost wholly conflated."[183] Redistribution of the world's goods would occur, said the social gospel in Canada: it would emerge as divine providence guided the spiritual engineering of individual and community.

It mattered also that the problem of inequality was the ethical dispensation of small proprietors, professionals, and other petit bourgeois, most of whom were men. They grappled with the issue of property and its rights, and they struggled to understand the capitalist hydra that had captured their world. They did so from a gendered perspective, in a society where proportionately many fewer women worked than in the United States and Europe. In Britain Hugh Dalton came to see that increasing women's wage rates might be a way to change the overall distribution of incomes. Although many Canadians might support mothers' allowances, pensions for widows, and even a limited form of minimum wage, Dalton's vision lay outside their frames.

In summary, a generation of Canadians from rural and small-town origins and from nineteenth-century Protestant homes struggled to understand the alien world of wage labour, industry, and urbanity. Inequality was a simplifying frame that made sense of this new world. They had been taught that faith meant charity, benevolence, and doing unto others. Their material world – in which the economies of family, farming, and commerce intersected – taught them the values of fair dealing and equitable exchange. They could see the struggle between capital and labour, and the appalling miseries so evident in the modern city, only as deep violations of these ethics and these values. Vast social problems made visible to them evils that fell under the sign of inequality, which ushered them into the new century to confront the perils of modernity.

The problem of inequality's political constriction cannot be the last word on the politics of spiritual engineering. It arose and persisted in a distinctive Canadian context, specifically within a complicated relationship between moral imperatives and social science, between faith and reason. Social gospellers tended to accept utilitarianism and secular social science in an opportunistic way, on condition that they served faith or higher ideals. But it was a truism, a common sense, that neither the social order nor any natural order furnished inherent regulatory or moral principles.[184]

John Clark Murray made the point when discussing secular political economy. "No man of sense," he said, would insist that prices in markets respond to only "the Law of Supply and Demand." Especially "pernicious" was the idea that it was "not only a natural, but also a moral law." Political economy was producing laws that purported to be about how "men ought to be governed" in their relations with one another. "Every mind of unperverted moral sensibility" must revolt from this moral corruption, said Murray.[185] Even if it did not yet translate into a coherent politics of distributive justice, his moral imperative was powerful and enduring, within and beyond the social-gospel era.

CHAPTER SIX

The Silence and Scope of English-Canadian Political Economy (1880–1920)

In the early twenty-first century, we may be forgiven for assuming that inequality is a subject mainly for economists. They are first in line when a public conversation occurs, and scholars from other disciplines usually play supporting roles. These include sociologists, who talk about social consequences, and political scientists, who offer informed commentary on the connections between inequality, political power, and the workings of democracy. Surely most scholars who study inequality would be unlikely to accept such disciplinary priorities. Inequality is the preserve of all disciplines in the humanities and social sciences, and none has priority. It might surprise editors and producers in the media to hear that the discussion of inequality began among philosophers, and it continues intensively among them. How often do television or radio programs invite them to talk about inequality? Their relative absence reflects, at the very least, a lack of connection between the academy and the media. Inequality, however one defines it and whatever its dimensions, is the subject of philosophy.

THE HERITAGE OF PHILOSOPHIC IDEALISM

This chapter begins with philosophers before proceeding to the preoccupations and elisions of the new breed known as political economists. In the small world of Canadian colleges and universities in the late nineteenth century, the problem of inequality emerged among philosophers. Economics, in so far as it existed as a category of knowledge, began as a branch of philosophy or "mental philosophy." Professorships in "political economy" did not appear until the 1880s.[1] The absence of clear distinctions by discipline should be no surprise. In the 1880s and 1890s professionalization was only beginning its complex and uneven transformation of scholarly practice, and the administrative exigencies that hatched modern disciplinary enclaves lay in the future. The branch of knowledge that dealt with material life, production, and wealth belonged to philosophers, to theologians, and to a handful of scholars who were beginning to be known as political economists. There were no boundaries to knowledge of humanity. Discipline-specific journals were starting to appear, but in Canada the main organs of scholarship were university-based journals, such as *Queen's Quarterly*, that printed articles in all subject areas, including the sciences. When my two grandfathers went to university to study sciences and medicine – one to McGill, the other to Queen's – they took courses in philosophy, and both were ordained ministers of religion. Such was the intellectual stage on which the problem of inequality appeared in Canadian universities.

Playing leading roles in that drama were scholars in the tradition of philosophical idealism. It requires an imaginative leap to enter that tradition. Today we dwell, or so we often hear, in an age of cynicism. We live in the aftermath or "afterlife" of idealism, after many other "isms" have contended with idealism or sought to absorb it (pragmatism, realism, materialism, postmodernism). In Britain philosophical idealism held sway in a time we cannot recover, before the world wars and before the twentieth-century clash of ideologies, in an era when it was still possible to believe that the evolving social organism contained resolutions to its many venalities and its class conflict. Recently many writers have tried to introduce us to that older idealism, and even to rehabilitate a politics of idealism.[2]

Philosophical idealism arrived in Canada with British-born disciples of T.H. Green and Edward Caird, most notably John Clark Murray, John Watson, and George Paxton Young (whose idealism preceded his contact with Green and Caird's works). A.B. McKillop and others have discussed the thought of Murray, Watson, Young, and other Canadian idealists who followed.[3] A summary of their ideas is neither possible nor necessary here, but a few points are in order. The teachings of these Canadian philosophers helped a generation of students to deal with troubling dualisms: spirit and matter, mind and body, mental and physical. Epistemological idealism said that, although there was an existence or "reality" independent of the mind, consciousness constructed knowledge of that reality in the mind's conception of order and relation. T.H. Green went further, to argue that the order of which we are aware is supra-individual: it is "an eternal intelligence realized in the related facts of the world," and the world is "a system of related facts rendered possible by such an intelligence."[4] Green opened the door to conceptions of collective consciousness, and he went still further when he collapsed the distinction between consciousness and the physical organism: "In the growth of our experience, in the process of our learning to know the world, an animal organism, which has its history in time, gradually becomes the vehicle of an eternally complete consciousness."[5]

John Watson (1847–1939) was the most influential Canadian follower of T.H. Green and Edward Caird. His "philosophical system" could accept evolutionary science without any diminishment of Christian spirituality.[6] It could assail empiricism that assumed a reality independent of the mind, while adopting the methods of scientific and rational inquiry. Such a schema, sometimes called "absolute idealism," reconciled reason and faith and embraced a progressive conception of history. The various stages of history "exhibit the progressive evolution of reason."[7] At the same time history exhibited the unfolding of a principle of spirituality – "the process by which man comprehends, and comprehends ever more clearly and fully, the spiritual unity which combines all existence."[8]

For students in Canadian universities around the turn of the century, such teachings could be deeply reassuring and inspiring. To suggest their "influence" would be to simplify; rather social science of the period became "idealist" in its inspiration and assumptions. As José Harris argues for the British context, "the cultural hegemony of idealism was established at many levels."[9] In Canada, as in Britain, idealism informed the thought of political and intellectual elites and social reformers. As a result, positivism and materialism made a slow appearance, or were ruthlessly attacked. Empiricism thrived, but usually in the service of altruism, ethical imperatives, and notions of common good. And political economy became a branch of ethics. Any interpretation of production and distribution that invoked autonomously "natural" laws or material forces, such as supply and demand, was suspect.

What happened when the idealist philosopher observed the world of production and distribution – what today we would refer to as "the economy"? John Clark Murray (1836–1917) offered a remarkable example. An immigrant from Scotland, Murray was professor of mental and moral philosophy at Queen's University 1862–72 and then at McGill University 1872–1903. Murray saw in Canada an "industrial kingdom" – a realm of land, labour, capital, production, and distribution. But crucially, he observed an industrial kingdom "*of God.*" His procedure was explicitly deductive: he sought to explain the "theoretical principles" that grounded "rules of conduct." He looked for "a moral guide" to human relationships within society. He was not, he said, engaging in "the declamation of vague moral platitudes." He was "inquir[ing] into the moral relations, into which men are brought as labourers, on the one hand, as owners of property, on the other."[10] Murray wrote these words in 1887: he referred throughout his manuscript *The Industrial Kingdom of God* to property rather than to capital, but he knew about monopoly, he had read Henry George, and he was well aware of the class conflicts of the 1880s. He was confronting directly the moral issues raised by the world of wage labour and capital.

On inequality, he stated the idealist position pellucidly. Referring to the branch of political philosophy known as political economy, he observed:

It has been too often assumed, implicitly if not explicitly, that these sciences deal, like the physical sciences, with certain inexorable laws of nature determining the social relations of men in a way which it is impossible for us to control ... These sciences are moral as well as physical; that is to say, they deal not only with the state of things that actually exists, but with a state of things that ought to be. This implies, however, that we are not the helpless spectators of the pitiless operation of a natural law which dooms the mass of mankind to irremediable poverty, and accumulates the wealth of the world in the hands of a few; for if there is anything that we *ought* to do, it follows that we *can* do something, to modify the existing condition of things.[11]

In order to arrive at "ought" we need a clear understanding of what *is*, or as Murray put it, "We must be acquainted with the facts."[12] His empirical observations related to moral relations between specific human constructions: labour, property, value, utility. He adopted a modified position on the relation between labour and value.

Whether referring to utility or to exchange value, economic value implied "an additional value which cannot belong to any object that may be procured without labour." But "there is another factor in the production of value besides labour" – land, which also comprised raw materials. The modification was crucial: it enabled a rejection of Marx and of socialism, and it shifted the discussion of "just reward" onto the terrain of rights and obligations. It was a "fundamental principle of 'justice' that the labourer has the enjoyment of the fruit of his labour," but not of "the whole of the product, to which his labour has contributed." Accordingly, there was no simple formula to measure just reward or "equitable proportion," especially vis-à-vis the relations between wage labour and capitalist enterprises. In the absence of an objective formula, Murray argued, the problem of "equitable share" was necessarily a matter of rights and obligations – those of labour and those of property – and of "a reciprocity of rights and obligations all through society."[13]

What he wrote next was a radical argument: not only a rejection of simple laissez-faire economics and market determinations of value, but also a broad claim to material entitlement for workers as human and spiritual beings. No distinction, he believed, was more profound than that between "person" and "thing." The worker's right to personhood did not stop when he or she sold labour power for a wage; the right was inalienable. Labour was *not* a commodity, and "the representation which describes the labourer's contract as simply an ordinary case of buying and selling" was merely a figure of speech that shielded an untruth.[14] Therefore the relation between employer and workers was one not of buyer and seller, but of co-partnership between human persons; in both justice and law, remuneration must reflect this fact.

Two questions followed for Murray. What material entitlement flowed from the rights of labour? And how to secure such rights? The first query relates to just distribution or "share": "The most perplexing problem of economical science, as well as of law and morality, is to devise a system of distributing the aggregate wealth produced in any community so as to give a perfectly just share to every member." A solution that avoided "the appalling inequalities of the present system" would be "the crowning achievement" of Christianity and of "social philosophy."[15] In Murray's idealism there was no simple formula or measure for just share. Having insisted that labour was not a commodity, and having detached just reward from a simple equivalence to labour contributed in production, he moved towards a minimum standard "guaranteeing ... necessaries and even the reasonable comforts and luxuries of our material civilisation," as well as "the required leisure for entering into the spiritual inheritance which humanity has already attained."[16] However imprecise, the standard was a high one, confirmed by Murray's egalitarian insistence that "the glories and enjoyments of the intellectual life" were not the privilege of any one class.[17]

And how to secure the material right of personhood? It was at this level that Murray's reasoning lacked precision and finality. A first answer was "the right to an equitable" share, which, historically, an accumulation of "the disadvantages of labour" had denied.[18] This answer was a sweeping rejection of the notion that poverty resulted from moral failings or lack of initiative on the part of the poor. Murray argued that environmental conditions, poor housing, poor nutrition, poor health, and "want of leisure" robbed the entire class of labourers of the power to assert "the right to an equitable share." It made sense therefore to say that poverty and inequality were self-perpetuating: people were poor because they lacked necessities.[19]

Murray's idealism also sustained an argument about power relations. He reminded us that notions of power – the differential distribution of collective capacities to secure material advantage, political influence, and influence over the fates of others – were not the particular preserve of materialist thought or philosophical realism. In Murray's idealism there was a keen insight into how embedded advantages and disadvantages impeded "a higher justice."[20] Labour's embedded – even structural – disadvantages included chronic surplus labour, trade unions' weak bargaining power, employers' ability to form combinations, the "legislative tyranny of wealth," capitalists' ability to exact "charges" from the community, and capital's benefitting from natural monopolies and creating artificial ones.[21]

This idealist diagnosis was more radical than its therapies. Murray spoke of devising a "system" to distribute wealth and of the need for "legislative efforts."[22] He argued that "regulations" and "concerted action" did not interfere with "the real freedom of individuals."[23] Yet he did not come close to a new liberal conception of the state, similar to those appearing in Britain. He feared the replacement of one legislative tyranny by another. His account of the "obligations of labour" implied that workers must fulfil their duties before any distributive reform, while his itemizing of the obligations of property seemed to evoke *noblesse oblige*. As for collective action, he supported cooperatives, courts of arbitration, and very limited forms of public ownership (municipal utilities and the post office).

On the subject of inequitable distribution, Murray had written the most radical study by a liberal idealist in late-Victorian Canada. Unfortunately *The Industrial Kingdom of God* did not appear in print until 1981 – ninety-four years after he wrote it. Instead he put its arguments into a series of shorter publications, speeches, and lectures at McGill. Any determined reader could have found his ideas. He had put inequality at the centre of political economy and ethics. His background was relevant to this achievement, as Nicholas Terpstra suggested in 1983.[24] He was the son of a cloth manufacturer in the industrial town of Paisley, Scotland. He witnessed at first hand the relations of capital and labour, and he saw the imprint of class relations on the urban landscape. In Glasgow he attended lectures in the middle of slums. He may be the first Canadian scholar to include life expectancies and physical stature in an analysis of inequality and its effects.[25]

Murray had presented – *sotto voce* – an immense challenge to Canadian scholars. How to reconcile individual rights and freedoms to social justice in the era of industrial capitalism? What level of inequality was consistent with justice and the common good? Even if one read only his 1893 article on "Philosophy and Industrial Life," and his 1899 essay on Shakespeare's *Merchant of Venice* as a parable of industrial ethics, Murray had placed before the emerging Canadian social sciences a profound but unresolved *problematique*.[26]

THE CONTRIBUTIONS AND SILENCES
OF POLITICAL ECONOMY

The next decades saw a litany of missed opportunities and evasions. More charitably, one might say that Canadians gave up certain opportunities to pursue others. Their scholars made useful, even seminal contributions to scholarship in specific fields; they published very little on economic inequality or distributive justice. The major university journals in the 1890s and 1900s – *Queen's Quarterly*, *Queen's University Journal*, and *University Magazine* – published no articles on these subjects.[27] One extended study of Canadian wealth and its concentration emerged in the Progressive era – Gustavus Myers's *History of Canadian Wealth* (1914). This volume by an American socialist said much about concentration, the political influence of corporations, and exploitation. Although it began with distribution – "less than fifty men … control more than one-third of Canada's material wealth" – it said little more about the subject and, as the word "control" suggested, focused on political influence and corruption.[28] Such was the dearth of scholarly work on such subjects in Canada that when Harold Innis in the early 1920s assigned a reading on corporate concentration in his economic-history class, he chose Myers's polemic.[29]

Canadian scholars did not ignore altogether the problem of inequality. The point is this: as we explore the issue in Canadian political economy in the Progressive era, we are seeking to explain specific iterations of the challenge, and also the remarkable silence. Particularly striking was academics' virtual non-engagement with the political economy of distribution in the transatlantic world. The silence pointed to a distinctive aspect of the inequality problem in Canada, and of the country's political economy more generally. The secular discipline was slow to address the economic, social, and political effects of the rise of wage labour and an industrial working class. The problem of inequality therefore remained mostly within the social and political discourse of social gospellers, agrarian populists, and a number of idealist philosophers. It endured as a moral imperative within an ethical political economy.[30]

Philosophical idealism survived in early-twentieth-century Canada, but even philosophers were losing interest in John Clark Murray's telling questions.[31] Professor George John Blewett (of Wesley College, Winnipeg, and later at Victoria University, in the University of Toronto) condemned waste, social injustice, and class oppression, and he influenced social gospellers. But his reconciliation of faith and reason, and his views on organic evolution, led him to accept the existing order. In that order he saw "no chaos, no dualism or pluralism of irreconcilable forces, but what reason demands it [the order] to be – an order one and intelligible."[32] This reconciliation of reason with the "light of God" was reassuring: "Out of the natural inequalities of human beings in the social order, compassion has arisen." One had only to compare present society with primitive societies, said Blewett, to see "the manifestation of the saving grace of God."[33] With Blewett and with James Ten Broeke at McMaster University (a Baptist institution, then in Toronto), the preoccupation

with Christian theology and reason – with theological accommodations to the philosophical tradition from Plato to Kant – directed
attention away from Murray's questions.

The two academics' books virtually ignored the concepts central to
the "new liberal" engagement with distributive justice: distribution,
equity, fairness, inequality, and wealth.[34] The two men's backgrounds
differed greatly from Murray's. They had little or no direct experience of industrial manufacturing: Blewett was the son of a farmer,
Ten Broeke the son of a town clerk in a small agricultural town. A
suggestion of Elizabeth Trott about Blewett is relevant: his preoccupation with nature was surely a response to his rural upbringing and
his experiences in western Canada.[35]

What of the emerging "political economy" scholars in English-
Canadian universities? Any account of their engagement with the
problem of inequality is necessarily complicated and tentative.
Between the 1880s and 1920s they displayed no singular pattern
and shared no theoretical basis for engagement with the problem:
there was no Canadian school of economics. Many came from the
United Kingdom; among the Canadian-born, most had U.S. training,
including many at Chicago. They all had some background in philosophy, and many had faced a choice between university lecturing
and a career in the church. Among those born in Canada, a rural
childhood was very common. Adam Shortt was born in the village of
Kilworth, Ontario, where his father operated a grist mill. Harold Innis
was from a family of farmers. Stephen Leacock was a native of rural
Hampshire, England, and spent much of his childhood on a farm near
Sutton, Ontario. O.D. Skelton was a small-town boy, born in Oran-
geville (population about 2,800). Growing up on a farm or in a small
town was one of the few characteristics the first two generations of
Canadian-born or -raised economists shared.

Canadian economic thought did not emerge de novo in these
decades. There were predecessors, as Craufurd Goodwin and Robin
Neill have shown. In the existing body of thought the new university-based economists could have found much to inspire an interest in the related issues of economic inequality, wealth distribution,
and distributive justice. Canada's most original nineteenth-century
economic thinker was John Rae, a Scots immigrant. In 1834 Rae
published his *New Principles of Political Economy*, a seminal work

on capital formation, the role of invention, and the role of the state. The volume was not popular, and copies were scarce; yet it was known and admired by English political economists, including Nassau Senior and J.S. Mill. A reprint in 1905 made it easily available to Canadians. Rae was a classical economist who assumed that "the wages of labor constitute an invariable quantity."[36] He accepted that wages must vary with the "vigor" and "skill" of workers; he did not mention societal-level inequality.

Nevertheless, Rae's *New Principles* offered at least two radical observations relevant to the later problem of inequality. First, while acknowledging that it was difficult to determine the laws governing distribution of revenue among its producers, he stated as "a general truth" that "the larger the share falling to labor the more rapid will be the increase of capital."[37] He did not touch the thorny problem of causal relations among wage levels, purchasing power, and capital formation; but here was a suggestion that Progressive thinkers in the early twentieth century might well have taken up.

Second, and even more provocative – had anybody been paying attention – was Rae's discussion of luxury consumption. Perhaps influenced by his Presbyterian faith, he offered a moral and economic condemnation of specific forms of luxury. He understood that vanity and display of superiority over others often motivated such purchase, and he cited historical examples. As a theorist of capital, he saw such consumption as diverting savings from formation of capital and spurring of economic growth. Rae had discovered conspicuous consumption, sixty-five years before Veblen's *Theory of the Leisure Class*.[38] Rae therefore had not developed an early version of the problem of inequality that emerged in the late nineteenth century; but he had offered a potentially persuasive economic rationale for the Protestant critique of wealth.

Another source for the articulation of inequality, of much wider import, appeared in the debates over free trade and protection – first in Europe and soon thereafter, as a matter of political urgency, in British North America. Distribution, as a problem of social justice, emerged when the politics of international trade intersected with "the social question" and the class tensions of the mid-nineteenth century. The British debate in the 1840s over repeal of the Corn Laws involved politics and economic interests and differing reactions to Chartism, the Irish famine, and poverty in general. Free traders presented themselves as anti-poverty advocates, arguing that lower bread prices would not reduce wages or displace agricultural labour. Protectionists also claimed to be on the side of the angels, and on the continent, as in England, their stance was in part a response to social tensions, addressing the inequalities that accompanied industry and the rise of the proletariat.[39] In the Canadas both sides in these debates claimed to be on the side of equality as well as freedom; "inequality" appeared as a by-product of misguided commercial policy, whether free trade or protectionist, and of subservience to past economists' mistakes.[40]

Debates in Canada over reciprocity in the early 1850s and the National Policy in the late 1870s helped to shift the meaning of distribution in economic discourse (they also encouraged the understanding of the economy as an organic system of interconnected parts and feedback mechanisms).[41] Distribution now referred not merely to the functional distribution of revenues or profits among land, labour, and capital, but also to the differential distribution of access to consumption goods, and the distribution of burdens, especially that of taxation. Government, said free traders, was making laws to benefit a small minority while imposing unequal burdens and higher costs on the majority. Protectionists responded with their own distributionist and egalitarian logic: protection for infant industries equalized opportunity for domestic labour and reduced the impact of unfair competition.

The consequences of this shift in meaning were ambiguous. These debates put distributionist rhetoric at the centre of politics, while also giving priority to trade policies that furthered economic growth, especially for specific economic sectors. John A. Macdonald's National Policy, after all, was part of a specific nation-building strategy; when its advocates proclaimed its employment benefits, they were not suggesting a vertical redistribution of political power, incomes, or wealth. Debates on trade policy put social questions and class relations into a narrow box, and only gradually did some labourite reformers join the socialists in arguing that trade was a red herring, and that neither protection nor free trade addressed the fundamental problems facing both farmers and workers.

The history and politics of trade and tariffs attracted political economists in late Victorian Canada, but they did not ignore industrialization.[42] A case in point: in 1898 a political economist at the University of New Brunswick published Canada's first major work on labour economics. Scots-born John Davidson had studied in Edinburgh and Berlin. *The Bargain Theory of Wages* (1898), though informed by the economics of marginal utility, was highly critical of existing theories on wage determination. Davidson rejected "productivity theory": the related ideas that the contribution of each factor of production was "determinate" and measurable and that each factor "should obtain as a return what it has contributed." The theory, he said, neither explained nor justified labour's actual remuneration "and cannot be treated as such unless we assume that the whole system of society is a monstrous iniquity."[43]

Davidson claimed originality for his "bargain theory" and thought that he had proved the irrelevance of simple curves of supply and demand. Wage levels, he said, were not the outcome of the supply price at which labour was offered and the demand price based on productivity or anticipated profits. "We must get rid altogether of the idea that there is an economic force which allots absolutely any share of the product, even the smallest, to any of the claimants. There is no absolute minimum and no absolute maximum for any share; and the amount at which the share is finally fixed is determined by a combination of forces."[44] These forces included the worker and the employer's estimates of the value of labour, which were a function of the two sides' respective utility functions. The shares that eventually resulted, however, flowed not from utility calculations alone, but also from "the comparative strength of the various claimants."[45] Hence the "bargain theory."

Davidson knew much about employers' strengths and workers' relative weaknesses (echoes here of John Clark Murray). He was obviously very well read on economic theory, and he cited progressive thinkers from the Webbs to J.A. Hobson. He perceived the advantages of employers in collective bargaining, and like Murray he saw that "the curse of the poor is their poverty, and the disabilities of labor are cumulative in their effect."[46] He believed that managers received more than their work was worth. Despite his clear awareness of labour's disabilities, he could at times be remarkably optimistic, and at one point he stated, without supporting evidence, that "the amount of capital employed" has grown faster than "the amount of the product" – "and that wages have increased in a higher ratio than either"![47] His book included well-researched analyses of workers' knowledge, machinery's effects on wages, labour mobility, and trade unions.

As a study of distribution, however, the book had its limits. Davidson saw a narrow range between maximum and minimum wage levels, which in turn reflected the estimates and forces available to employers and labour. Legislation should deal only with education and tariff protection. Davidson appears to have had no concept of a minimum wage. Thus he placed distribution within the frame of wage determination. Society-wide inequalities lay largely outside his frame, and the word "inequality" did not arise. Conspicuously absent too: any hint of philosophical idealism or the social gospel; this was a remarkably secular book. For all its limits, *Bargain Theory* was an original and provocative study of the conditions of labour and wages in Canada, a work of obvious interest to anybody thinking about inequality and distributive justice.

Perhaps the most remarkable thing about Davidson's book was the reaction, or absence of reaction, in Canada. The nation's first major economic study of labour met with almost total silence. According to Craufurd Goodwin, no Canadian journal reviewed the book.[48] Davidson remained unknown to social gospellers interested in labour and social justice. In the 1900s and 1910s a few major studies of labour relations and social justice appeared in Canada: foremost among these, W.L.M. King's *Industry and Humanity* (1918), Stephen Leacock's *Unsolved Riddle of Social Justice* (1920), and Robert M. MacIver's *Labor in the Changing World* (1919). None of these works mentioned Davidson or his book. Davidson's fate was not unlike that of John Rae and John Clark Murray – each disappeared in the great silence that befell inequality in secular Canadian political economy.

An absence is more difficult to explain than a presence, and of course it is never total. What we are observing was a relative lack of attention, a gaze in which what lay in the foreground obscured what lurked in the background. At one level the relative absence of inequality related to the dominant historicism among Canadian political economists. In his inaugural lecture as Professor of Political Economy and Constitutional History at the University of Toronto, W.J. Ashley endorsed the "scientific character" of the new political economy: "The direction for fruitful work is no longer in pursuit of the abstract deductive method which has done as much service as it is capable of, but in following new methods of investigation – historical, statistical, inductive."[49] By itself the historical approach did not preclude the study of distribution and distributive justice; Ashley himself opened the door to such studies.[50] But Canadian political economists, especially those born in this country, took the historical approach in particular directions. They concentrated on long-term factors in a developing colonial economy. Their approach, often influenced directly or indirectly by the German historical school, enabled them to reject much of classical political economy in favour of attention to technological, geographical, and institutional constraints on development.[51] The approach was also consistent with scepticism about neoclassical economic theory.

The historical approach went hand in hand with a gradual retreat from, or re-direction of, philosophical idealism. Idealism, where it retained an influence, now moved into public service or towards elevating social service into a personal and professional calling. The academic career itself became a kind of public service, and even a contribution to nation-building. And as is well known, many of the first few generations of Canadian economists became civil servants.[52] Idealism did not disappear from Canadian political economy; pragmatism refracted it. Pragmatism had many adherents and many variants. Put simply, it held that consciousness existed, but meaning arose when thought translated into action; truth had practical consequences, and the test of truth lay not in consistency with an absolute ideal but in the consequences of accepting it. Perhaps Canadian political economists – those who went into public service – agreed with the maxim of the American pragmatist Charles Peirce: "Consider what effects, which might conceivably have practical bearings, we conceive the object of our conception to have. Then, our conception of these effects is the whole of our conception of the object."[53] When political economists entered public service, they were reconciling idealism and pragmatism in their own lives. The outcome, for many, was a morally inspired and applied social science.

Pragmatism did not reduce their interest in social questions or the problem of inequality, as the career of John Dewey in the United States showed. Nevertheless, the further they moved from the idealism of Caird, Murray, or Watson, the less likely were they to confront the problem of inequality. We can detect the value of idealism for a sustained encounter with inequality by observing the effect of its loss or abandonment. The intellectual trajectory of James Mavor (1854–1925) offered a striking instance. Mavor was Ashley's successor at Toronto. As a young adult in Scotland he acquired a critical perspective on wealth and its distribution: he was a disciple of Caird's, joined the Social Democratic Federation and William Morris's Socialist League, stood unsuccessfully as a labour candidate for Parliament, investigated urban slums, and wrote about wage theories and labour.[54]

By the late 1880s, and especially after his arrival in Toronto in 1892, he abandoned idealism in favour of empiricism and positivism. While not denying the existence of a wide chasm between rich and poor, he emphasized the rising "standard of comfort" of the poor.[55] In his rigid empiricism, as S.E.D. Shortt has argued, moral questions about the collective responsibility of society became irrelevant. Certainly industrialism had brought social problems; but for Mavor these required targeted, pragmatic responses growing from scientific research, such as that of Charles Booth and other social investigators. As Shortt puts it: "The political economist became, in effect, a master mechanic tinkering with the machinery of society only to the degree required to maintain maximum stability and efficiency."[56] A strong but focused commitment to "applied economics" and public service followed: Mavor published studies of immigration policy, wheat marketing, public utilities, Ontario Hydro, workers' compensation, and arts funding. When (in 1935) Frank Underhill described economists as the "intellectual garage-mechanics of Canadian capitalism," Mavor was undoubtedly one of those in his sights.[57]

Other economists took parallel paths from idealism to empiricism and pragmatism. A preoccupation with nation-building smoothed those paths. It may be fair to say that economics in Canada emerged through the study of commerce and its adjuncts, banking and transportation, in their imperial context. Adam Shortt (1859–1931), often referred to as the father of Canadian economics, led the way: his many publications are in themselves a capsule of nation-building, encompassing banking, currency, imperial trade, transportation, and constitutional history. These interests were at once historical and political, and we may see them emerging within Shortt's personal trajectory. His life was a search for the stability that had eluded his father, a miller in the small village of Kilworth; his quest for security through education and hard work led him to his professorship at Queen's.[58] He rendered the personal and the spiritual political: "The distinctive characteristic of a moral people is the steady manifestation, on the part of the individuals, of self-control, self-respect and a strong sense of personal responsibility."[59]

Shortt, who had been a tutor working for Professor John Watson in 1886, was a Presbyterian moralist who believed that the university had a duty to raise the spiritual tone of the country. As Barry Ferguson argues, he moved between idealist humanism and empirical social science.[60] Our great aim, he said, must be human, allowing "the material and the commercial only insofar as these are human," part of "eternal progress with perfection as its goal."[61] This was the conservative Presbyterianism of individual conscience, with little foreshadowing of the social gospel. In Shortt's view, legislation could not promote morality directly; it could do so only indirectly, by suppressing vice and crime. Certainly Shortt's view of the state changed and expanded, but he remained suspicious of state intervention: history had taught him that government monopolies, as in New France, were dangerous intrusions on freedom.

This trajectory, from the rural village to the halls of academe, allowed the professor only short visits to the world of manufacturing industry and the urban proletariat. Although he wrote briefly about the relations between capital and labour, Shortt knew little about the subject. Writing about the First World War's economic effects, he asserted that all that the cities in the "newly settled" regions of the far west did was in the "distribution and transportation of goods"; there was "little manufacturing" except in lumber and some mining.[62] Although he had travelled west, he seemed unaware of the region's extensive pre-war manufacturing base. Little wonder that he saw "high earnings and high profits" leading to "increased expenditure" during the war and a growing taste for "luxuries." Only people on fixed salaries or annuities, he asserted, lost out when prices shot upwards.[63] There is no need to belabour the point – one more example will suffice. Here was an economist, writing in 1889, who still believed in the wage-fund theory and apparently did not realize that J.S. Mill and others had undermined the doctrine. "The capitalist is working for his profits, the labourer for his wages. Where both shares have to come out of the same fund, it follows that if one is increased the other must be diminished by just that amount."[64] From this theoretical and political vantage point the problem of inequality was unlikely to come into view.

POLITICAL ECONOMISTS ON SOCIALISM

The retreat from idealism helps to explain certain political economists' reaction to socialism. As we saw above, the problem of inequality was a liberal answer to the challenge of socialism, and one that took socialism very seriously. Philosophical idealism, of course, did not lead directly to socialism or social democracy. But idealism, as it evolved in Britain and Canada, facilitated accommodations and borrowings. Even where new liberals and Fabians sought to neutralize a revolutionary threat, their rebuttals recognized socialism as a well-thought-out response to capitalist industrialization. Canadian political economists, in contrast, did not allow for accommodation or compromise; they worked more to discredit socialism than to help solve the problem of inequality.[65] Two of them – J.E. Le Rossignol and O.D. Skelton – published major works on the subject. J.A. Estey added a doctoral thesis and a book on syndicalism.[66]

But we may begin with Adam Shortt, writing in 1897. In Shortt's caricature, socialism offered no serious threat, so "society has little to fear." This was because socialism lacked intellectual content: it was, according to Shortt, a type of "Dickens Christmas story," and its International Congresses showed it to be mere "babel and bedlam." Educated men who supported socialism – Shortt mentioned no names – were "sowing their philanthropic wild oats." In his account socialism was really about "the personal and material self-interest" of ignorant men. Therefore it did not require an alternative: it would dissolve of its own accord. Shortt rebuffed idealism: one set of ideals (socialism) required no liberal surrogate. He offered instead a complacent pragmatism: the modern corporation, far from being a locus of exploitation, expressed "the natural evolution" of the industrial system "in accordance with the changed conditions of machine production, capital investment and business competition." The "modern industrial combination," according to Shortt, also beneficially "does away with wasteful competition."[67] The need to respond to socialism was often a valuable inspiration for the problem of inequality; here our author was short-circuiting any such motivation.

James Edward Le Rossignol (1866–1959) was an Anglo-Quebecer, a philosopher and political economist educated at McGill, Leipzig, and Clark University in Worcester, Mass.[68] His early works, including studies of monopolies and of socialism, bore no apparent influence of idealism or the social gospel; they were historical and secular. His *Orthodox Socialism: A Criticism* (1907) was no mere polemic; it was a thoroughly researched critical analysis. Yet the conclusion was remarkable for its dismissive complacency. Orthodox socialism, as in Europe, was "a striking example of mental perversion" similar to certain theological doctrines that proclaim the dualism of absolute wickedness and absolute perfection. In North America, Le Rossignol argued, socialism was weakened because it confronted a widespread "spirit of compromise and common sense" that tended inexorably towards general welfare.[69] Here, as in his study of monopolies and trusts, Le Rossignol acknowledged the presence of inequality but erased it as a problem.[70]

Oscar Skelton wrote what may be the most comprehensive and intelligent Canadian critique of socialism in the twentieth century. An expanded version of his Chicago doctoral dissertation, *Socialism: A Critical Analysis* (1911), offered a vivid and eloquent survey of socialist thought from its origins through the utopian socialists to Marx and contemporary socialists in Europe and the United States. Inequality, and workers' growing consciousness of it, seemed to him central to socialism's origins and appeal. He saw how much industrialization had raised material standards, rendering yesterday's luxuries, he said, today's necessities. But "standards have advanced faster than incomes"; democracy has transformed economic as well as political expectations; "industrial democracy appeals as the inevitable complement of political democracy."[71] The gap between the modern millionaire and the tenement dweller may be less than the gap between the medieval lord and the peasant, Skelton argued; but the peasant did not compare himself with his lord. Literacy and print media had empowered the imaginative capacity for comparison; wage labour further made people aware of advantage and disadvantage; millionaires, unscrupulous, tax-dodging corporations, and price-gouging trusts confirmed that perception, and unbridled capitalism produced in socialism its egalitarian opposite.[72]

Skelton dismembered socialism's claims to redistributive justice. "The socialist cannot be permitted to denounce with voluble vigor the existing system of distribution, to base on its defects his strongest appeal to the discontented, and then himself to escape the test he has applied."[73] Skelton's critique then moved beyond its intended target, perhaps constricting liberal egalitarian responses to inequality. He proposed, first, that perfect or nearly perfect equality in distribution failed to meet any standard of need or merit, and it was not practicable. Second, the ideal that remuneration should be proportionate to the value of labour failed: evaluating each worker's labour was impossible; any attempt to do so would cause friction and discord. So too with making reward equivalent to "full product of one's labor" – an ideal that Skelton astutely saw as "a survival of primitive hand-icraft individualism."[74] Finally, what of the more common socialist test – from "each according to his capabilities, to each according to his needs"?[75] In his usual, judicious way, Skelton granted it "much to com-mend" and conceded its "limited" practicability. But the "needs" test set an impossible ethical standard: needs were appetites and desires, which were infinite, whereas the means of satisfying them were finite. Furthermore, the test placed no emphasis on "efficiency and desert."[76]

Skelton's critique, to be persuasive, required no elaboration of an alternative remedy to the problem of inequality. Nevertheless, his examination of the distributionist claims of socialism raised an obvious question: how would he address the resulting antinomy between an intellectually defensible socialism and its liberal-democratic foe? Could he envision a path between the extremes of unrestrained capitalism and its socialist opposite? His answer was tentative but not an evasion, and it reflected Canada's minimal scholarly grappling with the problem of inequality. Socialism, first of all, was not so serious a threat in Canada as it was in Europe, Skelton believed; a powerful U.S. socialist party seemed unlikely to him. He said little about Canada (and his book had an American publisher), but he did note that even in British Columbia socialists had so far won only a tiny fraction of votes in elections.[77]

His reassurances derived from a historical interpretation that restrained whatever impulse Skelton felt towards progressive reforms. In Canada industrialization had not advanced so far as it had in Europe. Agriculture dominated, said Skelton (he had a point, even if agriculture accounted for only between a third and 40 per cent of the measured labour force in 1911). He then trotted out the notion of equal opportunity in a resource-rich geography: "Widespread poverty is unknown; the gates of opportunity are open wide."[78]

Skelton's book did not do away with the problem of inequality; but the writer contained and reduced it as a social and moral evil. Private property and, with it, industrial capitalism would survive, he pre-dicted, because of "proved social utility," "state insistence on the rules of the game," trade unions' "sharing in determining the conditions of employment," and the "growing sense of the trusteeship of wealth."[79]

Here was a distinctively Canadian answer to the problem of inequality that said little about an expanding state, redistributive taxation, minimum living standards, or a future welfare state. It grew from a particular historical understanding of how geography, resources, and settler populations related: Canada was especially unbalanced: unlimited resources and too few people. From this imbalance the political economist deduced endless opportunity: "Here was wealth to employ and amply to reward the toil of unending millions."[80] And endless opportunity seemed to promise a uniquely Canadian freedom from inequality. "Gross inequalities of wealth" and "antagonism between rich and poor" were "the world's most pressing problem"; Canada was "fortunate above most lands" in its freedom from the problem.[81] This reading of the country's history was deeply political: it evaded the vast inequalities and the cavernous gulf between opportunity and reality. A highly intelligent, well-trained economist had come to believe that slum dwellers in Toronto and Montreal could efficiently move to the west and acquire the tools and knowledge sufficient to establish prosperous farms.

The logic made sense only in the presence of a particular ethics. Skelton was not a social gospeller. He was born into an Irish-origin Protestant family, the son of a small-town petit-bourgeois pro-imperialist.[82] The young Skelton retreated from the religious observance of his parents and in a debate with his father offered "anti-religious arguments" against Christian socialism.[83] His scholarly writings made little explicit reference to Protestant ethics. The philosophical idealism that he studied at university did not disappear, but his secular empiricism muted it, transforming Protestantism and idealism into secular humanism and a belief in individual responsibility. "Individual initiative" was a recurring theme in his critique of socialism. Within this ethic lay a view of human nature: no original sin, but an innate tendency to "weakness" and extreme variability. Of course, said Skelton, the influences of institutions on individuals were reciprocal; but human weakness must limit the achievement of an ideal social order. Mistaken attempts to realize such an order through state action risked crippling individual responsibility. Even old-age pensions tended "to release the individual from all responsibility" to provide for the later years. The state's role was to provide the conditions for individual initiative to flourish, "to help the individual to help himself."[84]

THE MANY TEMPERINGS OF IDEALISM

Even before Skelton moved from academic life to government, we can see pragmatism tempering his idealism.[85] He was a pragmatic supporter of progressive taxation.[86] On the subject of income tax he saw fiscal necessity working together with justice or, at least, "fair-ness."[87] Shifting taxes from consumption to income would more equitably distribute burdens between economic sectors and classes of producer and thus might redress societal-level inequities. But his reforms were cautious and always sensitive to administrative con-straints and the need to avoid limiting capital investment. He offered no plan to solve the problem of inequality: inequality, distribution, redistribution, and inequity were not operative concepts in his anal-ysis.[88] Skelton was Canada's most gifted and energetic economist. He was also a progressive. But his progressive liberalism did not lead to a sustained analysis of the problem of inequality.

Instead Skelton transferred "individual initiative" to the nation: its mature, adult independence within the British Empire was, he said, "my chief interest"; his wife termed it "a missionary call."[89] The growth and maturing of Canada, its attainment of responsible individuality within the empire, may be seen as an analogue of the ethic of responsibility. His scholarship, says Norman Hillmer, took a "practical bent" – "events shaped his thinking, not abstractions."[90] Here was idealism and secular humanism morphing into public ser-vice and an all-consuming personal commitment.

The analogue of personal ethic and national personhood may also be present in another Canadian political economist, sixteen years younger than Oscar Skelton – Harold Innis (1894–1952). Accord-ing to biographer Alexander John Watson, Innis undertook a vast, career-long project of individual and collective responsibility: a quest for responsible *intellectual* government on the periphery – to realize a home-grown, peripheral contribution to world knowledge.[91] The many faces of Innis – historian of staple trades, communications theorist, system theorist – need not concern us here. What follows is a brief comment relating to the virtual absence of the problem of inequality in the vision of Canada's best-known political economist.

Innis, like Skelton, was not a social gospeller. Introduced to philo-sophical idealism by James Ten Broeke and others, he may never have lost his early idealism: John Bonnett argues for a form of Platonic idealism in Innis's conception of historical change and his "complex adaptive systems."[92] Whether or not one concurs, idealism seemed to take a very different direction with Innis than it did among others, especially those within hailing distance of the social gospel. As with Skelton, his consistently secular language did not mean that religion was irrelevant. On the contrary, as Michael Gauvreau insists, it remained part of Innis's personal life. Innis was a conservative rural Baptist who considered becoming a Baptist minister.[93] He did not share social gospellers' passion for social activism. His commitment to a secular social science did not erase either his Christian ethical standards or his belief in a public role for the intellectual.

But in his view the public role must entail no compromise with intellectual independence and what he called the "philosophical approach." Perhaps it was a matter of one fundamentalism giving way to another – a strict, principled devotion to academic freedom, to the sacred role of disinterested research, and to "the university as the secularized heir to the monastic tradition that had kept Western culture alive during the Dark Ages."[94] Innis's principled rejection of what we would call ideologically driven research hardened in the 1930s. Writing in 1944, he deplored the "present-mindedness" that he believed had come to dominate research between the wars. Quoting the American economist Frank Knight, he argued that the effects of "preaching" about economic relations were "bad": "Christianity affords no concrete guidance for social action, beyond an urge to 'do good and avoid evil.'"[95]

Some later scholars would seek to reconcile parts of Innis's writings with progressive and even neo-Marxist theory.[96] Certainly Innis shared with progressive contemporaries a preoccupation with monopoly. But he mixed censure with acceptance.[97] A reform politics of welfare or distributive justice was beyond the scope of his proliferous theorizing and his *longue-durée* perspective. He did not use the words "inequality," inequalities," or "distribution of wealth" anywhere in his collection of essays, *Political Economy and the Modern State* (1946).[98] The problem of inequality was foreign to a scholar who had little contact with the urban working class. "Dirt research" took him across the country and into the far north, but not across Toronto.[99] Information theory, systems theory, communications, the relations of core and periphery – wherever one puts the emphasis when reading Innis, one finds only occasional room for the "social question."

Innis remained a farmers' son whose rigorous self-discipline and dedication to "personal betterment" probably owed much to his escape from youthful poverty and insecurity.[100] This background came together with evangelical Baptist rectitude in his reaction to ordinary soldiers in the First World War – one of the occasions when he had extended contact with working-class men. He became an artillery signaller, served at Vimy Ridge (April 1917), and was invalided out in July 1917 for a shrapnel wound in his thigh. Army life, he said, induced dependence, "lassitude," and a "cramping of individuality."[101] Postwar reconstruction must avoid promoting further dependence on government. Gauvreau suggests that his "revulsion against handouts of any kind" had not altered since his high-school essay that condemned giving food to tramps.[102] "Ethical social science" therefore led not towards a welfare state, but rather to a reinvigorated and scientific social service and the inculcation of the ethical practices so amply demonstrated by the iconic Canadian beaver – "hard work and provident saving."[103]

Idealism and Protestant humanism were present in Canadian political economy, but few adherents analyzed the distribution of income and wealth. Those who did came at the end of the First World War. In very differing ways, they were responding to the intensity of class conflict before, during, and after the war. That conflict, and the increasing number and strength of trade unions, caught the eye of a few Canadian political economists. One of these was not in academe, despite his doctorate in the subject. No Canadian in the first half of the twentieth century wrote more about labour and industrial relations than did W.L. Mackenzie King.[104] In his *Industry and Humanity* (1918) there was no retreat from idealism or Protestant humanism. Quite the opposite: the book applied "high ideals" and "the human factor" to industrial relations.[105] But it was precisely this untempered idealism that put King outside the company of political economists, and he said so: their discipline was entirely about wealth and "material considerations"; it had nothing to do with morality; it therefore had nothing to say about improving society. King, accordingly, did political economists the favour of ignoring all but a few of them.[106]

　　King's book is an extreme instance of channelling idealism into the pragmatism of personal public service. He took inequality seriously, and offered a commonplace description (King was skilled at picking up on contemporary preoccupations). "Everywhere there is vast inequality of circumstances ... In the changes industrial evolution has wrought, whilst the wealth of the world has vastly increased, its distribution has become increasingly disproportionate." "Unregulated competition" meant that "unto him that hath shall be given."[107] If his language seemed occasionally to damn the effects of industrialization on living standards, that was not his intention.

Inequality was instead a source of spiritual inspiration and a call to humane action. King was resolving the contest between material and spiritual through his faith in (as Reg Whitaker put it) "the essential order and pattern in the material world which could be discovered by human science but which was founded in a divine purpose which itself transcended the material world."[108] In that essential order "the more equitable distribution of wealth" had "already begun," announced King, and it had started in the cooperation that already existed between management and labour.[109] King did not mean worker co-ops; he was drawing on his own experience as a labour conciliator. Cooperation signified "right attitude" and personal effort. The parties to industrial relations were Labor, Capital, Management, and Community. "Co-ordination of function as regards the several factors is a small problem"; "the attitude of the parties toward each other is everything." "Assuming the existence of a right attitude" and the presence of a right-thinking investigator and conciliator, "the rest is so simple as to be almost a matter of mathematical calculation."[110]

Here was another Canadian response to the problem of inequality, which reduced it to one of industrial relations, to recurring compromise by labour, and to the simple remedy of human kindness. King's work, a source of continuing interest to historians, was both idiosyncratic and reflective of trends in Canadian political economy. It was not an original contribution to the discussion of inequality that ranged widely in social science and philosophy in Europe and North America. Though explicitly a study of "principles," and emulating "accepted methods of dispassionate research," it was a personal testament.[111]

A much more substantive and learned contribution to the problem of inequality came from within the Department of Political Economy at Toronto. Scotland-born Robert M. MacIver (1882–1970) taught at Toronto 1915–27, heading his department 1922–27, when he left for Columbia University. An eclectic scholar with a doctorate in classics, he became a distinguished political scientist and sociologist and a liberal theorist of the state.[112] He was in Canada but not of it – a twelve-year resident who wrote little about the country.

MacIver pushed liberal political thought to the outer reaches of its radical potential. His *Labor in the Changing World* (1919), ostensibly a study of industrial relations, offered in fact a wide-ranging analysis of economic and social conditions in the Western world. MacIver's humanist reaction to current social evils led him directly to the problem of inequality as the basis of those evils. Management–labour relations were indeed conflictual, but, he argued, only a symptom. "The profounder problem is one of distribution not of production."[113] The industrial system caused "intolerable waste due to the extreme disparity of the distribution of wealth." By waste he meant not simply economic loss, but a deep human and even "spiritual" loss, the "perverting and devitalizing [of] all healthy human instincts."

For his Canadian readers MacIver stated a well-known but (in Canada) seldom-heard principle of relative value: an additional dollar a week to a low-income family rendered more value than the same dollar to a well-off household. Thus "any redistribution of wealth which, without disastrous disturbance, rendered less unequal the shares of rich and poor, would increase the total service of wealth, that which alone justifies it or its pursuit, the contribution it makes to welfare."[114] He endorsed equality of opportunity and explained its absence: "The unequal distribution of power, dependent in democracies largely on the unequal distribution of wealth," was the cause of unequal opportunity.[115] Thus equal opportunity required some redistribution of wealth and power. As his language indicated, MacIver was working with a concept of social welfare – a notion of social well-being that involved more than maximizing individual utilities or happiness.

MacIver was putting redistribution of income and wealth at the forefront of a liberal conception of social justice. But how was redistribution achievable? MacIver proposed rebalancing power between capital and labour, mostly through expansion of trade unions and their role in labour markets. MacIver saw the industrial councils that Britain's Whitley Report (1917) proposed as no panacea. Such bodies, he opined, would do nothing to bridge capital and labour's fundamental differences.[116] Augmenting labour's power required elimination of unemployment through state-funded public works.[117]

MacIver did not use the term "reserve army," but he understood how unemployment and immigration tended to disempower organized labour. And the same applied to women: serving as a reserve army, women could limit labour's bargaining power. MacIver's logic led him to a radical position on women and family: empowering labour required equal pay for equal work. But wage equality by itself would achieve little without the organization of all women workers, "the emancipation of women from their economic dependence," and a sweeping redefinition of women's roles such that "the task of raising children is itself accounted an economic service."[118] MacIver's redistributive plan also called for unemployment insurance, legislated minimum wages for all workers (not merely the unskilled), and legal limits on working hours. He offered a supportive summary of the British Labour Party's position on postwar reconstruction, and he saw the redistributive power of taxation. "Progressive income taxes and inheritance duties" would tend "towards a more equitable distribution of wealth."[119]

By its very rarity, MacIver's writing on inequality and social justice exposed the lacuna in the Canadian political economy of his era. He himself pointed to a transatlantic difference: Britain's greater "sense of the need" for postwar reconstruction than Canada's. In North America "we are more complacent for the most part." Note a hint of impatience: "Needs are not to be measured by complacencies."[120] MacIver differed from his Canadian colleagues not so much by rejecting complacency as by his personal and intellectual background and his reconciling of idealism and empiricism. He was a Scots Presbyterian who knew something of both commerce and industry. His father was a merchant and tweed manufacturer. MacIver retreated from the strict piety of his father and embraced a humanist ethics that sought "deliverance" from the "selfishness," "slackness," "irresponsibility," and "monstrous evils" that seemed to pervade society.[121]

His debt to idealism was fully evident in his 1917 book on *Community* – an original, erudite study of the laws of community development and group interest.[122] Here he resisted the positivism that sought to turn sociology into science, and he rejected the metaphor of society as an organism. "Social science will never advance except by freeing itself from subjection to the methods and formulae of both physical and biological science."[123] His idealism was apparent in his distinction between "extrinsic" and "intrinsic" interests. The former included interest in power, prestige, and material possession; the latter, "all higher ideals, and, above all, the ideas of the common welfare."[124] The two types "inextricably mingled" in all human activity, said MacIver; but the extrinsic was the enemy of the intrinsic and tended to pervert all higher ideals. Hence his position on inequality: redistributing the "external conditions of inequality" could rebalance extrinsic and intrinsic, to construct a community "governed by considerations of social welfare."[125]

MacIver stood apart from Canadian political economy and its particular historicist frame. He also differed with most of his colleagues on the relationship between ethics and social science. Ethics had complex relations with economics in this period, with too many dimensions to neatly summarize here, and certainly no simple narrative of secularization will suffice. Practitioners were still a long way from the rigid position of many neoclassical economists later in the twentieth century – that economics, within its analytical confines, had nothing to do with morality, since it dealt with what is and not what ought to be.

These thinkers lived still in the world of John Neville Keynes. In 1890 this British philosopher and economist (the father of J.M. Keynes) sought to explain the distinction and relationship between ethics and economic science. He maintained that one could study material conditions and seek economic laws both inductively and deductively, without passing ethical judgments, but positive scientific explanations for phenomena could not settle the ethical question. Neither economic activities nor the laws explaining them could be independent of moral laws. These two positions were not in contradiction, because there was a reasonable ontological distinction between ethical science and economic science. Both were necessary; but they need not be systematically combined. Thus, Keynes said, one could study the influence of doctrines of usury on medieval trade without examining the doctrines' validity.[126] We can see Adam Shortt and W.J. Ashley groping towards similar positions at the same time. Probably most Canadian political economists in the coming decades would have accepted something like Keynes's compromise, preserving both the possibility of a value-free social science and the necessity of ethical inquiry.

In *Community*, MacIver exposed the problems inherent in this compromise. He accepted, but only as a practical necessity, that the "sphere of economics" was a "specific science." Its "main" concern was the study of such interrelated phenomena as production and distribution; its "partial" concerns or "series" were, first, the prior social determinants of economic phenomena and, second, the ethical and social consequences of these phenomena. MacIver then rejected the separation of main from partial concerns: "We must see that by their very nature these series form part of a greater system

within which they arise and without which they would be mean-
ingless."[127] Take the law of supply and demand, he suggested, as an
obvious example: its operation varied according to multiple conditions external to the law itself – type of commodity, custom, fashion,
social conditions, and the "realm" of morality. In other words, there
was no economic law independent of value. It was not possible to
study the effects of usury without taking a position on usury. For
MacIver, the ontological solution was to give pre-eminence to sociology, the science "that investigates all those social relations which are
too broad or deep or complex to fall within the scope of any one of
the specific social sciences." The integration of ethics with the study
of economics, politics, literature, history, and art was possible, he
argued: Plato did so in *The Republic*, "the first and the greatest of
sociological treatises."[128]

MacIver's intellectual and theoretical framework brought the
problem of inequality into view, rendering a political deliverance
conceivable. Applying it to the operative concepts of a liberal order –
individual, property, community – required considering their ethical
implications, and that meant exploring inequality and distributive
justice. This was especially so when MacIver was trying to reimagine
community while preserving private property and ethical regulation
of capital – the "live monster that is fruitful and multiplies" (he was
quoting Marx).[129] There was no escaping the problem of inequality,
and hence the state's role as "the great protector of the commonwealth," the guarantor of a minimum standard of material life for
everyone.[130]

There was more than one way to cling to idealism. MacIver engaged
directly and repeatedly with ancient and modern philosophers;
not all social scientists did so. More often scholars gave priority to
inherited but unexamined ideals, or to articles of faith and ethics,
and sought to apply such ideals to the real and the material. It was
easy to retain from one's reading of Plato the notion that ideas and
essences existed, and can be known, independent of any empirical
confirmation of their existence. Consider, as an example, one writer's expression of idealism: "You cannot depict love inside a frame
of fact. It needs a mist to dissolve in. You cannot tell a love story just
as it is – because it isn't. There is something else there, something
higher than our common selves and perhaps truer."[131] Then think of
"the sheer beautiful idealism" of Dickens: "It is of no consequence

whether *A Christmas Carol* is true to life. It is better than life."[132] We know what is of *value* – what is true – not because it conforms in some mechanical or evidentially provable way to the putative real world, but from our prior conceptions of truth and value. Here then was an idealist departure from much of political economy, by one who was still a practitioner: "The fault with economics was the assumption that what can only be done by the Spirit could be done by material interest."[133]

Now look, from this perspective, at the idea that "every man gets what he produces" – that "enormous salaries represent enormous productive services and that humble wages correspond to a humble contribution to the welfare of society." These notions – simplified and unqualified renditions of neoclassical wage theory (the author had been reading John Bates Clark) – were "not true."[134] That resounding "not true" was the voice of Stephen Leacock – and also in the previous paragraph. Leacock wrote one of the few books of the Progressive era in Canada that was entirely and explicitly about the problem of inequality.

The Unsolved Riddle of Social Justice (1920) was a work of political economy, even if its author was often contemptuous of the discipline and dismissive of his colleagues; and it was only a later, constricted definition of "economics" that labelled Leacock a humourist and political scientist rather than an economist.[135] A later economist might not have recognized his or her own discipline in Leacock's work because the writer integrated categories that later came to be separate: cost, goods, labour, price, production – joining these with good, human, justice, liberty, social (see the word cloud in Figure 3). *The Unsolved Riddle* was a work of idealist political economy. Leacock grounded it in a very Canadian configuration of idealism, with deep roots in nineteenth-century political and religious thought.[136]

Leacock's "not true" works at more than one level. First, at the empirical: wages, interest, rent, and profit do not conform to a natural law or a "simple law of natural justice." Wages are the product of a number of intersecting variables, each having its own historical context: these include the population of available workers, their state of organization, and whether the industry is monopolistic or competitive. Wages reflect relative "economic strength" (another reminder of Davidson's "bargain theory") in a condition of "unstable equilibrium."[137] Second, whatever specific conditions determine

Figure 3 | Word cloud of Stephen Leacock, *The Unsolved Riddle of Social Justice* (1920).

wages, and whatever general principles may seem to be in play, these factors have no direct correspondence to "social justice." To argue that a wage level represents a just reward – "every man gets what he produces" – is the dangerous "dream" of a "quietist" who knows nothing of justice.[138]

The complexity of wage determination is a specific instance of the larger problem of social justice that Leacock articulated in *Unsolved Riddle*. "Few persons can attain to adult life without being profoundly impressed by the appalling inequalities of our human lot. Riches and poverty jostle one another upon our streets. The tattered outcast dozes on his bench while the chariot of the wealthy is drawn by. The palace is the neighbor of the slum."[139] Leacock's style was evocative and epigrammatic, but his understanding of inequality was a standard one: industrialization, the "age of machinery," has produced the most perplexing "paradox ever presented in the history of mankind": beside "the vastly increased powers of production" lay the "apparent inability to satisfy for all humanity the most elementary of human wants."[140]

Leacock's book was one of the rare Canadian works that sought to explain the inequality that its author observed, to critique specific solutions, and to propose other answers. It fitted within the broad framework of idealism, but here too Leacock stood outside the pattern: his idealism was not that of Murray and other idealist philosophers, or that of Skelton or King. In Leacock we find a Tory idealism that echoed the thinking and the imagination of Thomas Carlyle while absorbing much of Mill and Veblen.[141] Leacock's "paradox" was that of Carlyle: "England is full of wealth, of multifarious produce, supply for human want in every kind; yet England is dying of inanition."[142] The echoes of Carlyle, as Gerald Lynch has pointed out, included a rejection of simple placebos and references to spiritual regeneration or "a higher public spirit." But these echoes appeared in theoretical reckonings with basic concepts – individual, liberty, community, the state – that long preceded *The Unsolved Riddle*.[143]

Leacock's understanding of inequality emerged from his wrestling with "the liberty of the individual." There was, he argued, no such thing as "natural liberty," if that implied the individual's unlimited right to do as he or she pleased. A self-consistent definition was that of France's Declaration of the Rights of Man in 1789: liberty consisted in the freedom to do whatever did not injure another. Such liberty, Leacock pointed out, necessitated the presence of coercive power – the forcible prevention of interference with the rights of others. By exercising this duty through law, the state brought liberty into being. "It does not follow, however, that it is the duty of the state to find the ideal of its action in the maintenance of individual liberty; that is to say, to confine its operating to enforcing non-interference."[144]

No – and at this point Leacock introduced another concept, that of community and its attendant "social" rights: the state had the right of "positive" as well as "negative" functions, because there was such a thing as community or "general good" within which liberty could exist. There was no such thing as an autonomous individual; there were only individuals exercising their freedoms while associating with others doing the same. Unfortunately, Leacock commented, certain ideas on the state originating with Kant, Fichte, and Wilhelm von Humboldt led to a form of "extreme individualism" in the early nineteenth century, where the individual and "the highest ends of his existence" were paramount; the existence of community was forgotten; and it followed that the state's only proper function was non-interference. Against Herbert Spencer's view of the state, Leacock followed Mill and Sidgwick in allowing it positive duties: national public education was merely one example that community interest and "social rights" justified.

To Leacock "laissez faire" was a particularly dangerous form of extreme individualism: "If individuals are left free to follow their own choice in the use of their capital, the sale of their labor, or the renting of their property, the liberty of each will be in the general interest of all." This model engendered an "equilibrium" or "harmony," rendering any interference by government "needless and necessarily noxious."[145] Such notions of individual liberty, Leacock argued, amounted to "a mechanical attempt to completely divorce individual and social rights." The attempt became a rationalization of injustice, oppression, and brutal injustices.

Leacock's position, which I summarized above with risky brevity, hinged on his deep sense of community – of the "social" – and of social rights and social justice. He did not develop a formal theory of social rights and of the state as their protector. He worked instead with a generalized but deeply held belief in an organic society of mutual obligations that could harness its better traditions to counter human fallibility. This was a very Canadian democratic toryism, reconciling liberty with order and tradition. This forward-looking, even progressive toryism abhorred extremes, such as individualism and socialism; it was, as Gerald Lynch puts it, "a secular version of the Anglican via media."[146] Thus, for Leacock, the origins of inequality lay not in capitalism, machinery, or industrialization, but in an extreme – the excessive individualism that accompanied industrialization as a parasitic ideological appendage – an extreme that he sought to expose and exorcize.

Hence Leacock's solutions. These may seem a program for a middle way between socialism and individualism, between the "cruel inequality" of the present system and "the dark gulf of social chaos."[147] Remedial actions included a full-employment policy, which the state could pay for if necessary, despite the risk of "the subsidizing of an army of loafers"; old-age pensions; a national "policy of social insurance" against illness and accident; a national expansion, "at whatever cost," of housing, sanitation, child welfare, and education; minimum-wage laws; legislation on shorter hours of work; and the maintenance of the "terrific engine of taxation" started in the war, including a progressive income tax and taxes on profits and inheritances.[148] He had derived a non-, even anti-socialist strategy of social security out of his moral assault on the evil of inequality.

This tory-democratic schema remained firmly within the Canadian liberal order: it included an explicit but very limited articulation of a principle of equality – not of condition, but "the broad general principle of equality of opportunity."[149] Leacock understood that principle required a material minimum: every child had the right to food, clothing, and education, irrespective of the lot of their parents.[150] Leacock's equality of opportunity was a far cry from liberal egalitarianism, of course. Here was a tory program to preserve liberty within "a sane, orderly, and continuous social reform."

In Leacock, idealism and tory humanism confronted the harsh realities of modernism, and recoiled. His response took the form of political economy and fiction, and the two were inseparable. *The Unsolved Riddle* (1920) did not stand alone. It is one of three of his works that shared moral and even political purpose and grew directly from his encounter with the problem of inequality. Two of those works were fictional: *Sunshine Sketches of a Little Town* (1912) and *Arcadian Adventures with the Idle Rich* (1914).

Whether one views Leacock from a historical perspective or through the lens of literary criticism, one cannot escape the coherence of vision and ethics that underlies two genres. *The Unsolved Riddle* contained a tory-progressive reform program within a critique of liberal individualism and materialism. *Arcadian Adventures* took the same critique but elevated it to a plane beyond mere legislative reform. Much has been written about Leacock's theories on humour and their limits. In the present context we can offer only a suggestion about the path by which the author conjoined political economy and tory humanism in a satirical representation of inequality.

Leacock differed from other theorists of humour in his insistence on humane kindliness and his view that humour had experienced a type of progress through history. At the same time he followed others in seeing incongruous juxtaposition and irony as basic to the comic. As to the value of humour, he held more than one position. Humour was escape, a release from the pains of a disillusioning world, from the "poor stuff" of "actual life," but its humanity – its capacity to bestow humane empathy and to set the spirit free – saved it from indifference and self-indulgence. Humour, so long as it did not lapse into cruel negativity, lifted the spirit. When humour took the form of satire, its negations suggested a humane alternative to the object of ridicule. Thus, despite his scepticism about tendentious reformism and crusading zeal in literature, Leacock applauded denunciations of social injustice, such as Thomas Hood's 1843 poem "The Song of the Shirt." His favourite humourist was Dickens – who, he said, had done more than any political reformer to "sweep away" removable cruelties and injustices. "The pen was mightier than the parliament." "He [Dickens] did it with laughter and the smiles that mingled even with anger."[151]

The Unsolved Riddle was about the great paradox of inequality. *Arcadian Adventures* was about incongruous juxtapositions rooted in the greed, vanities, and hypocrisies of the idle rich. Satire, observed Northrop Frye, is "militant irony." Leacock tempered his militancy, but the irony of *Arcadian Adventures* was relentless and ungentle. Unearned increment, frivolous luxury, self-serving piety, and political corruption – all these became ludicrous absurdities. While the focus was on the idle rich of Plutoria, the ironic gaze fell mercilessly on the many dimensions of inequality.

"In fact, if you were to mount to the roof of the Mausoleum Club itself on Plutoria Avenue you could almost see the slums from there. But why should you? And on the other hand, if you never went up on the roof, but only dined inside among the palm trees, you would never know that the slums existed – which is much better."[152] Throughout Plutoria the non-rich appeared, mostly silent and barely visible, their "daily toil" a recurring foil to the plutocrats' idleness: the "noiseless" waiters in the Mausoleum Club; the clerks, pages, and elevator boy in the Grand Palaver Hotel; the junior clerks in the business offices; the servants, chauffeurs, and gardeners; the staff who did all the work in law offices; and the poor, who were condemned as being of "no good" in the "splendid invective" of Rev. Uttermust Dumfarthing. There were miners, perhaps fortunate to hear "the distant murmur of the sea" while toiling in the coastal mines. And there were construction workers "blasting out the motor road" to Mr Newberry's estate. "I blew up two Italians on the last job," said Mr Newberry. "Hardy fellows, the Italians."[153] The book ended with inebriated millionaires – the city's "best" people – driving home after an all-night binge, and "the others – in the lower parts of the city" rising to their "daily toil."

It would be easy to dismiss the satire as having no political import, of value only as amusement. But only if one were to insist on literature's irrelevance to an understanding of the world in which we live. And only if one were to forget that humour can be a political weapon. *Arcadian Adventures* is astonishing in its durability. Its pertinence – its capacity to resonate with the present – has, if anything, grown in recent decades. Read *Arcadian Adventures* and the gated mansions and stock portfolios of the super-rich today look very different. No longer signs and symbols of worldly success and just reward, these become emblems of spiritual vacuity, self-indulgent narcissism, and political corruption. Nothing comparable has appeared in the great age of inequality that we live through today. And so it came about that Canada's most original, enduring, and distinctively Canadian contribution to the problem of inequality was a work of satire.

CHAPTER SEVEN

The Force and Frailty of Quebec's Social Catholicism (1930s–1950s)

Elsewhere in Canada, within a distinct intellectual heritage, there emerged a powerful and comprehensive assault on capitalism. This critique declared "the paradoxical condition of a world reduced to misery in the middle of abundance" to be at the heart of the crisis in capitalism in the 1930s.[1] This chapter reveals another Canadian current in the transatlantic stream and another version of the problem of inequality – the product of a specific Canadian religious tradition and its long struggle with the Enlightenment heritage – and explores four stages of thought on inequality in Quebec: the 1930s' critique of liberal capitalism, the movement for social regeneration via social corporatism, the political limitations on inequality in the mid-1940s, and its virtual demise by the late 1950s.

Today, when we address the problem of inequality in a secular language of economics and social epidemiology, it can be a shock to go back to writers who pronounced, repeatedly and incessantly, that economic failure and the paradox of poverty in a world of wealth constituted a "moral crisis."[2] And when we enter their time and place, a surprise awaits us: the apparently seamless fusion of spirit and matter in the very definition of economics. "When dealing with the economic order and the science that explains its laws, we must first point out this particular characteristic: that in this order one is placed within the two worlds into which creation is divided, the world of spirit and the world of matter. To achieve the object of his research, the economist must therefore consider at the same time the laws that govern the moral world and the laws that govern the physical world."[3]

In this intellectual culture neoclassical economics, with its pretensions to being a secular science, found little purchase in the 1920s

and 1930s, as Jonathan Fournier argues.[4] Its practitioners had forgotten, or never understood, that economics was a "moral science":
"The science of what is, does not detract from moving towards that
which must be. The scholar must, therefore, 'interpret' and 'emend'
reality."[5] This Catholic culture generated a critique of "scientific"
economics and of free-market ideology that sometimes sounds like
a challenge to today's free-market fundamentalism: "In the face of
the miseries of the world, in the face of the unreality of their fundamental hypotheses and their belief that respect for economic laws
and for non-intervention are synonymous, they have thrown before
almost all who believe that something ought to be done, a profound
suspicion of political economy."[6]

We have entered the world of social Catholicism in Quebec.[7] Its
responses to the presence of "*la misère*" cheek by jowl with "*la richesse*" fitted into a long tradition, which boasts descendants in our
own time.[8] They form part of the Catholic church's long struggle
with modernity and its many manifestations – the Enlightenment,
capitalism, liberalism, and democracy. From this struggle emerged
a searing critique of industrial capitalism, a Catholic tradition of
social reform, and a gradual, albeit critical, acceptance of capitalism.
This context animates the oft-repeated word "*misère*" and its moral
nuance, one missing from the English "poverty." *Misère* indicated
material deprivation but also "miserable situation," distress, and
wretchedness – the subject of the Miserere, Allegri's sublime setting
of Psalm 51: "*Miserere mei, Deus*" (Have mercy on me, Lord). The
contemporary *misère* was a specifically modern condition, product
"of a world reduced to *misère* in the middle of abundance."[9] As
the French philosopher Jacques Maritain put it: "Modern societies
exude *misère* as a normal product of their functioning."[10]

When entering this world, we may feel surprise not only at the
force of moral invective, but also at the use of terms and concepts
that we expect to hear from socialists. How could a critique of capitalism be both radical and conservative, and why would an appeal
for radical or even revolutionary change say little about the state's
role?[11] One thing should not surprise us: the distance between
English and French Canada's political-economy traditions. There
were few references across the ethno-linguistic divide, even among
scholars in the same city. The Québécois read and learned from their
peers in France and Belgium. When they discovered the problem
of inequality, they appeared not to borrow at all from their Anglo

compatriots. They seemed to take nothing from England's Catholic tradition that produced distributism, an economic philosophy associated especially with G.K. Chesterton and Hilaire Belloc.[12] We have entered a specifically Quebec domain within the wider world of social Catholicism.

Two papal encyclicals, forty years apart, propelled the paradox of inequality into the intellectual world of social Catholicism. Leo XIII's *Rerum novarum* of 1891, on the "new world" of industrialization and urbanization, framed the discourse and offered an authority that later, more secular generations chose to find in charts and tables on the distribution of income and wealth. *Rerum novarum* saw a spirit of revolutionary change and conflict between classes, not only in politics but in the "sphere of practical economics." Out of "the vast expansion of industrial pursuits" had come "the enormous fortunes of some few individuals, and the utter poverty of the masses."[13] This seminal document dealt not only with workers' conditions, but with relations between and mutual obligations of rich and poor, of capitalists and workers. It flowed from a conception of inequitable distribution: "A small number of very rich men have been able to lay upon the teeming masses of the laboring poor a yoke little better than that of slavery itself."[14]

Pius XI's *Quadragesimo anno* (1931) – forty years after *Rerum novarum* – expanded the paradox to associate inequalities of wealth and power with concentrations of financial capital: "In our epoch, what first captures our attention is not only the concentration of wealth, but also the accumulation of enormous power, a discretionary economic power in the hands of a small number of individuals, who are not usually the owners of capital, but the agents and managers who manage capital as they see fit."[15]

The paradox echoed through the writings of Catholic intellectuals and journalists in Quebec in the 1930s. They clearly distinguished the problem from the age-old plight of the poor. It is true that Christ said that the poor are always among us, wrote J.-E. Grégoire, professor of political economy at Laval. "But it is not entrusted to anybody to concentrate wealth in such a way as to multiply beggars alongside a handful of rich, privileged monopolists."[16] The Catholic archbishops and bishops of Quebec, Montreal, and Ottawa were not talking about poverty alone when in 1932 they reduced the basic causes of the Depression to two very modern conditions: "the concentration of wealth in the hands of a small number and unrestrained

luxury."[17] By 1934 the subject of "the distribution of wealth" had
such currency that the president of the Banque canadienne nationale,
Beaudry Leman, publicly objected to the "utopian" ideal of "the better distribution of wealth" and similar "deplorable confusions."[18] By
this time the problem of distribution had found its way into Quebec
politics. In 1933 a group of Catholic lay thinkers produced "Le
programme de restauration sociale." The text boldly affirmed government responsibility for better distribution: "We believe that the
State ... must intervene by legislative measures to put an end to economic dictatorship and to assure a better distribution of wealth."[19]
This program formed the basis of the Manifesto of l'Action libérale
nationale, which joined the provincial Conservatives to form the
Union nationale (which ruled the province 1936–39, 1944–60, and
1966–70). The manifesto began: "The present crisis is due in large
part to faulty distribution in the economic domain."[20]

THE CRITIQUE OF LIBERAL CAPITALISM

The political economist who stated most thoroughly the social
Catholic position on inequality was Esdras Minville (1896–1975).
A co-author of "Le programme de restauration sociale" (1933) he
placed inequality at the heart of the social crisis. "The general and
profound *misère* in the world of workers" was threatening capitalism itself, he argued. The "excessive concentration of wealth in
the hands of fewer and fewer individuals" was one of the primary
"abuses of capitalism," and it was connected to "the anarchic organization of production."[21] He returned to the theme in an article on
the 1935 federal election, which returned the Liberals under W.L.M.
King. Capitalism and liberalism, Minville insisted, had brought
immense progress, but they had done so "in a time when the most
pressing economic problems were those of production. That is no
longer the case: the present crisis is a crisis of distribution, our problems are problems of distribution."[22] The writer would return to this
theme through the 1930s.

Although Minville's proposals to solve the social crisis and the
problem of inequality resembled some of those of Anglo-Canadian
reformers, his logic followed a different path. His solutions were
rigorously consistent with his analysis of the origins of social crisis.
Likely he would have been appalled by any suggestion that his economics amounted merely to idealistic moral homily. He was treading

in the footsteps of Édouard Montpetit (1881–1954), the pioneer of empirical economics in Quebec and professor at Montreal's École des hautes études commerciales (HEC).[23] For these political economists the Catholic ethical framework was thoroughly consistent with rigorous empirical analysis and research-based historical knowledge. For Minville the defects in contemporary capitalism required empirical and historical confirmation. They were not incidental aberrations; they were demonstrably structural and organic.[24]

We are, however, a long way from any Marxist understanding of capitalism. Here then was a distinctive characteristic of Minville's thought: there were structural problems and inherent contradictions in the economic system, but they did not arise in capitalism itself. Capitalism was not intrinsically evil; it was not inherently exploitative. On the contrary, it was "the system most appropriate for ensuring the flourishing of economic life, as a precondition for intellectual, moral and social life."[25] How then had it become "a vicious regime," a deformed and corrupted perversion of itself? Minville's answer was that over the course of a century the economic system had been transformed "*de fond en comble*" (from top to bottom) by a profound and retrograde historical force: economic liberalism, which itself grew from "fundamental postulates of liberal theory." Minville cited as examples individual interest as the motor of economic activity; supposed natural laws working towards equilibrium and social harmony; and the pre-eminence of liberty among the principles of prosperity and civilization.[26]

Ironically Minville was denying the historical role of, and advocating collective rejection of, the very principles that had created the economic system that he praised. Resolving this conundrum was no simple matter; it was a problem for everyone who took seriously the papal encyclicals, which also rejected political and economic liberalism while endorsing private property. Solving the problem inspired enormous intellectual effort over a few generations. Minville attempted a complex reconciliation of private property and capitalism with Catholic ideals of social justice and common good.[27]

Minville's originality lay in applying Catholic thought to economics as an applied science in twentieth-century Quebec. He analyzed neither capitalism nor liberalism, but their historical conjuncture. His critique was far more comprehensive and radical than any Anglo-Canadian efforts. Capital, he said, obeyed only the law of profit; it never worried about equivalence between selling prices and purchasing power; it left the connection between production and consumption to "the free play of competition." It removed from sight "the supreme end of economic activity" – the common good and the flourishing of the human spirit. The result was disequilibrium in the "economic organism."[28]

Minville's analysis emphasized how dehumanized actors – capital, money, markets – became agents in the economic system. And this was the central defect, or "*abus*," of liberal capitalism. The French "*abus*" conveyed a moral opprobrium lacking in the English "abuse," with its narrow sense of "misuse"; it also implied corruption or violation. Liberal capitalism's misconception of labour constituted therefore a morally corrupting abuse. It made labour an input, Minville said – a commodity whose value reflected supply and demand. Its commodification of labour had led to "*la misère profonde*" and wealth flowing more and more to the few. Minville went even further. These "*abus*" amounted to alienation (although he did not use that word), turning workers into beasts of burden, depriving them of humanity, cutting them off from the higher part of themselves ("*amputés de la partie la plus haute d'eux-mêmes*").[29] Had labour, in capitalism, become a form of wage slavery? No, answered Minville, it was worse: having succumbed to this systemic "*misère*," labour was the victim of "a social scourge in a sense more degrading than slavery in the ancient world."[30]

To highlight elements of Minville's analysis in this way risks giving the impression that his work was stridently polemical, which it was not. His critique was deeply informed and historical. He acknowledged that workers' standards of living might have improved somewhat in the forty years since *Rerum novarum*; nevertheless, he saw more of the world's goods in fewer hands. One culprit was a fundamental contradiction in liberalism: it granted capital an absolute right of association, in the name of individual freedom, but denied it to labour, or severely limited it. Capital's total right permitted it to commit many abuses of power; it could, for instance, pool capital, fix prices, swallow up competitors, even suppress the supreme regulator of the capitalist system – the law of competition. The end of this process was monopoly and the "triumph of plutocracy."[31]

Minville's analysis of liberal capitalism and its contradictions tied in tightly with his economic nationalism. Seeking to balance agriculture and industry, and studying corporate capital's workings in his province, this nationalist knew that the "rule of the strongest, that is to say, of the richest" meant English Canadians and Americans. His nationalism nourished his keen insight into the overlap between wealth and political power, obvious under Quebec's Liberal Taschereau government and its alliance with big business.[32] Centralized wealth had led to systemic political corruption: "the hidden influences of the power of money over public authority." "And the capitalist dictators are too prudent, in truth, and too clever, not to play all the trump cards in their hands."[33] Minville noted the overlap of wealth and political power as individuals moved between politics and the heights of commerce, industry, and finance. It was also evident in the "enslavement of the press." Directly and indirectly, financiers and entrepreneurs submitted the newspapers to their will and turned them into propagandists of money.

Minville's critique of the power of plutocracy went even further. Capitalist "dictators" had pushed the state towards protectionist extremes, excluding foreign imports, thereby forcing consumers to pay higher prices. On the world stage the subjugation of politics to wealth had fostered "economic imperialism" (had Minville read J.A. Hobson?). As examples, he cited the long-standing penetration of American trusts into the Caribbean and South America. The United States, he wrote in 1927, was practising the most ingratiating, enterprising, and brazen imperialism that the world had ever known.[34] Does this analysis take us away from the subject of inequality? Not at all: liberal capitalism, faster concentrating of wealth, subordinating political to economic power, and capturing foreign resources all formed links in a single chain of logic.

In Minville we do not find the same focus on finance capital that existed in Social Credit's contemporary analyses of the economic system. For him it served as a telling example of the evil that flowed from economic liberalism and capitalists' unrestrained exercise of power. His language was heavy with moral censure: "Protected against the intervention of any public power ... the masters of finance and of business may plot in peace their profitable combinations and proceed in complete security with the fiddling of funds ... that a public, ill-informed or falsely guided by subservient newspapers, entrusts to their administration."[35]

Minville then used a weighty moral term – usury – calling it "one of the worst abuses of contemporary capitalism."[36] He did not mean that charging interest on loans was inherently sinful, but mentioning "usury" invoked long-standing Catholic reservations about interest.[37] Minville was condemning not interest in itself, but exorbitant and unearned profits from secret and dishonest machinations: "not just the sordid usury that hides itself in some smelly little office, but usury that has the façade of honesty, practised within the limits of the law, thanks to the complicated game of financial operations conducted in the inspiring silence of luxurious offices. We affirm – and this has never been denied because it is based on precise data – that one great Canadian enterprise [unidentified] pays an annual dividend of 70 percent on a capital investment that is thereby reimbursed four times. Did even the most money-grubbing usurers of the Middle Ages ever dream of such returns?"[38]

The Depression of the 1930s confirmed for Minville and many of his contemporaries the intellectual and moral bankruptcy of economic liberalism. The intellectual edifice was in decline. But what would replace it? Minville, though very much a public intellectual who never confined economics within the academy, was not a populist. His work was rigorously consistent and tackled difficult issues. He knew that economic liberalism had co-existed with the remarkable economic growth of the previous century; he grasped that its roots were deep. To change conditions that had deep historical roots would necessitate sweeping cultural, political, and economic changes. Modest state-initiated reforms would be mere palliatives; Minville believed that social-welfare legislation, such as minimum wages and unemployment insurance, failed to address the root causes of the social problem. Something more ambitious was essential.

CATHOLIC SOCIAL REGENERATION

Especially in the 1930s, nationalist, Catholic HEC professor Esdras Minville proposed sweeping reform embracing rural restoration, cooperativism, agricultural modernization, education reforms, and corporatism.[39] Working as an integrated whole, this radical program would address the multiple conditions of inequality endemic to French Canadians in Quebec. Minville created one of the most comprehensive schemas of reform ever conceived by a Canadian economist.

Towards the end of his intellectual biography of Minville, Dominique Foisy-Geoffroy offers an intriguing clue to the personal and intellectual roots of the economist's reform vision. Minville shared the rural or small-town roots of so many other Canadians who confronted the problem of inequality. He was born in 1896 to a poor fishing family in Grande-Vallée in the Gaspé region. He lived the economic conditions that he would describe three decades later. Grande-Vallée had been a multi-resource region, but over the nineteenth century access to land and forests was increasingly restricted. The "seigneury" fell into the hands of a rich elite, whom Minville described caustically as "seigneurs – millionaires – speculators – salmon fishing enthusiasts."[40] Rural families became increasingly dependent on fishing, the price of fish dropped, and the local people fell into an increasingly onerous "*misère.*" Eventually an Anglo company appropriated the forest resources. Here, in the place of his birth and childhood, Minville found a microcosm of the social crisis that would engulf his province, in which wealth coincided with immiseration and economic inequality was also an inequality of peoples. Minville's reform vision addressed both inequalities at once.

Minville considered and quickly rejected other radical alternatives available in the 1930s. He was not preoccupied with either socialism or communism; he would offer no sustained critique of either, and certainly nothing approaching O.D. Skelton's work on socialism. Communism was forfeiture (*"décheance"*) and destruction. Nazism was an "idolatry" prone to racist scapegoating. Italian fascism was excessively statist and tended to "diminish ... the human person." Italy and Portugal's "political corporatism" seemed to him little different from "statism."[41]

There remained, he said, only "social corporatism" or *"corporatisme d'association."* His corporatism was at once complex, detailed, and, as Foisy-Geoffroy suggests, nebulous. Its connection to the problem of inequality, however, was explicit. In his 1936 article "Libéralisme, Communisme? Corporatisme?" he introduced corporatism: "The problem before the world today is this. On the one hand, to ensure a better distribution of wealth created in ever larger volumes by an increasingly perfected production; on the other hand, to safeguard individual liberties in order to ensure the healthy development of the human person."[42] Individual liberty, in its liberal conception, cannot by itself assure the just distribution of wealth, Minville insisted.

His next step was to define liberty. It could not be the right to act as one pleased, free from all constraints. It was rather the right to act in accordance with a competent and recognized authority, and within the limits of justice. And what was that competent authority? It was not the state, which represented only political authority, and not the church, which represented only religious authority. It was "*la profession*" – a broad concept: not so much an occupation as a declaration of faith, belief, or knowledge, and embracing the associated body of those who share those principles. "This alone is competent in the domain of its jurisdiction."[43] The liberty of the individual emerged within the profession and within its interconnected association of religious, social, and political authorities, "each of these being limited in its power by the power of others." This plurality of authorities enabled action while limiting threats to the human person, including those Minville saw existing under economic liberalism. His concept of liberty owed little to Locke and nothing to Mill. Rather, the individual existed only in association with his or her community, and liberty, only within its constraints.[44]

The corporation therefore embodies "*la profession*." As usual, Minville confronted directly the challenging questions. One could not describe the corporation in the abstract, he said. So where did the institution exist, even in embryo? And how to integrate such institutions within the capitalist regime? Minville foresaw associations growing organically from shared interests and from the "ethnic genius" of French Canada, so different from that of Anglo-Saxons.[45] Corporations must emerge from social realities, as "the product of a general and profound conviction."[46] Examples included chambers of commerce, associations of merchants, the Collège des Médecins, the Union catholique des cultivateurs, and the *chambre des notaires*. "It is a question above all of widening their vision, in such a way as to temper, by social and national concerns, the strictly professional motives that have guided their formation and their action."[47] This process would be assisted on several fronts: by the educational efforts of the St-Jean Baptiste Society (with which Minville was already collaborating), by the universities, and by a complex administrative structure that the writer described in detail. This was social, not political or state corporatism, so the government's role was important but small – providing enabling legislation and protection.

How then would this structure of corporate bodies, emerging slowly, improve distribution of wealth? It would take questions of value and of remuneration out of the unregulated play of competition and short-circuit the class struggle that the state arbitrated.[48] It would provide an institutional context that would attach workers to their employer not merely by a wage, but by a new form of connection, or belonging: workers would own shares, and corporatism and cooperatism would merge – members would collectively own companies.[49] Sharing ownership would give employees a material stake in their company, but such an interest was never enough. To ensure that classes would spontaneously and willingly collaborate, the corporation would provide more: by enveloping and disciplining its public and private enterprises, it would render "*les grands patrons*" a minority, with no more influence than the small-business owners and the mass of wage earners.

Such a community would end the dictatorship that big capitalists imposed on so-called free markets. What would emerge was not "the singular point of view of one group or one class, but a social point of view, that of all groups and classes. One would thus have a chance of arriving at an equitable solution for all."[50] The argument had deep roots in the Catholic understanding of liberty and the spiritual necessity of community, outside which no liberty was possible. The community generated its own egalitarian concept of the human person, nourishing bonds that were far stronger than the sin of greed and the individual quest for material accumulation.

The question remained: given the entrenched power of vested interests, especially in financial and industrial capital, and because of the overlap between economic and political power – all of which Minville perceived clearly – how to persuade those interests to compromise and to forgo their share of profits, economic rent, and political power? This is the same question that confronts solutions to inequality today. It would seem pressing for Minville, because of his ambiguous attitude towards democracy.[51]

He confronted the question and answered it. Although he collaborated with L'Action liberale nationale and even worked for a time in the provincial civil service, he did not see his reforms as realizable through the democratic system, by the gradual pressure of progressive political interests working their way into and through political parties. His answer had its own persuasive force, even though it never materialized, even within Quebec, where alone it would apply. Minville invoked a historical force unavailable to Robert MacIver or others outside Quebec: nationalism. "Nobody doubts that the rising generation will no longer endure economic dictatorship, and will no longer consent to allow foreign capitalists the privileged position that they have used so far to our detriment."[52] If you objected, he argued, that similar efforts have failed elsewhere, as in Holland, well, the effort there was by a Catholic *minority*; in Quebec it would be the creation of a majority. Similar social problems existed elsewhere: desertion of the countryside, destruction of the middle class, proletarianization of the masses – but for Québécois these were "national problems first and foremost, since, situated as we are, they bring into play our national existence itself."[53]

Minville believed that French Canadians in Quebec were beginning to see the connection between inequality and nation. Unleash the force of national loyalty and national survival on the social crisis, and even the entrenched power of the capitalist class would yield to compromise. Within three decades the economic nationalism that Minville represented would move beyond the colleges and economic journals to seek political realization in the Quiet Revolution.[54]

What did distributive justice mean for Minville? What would a society that had overcome the problem of inequality look like? Minville's essay "La juste répartition des richesses" provided the clearest answers. The article began by formulating the great paradox of inequality in a novel way. Elsewhere, even in Minville's work, the paradox was that creation of unprecedented wealth had been accompanied by extensive poverty. In "La juste répartition" the crucial damage was the destruction of what allows people to enjoy whatever they have: "the spirit of justice, the understanding of the sacrifice that tempers covetousness, the human sensibility which is only human to the extent that it is inspired by the divine."[55] Within this formulation lay an ancient Catholic suspicion of wealth and materialism, which had deepened in the church's complex and often ambiguous responses to industrialization and to modernism. Although Minville believed that the last century had seen generally higher standards of living, he also believed that wealth creation had gone too far. Humanity was suffering, he said, not because so much was lacking but because there was too much of everything. A "new *misère*" had surfaced: "The *misère* of superabundance has become a greater scourge than the dearth of the past." Distress existed among so much opulence, he said, citing Pius XI, principally because of "the taste for lucre, cupidity, the thirst for riches." [56]

Distributive justice therefore should not mean a society-wide extension of cupidity. It meant that the working class had both duties and rights. Among the duties was acceptance of "the inevitable inequality of human conditions" and of the economic system, which one may legitimately seek to improve but not to overthrow. Justice required also that workers have the right to be treated as human beings, not machines and to associate to defend their interests. A working man who was "sober and honest" had the right to receive, in return for his labour, "sufficient revenue to assure the subsistence, in humane conditions, of a family of normal composition."[57] This right was recognized in principle, said Minville, in the concept of family wage and in legislation on minimum wages.

Minville's critique of liberal capitalism and its inequities was an analytical *tour de force*. His discussion of just distribution, in contrast, was a deflating balloon, at least to the reader from outside his moral world. His standard of subsistence-level earnings for working-class families took the solution away from the relative distribution of economic rewards, towards a minimal absolute standard, and a very low one at that. Did his "just distribution" in fact amount to any form of redistribution, and did it place any limit at all, other than the duty of honesty, on the capture of profit and economic rent by a tiny minority? He was, however, formulating just distribution in terms of both duties and rights. Social Catholic thought tended to give duty precedence, especially over any concept of social rights to be guaranteed by secular authority. In his study of the history of state welfare and of "social capitalism," Kees van Kersbergen traces this tendency to a contradiction in *Rerum novarum*. "The basic contradiction in *Rerum Novarum* as the expression of Catholic social theory, therefore, is found in the attempt to define a conception of justice while omitting a theory of correlative rights. In other words, the first social encyclical acknowledges only the right to private property. Only the duties of justice are clearly defined."[58]

But Minville did not fall into this trap, because he was clearly specifying social rights that belonged collectively to workers. However, he did not join these rights clearly to correlative duties, other than that of spiritual and ethical observance by employers. There appeared to be no agency of enforcement, other than that of moral suasion within the corporation. The right of association for workers was no solution at all, unless it came with an enforceable duty for employers to negotiate with trade unions.

There are answers to these objections. To apply such reservations to Minville's distributive justice is to bring us closer to its sources and the core of its message. For one thing, Minville would surely deny that he had missed the duties that correlated with workers' rights. And he would add that to reduce the social question to the level of material rewards or to quarrelling over details of labour law was to miss the point.[59] The level of material rewards to labour could be only one part of the solution to social crisis, and a minor part at that. The greater part lay at the moral and spiritual levels, where his answer was redistributive. Minville invoked the church's theory on private property – God originally gave the earth and its resources to all humanity, in a form of stewardship, to preserve and use for common benefit. Private property did not extinguish the duty of stewardship – using one's property for the benefit of others or for a common good.[60] For Minville, capitalists' duties included just remuneration for employees, reasonable hours of labour, humane working conditions, and Sunday rest. Above all stood the duty of humane caring – *caritas* – respecting the human dignity of employees. These duties were enforceable not through mere *voluntary* compliance or moral suasion. They were *necessary* actions, or commands, enforced by the highest of authorities – the church itself. The capitalist could not evade them. The program of reform was redistributive at the only levels that really counted.

Within this perspective lay a specific Catholic egalitarianism, and in Minville an ambiguity that Dominique Foisy-Geoffroy emphasizes. Minville's work was egalitarian, as was apparent in his faith in the masses' capacity to self-organize and to embody cooperative principles, and in his profound belief in the dignity of the human person. There was also the egalitarianism of the Christian believer: all human beings are equal in the sight of God.[61] Thus human beings, sharing a specific place in the natural order of things, were endowed with the light of reason, which was "an imprint on us of the Divine light," as Aquinas put it.[62]

Yet Minville's egalitarian impulse sat closely with his pervasive elitism. In corporatism, the "profession" – the company of the competent – was led by the elite possessors of knowledge, who communicated that knowledge to those who lacked it. In the education system an elite had the duty to help a wider population grasp its own true interests. At the national level, government must work with and through committees of elite specialists. Human beings did not share natural endowments equally. It was obvious to Catholic intellectuals in Quebec, as it was clear in Thomist theology, that people possessed very unequal abilities to acquire ethical knowledge and to act in the service of morally acceptable ends.[63]

The light of reason co-existed with differing capacities to apply reason. The deeply hierarchical vision helps to explain the rarity of the word "equality" and of its opposite, inequality, in social Catholicism. It was not just that Catholic reactions to the French Revolution expunged "*égalité*" from the discourse. The elision lay deeper, in Thomistic theology. Thus neither Minville nor his colleagues appear to have considered a more equitable distribution, or asked whether "*répartition*" would recalibrate equality. "*Égalité de chances*" and "*le manque d'opportunités*" were not part of their language; even "*l'équité*" appeared rarely. Minville's promotion of education did not contain the concept of equality of opportunity. Education for French Canadians was to nourish a consciousness of collective and national duties and combat individualism.[64] "Equality of opportunity" would contradict differential inherent endowments. It was also profoundly individualistic, aiming to level conditions among persons conceived as autonomous individuals.

The meaning of "just distribution" in Minville's thought crystallized in this context. Distributive justice could not aim at something so chimerical as equality. His rare mentions of "equality" and "inequality" excluded them as operating principles of justice. "Now given the irreducible inequalities that exist among men, a social order devoted to the common good must proceed, neither from liberty alone … nor from political dictatorship … nor from equality of material goods, which would destroy all forms of liberty; but from the justice that blossoms through charity (*la charité*)."[65]

THE POLITICAL CONSTRICTION OF SOCIAL JUSTICE

The limits to Minville's distributive justice became clear in the 1940s, when the Canadian state took significant steps towards a social-security system. In the 1930s, when his concern for the rich–poor paradox increased, Minville was ready to consider state intervention to further a more equitable distribution of wealth. The Programme de restauration sociale of 1933, which he helped to write, stated: "We believe that the state must intervene through legislative measures to put an end to economic dictatorship and to ensure a better distribution of wealth."[66] And in the 1930s he was prepared to accept a social-security system in principle. "The principle that seems a good one is to transfer to the collectivity a just measure of the benefits of machinery, of rationalization, and of the perfection of the means of production, from which only a handful have benefitted so far."[67] In a 1937 article on fascist Italy's corporatist and pro-natalist family allowances of 1934, Minville termed such payments "well adapted to the social exigencies of our epoch" and endorsed a targeted version as part of Quebec's rural restoration.[68]

By 1944 Minville's concern for the paradox of rich and poor had diminished, and his reservations about state-led social security had sharpened, especially if family allowances appeared as "gratuities": "It is important to rule out gratuities or a distribution of wealth for social considerations that for all practical purposes would appear to be gratuities in the eyes of the masses and would result in the same moral effects. Such as, at this time, our old age pensions; such as the family allowances planned by the federal government."[69]

His concerns were consistent with social Catholicism's resistance to an expanded role for the state. In the same article, he reported hearing on the radio a professor who argued that the tax system corrected the pre-tax distribution of income. This, Minville said, conjured away the problem "in the Anglo-Saxon way" and tackled the effects while assuming that the causes of inequity are beyond solution. "Well no! The responsibilities of the State regarding social security can be compared to those of the teacher for the child: not to do it for him, but to teach him how to do it for himself."[70]

State and citizen – educator and child: his analogy reflected both elitism and fear that state "gratuity" would pauperize recipients. Minville believed that to ameliorate the material condition of poor individuals was to remove individual responsibility and initiative; the "fatal consequences" would be to protect individuals from the "ordinary risks of life" and the results of incompetence, negligence, and feeble character. Underlying such fear was a deeply pessimistic view of the moral condition of most human beings, despite their innate capacity to reason: most "men" are basically lazy. "Man is inclined to the least effort, and even when he seeks more than what is strictly necessary for a certain comfort or ease, he more or less follows the idea that one can deal with risks only by trying to prevent them."[71]

The moral vision that drove Minville's assault on economic liberalism also impeded any chance of redistributive social justice. At the heart of his moral philosophy lay a tension, even a contradiction. He rejected liberal individualism: the individual did not exist except as part of collectivities, including family, nation, and, prospectively, corporation. Yet each person was "responsib[le] for his [sic] own life," and any dependence on others directly or indirectly threatened his or her liberty and dignity as a human being.[72] Minville seems to have been aware of the logical problem: liberal economists believed that individual interest helped drive the economic organism, and he substantially agreed. So what, then, was his quarrel? It was a weak moment in Minville's writing: the liberal mistake, he proposed, was to exaggerate individualism's reach,[73] which he then extended throughout society. Individual responsibility towards the social body and the social order was fundamental; anything that risked reducing personal initiative and effort must be avoided.

Clearly the mid-century Catholic understanding of social security placed a severe limit on the state's redistributive capacity, which should ensure enough material goods for the recipient to realize his or her spiritual being. As François-Albert Angers put it: "A minimum of goods is necessary for the practice of virtue [and] … for providing the fair family wage."[74] Ensuring this minimum – the "just family wage" – was the task of the male family breadwinner. "That is why Catholic social security, rather than being a program of redistribution, tends toward a politics of just distribution of revenues within the production process itself."[75] And so the Catholic doctrine kept the state out and threw just distribution back into the productive system. The (Édouard) Montpetit Commission on social security, reporting in 1932 and 1933, also rejected any state role in distributing wealth across society.[76]

By mid-century social Catholicism stood divided and uncertain before the progressive reforms of the emerging social-security state.[77] These included a widened and progressive federal tax regime, recognition of trade unions, compulsory collective bargaining through a state-regulated industrial-relations system, and family allowances. Minville's extensive economic and social reforms might have given Quebec more economic autonomy and increased income and wealth. Some of the actual reforms did contribute to such results, but only via the sort of *dirigiste* state that he opposed in the 1940s. None of Minville's proposals, or his reform program as a whole, even if implemented, would probably have helped reduce the extreme disparities of income and wealth that he condemned in the 1930s.

The paradox of inequality was being circumscribed by the very moral perspective that created it as a problem – perhaps most notably by the long-lived Victor Barbeau (1894–1994). His thought is difficult to categorize. Professor at Montreal's Hautes études commerciales, economist, journalist, and cultural critic, Barbeau is a reminder that Catholic intellectuals in interwar Quebec elude our usual ideological spectrum, from left to right, or conservative to progressive,[78] especially where attitudes (either interventionist or non-interventionist) towards state action have little relevance. Pierre Trépanier describes Barbeau as an "anarchist of the right."[79] The first page of Barbeau's *Pour nous grandir: Essai d'explication des misères de notre temps* (1937) formulated his idiosyncratic view of the paradox of inequality (although he avoided that word). The proletariat, he said, had been reduced for the most part to begging; above it were smaller middling social groups; at the top was a thin line of rich bourgeois, whose fortune scoffed at the collective distress beneath them.[80] The first chapter's title offered the rich–poor dichotomy as melodrama: "The Living and the Others."

What followed presented no sustained analysis of this social hierarchy, still less any discussion of wealth and income distributions; statistics, for Barbeau, were a fragile delusion of empiricism.[81] Instead the first page launched a polemic that spared nobody. Proletarian beggars and illiterate bourgeois were symptoms of a modern corruption that permeated all of society. In Barbeau's dark vision ideological "isms" inspired his penchant for ad-hominem aspersion. Conservatism was "a doctrine of the wilfully blind, of the magnificent powerless, of the credulous and the pusillanimous."[82] Liberalism, in its religious, economic, and political forms, was no better, and political liberalism was the servant of capitalism. Even worse, economic liberalism led to communism.[83] The current corruption, Barbeau argued, had distorted and robbed worthy principles of their meaning. Equality merely begged the question: equality before what? ("*Égalité devant quoi?*"). "In this individualism, which encourages each to play his or her own game well at the expense of common interest, who can recognize liberty? In this levelling of consciences and of brains who can recognize equality?"[84]

In Barbeau's intellectually aristocratic anti-modernism, poverty in the midst of wealth took on a meaning that had little to do with relative material condition. A conception of distributive justice was certainly present, but justice was about moral, not material condition. Simple "men of the earth" were at the base of society precisely because they were eaten away by anxiety and discomfort. The condition of the proletariat was indignity – the indignity associated with begging. The bourgeois may have been, in some sense, "at the top," but most of them were illiterate (*"en quasi-totalité illetrés"*); they invalidated all pretensions to an educated order in society.

Barbeau was describing moral *dis*order, not material injustice. His answer to such profound *"désordre"* began and ended at the spiritual level. This did not mean that he didn't want institutions to help detoxify society morally. "A doctrine of justice, order and hierarchy" must have an institutional form: "The professional organization contains all of that ... It does not destroy private initiative; it stimulates and prescribes it."[85] The spiritual priority remained intact, however: corporate institutions were enabling environments, but did not initiate moral and spiritual cleansing. The same applied to democracy itself. As Barbeau said of it: "We will have to detoxify it first and then organize it. By detoxify, I mean to get rid of ideologies that contradict facts and enfeeble common sense."[86]

If Barbeau's answer to the social crisis was conservative, it was so in large part because it relied on a return to a pre-modern French Canada. The moral wellsprings of detoxification, and hence of social justice, lay in the ineradicable character of French Canadians themselves. "We must erect barriers against the rising tide of repugnant materialism and of base appetites. If there is to be – implausible hypothesis – a small island in America where simplicity and moral sobriety persists, let it be ours. We have already given up too much to extravagance, to stupidity, to filth ... God willing, our distinction rests on something better. It rests not on flesh but on spirit. It is built on culture, beauty, wisdom, chivalry, rectitude. No matter that the France of today, plagued by the throes of metamorphosis, cannot offer us an exact measure! We know that this culture exists, that this flame burns. The rest is nothing but rot and decay."[87]

As for any problem of distribution in this analysis, the utopian reverie of national essence washed it away. The state's role was either diminished or denied. Grossly inequitable material conditions in society succumbed to the dream of moral metamorphosis.

Barbeau was a somewhat unusual Catholic social thinker of the 1930s. As historians of Quebec have shown, its intellectuals reacted to industrialization and to modernism in complex and varied ways, and "social Catholicism" was no procrustean bed. The fate of the problem of inequality is more easily traced in the work of François-Albert Angers (1909–2003), a disciple of Minville who took over the editorship of *Actualité économique* in 1938. With

Angers, the paradox of misery in the midst of wealth receded from
view: it almost disappeared from the journal in the 1940s.[88] The
waning of the problem of inequitable distribution preceded the
eventual dethroning of social Catholicism in economics and the
triumph of neoclassical economics within the discipline in Quebec,
a gradual and contested transformation Jonathan Fournier discusses at length.[89] Inequality therefore slowly disappeared within
social Catholicism during and after the Second World War – but
not simply because war-related topics took over space in *Actualité
économique*. The traditional topics survived: agriculture, cooperatives, corporatism, federal budgets, the forest sector. Issues of social
justice also received attention, especially as the war wound down.

It was Angers who prepared the journal's first table representing
income distribution in Canada. In an article in 1945 he presented,
for 1942, the percentage of employed persons in Quebec in each of
ten income levels, from less than $500 to more than $5,000. The
source, of course, was federal tax data. A simple arithmetical calculation would have shown him that the bottom third of employed
Canadians earned only about 15 per cent of all incomes, and the top
28 per cent, about 50 per cent. The result would not have said much
about distribution of incomes among all Canadians, because farmers
were left out, and so were the unemployed.

The point is that Angers had no interest in using his data for
any such purpose. He wanted to show how Quebec's distribution
of taxpayers across income categories compared with Canada's
as a whole and other provinces'. He was also keen to reveal the
distributions among married men, and he noted that their proportion in the lowest income levels was higher in Quebec than in all
of Canada. He also pointed out that the percentage of Quebecers
in the highest bracket was slightly higher than that for Canada,
and his conclusion revealed no concern that "senior personnel ...
take it upon themselves to reward their talents at the same level as
the rest of Canada."[90] The problem of inequality, so urgent a mere
ten years earlier, had evaporated. In April 1946 Angers presented
a much more detailed breakdown of taxpayer data, with tables
showing the national distribution of taxpayers by income level in
1937 and 1944.[91] Another table displayed the mean annual income
of taxpayers at each of twelve income levels, the mean taxes paid at
each level, and the mean after-tax incomes at each level. These data
were ripe for analysis. Once again Angers might have estimated

the share of total incomes held by those at each level; once again he did not.

Issues of social justice were not absent, however. Angers noted the many more taxpayers at the $1,000–$3,000 levels in 1944. Their numbers had grown much more than had those of the poorest, below $1,000, and than the total Canadian population. From this he inferred an increase in individuals' nominal incomes. This cautiously optimistic observation might have led him on to infer a significant shrinking in the gaps between rich and poor, especially since the top income levels had grown relatively slowly. But his attention lay elsewhere.

Angers's real concerns were first, the tax-generating capacity of each level of income, and second, the serious possibility of a deep moral offence – tax evasion. He noted that the proportion of all tax revenues coming from the lowest five income categories (not including those below $1,000) had shot up. In 1937 the wealthiest people contributed the bulk of tax revenues; by 1944 the burden had shifted to the lower income groups. The state, he argued, had a duty to ensure that the tax burden did not fall unduly on the poor. But how should it do so? Angers did not consider adjustment of taxation rates at different levels, or surtax on the highest incomes (which would merely encourage more tax evasion). The only effective way for the state to ensure tax fairness was to restrain its spending and hold it at "an appropriate level." The state must avoid "the politics of paternalism." It must not seek to remedy all social evils "by paying to the taxpayer family allowances, the means of health and hygiene, etc. that normally fall within the private mechanism of production and distribution."[92] There was a social justice in Angers's complaint that tax exemptions were greater for the rich than for the poor. But the paradox of systemic inequality between rich and poor had clearly receded from view.

In 1946, there was no hint of Angers's seemingly radical view, six years earlier, that "we are in the stage of economic dictatorship" in which only the possessors of capital directed the economy and the mass of workers had no choice but to obey. There was no echo of his call for "an evolution towards economic and social democracy."[93] Economists in Quebec were aware of the expansion of the tax system and federal taxation capacity during the war. But this realization did not encourage them to discuss the redistributive potential of taxation. The change more often reinforced their resistance to an expanded role for the state in the realm of social security.

POLITICAL AND MORAL DEFLATION

The disappearance of the paradox of inequality in social Catholicism was perhaps nowhere more apparent than in a remarkable
mid-century document on the condition of workers. In 1949 the
Commission sacerdotale d'études sociale issued a long pastoral letter entitled *La condition ouvrière au regard de la doctrine sociale
de l'Église*. This work, appearing soon after the Asbestos strike of
1949, earned favourable reviews from progressive groups and condemnation from conservative Catholics and the Duplessis government.[94] The authors were attempting to accept and to reckon with
the extent of industrialization and urbanization in Quebec. In their
focus on the industrial-relations system they endorsed a positive and
interventionist role for government. The state, they said, had a duty
to intervene to correct the instability of an economic regime whose
guiding principles were not always compatible with the common
good, and to protect the community against the abuses of a flawed
capitalism.[95] They endorsed, among other reforms, protections for
the right of association, worker participation in management and in
ownership of industrial enterprises, profit-sharing, and a ban on the
firing of workers for union activity.

Absent from the document was any direct and explicit reiteration
of the paradox of "*misère*" in the midst of wealth. This lacuna is all
the more remarkable because of the document's frequent quotations
from papal encyclicals and from recent papal letters on social issues.
The assertion in *Rerum novarum* that wealth was concentrating in
fewer and fewer hands was missing, except for vague references to
"the rich class" and "the poor class."[96] The document revealed how
much the perception of social problems had shifted in the 1940s,
in the context of war, falling unemployment, the growth of trade
unions, and the appearance of a legalized industrial-relations system.
The problems that moved the authors included those of affluence:
workers' increasing assertiveness and independence and increased
leisure; rising material expectations; and the plight of the consumer.
The problem now was "the separation of the consumer from the
producer," who, the writers asserted, was likely to exploit consumers
in the quest for profit. And the consumer society was producing a
new kind of paradox: the production of useless or harmful goods
when basic necessities were in short supply. "Who has not deplored
the absurdity of the abundant and lucrative production of trivial and

often harmful goods, while the scarcity of basic necessities causes unprecedented deprivation."[97]

Inequality occasionally resurfaced in Quebec economic writings in the 1950s, but no longer as a paradox, and its moral urgency had waned.[98] In 1954 Pierre Harvey became the first contributor in *Actualité économique* to show the percentage of all incomes earned by each quintile in the income distribution, and the first to present Lorenz curves (though not Gini coefficients). Harvey was not discussing Canada, however: he was using Simon Kuznets's data for the United States. He confirmed the popular idea that for the years between 1935–36 and 1950 there existed an extreme disparity in incomes. He made no mention of papal encyclicals and no suggestion of moral opprobrium in his tepid conclusions: inequality was perhaps a constant in the "law of the régime"; any rectification could be only partial; and those who believed in "natural laws" could rest assured that there would always be "the poor among us."[99] It is an irony worth noting that when the extent of the problem of inequality finally received empirical confirmation, that confirmation did not sustain a call for distributive justice.

The paradox of poverty in the midst of wealth had a short life in the political economy of social Catholicism in the first half of the twentieth century. The conditions of its fading help us to understand why it appeared in the 1930s. Social Catholicism and economic nationalism had to respond to the economic and social crisis of the Depression. Although, as Michael Gauvreau argues, many people would in theory have accepted a wider role for the state, both Quebec City and Ottawa's collaborations with secularism and external ethnic elites deeply compromised the state.[100] Those who rejected a place for government had read *Quadragesimo anno* selectively: they ignored the sections accepting an expanding role for the state in defending justice and common interest. "For it is rightly contended that certain forms of property must be reserved for the state, since they carry with them an opportunity of domination too great to be left to private individuals without injury to the community at large."[101] The encyclicals left open a wide range of interpretations of the state's role; redistribution was rarely part of it.

Catholic intellectuals were impelled to respond to the Depression because of the apparent resurgence in the 1930s of old threats, which they often conflated – most notably socialism, particularly in the form of the Co-operative Commonwealth Federation

(CCF), and communism. As Yvan Lamonde suggests, the Catholic church in Quebec had a massive investment in battling communism – reminiscent of its fight against that other modern evil, the French Revolution. One has the impression, says Lamonde, that the anti-communist forces felt they were fighting an omnipresent communism that was about to overthrow established authority and burn down the churches.[102] These groups linked the intellectual assault on inequality and on capitalism's abuses directly to their fear of communism, which, according to *L'Action nationale*, "is already firmly settled in the heart of our population," and we must lead with great vigour both the "battle against communism" and "the removal of the abuses of capitalism."[103]

Quebec's economists probably realized the very small numbers of communists in the province; their main target was another secular force, that of economic liberalism. Nevertheless, they were increasingly aware of the threat of the discontented masses. "Economic laws, free of constraint, have legitimized all ambition and justified the fortunes of the last century; but they have also provoked anxiety, revolt, and often hatred among those that were deprived while a small number grew rich."[104]

In the face of what appeared to be imminent chaos, economic writers reached back into their traditions and found a reassuring discourse. The basic structure of the economic system was sound; the fault lay in a perverse secular materialism and in economic liberalism. The language of the paradox – massive concentrations of wealth in a world of misery – seemed to reflect perfectly the current reality of foreign corporate elites existing beside masses of unemployed workers, overwhelmed urban relief programs, and broken families. Since the causes of the crisis lay not in the economic system, nor in the domain of secular politics, they must be moral – and the rich–poor paradox appealed precisely because it was moral. As the *Programme de restauration sociale* of 1933 stated: "We believe ... that the principal causes of the crisis are those of moral order, and that we will be healed above all by the return of the Christian spirit."[105] The solution to a moral crisis was not a materialist redistribution but a moral purification: "The environment of work and industry can have sanctifying effect."[106]

The Quebec economists who spoke of the paradox of poverty beside wealth did not define distributive justice coherently. They struggled to reconcile charity with government action and taxation's growing role in the distribution of income and wealth.[107] They knew that the state collected and distributed funds, but they saw it as infringing on the church's traditional role and the Christian obligation of giving. They sought alternatives to state-directed social justice, and many turned to social corporatism. As a means to realize distributive justice or common good, however, the corporation had little history in Quebec and no promising future. It was precisely in their own domain – collective or community action towards social justice – that Catholic social thinkers failed to respond convincingly to the social crisis. Government was already implementing economic change and social policy and intervening in class relations, but these observers tended to see it as merely a facilitator and regulator of non-state actors. A theory of distributive justice could not emerge via such a misreading of the state's substantial actual power and of the minimal potential of non-state organizations such as social corporations.

Under-theorized and ancillary to other agendas, the problem of inequality in social Catholicism rested on fragile foundations, as was already apparent in the 1930s. One small but revealing illustration came in conversations between a group of French-Canadian Catholic nationalist reformers and Anglo members of the CCF in 1938 and 1939. The groups differed over the national question and the role of the federal government, but also, at a deeper level, over any notion of distributive justice.[108] Following a talk that F.-A. Angers gave to members of the League for Social Reconstruction (LSR), Frank Scott wrote to Angers in October 1939. Scott, still hoping for common ground, noted apparent differences between the LSR and the French-Canadian reformers, especially on social issues. Economic inequities, not surprisingly, were central to his social analysis: "Human suffering, malnutrition, bad housing, and lack of leisure are inexcusable" and "most unjust" when they co-exist with "the wealth of certain sections of our population." Mutual incomprehension began over the state: "Another point that surprised many of our members was your attitude toward social legislation and the State. You seemed afraid of both." And in this context Scott stated the CCF position as a matter of ethics. "You left the impression that there was a superior ethical value in administration by the family or private agency over administration by the public body. Just why this superiority exists is not clear to people of our way of thinking."

In his six-page reply, Angers tried to articulate the ethical case for social security by non-state agents. But social Catholicism had given him a narrow theoretical base from which to respond, almost as though the primacy of the patriarchal family was self-evident, and so too the Catholic principle of subsidiarity – the smallest or least centralized competent authority should make social decisions. Quebecers did not support old-age pensions, said Angers, because they were demoralizing, diminishing the relevant authority – the family. Pensions subtracted from the debt that children owed to parents. Giving more power to the state risked giving politicians the power to bribe the electorate and to create dictatorship. The state must not become "the universal distributor of wealth" (a non sequitur, since neither Scott nor the CCF argued for such a role). Finally, Angers offered a confused, ambiguous dismissal of any laws that would increase workers' incomes: "I am not in principle opposed … to laws that would tend to increase the wages of workers, but I think that would be to start at the wrong end and be a disservice to the workers themselves." It was preferable – no hint why – that workers join cooperatives and use other means to cut their expenditures and increase their wages.[109] The solution to the problem of inequality therefore lay primarily with those in lower income groups. They should join co-ops, help to create corporations, and spend less money.

Such then was the distributive justice that flowed from the comprehensive critique that social Catholicism launched against the abuses of capitalism. There are lessons here for any serious effort to connect ethics to collective responsibility and action. Inequality is a collective or social condition; any set of remedies is necessarily collective, so must be applied through the institutions that society erects for collective ends. Many institutions may be necessary; but there is no solution that puts government at the margins of corrective action, for it was and remains the principal agent available to pursue common ends and able to realize them, including social justice. Any state action that responds to the problem of inequality contains a moral position at some level. It is equally true that any moral position on distributive justice that does not embrace state action is either inconsequential or an evasion of the moral position itself.

CHAPTER EIGHT

Idealism, Equality, and the End of Inequality
(1920–1945)

IDEALISM, PRAGMATISM, AND THE SELF

In the second quarter of the twentieth century philosophers in English Canada clung to an older idealism, even as its great British advocates left the scene.[1] The new analytic philosophy, variously embracing formal logic, analytical empiricism, mathematics, and eventually logical positivism, was slow to find followers in Canada. The small company of philosophers in the Dominion was a mixed lot, but many combined their idealism with a strong interest in pragmatism and a reading of the American pragmatists, including William James and John Dewey.[2] What emerged was a peculiarly Canadian pragmatic idealism: a tendency to shy away from large theoretical questions and to think instead about knowledge as practice, the operation of reason in the real world, and hence about the spread of rationality through education.[3]

These trends are important for the history of inequality. First, the boundaries between academic philosophy, reform activism, and politics were porous. In their study of Canadian philosophy before 1950, Leslie Armour and Elizabeth Trott point out that many practitioners were influential: they appeared on public platforms and in educational or service roles. More deeply, they reflected changes that were occurring in the society around them. Very often women and men who had read little or no philosophy debated serious philosophical issues in public, without realizing that they were doing so.[4] The movement in philosophy from absolute idealism to practical utilitarianism and pragmatism had its analogue in public discussions of rights, freedom, education, the role of the state, and much

more. The movement took Canadians towards a reformed liberalism, a new egalitarianism, and the welfare state. In this transition,
in the mutation and narrowing of the older idealism, the problem of
inequality came to an end.

To sustain this claim requires that we trace a circuitous and uneven
path of change that involved many actors. Philosophers, economists,
journalists, democratic socialists, and politicians all have a place in
the story. We tread on some well-covered ground, especially when
encountering the origins of social welfare.[5] The path is one where
ideas responded to material events and especially to the crucible of
two world wars and a deep crisis in capitalism. The wars challenged
notional separations of the individual, free-floating self and community. The first helped to shatter idealist beliefs in progress and in the
reconciliation of reason and religion. It became more difficult to see
social salvation as immanent; hope for the future must rest therefore
on incremental remedy and on practical and feasible antidotes – the
small victories of practical religion. The Depression of the 1930s also
encouraged a retreat from absolute idealism. It opened the door to
radical and revolutionary threats that Christian, conservative, and liberal thinkers struggled anew to contain. Containment was urgent, and
evolutionary progress, however real, was neither sure nor prompt.
Even where religion was the primary source of social inspiration, it
must be directed towards the practical and even the technical.

A further dimension of change, occurring in the intersection
of material and intellectual, was the more informed reckoning of
philosophers and theologians with the implications of industrial
capitalism and its class relations. Nineteenth-century pieties no longer sufficed. The "industrial revolution," the ubiquitous "machine,"
and industrial mammonism had transformed Canada. Divine providence was not going to be fully realized in a deeply flawed social
order subject to dangerous pathologies. It would not be easy to tame
the industrial beast, or even to contain it. In these contexts philosophers were bellwethers of change: they reacted directly to social and
economic conditions, and they led a broad transition from absolute
idealism to pragmatism.

Philosophers repeated the older idea of inequality – except that
it was no longer a paradox, an anomaly to remove in a sweeping
social restoration of natural order. Inequality came to be seen as
a malaise, a chronic social distemper that practitioners of social
health could treat. It was "an increased power to make profits for a

few individuals." "Society as we have known it reeks with inequalities."[6] "Economic inequality ... is the root of many social evils at the
present time," said Henry Wilkes Wright in 1925[7]; note, it is not a
structural anomaly. It was possible to treat the social evils without
extracting the root. Any one industry, said Wilfred Currier Keirstead,
could reap "larger gains" for a capitalist through exploitation; but
this was merely one of the "defects" of industry, not a structural condition.[8] Keirstead did not condemn inequality in toto – he wanted
a "removal" of specific inequalities "which arise from class restrictions and discriminations."[9] It followed, in his thinking, that "a more
just distribution of income" was merely one of a series of reforms
that a healthy democracy must pursue, along with "more planning
in production," reducing unemployment, conserving resources, and
eliminating "gambling in industry."[10]

A mixing of idealism and pragmatism turned philosophers away
from the great structural-historical paradox of inequality to a
non-structural issue – the individual and society. Of course this relationship had preoccupied social gospellers. But the philosophers of the
second quarter of the century were groping towards a new conception
of personality and the self. Briefly, they no longer saw individuals as
containing varying quantities of sin and virtue; the self was no longer something we were born with, possessing varying capacities for
improvement by experience or environment. Instead, philosophers
were struggling with the notion that the individual had an identity or
personality that was made reflexively. The self was not simply a set of
traits or observable characteristics; it was not what a person inherited
and contained. It was a being in constant thoughtful interaction with
a mediating world.[11] At the simplest level, we see philosophers puzzling over the relation between individual and community.

Reciprocal influences no longer shaped that relationship. The
social gospellers of the early twentieth century said: the miserable
conditions of the urban environment prevented moral improvement.
But this was to see the individual and the environment as autonomous entities that affected each other. W.C. Keirstead wrote: "The
individual and society as independent entities are fictions. Individuals
are as inextricably a part of society as any organ is of the body."[12]
Even this analogy did not satisfy everyone. Philosopher John Line
argued that the individual's relation to society was not that of a part
to the whole; the self was instead a being within a whole. "If he is
conscious of the social whole, he is also self-conscious."[13] The self

was the centre of "all conscious activity" – it was conscious activity
not in isolation but in association with others.[14] Gregory Vlastos
insisted that "the problem of personality is essentially a social problem": it was only within social relations that the individual became a
person.[15] In 1936 Rupert Lodge linked pragmatism to a new understanding of "the transient nature of the persona" and of "the power
of consciousness."[16]

This conception of self was a new way of denying laissez-faire
and the conception of "economic man" that underpinned it. Homo
economicus was a self-reliant accumulator moved by self-interest.
This, said Line, was a "static view of the self," "built on a substrate
of self-interest"; our modern view held the self to be a dynamic and
interactive "complex of possibilities," which could be either altruis-
tic or egoistic depending on tractable circumstances.[17] Vlastos saw a
direct link between inequality (understood as relative material deprivation), community, and personality: in a community – for example,
of workers – thwarted personalities were able to press for "a greater
share" of those material advantages "which are the conditions of
the spiritual values of personality." The "co-operative community"
was not, as in fascism, a "mystic unity of the whole"; nor was it
merely an ethical ideal to proclaim from pulpits. It was practical
action, said Vlastos – "a progressive discipline of interdependence
and co-operation."[18]

The malleable, reflexive self existed not in relation to society but
within community. This concept of self was inherently pragmatist. It
no longer made sense to reconstruct society according to some transcendent ideal, and thereby to liberate individuals from the conditions
of misery.[19] To confine thought and preaching to "general truths," said
Keirstead, would be "to furnish no insight into new problems." "For
when general truths or values are presented in a detached and abstract
manner, they are generally assented to, because they mean everything
in general and nothing in particular and lead to no definite and positive action." Instead the analyst must attend to actual ends and means
in the ordinary business of life and work, because "the moral virtues
were but the habits and ways of action" that we use to achieve specific
satisfactions. Even the minister of religion, said Keirstead, must be
an applied social scientist, interpreting the "ethical significance of the
economic life … through an earnest, careful, and intimate study of the
economic processes about him as interpreted by a knowledge of the
principles of economics and sociology."[20]

There was a direct connection between such concepts of the self and education. The school curriculum was a "medium," said Rupert Lodge, through which the student "may succeed in realizing his self."[21] Lodge proceeded to erect a philosophy of education on his concept of the social self and his integration of idealism and pragmatism. He was not alone: Canadian philosophers were pioneer theorists of education, and also of the emerging field of psychology.[22] Psychology itself was a pragmatist discipline. Was "serving the good of others" – the realization of social good – a utopian dream? No, said John Line: "Psychology now testifies to its practicability."[23] The mistake of previous philosophers, said Line, was "not in their particular representation of human nature but in their conceiving it to be morally anything at all as fixed or given." Psychology has made it clear – Line was quoting the American philosopher Wilbur Marshall Urban – that the human person was as much an altruist as an egoist.[24]

And so the problem of distribution – how to achieve "a more equitable share" – moved towards secular and pragmatic remedy. In the words of Henry Wilkes Wright, equitable share depended on "the growth of public spirit" and "the experience of the individual" – and these were "primarily a matter of education." The possibility of finding a solution in human nature, he said, depended on "the efficacy of our systems of general education."[25] For this grand agenda to succeed, education must be universal and open to everyone. And so Canadian philosophers followed John Dewey towards the great egalitarian claim for education – equality of opportunity.

We can see the connection between these developments and the changing conception of inequality perhaps most clearly in John Line, who taught at Victoria College, Toronto. Line was well aware of the "colossal inequalities" of the industrial era, although he did not frame the problem as a paradox. On the contrary, the modern problem of inequality emerged logically, he said, from the fate of "the eighteenth-century trilogy of liberty, equality, and fraternity."[26] The industrial revolution, he argued, privileged liberty above the other two ideals. The image of the individual as an egoistical accumulator whose freedom of action needed maximizing became enormously powerful. It overwhelmed the ideal of equality to such an extent that equality and individualism seemed to oppose each other. This set the individual loose to reap gains with a minimum of moral or legal constraint; the stronger used their initial superiority to acquire more, and the cumulative result over time was a "race of possessors" confronting a greater number of dispossessed.

Since inequality originated in a "false philosophy" that started with Bentham and Ricardo, the solution required a renovated liberalism. We must learn, said Line, from Rousseau's appreciation that the individual, and individual rights, rested on a doctrine of equality. It no longer made sense, he said, to see liberty as consisting of "a maximum of non-interference at the hands of others." Rather it meant that the individual functioned freely "to fulfill the ends of his being ... within a field of relations with others through which he contributes to communal self-fulfilment." Line was conjoining liberty, equality, and fraternity (community): "Equality and fraternity are not collateral with liberty but are components of it."[27] Equality was, he announced, essential to liberty. Line was not alone. In 1935 a history lecturer at Winnipeg's Wesley College, J.W. Pickersgill – later a prominent Liberal politician – argued that "nineteenth century Liberalism is dead," that liberty had given rise to "glaring economic inequalities" and plutocracy, and that equality was a core element of true liberalism.[28]

Canadian philosophers did not proceed to develop a theory of distributive justice. They may not have been aware of the axioms of distributive justice proposed by thinkers as various as Dalton, Hobhouse, Pareto, and Pigou.[29] Nor did they develop a systematic justification for social security. Nevertheless, the idealist-pragmatist strands of thought, which I summarize here, had analogues in wider political discourse. Philosophers in Canada were helping to create intellectual underpinnings for a widening acceptance of state-sponsored social security. The process began with a reframing of inequality. Inequality had become plural – a series of flaws or defects in an economy too long governed by outdated liberal principles.

There were practical remedies that could reconcile individual and community, liberty and equality. The ones that worked were those that gave opportunity to the self-reflexive, educatable individual. The answer to inequality therefore was "a universal diffusion of welfare" (Line)[30]; the provision of "material conditions of social welfare" (Wright)[31]; reduction of "dire poverty" through the guarantee of "minimum supply" or "secure supply" (Eric Havelock)[32]; "the guarantee of at least a minimum level of security" (J. King Gordon)[33]; "greater equality of opportunity for self-realization" through "social welfare" and "a minimum standard of well-being" (W.C. Keirstead).[34] John Macdonald believed that democracy had already made a beginning "in removing the grotesque discrepancies of income to be found in it"; the solution, he argued, was to guarantee educational opportunity and "economic security."[35] The coming welfare state already existed in the mental world of the philosophical pragmatist, and in the pragmatist's reworking of the problem of inequality.[36]

POLITICAL ECONOMY AND SCIENTIFIC POSITIVISM

Philosophers were not alone in these new liberal articulations, of course. It is remarkable, however, that they were in the forefront of thinking about social questions. The growing separation between philosophy and political economy was obvious (although there were those, such as Keirstead, who stood in both fields). But where were Frank Underhill's "garage mechanics"? The answer is that they had embarked on their own retreat from idealism. The acceptance of neoclassical economics remained slow, as did the impact of recent and current work by welfare economists and Keynes.

Nevertheless, a scientific positivism began to soften and eventually to silence the Christian humanist critique.[37] This positivism, which eventually turned mainstream economics into a form of applied mathematics, had enormous analytical power, but it came at a cost: an increasingly sophisticated dissection of macro- and micro-economic trends – the world as it is (or at least as statistical models represented it) took priority over the world as it might be, leaving little room for prescriptive modelling that used explicit articulations of social justice or equity.[38]

Two economists represent the beginnings of this transition: Ralph Evans Freeman (1894–1967), who taught at Western Ontario, and Duncan Alexander MacGibbon (1882–1969), an economics professor who became a senior civil servant.[39] Freeman's textbook *Economics for Canadians* (1928) introduced marginal utility, supply and demand, business cycles, and markets, with Canadian examples. The "marginal productivity theory of wages" appeared as a theory of long-run trends. "The factor of scarcity, whatever may be the cause, is the chief factor determining the price of labor. High wages come to a man chiefly because he is different from other people."[40] Yet the progressive and humanist moral vision was still present. It qualified

Table 1 | Number of individuals by size of income and amount of taxes paid under the Dominion Income Tax Act, fiscal year ended 31 March 1926

Income Class	Number	Amount
1,000 to 6,000	115,758	$2,836,490
2,000 to 6,000	76,687	$3,137,247
6,000 to 10,000	10,250	$2,888,189
10,000 to 20,000	4,976	$4,417,916
20,000 to 30,000	1,009	$2,433,720
30,000 and over	859	$8,252,215

Source: Ralph Evans Freeman, *Economics for Canadians*
(Toronto: Pitman and Sons, 1928), 237.

the theory of wage determination and allowed for "economic diseases and remedies," as well as "the problem of inequality."[41] "The unequal distribution of wealth is rightly condemned by economists and social philosophers."[42] Freeman used tax data to give his readers one of the first published tables on the distribution of incomes in Canada (Table 1).[43] Note, however, that he did not proceed to offer the key estimate of inequality: the percentage of total incomes accruing to each of his six income classes.

And what of Freeman's remedies? Instead of a manifesto for social justice, he articulated arguments against the redistribution of wealth that would reappear in every generation into the twenty-first century. The profit motive and the "lure of gain" were engines of growth, and "we cannot afford to weaken these incentives." Furthermore, we must not exaggerate the gains from redistributing income away from the "idle rich" (no doubt a conscious borrowing of Leacock's words). "Distribute the total income of the country equally amongst all the people, and the net gain to the poor might suffice to raise their incomes by 20 or 30 per cent." (What breathtaking myopia: at living standards below subsistence level, such a percentage gain would have been enormous). Better to "eliminat[e] waste" and increase productivity – "enlarging the product obtainable with a given expenditure of natural and human energy."[44] Freeman allowed for positive action by the state and for progressive taxation, but not for income redistribution: "It is not to be supposed that these activities are undertaken by the state with the conscious purpose of equalizing incomes."[45] Positivist economics had given its answer to Stephen Leacock and Robert MacIver.

The tension between neoclassical economics and the moral problem of inequality – and the resulting confusion – was even more evident in another 1920s' Canadian textbook.[46] Duncan MacGibbon's *Introduction to Economics* contained no moral critique of the new economics. It offered a secular account of the operation of markets, manufacturing industry, financial institutions, banking, transportation, and public finance. The deep historical perspective dear to Innis and others was missing.[47]

Production and distribution were two major sub-topics. Chapter 16 introduced "The Problem of Distribution" – the problem was not moral or social, however, but empirical: "What proportion of this fund of finished goods, available for consumption, is to be obtained by each individual who has contributed to its production?"[48] The issue resolved itself into one of pecuniary reward: "How much money should each receive in return for his services?" MacGibbon answered by reference to the market value of labour, "enterprise," or "service" – and his answer implied rejection of Mill's separation of distribution from production. "Whether the share will be large or small is determined by the value placed upon the services rendered." The "size of the reward" depended on the supply and demand for each human agent in the production process.[49] Unskilled labour was much in demand, but supply was substantial, because it required only strength and endurance rather than high intelligence or lengthy training. Since the supply was large, wages were low.[50]

In this framework, income or wealth inequality did not appear even in the context of distribution. A secular positivism was erasing the moral vision of both Leacock and Ralph Evans Freeman. Nevertheless, echoes of a Christian humanism surfaced, and when they did, they sat uncomfortably beside the detached analysis of distribution. The result was a tension, if not a contradiction. MacGibbon had an undeveloped concept of fairness – of just reward – and of its opposite, "unjust discrimination" (which he applied to railway freight rates).[51] Competition was a "ruling force," but it was, and should be, "regulated in the interests of fair play and social stability."[52] There was such a thing as a "fair wage," not determined by market forces alone. The empirical "is" – reward is determined by market value of labour – instead became a morally imperative should: "While the principle that wages should be paid on the basis of the value of the services that the labourer performs is clear enough, the application of this principle raises all sorts of difficult questions."[53] For one thing, the value of unskilled labour was a function not of supply and demand alone, but also of how different classes of labour related and of how they acted collectively, and the implication was that these relationships too were not a function solely of supply and demand. "It is not possible to determine exactly how much value each factor contributes to the whole."[54] MacGibbon then rejected his own general rule of reward determination: "No general rule can be laid down."[55]

Moral considerations also led MacGibbon to separate distribution from production vis-à-vis the state's role. Government did not need to maximize wealth or respond to market forces, although it had a duty to nourish these. "The individual aims to accumulate wealth, the state aims to render service."[56] And in doing so, the authorities sought fairness, welfare, and "balance," which MacGibbon did not define. He stopped well short of any notion that the state should redistribute wealth. A "high standard of living" for individuals, as for nations, depended, in his view, on being thrifty and avoiding extravagant consumption.[57] In the end, market forces must somehow be subject to higher moral principles; how he did not say. MacGibbon ended with a moral assertion from Aristotle's *Politics*: "Happiness, whether consisting in pleasure or virtue or both, is more often found with those who are most highly cultivated in their mind and their character, and have only a moderate share of external goods, than among those who have external goods to a useless extent, but are deficient in higher qualities."[58] MacGibbon grasped the distinction between moderate and immoderate shares of wealth; he knew that "lust" for material gain led away from virtue. Yet neither his ethics nor his economics let him reconcile "fairness" with the economic theory that he applied to Canada.

The era of humanist economics in Canada wound down mid-century. Following Freeman and MacGibbon, the next major economics textbook was Vincent Bladen's in 1941, with reprints following through the 1940s and 1950s. There was an echo of the earlier era in

Bladen's admissions that the absence of full employment was a "failure of the individualistic order" and that "great inequality ... is in most systems of ethics always on the defensive."[59] But he closed the door on any moral stance of his own: "Our primary task is explanation, not justification or condemnation."[60] By the 1950s and 1960s, introductory economics courses in Canada were turning from Canadian textbooks to Paul Samuelson's *Economics: An Introductory Analysis* (1948), still in print today. The problem of inequality survived in Samuelson's secular progressivism. In the first edition he referred to "improper distribution of income" as one of the three main "evils" of our capitalist system.[61] By the fifth edition, these words had gone, but there was an extended discussion of inequality, including new measures of income distributions, Lorenz curves, and references to Simon Kuznets. The conclusion was optimistic: both poverty and inequality were declining before the ameliorative powers of economic growth and the welfare state.[62] Readers of Thomas Piketty may recall a cheeky remark: "We might say that [nineteenth-century] economists' no doubt overly developed taste for apocalyptic predictions gave way to a similarly excessive fondness for fairy tales, or at any rate happy endings."[63]

By 1935 political economy in Canada had its scholarly journal – the *Canadian Journal of Economics and Political Science*. The journal tried to keep its readers abreast of developments elsewhere, and by 1937 one could even read about Keynes.[64] Inequality surfaced rarely, referencing subjects such as regional disparities or price spreads rather than national-level income distributions in Canada. Economists knew about Canadian tax data but ignored the opportunity they offered. The first appearance of the Gini coefficient was in 1954: the article, by a Californian, was about the inequality of prize distribution in lotteries.[65]

THE MORAL IMPERATIVES OF
DEMOCRATIC SOCIALISM

The intellectual burial of inequality in Canadian economics did not go unchallenged. As all Canadian historians know, there was a loud voice from within the economics professoriate that sustained an older idealism and Christian activism well into the twentieth century. Eugene Forsey was a lecturer in political economy at McGill from 1929 to 1941. What set him apart from so many of his contemporaries in political economy? In Forsey we find a rare, perhaps unique combination of interests and influences. A student of Stephen Leacock, he began by supporting "Tory democracy." He lived in Montreal and had personal knowledge of its class divisions; he observed the city's working class and studied its trade unions; in Nova Scotia he studied mining and labour relations; he absorbed John Watson's philosophy into his own uncompromising Christian idealism; he was suspicious of the empirical "relativism of the social sciences." All of this put him on a trajectory very different from that of most other economists. And then he went to Oxford – not Chicago. There he was influenced by the Fabian moral philosopher and activist A.D. Lindsay and by other followers of T.H. Green and Edward Caird, and he joined the Oxford Labour Club. He met G.D.H. Cole and absorbed his ideas on industrial democracy.[66]

More than any other Canadian writer, Eugene Forsey sustained a focus on the problem of inequality through the second quarter of the century. As Frank Milligan argues, Forsey's "major goal" through the Depression was to define inequalities, to "identify the mechanisms by which the 'vested interests' shaped the policies that produced those inequalities, and recommend how the system could be improved to eradicate, or at least minimize, those inequalities."[67] Forsey's analysis was a complex compound of Protestant activism, British idealism, materialism, and a very Canadian class analysis.

Forsey said that he rejected idealism in favour of materialism: "We cannot start from a mental picture of the kind of world we should like to live in and then try to mould the real world into a likeness of that idea ... We must start from the world as it really is."[68] Milligan tends to take Forsey at his word, especially when the latter insisted that he was not imposing an ethical judgment on capitalism but presenting "fact."[69] But we need to read Forsey's statements in context. And in our own time, when philosophers debate concepts such as transcendental materialism, we know that the relationship between idealism and materialism is not immediately transparent and not always simply dichotomous.[70] In Forsey's case, a durable idealism informed his materialism. Having disclaimed ethical judgment, he proceeded to imagine contemporary capitalism "from a Christian point of view." Capitalism, he said, had its own "beatitudes." To these he counterposed those of Jesus. His reading of capitalism was a blend of what ought to be (or ought not to be) and what was: "appalling waste"; monopoly capitalism as "the dilemma of profits or plenty"; "minority control" that subverted individual proprietorship; "irresponsible oligarchy"; absence of responsibility to the community; and price manipulation that robbed both workers and consumers.[71]

Forsey's answer to the problem of inequality came in two parts. First, he clearly equated capitalist exploitation with inequality. "Exploitation is not an excrescence on capitalism. It is capitalism." His next sentence was: "The truth is that rich and poor, secure and insecure, do not really belong to the same community at all."[72] In this thinking, class and inequality were not cause and effect: they were conjoined conditions. In Forsey's socialism, private property "in the means of production" must end: "Only the capture of political power and the transfer to the state of at least the main industries and services now in capitalist hands can bring in the new economic order."[73]

The second part of Forsey's answer, not inconsistent with the first, was gradualist. The socializing of industries, though necessary, could not occur "overnight"; it did not mean "confiscation" or nationalization of land. For industry it would occur through "prudent investment" by the state, financed by steeply graduated income taxes and inheritance taxes. There was no reason, he said, to deprive children, the aged, and the disabled of any "reasonable security" that capitalism might give them.[74] He did not elaborate a theory of historical change leading to socialism.[75] This was Canadian democratic socialism, and it had much of Mill, something of Marx, and plenty of a Protestant ideal popular in the 1930s – "Christian fellowship in community."[76] In this sometimes-awkward harmony of traditions, the problem of inequality lived on.

Eugene Forsey was hardly alone in bearing an older idealism and its moral imperatives into the second quarter of the century. He shared a common pattern with his collaborators: the lasting influence of a Protestant church-going childhood; studies at Oxford and exposure to latter-day Oxford idealists; the reading of R.H. Tawney and G.D.H. Cole; and association with Christian socialists.[77] The League for Social Reconstruction was one of Forsey's many homes. Often referred to as a Canadian version of the Fabian Society, despite notable differences, the LSR criticized the churches for becoming "middle class," for succumbing to the spirit of capitalism, and for losing contact with workers.

The LSR was resolutely idealist in its moral imperatives and its commitment to social engineering. As James Naylor has argued, it was a distinctly "non-proletarian" assembly that remained distant from the working-class interests the earlier labour parties had espoused.[78] The Protestant critique of wealth was alive and well here, and so was a nineteenth-century term – privilege: "The great condemnation of our system," said *Social Planning for Canada* (1935), "is that it makes an interest in 'things' the major interest to the almost complete exclusion of an interest in values. The basis of privilege is wealth, the creed of privilege is a belief in the making of money. The measure of human achievement is a monetary yardstick. This philosophy of acquisition renders impotent the finer impulses."[79] Christian teaching, said the LSR, inculcated social justice: throughout capitalism's development "prophetic voices have been raised in the name of a high ethical religion against some of the more flagrant forms of social injustice."[80]

The LSR's analysis of the Canadian economy rested on two related assumptions. First, "the present economic order is unjust, cruel, wasteful, and inefficient." Second, it was "the legacy of an unplanned, haphazard expansion by and for private enterprise."[81] These were ethical judgments: privilege – the unearned advantage of wealth – was injustice, and waste was a sin against providence and against honest labour. Inequality was central to this ethical economics: maldistribution of income was an "essential" defect – part of "the nature of our economy." The old paradox was intact: "Paradoxically the creation of plenty has brought forth calamitous scarcity."[82] It long preceded the Depression. But there was something new in the 1930s. The ethical indictment came from intellectuals who sought the support of social science. The LSR idealists were empiricists.[83] They knew that censuses and income taxes had created repositories of evidence that could prove the extent of injustice. The failure of the federal government to display the evidence became part of the LSR's ethical critique: "There seems to be a concern on the part of our federal authorities to protect the humble and God-fearing members of our society against the vulgar display of the wealth of its privileged group."

The LSR put the evil of "maldistribution" into two tables in *Social Planning for Canada* – four decades after U.S. scholars had produced similar data. The number of income earners and the percentage of all income earners at different income levels, and the percentage of total income earned at each level, all constituted ethical statements. "56.2% of Canadian income receivers have incomes of less than $1,000 a year, and their total incomes constitute only a fourth of the total." "20% of the income receivers secure almost half of the total national income." And another bit of evidence: in 1929 the 1,646 individuals earning the most received more than all the 105,504 workers in Canada's textile industry.[84] The estimates were crude, and they certainly understated the share of top income groups in the total national income. Nevertheless, the LSR had added a new empirical dimension to the problem of inequality.

The path of redemption would lead to centralized planning, and also to an array of social-democratic reforms – a mix of public ownership, new labour codes, public health services, and much more. But something major was happening to the problem of inequality. Displaying it empirically as never before also diminished it. Neither the LSR nor the emerging Co-operative Commonwealth Federation (CCF) moved from inequality to a theory of distributive justice (and neither did Social Credit, within its different ethical and economic trajectory).[85] They knew that existing levels of maldistribution were evil. But what did the LSR mean by "an approximate economic equality among all men"? – a phrase from its 1932 *Manifesto* that reappeared in its *Democracy Needs Socialism* (1938).[86] Its answer was "fair differentials" within a narrow range, but only for salaries and wages, and it offered no supporting theory of distributive justice. The LSR did not discuss redistribution of income or wealth: the word "redistribution" appeared only twice in *Social Planning for Canada* (1935), and not referring to vertical redistribution.[87]

The LSR's answer to inequality turned instead towards absolute, not relative poverty and "standards of living." Again the empiricist impulse. From the census, the LSR gave the percentage of male and female wage earners above and below specific levels of annual earnings, and the minimal family budgets from the Department of Labour. The conclusion? In 1930 "the majority of Canadian families ... were living below the bare standard of decent livelihood," and low-income earners needed at least 50 per cent more.[88] The LSR was giving its answer to inequality: not redistribution, but "the achievement of economic security, possession of the means of participation in the material advantages of an advanced industrial society," and "freedom from the threat of poverty."[89] Probably most Canadian social democrats had read R.H. Tawney's influential book *Equality* (1930) but had skipped over the sections on "the means of redistribution." Nothing in the writings of Canadian philosophers gave them any assistance, and most of the work by

Canadian economists was either irrelevant or positivist apologia for inequality.

There was, however, another answer to the problem of inequality in the LSR's two books, and it had clear affinities with what philosophers were saying. They rejected the idea of homo economicus, the individual as maximizer of utility. They saw the individual as self-reflexive and educatable, a person in quest of "the fulfilment of human personality."[90] Extreme material inequality, when it led to debilitating poverty, aborted this quest. Hence the LSR's repeated invocation of "self-sufficiency." The solution therefore was equality – a more equal distribution of the conditions people needed to realize personhood. And that meant specific types of equality, including especially the extension of equal rights within the realm of industry, and equality of opportunity. The LSR writers were seeking to revive "the lingering democratic predisposition in favour of equality," to "make democracy effective" through "greater equality of opportunity."[91] For all their emphasis on socialism, they were part of the wider elevation of equality in liberal political culture in the second quarter of the twentieth century.

THE WARTIME RHETORIC OF EQUALITY

The 1940s saw a rhetorical surge in references to "equality," in British English, in American English, and in Canadian journalism (I draw here especially on Toronto's *Globe and Mail* newspaper between the 1910s and 1950s). "Inequality" also increased in frequency, but not so much. The *Globe and Mail* shows us contexts that gave "equality" meaning and normative currency.[92] Such language appeared in many subject areas where writers felt that individual freedom and self-realization required a new equality of rights or of condition. Such usage also reflected what some have called a new political modernity: the gradual acceptance, crossing ideological lines, that every individual is part of a community and has an obligation to it.

Pierre Rosanvallon sees the First World War as a "turning point in democratic modernity." The conflict universalized the idea of social debt to community and thereby restored an older idea of equality: the war, like a battle, was equal for all citizens and spared no one.[93] Although Canada's mobilization may not have been as total as Europe's, the world wars reconfigured collective obligation and sharpened awareness of departures from it. "The rich ... should give to such an extent that it will hurt": as David Tough argues, despite partisan differences, a shared understanding grounded the demand that everyone should sacrifice and that some were able to do more than others, especially if they were not risking death.[94] Specific forms of equality expressed the demand: equality of sacrifice, of service, of responsibility, of effort. Military conscription, conscription of wealth, the inequalities of war finance, the new war income tax – these and other issues fuelled the rhetoric of equality.[95]

By the early 1940s, when wartime mobilization and centralized planning attained unprecedented levels, the rhetoric of collective obligation and equality transformed political discourse. "Equality of service and sacrifice in times of great national emergency" became a popular common sense.[96] It was easy to accept that citizens, women and men, could serve in different ways. But was it fair that some of them give more than others? "Equality of service" answered the question by saying that justice, or fairness, required roughly comparable sacrifice or comparable burden. As a principle of justice, however, equality posed an obvious problem: how did one compare one service or sacrifice with another? Some people were willing to offer the ultimate sacrifice of life itself, and no contribution of labour or money was comparable to death. "Equality of sacrifice" was impossible in wartime, Canadian War Services Minister J.T. Thorson concluded; but he was whistling vainly into the gale.[97] A commonplace solution was the principle of service according to capacity or ability. Those who had the capacity to fight would offer that capacity; those who had great wealth would contribute a large share of that wealth. The slogan was "Let him pay who can."[98]

For some observers, and especially for organized labour, that meant conscription of wealth or conscription of capital from the rich. In rejecting that idea, the federal government followed a different principle: "equality of sacrifice on the basis of ability to pay."[99] This principle served to cloak a huge expansion of the taxpayer population within a principle of equity. "We tax higher incomes more heavily than lower incomes," Finance Minister J.L. Ilsley told the Trades and Labor Congress.[100] He also noted that by 1941–42 the excess-profits tax was generating more revenue than the income tax.[101] Price controls also served the claim to equality: they would protect workers and farmers against rising costs of living and against "an unfair distribution of the costs of the war."[102] Such claims merely invited counterclaims. Wartime wage controls fuelled controversy around the meaning of equality, when Ottawa limited wage increases to the removal of "gross inequalities or injustices."[103] Labour leaders accepted the invitation and brought forth a host of inequalities and injustices.

In deploying the motif of equality, the government was amplifying a popular wartime theme. The motif spread.[104] Rationing became a question of equality of distribution and of treatment. In the name of "equality between all classes in our community" ration books must be the same for all citizens.[105] Equality was demanded in the distribution of canned vegetables and of sugar for canning purposes.[106] The contributions of soldiers and their dependants led to an array of appeals for equal treatment. "Inequalities" in gratuities for widows of soldiers violated the doctrine of equality of sacrifice.[107] Where women accepted equal responsibility for participation in the services, there must be "equality of pensions."[108] Occasionally pensions and dependants' allowances prompted serious ethical debate. Should the same allowance go to all dependants of servicemen – the same reward for the same sacrifice? Or should the amount depend on their level of pre-enlistment support?[109] And what about compensating for war damage to residences? The war-insurance bill provided none if the amount was less than fifty dollars: surely this introduced a new "inequality," since owners of small homes would get nothing, whereas those with big houses would get full compensation.[110]

What about disabled soldiers? Did "equal treatment" mean that pensions should figure in only the length of their service, or the length of treatment they required for the disability?[111] The power of the principle became clear in a government decision on repatriating the bodies of dead soldiers. The Imperial War Graves Commission received requests from families who were willing to pay the costs. The equality principle took precedence: "Private repatriation of a few individuals who could afford the cost would be contrary to that equality of treatment which is the underlying principle of the commission's work."[112]

With the expansion of taxation systems in both world wars, especially in the second, consciousness of "inequalities" expanded and went beyond question of war-related taxation. Were the income-tax authorities giving equality of treatment to United Church ministers and Catholic priests?[113] Churches were exempt from property taxes; did equal treatment make people who rented property to churches also exempt?[114] Tax exemption for cooperatives was a monstrous "inequality," according to their business competitors.[115] The war tax on Ontario Hydro bills was an evident "inequality and unfairness," claimed one taxpayer.[116] Alleged inequalities in property assessments within urban places – and even among them – were a preoccupation, before and after the war. What accounted for the "inequality" between Montreal and Toronto's taxation of street tramways?[117]

Women's war efforts amplified the rhetoric, without leading to many egalitarian solutions. "Equality of status" and "equality of opportunity" for women were popular refrains.[118] Equal-sacrifice demands of "equal pay for equal work" extended far beyond war-related service.[119] The war saw, for instance, a new campaign for equal pay for women teachers. Vastly varying teachers' salaries became an issue during the war, as did women's right to continue teaching after marriage. Where husband and wife both worked, did equity require separate tax exemptions on each income or a single exemption based on the sum of both?[120]

There was scarcely a public issue in which equality was not in the foreground. It was rarely a formalized concept – rather a popular idiom or meme, a normative ideal assumed to be a positive social good that everybody shared. A consistent and coherent meaning was not available. Certain underlying assumptions were discernible. It extended beyond political rights and the law. It referred to a type of fairness – "equality of treatment." This usually implied sameness: one person or group should get the same deal as another. It also referred to opportunity: any group should have the same or similar chance to participate (most obviously, in education). Equality of sacrifice during the war must, many people said, lead to equal opportunity after it ended. Occasionally we can detect an awareness that equal treatment did not always require sameness. It might mean difference of treatment – as when the state accorded special protection to specific groups or units (separate schools, distinct language communities).[121]

Equality was understood to be consistent with – even a pre-condition for – individual freedom. To realize one's identity as an individual required, for instance, access to education – hence equal opportunity in schooling. Thus the "equality" discourse increasingly moved away from the goal of reducing income or wealth differentials. It could even be a way of sanctioning inequality. Once equal opportunity came about, or appeared to, then any inequalities that remained were the consequence of innate natural differences in ability, differences in effort, or choice.

"Equality of treatment" severely reduced the meaning of equality and of its absence, inequality. The principle referred to a fairness between two comparable entities that stood within the same horizontal sphere. It made no sense to call for equal treatment between fish-plant workers and orchestra musicians; it did make sense to demand equal wage rates for meat packers in Ontario and their counterparts in Quebec.[122] Substantial differences in pay between two such comparable groups could be seen as "inequality" and hence unjust – different rewards for the same labour.

Reducing inequality to such horizontal disparities downplayed vertical inequalities. Such obvious corollaries of the evolving discourse appear to have evaded notice, even among philosophers. The main point is this: even if all such horizontal disparities were removed, the effect on vertical income inequality could be non-existent or even negative (since equality could be achieved by setting all wage rates at the level of the lowest unit).

The popular formulations also ignored the question of what was being equalized, other than opportunity or wage rates. Take the example of meat packers. Let us suppose that their wage rates were standardized for each job classification across the country. Obviously that outcome could leave them all unequal to workers in most other occupations. Moreover, wage rates were not the only pertinent measure. We cannot assume that different categories of worker placed equal value on the same marginal increase in wages, or that they all had the same utility functions or preferences (British economists had made the point decades earlier). How did meat packers perceive themselves? They might have wage rates similar to janitorial workers; their assessment of the social value of their labour might lead them to demand the wage levels of railway engineers. In this case inequality would not disappear until the subjective levels of satisfaction – and even of status – of different classes of worker were equal. A serious discussion of equality claims – and hence of inequality – required a discussion of what to equalize.

Furthermore, was personal utility or satisfaction the appropriate measure? What of higher social goods or values? Heroin addicts and thieves' utility functions differ greatly from those of teachers and nurses; does equality mean equalizing the marginal utilities of all? If utility is not a good measure of equality, or the reduction of inequality, then what principle of distributive justice does society want to share and to apply? In so far as the wartime rhetoric of equality contained a principle of distributive justice, it was a secular principle of universal entitlement to minimal subsistence, or satisfaction of "want." References to scriptural authority were infrequent. When they did appear, they did not cite the older sanctions against wealth ("It is easier for a camel to pass through the eye of a needle …"). Instead we read a command that linked equality to reciprocal obligation and supply of want: "But by an equality, that now at this time your abundance may be a supply for their want, that their abundance also may be a supply for your want: that there may be an equality" (2 Corinthians 8:14).[123]

It would be ahistorical to expect any Canadian in the 1940s to anticipate philosophers' arguments about distributive justice several decades later. Nevertheless, it was easy for contemporaries to see a problem with the older labour theory of value and its derivatives – and these were still present in the 1940s, especially in labour circles. Should rewards be commensurate with labour and effort? Or should simply being a citizen, or a human being, justify a minimal living standard?[124] The principle of equality of opportunity invited similar questions. If vast inequalities persisted even alongside equal opportunity, and reflected differences in talent and ability, was that justice at all? It was no fault of some people that they were born with lesser abilities. Why should they be poor? Such were the problems that were evaded, both in popular discourse and in Canadian philosophy (and, needless to say, in Canadian economics). The Canadian conversation rarely went beyond the simple axioms – equality of treatment, of sacrifice, and of opportunity.

So powerful was the rhetoric of equality that it was easy to draw the conclusion that equality had already arrived in Canada. "Canada's development has been on a sound democratic basis with equality of opportunity," declared the president of the Toronto Board of Trade in October 1942.[125] Trade unions already had enormous power and "the tyranny of numbers."[126] We are on "the path of equality" Prime Minister King told the American Federation of Labor in 1942: and he explicitly connected freedom, equality, and "social security."[127] This trifecta was the perfect answer to communists and their fellow travellers. They and socialists claimed to know the path to equality; but "the Canadian way of life has already been based on economic and social equality."[128]

Equality, in all its perverse elasticity and ambiguity, was central to Canadian liberal thought by the second quarter of the century, if not before. Much more could be said about the discourse and about its cultural and political reverberations. It was certainly fundamental to social security and, most clearly, to the debates over family allowances. The ideological barriers to the latter were high, even in 1944. A generation earlier, such a universal transfer, seeming to shift responsibility from the individual and the family to the state, would have been highly improbable. It would not have been acceptable to a federal government, to Parliament, or to large sections of the media and the public, in the absence of a powerful ideological and rhetorical rationale. Equality, especially of opportunity, emerged as central to that rationale during the war. It became a common sense, a shared perception of moral right, that so many held so deeply as to require no explanation. Challenged in cabinet, King insisted: "My Liberalism was based on getting for men equality of opportunity."[129] Family allowances were explicitly an answer to the problem of inequality, but in specific and narrow senses: they helped to reduce the effect of poverty on low-income families; they helped to equalize burdens of cost between large and small families.[130]

THE LIMITED DISTRIBUTIVE JUSTICE
OF SOCIAL SECURITY

The family-allowance debates highlighted another feature of Canadian liberalism by the 1940s. The ubiquitous equality discourse overwhelmed and stifled any politics of redistribution. There is more than one sense to the word "redistribution," of course. In the Canadian context it often referred to possible changes in the distribution of tax revenues between the federal government and provinces, and among provinces, and in this sense the word appeared frequently from the time of the Rowell-Sirois Commission (1937–40) to the tax-equalization agreements of the 1950s. This horizontal revenue distribution helped reduce economic disparities among provinces and in complex ways limited, if not reduced, vertical inequalities in income distribution. Redistribution may also refer to the movement of funds or tax benefits from one location or segment of the population to another. Thus the tax system collected revenues and disposed of them in specific ways, including transfers to corporations or to individuals. In this sense it was distributing or "redistributing" money, and this was happening in the 1940s.[131]

In the equality discourse surrounding family allowances, there was a remarkable absence. Canada's first universal security benefit did not evoke a discussion of redistribution – the net shift in resources or incomes from one income level to another, or from rich to poor. The word hardly ever appeared in the debates over family allowances. When it did, it was usually in the mouths of opponents, such as Charlotte Whitton. She argued that the benefit represented "redistribution of income on the crude basis of birth rate": the result, she said, would be "the economic and social submersion of British and Scandinavian stocks."[132] Critics were aware that family allowances differed from unemployment insurance or old-age pensions. Insurance schemes took funds from eventual beneficiaries and gave them back in time of need; old-age pensions were a type of saving, transferring spending power from recipients while young to when they were old. Family allowances, by contrast, did neither. They could be justified as a reward to parents for familial labour, but even so, they were unconditional transfers to all mothers.

The effect of social-welfare systems on income distributions is a complex subject. We need to separate the fledgling security provisions of the 1940s and 1950s from the larger and more complex tax and transfer systems that emerged later in the century. In the Canadian tax system as a whole, as it existed in the third quarter of the century, the incidence of taxation, including all indirect taxes, was quite even: all income categories paid roughly the same percentage of income in taxes.[133] The actual redistributive effects of the new family allowances, by themselves, were likely negligible, though impossible to estimate in 1944, given the underdeveloped state of Canadian income data.[134] It would have been easy to overestimate their redistributive effect.

Intention is different from effect, of course, and, remarkably, politicians justifying family allowances omitted "redistribute" and "redistribution" from their vocabulary – whether deliberately or unconsciously – perhaps hoping to reassure affluent voters that confiscatory or redistributive transfers from rich to poor were not on the agenda. There is a striking contrast with the United Kingdom, where redistribution was fully part of the rhetoric of postwar reconstruction.[135] As a writer in the *Canadian Journal of Economics and Political Science* perceptively observed in 1953, federal politicians rejected "the idea of vertical redistribution" through tax-funded welfare payments. They insisted that even family allowances respected the "universal contributory" principle. "Social security," said Prime Minister Louis St Laurent in 1952, "while desirable in itself, has to be paid for and must be proportionate to what is taken out of the pockets of those who benefit from it."[136] Keith Banting has concluded: "The primary goal of the postwar welfare state was less redistribution from rich to poor than economic security for the population as a whole."[137]

In March 1943 the Special Select Committee on Social Security of the House of Commons received Leonard Marsh's *Report on Social Security for Canada* – probably the pivotal document in the development of social welfare in Canada. Marsh had co-written the League for Social Reconstruction's *Social Planning for Canada* (1935), which placed the LSR *Manifesto* of 1932 within an analysis of "maldistribution" of incomes and the "privilege" of wealth. Marsh had also thoroughly surveyed the country's occupational structure: *Canadians In and Out of Work* (1940).[138]

His 1943 report – the major statement of progressive liberal thought on social security – was notable for what it said and for what it did not say. Maldistribution, inequality, and privilege were missing. Marsh gave four main reasons to extend social security: maintain purchasing power, stabilize the economy, equalize conditions between returning veterans and civilians, and provide "one of the things [social security] for which the peoples of the world are fighting."[139] He acknowledged that all social-insurance schemes involved "a redistribution of existing income" and that there might be a redistribution "to some extent from the wealthier to the poorer members of society," but this effect was not social security's major goal. It was strictly about providing a basic minimum of material security. "It would not be reasonable to expect a social insurance system to iron out all the inequalities of income distribution except so far as basic minima are concerned."[140] Marsh's blueprint for Canadian social security was an epitaph for the problem of inequality.

Fundamental to establishing social security was a broad strategy to stabilize society, contain socialism and communism, and ease class conflict. Such purposes are explicit in another wartime publication on the subject: Harry Cassidy's *Social Security and Reconstruction in Canada* (1943). Social services in wartime constituted "an indispensable element in the full mobilization of the nation." But social security had "broader implications," Cassidy argued. Poverty, insecurity, and lack of opportunity made possible the growth of both fascism and communism. In Canada the threat of "internal strife" would increase after the war, Cassidy feared: there was more expectation of security and "public fear of depression."[141] Unless Canada provided social security, it risked "resumption in more acute form of the social struggles of the 1930s, with the ever-present possibility that these conflicts will lead to violence."[142] The writer said little about taxation for the purpose, but proposed that "the prospective beneficiaries" should bear most of the costs. He was conflating social security and insurance. "Social insurance is not primarily a device for transferring income from the rich to the poor, although it may properly perform this function to some extent. Its great function is to spread income from gainful employment ... over the whole period of life."[143] Social security answered the problem of inequality by extinguishing it.

Social security and its great correlate, equal opportunity, were the ultimate expression of the marriage of idealism and pragmatism. Philosophy proposed the marriage, politics consummated it. This outcome occurred in a political economy undergoing slow and uneven industrial development in a predominantly rural and small-town archipelago, which dispersed equality and inequality and gave them a range of foci. By the 1940s, if not before, one could not predict, on hearing or reading the words "inequality" or "inequalities," the exact referent. The great issues of social justice and class relations became thoroughly enmeshed in the challenge of federal–provincial relations and the distribution of powers in a federation. In the 1940s, more urgently than ever before, equality and inequality also arose in the arena of gender and changes in the roles of women as citizens, workers, taxpayers, and marriage partners. The relationship between these and other inequalities and the vertical distribution of incomes and wealth attracted little examination.

This is not to deny the value or beneficial consequences of state-sponsored and state-legislated security and health systems. As an answer to the social problems and costs accompanying industrial-capitalist growth, they proved their value many times over, in Canada and elsewhere. They continue to demonstrate their worth as we observe the terrible costs of their erosion. The rise of inequality in recent decades correlates clearly with the weakening of the social-security and industrial-relations systems that emerged after 1945. A small victory over inequality had been won, and it was better than none at all. In a capitalist economy there is no complete solution to inequality; the small, tenuous remedy is precious.

While acknowledging these things, we need to remember that the material problem of inequality – the vast distances between the conditions of rich and poor – remained. Even mid-century – an era that some observers call the "great compression" – when income inequalities in Canada were much smaller than earlier in the century, and smaller than they are today, those inequalities remained extreme and remarkably rigid. While offering a modest protection to the disadvantaged, social-welfare systems did not solve the inequality problem, and it is not clear that they were even intended to do so.

CHAPTER NINE

Fractured Echoes of Inequality in the Welfare Era (1940s–1960s)

Inequality is the inverse of a core liberal value – equality. Inequality is resilient but fragile, durable yet ephemeral, its origins difficult to discover and to predict. It is the child of many parents in Canada, but its intellectual maturation was slow. The idea contributed to many reform causes. The perception of extreme inequalities of income and wealth could inspire anger and protest. Yet it was never the coherent ideological core of any social or political movement. Can the idea of inequality, in whatever form it may be revived, contribute to a future release from the problem that it addresses? And what, if anything, can the history of inequality contribute to a politics of hope – to the revival of the revolutionary politics of equality that Pierre Rosanvallon has called for?[1] The problem that inequality idealists addressed was real and persistent, and today it has become more pressing than at any time since the so-called Gilded Age of the late nineteenth century. If we are to engage with the problem, intellectually and politically, our effort must begin with the twin ideals of equality and common good.

Equality is the uncharted ideal of the Canadian liberal order. In that schema's trinity – property, liberty, and equality – at least as Ian McKay initially laid it out, equality is firmly present but not well developed.[2] This should be no surprise, since its place and priority in histories of liberal thought are also uncertain. Those histories tell us that it cannot be merely a value deriving from a sacred right to property; nor can we reduce it to equality before the law, central as that may be. If liberalism is a specific set of values, they cohere in dimensions that are unstable and historically contingent. The coherence itself is fragile and often contested. On the one hand, property is indispensable to liberty; yet certain accumulations or concentrations of it may infringe on liberty – and also on equality, even equality before the law. It may be that liberalism is neither theory nor even ideology, but rather a collection of values centring on individualism, which have variously attached themselves to Western institutions and politics.[3] However we see it, if we focus our gaze and accept for the moment the idea of liberal order as a Canadian project of rule, we must surely see that egalitarianism – the primacy of equality – was central as never before in mid-twentieth-century Canada.

In that centrality specific themes emerge, to be pursued in this chapter: women's rights, the myth of a classless society, the role of statisticians, the Canadian conception of welfare, and the appeal of a specific egalitarian ideal – equality of opportunity. As the liberal order triumphed, it also fractured, and the problem of inequality resurfaced only briefly, among a few brave heirs to the idealist tradition.

WOMEN, RIGHTS, AND INEQUALITY

There is one vast area of historical inquiry that has explored equality and inequality, and egalitarian politics, deeply and extensively. That field – the related histories of women, men, gender, and politics – demands our attention, however tremulous and speculative our foray may be. Gender inequalities lie in a dimension different from that of vertical inequality in the distribution of wealth or income in a society. The former exist as multiple differences between culturally constructed identities or subsets within a population; the latter are measurable, material differences across the whole of a population. To reduce inequality in one of these dimensions does not necessarily affect inequality in the other. Thus shrinking the gap between female and male incomes does not by itself reduce vertical or "total" income inequality.[4] Any relationship between the two dimensions is not binary; it requires imaginative and analytical ingenuity to connect them. It is little wonder that few historians have made those leaps. The two inequalities share a common frailty – the tendency to frame solutions around equality of opportunity (always a contested and, by itself, incomplete panacea).[5]

Let us begin by asking: was there a connection between feminism and the problem of vertical inequality? A preliminary answer requires that we return to the early twentieth century. The main reform causes of that era's first-wave feminists seem to have had no direct link to macro-level distributions of income and wealth. The political economy of vertical wealth distribution stood at a distance from such issues as dower, marital property, the status of the farm wife, the liquor question, and votes for women. The gaze of women reformers, moreover, focused on the politics of a property-owning middle class. When the Women's Labour League and others supported minimum wages for women, they were seeking specific protections for vulnerable women, not a radical change to distributions of work or income.[6]

We have learned, however, that feminism was a diverse and complex insurgency. We cannot confine it within a small ideological box. As Joan Sangster has argued, the suffrage movement was about "intersecting inequalities" and "multiple versions of equality."[7] First-wave feminists forged a great crucible of egalitarian thought: even where their values may seem to indicate a cautious acceptance of "liberation deferred," feminists were asking about the meaning of inequality and equality in vast domains of human experience: work, marriage, and family.[8] The right to vote was not an end in itself; neither was prohibition.[9] Suffragists in Canada and elsewhere discussed at some length the new society that would emerge with the political empowerment of women. Many anticipated a social democracy that would reduce, if not eliminate, all inequalities. "Commercialized autocracy" stalks the land, wrote the editor of *Western Woman's Weekly* in 1919. "The principles of democracy fail utterly as long as there are very rich people and very poor people." In the coming "True Democracy" there will be a living for everyone.[10]

Canadian reformers did not produce an original theory that connected "the woman question" to the distribution of income and wealth. Where some did imagine such a link, they often borrowed and spoke others' ideas. A striking example is the oft-heard voice of the South African Olive Schreiner, whose widely read book, *Woman and Labour*, was published in Toronto in 1911. In the ancient world, said Schreiner, women largely controlled economic activity. "Civilization" subjected women to a long historical process of dispossession as males took over economic roles and economic power. The resulting "female parasitism" – the dependence and enervation of women – though gendered, was part of wider repressions, which started with "the subjugation of large bodies of other human creatures, either as slaves, subject races, or classes." Female parasitism therefore facilitated the "accumulation of unearned wealth in the hands of the dominant class or race." "The wealthier the males of a society become, the greater the temptation, both to themselves and to the females connected with them, to drift toward female parasitism."[11] The solution, Schreiner maintained, was not merely a more equitable distribution of wealth among men. She envisioned women's recapturing productive labour, within a complex world of companionate marriage, women and men's common interests, and female escape from dependence on sexual function. Schreiner was widely read and admired in Canada, by feminists of various political orientations.[12]

It may be that the maternal feminist valorization of women's domestic labour offered its own appreciation of the labour theory of value. Children were the real wealth, and women were "children bearers" of the nation.[13] The product and its value were vital to the country and stemmed from women's labour, which carried no market price. Here was a world of value remote from market determinations and from the emerging neoclassical political economy. It maintained Protestant strictures on wealth, but with a particular slant: "Many of our laws are not framed from a belief in the doctrines Christ taught but from a worship of Mammon," wrote Margaret M. Dickson. The laws were there "to protect the interests of the rich" – she did not need to point out the obvious, that the rich and the lawmakers were all men.[14] Readers of the *Grain Growers' Guide* knew that in the cities men became rich through no effort, while women were slaving to sustain farm and family. A question of justice followed: "By what moral right should a man be permitted to inherit a million or more while thousands of his fellow beings are starving?"[15] Here was an egalitarianism that was expanding far beyond political rights. "Do I really have a right to two coats when my brother only has one?" asked Flora Denison. "Have I a right, even as mistress of a Government House[,] to 500 gowns, while my sister has not enough to cover her nakedness, she having done more in her life to produce wealth than I?"[16]

This was an egalitarianism that easily accepted ideals of common good and society as an organism. Most of the work of women was not about maximizing self-interest or fulfilling individual aspiration. It was always about collective goals: those of family or community. It followed that the individual existed only as part of a community. On incentives and rewards, most Canadian feminists would have taken for granted the observations of Charlotte Perkins Gilman.

"Collective man," she wrote, must necessarily labour "as individual." "But it is *their* living which they work for; the effort and the result are in common, and to the individual is supplied the great organic energy to work with. The normal goal to labour for, in a highly socialized race, is the common interest, a far stronger attraction than the personal interest."[17] Flora Denison made a similar point when she lampooned an imaginary "League of Personal Liberty," in which wealth and waste hid behind the justification of "Personal Liberty." The real inspiration of the League, she said, was not liberty but "vested interests." Remember, she added, "that your Personal Liberty stops just where society's Personal Liberty begins."[18] In the presence of such understandings of liberty and community, the later neoclassical image of homo economicus made no sense. Canadian women activists in the early twentieth century did not say a great deal about society-wide distributions of income and wealth. But they were challenging inequalities on a broad front and claiming equality beyond legal and political rights. If they could challenge the hierarchy of gender, then all hierarchies were open to interrogation.[19] Yet – an important historical point – the cultural and intellectual defences of inequality could erode in the absence of a direct and explicit rhetorical assault on the concept. At the very least, and however incomplete their success, feminist claims to equality – and the insurgency did not cease after women won the vote – had embedded themselves into the Canadian liberal order by mid-century. The durability of the male-breadwinner norm was merely one reminder of that incompleteness. Equality claims, though often inconsistent and incoherent, are resilient and portable across "equality of what?" dimensions. Egalitarianism is not a coherent ideology. We grasp today what some early feminists intuited: the political and economic empowerment of women helps reduce inequality across the economy, however complex the link may be.[20]

In the wake of the Second World War there was another egalitarianism that we cannot ignore here, for all its uncertain connection to economic inequality: that of human rights. At both Canadian and international levels, egalitarianism became more inclusive in the 1940s, at least in principle. The United Nations' Universal Declaration of Human Rights of 1948 – drafted by a Canadian (John Peters Humphrey) – "epitomizes the historical moment when an inclusive concept of modern equality acquired the status of a global value." In principle, the ideal no longer stopped at racial or gender boundaries, and scientific racism was dead in the "family of man."[21] Inclusive egalitarianism had already forged connections, albeit imperfectly, to material equality. An International Labor Organization declaration of 1944 affirmed the right to economic security and equality of opportunity irrespective of race, creed, or sex.[22] The UN Declaration of Human Rights, though not condemning inequality, expanded equality to include economic rights: the right to social security, the right to "just and favourable remuneration," equal pay for equal work, and more.[23]

This universal and inclusive egalitarianism provoked reactions, many of which prevaricated with its anti-racist and decolonizing thrust. Andrew Lui has documented the official Canadian opposition to the declaration and efforts to maintain exclusions.[24] Reactions in Canada and beyond also included a backlash against egalitarianism and a project of containment that sought to neutralize any egalitarian implications for economic distributions. It is no coincidence that neoliberalism emerged in the 1940s. The Mont Pelerin Society, for instance, sought to contain the egalitarian tendencies in democracy, which were shifting the priorities in liberalism away from individual freedom and towards equality, redistribution, and state intervention to "plunder the rich."[25] Neoliberalism offered sustained resistance to "utopian egalitarianism."[26]

The complex history of human rights in Canada since the 1940s indicates an ongoing failure to connect material inequality and distributive justice to the egalitarian politics of human rights and anti-racism. Human-rights law failed to address systemic inequality, argues Dominique Clément, writing about British Columbia. The "apparent neutrality of the human rights state reproduced the same inequalities of the society that it served ... Human rights legislation ... was never designed to deal with the inequitable distribution of wealth."[27] In *Not Enough: Human Rights in an Unequal World*, Samuel Moyn concludes: "Human rights guarantee status equality but not distributive equality."[28] The expanding inclusivity of equality created a historical watershed; its potential for the problem of inequality went unrealized.

EQUALITY AND THE MID-CENTURY MOSAIC

In Canada equality – for all its fragility and its enduring hermetic limits – became a core value in the liberal order. Proclaimed loudly and persistently by politicians, educators, and journalists, equality took its place in the historical succession of first-wave feminism, Depression, war, and postwar economic growth. The media celebrated the individual's decision-making autonomy, equal in his and her freedom to live, to work, and to consume. That equality was all the more acclaimed, a value to cherish and celebrate, when the Cold War pitted it against the alleged equality of the communist world. A by-product was a motif, even a myth – Canada as a "classless society."[29] Walter Gordon, then chairing the Royal Commission on Canada's Economic Prospects, made the point clearly in 1957: "Canada is fortunate to have virtually a classless society where the great majority of those able and willing to work can attain what in Europe would be called a middle-class, property-owning standard of living." The elements of the assumed equality were all there: ability to work, equal opportunity to work, a possible "middle-class" living standard, and perhaps owning property.

For many Canadians, of course, lived experience was radically different. Real material inequality persisted, poverty (however defined) was widespread, trade unionists battled to secure the "middle-class" life for their members, official unemployment rates stood at 5 to 7 per cent between 1958 and 1963, and in 1957 and 1961 the unemployed protested outside the BC legislature.[30] The contradiction between reality and myth was painfully apparent to many Canadians. So long as it persisted, it made revival of the idea of inequality possible, even immanent. But how to realize that immanence? In the scholarly world, how could the idea of inequality resurface, out of the complacent optimism and abstracted empiricism of Canadian social science?

From the history of inequality in Canada we may derive a prescription. If inequality were to revive at all, it might be by a Canadian thinker of Protestant upbringing who

- exchanged Christian piety for a fervent secular humanism;
- lived in poverty as a youth;
- spent time in England, observing directly the English class structure;
- studied at the home of both Fabianism and radical liberalism – the London School of Economics;
- absorbed an older idealist philosophy and studied with the

disciples of L.T. Hobhouse, J.A. Hobson, and other intellectual heirs of T.H. Green;
- and joined the older liberal quest to reconcile individual rights with common good in society understood as an evolving organism.

He might be a Canadian who had absorbed so deeply the ideal of egalitarian community that, at the age of twenty-one, he could write the following:

We are tied in one vast continent of life
Each to the other indispensable ...
Each man is part of everyman
Here and beyond.
There are no colours, classes,
Creeds, sexes, nationalities,
Schools of thought;
No possessions, no destitution,
No power, no weakness –
All men shall be one.[31]

If such a Canadian existed in the 1950s, and then sought to reconcile his idealism with pragmatism – with "rational" and practical ethics – then such a thinker might expose and demolish the myth of classless equality.

Such a scholar existed. John Porter crafted one of the most influential Canadian studies of inequality ever: *The Vertical Mosaic*. His book, conceived in 1952 and published in 1965, was explosive in no small part because it confronted and demolished the myth of Canada as a classless, egalitarian society. Porter's decision to study class, inequality, and power in Canada followed from a conversation with his teacher at LSE, Morris Ginzberg, a philosopher of ethics, a sociologist, and one of the last disciples of L.T. Hobhouse. In his biography of Porter, Rick Helmes-Hayes traces Porter's intellectual roots in new liberalism and in doing so presents clear evidence of philosophical idealism. Late in his career Porter wrote: "The major task of social science is to abstract from the confused flow of events perspectives which clarify and which permit some judgment about society in the light of moral principles." There was no such thing as a "neutral position" from which social issues "can be analysed objectively." "If we are not concerned with questions of value," he said, then sociology will return to a "condition of aimless empiricism and laborious webs of theory spinning."[32]

What values informed Porter's social science? A thorough answer would require a long essay. It suffices to repeat Helmes-Hayes's emphasis on the new liberals' reconciliation of the liberal values of freedom and equality with "mutuality," community, and common good or "social good." "The underlying value that has always guided me is ... individual equality," Porter wrote.[33] It followed that Canadian democracy was riven by a deep contradiction: it celebrated equality, in Porter's view, when no real equality existed. He revived and repeated an old word – privilege, the possession of position or status that bore no relation to real contribution, merit, or desert.[34] His lengthy analysis of elites and elite power followed, as empirical confirmation of privilege, and so too did his analysis of income. Chapter 4 of *The Vertical Mosaic* was about income distributions; though only a little over 5 per cent of the book, it was one of very few extended discussions of income inequality by a university-based scholar in Canada (evidence on the size distribution of farms also appeared, in chapter 5).[35] It presented no broad temporal analysis: the data came mainly from the Department of National Revenue's Taxation Statistics for 1955 and 1959. Canadian readers – most of them undoubtedly for the first time – read about Lorenz curves. Only the more attentive may have spotted Porter's brief but valuable conclusion: welfare measures, even where aiming to redistribute income and wealth (as in the United Kingdom), "have had very little effect on the structure of inequality."[36]

For Porter, "distributive justice" was a value in itself, and it had a particular meaning. It was the guiding principle of a "thorough-going democracy"; it meant "a sense of shared social purpose and collective participation in achieving social ends."[37] And that in turn meant equality of opportunity, especially realizing it in a democratic education system. Income inequality occupied a small proportion of the book, in part because Porter saw it not as an evil in itself, but as one of several barriers to equality of opportunity. The priority also reflected his heightened sense of "waste": the problem with inequality was its deep social inefficiency. It disconnected talent, effort, or merit from status or power, building in inefficiency. The most valuable of all resources – "human talent" (a later writer might have said human capital) – "is being squandered."[38] Inequality, far from being a result of just reward and fair returns to talent, was a primary source of inefficiency and social-psychological pathologies.

From this perspective Porter made mincemeat of the self-serving "ideologies" of Canada's corporate elite. He heard their old canard that "welfarism" was a demoralizing form of charity that eroded incentives to hard work. His response combined ethics with social science: "The arguments put forth in the corporate ideology can be neither refuted nor supported because they are mainly propositions about other people's states of mind and motivations. Even where some of them could be put to some empirical test there is never any empirical evidence to support such statements about increasing indolence or other alleged consequences of the extension of welfarism."[39] In fact Porter was refuting the disincentive thesis. The spread of education, he argued, correlated positively with social mobility, productivity, and economic growth. Here he was advancing older "new liberal" arguments in the language of the new empirical and statistical social science.

There was more originality in Porter's impressive empirical edifice than in any principles of distributive justice or any politics that he derived. As commentators have observed, his political stance was shifting in the 1960s, and the book's conclusions were brief and tepid. He had begun by asserting his strong belief in "the creative power of politics" and "the importance of political institutions as the means through which the major goals of society can be achieved."[40] Turn to the last page, however, and we find a rejection of older liberal models, and in their place little more than a plea for "open recruitment from all classes into the elites" and for "very great changes and institutional experimentation."[41] Politics was not absent here. The insistence on institutional and educational reforms to further equalize opportunity fitted firmly within a long tradition of reformist liberalism. It was consistent, as Michael Ornstein has noted, with a pluralist conception of power – power as an elastic property of "functionally defined elites in the economic, labour, political, bureaucratic, and ideological realms."[42] Elites, in this politics, were a necessity of power and decision-making, and governments must strive to maximize "open recruitment" into the elites.

Put simply, Porter's answer to the problem of inequality was that material inequality was inevitable and acceptable, so long as society maximized the opportunities for mobility, or made them as equal as possible, across the population. Porter himself had shown why this answer said nothing about reducing overall inequality: the entrenched power of elites and of the wealthy gave their children privileged access to education and to elite occupations. Nothing in his analysis or his recommendations would diminish that power and its associated privileges. Instead he directed attention to the barriers facing lower-income groups and proposed easing them. Inequality, in effect, was a problem of the poor, not of the rich. He implicitly evoked the old notion that a rising tide lifts all boats. The problem was that the rising boats did not touch the structure of inequality.

Porter's great book invites questions about how positivist social science, ethics, and politics connected in the mid-twentieth century. That relationship has spawned its own literature. In 1956 Peter Laslett voiced the controversial position that political philosophy was dead and that the main culprit was logical positivism, because it "called into question the logical status of all ethical statements."[43] The social scientist, like the scientist, was uncovering the immutable laws of matter and society, rendering normative statements or ethical judgments extraneous, or merely logical derivatives of scientific inquiry. The strong version of this interpretation suggested that political ethics weakened until John Rawls rescued it from the positivist trap in 1971. Laslett's hypothesis has indeed faced many questions, and it is no longer possible to argue that mid-century "high modernist" positivism stifled political ethics.[44]

Nevertheless, a more modest conclusion may be appropriate for Canada. In the 1950s and 1960s social-science scholarship reflected a wider cultural and political faith in the redemptive powers of education, which itself embodied – even inculcated – positivist, value-free, scientific knowledge. Education for everyone was an answer to the problem of inequality. But it was evasive, tending to supplant rather than solve the problem.

STATISTICIANS, NATIONAL INCOME, AND INEQUALITY

Does a single-minded focus on empirical measurement of social trends preclude ethical statements? In one crucial centre of social research in Canada we may find an affirmative answer. The country's major source of social and economic data was the Dominion Bureau of Statistics (renamed Statistics Canada in 1971). Statisticians at the Bureau published statistical representations of income distributions, and they did so before *The Vertical Mosaic* (which did not cite their work). DBS statisticians sought to exclude all normative statements from their analysis, and even to de-valorize the word "inequality."

How then did income distributions appear in this location at all? Briefly, they emerged as a by-product of the gradual creation of national income accounts. These constructs offered a set of basic macro-economic tools for measuring total economic activity, one being the total of all incomes in the economy. Canada was late to develop these tools, and when the Royal Commission on Dominion–Provincial Relations (Rowell-Sirois) in the late 1930s wanted provincial breakdowns of national income, it had to commission its own analysis.[45] From their beginnings in the 1930s the authors of national-income studies refrained from any commentary for fear that any "interpretation" might compromise the "objectivity of the estimates."[46]

Wartime estimates of national income failed to meet the multiple and expanding requirements of both the state and private enterprise. Ottawa and the provinces needed not just the provincial shares of national income but the distribution of incomes across the population, especially vis-à-vis taxes, which increased during the war.[47] Officials had to know the number of earners at all income levels. Particularly after the war, business wanted more precise levels and locations of personal incomes, which represented purchasing power. Government and business also sought a reliable consumer price index; such an instrument required adjusting for expenditure patterns by family size and income level, which depended on details about the number of individuals and families at each income level.

In the 1940s DBS started its first estimates of the "size distribution" of national income[48] – the aggregate number of income recipients by income level and by province, and total incomes by province and by industry. It did not yet involve the percentage *share* of all incomes accruing to persons at various levels of income, or the share going to quintiles or deciles of the population.[49] Thus it did not relate to inequality; still less to poverty, at least directly.[50]

Inequality – the share of total income going to different income cohorts – finally appeared in 1955. In that year two Bureau statisticians, Simon Goldberg and Jenny Podoluk, presented a paper to the fourth conference of the International Association for Research in Income and Wealth (the body for researchers who studied national accounts). The paper, published in 1957, used Dominion census returns for 1931 and 1951, deployed Lorenz curves, and applied the word "inequality" to the vertical distribution of wages and salaries, mainly by quintile (one table showed the income share for each of the top five percentiles). The estimates give us the first measures of Canada's version of the "great compression" – the mid-century narrowing of inequality. In 1930–31 the lowest fifth of earners took home only 2.1 per cent of all earnings; by 1951 its share had risen to 3.9 per cent. The decline in the top fifth's share was even more striking.[51] The authors concluded that "a considerable decline occurred in income inequality," and they suggested, very cautiously, that it might reflect, "in part at least, longer-term tendencies."[52]

In retrospect it seems surprising that Podoluk and Goldberg did not say more – they appear not even to have appreciated how original their conclusion was. They might have used the data to suggest an expanding economy, the beneficent hand of government, and a long-term tendency towards social justice. Their data on the rise of earnings in constant dollars would have supported that more upbeat conclusion. The authors betrayed no such optimism. Their reticence was all the more remarkable because they already knew about one of the most original contributions ever to the study of inequality.

In 1954 the American expert on national income, Simon Kuznets, gave a lecture on "Economic Growth and Income Inequality" (it appeared in print in 1955).[53] This paper was the source of the famous Kuznets curve: historically, inequality of income assumed the shape of a bell curve; inequality rose early as a society industrialized and then declined as capitalism developed and more of the population shared in the resulting wealth. The author offered plausible, if tentative, explanations for these trends. His hypothesis offered, if nothing else, a comforting reassurance that capitalism was trending towards greater material equality, and he explained the political value of his hypothesis during the Cold War. Goldberg and Podoluk used his paper, but merely to help justify focusing income surveys on family rather than on individual earnings, and they said nothing about his optimistic historical interpretation.[54]

In fact, the two DBS statisticians tried to seal their observations within a value-free box. They knew, of course, that other economists would make use of their data, but they tried to leave all political and social lessons and inferences to others. In presenting data on income size distributions, they were responding to "strong demand for data" and trying to anticipate more to follow. It came, they said, from business, marketing research agencies, and government departments and non-government agencies interested in living standards, housing, social-security payments' effects on families, women's participation in the labour force, and seniors' economic position.[55] This was the context in which Podoluk and Goldberg put forward preliminary inequality measures and Lorenz curves. They were presenting a "survey" of what their current sources could offer; they were also testing the limits of what could be said and reiterating a plea that was old even in 1955 – still heard today – for more and better Canadian data on economic and social trends.[56]

Is there contradiction in the thesis that I present here? The problem of inequality resurfaced in very specific ethical and political contexts, such as John Porter's intellectual trajectory. Yet outside any such realm, DBS had prepared a telling version of "inequality" and original measures of it. The Bureau's account of income distributions, however, did not touch the inequality "problem." The only issue it presented was statistical: how to refine measurement techniques in order to reduce apparent anomalies and to limit the effect of flaws in the source base.[57] Its abstracted empiricism underscored powerfully the centrality of ethics and politics in the conception of inequality. The measured distribution did not become inequality in the absence of ethics and politics.[58]

The data remained almost entirely sealed within the Bureau. Far from sparking a debate over poverty, social justice, or the impact of social security, Goldberg and Podoluk's findings did not even make it into the pages of the *Canadian Journal of Economics and Political Science*.[59] Their observations could have supported a pessimistic interpretation, just as easily as Kuznets's optimism. Even if average real wages and living standards were rising between 1931 and 1951, relative poverty remained remarkably durable. The top fifth of wage and salary earners took home 40 per cent of all earnings – and that excluded earnings from investments, rental income, and other non-employment sources. The inequality that Goldberg and Podoluk observed was certainly an underestimate. Better figures did not appear for years, while Canadian scholars moved on to other subjects. Inequality was succumbing to the economic problems of affluence – Canadian-born John Kenneth Galbraith's subject in *The Affluent Society* (1958) – and to what the Canadian economist Harry G. Johnson called "the political economy of opulence."[60]

Amid the celebrations of affluence, there were contrary voices. In 1962 Michael Harrington's popular book *The Other America* uncovered the "invisible poor" and showed that a quarter of Americans were living in poverty.[61] His study became well known in Canada, where journalists were already expressing concern about poverty and the effectiveness of the welfare state. The Canadian "war on poverty" took place on several fields of battle. At the federal level, it began as a response by the Liberal Party and a few welfare organizations to anxieties about the welfare state's workings, and it was, says David Tough, "an examination or evaluation of postwar prosperity."[62] DBS was pulled, somewhat reluctantly, into the examination. In December 1959 its statisticians met with representatives of the Canadian Welfare Council, who presented what Simon Goldberg described as an "overwhelming" list of suggested research on welfare. This alarmed the statisticians. How could they respond to concepts such as "unmet needs," "adequate income," and even poverty? Jenny Podoluk concluded: "This type of analysis involves a substantial extent of value judgment right down the line." "The type of research envisaged in these suggestions is not feasible for D.B.S.*"[63] There is a fascinating story for someone to tell about the resulting struggle between "value-free" statistics and the demands of poverty analysts. A major and durable outcome was the "low-income cut-off" (LICO) Jenny Podoluk devised in 1961.[64] The LICO was not a measure of either inequality or absolute poverty but indicated the income level at which a family's spending on food, clothing, and shelter might meet or exceed its income.[65] Despite Podoluk's insistence that it was not a measure of poverty, the cut-off acquired currency as a "poverty line."[66]

Podoluk objected to reductionist and simplistic uses of the measure that she had created, but as a statistician, not an ethicist.[67] The complex problems of distribution and poverty allowed for no simple definition and diagnosis. As if to prove the point, Podoluk produced the most comprehensive and sophisticated study of income distributions yet to appear in Canada. Theorists (and presumably also philosophers) would deny the possibility of perfect answers, she said, and propagandists would use whatever serves their purposes (she was quoting the American Dora Brady); the better path lay in secure knowledge of the real world. Podoluk's better path was *Incomes of Canadians* (1968), a 356-page study in the DBS monograph series that grew out of the 1961 census. She presented her analysis as a "statistical study" of census and survey data, without value judgments and explicit political inferences. In effect, she was saying to all poverty analysts and activists: you are swimming in very deep and treacherous waters; to make any progress at all you need "objective criteria" and solid data.[68]

Podoluk's book summarized the state of knowledge of incomes in Canada by the late 1960s. It reflected the enormous gaps in knowledge, especially by comparison with great advances south of the border. On income inequality, Podoluk offered cautious hope – inequality in money incomes had shrunk somewhat among quintiles between 1931 and 1951 – that she immediately qualified: "The lack of comprehensive income data for the prewar period makes a comparison of prewar and postwar inequality impossible."[69] She also noted that her data indicated no further shrinking of inequality between 1951 and 1961.

But her caution ran even deeper. *Incomes of Canadians* seemed to shout an extended warning about the very meaning of income inequality. First, income: it could not mean only wage or salary earnings: people received material returns by methods that varied across space and time and for which existing measuring tools did not account. And what of inequality? Its presence and extent depended entirely on its referent or "basis": a distribution that showed equality on one basis might indicate inequality on another.

Furthermore, it was risky, she warned, to make inferences about "economic well-being" from data on income distribution. One obvious example made her point: much of the low-income quintile consisted of the elderly; but far more proportionately of the elderly than of younger adults owned their homes free of debt, so might actually be "better off" than their younger counterparts in the same quintile. What about being very much "better off"? Placing people in the top money-income quintile, or even the top 1 per cent, missed much of their relative advantage: free automobiles, club memberships, stock options, pension plans that allowed deferral of income until after retirement, income from capital gains, and "various types of tax-escape income." To read Podoluk is to learn that all quantitative measures of material distribution are incomplete as references to inequality. At best, "they may not be too unsatisfactory as indicators of trends in inequality."[70]

Podoluk's data had useful political implications, if anybody had chosen to look for them. The limited social-security system in existence by the 1960s raised a critical question: what was the effect of the tax system that had expanded in the war, and how were tax-funded transfer payments affecting families and individuals? For all her cautions and qualifications, and her insistence that measuring tax incidence by income level was "exceedingly difficult," Podoluk offered a remarkably firm conclusion. The combined effect of taxes and transfers was redistributive – "a substantial levelling effect on the income distribution."[71] And the transfers were significantly helping the poorest families to maintain their income.[72] Even readers puzzled by her Gini coefficients could have understood her conclusion: the welfare state was a major change in the long history of inequality. Furthermore, there was a necessary connection between transfer payments and redistribution through the tax system. Economic growth alone would not have achieved what transfers were doing for the lowest income groups. The alleviation or prevention of extreme poverty required redistribution through the tax system. The politics of poverty were inseparable from the politics of inequality. Nobody noticed. *Incomes of Canadians* received almost no attention, and the few references in the media focused on issues other than inequality.[73]

POVERTY AND SOCIAL RIGHTS

We need a new book-length study of poverty and poverty debates in Canada in the era of the welfare state. In the present context, we can draw a very useful conclusion: the connection between inequality and absolute poverty, however we define it, was being severed in post-1945 Canada. As Jenny Podoluk observed: "Poverty to an increasing extent is becoming associated with specific groups rather than a characteristic widely associated with all segments of the population."[74] She was right: poverty was repositioning itself as a problem of the poor; it was not a contingent outcome of societal inequality. The task of statisticians and social analysts was to locate the poor and to identify their inadequacies and deficiencies. The rising tide was lifting almost all boats, or so it was assumed; the task at hand was to plug the leaks in the minority that were not rising.[75]

The connections between inequality and poverty were easy to sever because the Canadian welfare state's intellectual foundations failed to connect them effectively. Its social vision lacked a universal or even a wide embrace; as Antonia Maioni says, "the idea" was "relatively short-lived" in Canada.[76] It depended on a specific and narrow set of values: helping people with short-term needs; supporting the male-breadwinner family; and above all, equalizing opportunity, especially in education.[77]

Alternative justifications were available in the third quarter of the century, even within a liberal framework. One was the philosophical and legal concept of "social rights," which had far more purchase in Europe than in Canada. T.H. Marshall, the prominent English theorist of welfare, articulated his vision of civil, political, and social rights in his *Citizenship and Social Class* in 1950.[78] He saw a historical evolution in which those three elements built on each other. Social rights of citizenship incorporated "the whole range from the right to a modicum of economic welfare and security to the right to share to the full in the social heritage and to live the life of a civilised being according to the standards prevailing in the society."[79] Inequality was central to Marshall's analysis, and he insisted that social citizenship was not the same as equality of opportunity. His sweeping vision of structural change contrasted sharply with Canadian visions: "Class-abatement is still the aim of social rights, but it has acquired a new meaning. It is no longer merely an attempt to abate the obvious nuisance of destitution in the lowest ranks of society. It has assumed the guise of action modifying the whole pattern of social inequality. It is no longer content to raise the floor-level in the basement of the social edifice, leaving the superstructure as it was. It has begun to re-model the whole building."[80]

Another seminal work was *The Bill of Social Rights* (1944) by the Russian-French sociologist Georges Gurvitch. He was attempting a sustained and complicated reckoning with inequality, with social rights as the "jural negation ... of all inequality." Gurvitch appears to have been almost unknown in Canada.[81]

The narrow theorizing of social security in Canada, and its evasion of inequality, reflected deeper absences. The comparative template I offer above in chapter 1 now acquires its full analytical value. Canadian scholars seemed blithely unaware of the seminal, Progressive-era principles of distributive justice from Britain and the United States, even though the problem of inequality was still present in Canada. They scarcely knew Dalton, Gini, Pareto, and Pigou; they glimpsed J.A. Hobson occasionally; they ignored John A. Ryan.[82] The absences reflected a kind of parochialism, but they emphatically did not connote an intellectual abdication or any *trahison des clercs*. Canadian philosophers and political economists stood on public platforms, and many entered the corridors of political power. In doing so they were acting on their distinctively domestic translation of idealism into pragmatism. Their social justice, in all its strengths and weaknesses, stood within a national heritage of Christian economics and its moral imperative of commutative justice.

The concept of social citizenship or social rights was almost entirely absent in the platforms of Canada's social-democratic Co-operative Commonwealth Federation. The party's vision of social and economic democracy went beyond social security, until the 1940s at least. Social insurance and social security, David Lewis and Frank Scott argued in *Make This Your Canada* (1943), could not be "an adequate national objective." Their vision of the "rebirth" of democracy saw "social ownership" replacing "capitalist ownership."[83] This socialism presented the older paradox of inequality – "want and despair" in the midst of wealth – as prime evidence of social injustice within capitalism and "the undemocratic nature of monopoly control" of the economy.[84] But it hovered, as James Naylor argues, precariously between class analysis and the leftist populism of "political action for the 99%."[85] "The basic struggle today," posited Lewis and Scott, "is between the 99% who are reaching out for the economic and political power which the 1% now effectively control."[86]

In the decades that followed, as both class analysis and labour socialism gave way to incremental social welfare and trade-union rights in a mixed economy, the paradox of inequality also waned. The CCF's Winnipeg Declaration of 1956 linked wealth with opportunity in its brief reference to inequality: "Canada is still characterized by glaring inequalities of wealth and opportunity." Its principled responses included "social planning," equality of opportunity, "the highest available standard of living," and "maximum opportunities for individual development." There was no mention of progressive taxation, transfer payments, or social rights.[87] In the 1961 "Draft Program" of the "New Party" (the New Democratic Party) inequality had disappeared. It promised "to distribute the wealth produced by Canadians to assure to them all a decent standard of living." The decent standard lacked a precise definition, as did the "moral principles" behind "our social goals."[88] By the 1960s, as Murray Cooke astutely observes of the NDP, "inequality was recognized as a problem, but it was understood as a challenge of including all within the booming economy and the growing consumer society."[89]

*

Seven years after the party's founding, one of its unorthodox supporters did something that nobody else had ever accomplished – not the NDP, not Jenny Podoluk, and not John Porter. He connected inequality, poverty, and social rights and did so for a very wide public. The result was the most controversial book on inequality any Canadian ever penned.

The author of *The Smug Minority* (1968) was Canada's prolific writer of popular histories, Pierre Berton. His "smug minority" was the wealthy elite, mainly the corporate executives and bankers represented by chambers of commerce and the Canadian Manufacturers' Association. Berton clearly enjoyed poking a stick in their eyes and exposing hypocrisies. Almost buried behind the fun was his serious commentary on the meaning of poverty that borrowed from major studies in the 1960s. Did welfare create disincentives ("laziness")? He answered that poverty itself was disincentive: it destroyed capacity, opportunity, and freedom. He also argued that the motives and incentives behind all labour were complex; they were never merely about monetary gain, although for many that must be primary. Beyond a certain level of accumulation, monetary gain was never the main incentive to work, innovation, or creative entrepreneurship. The poor were not lacking in incentives, Berton insisted. They were given not to laziness but to "back-breaking toil"; they lacked cash, not character. Berton understood that the social cost of poverty was "staggering"; society would pay its costs – disease, disability, delinquency, crime, and so on. The question was not whether society would pay the cost, but when and how, and by what principles of justice.[90]

Berton proposed that "basic security" was a social "right," which government must recognize through a guaranteed annual income, paid for by redistributive taxation.[91] He also suggested a minimum annual income – "it should not be less than $3,500" – but did not explain that number.[92] He clearly intended such a measure to be a social right of citizenship, in order to get rid of the word "welfare" and its stigma. His discussion of social rights was fleeting and undeveloped, having the feel of an accidental discovery. He absorbed and reflected progressive notions, and he cited social scientists, including John Porter.[93] If a concept of social rights had been readily available in the intellectual milieu of a curious Canadian journalist, he would have found and cited it. In the last of the book's four section, he turned to education, universities as "pastures for the privileged," and the solution: equality of educational opportunity. Berton's polemic sounded radical; his solutions were not.

The Smug Minority provoked both enthusiasm and hostility. It sold over 100,000 copies in a few years, making it a Canadian bestseller. Berton's biographer, A.B. McKillop, has summarized the responses and reviews, most of which ignored the serious arguments about the nature of poverty, freedom, government planning, and education.[94] While opinion divided, mainstream attacks were fierce and often personal. Unintentionally they confirmed Berton's claims that false assumptions, ignorance, and fear enveloped poverty, inequality, and the welfare state. Well before the rise of neoliberalism in the last decades of the century, the welfare state had prompted widespread hostility.[95] The hostility certainly had links to the "conservative populist mobilization" of the 1960s against taxation that Shirley Tillotson discovered.[96] The era's intellectual justifications for the welfare state were not consistent and secure; they did not win the social and cultural acceptance necessary to withstand the attacks then, let alone the neoliberal onslaught that followed.

THE TRIUMPH OF EQUALITY OF OPPORTUNITY

In that decade of discordant voices and contested values, a resurgent egalitarianism sustained many progressive causes. Pierre Berton's anti-elitist polemic resonated with that position. Within the youth counterculture a politics of "justice and equality" guided organizations such as SUPA (Student Union for Peace Action) towards participatory, anti-hierarchical structures.[97] Beyond the offices of Ottawa mandarins a wider war on poverty proclaimed ideals of justice and equality. Activist supporters of Indigenous peoples proclaimed a new equality, especially after the widely publicized "discovery" of Indigenous material inequality.[98] An "abstract ideal of human equality" animated participants in the battle against global poverty (so argues William Langford in a very helpful doctoral thesis). Poverty in "developing" countries enabled a "new legibility of inequality," and many Canadians proclaimed a new equality as they supported parallel liberation struggles at home and abroad.[99]

Many joined the bandwagon of equality; discord and inconsistency prevailed. Within the many-sided wars on poverty, the liberal–New Left divide was never resolved. Canadian anti-poverty activism abroad fell within a development model that worked against the ideal of social equality.[100] At home, federal programs intending to introduce greater equality for Indigenous peoples reinforced existing inequities, as Justice Thomas Berger noted in 1977.[101] The 1969 federal White Paper on "Indian Policy" blew open the contradictions of equality and its meaning. The ideal of "an equitable distribution of income" did not evaporate in Ottawa, but the liberal stance diminished to maintaining income for the poor or alleviating regional disparities.[102] Summing up the post-1945 decades, Alvin Finkel underlines the limits in the liberal order. This "heyday of Canadian commitment to creating greater equality among its citizens" depended on "an expanding economy and an ability to distribute monies to the poor without attacking the privileges of either the rich or a growing middle class."[103]

Other people made Finkel's point at the time. A perspective outside the liberal order could detect the slender foundations of Canadian welfarism and its tenuous connection to income inequality. In 1972 the labour economist Cy Gonick cited Podoluk's table on the percentage distribution of family income by quintile in the 1950s and 1960s. But he was using the data not to argue for redistributive remedy but to challenge official definitions of poverty: the proportion of poor in the population might have dropped, but only by measures that ignored changing standards or expectations and dismissed poverty as a relative condition.

Poverty, said Gonick, remained an incoherent concept. Poverty – as in John Kenneth Galbraith's 1958 book *The Affluent Society* – increasingly appeared to result from deficiencies or "peculiar qualities" among the poor: lack of education, mental deficiency, attachment to regions that could not support them. This perception confused causes and symptoms, Gonick insisted. It denied the reality: "Poverty does not lie outside our political economy – it is produced by it." "Equality of opportunity" was a vacuous concept, Gonick said. A guaranteed annual income would not solve poverty; "at best it is a cheap way to administer a welfare program." Of course we should support measures that lighten the burden of the poor, but we must not let the official panoply and the moral outrage of speechmakers hide the reality.[104] These will not defeat either poverty or inequality. Gonick was an intellectual descendant of earlier socialists who had rejected the distributive palliatives of liberal reformers.

The problem of inequality staggered on in the 1960s, but usually as a deficit of opportunity – by then the dominant form of equality in Canadian political culture. This result had, according to Pierre Rosanvallon, "the paradoxical consequence of ending in the consecration of inequality."[105] Where most people assumed equality of opportunity existed – as in Canada by the 1960s and 1970s – any remaining inequalities appeared inevitable, even justifiable. Making equal opportunity the realization of social justice sanctioned inequality of outcome. So did the principle of a minimum standard of living for everyone. As a matter of egalitarian justice, it was an evasion: it did not answer the problem of inequality. To offer "minimum standard" as the sole or primary answer was to consecrate any level of inequality that might exist beside that minimum.

Although equal opportunity became a mantra of Canadian liberalism, it actually constricted equality. Few Canadians grasped its limits, so Pierre Berton and John Porter were hardly alone in missing this fact (to his credit, Porter eventually recanted).[106] Although both writers self-identified as social democrats, neither *The Vertical Mosaic* nor *The Smug Minority* cited the era's most famous revision of social-democratic thought: Anthony Crosland's *The Future of Socialism* (1956). The long-time British Labour MP included a chapter on "Is Equal Opportunity Enough?"[107] He cast a critical eye on the principle and questioned it. The ideal had seductive appeal, he noted: it would mean that any poor-born genius might rise to wealth or power; it would end the deeply felt injustice of hereditary privilege. Crosland agreed that its absence was "a denial of democratic rights" and its realization a desirable objective.[108] Nevertheless, "class stratification goes too deep to be uprooted merely by equalising opportunities." The pursuit of that goal "cannot absolve us from a direct attack on other inequalities."[109] To open elite schools to competitive examination did not by itself reduce inequality; it did not even equalize opportunity. Crosland offered an early and simple version of "luck egalitarianism": equal opportunity rewarded merit and allowed the meritorious to win advantage; but merit reflected qualities that luck endowed – personality traits or qualities "implanted from outside."[110] Why should such good fortune make a few people rich while many were poor? Equal opportunity, Crosland concluded, was inadequate as a principle of justice. It must be combined with other means of reducing inequalities of condition.

Liberal Prime Minister Pierre Trudeau repeated the mantra of "equality of opportunity" when he announced his "Just Society" in 1968. He even offered a faint echo of the idea of inequality: Canada "must move forward towards a more equal division of our abundance."[111] Many in the labour movement scoffed: "The Just Society – Just for the Rich."[112] As Christo Aivalis has shown, Trudeau's "just society" rhetoric quickly evaporated. For Trudeau, distributive justice meant a better distribution of support for economic growth among regions. It also meant a secure distribution of the guarantee of individual rights across regions and ethno-cultural groups. In this strong but much-debated iteration of liberalism, distribution and redistribution of incomes fell from any tiny perch they may have had in federal politics. In other areas of state action in the 1960s and 1970s – including tax policy – the retreat from distributive justice was apparent.[113] The social democrats clung to the idea of inequality, and the New Democratic Party turned it into a catchy slogan about "corporate welfare bums," but even in its ranks the problem was usually reduced to support for social security and equality of opportunity.

RETHINKING PROPERTY AND JUSTICE
IN THE NEOLIBERAL ERA

In the world of ideas and ideology, we may observe a paradox: in the same quarter-century when Canada constricted or displaced the older problem of inequality, there occurred a vast and enduring rethinking of distributive justice and, with it, of the history and meaning of liberalism. Multiple fracturings followed, including the rise of a "neoliberalism." The history of distributive justice, before and after the seminal works of John Rawls, is a vast arena and the subject of continuing study. In Canada, the problem of inequality was separating from distributive justice, in so far as that was possible. Less often did philosophers and ethicists begin their discussions of distributive justice by referring to a pressing problem of gaps between rich and poor. And for those political activists dealing with either poverty or inequality, the growing literature on distributive justice remained remote, something to contact, if at all, in university courses.

From the contested worlds of distributive justice and revisionist liberalisms in the third quarter of the twentieth century, one Canadian intervention may resurface in our own time. Or so some have argued.[114] C.B. Macpherson did not write, in a long-standing and explicit way, about the problem of inequality, and the concept did not have an initiatory place in his thought. It was none the less present throughout his writings on property and on "the life and times of liberal democracy." To read Macpherson is to revisit much of the philosophical idealism that he encountered in his formative years in Toronto and at the London School of Economics. In his lectures on *The Real World of Democracy* (1965) we hear his lucid summaries of the new liberals' decades-old case against inequality, laissez-faire liberalism, and utilitarianism. At the same time he cast a new and unfamiliar gaze on the problem of inequality and the associated distributive justice. It is almost as though his *longue-durée* perspective and his absorbing of both idealist and materialist traditions and of their sometimes-awkward juxtapositions and reconciliations had all worked to move this author to a distant vantage point, far above the fractious divisions of his time. And from that eyrie he was able to pose simple but often unasked questions.[115]

What *was* this equality of opportunity that was so often proclaimed in the triumph of mid-century liberalism? If it referred to a right, it could mean an equal right for a fully human life for everyone. Or it might signify "an equal right to get into the competitive race for more for oneself."[116] It is this second right that has come to prevail. Macpherson understood, more clearly than Anthony Crosland, that the right, in the second sense, was vacuous and evasive. It assumed falsely that everybody entered the race – or the educational system – on equal terms or from a similar starting point. Equal opportunity did not deliver on its promise of equality: even if it were attainable, it would simply allow more mobility between unequal classes.[117]

Did a generous welfare state solve the problem of inequality? Perhaps its transfers from rich to poor changed the overall distribution so as to reduce inequalities. Macpherson's answer had nothing to do with measuring redistribution; it had to do with the logic of power. "Any welfare state transfers from owners to non-owners cannot offset the original and continuing transfer in the other direction."[118] Defenders of capitalism admitted this, pointing out that if welfare transfers were so large as to eat up profits, there would be no incentive to capitalist enterprise, which would cease to exist. And so welfare transfers could not change the original distribution, which was one of power.

But surely inequalities were inevitable, and they were justifiable if they could be shown to help everybody? Today a negative answer is likely to rest on empirical grounds: with few political controls on the growth of inequality and enormous resulting social costs readily observable, inequality does not work to everyone's advantage.

Macpherson answered at a different level, at once simpler and more direct: advantage compared to what?[119]

The advantage the question implied was that of people as consumers in capitalist markets (economic growth together with a welfare system gave everyone this leg up, however unequal). Such a view narrowed distributive justice to material advantage in capitalist markets. It reduced the human person to homo economicus, a maximizer of material utility. It left out the relative strengths and weaknesses of human persons "as exerters and developers of all their human capacities."[120] Of course material condition affected the way people developed their capacities. But, Macpherson was saying, the reducing of material disadvantages did not compensate for – or even address – the remaining challenges that the distribution of power assigned to everyone. At another level, he was telling us: we do not need to grant to those who justify inequality the premises on which their defences rest – that the individual is mere homo economicus.

Was not the right to private property basic not only to economic growth, but also to freedom in a liberal and democratic society? Even if it involved, maybe even required, unequal material rewards? Macpherson's answer, though complex, was pellucid. His sustained and profound examinations of property and "possessive individualism" had a direct bearing on the problem of inequality. "All roads lead to property."[121] And what was property? Look at it in a *longue durée*, from Aristotle and Aquinas to the Enlightenment thinkers and those who followed. Property was not material object. It consisted of relationships that human beings constructed in law, and ultimately therefore in politics, economics, and culture. Private property – that is, property as a right, the enforceable claim of an individual owner – was not the only form of property, and not always the dominant one. Even if we focus on this particular form, there are historical variations, as, for example, in the nature and extent of the right. For Aristotle and for Aquinas the right was limited, "justified as a means to some ethical or ontological end."[122] Property, whether natural or from God, was a means, not an end, and the justificatory end must be specified for the right to exist.

In Macpherson's history of property (impossible to summarize briefly), a radical change occurred with Bentham and his utilitarian followers.[123] They equated not only collective good with maximizing aggregate utilities, but money with utility – money as the measure of quantities of pleasure and pain. A much wider ethos developed:

property as an individual right, and unlimited accumulation of it as ethical in itself. That ethos buried older ideas of common property.

It also weakened the idea of conditions governing the owner's right to private property. The unlimited right served the capitalist economy perfectly: "freedom" gave free rein to private property in markets, which could allocate labour, resources, and rewards.[124] This "freedom" led to economic growth, further inequality, and the investing of social justice in markets. "Not only would this maximize the product, it would also distribute the whole product among all the individuals exactly in proportion to their contribution to it."[125] This evolution of property not only led to inequality, but limited freedom itself to the right to maximize material accumulation. It had detached freedom from the right to fulfil human needs, realize human capacities, and enjoy and cultivate what Macpherson (following Aristotle) sometimes called "human essence."

From his vantage point, Macpherson did not propose policy or political solutions. Yet we can see him seeking a "way out" of the contradictions and "vicious circles" that the nexus of liberal democracy and capitalism had created. Essential to his exit strategy was a collective rethinking of property – reconceptualizing it as "the right not to be excluded" from "a full and free life."[126] This would anchor the social right to realize individual capacities in a re-imagined right of property.

We would do well, he suggested, to remember the seventeenth-century writers who spoke of property not only as rights in material things, but as rights to life, person, faculties, liberty, conjugal affection, and much more.[127] The vision may seem utopian, as Ian McKay has said. But Macpherson rescued it from an excess of optimism by his understanding that change was never smooth, elites would probably not convert to a new moral order, and revolution was unlikely. There would instead be periodic crises in capitalism, "partial breakdowns" of political order, and "partial break-throughs of public consciousness." The fractures and advances would be responses to the increasing costs of economic growth, including "the likelihood of irreversible ecological damage" (today: certainty).[128] Also impelling them: growing doubts about capitalism's ability to reconcile growth with popular expectations in "the present degree of inequality." "Capitalism reproduces inequality," Macpherson said. And any escape would require the injection of coherent principles of justice into movements of "participatory democracy."[129]

Macpherson was a liminal thinker, whose search for reconciliations and mediations has much to teach us. He echoed R.H. Tawney and Harold Laski; and he looked ahead, as Ian McKay notes, to Amartya Sen's discussions of property as politics and to Sen's principle of "capability."[130] In one other striking way he pointed to our own time. His references to the costs of economic growth and to ecology came well before our deeper awareness of our species' impact on the planet and its ecosystems in the age of the anthropocene. Nevertheless, he was anticipating the end of economic growth and its consequences. One old and oft-repeated justification labelled inequality a tolerable or even necessary trade-off: in return for unequal material conditions, everyone would benefit from economic growth. But what if that ended, killing the trade-off? What principles should guide us then? Macpherson was at least proposing such questions.

A half-century later, the same questions are loud and desperately urgent. What if economic growth really does cease? What if the reward for previous (and any future) economic growth, for the holy grail of "maximization," is unending disaster, perhaps even extinction? At that point all previous bargains and compromises end. The termination will be brutally apparent. At that point principles of distributive justice are no longer matters of debate among philosophers. They are tools of survival.

To pose the questions in this way is to measure the distance between Macpherson's time and our own. In his time the egalitarian values of liberalism were already under attack, although few predicted the extent to which "free market" ideology would colonize politics. Economists became oracles of progress, analysts of economic downturns, solvers of problems – ushers in of the new Gilded Age of inequality that began in the 1980s. The rise of neoliberal, pro-business think tanks, and their success in shaping political conversations, helped to contain an egalitarian ethic such as Macpherson was proposing.

To read the newspapers of the 1970s and 1980s is to remember the force of preoccupations at odds with Macpherson's reckonings with property and inequality. In Canada "inequality" referred to disparities of income and economic power among provinces and regions – and to wage disparities between Quebec and other provinces. "Rich and poor" as often as not involved gaps between wealthy and developing nations. Progressive thinkers and some politicians worried about multinational corporations and the constraints they imposed on Canadian independence. Second-wave feminism had much to say about the politics of pay equity and about male privilege in politics and the economy. There followed the debates around a federal charter of rights, which privileged individual rather than collective or social rights. At another level, political culture in the era of "postmodern anxieties" worked against a revival of egalitarian critiques of property, income, and wealth. The politics of identity, the epistemology of deconstruction, the existential quest of the de-centered self – these pushed onto the intellectual sidelines the socialist politics of class, and stood in unresolved relationship to the scholarship on macro-level inequality and distributive justice. Scholars connected race and gender to material inequalities at many levels, but the connections with macro-level vertical income distributions were under-theorized even where they were known.[131]

At this time in Canada there was a political philosopher, an expert on John Stuart Mill, who was also a politician. In 1973 Edward Broadbent asked: who now will listen to the old Fabian song? And where now can we find "the moral and philosophical case for an egalitarian society"?[132] His question came from a fading past. And it is a question for our own time.

CONCLUSION

To Explore and to Know Again

Many Canadians have spoken of inequality, in different voices and tones. In the nineteenth and early twentieth centuries, they were confronting what many saw as new and alien corruptions and social evils. They believed these evils had connections somehow to the same forces – commerce and industry – that were producing great wealth. Most Canadians were seeing commercial and industrial capitalism for the first time. First sightings through innocent eyes revealed shapes and contours in a stark clarity often inaccessible to later witnesses. These newcomers saw through a moral lens framed in secular and especially religious traditions. Thus when they began to speak of inequality, they did so with a home-grown accent reflecting moral imperatives more than secular political economy. They borrowed from sources in the transatlantic world, but selectively, choosing those that upheld their own distinctive mixture of idealism and pragmatism. We can learn from their ideas of inequality and from the moral imperatives that inspired them. Our historical reconnaissance may help to inspire a renewed moral vision without which there is no path into the future.

To start at the beginning: the idealist philosopher tells us, in sharp clarity, that the science of political economy (what we call economics) can make no distinction between ethics and science. There are no inexorable laws that determine social relations outside human control, and hence beyond the sphere of ethical choice. The "market," for instance, was a choice-based creation of human beings as they related through production, distribution, and exchange. It was also a construct of the state and of government policy, as Karl Polanyi taught us long ago.[1] It followed, John Clark Murray said, "that we are not the helpless spectators of a natural law which dooms the mass of mankind to irremediable poverty, and accumulates the wealth of the world in the hands of the few."[2]

SHOULD WE CARE?

Two questions follow. First, was Murray's description accurate? Did society in his time, and does it today, display extremes of poverty and of wealth? As our nineteenth-century forbears taught us, there is no purely empirical answer, standing outside a frame of value. The value judgment – the affirmative answer – came first; the empirical data followed, often much later, and confirmed the moral critique. John Clark Murray witnessed the extreme disparities of income and wealth in the Gilded Age, and many in his time tried to measure them. Today a plethora of studies confirm the rapid rise of such imbalances in many (but not all) countries, including Canada, beginning in the 1980s.[3]

The second question, wrapped in the first, is: should we care? There is no affirmative answer that our predecessors did not anticipate a century and more ago. The "Yes" response then, as today, rested on the perception and documentation of the evil consequences of inequality: crime, poor health, high mortality, poor education, lack of opportunity, demoralization, and more. Richard Wilkinson, Kate Pickett, and a legion of social epidemiologists have documented what labour activists and social gospellers knew and said long ago.[4] They also understood that charity was no answer: it was of greater spiritual benefit to the giver than of material benefit to the recipient.

Is it an answer to say that the real problem is poverty, not inequality, and that attention should focus on the former? Harry Frankfurt and others answer "Yes" (and here I begin my comments on the six quotations that concluded the Introduction).[5] Historically, this was the political answer that Canadians offered in creating a social-security system in the twentieth century: guarantee a minimum basic standard, an escape from the worst extremes of poverty, and that solves the problem. The system's value and necessity are not in doubt: in Canada it was a precious triumph for an egalitarian ethos, and for those who had long since confronted the problem of inequality. It was a victory, even if comparative analysis suggests its inadequate theorization and political vulnerability.[6]

But social security was at best a partial solution to the inequality problem. It helped to support the material conditions and health of many people, but it did not eliminate the vast extremes of income distribution, and it may have even facilitated the increase in inequality that followed. This history confirms what Phillips Thompson and many others in the late nineteenth century grasped: poverty and inequality are symbiotic, each a condition of the other. Society has a clear choice: either prevent the accumulation of great wealth that the production process allows, or redistribute the resulting incomes and wealth.

Our nineteenth-century forbears saw another connection: great wealth was a form of political power that corrupted the political process and negated the democratizing impact of an expanded suffrage. It was no accident or coincidence that corporate and capitalist interests captured and took control of political parties and electoral advantage during or just after the expansion of political rights. Such inequality eventually relegated poverty and unemployment to the margins of state concern and action.

The answer to the question "Should we care?" did not – and should not today – rest only on an appreciation of the vast social costs of inequality. Our predecessors' moral visions (and there was obviously more than one) led them to see that the accumulation and spending of vast wealth *in themselves* constituted an evil. Does it matter, asks Anthony Atkinson, that some folks can spend huge sums buying tickets for space travel while others are queuing at food banks?[7] Did it matter that plutocrats could spend fortunes on extravagant personal luxuries, the production of which yielded few if any jobs or wider social benefits, while blocks away people lived in squalor and died of poverty-related illnesses? The labour theory of value, for all its limitations, enabled one clear and potent affirmative answer: it mattered, because the millions were not theirs to spend. In different ways, both the Protestant critique of wealth and social Catholicism sustained another answer: it mattered, because wealth was a trust that people held in beneficial obligation; to squander that wealth in purely personal satisfactions was to refuse a divinely ordained obligation.

NINETEENTH-CENTURY RECKONINGS WITH VALUE

There were other answers in the nineteenth century. The concepts of rent and unearned income were creations of classical economics. Rent, let us recall, refers to the revenue accruing to a resource whose supply is fixed; it is an amount above what the owner needs to keep it productive, in its present use. An obvious example is the revenue the landowner receives from possessing land rather than through any of his labour. Rent extraction is greater for good land or for land in a good location that appreciates in market value. Henry George used the theory of rent to great effect, but he was deploying a concept that was well known. David Ricardo associated rising rent with high prices, economic stagnation, and a drag on capitalist growth. Rent was therefore unproductive; it was also a type of unearned income – getting something for nothing. Behind the theory of rent extraction, as Mariana Mazzuccato has argued, lay a theory of value – a way of assigning value to economic activity that yielded new goods and services (production), to sharing across the economy (distribution), and to productive use of earnings (reinvestment).[8] Classical economists had a value system that allowed them to assess whether activity was or was not productive. They could distinguish, for instance, productive reinvestment from unproductive circulation. As Mazzuccato says, they would have understood that today's venture-capital industry extracts value by shifting money around rather than creating value.[9]

We have lost, and not re-created, a value system that identifies and names economic parasitism. We have also discarded any sense of something that the first great Canadian economist – John Rae – understood: "waste." Waste destroyed value and was most obvious in luxuries: labour and capital invested in "the formation of luxuries" was "direct loss to the community" because it diverted capital and knowledge from productive activity, and any spin-off benefits were at best indirect or accidental.[10] Such diversion was parasitic: it sucked value from the community's productive capacity.[11] Where luxuries existed they justified and required state intervention in the form of taxation.

"Is it not lawful for me to do what I will with mine own?" (Matthew 20:15). An answer came in the tradition of idealist philosophy – the thought of T.H. Green, John Clark Murray, John Watson, and others. This tradition gave a "No" answer flowing from emerging conceptions of common good. Rights were not individual: they were the creation of society. "There can be no right," said T.H. Green, "without a consciousness of common interest on the part of members of a society."[12] There was a right to acquire wealth, said Green; but not to do as one wished with one's gifts.[13]

John Watson was a successor to Green when he rejected Kantian individualism and "theories of hedonism." "Each individual is a member in an organism, and realizes himself only as he makes the common good his end."[14] Of course, said John Clark Murray, a man might *legally* do as he wished with his property, so long as he did not injure others. But "most men" would rightly consider it an insult to suggest that "they can conceive of no higher restrictions on their conduct than those which are imposed by the mere letter of the law." And even the law assumed no absolute right over property that was legally one's own: law assumed that owners held property "in subordination to the general good." "Law, therefore, as well as justice, refuses to recognise a man's right to dispose of his property as he pleases without any regard to the interests of society."[15] As if to buttress the case, the idealist philosopher, echoing Protestant contemporaries, insisted that indulgence in personal luxury cramped "the moral intelligence" and blunted "the spiritual sensibilities of our nature."[16] This moral sensibility offered a clear answer to Anthony Atkinson's question. Look through this moral lens: space travel as pure tourist adventure is anti-social narcissism and amoral hedonism.

Idealist philosophers and new liberals never fully resolved the dilemmas that followed from their attempts to reconcile individual rights, especially to property, with common good. There was an obvious dilemma: what power, or what historical forces, would apply the "higher restrictions" on individual rights that common good required? Perhaps Christianity? Protestants and Catholics faced the terrible prospect that the institutional church's moral force and social controls might not be sufficient to defeat the hydra-headed monsters emerging from capitalism's underworld. Among those horrors was socialism, a secular ideology offering an answer that many people found persuasive. Socialism, and later communism, demanded responses that would preserve the rights on which individual freedoms and economic growth seemed to rest. The outcome – much later among Canada's Catholic thinkers – was acceptance of the state's necessary role in realizing common good and addressing the extremes of inequality.

Did social gospellers and new liberals struggle against laissez-faire ideology? Did they tend to assume that self-interest, or even greed, if left unimpeded, would empower economic innovations and investment so that everyone benefitted from the results?

In Canada, certainly, laissez-faire positions had a tenuous hold. Adam Smith's "invisible hand" metaphor – now a catchphrase – was almost certainly unknown to the many Protestant, Catholic, and new liberal thinkers who appear in this book.[17] Smith never used the argument to justify leaving everything to the market; only in later selections from his work did such a position appear. When he placed government on the unproductive side of a productive / unproductive dichotomy, he was far from saying that the state had no role in promoting the enrichment of society and the nation-state.[18]

Take, for instance, the case of Robert MacIver, who in the 1910s was in the process of becoming a major liberal theorist of the state. Neither Adam Smith, nor any popularized notions of laissez-faire, prevented MacIver from seeing clearly that unrestrained competition yielded costs as well as benefits, and that the healthy development of community required "the growth of co-operation at the expense of antagonism and competition."[19] The realization of community and its common values, he said, required government: "The State possesses the most complete, powerful, and centralised of all organisations. There seems no reason why the community should not take advantage of the greatest organisation it has built."[20]

MacIver was not alone. It was a common view in Canada that commerce and industrial capitalism had encroached on community and the bonds that held it together. Capitalism's untamed forces had thrown up systems of value that stood outside, and seemed to threaten, those of the churches and morality. They also intruded on the state's role, most obviously when monopolists and plutocrats purchased political influence and turned government to their ends (recall Phillips Thompson's proposition that the business corporation had become the real authority). Such was the broad perspective of rural romantics, social gospellers, and labour radicals, however much they differed on politics and policy. The response to the problem of inequality was to recapture power from the unregulated forces that produced poverty in the midst of unprecedented wealth. That answer recovered an old republican wisdom: politics and government created economic relationships, and those who seek to erode the protective power of the state must meet defiance. The modern corporation, and its markets, were substantially creatures of the modern state and its laws; to argue that they were the product of natural laws was, said Thompson, delusion and fanaticism.[21]

INCENTIVES AND INEQUALITY

Much deeper than laissez-faire, and enduringly difficult to dislodge, was the "incentives" argument. People required them, it assumed – extrinsic motivators or enticements to action – especially to work hard and to deploy fully their mental and physical faculties. In their absence, human beings would lose motivation, energy, and creativity. In our time, incentives have become virtually synonymous with rewards: rewards *are* an incentive; an incentive *is* the reward that flows from effort. It followed that inequality was inevitable, because if all rewards were the same or similar, there would be no incentives. An instinctive, popular response to greater equalizing of material reward (whether income or wealth) was: "But what about incentives?" In the nineteenth century the argument appeared in a different form and vocabulary: an excess of charity would induce pauperism, or demoralizing dependence; there were folks who deserved assistance and those who did not; in general the poor were inescapably poor, as a consequence of their lesser skills, occupations, or inherited status. Furthermore, poverty was a source of moral inspiration and social conscience. Samuel Fleischacker was surely right: the main obstacle to developing a modern conception of distributive justice was the belief in the necessity and value of keeping the poor in poverty.[22]

The incentives argument is all too often a tendentious ideological ruse. Our forbears of a century and more ago answered it. For many, including those who spoke for labour, the idea required no substantial response because it made no sense. Wealth did not arrive through talent or effort, but by capture of rent, parasitism, systematic robbery, or the accident of birth. No one could become rich through hard work and skill. In any case, there was another incentive to hard work, having nothing to do with the prospect of wealth, and all workers knew it: the need to provide for oneself and one's family. As for the "self-made man" ideal – the notion that social mobility was possible and open to those who responded to incentives and worked hard – this was a confidence trick. "Mere industry will make no man wealthy. Saving what is earned by hard Labor will not enable any man to rank among the rich and influential."[23] As for pauperism and the inevitability of poverty: in the social-gospel era, these nostrums now had to sit, often uncomfortably, beside a newer sociological wisdom. This last held that lack of food, clothing, and shelter severely damaged mental and moral life; it was a symptom of inequality.[24] Inequality impaired or destroyed incentives.

Nobody would do something for nothing; monetary rewards were essential; therefore inequality was indispensable. Today a critic can point to the unexamined assumptions behind such simplistic logic. Why assume, for instance, that inequality is essential to incentives, when it is not clear, psychologically, that the prospect of more income really does inspire harder or better work?[25] Furthermore, the argument is merely a variant of homo economicus (humans as rational and self-interested agents in pursuit of preferences or subjectively defined ends), a model that behavioural economics and psychology have savaged.[26] In the nineteenth and early twentieth centuries, Canadians did not know homo economicus and rarely heard the simple incentives argument. To the extent that they knew about the latter, social gospellers and idealist philosophers dismissed such logic as gross materialism and a facile misunderstanding of human motivation. They knew that the great spurs were duty, discipline, passion for one's work, a sense of responsibility for others, loyalty to family, and faith in God. "An intelligence trained for doing skilfully whatever work may be assigned to it in life; a taste so refined that it will be shocked with work that is not done with neatness and, if possible, even with some charm of beauty; habits so disciplined as to shrink equally from the shame of sensual excesses and the tricks of dishonesty" – these and related qualities of character were "the most efficient instruments for producing wealth," wrote John Clark Murray.[27]

The equation of incentives, rewards, and inequality was a gross reductionism. Long ago, ethics and social science were combining to produce a new logic: inequality weakened or destroyed incentives. But would not equality throttle the engine of growth? If we levelled the distributions that resulted from "enterprise," "industry," or "thrift," argued O.D. Skelton in 1911, then we risked plunging society into "an equality of misery."[28] And here is Harry G. Frankfurt in 2015: "Economic equality is not in its own right a morally compelling social ideal."[29] Such anti-egalitarian statements, common a century ago in opposition to socialism, and more recently in use against liberal egalitarianism, are red herrings. No critic in Canada a century ago was suggesting perfect economic equality; the socialist formula – from each according to ability, to each according to need – rejected it. No liberal theorist of distributive justice in recent decades says that "it is desirable for everyone to have the same amounts of income and of wealth."[30] The question of labour radicals a hundred years ago was: how to rid society of the waste and unearned increment that contributed nothing to the economy while producing social injustice? They also asked: what was a fair equivalent for the value of labour, and how to achieve that fairness?[31] Neither question implied perfect equality as a desirable outcome.

It was much easier to pose such questions that to answer them. There was no agreement on what a "fair equivalent" looked like or how to estimate it. Nobody tried to construct a table of incomes appropriate to each level in an economy-wide job-classification model. To the extent that one could determine a fair income, it could arrive only after a radical transformation: set perhaps by worker-employer co-managers in an industrial democracy, or a national-level committee of wise technocrats, or state managers who used the tax system to achieve fair after-tax incomes.

In the social-gospel era the liberal and labourite critiques of inequality ran up against unresolved dilemmas and impossibly difficult questions. How to reduce inequality without infringing on the right of private property, which seemed basic to freedom? How to limit concentrated accumulation of wealth without stifling the engines of growth? In Canada neither philosophers nor economists developed a theory of justice in response; principles emerging elsewhere remained largely unknown; in Canada, at least, John Rawls had no antecedents. Finding no solid and enduring answers in theology, philosophy, or social science, Canadians fell back instead on pragmatism: the satisfying activism of social service, and the search for basic or minimal support for those in most dire need. Many in the social-gospel world also took comfort in the assurance that justice was immanent in an emerging new Christian order.

IDEALISM, REALISM, AND POWER

It may be that, at a deeper level, philosophical and religious idealism was confronting the insuperable realities of economic and political power. The Platonic ideal of a merging of ethics and politics was impossible, or so realists through the ages have maintained. In the first half of the twentieth century, the idealist's vision of a new social order fell victim to the entrenched power of the wealthy and their allies – the very power that critics of inequality had identified and condemned. Salem Bland's vision of the inevitable replacement of capitalism by a new Christianity may seem, in retrospect, a naïve dream. In our own time, capitalism is transcendent and expanding, and so are rent extraction, finance capitalism, and inequality. New forms of rent extraction spring up like mushrooms: "surveillance capitalism" renders even human experience an object to commodify, purchase, and sell in virtual markets; a new material inequality may have appeared with this dispossession of human experience.[32]

Scholars differ over what the future may hold, but realists and pessimists have plenty of evidence. Thomas Piketty has argued that, under specific assumptions, capital's share in national income is likely to rise and that, without powerful corrections, so will inequality.[33] Population ageing and rising dependency ratios may increase inequality even in countries with relatively low levels of it. Some theorists point out that mass migration and declining ethnic homogeneity within nation-states may put more pressure on social-security systems. Automation and artificial intelligence may displace occupations and increase unemployment, or so some maintain. Even genetic engineering may expand disparities by giving new genetic advantages to the wealthy.

In the face of the entrenched economic and political power of capital and the defenders of inequality, remedial policy proposals seem unlikely to succeed. Thomas Piketty proposed a "logic of rights," building on "various national political and philosophical traditions," and a modernizing of the social state. His logic led him to consider higher marginal tax rates on top incomes and a global tax on capital, among other proposals. More recently, with even more radical solutions, he pushes vigorously for "participatory socialism" and "participative and egalitarian democracy."[34] In *Capital in the Twenty-first Century* he admitted that his specific proposals were unlikely to see adoption soon and that a global tax on capital is "a utopian idea."[35] The basic political question remains: how are we to get there? Anthony Atkinson's fifteen proposals to reduce inequality include employment guarantees, a national pay policy, a more progressive tax structure, and a renewal of social insurance.[36] His powerful schema carries the weight of great authority and is worthy of serious consideration by anybody who thinks about the inequality problem. Yet he too notes that the rise in inequality in recent decades has reinforced the opposition to redistribution and has strengthened support for policies that contribute to inequality. Economists have given us a range of tools, as well as economic and even ethical justifications, to reduce inequality, but they do not tell us where to find the "political leadership," even where there is "appetite for action."[37]

A century ago, labour leaders and socialists saw a material-political force that would empower justice in the real world – namely the working class, its full power yet to be realized. Here was an immanence – a force clearly extant in recent and current historical developments – that gave credibility to the ideals of economic democracy and lower inequality. If there is such an immanence in the world today, it remains to be identified and mobilized. And the four "horsemen of apocalyptic levelling" that Walter Scheidel identifies in history – mass-mobilization warfare, transformative revolution, state failure, and pandemics – are, he argues, unlikely to return soon – although the coronavirus pandemic of 2020 may undermine part of his case.[38] The conditions necessary to reduce inequality in the twentieth century – communist revolutions, the great Depression, world wars – may not recur.

To this catalogue of realism one may add another key lesson from Canadian history. Inequality by itself is unlikely to be the ideological core of a movement of social change. It was always – whether as measurable disparities or the perception of a problem – an epiphenomenon, a symptom of other historical conditions. Labourite reformers in the 1910s produced a program of equalization, but they knew that inequality was a symptom of their disempowerment in the economy and in politics. Their movement arose around class empowerment through collective organization and some form of industrial democracy. The reduction of inequality would follow from the achievement of these specific goals. Later movements that emphasized extreme inequality, such as Occupy Wall Street in 2011–12, failed to attach themselves to a coherent ideological or organizational base. It is never enough to rage against inequality.[39]

The realist catalogue is not the end of our story. Its problem lies in its history – the way that it connects past to future. It selects certain past conditions and declares them to be limits on future directions. Thus, argues Scheidel, the four necessary conditions of levelling are unlikely to recur; therefore future levelling is doubtful.[40] But the pessimistic conclusion does not follow from the premise, because the past never repeats itself in identical or even similar forms. In Canada awareness of inequality as a problem arose in great historical disruptions, but those were not the same in the 1910s as they were in the 1830s. The "great compression" – the reduction of income inequality in the 1950s and 1960s in Canada – occurred in part because the close conjunction of depression and war eroded capital and its economic and political shares. But those conditions are not repeatable and hence are not necessary parameters of future levelling.

We should accept that extensive disruption is a necessary condition of change in the direction of greater equality. We should also grasp that massive and even unprecedented disruptions are imminent and unfolding. Consider the long history of economic growth in Western countries, lasting almost two centuries, albeit with huge interruptions. That growth went hand in hand with extreme inequality, but also rising average material standards across generations. These changes contained a kind of historical bargain: accept the presence of inequality, and even members of lower-income cohorts will share in the benefits. In Canada, as elsewhere, it was a reasonable expectation, especially in the twentieth century, that your children and grandchildren would enjoy higher material standards than you did. But what happens if that sustained economic growth ceases? Robert J. Gordon proclaimed the end of American growth in his 2016 book, and he was not alone.[41] The interaction of inequality with productivity and growth, both as cause and effect, remains a subject of ongoing debate.[42] But the point stands: stagnant growth cancels the great historical bargain, and one of the standard defences of inequality collapses.

Relating to the end of growth, and a cataclysm already in progress, is the impact of climate change and global heating.[43] We are witness to capitalism undermining the conditions of its existence. At the very least, the climate catastrophe will see unprecedented destructions of capital and wealth. The net effects on income and wealth distributions are impossible to predict accurately. We will certainly see the wealthy homo munitus – "barricaded human" – retreat even further from society into air-conditioned enclaves, while the poor and displaced migrate for shelter or perish in ever-increasing numbers. In that moment any separation between economic decisions and ethical choice becomes impossible to sustain.

Canadians will be profoundly affected, but we will also be observers, as we were a century and more ago. Our intellectual and political responses will interact with those elsewhere. A home-grown response is none the less urgent. In formulating it we would do well to engage with our idealist forbears. When they attached their ideals to political programs, they achieved results and a partial victory over inequality. And in our era of delusive and self-serving idealisms, theirs no longer seem so naïve. The neoliberal idea that competitive markets allocate resources efficiently and return value in proportion to inputs – including labour – is an escapist fairy tale. An outdated free-market environmentalism, which held that private property rights, markets, and torts are efficient in reducing environmental degradation and costly externalities, was the ultimate naïveté. The philosophical idealist, by contrast, is a realist, firmly grounded in the reality of choice and free will. "We are not the helpless spectators of the pitiless operation of a natural law which dooms the mass of mankind to irremediable poverty, and accumulates the wealth of the world in the hands of a few; for if there is anything that we ought to do, it follows that we can do something, to modify the existing condition of things."[44]

TOWARDS A CANADIAN DISTRIBUTIVE JUSTICE

In those great disruptions, distributive justice resurfaces, in both theory and politics. In our time, the long reach of John Rawls and his theory of justice approaches its limits. His principle of justice as fairness, and the conditions for inequality in his "difference principle," reflected the values and politics of his era, even though Rawls was a critic of welfare capitalism: the distribution that maximized the income of the least advantaged was the just one, he said. As critics have shown, that principle is consistent with high levels of inequality.[45] Rawls is often credited with reviving liberal political philosophy and placing liberal justice on new foundations. His 1971 book stood at the beginning of a decades-long debate in political philosophy. The extent of his influence beyond the academy is less certain, prompting widely differing opinions. His liberalism was radical in its political implications, but his work soon stood in the face of a neoliberal gale that his theory of justice did little to abate (more in tune with the neoliberal ethos was Robert Nozick's libertarian defence of a minimal state).[46]

We cannot say the same so definitively for Rawls's great predecessors, beginning with T.H. Green, in the era of new liberalism more than a century ago. Two generations of philosophers and political economists deliberated over social justice and drove a new conception of the liberal state. Many entered politics or became advisers to politicians. Of course they met opposition, and they were one fragment among many catalysts of change. But these scholars and the intellectual formation of which they were part helped shape British political history in the first half of the twentieth century. In a similar way, despite many Canadian intellectuals' indifference to the problem of inequality, the history of the emergent Canadian welfare state requires reference to them. Ideas matter.[47]

In the great disruptions that are immanent, a new encounter with inequality and distributive justice will occur. In that engagement we may learn from our idealist forbears, for all the fragility and incompleteness of their reasoning on social justice. Learning does not mean uncritical acceptance. Most obviously, new liberals, social gospellers, social democrats, and many others who addressed the problem of inequality failed to transcend the limits of their own class position and their liberal assumptions.

Their problem of inequality did not reside securely in the ideological core of any movement of transformative change. The solution – greater equality in some form – was forever swirling within the unresolving tension between the ideal of equality and its liberal consorts, individual liberty and the right of private property. Reconceptualizing distributive justice means deploying a new egalitarianism while thinking outside the liberal box, and engaging with theoretical and political alternatives that appear with the discrediting of neoliberalism.[48] In the hard work of rethinking, we must remember and seek to transcend the seminal principles that emerged in the first great age of inequality a century ago, the principles of justice (which I summarize in chapter 1) that our Canadian forbears too often ignored.

Beyond the reach of neoclassical economic models and neoliberal ideology lie the pro-social and egalitarian values of workers and the dispossessed. Protests against injustices of inequality and against racism in many countries are already recovering and mobilizing these values.[49] Community, common good, and reciprocity: these are egalitarian values sacred to communities and the social movements that emerge from community. There is no trade-off between equality and individual liberty; community realizes both. Community, common good, and reciprocity are also recoverable from our philosophical traditions, ready to redeploy in a new, heterodox economics and a new politics of equality.

Reciprocity – the active agent of community – began with Kant and Hegel and proceeded through T.H. Green to find its place among Canadian idealist philosophers a century ago.[50] It was, for Green, "the reciprocal claim of all upon all to be helped in the effort after a perfect life."[51] John Clark Murray said: all actions bring men and women into "manifold reciprocity" with their fellows; it is the "imperious necessity" of community.[52] Robert MacIver said: the "law of reciprocity" is the "deepest question of social philosophy."[53] And so to our own century, when another Canadian political philosopher said: "Communal reciprocity is the antimarket principle according to which I serve you not because of what I can get in return by doing so but because you need or want my service, and you, for the same reason, serve me."[54] Gerald Cohen may not have been aware that his communal reciprocity echoed another Canadian anti-market praxis: *reciprocity* – the practice of exchanging with others in community for mutual benefit – is part of Indigenous knowledge in Canada, and hence part of an ancient wisdom from which all Canadians may draw.[55] It occupies a moral and political plane far beyond the heritage of utilitarianism and its intellectual descendants.[56] And it is not just another form of moral aspiration or injunction; it is a potent immanence. Equality, community, reciprocity: among the displaced, the dispossessed, and the unhoused, the principles are necessities.[57]

In the rethinking of equality and community we Canadians have much to draw on, especially when we seek to offer intellectual and ideological resources to agents of social and political reform, including the dispossessed and the displaced. A robust popular egalitarianism exists, and it resists the well-funded efforts of anti-egalitarians and neoliberals to erode it. At the end of the twentieth century, Canadians were asked what they thought about social inequalities. "In Canada, are income differences too large?" 70.6 per cent agreed or strongly agreed; only 13.8 per cent disagreed or strongly disagreed. The majority disagreed that "large income differences are necessary for a country's prosperity." When informants were asked to state, for a range of occupations, what they thought people "do earn" and what they "should earn," Lars Osberg and Timothy Smeeding reported a substantial gap, especially for high-earning occupations – "do earn" was much higher than "should earn." As well, respondents seriously underestimated CEOs' earnings, but still thought them too high. They could accept a "fair" level of inequality, but it was much smaller than Canadians thought the level to be – and even less than it actually was.[58] More recent surveys provide similar results.[59]

Canadian egalitarianism has a long history, despite the relative absence of a revolutionary canon proclaiming liberty and equality. In the Canadian origin story – as it is often told today – newcomers, beginning with their interactions with Indigenous peoples, entered a long and continuing history of accommodation with strangers and conciliation among peoples of distinction and difference. Even when these adaptations involved conflict, the relationships were those of rights, duties, and mutual obligation. In other words, people related in terms of commutative and distributive justice. Even when Europeans assumed natural laws of subordination and superordination, and their own superiority under those laws, they had to compromise and to accommodate. This was a long way from any acceptance of equal status or any modern conception of equality. There was, however, an ongoing search for middle and level grounds of encounter, enabling a ritualized theatre and discourse of equity, if not equality: we accept your rules of trade as ours; we will give an amount equal to what we receive; we are your brothers.

In the nineteenth and twentieth centuries other accommodations followed that, however imperfect, put specific equalities into the forefront of politics: equal rights in religion; equality of language; equal rights to schooling; equality of political rights; and eventually, equality of right, status, and condition by gender, race, and other forms of identity. A distinctive characteristic of Canadian egalitarianism is the importance of collective rights – the rights of regions or ethnic groups, for instance. Canada's distinctive multiculturalism, embedded in our law, politics, and Charter of Rights, entails a peculiar, often contested form of equality. There is of course no consensus on the meaning of equality, and egalitarianism co-exists and collides with multiple inequalities and enduring racism. But equality is a core value deep in our history, a value to which we return, especially in times of crisis, as we did in two world wars. When the big history of Canadian political thought is written, equality will be at the heart of that story. And the quest for a society of equals will be found to have its own historical trajectory; it does not arise directly from the assault on inequality, as we saw in chapter 8. Egalitarianism is nevertheless the beginning to any political answer to inequality. The "great compression" between the 1950s and 1980s was a small victory – a reduction of inequality, however brief. To the extent that it depended on policy and state action, we cannot separate it from a resurgent egalitarian sensibility.[60]

In the early twenty-first century we have seen threats to democracy, backlashes against immigration, systemic racism, and even an alleged clash of civilizations. Economic crises and climate change may exacerbate such trends. Yet we witness expansions of egalitarian inclusivity and movements of reconciliation and anti-racism. Over the last fifty years, most OECD countries have become more inclusive – more accepting of diversity as consistent with national membership.[61] And furthermore: a universal and inclusive existential threat creates its own egalitarian sensibility and its own inclusivity. Where none can escape the threat, there is a new answer to "equality of what?": equality of the experience of risk and loss, even where the losses differ in quantity and type. When humanity itself is under siege, difference and distinction are less likely to put the "other" in a category outside the community of relation. A long-standing barrier to redistribution was the "desert" or "deservingness" idea: some people were less deserving than others, it maintained, and redistribution did not recognize or reward desert. This barrier collapses in the face of catastrophic climate-change destruction, which affects us all, and none is more or less deserving.

"The prospects for a more equal and inclusive society depend in part on whether we can sustain the move toward inclusive national membership while avoiding the potential for exclusionary and stigmatizing judgments."[62] When it comes to realizing such prospects, Canadians have an advantage relating to our history of conflict, our accommodations of difference, and our pluri-nationality. By most measures we are relatively accepting of diversity. We do not reduce equality to sameness of treatment (equality among provinces, for instance, does not mean sameness of rights or responsibilities). We know – or we have heard many times – that equality of opportunity by itself is inadequate as a standard of social justice.[63] By all measures, our inequalities are less extreme than those in the United States, and we must remember the difference. We are able to, and often do, connect specific harms relating to origin, race, and gender to societal-level economic inequalities. The absence of safe water on many First Nations reserves; the terribly high rates of suicide in some communities; the differential access to education by class, race, location, and other measures; the continuing presence of "glass ceilings" and other exclusions (one could go on) – these are denials of equality and of freedom that we cannot separate from parasitic accumulations of water, longevity, educational access, ceilings, and gated luxuries at the tax-evading top end of the income and wealth distributions. These conditions are constituent elements of the distributions of economic and political power. Equality is not an ineffectual abstraction. Its potential can be realized when we interrogate, refine, and expose its tendency to exclusiveness. As Siep Stuurman says: "Bringing into existence social dreams and imagined futures, equality-thoughts create their own reality."[64]

In the future existential crisis (as in the Second World War), old principles surface in new contexts. The autonomous individual, the sovereign consumer, market-driven incentives – these give (gave) way to the higher demands of common good and survival. Economic growth is (was) no longer the first goal and the guarantor of collective well-being. The right of capital to profit exists but is (was) circumscribed and contingent, dependent on service to a higher good not defined by owners of capital alone. Production is for use (or survival) and not for profit. Property and capital exist under the protection of law and the state; they pay in proportion to that need for protection, even if that necessitates marginal tax rates of 80 per cent and more. In the face of existential threat, "equality of what?" takes a specific and urgent answer: equality of sacrifice. Community is an imperious master: when society has to mobilize, then everyone participates and everyone must pay. How to apportion sacrifice equally, and what does equality mean? It means, among other things, sacrifice in accordance with ability to pay, which increases as income exceeds reasonable personal need.[65] Taxation, if truly progressive, is not a burden but a gain, a necessary means of survival.[66] Equality demands that people pay taxes and not evade them.[67] Extravagant personal luxuries are waste; waste will be eliminated or taxed. Equality demands that the fiscal anchorites, the possessors of great wealth who withdraw from community, be recovered and deployed for common good and survival. The state and its many institutions are the most powerful agents that society has created to serve its needs and to protect itself; that power includes rights of control and ownership when capital fails or becomes a threat.

Such were the egalitarian principles that Canadians, however imperfectly, put into political practice. The ideal realizes itself in the material world, and a small victory over inequality is won.

Notes

INTRODUCTION

1 "Distribution" has more than one meaning. It may refer to dispensing or sharing: the process of supplying goods among recipients, including persons, groups, or regions. In statistics it relates to a listing of all possible values or intervals and the number of times each appears. In Canada, a value-laden or normative meaning concerns the volume of goods or services in each of several regions. On the meaning of "redistribution," see note 40 below.

2 Examples include the percentage of all income earners in each of several vertical groupings, such as quintiles. Several statistical measures allow comparison of various society-wide distributions: for example, the Gini coefficient, or index (defined in chapter 1). Measuring distributions of income and wealth is not a new challenge. A valuable rethinking began with Anthony B. Atkinson, "On the Measurement of Inequality," *Journal of Economic Theory* 2, no. 3 (1970): 244–63. The now-voluminous literature embraces several disciplines, and there are many summary statistical measures (including Atkinson's index, the Gini index, the Hoover index, the McLoone index, the Range ratios, and Theil's T statistic).

3 Thomas Piketty, *Capital in the Twenty-first Century*, trans. Arthur Goldhammer (Cambridge, MA: Harvard University Press, 2014).

4 Thomas Piketty, *Capital et idéologie* (Paris: Éditions du Seuil, 2019); *Capital and Ideology*, trans. Arthur Goldhammer (Cambridge, MA: Harvard University Press, 2020). This book explores the ways in which inequality is justified and structured.

5 Most of the economics literature focuses on the rise of inequality that began in Canada in the 1980s; the weight that one gives to various factors

in explaining that rise will necessarily affect the weighting of factors in accounting for the preceding decline.

6 Emmanuel Saez and Michael R. Veall, "The Evolution of High Incomes in North America: Lessons from Canadian Evidence," *American Economic Review* 95, no. 3 (2005): 837.

7 Measured inequalities differ in Canada and the United States in recent years: in Canada any future changes begin from another starting point. Essential sources include ibid.; Michael R. Veall, "Top Income Shares in Canada: Recent Trends and Policy Implications," *Canadian Journal of Economics* 45, no. 4 (Nov. 2012): 1247–72; David A. Green, W. Craig Riddell, and France St-Hilaire, *Income Inequality: The Canadian Story* (Montreal: Institute for Research on Public Policy, 2016); Lars Osberg, *The Age of Increasing Inequality: The Astonishing Rise of Canada's 1%* (Toronto: James Lorimer, 2018); David A. Green and Jonathan R. Kesselman, eds., *Dimensions of Inequality in Canada* (Vancouver: UBC Press, 2006); Keith Banting and John Miles, *Inequality and the Fading of Redistributive Politics* (Vancouver: UBC Press, 2013).

8 Amartya Sen, "Equality of What?," Tanner Lectures on Human Values, Stanford University, 1979, at http://www.ophi.org.uk/wp-content/uploads/Sen-1979_Equality-of-What.pdf, accessed 27 March 2019, and *Inequality Re-examined* (Cambridge, MA: Harvard University Press, 1992).

9 There is an enormous literature. The indispensable survey is Serena Olsaretti, *The Oxford Handbook of Distributive Justice* (Oxford: Oxford University Press, 2018). Particularly useful for historians is Samuel Fleischacker, *A Short History of Distributive Justice* (Cambridge, MA: Harvard University Press, 2004).

10 Eric W. Sager, "The Working-Class Peace Movement in Victorian England," *Histoire sociale / Social History* 12, no. 23 (May 1979): 122–44; "The Social Origins of Victorian Pacifism," *Victorian Studies* 23, no. 2 (winter 1980): 211–36; "Religious Sources of English Pacifism from the Enlightenment to the Industrial Revolution," *Canadian Journal of History* 17, no. 1 (April 1982): 1–26. For a very different perspective: Martin Ceadel, *The Origins of War Prevention: The British Peace Movement and International Relations 1730-1854* (New York: Oxford University Press, 1996), and other works by Ceadel.

11 Quentin Skinner, "Meaning and Understanding in the History of Ideas," *History and Theory* 8, no. 1 (1969): 500.

12 A valuable collection is James Tully, ed., *Meaning and Context; Quentin Skinner and His Critics* (Princeton, NJ: Princeton University Press, 1988).

13 James Tully, "Political Philosophy as Critical Activity," *Political Theory* 30, no. 4 (2002), 535.

14 E.A. Heaman, *Tax, Order, and Good Government: A New Political History of Canada, 1867–1917* (Montreal and Kingston: McGill-Queen's University Press, 2017); Shirley Tillotson, *Give and Take: The Citizen Taxpayer and the Rise of Canadian Democracy* (Vancouver: UBC Press, 2017). David Tough argues that a "modern political imaginary" emerged in which "politically engaged people" tended to position themselves "along a spectrum, left to right, on the basis of the extent to which they wanted the state to intervene in the distribution of income." David Tough, *The Terrific Engine: Income Taxation and the Modernization of the Canadian Political Imaginary* (Vancouver: UBC Press, 2018), 147.

15 Another chapter could be written about twentieth-century reactions to inequality by people in the labour movement and by socialists of various orientations. I include specific moments in the history of Lower Canada and Quebec, but my attention to French Canada is narrow and episodic. I do not focus on the changing justifications for inequality; this is not a history of a "*régime inégalitaire*" as is Piketty, *Capital and Ideology*.

16 I am drawing on Takashi Shogimen, "The Elusiveness of Context," *History and Theory* 55, no. 2 (May 2016): 233–52; Michelle T. Clark, "The Mythologies of Contextualism: Method and Judgment in Skinner's *Vision of Politics*," *Political Studies* 61, no. 4 (2013): 767–83; Robert Lamb, "Recent Developments in the Thought of Quentin Skinner and the Ambitions of Contextualism," *Journal of the Philosophy of History* 3, no. 3 (2009): 246–65; Joseph V. Femia, "A Historicist Critique of 'Revisionist' Methods for Studying the History of Ideas," in James Tully, ed., *Meaning and Context; Quentin Skinner and His Critics* (Princeton, NJ: Princeton University Press, 1988), 156–75; and Ian McKay, "A Half-Century of Possessive Individualism: C.B. Macpherson and the Twenty-first-Century Prospects of Liberalism," *Journal of the Canadian Historical Association* 25, no. 1 (2014): 319–21.

17 Fernand Braudel, "History and the Social Sciences: The *Longue Durée*," in Braudel, *On History*, trans. Sarah Matthews (Chicago: University of Chicago Press, 1982), 37.

18 While dissenting from much that I find in Guldi and Armitage's manifesto, I support the general direction of their appeal to historians: Jo Guldi and David Armitage, *The History Manifesto* (Cambridge: Cambridge University Press, 2014).

19 Among the first of several timely warnings is Tim Hitchcock, "Confronting

the Digital: or How Academic History Writing Lost the Plot," *Cultural and Social History* 10, no. 1 (March 2013): 9–23. A valuable survey up to 2018 is Chad Gaffield, "Words, Words, Words: How the Digital Humanities Are Integrating Diverse Research Fields to Study People," *Annual Review of Statistics and Its Application* 5, no.1 (2018): 119–39.

20 Though granted electronic access to the Canadiana collection as a single corpus, I do not use it as such; for lack of time and expertise, I stick to simple keyword searches.

21 See, for instance, Charlotte Perkins Gilman, *Women and Economics* (London: G.P. Putnam, 1905), 13–14, 99–100. I offer speculative suggestions at the beginning of chapter 9.

22 Dalton is discussed in chapter 1, below.

23 Alan Ryan can explore liberalism since the Enlightenment; Larry Siedentorp, "the individual" over centuries; and Pierre Rosanvallon, equality in Europe and America since the eighteenth century. See, respectively, Alan Ryan, *The Making of Modern Liberalism* (Princeton, NJ: Princeton University Press, 2012); Larry Siedentorp, *Inventing the Individual: The Origins of Western Liberalism* (London: Allen Lane, 2014); and Pierre Rosanvallon, *The Society of Equals* (Cambridge, MA: Harvard University Press, 2013).

24 "The Enlightenment was marked by the double invention of modern equality and modern inequality": Siep Stuurman, *The Invention of Humanity: Equality and Cultural Difference in World History* (Cambridge, MA: Harvard University Press, 2017), 557.

25 I am drawing on Samuel Fleischacker, *A Short History of Distributive Justice* (Cambridge, MA: Harvard University Press, 2004), 55–61; Andrew Geoffrey Billing, "Rousseau's Critique of Market Society: Property and Possessive Individualism in the *Discours sur l'inégalité*," *Journal of European Studies* 48, no. 1 (March 2018): 3–19; and James David, "Reading Rousseau's Second Discourse in the Light of the Question: What Is the Source of Social Inequality?" *European Journal of Philosophy* 26, no. 1 (March 2018): 238–60.

26 Immanuel Kant, *Lectures on Ethics*, trans. Peter Heath (Cambridge: Cambridge University Press, 1996), cited in Fleischacker, *Distributive Justice*, 82.

27 Henry Phelps Brown, *Egalitarianism and the Generation of Inequality* (Oxford: Clarendon Press, 1988), 87; Iain McLean and Fiona Hewitt, eds., *Condorcet: Foundations of Social Choice and Political Theory* (Cheltenham, England: Edward Elgar, 1994).

28 Fleischacker, *Distributive Justice*, 75–9.

29 Adam Smith, *Lectures on Justice, Police, Revenue and Arms* (1766), in Robert L. Heilbroner, ed., *The Essential Adam Smith* (New York: W.W. Norton, 1986), 46.

30 Samuel Moyn, *Not Enough: Human Rights in an Unequal World* (Cambridge, MA: Harvard University Press, 2018), 12–13, 20–3.

31 John Locke, *Two Treatises*, sec. 48, cited in Alan Ryan, *The Making of Modern Liberalism*, 535.

32 David Hume, *Of Justice* (1753), cited in Phelps Brown, *Egalitarianism*, 159.

33 Fleischacker, *Distributive Justice*, 37.

34 Gertrude Himmelfarb, *The Idea of Poverty* (New York: Alfred A. Knopf, 1984), 46. "The fundamental departure point for Smith's defense of commercial society is its capacity to provide for the poor": Ryan P. Hanley, *Adam Smith and the Character of Virtue* (Cambridge: Cambridge University Press, 2009), 18. See also Dennis C. Rasmussen, "Adam Smith on What Is Wrong with Economic Inequality," *American Political Science Review* 110, no. 2 (May 2016): 342–52.

35 No short, published summary exists. The best introduction is Samuel Fleischacker, *Distributive Justice*. Christopher Brooke is working on a new history of the subject (referred to in Moyn, *Not Enough*, 224n3).

36 Daniel Rodgers deals with social security, poverty, minimum wages, and related subjects, but does not explore inequality or wealth distribution. Daniel T. Rodgers, *Atlantic Crossings: Social Politics in a Progressive Age* (Cambridge, MA: Belknap Press, 1998).

37 Piketty, *Capital in the Twenty-first Century*, 20.

38 Classic statements on ethics and economics include: John Neville Keynes, *The Scope and Method of Political Economy* (London: Macmillan, 1897); Frank H. Knight, "Ethics and Economic Interpretation," *Quarterly Journal of Economics* 36, no. 3 (May 1922): 454–81; Lionel Robbins, *An Essay on the Nature and Significance of Economic Science* (London: Macmillan, 1932); Kenneth Boulding, "Economics as a Moral Science," *American Economic Review* 59, no. 1 (March 1969): 1–12; Amartya Sen, *On Ethics and Economics* (New York: Basil Blackwell, 1987); and Jonathan Aldred, *The Skeptical Economist: Revealing the Ethics inside Economics* (Abingdon, England: Earthscan, 2009). Robbins's book is often seen as a key moment in the break-up. He saw the two fields associated in juxtaposition only, but not in the same plane of discourse. A recent bestseller is Michael J. Sandel, *What Money Can't Buy: The Moral Limits of Markets* (New York: Farrar, Straus and Giroux, 2012).

39   Steven D. Levitt and Stephen J. Dubner, *Freakonomics: A Rogue Economist Explores the Hidden Side of Everything*, rev. ed. (Toronto: HarperCollins, 2009), 11.

40   As Colin Macleod has reminded me, one must specify the meaning of "redistribution." It does not mean taking money or goods from one person or group and giving these to others. It refers to a change over time in the allocation of resources. For Arthur Pigou, in his seminal book on welfare, redistribution was equivalent to a "transference" of economic dividend "between certain different uses." The absence of such a transference leaves portions of the dividend for goods consumable by the rich, for reinvestment in machines to assist future production, and for goods consumable by the poor. Redistribution alters allocations among such uses. Pigou knew that such redistribution did not mean a net loss to one use (or group) and a net gain to another, partly because it could affect the overall "magnitude of the dividend." A.C. Pigou, *The Economics of Welfare* (London: Macmillan, 1920), 773–4.

41   This question is pre-eminent in Carsten Jensen and Kees van Kersbergen, *The Politics of Inequality* (London: Palgrave, 2017), 8–20.

42   Harry G. Frankfurt, *On Inequality* (Princeton, NJ: Princeton University Press, 2015), 3.

43   Anthony Atkinson, interviewed by *Prospect Magazine* (2015), cited in Jensen and van Kersbergen, *Politics of Inequality*, 12.

44   Daron Acemoglu, "The Crisis of 2008: Structural Lessons for and from Economics," Centre for Economic Policy Research, *Policy Insight* no. 28 (2009), cited in Jean Tirole, *Economics for the Common Good*, trans. Steven Rendall (Princeton, NJ: Princeton University Press, 2017), 48–9.

45   "Branko Milanovic: Beware Rising Inequality within Countries," in BBC News, "How Much Inequality Is Too Much?," 8 January 2016: https://www.bbc.com/news/business-34987474. Milanovic also discusses the negative effects of inequality. A leading authority on inequality, he wrote *The Haves and the Have-Nots; A Brief and Idiosyncratic History of Global Inequality* (New York: Basic Books, 2011) and *Global Inequality: A New Approach for the Age of Globalization* (Cambridge, MA: Harvard University Press, 2016).

46   Walter Scheidel, *The Great Leveler: Violence and the History of Inequality from the Stone Age to the Twenty-first Century* (Princeton, NJ: Princeton University Press, 2017), 443.

47   John Rawls, *Justice as Fairness: A Restatement*, ed. E. Kelly (Cambridge, MA: Harvard University Press, 2001), 42–3. Rawls stated the difference

principle initially in his *A Theory of Justice* (Cambridge, MA: Harvard University Press, 1971).

CHAPTER ONE

1 Jonathan Israel, *Radical Enlightenment: Philosophy and the Making of Modernity, 1650–1750* (Oxford: Oxford University Press, 2001), 79.
2 Boyd Hilton, *The Age of Atonement: The Influence of Evangelicalism on Social and Economic Thought, 1795–1865* (Oxford: Clarendon Press, 1988), 36.
3 I have reluctantly omitted many major scholars who addressed questions of inequitable distribution and distributive justice. These would include Thomas N. Carver, *The Distribution of Wealth* (New York: Macmillan, 1904); G.A. Kleene, *Profit and Wages: A Study in the Distribution of Income* (New York: Macmillan, 1916); William Smart, *The Distribution of Income* (London: Macmillan, 1899); and Westel Woodbury Willoughby, *Social Justice: A Critical Essay* (New York: Macmillan, 1900). Perhaps my most conspicuous omission is the Catholic distributist tradition, especially Hilaire Belloc and G.K. Chesterton. The English Fabians applied a Ricardian theory of rent to non-land factors of production and derived a theory of monopoly power and inequitable distribution: see Noel Thompson, *Political Economy and Socialism: The Economics of Democratic Socialism* (London: Routledge, 1996), 23–4.
4 David Wootton, *Power, Pleasure, and Profit: Insatiable Appetites from Machiavelli to Madison* (Cambridge, MA: Harvard University Press, 2018), 2–5, 231.
5 Branco Milanovic, *The Haves and the Have-Nots: A Brief and Idiosyncratic History of Global Inequality* (New York: Basic Books, 2011), 3.
6 Wootton refers to "a striking intellectual failure on the part of Adam Smith: his failure to recognize the possibility of starvation in the midst of plenty." Wootton, *Power, Pleasure, and Profit*, 188.
7 Samuel Fleischacker, *A Short History of Distributive Justice* (Cambridge, MA: Harvard University Press, 2004), 62–8.
8 Dennis C. Rasmussen, "Adam Smith on What Is Wrong with Economic Inequality," *American Political Science Review* 110, no. 2 (May 2016): 349. Less persuasively, in my view, Deborah Boucoyannis argues that Smith's economic system, if implemented, would not allow steep inequalities to arise: Boucoyannis, "The Equalizing Hand: Why Adam Smith

Thought the Market Should Produce Wealth without Steep Inequality," *Perspectives on Politics* 11, no. 4 (Dec. 2013): 1051–70.

9   Wootton, *Power, Pleasure, and Profit*, 175.

10   Fleischacker, *Distributive Justice*, 103.

11   William Thompson, *An Inquiry Into the Principles of the Distribution of Wealth, Most Conducive to Human Happiness* (London: Longman, Hurst, 1824). Thompson was also a political feminist: James Jose, "Feminist Political Theory without Apology: Anna Doyle Wheeler, William Thompson, and the Appeal of One Half of the Human Race, Women," *Hypatia* 34, no. 4 (Nov. 2019): 827–51.

12   S.T. Coleridge, *The Statesman's Manual; or the Bible the Best Guide to Political Skill and Foresight* (1816), cited in Hilton, *Age of Atonement*, 50.

13   The absence of Bentham and of utilitarianism is noticeable in A.B. McKillop, *A Disciplined Intelligence: Critical Inquiry and Canadian Thought in the Victoria Era* (Montreal and Kingston: McGill-Queen's University Press, 1979).

14   J.C.L. Simonde de Sismondi, *Nouveaux principes d'économie politique, ou de la richesse dans les rapports avec la population* (Paris: Chez Delaunay, 1819); M. de Sismondi, *Political Economy and the Philosophy of Government* (London: John Chapman, 1847). John Rae was aware of Sismondi but appeared to make no use of his work, except for a tangential reference; Rae, *The Sociological Theory of Capital, being a complete reprint of The New Principles of Political Economy, 1834* (New York: Macmillan, 1905), 452 (Appendix). Another early critique of luxury and inequality was George Ramsay, *An Essay on the Distribution of Wealth* (Edinburgh: Adam and Charles Black, 1836). An anti-Ricardian defence of the labour theory of value appeared in Thomas Hodgskin, *Labour Defended against the Claims of Capital* (London: Knight and Lacey, 1825), and *Popular Political Economy: Four Lectures Delivered at the London Mechanics' Institution* (London: C. Tait, 1827). Wakefield cited "extreme inequality of conditions" in Britain and relief from poverty as part of his justification for colonization: see, for instance, Edward Gibbon Wakefield, *England and America; A Comparison of the Social and Political State of Both Nations* (London: Richard Bentley, 1833), vol. 1, 134, 147.

15   John Stuart Mill, *Principles of Political Economy* (London: J.W. Parker, 1848), vol. I, book II, 239–40.

16   Hans E. Jensen, "John Stuart Mill's Theories of Wealth and Income Distribution," *Review of Social Economy* 59, no. 4 (Dec. 2001): 506.

17   Mill did not propose leaving equitable distribution to taxation or state action alone. But a "better distribution" might emerge from "a system of

legislation favouring equality of fortunes, so far as is consistent with the just claim of the individual to the fruits, whether great or small, of his or her own industry. We may suppose, for instance … a limitation of the sum which any one person may acquire by gift or inheritance, to the amount sufficient to constitute a moderate independence." Mill, *Principles of Political Economy* (London: Longmans Green, 1911), book IV, chap. VI, 454.

18 Marx, *Critique of the Gotha Program*, 1875, 1891, in Robert C. Tucker, *The Marx-Engels Reader*, 2nd ed. (New York: W.W. Norton, 1978), 531–2.

19 Louis Blanc, *Socialism: The Right to Labour, in Response to M. Thiers* (London, 1848). See also Blanc, *The Organization of Labour* (London: H.G. Clarke, 1848). A widely available critique of simple distributionist solutions appeared in the pamphlet by Friedrich Sorge, *Socialism and the Worker* (first pub. 1876) (London: Justice Printery, 1890).

20 Arnold Toynbee, *Lectures on the Industrial Revolution in England: Popular Addresses, Notes and Other Fragments* (London: Rivingtons, 1884).

21 The economists' interest in inequality often went hand in hand with concern for poverty. The Englishman Alfred Marshall (1842–1924) was one example. A joiner of social causes, he began to study economics largely because of his concern for problems of poverty. At the start of his *Principles of Economics* (1907 edition) he asked a question that would have surprised no economist of his time: "May we not outgrow the belief that poverty is necessary?" Was it really impossible that everyone should start life with a fair chance of being "free from the pains of poverty"? The answer, he reported, lay in great measure "within the province of economics, and this it is which gives to economic studies their chief and their highest interest." Alfred Marshall, *Principles of Economics* (first pub. 1890), 5th ed. (London: Macmillan, 1907), 3–4. See Peter Groenewegen, *Alfred Marshall, Economist 1842–1924* (Basingstoke, England: Palgrave Macmillan, 2007), 121ff.

22 J.S. Mill, *Principles of Political Economy*, 3rd ed. (London: J.W. Parker, 1852), vol. II, book IV, chap. VI, 318–19.

23 Henry Phelps Brown, *Egalitarianism and the Generation of Inequality* (Oxford: Clarendon Press, 1988), 176–93.

24 Toynbee, *Lectures*, 219.

25 Henry Sidgwick, *The Principles of Political Economy* (London: Macmillan, 1883), 519.

26 The utilitarian argument that the marginal utility of income decreases as income rises was stated by Francis Edgeworth in 1877: F.Y. Edgeworth,

New and Old Methods of Ethics (Oxford: James Parker and Co., 1877), 60–2. Sidgwick was acutely conscious of "drawbacks and disadvantages" of government intervention: "corrupt purposes"; assistance to powerful groups; and "wasteful expenditure under the influence of popular sentiment." Yet perhaps, he hoped, improving the organization and working of government departments might make state action more popular. Sidgwick, *Principles*, 419–20. See also Steven G. Medema, *The Hesitant Hand: Taming Self-Interest in the History of Economic Ideas* (Princeton, NJ: Princeton University Press, 2009), 48–50. The concern that government action involved a mix of good and evil was widely shared. Alfred Marshall, while arguing that government could confer great economic benefits, was deeply conscious of the risks of corruption, the influence of sectional interests, and the operation of bureaucracies. See Medema, *The Hesitant Hand*, 56–8.

27 Keith Tribe, "Henry Sidgwick, Moral Order, and Utilitarianism," *European Journal of the History of Economic Thought* 24, no. 4 (2017): 924; Martin Daunton, "Welfare, Taxation, and Social Justice: Reflections on Cambridge Economists from Marshall to Keynes," in Roger E. Backhouse and Tamotsu Nishizawa, eds., *No Wealth But Life: Welfare Economics and the Welfare State in Britain, 1880–1945* (Cambridge: Cambridge University Press, 2010), 66–7. I avoid discussion of Sidgwick's position on utilitarianism, but see David Weinstein, *Utilitarianism and the New Liberalism* (Cambridge: Cambridge University Press, 2007). Following Jevons, Sidgwick raised the problem of how to sum individual utilities, especially as price did not convey a good's utility. Keith Tribe summarizes Sidgwick's problem with distribution: "Given that there could be in effect no intersubjective comparison of 'happiness', how could we move from the level of the rightness of individual action to the welfare of society as a whole?" (Tribe, "Henry Sidgwick," 921). Sidgwick was no longer equating wealth with welfare, so how could one compare wealth across time or space with no common measure of value?

28 Sidgwick, *Principles*, 517. One obvious problem with the principle is its apparent conflation of "Deserts" with the work of exertions.

29 For instance, Matt Carter, *T.H. Green and the Development of Ethical Socialism* (Exeter: Imprint Academic, 2003). Peter Clarke opposes the view that Green was a collectivist: "Green's politics of moral regeneration did not envisage anything like a welfare state." Peter Clarke, *Liberals and Social Democrats* (Cambridge: Cambridge University Press, 1978), 15, and *Hope and Glory: Britain 1900–1990* (London: Penguin, 1996), 44. There is now a substantial literature on T.H. Green. His egalitarianism did not

extend to a radical condemnation of inequalities, which in his view were not inconsistent with common good. On the growth of an impoverished proletariat, he wrote: "It is not then to the accumulation of capital, but to the condition, due to antecedent circumstances unconnected with that accumulation, of the men with whom the capitalist deals and whose labour he buys on the cheapest terms, that we must ascribe the multiplication in recent times of an impoverished and reckless proletariat." R.L.Nettleship, ed., *Works of Thomas Hill Green*, vol. II (London, 1890), 531. He did, however, argue that modern legislation on labour, health, and education was justified, despite its interference with freedom of contract, for the state must "maintain the conditions without which a free exercise of the human faculties is impossible." Green, "Lecture on Liberal Legislation and Freedom of Contract" (1881), in P. Nicholson, ed., *Collected Works of T.H. Green*, vol. 3 (Bristol: Thoemmes Press, 1997), 374, cited in Yuichi Shionoya, "The Oxford Approach to the Philosophical Foundations of the Welfare State," in Roger E. Backhouse and Tamotsu Nishizawa, eds., *No Wealth But Life: Welfare Economics and the Welfare State in Britain, 1880–1945* (Cambridge: Cambridge University Press, 2010), 102.

30 Avital Simhony, "T.H. Green: The Common Good Society," *History of Political Thought* 14, no. 2 (summer 1993): 225–6.

31 Shionoya, "The Oxford Approach," 99. On Green's variable senses of common good see Avital Simhony, "T.H. Green's Common Good: Between Liberalism and Communitarianism," in Avital Simhony and David Weinstein, eds., *The New Liberalism: Reconciling Liberty and Community* (Cambridge: Cambridge University Press, 2001), 49–68.

32 Much has been written about the limits Green applied to state action. For instance, he agreed that landowners reaped an unearned benefit from the increase in the value of their land; but he argued that the relationship between earned and unearned increment was so complicated that the state could not appropriate the latter without lessening the incentive to improve the land. T.H. Green, *Lectures on the Principles of Political Obligation* (London: Longmans Green, 1901), 229.

33 David G. Ritchie, *Natural Rights: A Criticism of Some Political and Ethical Conceptions* (first pub. 1895) (London: Swann Sonnenschein, 1903), 217, 260. See also David G. Ritchie, *The Principles of State Interference: Four Essays on the Political Philosophy of Mr Herbert Spencer, J.S. Mill, and T.H. Green* (London: Swan Sonnenschein, 1891).

34 Edward Caird, *Individualism and Socialism: Being the Inaugural Address to the Civic Society of Glasgow* (Glasgow: J. Macelhose, 1897), 15.

35 L.T. Hobhouse, *Liberalism* (first pub. 1911) (New York: Oxford University Press, 1964), 70. It is my privilege to be using a copy of this book previously owned by Peter F. Clarke and signed by him on the inside cover – part of his donation of books to the University of Victoria.

36 Hobhouse, *Liberalism*, 70.

37 Ibid., 103.

38 James Meadowcroft, "Neutrality, Perfectionism, and the New Liberal Conception of the State," in Avital Simhony and David Weinstein, *The New Liberalism: Reconciling Liberty and Community* (Cambridge: Cambridge University Press, 2001), 124–5.

39 Hobhouse, *Liberalism*, 70. See also Hobhouse, *The Elements of Social Justice* (New York: Henry Holt, 1922), 208–9.

40 Hobson's intervention was neither sudden nor singular. Educated at Oxford and usually working within the Oxford tradition, Hobson was unorthodox. He used utilitarian arguments, but sought to create a "new utilitarianism." A prolific writer, between 1889 and 1914 he produced a series of works dealing directly or partially with the "distribution of wealth" problem. These included: *The Physiology of Industry* (1889, written with A.F. Mummery), *Problems of Poverty* (1891), *The Evolution of Modern Capitalism* (1894), *The Economics of Distribution* (1900), *The Industrial System: An Inquiry into Earned and Unearned Income* (1909), *The Science of Wealth* (1911), and *Work and Wealth* (1914). He is best remembered today for *Imperialism: A Study* (1902).

41 Among others: John Allett, *New Liberalism: The Political Economy of J.A. Hobson* (Toronto: University of Toronto Press, 1981); P.J. Cain, *Hobson and Imperialism: Radicalism, New Liberalism, and Finance 1887–1938* (Oxford: Oxford University Press, 2002); (Peter F.) Clarke, *Liberals and Social Democrats*; and Michael Freeden, *J.A. Hobson: A Reader* (London: Unwin Hyman, 1988), *Reappraising J.A. Hobson: Humanism and Welfare* (London: Unwin Hyman, 1990), and *The New Liberalism: An Ideology of Social Reform* (Oxford: Clarendon Press, 1978).

42 Economic rent refers to the revenue above what is needed to keep the resource productive, in its present use. An obvious example is the revenue the landowner receives from owning land rather than working it.

43 In the 1890s we see Hobson exploring the issue of rent as a ubiquitous and complicating factor in markets and price determination. J.A. Hobson, "The Law of Three Rents," *Quarterly Journal of Economics* 5, no. 3 (April 1891), 263–88. I could here explore Hobson's friends the Fabians, especially Sidney Webb, who focused on monopolies' accumulation of rent and urged that the state tax it away. D.M. Ricci, "Fabian Socialism: A Theory

of Rent as Exploitation," *Journal of British Studies* 9, no. 1 (1969): 105–21. Another Fabian theorist of rent was William Clarke: Peter Weiler, "William Clarke: The Making and Unmaking of a Fabian Socialist," *Journal of British Studies* 14, no. 1 (Nov. 1974): 77–108.

44 Hobson rebutted the marginal theory of distribution in his *The Industrial System: An Inquiry into Earned and Unearned Income* (London: Longmans, Green, 1909), 106–14. "Regarded as a theory of distribution of the product, the marginal productivity theory is a misapplication of an unsound and unprofitable assumption. The assumption is that we may profitably treat the industrial system as composed of factors of production, infinite in quantity and absolutely fluid and competitive in character, afterwards making some allowance for their not being what we have supposed them to be" (112).

45 J.A. Hobson, *The Economics of Distribution* (London: Macmillan, 1900), 359–61. These terms are bafflingly complex. Context gave "unearned income" varying meanings – economic, political, and ethical. Some contemporaries were well aware of its varying meanings and their political implications. An insightful survey of the term, from J.S. Mill to Hobson, is in J.C. Stamp, "The Meaning of 'Unearned Income,'" *Economic Journal* 25, no. 98 (June 1915): 165–74.

46 It was non-Marxist because Hobson did not connect it to a theory of exploitation and class relations in production; his surplus value related not at all to a labour theory of value.

47 "So far from competition being free, it is fettered and impeded everywhere by the growth of innumerable forms and degrees of monopolies and forced gains. The theory that the enlightened self-interest of producers keeps down normal prices to the bare expenses of production, and that in consequence the whole gain of modern industrial improvements filters down to the community in their capacity of consumers, is seen to be quite unwarranted. Indeed, the whole notion of the consumer as residuary legatee is as groundless in theory as in practice. There exists no such fourth party in the working of distribution: the various owners of land, capital, and labour take each according to his strength. Thus emerges the true surplus value, derived not from some vague, unintelligible idea of tyranny, but from the various hindrances to perfect equality of bargaining-power in the owners of the various factors of production and the consequent establishment of different forms and pressures of economic force." Hobson, *Economics of Distribution*, 360.

48 Hobson anticipated the objection that production created income of equivalent value, and that if all income was spent all production could be

sold. By way of answer he referred to "the refusal of owners of consuming power to apply that power in effective demand for commodities." He also noted "recurrent gluts and consequent depressions of modern industry … The general character of the excess of producing power is proved by the existence at such times of large bank stocks of idle money seeking any sort of profitable investment and finding none." J.A. Hobson, *Imperialism: A Study* (first pub. 1902) (New York: Gordon Press, 1975), 81–2. See also E.K. Hunt and Mark Lautzenheiser, *History of Economic Thought: A Critical Perspective*, 3rd ed. (Armonk, NY: M.E. Sharpe, 2011), 354–5.

49 Hobson, *Imperialism*, 81.

50 Hobson, *The Industrial System*, 307. Like so much of his writing, the study is bold, speculative, and weak in empirical evidence.

51 John Ruskin (1819–1900) critiqued political economy, laissez-faire, utilitarianism, and the dehumanizing effects of industrial capitalism. He was not an egalitarian. Writers seeing some of his ideas as anticipating aspects of the welfare state have risked anachronism. J.A. Hobson wrote a study of Ruskin: *John Ruskin Social Reformer* (London: James Nisbet, 1898).

52 J.A. Hobson, *The Science of Wealth* (London: Williams and Norgate, 1911), 14.

53 Hobson presented an extended critique of scientific management in his *Work and Wealth: A Human Valuation* (first pub. 1914) (New York: Macmillan, 1926), 202–27.

54 In Hobson's definition of "vested interests" or "classes" as including a range of propertied interests, P.J. Cain sees him anticipating Gramsci's ideas of "historic bloc" and hegemony: Cain, *Hobson and Imperialism*, 117.

55 Hobson tended to reduce economic problems to absences of opportunity in his *Imperialism*. "If the industrial revolution had taken place in an England founded upon equal access by all classes to land, education, and legislation," he argued, manufacturing would not have specialized so much and all portions of the population would have been more prosperous (88–9). "The chief economic source of Imperialism has been found in the inequality of industrial opportunities by which a favoured class accumulates superfluous elements of income" (361).

56 The obvious should not escape our attention: in this era, one's acceptance (or not) of the economics of marginal utility was not a sure predictor of one's position on wealth distribution or the state's role. It would be simplistic and perhaps anachronistic to assume that acceptance of marginal utility indicated a certain kind of "laissez-faire" market fundamentalism. On Hobson's break with marginalism in the early 1900s see Roger E.

Backhouse, "J.A. Hobson as a Welfare Economist," in Roger E. Backhouse and Tamotsu Nishizawa, eds., *No Wealth But Life: Welfare Economics and the Welfare State in Britain, 1880–1945* (Cambridge: Cambridge University Press, 2010), 115–16. Alfred Marshall was keen to avoid some of the classical economists' naïve laissez-faire views, which often resurfaced in the nineteenth century. John Maynard Keynes concluded that Marshall's "proof that laissez-faire breaks down in certain conditions *theoretically*, and not merely practically, regarded as a principle of max-imum social advantage, was of great philosophical importance." Keynes, in A.C. Pigou, ed., *Memorials of Alfred Marshall* (London: Macmillan, 1925), 44, cited in Medema, *The Hesitant Hand*, 56. Furthermore, it does not follow that rejecting neoclassical economics predisposed one to endorse redistribution. William Cunningham, the pre-eminent exponent of the historical approach in economics in Alfred Marshall's time, argued against redistribution through state action. William Cunningham, *Modern Civilisation in Some of Its Economic Aspects* (London: Methuen, 1896), 12–13, 212–14. Reducing the wealth of the very rich, he said, seemed "plausible" to many people because it would remove "great inequalities." But, he argued, diverting wealth from landlords and potential investors into the state's coffers would not necessarily benefit the public or ensure its productive investment. Cunningham, *Christianity and Social Questions* (London: Duckworth, 1910), 97–8, 146–7.

57 J.A. Hobson, *Canada To-Day* (London: Fisher Unwin, 1906).

58 Backhouse, "J.A. Hobson as a Welfare Economist," 116.

59 His frequent references to selfishness and greed, and his emphasis on eco-nomic waste, might suggest a residual influence of his Anglican upbringing in Derbyshire and the "humanism" of "a religious heretic" (*Confessions of an Economic Heretic* [New York: Macmillan Company, 1938]), 20–1). Hobson was associated for a time with the London Ethical Society and the Charity Organisation Society. He had contacts with prominent Liberals and with Fabians.

60 J.A. Hobson, *The Social Problem* (London: Nisbet, 1901), 20, cited in Backhouse, "J.A. Hobson as a Welfare Economist," 121.

61 J.A. Hobson, *Work and Wealth: A Human Valuation* (first pub. 1914) (New York: Macmillan, 1926), vi.

62 Hobson was so prolific that selective borrowings could move in many dir-ections. As Shionoya points out, one can see Hobson criticize classical eco-nomics for its distinction between fact and value; reject hedonistic utilitarianism; reject Pigou's identification of national income with eco-nomic welfare; conceive of virtue as being pluralistic, so allowing different

ways to evaluate human conduct; and grasp historical evolution as basic to economic conditions (Shionoya, "The Oxford Approach," 107). Each of these positions could shape the conceptual configuration of income and wealth inequality.

63 Hobson, *Work and Wealth*, vii, 163–4. It is not clear why Hobson used "power" instead of "ability" (as Louis Blanc or Marx did).

64 Hobson did, however, connect needs to "social utility" and efficiency. "Only by satisfaction of genuine needs can an individual be kept in a position to serve society by efficient labor 'according to his powers.'" Hobson, *The Social Problem*, 162.

65 Money was elected as a Liberal MP in 1906. He advised David Lloyd George (Liberal prime minister 1916–22) on national insurance. He joined the Labour Party after the First World War. Jose Harris describes him as a "New Liberal economist": Harris, *Private Lives, Public Spirit: Britain, 1870–1914* (New York: Penguin, 1993), 99.

66 L.G. Chiozza Money, *Riches and Poverty* (first pub. 1905), 8th ed. (London: Methuen, 1908), xvii, 41–2. The estimates prompted some scepticism: Edwin Cannan, "Riches and Poverty by L.G. Money," *Economic Journal* 16, no. 61 (March 1906): 85–90.

67 Money, *Riches and Poverty*, 97.

68 The words appeared several times: ibid., 138, 146, 149, 254, 255.

69 "We must strike at the Error of Distribution by gradually substituting public ownership for private ownership of the means of production." Ibid., 240–1, 323.

70 A revised version appeared as *The Economics of Welfare* (London: Macmillan, 1920).

71 In some sections "inequality" took on an expansive meaning, consistent with older nineteenth-century formulations that juxtaposed misery and luxury. "The misery and squalor that surround us, the injurious luxury of some wealthy families, the terrible uncertainty overshadowing many families of the poor – these are evils too plain to be ignored": Pigou, *Wealth and Welfare* (London: Macmillan, 1912), 488. Elsewhere inequality referred to the absence of mathematical equality between marginal net products. Pigou also possessed a deep sense of the way in which material inequality was different from, but inflected by, other inequalities – as in the unequal distributions in satisfactions to be had from income. Furthermore, comparative income and absolute income could yield different kinds of satisfaction. Hence the ambiguous meaning of both inequality and its reduction; any analysis required careful control of assumptions (24–5). Pigou was also sensitive to the way in which culturally

conditioned predispositions affected judgments on inequality. We might
deem some satisfactions of the rich (such as "luxurious sensual enjoyment") ethically objectionable and inferior, for instance, to the satisfaction
of physical needs by the poor; and other satisfactions for the rich (perhaps
literature and art) superior (10–11). Among the many studies of Pigou and
his contributions, a gem is Ian Kumekawa, *The First Serious Optimist:
A.C. Pigou and the Birth of Welfare Economics* (Princeton, NJ: Princeton
University Press, 2017).

72 The idea of market failure long antedated Pigou. See, for instance, Steven
   G. Medema, "Harnessing Self-Interest: Mill, Sidgwick, and the Evolution
   of the Theory of Market Failure," in Medema, *The Hesitant Hand:
   Taming Self-Interest in the History of Economic Ideas* (Princeton, NJ:
   Princeton University Press, 2009), 26–53.

73 Edwin Cannan, in a book review in *Economic Review* (July 1913), 333,
   quoted in Pigou, *The Economics of Welfare*, 112; cited in Steven G.
   Medema, "Pigou's 'Prima Facie Case': Market Failure in Theory and
   Practice," in Roger E. Backhouse and Tamotsu Nishizawa, eds., *No Wealth
   But Life: Welfare Economics and the Welfare State in Britain, 1880–1945*
   (Cambridge: Cambridge University Press, 2010), 45.

74 Marginal private net product is defined as the portion of product that
   accrues to the person investing resources in the process or in economic
   activity. Marginal social net product was, according to Pigou, the total
   net product of physical things or objective services due to the marginal
   increment of resources in any economic activity, regardless of any private
   return that might accrue. Medema, "Pigou's 'Prima Facie Case,'" 46;
   Medema, *The Hesitant Hand*, 60–1.

75 Other divergences between private and social net products occured, for
   instance, when private firms were allowed to operate public utilities but
   lacked incentives to make capital improvements. In this case private was
   greater than social net product. There could also be positive externalities,
   when private net product was less than social net product; Pigou's examples
   included lighthouses, parks, roads, tramways, street lighting, and scientific
   research. He argued that the state could intervene to apply incentives or
   restraints to remove the divergence. Medema, *The Hesitant Hand*, 62. Pigou
   did not invent *de novo* the concept of externalities. Alfred Marshall, in his
   discussion of external economies and diseconomies, is often so credited:
   Agnar Sandmo, *Economics Evolving: A History of Economic Thought*
   (Princeton, NJ: Princeton University Press, 2011), 228–30.

76 Ian Kumekawa discusses the shifts in Pigou's thought between *Wealth and
   Welfare* (1912) and *The Economics of Welfare* (1920), and later, further

changes. For one thing, Pigou softened the ethical starting point, the optimism, and the calls to action. Kumekawa, *The First Serious Optimist*, 119–21.

77 Marshall had proposed that welfare spending could be self-financing: it would so raise the "character" of the people that they would do much more work. Peter Groenewegen, *A Soaring Eagle: Alfred Marshall, 1842–1924* (Cheltenham, England: Edward Elgar, 1995), 33.

78 Pigou, *Wealth and Welfare*, 24.

79 Hugh Dalton, "The Measurement of the Inequality of Incomes," *Economic Journal* 30, no. 119 (Sept. 1920): 351–2.

80 The principle assumed even transfers and in doing so limited redistributive effects; transfers proportionate to the income levels of donor and beneficiary could increase social welfare. The principle was initially about not distributions but transfers, whose relationship to measured distributions proved immensely complex, despite the principle's origins in an article about measurement. A recent defence is Matthew D. Adler, "The Pigou–Dalton Principle and the Structure of Distributive Justice," 11 May 2013, at https://scholarship.law.duke.edu/cgi/viewcontent.cgi?article=5746&context=faculty_scholarship. A retrospective on Hugh Dalton is Anthony B. Atkinson and Andrea Brandolini, "Unveiling the Ethics behind Inequality Measurement: Dalton's Contribution to Economics," *Economic Journal* 125, no. 583 (March 2015): 209–34.

81 Hugh Dalton, *Some Aspects of the Inequality of Incomes in Modern Communities* (London: Routledge, 1920), 33–158. A briefer history occurs in Edwin Cannan, *A History of the Theories of Production and Distribution in English Political Economy from 1776 to 1848* (London: Rivington, Percival, 1894).

82 Dalton, *Some Aspects*, 267.

83 Ibid., 268–70, 352. To the idea "many men" held that women were by nature "less efficient" workers than men, Dalton replied that the idea was "mere hypothesis," capable of proof only when opportunities had been equalized.

84 James L. Huston, *Securing the Fruits of Labor: The American Concept of Wealth Distribution 1765–1900* (Baton Rouge: Louisiana State University Press, 1998), xiv (where Huston summarizes the "four axioms"). On the population axiom and its oddity see his pages 50–3: the population ratio was not subject to legislative control in the way that the other three axioms were.

85 Ibid., 356.

86 Russell H. Conwell, *Acres of Diamonds* (first pub. 1890) (New York: Harper, 1915), 18.

87　Ibid., 21.

88　Carnegie repeated the old wisdom about the evils of British landlordism
and the virtues of republican equality. He acknowledged serious costs to
the factory system and the "law of competition," including inequality and
social "friction"; but he rejoiced that the poor in his time were so much
more affluent than those in previous centuries, and he saw solutions to
inequality in death duties and expanded philanthropy. Andrew Carnegie,
The Gospel of Wealth (London: F.C. Hagen, 1889), 1, 5, and *Problems of
Today: Wealth – Labor – Socialism* (New York: Doubleday, Page, 1908),
44–5, 108–9.

89　George Gunton, *Wealth and Progress: A Critical Examination of the
Wages Question and Its Economic Relation to Social Reform* (New York:
D. Appleton, 1890), 4–10.

90　Ibid., 8. Gunton was not so naïve as to believe that abundance by itself
ensured more equitable distribution. The solution also required what he
called "social opportunity" – a vast expansion of working-class access to
education, culture, social contacts, and geographical mobility. And social
opportunity required shorter hours: Gunton's celebration of economic
growth and social opportunity was an elaborate argument for the eight-
hour movement. Whatever the egalitarian benefits of shorter hours,
Gunton had done more to erase the problem of inequality than to solve it.
Ibid., 203 ff.

91　Gary Dorrien makes this point about the American social-gospel movement in his *Economy, Difference, Empire: Social Ethics for Social Justice*
(New York: Columbia University Press, 2010), xi.

92　Charles B. Spahr, *An Essay on the Present Distribution of Wealth in the
United States* (New York: Thomas Y. Crowell, 1896). Robert Giffen, *The
Progress of the Working Classes in the Last Half Century* (London:
George Bell, 1884).

93　Spahr. *Essay*, also quoted (54) the valuable article on wealth by statistician
George K. Holmes, "The Concentration of Wealth," *Political Science
Quarterly* 8, no. 4 (Dec. 1893): 589–600. On the connection between
ethics, social surveys, and statistics see Bradley W. Bateman, "Make a
Righteous Number: Social Surveys, the Men and Religion Forward
Movement, and Quantification in American Economics," *History of
Political Economy*, Annual Supplement to vol. 33 (2001): 57–85. On the
birth of labour statistics: Margo Anderson, "Standards, Statuses, and
Statistics: Carroll Wright and the American Standard of Living,"
Advancing the Consumer Interest 9, no. 1 (spring 1997): 4–12; Lauren
Coyle, "The Birth of the Labor Bureau: Surveillance, Pacification, and the

Statistical Objectivity Narrative," *Rethinking Marxism* 22, no. 4 (2010): 544–68.

94 Spahr, *Essay*, 69, 129. Biographical information on Charles Barzillai Spahr is scarce. He had a doctorate from Columbia University. He was for a time the editor of the *Outlook*, a social-gospel magazine in New York, and belonged to that city's Social Reform Club. His wife, Jean Fine, was a prominent activist in the settlement movement. Anne M. Filiaci, "Wald and the Social Reform Club," at http://www.lillianwald.com/?page_id=489, accessed 13 December 2017.

95 Richard Mayo-Smith wrote a hostile review in *Political Science Quarterly* 12, no. 2 (June 1897): 345–8.

96 A similar upward trend appeared in British English after 1900, but "distribution of wealth" was much less frequent there than in American English.

97 Clark's key works were *Capital and Its Earnings* (1888); *The Philosophy of Wealth* (1894); and *The Distribution of Wealth* (1899). Thomas Nixon Carver, a student of Clark's, produced another marginalist study of wealth distribution and added an explicitly Malthusian approach to the determination of wages. Procreation, he argued, was related to the standard of living, which, it followed, determined the abundance or the scarcity of labor, and indirectly, the rate of wages. T.N. Carver, *The Distribution of Wealth* (first pub. 1904) (New York: Macmillan Company, 1921), 171.

98 A reviewer in Toronto's *Globe* in 1904, in one of the rare Canadian references to Clark's work, assumed that he too opposed the oppressive power of corporations. "The Library Table," *Globe*, 20 Aug 1904. On Clark's defence of oligopoly in 1887 see John F. Henry, *John Bates Clark: The Making of a Neoclassical Economist* (New York: St Martin's Press, 1995), 30.

99 Guglielmo F. Davanzati, *Ethical Codes and Income Distribution: A Study of John Bates Clark and Thorstein Veblen* (London: Routledge, 2006), 36–52.

100 Clark's theory drew on previous productivity theories of distribution. As George Scrope wrote in 1833: "In whatever proportions the several classes of labourers, capitalists, and landowners contribute their quota to the production of wealth, in that proportion have they clearly an equitable title to share in the wealth produced." George Scrope, *Principles of Political Economy* (first pub. 1833) (New York: Augustus M. Kelley, 1969), 227; cited in Henry, *Clark*, 50.

101 Clark, "The Law of Wages and Interest," *Annals of the American Academy of Political and Social Science* 1 (July 1890): 43; cited in Henry, *Clark*, 52. "The ultimate end of political economy is not, as is generally assumed, the

mere quantitative increase of wealth. Society, as an organic unit, has a higher economic end. That end is the attainment of the greatest quantity, the highest quality, and the most just distribution of wealth": John B. Clark, *The Philosophy of Wealth: Economic Principles Newly Formulated* (Boston: Ginn & Co., 1894), 205.

102 Clark, *The Distribution of Wealth: A Theory of Wages, Interest and Profits* (New York: Macmillan, 1899), 1.

103 Hunt and Lautzenheiser, *History of Economic Thought*, 302–5; Henry, *Clark*, 71–88.

104 Clark next had to reconcile the assumption of competition with the non-competitive reality of trusts. He proposed that trusts did not completely suppress competition; the appearance of monopoly profits would encourage new entrants into the industry, causing prices to fall and competition to resume. He also suggested that an economy of pure monopoly could benefit the public. Henry, *Clark*, 67.

105 Clark's challenge to the Protestant critique of wealth may not have been obvious, and he may not have seen it at all, since he continued to believe that corruption was endemic in modern capitalism and that "wealth is the corrupting element." Clark, "Gifts and the Moral Law," *Congregationalist and Christian World* (29 April 1905), 575; cited in Henry, *Clark*, 138.

106 Henry suggests that Clark, through his convoluted argument about the measurement of labour, reverted to a labour theory of value (*Clark*, 86). Henry may not convince all his readers.

107 Clark also rejected Henry George's ideas: he himself saw nothing special about land, and no sustained "unearned increment" appropriated by landowners, because land, like other factors of production, earned the equivalent of its marginal product.

108 Clark, *Essentials of Economic Theory* (New York: Macmillan, 1907), 257–8.

109 Henry, *Clark*, 53. Clark, according to Henry, wrestled with the tension between dynamic analysis and his model's assumption of static equilibrium. This tension was controversial; Alfred Marshall stated, cautiously and respectfully, his disagreement: Marshall, *Principles of Economics* (1907), xii n 1.

110 Henry, *Clark*, 148.

111 Clark, *Essentials of Economic Theory*, 255.

112 Clark's inconsistency on ethics was fully apparent by 1899. "Work according to ability and pay according to need, is a familiar formula," he wrote. "This rule ... would violate what is ordinarily regarded as a property right. The entire question whether this is just or not lies outside of our

inquiry, for it is a matter of pure ethics." Clark, *Distribution*, 8. Yet Clark did reason from an ethical perspective and did say that justice was met when factors were rewarded according to their productivities: Henry, *Clark*, 73–4.

113 Reactions varied outside the United States as well. The marginal theory of income distribution did not always entail an ethical justification of market-determined distributions, as the Swedish economist Knut Wicksell (1851–1926) showed. For Wicksell, explaining wage formation and income distribution was not the same as defending them as just. Agnar Sandmo, *Economics Evolving: A History of Economic Thought* (Princeton, NJ: Princeton University Press, 2011), 274–5.

114 Problems Clark failed to resolve included the frictionless assumption; the conflict between dynamic and static analysis of distribution; and how to measure capital (specifying the contribution of an additional unit of capital or of labour to output while holding other inputs constant) (Henry, *Clark*, 61–3). Eugen von Böhm-Bawerk criticized Clark's concept of capital (ibid., 64–6). Also, how to relate returns to the last unit of production?: previous units of labour represented greater productivity; if they received a wage determined by the last unit, that was less than their contribution to output.

115 John R. Commons, *The Distribution of Wealth* (New York: Macmillan, 1893), 252.

116 "Now instead of the profits being due to the powerful exertions and abilities of the captains of industry, they are due to certain fixed social relations and rights." Ibid., 236. Robert Hunter's *Poverty* (New York: Macmillan, 1904) cited Commons, who helped him with the book.

117 Veblen dismissed Clark as follows: "The 'natural' system of free competition, or, as it was once called, 'the obvious and simple system of natural liberty,' is accordingly a phase of the development of the institution of capital; and its claim to immutable dominion is evidently as good as the like claim of any other phase of cultural growth. The equity, or 'natural justice,' claimed for it is evidently just and equitable only in so far as the conventions of ownership on which it rests continue to be a secure integral part of the institutional furniture of the community; that is to say, so long as these conventions are part and parcel of the habits of thought of the community; that is to say, so long as these things are currently held to be just and equitable." Veblen, "Professor Clark's Economics," *Quarterly Journal of Economics* 22, no. 2 (Feb. 1908): 154.

118 Thorstein Veblen, *Theory of the Leisure Class* (first pub. 1899), ed. Martha Banta (Oxford: Oxford University Press, 2007), 135.

119 Ibid.

120 Ibid., 136.

121 Ibid., 29.

122 "Under the conditions prevalent in the era of handicraft, the rights of ownership made for equality rather than the reverse, so that their exercise was in effect not notably inconsistent with the ancient bias in favour of mutual aid and human brotherhood." Veblen, "Christian Morals and the Competitive System," *International Journal of Ethics* 20, no. 2 (Jan. 1910): 183–4.

123 As industrial development proceeds, he said, "property becomes massed in relatively fewer hands." Veblen, *Leisure Class*, 41.

124 Sidney Plotkin and Rick Tilman, *The Political Ideas of Thorstein Veblen* (New Haven, Conn., and London: Yale University Press, 2011), 85.

125 Matthew Watson, "Desperately Seeking Social Approval: Adam Smith, Thorstein Veblen and the Moral Limits of Capitalist Culture," *British Journal of Sociology* 63, no. 3 (2012): 491–512.

126 Had they noticed it, Veblen's tendency to pessimism might have puzzled labour reformers and socialists. In one of his rare mentions of "inequality," he was observing its cultural acceptance across classes. He noted in 1921 "some irritation and fault-finding" with "what is felt to be an unduly disproportionate inequality in the present distribution of income." But, he said, the "main fact" was that "absentee ownership after all is the idol of every true American heart." "To get something for nothing, at any cost," was a universal ambition, and there seemed no immediate prospect that Americans would outgrow "this commercialized frame of mind." Veblen, *The Engineers and the Price System* (New York: B.W. Huebsch, 1921), 161–2. This was a later work, easily ignored by readers who found inspiration in Veblen's books of 1899 and 1904.

127 M.O. Lorenz, "Methods of Measuring the Concentration of Wealth," *Publications of the American Statistical Association* 9, no. 70 (June 1905): 217. On the evolution of the graph and its status as "archetype" see Laurent Derobert and Guillaume Theriot, "The Lorenz Curve as Archetype: A Historico-Epistemological Study," *European Journal of the History of Economic Thought* 10, no. 4 (winter 2003): 573–85.

128 Lorenz, "Methods of Measuring," 217.

129 Willford I. King, *The Elements of Statistical Method* (New York: Macmillan, 1912), 156.

130 Lorenz's influence is evident in Ely's discussion of distribution in Richard T. Ely, *Studies in the Evolution of Industrial Society* (New York: Macmillan, 1906), 256–68.

131 Richard T. Ely, Thomas S. Adams, Max O. Lorenz, and Allyn A. Young,
     Outlines of Economics (New York: Macmillan, 1908), 114. The authors
     also rejected a labour theory of value: the equation of just reward with
     amount of labour failed – how was one to measure labour's productive
     contribution in occupations as varied as shoemakers, physicians, and
     presidents of life-insurance companies (115)? A measurement problem
     answered an ethical claim: the former had defeated the latter.
132 Ibid., 209, 552.
133 Ibid., 116.
134 Thomas N. Carver made the same point in his review of Clark's
     Distribution of Wealth in *Quarterly Journal of Economics* 15, no. 4
     (Aug. 1901), 579.
135 Ely et al., *Outlines of Economics*, 328 n1.
136 Ibid., 344.
137 Ibid., 115.
138 Ibid., 345.
139 Ibid., 114.
140 Ibid., 665.
141 Ibid., 116.
142 Bruce Baum, *Rereading Power and Freedom in J.S. Mill* (Toronto:
     University of Toronto Press, 2000), 273–4. T.H. Green wrote: "We rightly
     refuse to recognise the highest development on the part of an exceptional
     individual or exceptional class, as an advance towards the true freedom of
     man, if it is founded on a refusal of the same opportunity to other men."
     "Lecture on Liberal Legislation," 371. See also Matt Carter, *T.H. Green
     and the Development of Ethical Socialism* (Exeter: Imprint Academic,
     2003). Green offered a good example of how justification for inequality
     may co-exist with equality of opportunity that exonerated inequality.
143 The words do not appear in Google NGrams before the 1880s, in either
     British or American English. The frequency increased in the 1890s and
     then shot upwards between 1900 and the 1920s.
144 Ely et al., *Outlines of Economics*, 210.
145 Ibid., 209.
146 Ibid., 379, 394.
147 Public education was central to Progressive reform politics. The connec-
     tions between distribution of wealth and education reform operated across
     many reciprocal paths. The Progressive educator John Dewey, for instance,
     was a strong supporter of Henry George. For Dewey, education was a
     "democratic ideal," requiring school facilities in "such amplitude and effi-
     ciency" as to "discount the effects of economic inequalities, and secure to

all the wards of the nation equality of equipment for their future careers." Dewey, *Democracy and Education: An Introduction to the Philosophy of Education* (first pub. 1916) (New York: Macmillan, 1930), 114.

148 Pareto did not appear in the 1908 edition of Ely et al.'s *Outlines of Economics* but surfaced in the expanded bibliography in the 1917 edition, together with other European scholars.

149 F.D. Merritt, "Cours d'Économie Politique," *Journal of Political Economy* 6, no. 4 (Sept. 1898): 549–52; H.L. Moore, "Cours d'économie politique," *Annals of the American Academy of Political and Social Science* 9, no. 3 (May 1897): 444–7.

150 Pareto accepted the provisional status of his "law," since it was an empirical observation. "I should not be greatly surprised if some day a well-authenticated exception were discovered." Pareto, "The New Theories of Economics," *Journal of Political Economy* 5, no. 4 (1897): 501.

151 James Alexander, "Pareto: The Karl Marx of Fascism," *Journal of Historical Review* 14, no. 5 (1994): 10–18. See also John Cunningham Wood and Michael McLure, eds., *Vilfredo Pareto: Critical Assessments of Leading Economists*, vol. III (London and New York: Routledge, 1999); David Ingram, *Reason, History and Politics: The Communitarian Grounds of Legitimation in the Modern Age* (Albany: State University of New York Press, 1995).

152 Hunt and Lautzenheiser, *History of Economic Thought*, 384.

153 Giovanni M. Giorgi and Stefania Gubbiotti, "Celebrating the Memory of Corrado Gini: a Personality Out of the Ordinary," *International Statistical Review* 85, no. 2 (2017): 336.

154 "Intensità" was Gini's word. Gini, "Sulla misura della concentrazione e della variabilità dei caratteri," *Atti del R. Istituto Veneto di Scienze, Lettere ed Arti* 73, no. 2, 1203–48. Michael Schneider, "Measuring Inequality: The Origins of the Lorenz Curve and the Gini Coefficient," at https://econpapers.repec.org/paper/ltrwpaper/2004.01.htm, accessed 9 January 2018.

155 Willford Isbell King, *The Wealth and Income of the People of the United States* (New York: Macmillan, 1917).

156 Ibid., 231.

157 The following words did not appear in King's book (ibid.): "Christian," "ethics," "ethical," "moral," and "morality." King had a notion of class, but entirely Weberian: his references to "poorest class," "middle class," and "richest class" followed directly from his tabular representations of income shares by income category.

158 Ibid., 54–60.

159 Ibid., 251.
160 Positive checks included delayed marriage, control of lust, and "war, starvation, disease and pestilence" (ibid., 242).
161 Ibid., 249, 254.
162 "The underpaid labor, the prolonged and grovelling drudgery, the wasted strength, the misery and squalor, the diseases resulting, and the premature deaths that would be prevented by a just distribution of the products of labor, would in a single year outweigh all the so-called 'crime' of a century." Ward, "False Notions of Government," *Forum*, 3 (June 1887), cited in Henry Steele Commager, *Lester Ward and the Welfare* State (Indianapolis: Bobbs-Merrill, 1967), 112.
163 Ward, *Dynamic Sociology or Applied Social Science* (first pub. 1883) (New York: Greenwood Press, 1968), vol. I, 507–8, where he defined intelligence. Evolution appeared often in this book; Ward's rejection of Spencer was in chapter 2, 139–219. On Ward's evolutionary views see Commager, "Introduction," in Henry Steele Commager, *Lester Ward and the Welfare* State (Indianapolis: Bobbs-Merrill, 1967), xxviii. See also Edward C. Rafferty, *Apostle of Human Progress: Lester Frank Ward and American Political Thought, 1841–1913* (Lanham, Md.: Rowman & Littlefield, 2003).
164 The "under-government" argument became most explicit in Ward's critique of plutocracy: Ward, "Plutocracy and Paternalism," *Forum* 20 (Nov. 1895), quoted in Commager, *Lester Ward and the Welfare State*, 184. As Commager argues, Ward took a pragmatic rather than a theoretical position on the state's role. Good legislation was that which contributed to the public's material, intellectual, and spiritual welfare. Commager, "Introduction," xxxv. There may be a parallel here to Arthur Pigou's later pragmatism on the state's role, as Medema outlined in "Pigou's 'Prima Facie Case,'" 50–1. Pigou's positions developed later, in the 1930s, and reflected a much deeper consideration of the criteria and principles to apply to state action, given the challenge of anticipating probable outcomes of policy options.
165 Ward, *Dynamic Sociology*, vol. I, 519, 522.
166 Wootton, *Power, Pleasure, and Profit*, 5.
167 Ryan, *Living Wage; Its Ethical and Economic Aspects* (New York: Grosset and Dunlap, 1906), 53.
168 Ibid., 58–61. In chapter 3 Ryan justified his natural-rights approach and critiqued others' approaches to rights.
169 Ibid., 67.

170 This is not to deny problems with Ryan's natural-rights position. Questions arise, of course, over the content in ibid. of key words ("essential needs," "reasonable maintenance").

171 For Ryan's "concrete estimate of a living wage" see ibid., 123–50.

172 Ibid., 302.

173 The duty did not end with a living wage. It included also pensions for the incapacitated and the elderly. Ibid., 320–2.

174 Studies of Ryan include Harlan Beckley, *Passion for Justice: Retrieving the Legacies of Walter Rauschenbusch, John A. Ryan, and Reinhold Niebuhr* (Louisville, KY: Westminster / John Knox, 1992); Francis L. Broderick, *Right Reverend New Dealer: John A. Ryan* (New York: Macmillan, 1963); and Robert G. Kennedy et al., *Religion and Public Life: The Legacy of Monsignor John A. Ryan* (Lanham, MD: University Press of America, 2001).

175 So proposes Kenneth Himes, "Catholic Social Teaching on Building a Just Society: The Need for a Ceiling and a Floor," *Religions* 8, no. 4 (2017): 1–11.

176 Ryan's justice entailed certain limits and compromises. He did not specify any maximum income; he suggested that businessmen using "fair business methods" might "take indefinitely large profits." Ryan, *Distributive Justice: The Right and Wrong of Our Present Distribution of Wealth* (New York: Macmillan, 1916), 255.

177 "The duty of distributing superfluous wealth" was the subject of chapter 21 in ibid., 303–22.

178 Ibid., 298.

179 Ibid., 293.

180 On the place of expediency and prudence in Ryan's economics see Harlan Beckley, "Theology and Prudence in John Ryan's Economic Ethics," in Robert G. Kennedy et al, *Religion and Public Life: The Legacy of Monsignor John Ryan* (Lanham, MD: University Press of America, 2001), 35–60.

181 Alfred Marshall, a very cautious social reformer, estimated in 1907 that three-quarters of Britain's national income went to purposes that made for "happiness and the elevation of life" – leaving over a very large "margin" that might yet be "diverted to social uses without causing any great distress to those from whom it was taken." Alfred Marshall, "The Social Possibilities of Economic Chivalry," *Economic Journal* 17, no. 65 (March 1907): 9.

182 J.A. Hobson, *Canada Today* (London: Unwin, 1906), 5–6.

CHAPTER TWO

1 Amury Girod, *Notes diverses sur le Bas-Canada* (Village Debartzeh [Lower Canada]: J.P. Boucher-Belleville, 1835), 63. Girod was born in Switzerland and migrated to Canada in the early 1830s.
2 Editorial in *La Minerve*, 10 août 1835.
3 Augustin-Norbert Morin in Assembly debates, *La Minerve*, 28 August 1837.
4 Yvan Lamonde, *The Social History of Ideas in Quebec 1760–1896* (Montreal and Kingston: McGill-Queen's University Press, 2013), 67.
5 Ibid., 365–7.
6 Aquinas, *Summa theologica*, q. 78, art. 1, quoted in Peter Dominy, *Decoding Mammon: Money as a Dangerous and Subversive Instrument* (Eugene, OR: Wipf and Stock, 2012), 23; see also Alan S. Kahan, *Mind vs. Money: The War between Intellectuals and Capitalism* (London: Transaction Publishers, 2010), 48.
7 Benedict XIV, *Vix pervenit* (1745), cited in William M. Woodyard and Chad G. Marzen, "Is Greed Good? A Catholic Perspective on Modern Usury," BYU *Journal of Public Law* 27, no. 1 (2012): 200. See also John T. Noonan, *The Scholastic Analysis of Usury* (Cambridge, MA: Harvard University Press, 1957).
8 John T. Noonan, "Development in Moral Doctrine," *Theological Studies* 54, no. 4 (Dec. 1993): 662.
9 Christine Hudon, "Prêtes et prêteurs au XIXᵉ siècle," *Histoire sociale / Social History* 26, no 52 (Nov. 1993): 231–8.
10 Amintore Fanfani, *Catholicism, Protestantism, and Capitalism* (New York: Sheed and Ward, 1955), 122. Much of this paragraph and the next is indebted to Fanfani's chapter "Catholicism and Capitalism" in ibid., 119–59.
11 Aquinas, *Summa theologica*, 2a2ae, in Brian Davis, *The Thought of Thomas Aquinas* (Oxford: Clarendon Press, 1992), 181. On Aquinas and property see Rachael Walsh, "Property, Human Flourishing and St. Thomas Aquinas," *Canadian Journal of Law and Jurisprudence* 31, no. 1 (Feb. 2018): 197–222.
12 Henry of Langenstein, *Tractatus bipartitus* (1392–93), cited in Fanfani, *Catholicism*, 129.
13 R.H. Tawney, *Religion and the Rise of Capitalism: A Historical Study* (London: John Murray, 1926), 35.
14 *Mirari vos: On Liberalism and Religious Indifferentism* (1832). Papal encyclicals available at http://www.papalencyclicals.net, accessed 22 May 2020.

15 Leo XII, *Charitate Christi* (1825), at http://www.papalencyclicals.net, accessed 22 May 2020.

16 "Lettre d'un curé du Canada," *Bulletin des recherches historiques* 17, no 1 (1911): 3–15; quoted in Lamonde, *Social History of Ideas*, 75-6.

17 Frank A. Abbott, *The Body or the Soul? Religion and Culture in a Quebec Parish, 1736–1901* (Montreal and Kingston: McGill-Queen's University Press, 2016), xix; Peter N. Moogk, *La Nouvelle France: The Making of French Canada – A Cultural History* (East Lansing: Michigan State University Press, 2000), 253.

18 Abbott, *The Body*, 242. The idea that religion was an imposed force, and that the church–parishioner relationship was one of domination and submission, has long ago been revised. For instance, Louis Rousseau, "À propos du 'réveil religieux' dans le Québec au XIXᵉ siècle: où se loge le vrai débat?" *Revue d'histoire de l'Amérique française* 49, no 2 (autumn 1995): 223–45.

19 Abbott, *The Body*, 125.

20 Ollivier Hubert, *Sur la terre comme au ciel: La gestion des rites par l'Église catholique du Québec (fin XVIIᵉ–mi-XIXᵉ siècle)* (Quebec: Les Presses de l'Universite Laval, 2000), 265.

21 Ibid., 269–71, 275–6, 299.

22 The intrusion of the market revolution is an old subject in U.S. history, going back to the work of De Tocqueville. A seminal interpretation is Charles Sellers, *The Market Revolution: Jacksonian America, 1815–1846* (New York: Oxford University Press, 1991). Sellers posits that the market revolution deeply divided the early republic, substantially because of religion.

23 Many sources note the increasing rural diversity and the rise of an *habitant "gentilité*," and a wide range of studies deal with market penetration. For instance, Gilles Paquet and Jean-Pierre Wallot, "Stratégie foncière de l'habitant: Québec (1790–1835)," *Revue d'histoire de l'Amérique française* 39, no 4 (1986): 556. See also Christian Dessureault, John A. Dickinson, and Joseph Goy, *Famille et marché, XVIᵉ–XXᵉ siècles* (Sillery: Septentrion, 2003).

24 Allan Greer, *The Patriots and the People: The Rebellion of 1837 in Rural Lower Canada* (Toronto: University of Toronto Press, 1993), 63–4.

25 *Quebec Mercury*, 27 Oct. 1806, cited in Lamonde, *Social History of Ideas*, 31.

26 Louis-Joseph Papineau, *Adresse à tous les électeurs du Bas-Canada* (Montreal, 1827), 7.

27 *Relations historique des événements de l'élection du comté du Lac des Deux Montagnes en 1834* (Montreal, 1835; reissued 1968), 7–8.

28 Girod, *Notes diverses sur le Bas-Canada*, 63, 65.

29 There is an impressive literature behind this sentence. Among other works: Robert Richard, "Bank War in Lower Canada: The Rebellion and the Market Revolution," in Maxime Dagenais and Julien Mauduit, eds., *Revolutions across Borders: Jacksonian America and the Canadian Rebellion* (Montreal and Kingston: McGill-Queen's University Press, 2019), 58–87; Albert Schrauwers, "'The Road Not Taken': Duncombe on Republican Currency: Joint Stock Democracy, Civic Republicanism, and Free Banking," in ibid., 174–205; Louis-Georges Harvey, "Banques, société et politique dans le discours politique d'Edmund Bailey O'Callaghan, 1833–1837," *Cahiers de dix* 69 (2015): 251–79. The connection between hard currency, credit, and the concentration of both wealth and political power is a recurring theme in Charles Duncombe, *Duncombe's Free Banking: An Essay on Banking, Currency, Finance, Exchanges and Political Economy* (Cleveland, OH: Sanford & Co., 1841). A bestseller, widely read in the British North American colonies, was William M. Gouge, *A Short History of Paper Money and Banking in the United States* (Philadelphia: T.W. Ustick, 1833). On Gouge see Richard, "Bank War in Lower Canada," 69–73.

30 Louis-Georges Harvey, *Le printemps de l'Amérique française: Americanité, anticolonialisme et républicanisme dans le discours politique québécois, 1805–1837* (Quebec: Boréal, 2005), 55.

31 J.G.A. Pocock, *Virtue, Commerce and History: Essays in Political Thought and History, Chiefly in the Eighteenth Century* (Cambridge: Cambridge University Press, 1985), 48.

32 "Observateur," *Le Canadien*, 12 Dec. 1807.

33 Ibid.

34 "À Verax," by "Un spectateur désenteressé," *Le Canadien*, 5 Dec. 1807.

35 Article by Canadensis, ibid., 5 Dec. 1807. See also ibid., 24 Oct. 1807: "The fur trade, which enriches the big capitalists of Montreal and Quebec, is for Lower Canada a seed of depopulation and destruction; it preoccupies and excites our youth, who indulge in debauchery with the lascivious Savages; there they lose all idea of religion and of decency."

36 "Canada can never be a commercial country or state ... Canada can never achieve a great degree of prosperity through commerce." Canadensis, ibid., 23 Jan. 1808.

37 Lamonde, *Social History of Ideas*, 31–2.

38 Caius, *Le Canadien*, 22 Nov. 1806.

39 *Le Canadien*, 7 May 1808. See also the article by "Un du people" in ibid., 28 Feb. 1807, for a rare appearance of the word "*inégalités*" in a

suggestion that the poor actually pay much more in taxes than the rich, because parishes differ in wealth: "For the comparative inequalities of wealth among parishes and in the proportion of poor in each, are too great to allow the imposition of a separate tax on each parish."

40 Lamonde, *Social History of Ideas*, 85, 92.

41 Michel Ducharme observes "a quintessential feature of republican argumentation: that liberty and equality go hand in hand." Michel Ducharme, *The Idea of Liberty in Canada during the Age of Atlantic Revolutions, 1776–1838* (Montreal and Kingston: McGill-Queen's University Press, 2014), 102. Mark Olsen and Louis-Georges Harvey, "Computers in Intellectual History: Lexical Statistics and the Analysis of Political Discourse," *Journal of Interdisciplinary History* 18, no. 3 (winter 1988): 449–64.

42 Even reformers could modify the principle of equality to apply it to some British subjects and not to other subjects. According to Étienne Parent, "as soon as an inhabitant of the country shows that he really is a citizen, no distinction is made any more." This principle applied only to *citoyens*, which not all residents were, in Parent's view. Lamonde, *Social History of Ideas*, 95.

43 Papineau in Assembly debates, 10 Jan. 1833, *La Minerve*, 24 Jan. 1833. Substitution refers to the designation of an alternate legatee.

44 Papineau, *Adresse à tous les électeurs du Bas-Canada*, 3–4, cited in Harvey, *Le printemps* 97–8.

45 Ibid., 98.

46 Quotations from the Ninety-two Resolutions are from W.P.M. Kennedy, *Statutes, Treaties and Documents of the Canadian Constitution, 1713–1929* (Toronto: Oxford University Press, 1930), 270–89. The context made clear that "fortune" referred to wealth rather than to a beneficent fate or *fortuna* (thanks to Michel Ducharme and Robert Griffiths for their clarifications).

47 It was gender-specific in Upper Canada, of course. On manly virtue, independence, and public life see Cecilia Morgan, *Public Men and Virtuous Women: The Gendered Languages of Religion and Politics in Upper Canada, 1791–1850* (Toronto: University of Toronto Press, 1996), 77ff.

48 "Adresse de la Confédération des Six Comtés au people du Canada 23–24 octobre 1837," *Le Canadien*, 13 Nov. 1837. The address is widely reprinted, as in Yvan Lamonde and Claude Corbo, *Le Rouge et le Bleu: Une anthologie de la pensée politique au Québec de la Conquête à la Révolution tranquille* (Montreal: Presses de l'Université de Montréal, 1999), 109–16.

49   A writer in *Le Canadien* (18 June 1838) referred to "a deep vice in the political order: this vice is the rise of an oligarchical principle in government, a principle of privilege, favoritism and monopoly and their accompaniments."

50   "Adresse de la Confédération des Six Comtés."

51   Ibid.

52   Étienne Parent, "À propos des 92 Resolutions," *Le Canadien*, 26 Feb. 1834, in Yvan Lamonde and Claude Corbo, *Le Rouge et le Bleu: Une anthologie de la pensée politique au Québec de la Conquête à la Révolution tranquille* (Montreal: Presses de l'Université de Montréal, 1999), 95.

53   Parent, "Adresse au public canadien," *Le Canadien*, 7 May 1831, in Jean-Charles Falardeau, *Étienne Parent 1802–1874* (Montreal: Les Éditions la Presse, 1975), 73.

54   Parent, "Le vrai histoire du Bas-Canada," *Le Canadien*, 7 Oct. 1839, cited in Falardeau, *Étienne Parent,* 95; "Les pouvoirs politique selon la Constitution," *Le Canadien*, 8 Sept. 1824, in Falardeau, *Étienne Parent,* 66.

55   Parent, "La vraie histoire," in Falardeau, *Étienne Parent,* 97.

56   Daniel Wickberg, "What Is the History of Sensibilities? On Cultural Histories, Old and New," *American Historical Review* 112, no. 3 (June 2007): 662. Among many examples: Damien Boquet and Piroska Nagy, *Medieval Sensibilities: A History of the Emotions in the Middle Ages* (Malden, MA: Polity Press, 2018); Joseph S. Moore and Jane G.V. McGaughey, "The Covenanter Sensibility across the Long Atlantic World," *Journal of Transatlantic Studies* 11, no. 2 (2013), 125–34.

57   There is a literature on both the play and the opera, of course, but see a succinct statement of the sensibility thesis by Geoffrey O'Brien in *New York Review of Books* (20 Nov. 2014), 42–3; see also Samuel Fleischacker, *A Short History of Distributive Justice* (Cambridge, MA: Harvard University Press, 2004), 53–4.

58   Pierre Rosanvallon, *The Society of Equals* (Cambridge, MA: Harvard University Press, 2013), 52–3.

59   Fleischacker, *Short History of Distributive Justice*, 53–5.

60   Rosanvallon, *Society of Equals*, 53.

61   Patricia Crone, *Pre-industrial Societies* (Oxford: Basil Blackwell, 1989), 104. See also Rosanvallon, *Society of Equals*, 52–4, 66–8.

62   Catharine Anne Wilson, *Tenants in Time: Family Strategies, Land, and Liberalism in Upper Canada, 1799–1871* (Montreal and Kingston: McGill-Queen's University Press, 2009), especially chap. 2, pp. 23–46.

Peter Baskerville's forthcoming book on land and settlement in nine-teenth-century Perth County promises to further complicate the meanings of property and rights of possession in Upper Canada / Ontario.

63 Catherine Parr Traill, *The Backwoods of Canada: Being Letters from the Wife of an Emigrant Officer* (London: M.A. Nattalli, 1849), 126.

64 Quoted in Peter A. Russell, *Attitudes to Social Structure and Mobility in Upper Canada 1815–1840* (Lewiston, NY: Edwin Mellen Press, 1990), 23. Robert Gourlay claimed that Upper Canadians also compared their situa-tion to that of Americans. "Every where I found the people well disposed to Government, but quite disappointed and dispirited with occurrences that might have been prevented. They see the property of their neighbours in the United States advancing in value, while their's [*sic*] is on the decline. They see everything in motion there, while all here is at a stand." Robert Gourlay, *Statistical Account of Upper Canada* (London: Simpkin & Marshall, 1822), vol. II, 462–3.

65 S.F. Wise, "Sermon Literature and Canadian Intellectual History," in A.B. McKillop and Paul Romney, eds., *God's Peculiar Peoples: Essays on Political Culture in Nineteenth Century Canada* (Ottawa: Carleton University Press, 1993), 17.

66 John Clarke, *Land, Power, and Economics on the Frontier of Upper Canada* (Montreal and Kingston: McGill-Queen's University Press, 2001), 457.

67 Ibid., 461.

68 Ibid.

69 Traill, *The Backwoods of Canada*, 103.

70 Montreal Society for the Attainment of Religious Liberty and Equality in British North America, *Sequel to the Prospectus ... [on] the Cause of Religious Liberty ...* (Montreal, 1837), 14.

71 Susanna Moodie, *Roughing It in the Bush* (first pub. London 1852) (Toronto: McClelland and Stewart, 1970), 140–2. Catherine Parr Traill thought that shopkeepers "maintain a rank in society which entitles them to equality with the aristocracy of the country." She concluded that "it is education and manners that must distinguish the gentleman in this coun-try, seeing that the labouring man, if he is diligent and industrious, may soon become his equal in point of worldly possessions." Traill, *The Backwoods of Canada*, 81. On the speed with which established farmers "consider themselves on an equality with those to whom, in former times, the hope of gain would have made them crouch like slaves," see John Howison, *Sketches of Upper Canada* (Edinburgh: Oliver & Boyd, 1821), 137. Howison also commented on the democratic egalitarianism of the Talbot Settlement in southwestern Upper Canada: 173–4.

72 J.R. Pole, *The Pursuit of Equality in American History* (Berkeley and Los Angeles: University of California Press, 1978), 111.

73 On the complexities of establishment and church–state relations in the colonies see Denis McKim, *Boundless Dominion: Providence, Politics, and the Early Canadian Presbyterian World View* (Montreal and Kingston: McGill-Queen's University Press, 2017), 123–34.

74 John Webster Grant, *A Profusion of Spires: Religion in Nineteenth-Century Ontario* (Toronto: University of Toronto Press, 1988), 85–8.

75 Carol Wilton, *Popular Politics and Political Culture in Upper Canada, 1800–1850* (Montreal and Kingston: McGill-Queen's University Press, 2000), 52.

76 Ibid.

77 Grant, *Profusion of Spires*, 98.

78 Larry Siedentop discusses "the defence of egalitarian moral intuitions" in *Inventing the Individual: The Origins of Western Liberalism* (London: Allen Lane, 2014), 293–305.

79 On the way in which the Children of Peace adapted music to the egalitarian theology of Inner Light see Albert Schrauwers, *Awaiting the Millennium: The Children of Peace and the Village of Hope, 1812–1889* (Toronto: University of Toronto Press, 1993), 65–7; W. John McIntyre, *Children of Peace* (Montreal and Kingston: McGill-Queen's University Press, 1994), 92–4. On Presbyterian psalm-singing: McKim, *Boundless Dominion*, 49. An egalitarian impetus appeared in the suspicion of hierarchical church governance (often associated with Catholicism), and also occasionally in the issue of selection of ministers. McKim, *Boundless Dominion*, 145.

80 This paragraph is indebted to Grant, *Profusion of Spires*, 101ff, and William Westfall, *Two Worlds: The Protestant Culture of Nineteenth-Century Ontario* (Kingston and Montreal: McGill-Queen's University Press, 1989), 36–45.

81 Westfall, *Two Worlds*, 42–3.

82 Montreal Society, *Sequel to the Prospectus*, 29.

83 Montreal Society for the Attainment of Religious Liberty and Equality, *Prospectus of the Plan and Principles of a Society ... for the Attainment and Security of Universal and Perfect Religious Liberty and Equality* (Montreal, 1836), 8.

84 Ibid., 6.

85 Ibid., 23.

86 Montreal Society, *Sequel to the Prospectus*, 5.

87 Mackenzie's appeal to arms is in Colin Read and Ronald J. Stagg, eds., *The Rebellion of 1837 in Upper Canada: A Collection of Documents* (Toronto: Champlain Society, 1985), 110–13.

88 William Perkins (1558–1602), quoted in Charles Taylor, *Sources of the Self: The Making of the Modern Identity* (Cambridge, MA: Harvard University Press, 1989), 225.

89 Albert Schrauwers, *"Union Is Strength": W.L. Mackenzie, The Children of Peace and the Emergence of Joint Stock Democracy in Upper Canada* (Toronto: University of Toronto Press, 2009), 17.

90 Ibid., 46.

91 Jeffrey L. McNairn, *The Capacity to Judge: Public Opinion and Deliberative Democracy in Upper Canada, 1791–1854* (Buffalo, NY: University of Toronto Press. 2000), 68–9; Schrauwers, *"Union Is Strength"*, 22.

92 The words were those of the seventeenth-century French writer Jean de la Bruyère, quoted in *Le Canadien*, 7 March 1807.

93 Rev. Christophorus Atkinson, *Interesting Extracts, Etc., on Religious and Moral Subjects* (Sheffield, England: J. Pearce, 1850), 256.

94 Westfall, *Two Worlds*, 37. McNairn believes that perceived social differences between Upper Canada and Britain could strengthen support for the idea of a mixed and balanced monarchy: McNairn, *Capacity to Judge*, 41.

95 *Church*, 3 March 1838, quoted in Russell, *Attitudes to Social Structure*, 194.

96 John Strachan, *A Discourse on the Character of George the Third* (1810), quoted in Ducharme, *The Idea of Liberty*, 129.

97 Francis Bond Head, *A Narrative* (London: John Murray, 1839), 465.

98 *Canadian Christian Examiner*, quoted in Russell, *Attitudes to Social Structure*, 187–8.

99 Glenelg, quoted in Read and Stagg, eds., *The Rebellion of 1837 in Upper Canada*, 321.

100 Thomas Dalton, in the *Patriot*, cited in Russell, *Attitudes to Social Structure*, 199.

101 Abbé Lartigue in 1812, cited in Lamonde, *Social History of Ideas*, 42.

102 Simcoe, in *Journals of the House of Assembly*, 15 Oct. 1792, 18, cited in McNairn, *Capacity to Judge*, 23.

103 *Correspondent & Advocate*, 11 April 1836, cited in McNairn, *Capacity to Judge*, 39–40.

104 Suspicion of unrestrained American individualism and materialism could lead some people to reject egalitarianism – for example, Parti canadien leader Pierre Bédard. The stereotypical frontier American was, he wrote in 1808, the opposite of "the virtuous citizen embodied in the small farmer"; U.S. citizens were "infected by the poison of equality." *Le Canadien*, 17 Dec. 1808, cited in Harvey, *Le printemps*, 72, 74. Clearly equality was a

contingent, context-dependent idea: its political uses were always limited, and in the 1830s "equality" had changed since Bédard's context in 1808. The traditionalist Denis-Benjamin Viger shared the aversion to American ideas and institutions: Maxime Raymond-Dufour, "Denis-Benjamin Viger en 1809 et en 1831: de la répétition de l'histoire au crescendo de l'inacceptable," *Revue d'histoire de l'Amérique française* 71, no 3–4 (winter–spring 2018): 13–39.

105 McNairn, *Capacity to Judge*, 43–4. Opponents of responsible government could acknowledge explicitly that it constituted a claim to "terms of equality." Ibid., 46.

106 Ibid., 58. According to Hartwell Bowsfield, Gourlay "did not indulge in the radical democracy of Cobbett or Hunt. He sought control of the arbitrary power of the executive rather than a democracy of numbers or of equality." Nevertheless, Gourlay's township meetings helped stir up popular politics in the colony. Hartwell Bowsfield, "Upper Canada in the 1820s: The Development of a Political Consciousness" (PhD dissertation, University of Toronto, 1976), 146.

107 Caius, in *Le Canadien*, 22 Nov. 1806.

108 Letter of "Ex Colonist," Montreal *Vindicator*, 21 Jan. 1837.

109 Meeting of the Freeholders of Terrebonne, 10 June 1837, in ibid., 16 June 1837.

110 Greer, *The Patriots and the People*, 268.

111 Harvey, *Le printemps*. Historians debate about Patriote ideology, its debt to civic nationalism or republican ideas, and its relationship to liberal thought: Ducharme, *The Idea of Liberty*, 122–3.

112 "Adresse de la Confédération des Six Comtés, 24 octobre 1837," in Jean-Paul Bernard, *Assemblées publiques, résolutions et déclarations de 1837–1838* (Montreal: VLB Éditeur, 1988), 277–8. See also "Address of the Confederation of the Six Counties to the People of Canada, 24 October 1837," in Montreal *Vindicator*, 27 Oct. 1837. See as well S.D. Clark, *Movements of Political Protest in Canada 1640–1840* (Toronto: University of Toronto Press, 1959), 302. The words of the U.S. Declaration of Independence also appeared in Upper Canada, as in the meeting of the inhabitants of Yarmouth in September 1837 (Clark, *Movements*, 382).

113 James L Huston, *Securing the Fruits of Labor: The American Concept of Wealth Distribution* (Baton Rouge: Louisiana State University Press, 1998), 233. Mackenzie referred with approval to Jackson's refusal to re-charter the U.S. Bank in *Colonial Advocate*, 21 Feb. 1833.

114 Jackson's statement is quoted in Huston, *Securing the Fruits of Labor*, 232–3.

115 Kennedy, *Statutes, Treaties and Documents*, 270–89.

116 *La Minerve*, 31 déc. 1827, cited in Clark, *Movements*, 262–3.

117 Quoted in Wilton, *Popular Politics*, 92.

118 Charles Duncombe to Robert Davis, 24 Oct. 1837, in Read and Stagg, eds., *The Rebellion of 1837 in Upper Canada*, 88.

119 Capitalists exploited labour in England, according to Mackenzie. Farm servants, weavers, and mechanics worked in poverty and neglect, he reported from that country in 1833, and the unemployed "become the slaves of a capitalist's interest." *Colonial Advocate*, 27 June 1833.

120 Read and Stagg, eds., *The Rebellion of 1837 in Upper Canada*, 110–13.

121 This discussion of primogeniture is indebted to Ducharme, *The Idea of Liberty*, 103–4, and McNairn, *Capacity to Judge*, 360–410.

122 McNairn, *Capacity to Judge*, 407.

123 *Mr Bidwell's Speech on the Intestate Estate Bill in the Provincial Assembly of Upper Canada*, 24 Jan. 1831, 2–5 (Canadian Institute for Historical Microreproduction [CIHM] Microfiche No. 21341). On Bidwell's speech see also Ducharme, *The Idea of Liberty*, 103.

124 The ideal of independent smallholding was intact when an Intestate Estates Bill came before the Legislative Assembly of the United Province of Canada in January 1845. Speaking against primogeniture, John Philip Roblin said that, even if its abolition led to division of properties into "small pieces," the evil "would not be equal to the opposite effect, namely, of placing all the lands in the country in the hands of a few ... The man who is rich, and owns an immense tract of land, becomes proud and will spend much of his wealth in ornamenting his estates, indifferent whether they produce much or not ... A thousand acres of land owned by five persons will produce much more than the same number of acres in the hands of one man." *Debates of the Legislative Assembly of United Canada 1841–1867* (Quebec: Centre d'Étude du Québec, 1970), vol. IV, part I (1844–45), 1227. John Prince, speaking in both French and English, said: "He knew no greater curse to a country like Canada than a large landed aristocracy. It was the absence of this inequality which constituted the happiness of the habitants in Lower Canada, who were the happiest and most contented people in the world." *Debates*, 1844–45, 1231.

125 Huston, *Securing the Fruits*, 257.

126 A "loco-foco" was a type of match used to light candles. When the gas-lights went out in a contentious meeting in New York's Tammany Hall in 1835, people used such matches to light candles so that the event could continue. Carl N. Degler, "The Locofocos: Urban Agrarians," *Journal of Economic History* 16, no. 3 (Sept. 1956): 322–33. Also Andrew Bonthius, "The Patriot War of 1837–38: Locofocism with a Gun?" *Labour / Le travail* 52 (fall 2003): 9–43.

127 Montreal *Vindicator*, 7 Nov. 1837 (reprint of article from New York *Evening Post*).

128 J.K. Johnson, "'Claims of Equity and Justice': Petitions and Petitioners in Upper Canada 1815–1840," *Histoire sociale / Social History* 28, no. 55 (1995), 239. For Lower Canada see Jean-Marie Fecteau, "Between the Old Order and Modern Times: Poverty, Criminality, and Power in Quebec, 1791–1840" in Susan Lewthwaite, Tina Loo, and Jim Phillips, eds., *Essays in the History of Canadian Law, Volume V: Crime and Criminal Justice* (Toronto: University of Toronto Press, 1994), 293–323.

129 Rainer Baehre, "Paupers and Poor Relief in Upper Canada," *Historical Papers* (Ottawa: Canadian Historical Association, 1981), 57–80; Jean-Marie Fecteau, *The Pauper's Freedom: Crime and Poverty in Nineteenth-Century Quebec*, trans. Peter Feldstein (Montreal: McGill-Queen's University Press, 2017), 121–2.

130 Petition of William Lyon Mackenzie to the House of Commons, in *Colonial Advocate*, 25 April 1833.

131 Ducharme, *The Idea of Liberty*, 105.

132 Ex Colonist, in Montreal *Vindicator*, 20 Jan. 1837.

133 John Prince, in *Debates of the Legislative Assembly*, 1844–45, 1231.

134 Mackenzie, *Sketches of Canada and the United States* (London: Effingham Wilson, 1833), 19.

135 McNairn, *Capacity to Judge*, 72–9.

136 Ibid., 55.

137 *Advocate*, 25 Jan. 1834.

138 Ducharme, *The Idea of Liberty*, 105-7, to which pages my paragraph is clearly indebted.

139 Cited in Stéphane Kelly, "Le lion ne s'informe jamais du nombre des moutons," in Charles-Philippe Courtis and Julie Guyot, eds., *La culture des Patriotes* (Quebec: Septentrion, 2012), 181.

140 Rosanvallon, *Society of Equals*, 188.

141 William Paley, *The Principles of Moral and Political Philosophy* (first pub. 1785); *Paley's Moral Philosophy Abridged and Adapted to the Constitution, Laws and Usages of the United States of America* (New York: Collins & Hannay, 1828), 144.

CHAPTER THREE

1 Thomas Ritchie, *The Unequal Distribution of Wealth. A Lecture Delivered before the Knights of Labor in the Opera House, Belleville* (Belleville, ON: Daily Intelligencer, 1889), 3, 5, 6.

2 The American J.N. Larned saw "a larger social philosophy – an ethical economy, so to speak – which embraces political economy and extends far outside of it." J.N. Larned, *Talks about Labor, and Concerning the Evolution of Justice between the Laborers and the Capitalists* (New York: D. Appleton, 1876), 56.

3 Ritchie, *Unequal Distribution*, 2.

4 The conflicted reactions of American Protestants to wealth and market capitalism are an old subject in U.S. history. See Mark A. Noll, "Protestant Reasoning about Money and the Economy, 1790–1860: A Preliminary Probe," in Mark A. Noll, ed., *God and Mammon: Protestants, Money, and the Market 1790–1860* (New York: Oxford University Press, 2002), 265–95.

5 Ritchie, *Unequal Distribution*, 14, 21.

6 Michael Gauvreau, *The Evangelical Century: College and Creed in English Canada from the Great Revival to the Great Depression* (Montreal and Kingston: McGill-Queen's University Press, 1991), especially 17–19, 27–31.

7 Neil Semple, *Faithful Intellect: Samuel S. Nelles and Victoria University* (Montreal and Kingston: McGill-Queen's University Press, 2005), especially chap. 7, 175–203; Marguerite Van Die, *An Evangelical Mind: Nathanael Burwash and the Methodist Tradition in Canada, 1839–1918* (Montreal and Kingston: McGill-Queen's University Press, 1989), 43–7, 57–8, 181–2.

8 Gauvreau, *Evangelical Century*, 33.

9 Van Die, *An Evangelical Mind*, 47.

10 Semple, *Faithful Intellect*, 35–8.

11 William Westfall, *Two Worlds: The Protestant Culture of Nineteenth-Century Ontario* (Montreal and Kingston: McGill-Queen's University Press, 1989), 79. See also Denis McKim, *Boundless Dominion: Providence, Politics and the Early Canadian Presbyterian Worldview* (Montreal and Kingston: McGill-Queen's University Press, 2017), 153–61.

12 Westfall, *Two Worlds*, 80.

13 Henry Wilkes, *Purity of Communion, Its Importance, and the Best Means of Promoting It: An Essay* (Montreal: John Dougall, 1854), 5.

14 Newton Bosworth, *Hochelaga Depicta: The Early History and Present State of the City and Island of Montreal* (Montreal: William Greig, 1839), 186.

15 Ibid., 195.

16 F.H. Armstrong, "Rev. Newton Bosworth – Pioneer Settler on Yonge Street," *Ontario History* 58, no. 3 (Sept. 1966): 165.

17 Newton Bosworth, *The Aspect and Influence of Christianity upon the Commercial Character: A Discourse* (Montreal: William Greig, 1837), 8, 13, 14.

18 Ibid., 17.

19 Van Die, *An Evangelical Mind*, 46.

20 William Case, *Jubilee Sermon Delivered at the Request of and before the Wesleyan Canada Conference* (Toronto: G.R. Sanderson, 1855), 60; cited in Westfall, *Two Worlds*, 79. Historians of religion have discussed the anti-materialism of the churches in the nineteenth century. See, for instance, Westfall, *Two Worlds*, 79–80, 130; Van Die, *An Evangelical Mind*, 75–7.

21 Was the critique of wealth stronger among specific denominations? My impressionistic comparison of religious journals suggests that the critique may have appeared more often among Methodists, but a confident answer is not possible. The confluence of conditions associated with the critique existed in all denominations.

22 Despite many writers' reservations about the way in which wealth was gained and used, it was possible to associate the economic success of Britain with the influence of Christianity. As Nathanael Burwash said: "Under the pure influence of Christianity has the commerce of England & almost the entire commerce of the world in modern times grown up." Burwash, Notebook, 3 July 1863, cited in Van Die, *An Evangelical Mind*, 76.

23 Francis Wayland, *The Elements of Moral Science*, ed. Joseph L. Blau (first pub. 1835) (Cambridge, MA: Harvard University Press, 1963), 174.

24 Ibid., 175.

25 Jonathan I. Israel, *Radical Enlightenment: Philosophy and the Making of Modernity*, 1650–1750 (Oxford: Oxford University Press, 2001).

26 Egerton Ryerson, *Canadian Methodism: Its Epochs and Characteristics* (Toronto: William Briggs, 1882), 130.

27 Wayland, *The Elements*, 213.

28 Ibid., 210.

29 R.B. Wiggins, *The Tenure of Property, and the Nature and Quality of Evil* (Saint John, NB: J. & A. McMillan, 1863). In 1851 Richard Berrian Wiggins retired from, or was removed from, a curacy in Saint John, when he was suspected of holding Swedenborgian views and denying the Trinity.

Rev. I.W. Gray, *A Reply to the Statement of the Rev. Mr. Wiggins, A.M.* (Saint John, NB: J. & A. McMillan, 1851).

30 Wiggins, *The Tenure of Property*, 3–5.

31 Ibid., 4.

32 Ibid., 11.

33 James Bennet, *Sermon on Labour, Its Rights and Duties* (Saint John, NB: Barnes and Co., 1861), 8, 12, 14.

34 On the complicated relations between religion and socialism, and the ways in which Christian belief could be one path to leftism, see Ian McKay, *Reasoning Otherwise: Leftists and the People's Enlightenment in Canada, 1890–1920* (Toronto: Between the Lines, 2008), 213–78.

35 "To Merchants" (a sermon by T. Dewitt Talmage), *Christian Guardian*, 28 March 1877.

36 "The Morals of Trade," ibid., 22 Nov. 1876.

37 "Profit and Loss," ibid., 16 Oct. 1878.

38 "Extravagance," ibid., 14 Nov. 1877.

39 C.C. Bonney, "Unconsecrated Capital," ibid., 20 Jan. 1886.

40 As James Bennet commented: "Our business is with these [Christian] principles as they relate to the duty of those who enter into voluntary contracts. And we say they apply to the making – the very terms of these contracts – as well as to their fulfillment. In the making of them as well as in the execution of them there should be a view to that which is fair, just, equal." Bennet, *Sermon on Labour*, 12.

41 "Laws and Counsels of God," *Christian Guardian*, 28 Aug. 1872.

42 "Commercial Morality," ibid., 24 Jan. 1872.

43 "Systematic Beneficence," ibid., 10 Aug. 1870. The duty of the wealthy to battle greed was all the more urgent because of a known psychological tendency for accumulation to induce selfishness rather than generosity. "Who ever heard of a man who was naturally greedy when poor, becoming truly liberal when rich? None." *The Home and Foreign Record of the Canada Presbyterian Church* 1, no. 2 (Dec. 1861), 34.

44 Ibid.

45 T. Dewitt Talmage, "All for the Best," *Christian Guardian*, 25 Sept. 1878.

46 "Systematic Beneficence," ibid., 10 Aug. 1870.

47 Thomas Wilson, *The Perfection of the Atonement* (Toronto: Adam, Stevenson & Company, 1869), 150–1. On atonement see also Stephen Card, *The Atonement and Modern Liberalism* (Toronto: William Briggs, 1892); "The Rev. J.S. Evans on the Doctrine of the Atonement," *Christian Guardian*, 22 April 1885. See also Boyd Hilton, *The Age of Atonement:*

The Influence of Evangelicalism on Social and Economic Thought, 1795–1865 (Oxford: Clarendon Press, 1988), 179–83.

48 Westfall, *Two Worlds*, 204.

49 "Labor and Capital," *Christian Guardian*, 25 Feb. 1885; "Profit Sharing," ibid., 14 Sept. 1887.

50 Larry Siedentop, *Inventing the Individual: The Origins of Western Liberalism* (London: Allen Lane, 2014); Steven Lukes, "Religious Individualism," in Lukes, *Individualism* (Colchester, England: ECPR Press, 2006), 84–7.

51 Rev. George S. Bishop, *The Atonement* (Toronto: S.R. Briggs, 1881), 14.

52 "Profit Sharing," *Christian Guardian*, 14 Sept. 1887; "Justice for the Working Classes," ibid., 19 Nov. 1890; "Labor and Capital," ibid., 25 Feb. 1885. An article on "Socialistic Theories" in 1886 proposed that a "healthy Christian socialism" would help to reduce poverty among workers: ibid., 31 March 1886. There were, of course, radical pro-labour reformers among the clergy. Homel cites the example of the Anglican Rev. Charles H. Shortt in Toronto in the 1880s and 1890s: Gene Howard Homel, "'Fading Beams of the Nineteenth Century': Radicalism and Early Socialism in Canada's 1890s," *Labour / Le travail* 5 (spring 1980): 15–16.

53 "'Q. What is the least that we should give? A. Of all that thou shalt give me, I will surely give the *tenth* unto thee.' Gen. xxviii, 22." *Presbyterian Record of the Dominion of Canada* (Oct. 1883), 277.

54 "Wealth and Education," *Christian Guardian*, 18 July 1888.

55 "Too Much and Not Enough," ibid., 1 June 1887.

56 "The Fight against Poverty," ibid., 6 July 1887. "If you equalize the distribution of the profits of labor … you strike at the root of the energy and self-restraint which are the conditions of moral elevation," said an article on socialism: "Christianity and Socialism," ibid., 22 Jan. 1890. The article was quoting the English divine Edward Plumptre, dean of Wells.

57 Samuel Fleischacker, *A Short History of Distributive Justice* (Cambridge, MA: Harvard University Press, 2004), 126.

58 Thomas-Aimée Chandonnet, *Discourses Delivered at Notre-Dame de Quebec … on the 21st, 22nd & 23rd December 1863*, cited in Jean-Marie Fecteau, *The Pauper's Freedom: Crime and Poverty in Nineteenth-Century Quebec*, trans. Peter Feldstein (Montreal and Kingston: McGill-Queen's University Press, 2017), 232. Agnes Buchanan wrote a fable on the theme "and having nothing, yet hath all": *The Treasures of Hassan* (Hamilton, ON: Spectator Printing, 1890). Buchanan was the wife of Isaac Buchanan, the advocate of protective tariffs.

59 "Joseph Cook on Bellamy," *Christian Guardian*, 9 April 1890; "The Origin of Great Corporations," ibid., 7 Sept. 1887.

60 "Bellamy's Utopian Dream," ibid., 19 Feb. 1890.

61 "Profit Sharing," ibid., 14 Sept. 1887. "Property is but liberty realized": "What Socialism Really Means," ibid., 5 Feb. 1890.

62 "Individualism vs Socialism," ibid., 12 Feb. 1890.

63 Christopher Pierson, *Just Property, Volume 2: Enlightenment, Revolution, and History* (Oxford: Oxford University Press, 2016), 6–7. Mandeville's *Fable of the Bees; or Private Vices, Publick Benefits* was first published in 1714.

64 "The False Ideal," *Christian Guardian*, 10 Sept. 1890.

65 "Christianity and Wealth," ibid., 18 Jan. 1888.

66 "Materialism in America," ibid., 15 Aug. 1888. When Nathanael Burwash encountered wealthy people distinguished for their philanthropy, he applauded them for their Christian stewardship; Van Die refers to his "veneration of the wealthy." Van Die, *An Evangelical Mind*, 84.

67 Lynne Marks, *Revivals and Roller Rinks: Religion, Leisure and Identity in Late-Nineteenth-Century Small-Town Ontario* (Toronto: University of Toronto Press, 1996), 64.

68 "Riches and Poverty," *Christian Guardian*, 4 March 1885.

69 T. Dewitt Talmage, "Distribution of Rewards," ibid., 26 Jan. 1887.

70 Randy William Widdis, "Belleville and Environs: Continuity, Change and the Integration of Town and Country during the 19th Century," *Urban History Review* 19, no. 3 (Feb. 1991): 197, 202.

71 M.C. Urquhart and K.A.H. Buckley, *Historical Statistics of Canada*, 2nd ed. (Ottawa, 1983), series D1–7.

72 Ibid., series A67–9; R.W. Sandwell, *Canada's Rural Majority: Households, Environments, and Economies, 1870–1940* (Toronto: University of Toronto Press, 2016), 9–10.

73 Lancefield was, at various times, printer, clerk, bookseller, librarian, copyright advocate, and manager of publicity for Grip Printing in Toronto.

74 Richard T. Lancefield, *Why I Joined the New Crusade: A Plea for the Placing of Taxes on Land Values Only* (Toronto: Grip Printing, 1888), 8–9.

75 Ibid., 10.

76 Ibid., 22–3.

77 Ibid., 28. The assumption that land was readily available to everyone in Canada was shared, of course, by the Protestants who wrote about poverty. "If the poor man cannot live in the city, he can at least fly to the

forest, and invoke the bounteous mother with axe and plough, and find support," opined James Bennet in his *Sermon on Labour*, 23.

78 "Our Land Laws," a letter to the *Christian Guardian*, 17 Aug. 1887.
79 Lancefield, *Why I Joined*, 16–17, 28.
80 Ritchie, *Unequal Distribution*, 18.
81 Ibid., 18–19.
82 Ibid., 25.
83 Ibid., 15.
84 Ibid., 42.

CHAPTER FOUR

1 James L. Huston, *Securing the Fruits of Labor: The American Concept of Wealth Distribution 1765–1900* (Baton Rouge: Louisiana State University Press, 1998), 263.
2 For what it is worth, Google Ngrams indicates that "inequality" became less common in American English between the 1820s and 1830s and century's end; it fell even more sharply in British English. Use of "distribution of wealth," in contrast, rose dramatically in the 1880s.
3 In 1690 John Locke linked labour and property in a definitive manner: "Though the Earth, and all inferior Creatures be common to all Men yet every Man has a *Property* in his own *Person*. This no Body has any Right to but himself. The *Labour* of his Body, and the *Work* of his Hands, we may say, are properly his. Whatsoever then he remove out of the State that Nature hath provided, and left it in, he hath mixed his *Labour* with, and joined to it something that is his own, and thereby makes it his *Property*." John Locke, *Two Treatises of Government* (first pub. 1690), ed. Peter Laslett (Cambridge, 1988), Second Treatise, 287–8, in Huston, *Securing the Fruits*, 10.
4 Patriot constitution, cited in Stanley B. Ryerson, *1837: Birth of Canadian Democracy* (Toronto: Francis White, 1937), 75.
5 David Montgomery, *Citizen Worker: The Experience of Workers in the United States with Democracy and the Free Market during the Nineteenth Century* (New York: Cambridge University Press, 1993), 10.
6 Craig Heron, "Factory Workers," in Paul Craven, ed., *Labouring Lives: Work and Workers in Nineteenth-Century Ontario* (Toronto: University of Toronto Press, 1995), 491.
7 Robert B. Kristofferson, *Craft Capitalism: Craftworkers and Early Industrialization in Hamilton, Ontario[,] 1840–1872* (Toronto: University of Toronto Press, 2007), 13–14.

8 *Daily Globe*, 23 March 1872, in ibid., 137.

9 *Spectator*, 3 Dec. 1872, in ibid., 144.

10 Saint John *Morning News*, 28 May 1849, in Richard Rice, "A History of Organized Labour in Saint John, New Brunswick, 1813–1890" (MA thesis, University of New Brunswick, 1968), 25.

11 *Workingman's Journal*, 18 June 1864, in Bryan D. Palmer, *A Culture in Conflict: Skilled Workers and Industrial Capitalism in Hamilton, Ontario, 1860–1914* (Montreal: McGill-Queen's University Press, 1979), 106.

12 Knights of Saint Crispin *Annual Meeting*, 1869, 16, in Eugene Forsey, *Trade Unions in Canada 1812–1902* (Toronto: University of Toronto Press, 1982), 33.

13 Brantford *Equalizer*, Dec. 1879, in Forsey, *Trade Unions*, 46.

14 *Morning Chronicle*, 11, 14 July 1866, in J.I. Cooper, "The Quebec Ship Labourers' Benevolent Society," *Canadian Historical Review* 30, no. 4 (Dec. 1949), 341.

15 *Evening Express and Commercial Record*, 9 April 1869, in Forsey, *Trade Unions*, 63. George Brown made the same argument when responding a few years later to the nine-hours advocates: Christina Burr, *Spreading the Light: Work and Labour Reform in Late-Nineteenth-Century Ontario* (Toronto: University of Toronto Press, 1999), 16.

16 The speaker was John McCormack of Toronto, cited in Charles Lipton, *The Trade Union Movement in Canada 1827-1859*, 3rd ed. (Toronto: NC Press, 1973), 53 (original source not given).

17 *Ontario Workman*, 13 June 1872, in Palmer, *A Culture in Conflict*, 145.

18 Wage-fund theory has a long history in economic thought, going back to the eighteenth-century Physiocrats. A review of the nineteenth-century literature is by Francis A. Walker, "The Wage Fund Theory," *North American Review* 120, no. 246 (Jan. 1875): 84–119.

19 The zero-sum assumption surfaced in the labour press: "Now if one man has more than his share, others must have less." *Palladium of Labor*, 3 April 1886.

20 Toronto *Globe*, 15 Feb. 1872, in Gregory S. Kealey, *Toronto Workers Respond to Industrial Capitalism 1867–1892* (Toronto: University of Toronto Press, 1980), 129.

21 Jeffrey G. Williamson and Peter H. Lindert, *American Inequality: A Macroeconomic History* (New York: Academic Press, 1980), 38–9, and *Unequal Gains: American Growth and Inequality since 1700* (Princeton, NJ: Princeton University Press, 2016), 166–73. David Burley shows that in Brantford, Ontario, the share of assessed wealth held by the top 5 per cent increased between 1851 and 1880: David G. Burley, *A Particular*

Condition in Life: Self-Employment and Social Mobility in Mid-Victorian Brantford, Ontario (Kingston and Montreal: McGill-Queen's University Press, 1994), 137.

22 Urban spatial distribution of population is a much-studied topic; in Canada Hamilton has received deepest scrutiny. In the pre-industrial era there the "juxtaposition" of rich and poor was striking: Ian Davey and Michael Doucet, "The Social Geography of a Commercial City ca. 1853," in Michael B. Katz, *The People of Hamilton Canada West: Family and Class in a Mid-Nineteenth-Century City* (Cambridge, MA: Harvard University Press, 1975), Appendix One, p. 340. Craig Heron notes the clustering of working-class residents in Hamilton by the early twentieth century: Heron, *Lunch-Bucket Lives: Remaking the Workers' City* (Toronto: Between the Lines, 2015), 51–4. See also Eric W. Sager, "Canada's Immigrants in 1911: A Class Analysis," in Gordon Darocch, ed., *The Dawn of Canada's Century: Hidden Histories* (Montreal and Kingston: McGill-Queen's University Press, 2014), 437–44. In early 1870s Hamilton the dwellings of masters, even of large workshops, tended to be close to their workplaces and hence readily visible to workers: Kristofferson, *Craft Capitalism*, 133.

23 *Ontario Workman*, 13 March 1873, in Lipton, *The Trade Union Movement*, 52. James Huston states that the labour press was the only pre–Civil War source that even tried to quantify the distribution of U.S. wealth or income. Huston, *Securing the Fruits*, 260 n 3.

24 I do not know where Hewitt acquired his estimate of 2 per cent. Historical research a century later suggests that it is not far-fetched. In the United States in 1870 the richest 1 per cent held 27 per cent of all wealth; the richest 10 per cent, 70 per cent. Williamson and Lindert, *American Inequality*, 38–9 (Tables 3.1, 3.6).

25 The question of whether poverty was increasing as wealth grew prompted debate in the late 1880s and early 1890s. A controversial intervention was that of George Munro Grant: while rebutting Henry George's arguments in a speech in 1891 and in an article in the *Presbyterian Review* in April 1888, he denied rising inequality. Ramsay Cook, *The Regenerators: Social Criticism in Late Victorian Canada* (Toronto: University of Toronto Press, 1985), 116–17; Burr, *Spreading the Light*, 85.

26 John Battye, "The Nine Hour Pioneers: The Genesis of the Canadian Labour Movement," *Labour / Le travail* 4 (1979): 25–56.

27 James Ryan, quoted in Battye, "Nine Hour Pioneers," 28, 39.

28 Battye, "Nine Hour Pioneers," 40. In the United States the argument was also commonplace, as in the writings of Ira Steward: David Montgomery, *The*

Fall of the House of Labor: The Workplace, the State, and American Labor Activism 1865–1925 (New York: Cambridge University Press, 1987), 193.

29 Kristofferson, *Craft Capitalism*, 225; Burr, *Spreading the Light*, 20–2.

30 Battye, "Nine Hour Pioneers," 40. A letter on the Nine Hours movement in *Ontario Workman*, 16 May 1872, was signed "Social Elevation." On the egalitarian and distributive consequences of shorter hours see T. Phillips Thompson, *The Politics of Labor* (New York: Belford Clarke and Co., 1887), 188–90.

31 *Globe*, 8 April 1872, cited in Kealey, *Toronto Workers Respond*, 133.

32 *Ontario Workman*, 15 May 1873.

33 Ibid.

34 *Labor Union*, 24 Feb. 1883.

35 *Ontario Workman*, 3 April 1873.

36 The question was explicit. Referring to two women in San Francisco who sent an order to Paris for eighty-five dresses, an article in *Ontario Workman* commented: "It may be said that a woman has a perfect right to waste her substance in purchasing a flimsy tissue, or in any other manner congenial to her desires. To this we reply that our objection does not extend so much to the manner in which the substance was wasted, as to the manner in which it was originally obtained." *Ontario Workman*, 15 May 1873, reprinting an article from *Cooper's Journal*.

37 *Palladium of Labor*, 21 Aug. 1886. Thompson, *Politics of Labor*, 109. Thompson quoted Connecticut's commissioner of labour statistics, Arthur Hadley, on the distribution of returns from production (p. 111). In these bureaux, said Thompson, "we have the starting point of a new departure – the germs of social evolution."

38 Forsey, *Trade Unions*, 445.

39 Reprinting articles from American journals was common. "Five per cent of our population own sixty per cent of the national wealth, and this wealth is unceasingly devouring the substance of the producing classes … If five per cent of the people now own sixty per cent of the national wealth, and if at seven per cent their wealth doubles in ten years, they will practically own nearly the whole country, or be in a fair way of being able to control the wealth and power of the nation." *Cooper's Journal*, in *Ontario Workman*, 4 Sept. 1873.

40 Thomas Galbraith, *Bensalem; or The New Economy. A Dialogue for the Industrial Classes on the Financial Question* (New York: Thomas Galbraith Jr, 1874), 9–18.

41 Ian McKay, *Reasoning Otherwise: Leftists and the People's Enlightenment in Canada, 1890–1920* (Toronto: Between the Lines, 2008), 31.

42 *Palladium of Labor*, 24 April 1886.

43 Ibid., 10 Jan. 1885, quoting an article in the *Bobcaygeon Independent*.

44 *Palladium of Labor*, 12 April 1884.

45 Ibid., 10 Jan. 1885.

46 Henry George, *Progress and Poverty: An Inquiry into the Cause of Industrial Depressions and of Increase of Want with Increase of Wealth: The Remedy* (London: C.K. Paul, 1881). McEvoy's concordance records thirty appearances of "inequality" or "inequalities." Helena Mitchell McEvoy, *A Complete Concordance to the Twenty-fifth and Fiftieth Anniversary Editions of Progress and Poverty* (Chicago: Ability Press, 1958.

47 Edward T. O'Donnell, *Henry George and the Crisis of Inequality: Progress and Poverty in the Gilded Age* (New York: Columbia University Press, 2015), 152–8.

48 Ian McKay, *Reasoning Otherwise*, 85.

49 Kristofferson, *Craft Capitalism*, 144.

50 Ian McKay, *Reasoning Otherwise*, 322; Burr, *Spreading the Light*.

51 Kristofferson, *Craft Capitalism*, 212–13.

52 E.A. Heaman, *Tax, Order and Good Government: A New Political History of Canada, 1867–1917* (Montreal and Kingston: McGill-Queen's University Press, 2017), 151ff.

53 *Palladium of Labor*, 23 Oct. 1886.

54 Ibid., 16 Oct. 1886.

55 *Labor Union*, 3 March 1883.

56 *Labor Advocate*, 24 July 1891.

57 Stating the argument at length: the American J.N. Larned, *Talks about Labor, and Concerning the Evolution of Justice between the Laborers and the Capitalists* (New York: D. Appleton, 1876), 47–9.

58 *Labor Advocate*, 24 July 1891.

59 Andrew Carnegie, *The Gospel of Wealth and Other Timely Essays* (New York: Century Co., 1901), 10–11; the essay appeared first in the *North American Review*, June and Dec. 1889.

60 *Ontario Workman*, 24 July 1873.

61 Ibid., 10 April 1873.

62 Ibid., 24 July 1873.

63 Ibid., 22 May 1873.

64 Sources on Thompson include John David Bell, "The Social and Political Thought of the Labor Advocate" (MA thesis, Queen's University, 1975); Ramsay Cook, *The Regenerators: Social Criticism in Late Victorian Canada* (Toronto: University of Toronto Press, 1985), 50–3 and 161–73;

Russell Hann, "Brainworkers and the Knights of Labor: E.E. Sheppard, Phillips Thompson, and the Toronto News, 1883–1887," in Gregory S. Kealey and Peter Warrian, eds., *Essays in Canadian Working-Class History* (Toronto: McClelland and Stewart, 1976), 35–57; and Ian McKay, *Reasoning Otherwise*, 90–7, 113–16.

65　Thompson, *Politics of Labor*, 5. The words "inequality" and "inequalities" appeared ten times in the book; "distribution," twenty-nine.

66　Ibid., 159.

67　Ibid., 150–1.

68　Ibid., 152. Writing in 1886 as "Enjolras" (a revolutionary figure in Victor Hugo's *Les Misérables* [1862]), Thompson assailed the myth of the self-made man and the idea that the opportunity to become rich was a stimulus to virtue and enterprise: *Palladium of Labor*, 24 April 1886.

69　Thompson, *Politics of Labor*, 93.

70　Today one thinks of the often-secret campaign by certain sections of capitalism to increase economic and political inequality and to limit democracy. For instance, see Nancy MacLean, *Democracy in Chains: The Deep History of the Radical Right's Stealth Plan for America* (New York: Viking, 2017).

71　Thompson, *Politics of Labor*, 101–2.

72　It is not clear how far Thompson would extend this understanding of the corporation beyond "railroads, telegraphs, telephones, banks, insurance companies, and the like." His next paragraph referred to "the modern corporation" (ibid., 112–13). He did not develop an expansive conception of the state such as that of Lester Frank Ward (see chapter 1, above).

73　Ibid., 39.

74　Ibid., 137.

75　Ibid., 138.

76　Ibid., 140.

77　Ibid., 198–9.

78　Ibid., 202, 207.

79　Ibid., 53–5.

80　Elsewhere Thompson proposed that "unearned increment" referred not only to increases in the value of land, but also to "accumulations of wealth by speculation and in commerce." "The larger share of great commercial accumulations belongs to the public." T. Phillips Thompson, "Thoughts and Suggestions on the Social Problem and Things in General," ed. Deborah L. Coombs and Gregory S. Kealey, *Labour / Le travail* 35 (spring 1995): 250.

81　Ibid., 271.

82 Ian McKay, *Reasoning Otherwise*, 94.
83 *Palladium of Labor*, 12 Sept. 1885; Thompson, *Politics of Labor*, 55.
84 Although he did not address the problem of inequality or wealth distribution at length, Colin McKay was a critic of reformist and distributionist rhetoric. In 1899 he rejected the commonplace moral explanations for poverty while directing the moral critique at the rich: "The social question is the outcome of idleness, gluttony, drink, waste, profligacy, indulgence, etc., among the rich more than the poor." But his main concern was the discovery of a "science of economics" that would transcend the "iron law of wages" and address "the great social problems of the day." "The Secret of Poverty," 1899, in Ian McKay, ed., *For a Working-Class Culture in Canada: A Selection of Colin McKay's Writings on Sociology and Political Economy, 1897–1939* (St John's, NL: Canadian Committee on Labour History, 1996), 34–8. Colin McKay is relevant because he showed how an evolving socialism and materialism, while retaining a form of Christian idealism, eschewed maldistribution of wealth, except as a symptom of exploitation. Yet in 1899 McKay's rejection of individualist liberalism led him to predict the rise of a collectivist social conscience. "The rich and strong owe a duty to the poor and unfit, and many are beginning to realize and accept the responsibility. In obedience to the imperative impulse of the spirit of Christianity the 'social conscience' is awakening among men." "The Duty of the Rich to the Poverty-Laden" (1899), in Ian McKay, *For a Working-Class Culture*, 160.
85 Ian McKay, *Reasoning Otherwise*, 108.
86 John Spargo, *Where We Stand* (Chicago: Charles H. Kerr, 1908), 5.
87 Ibid., 12.
88 Ibid., 21–4.
89 "Classes in America," *Wilshire's Magazine* (March 1903), 5. The periodical was published at various times in Los Angeles and Toronto by H. Gaylord Wilshire, the so-called millionaire socialist. He ran for the Canadian Socialist League in the Ontario provincial election in 1902. See Ian McKay, *Reasoning Otherwise*, 145–6.
90 "Classes in America," 5.
91 Ibid., 6. Similar reasoning appeared in Murray E. King, "New Zealandism and Socialism," *Wilshire's Magazine* (April 1903), 35; W.U. Cotton, *Cotton's Compendium of Facts* (Cowansville, QC: Cotton's Co-operative Publishing Co., 1913).
92 Edward Bellamy, "Parable of the Water Tank," in Bellamy, *Equality* (New York: D. Appleton, 1897), chap. 23, 195–203.
93 Spargo, *Where We Stand*, 13–14.

94 *Palladium of Labor*, 13 Sept. 1884.

95 Ibid., 7 June 1884.

96 Ibid., 11 Oct. 1884.

97 "Graduated income tax" was one of several solutions to the concentration of wealth, including nationalization of land, in the *Palladium of Labor*, 23 Oct. 1886.

98 Ibid., 16 Oct. 1886.

99 Hatheway had experimented with profit-sharing schemes for his employees. Peter J. Mitham, "Hatheway, Warren Franklin," *Dictionary of Canadian Biography*, XV (1921–1930).

100 W. Frank Hatheway, *Poorhouse and Palace: A Plea for a Better Distribution of Wealth* (Saint John, NB: N.p., 1900), 12.

101 Ibid., 17–20.

102 Ibid., 21.

103 Heaman, *Tax, Order and Good Government*, 287.

104 Hatheway, *Poorhouse and Palace*, 44.

105 Ibid., 30.

106 Ibid., 39. He was quoting William Fessenden, Abraham Lincoln's secretary of the treasury.

107 Ibid., 40, quoting the Swiss political economist Jean Charles de Sismondi.

108 "Equality of taxation, therefore, as a maxim of politics, means equality of sacrifice. It means apportioning the contribution of each person towards the expenses of government so that he shall feel neither more nor less inconvenience from his share of the payment than every other person experiences from his." J.S. Mill, *Principles of Political Economy*, book V, chap. II, v. 2.7. Hatheway quoted only the second sentence: *Poorhouse and Palace*, 41.

109 According to Ian McKay "much of the Marxist commentary" was influenced by a kind of "miserabilism" or "catastrophism" and an emphasis on the idea that "the workers were steadily becoming more and more pauperized." Ian McKay, *Reasoning Otherwise*, 49.

110 Karl Marx, *Wage-Labor and Capital, with an Appendix by Frederick Engels* (Vancouver: Whitehead Estate, 1919?), 31. "Every invention, every improvement in production, goes to the capitalist, and thus the worker becomes relatively exploited more and more as capitalism progresses." A.P. Hazell, "Summary of Marx's Capital," *Western Clarion*, 16 April 1910.

111 "The Standard of Living," *Western Clarion*, 15 Feb. 1923.

112 The Platform appeared frequently in ibid., 5 April 1913, 1 March 1921.

113 Marx, *Wage-Labor and Capital*, 31, 59.

114 *Western Clarion*, 1 June 1920 (an article entitled "A Philosophical Retrospect"). "Dub" is American slang for a naïve or unskilled person.

115 Ibid., 14 May 1910.

116 BC *Federationist*, 6 July 1917.

117 "A Basis for Correct Action," *Western Clarion*, 26 May 1906. By contrast, J.S. Woodsworth kept distribution separate from production. The latter had been solved, he announced in 1918; now we need to get busy on the former: BC *Federationist*, 11 Oct. 1918.

118 Gerald Desmond, *The Struggle for Existence* (N.p.: Socialist Party of Canada, 1911), 16.

119 *Western Clarion*, 1 March 1923. Progressive income taxation would not be redistributive, because capitalists would always find a means to evade the tax: *Canadian Forward*, 2 Dec. 1916.

120 *Canadian Forward*, 10 July 1917.

121 Morris Hillquit, *Socialism in Theory and Practice* (New York: Macmillan, 1912), 117.

122 Ibid., 117.

123 The labour theory was a problematic principle if "to each" was in proportion to "from each." "If any man will not work, he shall not eat." 2 Thessalonians 3:10, cited in Richard Allen, *The Social Passion: Religion and Social Reform in Canada, 1914–28* (Toronto: University of Toronto Press, 1971), 86.

124 "All socialism involved slavery," Spencer wrote. Herbert Spencer, *The Man versus the State* (London: Williams and Norgate, 1902), 34.

125 "Socialism and the Individual," BC *Federationist*, 30 May 1924.

126 Yet there could be ambiguities and pragmatic compromises: for example, one Canadian socialist mixing moral non-compromise and political pragmatism was James Simpson (1873–1938), sometime mayor of Toronto: Ian McKay, *Reasoning Otherwise*, 193–8.

127 Craig Heron, "Labourism and the Canadian Working Class," *Labour / Le travail* 13 (spring 1984): 50.

128 *Industrial Banner*, 28 Dec. 1917. The poem was of earlier origin and appeared in differing variations, as in Marie Joussaye, *Selections from Anglo Saxon Songs* (Dawson, Yukon: Dawson News Publishing Company, 1920), 14–15.

129 "'Reorganization' rather than 'reconstruction' of society is essential": *Reconstruction Program for Canada* (Winnipeg: Dominion Labor Party, 1919). For the same point: *Industrial Banner*, 2 May 1919. See also James Naylor, "Southern Ontario: Striking at the Ballot Box," in Craig Heron, ed., *The Workers' Revolt in Canada 1917–1925* (Toronto: University of Toronto Press, 1998), 158.

130 *Canadian Forward*, 10 Nov. 1917.

131 "The war brought the craftsworkers' outrage to its sharpest point," says Heron, "Labourism and the Canadian Working Class," 74. On conscription of wealth see, among others: Heaman, *Tax, Order and Good Government*, 414–16, 420–2; Heron, *Workers' Revolt*, 21–2, 31, 122; Ian McKay, *Reasoning Otherwise*, 134, 433–4; and David Tough, "'The rich … should give to such an extent that it will hurt': Conscription of Wealth and Political Modernism in the Parliamentary Debate on the 1917 Income War Tax," *Canadian Historical Review* 3, no. 3 (Sept. 2012): 382–407.

132 *Industrial Banner*, 5 July 1918, quoting George Bernard Shaw. Shaw's words would have been available to Canadian readers in Upton Sinclair, *The Cry for Justice: An Anthology of the Literature of Social Protest* (New York: Upton Sinclair, 1915), 212.

133 *Grain Growers' Guide*, 23 Feb. 1916.

134 BC *Federationist*, 6 July 1917.

135 *Grain Growers' Guide*, 8 Nov. 1916.

136 *Industrial Banner*, 8 June 1917.

137 BC *Federationist*, 6 July 1917. The Western Canada Labour Conference in Calgary in March 1919 passed a motion supporting "organization on industrial lines" to secure for producers "the full fruits of their industry and the most equitable distribution thereof." *Western Labor News*, 4 April 1919.

138 Cotton, *Cotton's Compendium of Facts*, 36, 93, 104.

139 BC *Federationist*, 3 Jan. 1919.

140 *Industrial Banner*, 18 April 1919. U.S. tax data were also cited in ibid., 28 Jan. 1919. See also the *Edmonton Bulletin*, 23 Nov. 1918, and the article on "Distribution of Wealth," *Strathmore Standard*, 30 Jan. 1918 (reprinted in several other newspapers). On wealth and income distributions, Joseph Naylor cited the British authority Leo Chiozza Money in an article in the BC *Federationist*, 8 June 1917.

141 Heron, "Labourism and the Canadian Working Class," 73.

142 Among many discussions of British Labour Party conferences and programs: BC *Federationist*, 5 July, 16 Aug., 18 Oct. 1918, 30 Jan. 1920; *Western Labor News*, 6, 14 June 1919; J.S. Woodsworth, *War: Clippings from a War-time Scrap-book* (Winnipeg: Labor Church, 1920). Alvin Finkel notes that at its founding convention in January 1919 the Alberta branch of the Dominion Labor Party adopted as its own the program of the British Labour Party. Finkel, "The Rise and Fall of the Labour Party in Alberta, 1917–1942," *Labour / Le travail* 16 (fall 1985): 68. See also Norman Angell, *The British Revolution and American Democracy: An Interpretation of British Labour Programmes* (Toronto: McClelland,

Goodchild and Stewart, 1919); this English author later served as a Labour MP and won the Nobel Peace Prize.

143 *Industrial Banner*, 2 May 1919.

144 BC *Federationist*, 20 Dec. 1918.

145 A more flexible definition of utopia includes any text that "proposes and enacts a better order that does not yet exist anywhere," which can dismiss almost any reform agenda as utopian. Dohra Ahmad, *Landscapes of Hope: Anti-colonial Utopianism in America* (New York: Oxford University Press, 2009), 68; cited in Michael Robertson, *The Last Utopians: Four Late Nineteenth-Century Visionaries and Their Legacy* (Princeton, NJ: Princeton University Press, 2018), 13.

146 *Industrial Banner*, 6 June 1919. The phrase originated with Ralph Waldo Emerson.

147 Thomas De Quincey, "Milton vs. Southey and Landor," in *The Works of Thomas De Quincey: The Riverside Edition*, vol. IV (New York: Hurd and Stoughton, 1876), 456.

148 *Industrial Banner*, 2 Aug. 1918.

149 *Western Clarion*, 1 Oct. 1920.

150 *Industrial Banner*, 2 Aug. 1918. The article was by Thomas Mufson.

151 Ibid., 2 Feb. 1917.

152 Ibid., 24 Aug. 1917. The article was quoting the American Federation of Labor leader James William Sullivan.

153 Ibid., 24 Aug. 1917.

154 Harriet Dunlop Prenter, for instance, put the case for land taxation in *Industrial Banner*, 11 Oct. 1918. W.A. Douglass, the single-taxer, was still arguing that an income tax would penalize workers: ibid., 17 Aug. 1917.

155 Ibid., 3 Aug. 1917. Proposals for taxation were wide-ranging. Before the war R.J. Watters of Winnipeg argued that the "gross inequality" between rich and poor was largely due to the unrestricted use of machinery, which should therefore be "taxed in proportion to its displacement of human labor." BC *Federationist*, 1 May 1914.

156 In 1917 the Labor Education Conference in Ontario passed a motion favouring an exemption level at $2,500 per year for householders and $1,200 for non-householders, and an allowance of $240 per annum for workers whose occupation required them to travel. *Industrial Banner*, 15 June 1917. On the independent labour parties and taxation see Heaman, *Tax, Order and Good Government*, 322, 404, 420, 434.

157 There was awareness of Judge Henry Neil, the American "father of

mother's pensions," and perhaps some exaggeration about his proposals. The *Industrial Banner* (3 Aug. 1917) cited Neil in support of "a universal mothers' pension system" for "the care of every child," which sounds much broader than a pension plan for widows.

158 The platforms of the Independent Labor Party of Ontario appeared in *Industrial Banner*, 13 July 1917 and 20 Feb. 1920. One plan for very extensive "common ownership" originated with James McArthur Conner, *Public Ownership* (Toronto: Central Executive of the Independent Labor Party of Toronto, n.d.).

159 Woodsworth considered a living wage one that provided for "a normal standard of living," including education, recreation, dependent children, and saving for old age; he clearly assumed a male breadwinner. J.S. Woodsworth, *Reconstruction from the Viewpoint of Labor* (Winnipeg: Hecla Press, 1919). His pamphlet was circulated by the Dominion Labor Party and the Winnipeg Labor Church. His proposal was certainly more expansive than others in his time, and it was unclear whether writers thought that either a "minimum" or a "living wage" would be redistributive.

In a rare discussion of the work of a Canadian political economist, the *Industrial Banner* quoted the politically progressive Professor Louis A. Wood (of Western University in London, Ontario) as endorsing a living wage that would guarantee much more than "the subsistence wants of the workers," "raise the standard of living," and eliminate "sweating." Wood actually proposed a minimum wage equivalent only to "the lowest rate which can be paid to a worker in any given trade." *Industrial Banner*, 21 March 1919.

The gap between labour expectations of "fair wage" and the minimum wages the state proposed is an old story. Margaret E. McCallum, "Keeping Women in Their Place: The Minimum Wage in Canada," *Labour / Le travail* 17 (spring 1986): 29–56; Bob Russell, "A Fair or Minimum Wage? Women Workers, the State, and the Origins of Wage Regulation in Western Canada," *Labour / Le travail* 28 (fall 1991): 59–88.

160 *Reconstruction Program for Canada* (Winnipeg: Dominion Labor Party, 1919).

161 Labor Party of Toronto, *Municipal Elections, 1920: Platform of the Labor Party* (Toronto: Banner Press, 1920), n.p.

162 Woodsworth, *Reconstruction*, n.p.

163 Shirley Tillotson, *Give and Take: The Citizen-Taxpayer and the Rise of Canadian Democracy* (Vancouver: UBC Press, 2017), 214.

CHAPTER FIVE

1   Owen E. McGillicuddy, *The Making of a Premier; An Outline of the Life Story of the Right Hon. W.L. Mackenzie King* (Toronto: Musson, 1922), 9–10; R. MacGregor Dawson, *William Lyon Mackenzie King: A Political Biography* (Toronto: University of Toronto Press, 1958), 9–10, 12.

2   For the account of Berlin in this and subsequent paragraphs I am indebted to W.V. Uttley, *A History of Kitchener, Ontario* (first pub. 1937) (Waterloo, ON: Wilfrid Laurier University Press, 1975).

3   Ibid., 13–15.

4   Ibid., 194.

5   Ibid., 189.

6   Ibid., 32.

7   Ibid., 214.

8   R.W. Sandwell, *Powering Up Canada: A History of Power, Fuel and Energy from 1600* (Montreal and Kingston: McGill-Queen's University Press, 2016); Sean Kheraj, review of *Powering Up Canada* in *Ontario History* 109, 2 (fall 2017): 278–9.

9   Kenneth M. Sylvester, "Rural to Urban Migration: Finding Household Complexity in a New World Environment," in Eric W. Sager and Peter Baskerville, eds., *Household Counts: Canadian Households and Families in 1901* (Toronto: University of Toronto Press, 2007), 167–9.

10   William Westfall and Malcolm Thurlbury, "Church Architecture and Urban Space: The Development of Ecclesiastical Forms in Nineteenth-Century Ontario," in David Keane and Colin Read, eds., *Old Ontario: Essays in Honour of J.M.S. Careless* (Toronto: Dundurn Press, 1990), 118–45.

11   William Lyon Mackenzie King, *Industry and Humanity: A Study in the Principles Underlying Industrial Reconstruction* (Toronto: Thomas Allen, 1918).

12   Ibid., 149–52.

13   R.D. MacDonald, "Small Town Ontario in Robertson Davies' *Fifth Business*: Mariposa Revisited?" *Studies in Canadian Literature* 9, no. 1 (1984): 61–77.

14   Adam Crerar, "Ties That Bind: Farming, Agrarian Ideals, and Life in Ontario, 1890–1930" (doctoral dissertation, University of Toronto, 1999).

15   Norman Knowles, *Inventing the Loyalists: The Ontario Loyalist Tradition and the Creation of Usable Pasts* (Toronto: University of Toronto Press, 1997), 34–8.

16   Edith Marsh, "The County History as a Factor in Social Progress,"

Ontario Historical Society Papers and Records (1915), 53, 56, cited in Crerar, "Ties That Bind," 84.

17 Peter McArthur, *Sir Wilfrid Laurier* (Toronto: J.M. Dent, 1919), 146.

18 Peter McArthur, *In Pastures Green* (Toronto: J.M. Dent, 1915), 49.

19 Ibid., 95.

20 Ibid., 293.

21 Ibid., x.

22 Ibid.

23 Ibid., xi. The anti-intellectualism was unapologetic. He tried to read Thorstein Veblen's *Theory of the Leisure Class*, admitted to doing so hastily while "skipping many passages," but announced confidently in the *Globe* that "this book was all a sick joke." McArthur, "After Harvest," *Globe*, 9 Nov. 1912. Apart from a book advertisement, this appears to be the only reference to Veblen in the *Globe* between 1890 and 1930. See also McArthur's contemptuous dismissal of Pyotr Kropotkin in his *The Affable Stranger* (Toronto: Thomas Allen, 1920), 119–20.

24 McArthur, *In Pastures Green*, x–xi.

25 Ibid., 332.

26 McArthur, *The Last Law – Brotherhood* (Toronto: Thomas Allen, 1921), 10–11.

27 Ibid., 47.

28 Peter Baskerville, "The Worth of Children and Women: Life Insurance in Early Twentieth-Century Canada," in Gordon Darroch, ed., *The Dawn of Canada's Century: Hidden Histories* (Montreal and Kingston: McGill-Queen's University Press, 2014), 452–80.

29 Canada, Senate, *Journals of the Senate*, vol. 47 (1911–12); Crerar, "Ties That Bind," 2.

30 John MacDougall, *Rural Life in Canada: Its Trend and Tasks* (Toronto: Westminster Company, 1913), 30–2.

31 Ibid., 64.

32 Ibid., 70.

33 Ibid., 70–1.

34 Ibid., 75.

35 Ibid., 90.

36 Ibid., 116.

37 Ibid., 147.

38 Ibid., 158.

39 Ibid., 159–60.

40 I take the term from Arthur Barner, "Spiritual Engineering," *Christian Guardian*, 3 Dec. 1919.

41 Unattributed quotation on the prefatory page of Charles C. James, *Agriculture* (Toronto: George N. Morang, 1899). James was Ontario's deputy minister of agriculture.

42 Farmers' Platform, 1910, in W.L. Morton, *The Progressive Party in Canada* (first pub. 1950) (Toronto: University of Toronto Press, 1971), 297.

43 Kerry Badgley, *Ringing in the Common Love of Good: The United Farmers of Ontario, 1914–1926* (Montreal and Kingston: McGill-Queen's University Press, 2000), 52, 56.

44 Of course there was a temporal overlap between agrarian populism and the growth of organized labour in the United States. The literature on Canada, of course, is vast. On populism there is David Laycock, *Populism and Democratic Thought in the Canadian Prairies, 1910 to 1945* (Toronto: University of Toronto Press, 1990). The substantial literature on religion and politics in Canada's prairie west includes Richard Allen, "The Social Gospel as the Religion of Agrarian Revolt," in Carl Berger and Ramsay Cook, ed., *The West and the Nation: Essays in Honour of W.L. Morton* (Toronto: McClelland and Stewart, 1976), 174–86; Clark Banack, *God's Province: Evangelical Christianity, Political Thought, and Conservatism in Alberta* (Montreal and Kingston: McGill-Queen's University Press, 2016); David R. Elliott and Iris Miller, *Bible Bill: A Biography of William Aberhart* (Edmonton, AB: Reidmore Books, 1987); Kenneth McNaught, *A Prophet in Politics: A Biography of J.S. Woodsworth* (Don Mills, ON: Fitzhenry and Whiteside, 1979); Allen George Mills, *Fool for Christ: The Political Thought of J.S. Woodsworth* (Toronto: University of Toronto Press, 1991); and Sam Reimer, *Evangelicals and the Continental Divide: The Conservative Protestant Subculture in Canada and the United States* (Montreal and Kingston: McGill-Queen's University Press, 2003).

45 The speaker was Thomas McMillan, representing the Dominion Grange of Ontario. G.F. Chipman, ed., *The Siege of Ottawa* (Winnipeg: Canadian Council of Agriculture, 1910), 53.

46 Ibid., 63.

47 The 1910 platform is in Morton, *The Progressive Party*, 297–8.

48 Ibid., 298.

49 The Farmers' Platform, 1916, reproduced in ibid., 300–1.

50 Ibid., 301.

51 Together with E.C. Drury, Good and Partridge drafted the constitution of the Canadian Council of Agriculture in 1909. Good helped to organize the United Farmers of Ontario, was a Progressive MP in Ottawa 1921–25,

and served as president of the Co-operative Union of Canada 1921–45. Partridge was the first president of the Grain Growers' Grain Company and the first editor of the *Grain Growers' Guide*, the voice of prairie farmers.

52 W.C. Good, *Production and Taxation in Canada from the Farmers' Standpoint* (Toronto: J.M. Dent, 1919), 67.

53 Ibid., 61.

54 Ibid., 62, 63–4.

55 Ibid., xi, quoting James W. Robertson.

56 Ibid., 82–3, 106.

57 Ibid., 90.

58 Ibid., 64–5.

59 Ibid., 88–9.

60 Ibid., 132–3.

61 Ibid., 19, 22, 132–3.

62 "Strange mixture": Ian MacPherson, "Edward Alexander Partridge," *The Canadian Encyclopedia*, at http://www.thecanadianencyclopedia.ca/en/article/edward-alexander-partridge/, accessed 26 May 2020; Carl Berger, "A Canadian Utopia: The Cooperative Commonwealth of Edward Partridge," in Stephen Clarkson, ed., *Visions 2020* (Edmonton: Hurtig Publishers, 1970), 257. For a very different perspective on the book see Murray Knuttila, *"That Man Partridge": E.A. Partridge, His Thought and Times* (Regina, SK: Canadian Plains Research Center, 1994).

63 Michael Löwy and Robert Sayre, *Romanticism against the Tide of Modernity* (Durham, NC: Duke University Press, 2001); Michael Löwy, *Redemption and Utopia; Jewish Libertarian Thought in Central Europe* (first pub. 1992) (London: Verso, 2017), and "Utopia and Revolution: The Romantic Socialism of Gustav Landauer and Martin Buber," *Value Inquiry Book Series* vol. 274 (2014), 49–64. See also Yossef Schwartz, "The Politicization of the Mystical in Buber and His Contemporaries," in Michael Zank, ed., *New Perspectives on Martin Buber* (Tubingen, Germany: Mohr Siebeck, 2006), 205–18.

64 E.A. Partridge, *The War on Poverty: The One War That Can End War* (Winnipeg: Wallingford Press, 1925), 14.

65 Perhaps the best example was the American social gospeller Vida Scudder, who wrote scholarly studies of poetry. Gary Dorrien, *The Making of American Liberal Theology: Idealism, Realism and Modernity 1900–1950* (Louisville, KY: Westminster John Knox Press, 2003), 132–4. Partridge's use of poetry to communicate meaning was suggestive of "theopoetics," a concept that emerged in the 1960s and 1970s merging theology with

poetic imagination. Amos N. Wilder, *Theopoetic: Theology and the Religious Imagination* (Philadelphia: Fortress, 1976).

66 Scholars have explored the connections between anti-modernism and the communitarian impulse, including T. Jackson Lears, *No Place of Grace: Antimodernism and the Transformation of American Culture 1880–1920* (New York: Pantheon Books, 1981), 95–6.

67 Partridge, *War on Poverty*, 80. "Capital ... shall not be individually owned, even by the worker who must use it ... but by a communal socio-economic unit engaged in providing by organized local effort all or as nearly all as may be, of the goods and services to meet the basic needs of the unit." Ibid., 194.

68 Ibid., 150.

69 Ibid., 85–6, 135.

70 Ibid., 29–32. Before we scoff, we should remember that only a decade earlier Carl Jung formulated his concept of the "collective unconscious." There is no evidence that Partridge had read his work.

71 Löwy, "Utopia and Revolution," 50.

72 Ibid., 54.

73 Partridge, *War on Poverty*, 172.

74 Ibid., 120.

75 As Ruskin said: "Every person who tries to buy an article for less than its proper value, or who tries to sell it at more than its proper value, – every consumer who keeps a tradesman waiting for his money, and every tradesman who bribes a consumer to extravagance by credit, is helping forward, according to his own measure of power, a system of baseless and dishonourable commerce, and forcing his country down into poverty and shame." Quoted in Partridge, *War on Poverty*, 223. The quotation is from John Ruskin, *The Political Economy of Art* (New York: John Wiley, 1872), 124–5.

76 Ian McKay, *Reasoning Otherwise: Leftists and the People's Enlightenment in Canada, 1890–1920* (Toronto: Between the Lines, 2008), 263.

77 Partridge, *War on Poverty*, 37. He is quoting a poem by Ella Wheeler Wilcox.

78 In Partridge's *War on Poverty* we may see a series of double and overlapping meanings of a kind that Dewey understood. The word "fair," for instance, referred to both an aesthetic value and an ethical value. The literature on Dewey's aesthetics and ethics is vast, and includes Scott R. Stroud, *John Dewey and the Artful Life: Pragmatism, Aesthetics, and Morality* (University Park: Pennsylvania University Press, 2011).

79 Partridge was attracted to the transcendentalism of Ralph Waldo Emerson.

Quoting Emerson, he asked why we should not enjoy "an original relation to the universe" and "a religion by revelation to us." Partridge, *War on Poverty*, 11. Transcending "the narrow limits of our positive knowledge" happened in an act of mystic revelation of the kind that Tennyson articulated in "The Ancient Sage" (1885): Partridge, *War on Poverty*, 12.

80 Partridge, *War on Poverty*, 135. Since it was not yet translated into English, Partridge would not have known the work of Ernst Bloch, *Geist der Utopie* (Spirit of Utopia), 1918. On Bloch's spirituality and Marxism and his "anticipatory consciousness" see Peter Thompson, "Ernst Bloch and the Spirituality of Utopia," *Rethinking Marxism* 28, no. 3–4 (2016): 438–52.

81 Partridge, *War on Poverty*, 141. Elsewhere the key to the transformative "psychological moment" lay in education: there was enough, he said, of "divine discontent, social spirit, sympathy, love of justice and idealism among us today, that, reinforced by moral impulses and intellectual powers now dormant in the mass of citizenry for lack of education, would make the creation of a happy social organization possible within a few short years," and, he added, the change could come without violence or pain (23–4).

82 In Burnaby, BC, Laura Jamieson and her colleagues in the "Army of the Common Good" drew inspiration from Partridge's book: Veronica Strong-Boag, *The Last Suffragist Standing: The Life and Times of Laura Marshall Jamieson* (Vancouver: UBC Press, 2018), 96.

83 The word "rich" appeared sixty-three times, and "riches" twenty. "Wealth" surfaced sixty-nine times, and "poor" seventy-nine. "Inequality" (or "inequalities") showed up nine times.

84 Partridge, *War on Poverty*, 43, 120, quoting Ruskin.

85 He called his utopia Coalsamanao, using the first letters of [British] Columbia, Alberta, Saskatchewan, and Manitoba, adding the "o" for a part of Ontario.

86 Partridge, *War on Poverty*, 139.

87 *Wetaskiwin Times*, 13 July 1933.

88 Partridge, *War on Poverty*, 173, 216.

89 Richard Allen, *The Social Passion: Religion and Social Reform in Canada, 1914–28* (Toronto: University of Toronto Press, 1971), 201; Allen, *Beyond the Noise of Solemn Assemblies: The Protestant Ethic and the Search for Social Justice in Canada* (Montreal and Kingston: McGill-Queen's University Press, 2018), 166–78. As is well known, the social gospel had notable regional variations. In its complex reckoning with social change and class relations, Protestantism was very different in Ontario than in Alberta, for instance. The focus here is very much on the Ontario context.

90 This applies to virtually all prominent Canadian social gospellers. S.D. Chown was unusual, having been born in a relatively large town – Kingston.

91 Allen, *The Social Passion*, 208. In the absence of the social gospel or of a theology of immanence, inequality was less likely, even where some people had an interest in the poor and in political reform. An example was Herbert Brown Ames: he did not use the words "inequality" and "inequalities" in *The City below the Hill: A Sociological Study* (first pub. 1897) (Toronto: University of Toronto Press, 1972).

92 On the Kingdom concept, the oft-cited source was Walter Rauschenbusch, *Christianity and the Social Crisis* (New York: Macmillan, 1907), especially 57–65. On Kingdom theology and the social gospel: Dorrien, *The Making of American Liberal Theology*, 109–17. Immanentalism, not without its ambiguities, reflected the intellectual heritage of neo-Hegelian idealism. It held that the material world was the expression of God's will; that theology could apprehend the workings of God's mind and intentions; and that in divine intentions there lay a spiritual "nearness" to God that included brotherhood, mutual understanding, and shared burdens. While science and philosophy could contribute to good theology, immanence, since it was of divine origin, could not be apprehended outside spiritual acceptance of the redemptive power of God. Dorrien, *The Making of American Liberal Theology*, 296–8, 529–31. Michael Gauvreau explores Kingdom theology and immanentalism in *The Evangelical Century: College and Creed in English Canada from the Great Revival to the Great Depression* (Montreal and Kingston: McGill-Queen's University Press, 1991), 201–14. A.B. McKillop discusses the affinity between idealism and evolutionary naturalism: *A Disciplined Intelligence: Critical Inquiry and Canadian Thought in the Victorian Era* (Montreal and Kingston: McGill-Queen's University Press, 2001), 183–6, 215–16.

93 Readers may ask how the argument here about the fate of the inequality problem related to debates about secularization and to the literature on the churches and social welfare. I do not intend this history of an idea to further qualify the secularization thesis. I have reservations about the idea that religion was ubiquitous and that, for instance, neoclassical economics was a type of religion; or that the Bolshevik revolution was a millenarian event and Marxism a fusion of religious millenarianism and Enlightenment rationalism (I am referring to Yuri Slezkine, *The House of Government: A Saga of the Russian Revolution* [Princeton, NJ: Princeton University Press, 2017]). Nevertheless, Christie and Gauvreau have convinced me that churches and popular piety were resurgent in Canada in

the first half of the twentieth century: Nancy Christie and Michael Gauvreau, *A Full-Orbed Christianity: The Protestant Churches and Social Welfare in Canada, 1900–1940*, McGill-Queen's Studies in the History of Religion, Number 22 (Montreal: McGill-Queen's University Press. 1996). I also accept that the churches and church representatives (lay and clerical) were so deeply immersed in the domains of social and political reform that notions of "influence" would be otiose. Beyond the elites, popular piety had deep connections to politics and culture that we are beginning to perceive, thanks to the work of Christie and Gauvreau and others. Secular and religious were so thoroughly interwoven that the very use of the terms to imply a distinction or possible separation seems increasingly unhelpful. Having said that, I would note this chapter's limited focus: it is not about popular piety, but about specific thinkers within the elites of specific religious-political movements, which constituted the intellectual context for the idea of inequality.

94   Albert R. Carman, "The Gospel of Social Justice," *Canadian Methodist Quarterly* 3, no. 3 (July 1891): 286–306. Ramsay Cook attributes the essay to Albert Carman (1833–1917), the general superintendent of the Methodist church in Canada: Ramsay Cook, *The Regenerators: Social Criticism in Late Victorian Canada* (Toronto: University of Toronto Press, 1985), 192. The essay was the work more likely of his son, Albert R. Carman (1865–1939), which is the journal's attribution – the son always used the middle initial. On this point see Daniela Janes, "Brainworkers: The Middle-Class Labour Reformer and the Late-Victorian Canadian Industrial Novel," *Canadian Literature* 191 (winter 2006): 83 n 12. Of course other thinkers in the 1890s were confronting the related problems of inequality, "unearned increment," and combines and trusts. Richard Allen notes Salem Bland's optimistic belief that past societies based on inequality were gradually giving way to those founded on wider equalities: Allen, *The View from Murney Tower: Salem Bland, the Late Victorian Controversies, and the Search for a New Christianity* (Toronto: University of Toronto Press, 2008), 229–30. American social gospellers had anticipated Carman's questions: for instance, Washington Gladden discussed growing inequality and raised questions about the role of the state and taxation in his *Applied Christianity: Moral Aspects of Social Questions* (Boston: Houghton Mifflin, 1887), 13–22.

95   Carman, "The Gospel of Social Justice," 300.

96   Ibid., 294.

97   Ibid., 298.

98   Ibid., 298, 303. J.B. Silcox also gave sermons anticipating social-gospel

preoccupations. Why did great nations fall in the past? he asked. "Because their political economies nursed wealth and concentrated it in the hands of a few while it drained and degraded the many whose labor produced the wealth." Rev. J.B. Silcox, *The Sacredness of Man* (Montreal: Norman Murray, 1893), 10.

99 Carman, "The Gospel of Social Justice," 295–6.

100 A more profound anticipatory challenge was that of John Clark Murray, · written a few years earlier than Carman's essay. For Murray's *Industrial Kingdom of God* (first pub. 1887), ed. Leslie Armour and Elizabeth Trott (Ottawa: University of Ottawa Press, 1981), see chapter 6 below.

101 Carman, "The Gospel of Social Justice," 299.

102 Ibid., 300.

103 Ibid., 305.

104 Marlene Shore, *The Science of Social Redemption; McGill, the Chicago School, and the Origins of Social Research in Canada* (Toronto: University of Toronto Press, 1987); Christie and Gauvreau, *A Full-Orbed Christianity*, especially chap. 3, 75–130.

105 Christie and Gauvreau, *A Full-Orbed Christianity*, 88–90.

106 For reviews of Ryan's *Distributive Justice: The Right and Wrong of Our Present Distribution of Wealth* (New York: Macmillan Co., 1916), see the *Catholic Record*, 10, 17 Feb. 1917; 23 March 1918; and 6 Dec. 1919. There was a short notice in the *Monetary Times*, 9 Feb. 1917. Ryan's *A Living Wage: Its Ethical and Economic Aspects* (New York: Macmillan Co., 1906) was reviewed in the *Catholic Record*, 5 Sept. 1914.

107 A good example of the resulting ambiguities came from Rev. James Cook Seymour, writing a decade after Carman's 1891 "Gospel of Social Justice." Seymour asked: "Did God intend one man to own two hundred millions and another man scarce two hundred cents?" His answer was an unequivocal "No." Yet the rich were not to be denounced, so long as their wealth derived from "honest industry." "If the rich mean to keep their wealth they will have to give it away." James Cook Seymour, "Wealth and Its Uses," *Methodist Magazine and Review* 53, no. 4 (April 1901): 312–15.

108 Here as elsewhere I make general statements about a large and diverse population awkwardly grouped as social gospellers. To every statement experts will be able to find an exception. The group's uncertain and often sceptical response to philosophy has been well documented, however. Even the most intellectual of social gospellers, Salem Bland, was at first "put off systematic philosophy," says Richard Allen, until he encountered John Watson's way of reconciling idealism, revelation, and processes in the real

world (as well as Watson's repudiation of economic individualism). Allen, *View from Murney Tower*, 219–28.

109 McNaught, *A Prophet in Politics*, 20.

110 Woodsworth had read Carlyle, Darwin, Richard Ely, Edward Gibbon, F.D. Maurice, J.S. Mill, John Ruskin, W.T. Stead, and many more writers. His required reading at Winnipeg's Wesley College in the 1890s had included Locke, Kant, Mill, and Henry Sidgwick. Allen Mills, *Fool for Christ: The Political Thought of J.S. Woodsworth* (Toronto: University of Toronto Press, 1991), 12. By the early twentieth century, however, as Christie and Gauvreau state, Woodsworth lacked familiarity with more modern writings by economists and sociologists: Christie and Gauvreau, *A Full-Orbed Christianity*, 88.

111 In his biography of Woodsworth, Kenneth McNaught suggests that Caird's philosophy "would not repel" the young Canadian Methodist. His reaction was more likely to have been enthusiastic and relieved acceptance. McNaught, *A Prophet in Politics*, 16. Mills mentions Caird briefly in *Fool for Christ*, 11, 13. For the wider influence of Edward Caird and his "collectivist liberalism" see Brian J. Fraser, *The Social Uplifters: Presbyterian Progressives and the Social Gospel in Canada, 1875–1915* (Waterloo, ON: Wilfrid Laurier University Press, 1988), 3–8; and McKillop, *A Disciplined Intelligence*, 183–5, 210–12.

112 Caird, *Individualism and Socialism* (Glasgow: James Maclehose, 1897), 20, and *Lay Sermons and Addresses Delivered in the Hall of Balliol College, Oxford* (Glasgow: James Maclehose, 1907), 101, 110, 146, 153.

113 Caird, *Individualism and Socialism* 20.

114 Ibid., 15.

115 Caird, *Lay Sermons*, 68.

116 The "consolation" of redemptive change, said Caird, was also a call to action: those who "are willing to sacrifice themselves for others" would see their reward "in the higher honesty and justice of our politics" and "in the realisation of the Kingdom of God among men in this present world." Ibid., 69–70.

117 J.S. Woodsworth, *Strangers within Our Gates, or Coming Canadians* (Toronto: F.C. Stephenson, 1909), 30.

118 Ibid., 226, 231.

119 J.S. Woodsworth, *My Neighbor: A Study of City Conditions*, 2nd ed. (Toronto: Missionary Society of the Methodist Church, 1913), 76.

120 Woodsworth was referring to inequality in Britain; the only evidence available was American – on distributions: Charles Spahr's *Essay on the Present Distribution of Wealth in the United States* (1896). The economist

whom Woodsworth quoted on the unequal distribution of wealth was the Irish economist John Elliott Cairnes, one of the last defenders of wage-fund theory, whose *Leading Principles* of 1874 was long out of date by 1911.

121 Woodsworth, *My Neighbor*, 14–15. *Sartor Resartus* also appealed to a young Salem Bland: Allen, *View from Murney Tower*, 49.

122 Woodsworth, *My Neighbor*, 278, 279.

123 Ibid., 338.

124 An especially revealing instance of the path from inequality to social service was the essay by George Pardon Bryce, *The Love of God in Relation to Social Service* (Ottawa, 1909). Bryce began by positing that social service presupposes "social need," which derived from "inequality in advantages, in opportunity, in the supply of economic valuables" (5). Bryce offered a short history of inequality in Western civilization and suggested that the enormous wealth-creating power of industrial machinery had created an entirely new form of inequality that manifested itself as "social cleavage," which was most apparent in the modern city (7). Two great movements had arisen in response – socialism and humanitarianism. The task of the church, he argued, was not merely "to point the way to others" or "rescue the individual soul in the city slum without changing the environment." Altering the environment required the vast collective effort of a "socialized church," and that meant social service (25).

An American example, printed in Canada, was Samuel Zane Batten, *The Social Task of Christianity* (New York, Toronto: Fleming H. Revell, 1911). Batten maintained that it was social workers' "duty" to aim for "a better distribution, not of wealth, but of the bare means of comfort, leisure and security" (141–2). Despite his claim that Mosaic law provided for equitable distribution, he did not conclude that the modern solution lay in distributive legislation.

On the ease with which social evangelicalism transitioned into social service and settlement work in Toronto see Sara Z. Burke, *Seeking the Highest Good: Social Service and Gender at the University of Toronto, 1888–1937* (Toronto: University of Toronto Press, 1996), 28–40. On social work: Christie and Gauvreau, *A Full-Orbed Christianity*, especially chap. 4.

125 J.S. Woodsworth, *The First Story of the Labor Church and Some Things for Which It Stands* (Winnipeg, 1920).

126 *Proceedings of the Fourth Ecumenical Methodist Conference*, with an introduction by H.K. Carroll and James Chapman (Toronto: Methodist Book and Publishing House, 1911), 221. The speaker was Rev. S.S. Henshaw.

127 Ibid., 390. The speaker was Rev. J.E. Radcliffe.

128 Ibid., 321, quoting an essay by T. Snape.

129 Ibid., 210. The speaker was Thomas R. Ferens, a British member of Parliament.

130 Ibid., 405. The speaker was Rev. William Bradfield.

131 Ibid., 375; an essay by Rev. Gross Alexander.

132 Ibid., 382. The speaker was Rev. B. Haddon of Gateshead-on-Tyne, England. On the complex reactions to socialism see Christie and Gauvreau, *A Full-Orbed Christianity*, 16–17, 20, 58.

133 *Proceedings of the Fourth Ecumenical Methodist Conference*, 382.

134 Ibid., 372. An essay by Rev. Gross Alexander.

135 Ibid., 212. The speaker was T.R. Ferens, British MP.

136 Ibid., 227.

137 There were, of course, many paths from both the new liberalism and the social gospel to active social service and social work. At the professorial level, Christie and Gauvreau discuss the different routes of E.J. Urwick and Robert MacIver in *A Full-Orbed Christianity*, 145–8, 152–6. On the subject of social service their study remains indispensable.

138 Social-service workers who reflected on their observations of urban poverty made the connection to societal-level inequality. An example was Frank N. Stapleford. "The system of distribution is based on the idea that the spoils go to the strong." What was the result of this idea?, the writer asked. Coal, he answered – a "mundane matter," but the absence of coal meant that children in Toronto were crying from cold and entire families were living in places "unfit for human habitation." Stapleford, "The Marks of the Modern Preacher," *Christian Guardian*, 28 Oct. 1918.

139 The church colleges reacted against what they saw as esoteric intellectualism and arid scholasticism: Christie and Gauvreau, *A Full-Orbed Christianity*, 6–8.

140 *Proceedings of the Fourth Ecumenical Methodist Conference*, 188.

141 *Social Service Congress, Ottawa, 1914: Report of Addresses and Proceedings* (Ottawa: Social Service Council, 1914), 3. This phrase did not make it to the Council's later "Principles and Programme": see *Social Welfare*, Nov. 1918 and Dec. 1918. On the origins of the Social Service Council see Allen, *The Social Passion*, 13. Allen also describes the 1914 Congress (19–23). Half of the speakers were clergymen, although not all were social gospellers. Allen says that the event was "overwhelmingly a professional man's conference," with a sprinkling of labour representatives and farmer or cooperative delegates (including W.C. Good and E.C. Drury).

142 Laurier said that he understood that the aim was not merely to help through charity, but "to work for a larger and more equitable share of the wealth of the earth." *Social Service Congress*, 8. W.C. Good declared: "There has been also a great increase in inequality, with growing lavishness and folly in methods of living on the part of the very rich" (289). Rev. J.W. Atkins of Toronto said: "A proper estimate of the worth of the individual would also lead to a more equitable distribution of the natural resources of the earth" (42). Rev. S.W. Dean of Toronto, in his address on city slums, insisted: "The right to a living wage must be proclaimed by the Church as the moral right of every honest toiler. More than that, she must proclaim the right of the toiler to a more equitable share in the wealth which he or she produces" (132). Charles Stelzle, the "consulting sociologist" from New York, declared that the labour problem was "not so much a question of production as a question of distribution," and proceeded to tell a clumsy joke about a Jewish man who divided a fish with his friend, giving his friend only tail and bones (63). The story was intended to illustrate wider social inequities.

143 Ibid., 192–6.

144 Ibid., 185–7.

145 Ibid., 187.

146 A remarkable exception was a pamphlet by the Methodist Rev. Wilbur W. Andrews, the first president of the Methodist Regina College. "The supreme work of the Church should be to realize social justice"; that work required a solution to the problems of "exploitation," "unearned increment," and "glaring inequalities." Andrews's optimism – "a new day is dawning" – did not preclude an egalitarian politics. "The supreme virtue in a democracy is loyalty to one's equals for the sake of common ends." The defeat of "moneyed aristocracy" required graduated income and inheritance taxes; "Christian statesmanship" would determine how to appropriate unearned increment to "public uses." W.W. Andrews, *Our National Sin: Something for Nothing* (Toronto: Department of Social Service and Evangelism of the Methodist Church, n.d. [between 1915 and 1925]).

147 The conclusions are from Google NGrams and from frequency distributions in the BC Historical Newspapers corpus, University of British Columbia Library, Vancouver. I am indebted to Luis Meneses for his assistance with the BC newspapers. Of course the increasing frequency indicates nothing about the content or direction of the contexts. Newspapers in western Canada reprinted stories from U.S. newspapers that discussed American and British wealth distributions.

The stories often contained numerical data on income and wealth distributions of the kind not available for Canada. An influential source was the (U.S.) Commission on Industrial Relations (John R. Commons [see chapter 1, above] was a commissioner), which emphasized "the existing system of the distribution of wealth" as a cause of unrest and presented estimates. "The 'rich,' 2 per cent of the people, own 60 per cent of the wealth." *Final Report ... by the Commission on Industrial Relations*, vol. I (Washington, DC: Government Printing, 1916), 33, 163. BC *Federationist*, 3 Jan. 1919; *Edmonton Bulletin*, 23 Nov. 1918; *Strathmore Standard*, 30 Jan. 1918; *Western Labor News*, 28 Jan. 1921.

148 "The Social Ideals of the New Day in Canada," *Social Welfare*, 1 Jan. 1919.

149 The words are from Methodist Church, *The Church, the War, and Patriotism: Report Adopted by the General Conference at Hamilton*, 1918 (N.p.: Army and Navy Board of the Methodist Church, 1918); cited in *Social Welfare*, 1 Aug. 1919.

150 Methodist Church, *The Church, the War, and Patriotism*, cited in *Social Welfare*, 1 Aug. 1919. See also "Co-operation: A National Policy," *Christian Guardian*, 1 Jan. 1919.

151 "Unearned Incomes," *Christian Guardian*, 6 Aug. 1919.

152 *Social Welfare*, 1 Jan. 1919. For a historical analysis that draws a lesson on the inevitable victory of freedom over privilege and of economic equity over profits and competition see Jonas E. Collins, "The Conflict of Many Centuries," *Christian Guardian*, 3 Sept. 1919. On the optimistic belief in transformation see also "The Coming Democracy" and "The New Earth," *Christian Guardian*, 16 May 1917; "Brotherhood Better than Wealth," *Christian Guardian*, 17 Dec. 1919; "Not Wholly a Matter of Money," *Christian Guardian*, 10 Sept. 1919; H.G. Cairns, "The Biggest Interest of All," *Christian Guardian*, 3 Oct. 1917; and Rev. S.W. Fallis, "The Millennial Hope," *Christian Guardian*, 13 Feb. 1918. Frank N. Stapleford, a Methodist minister and social worker, wrote regularly in the *Christian Guardian*. Not given to utopian visions, he understood the distinction between absolute and relative poverty. He argued that workers' minimal standards of living had risen in the previous century, but that the gaps between rich and poor had widened: "Causes of Poverty," *Christian Guardian*, 16 April 1919. Stapleford, cautious and informed as he was, nevertheless was capable of optimistic conclusions. "The more just distribution of wealth," he wrote, was "not for academic discussion" but for action, and "far-reaching changes are coming, fraught with peril and hope": *Christian Guardian*, 12 Feb. 1918. The process of enlarging

economic opportunity for everyone and curtailing privilege, he proclaimed, was "not something which *may* take place in the remote future,
but is something which is actively *going on* at the present time":
"Economic Revolution and Great Britain," *Christian Guardian*, 14 Aug.
1918.

153 Shore, *The Science of Social Redemption*, 69, 104; Christie and Gauvreau,
    A Full-Orbed Christianity, chap. 5, 165-96.

154 Social Service Council, *The Community Survey, A Basis for Social Action*
    (Toronto: Social Service Council, 1919), 5.

155 Frank N. Stapleford, "The High Cost of Living – A Present Social
    Menace," *Christian Guardian*, 18 April 1917.

156 On the reconstruction proposals of the churches: Christie and Gauvreau,
    A Full-Orbed Christianity, 91ff; Allen, *Social Passion*, 66-8, 73-5, 79-80.

157 On the debate see Allen, *Social Passion*, 74-9, 123-4.

158 Ibid., 78.

159 *Globe*, 29 May 1919.

160 J.H. Philp, "Lights and Shadows of Our Social Programme," *Christian
    Guardian*, 19 March 1919.

161 Ian McKay discusses Bland's "sweeping cosmic vision" in *Reasoning
    Otherwise*, 232-7. A.E. Smith offered a different example of movement
    from the social gospel to socialism. As a Methodist minister Smith's
    acceptance of immanentalism and evolutionary progress was consistent
    with political gradualism; by 1923 he was expressing a secular and
    Marxist position on class struggle and had shed the "optimistic verities"
    (ibid., 150) of the social gospel. He joined the Communist Party in 1925.
    Tom Mitchell, "From the Social Gospel to the 'Plain Bread of Leninism':
    A.E. Smith's Journey to the Left in the Epoch of Reaction after World War
    I," *Labour / Le travail* 33 (spring 1993): 125-51.

162 Salem Goldworth Bland, *The New Christianity, or the Religion of the
    New Age* (Toronto: McClelland and Stewart, 1920), 47.

163 Ibid., 48-9.

164 Ibid., 26.

165 Ibid., 93.

166 Ibid., 96.

167 Ibid., 168.

168 Ibid., 100.

169 The attack on privilege and concentration of power and wealth continued
    in the social-gospel student movement and the American-origin Fellowship
    for a Christian Social Order. See *Canadian Student*, Feb. 1924, 131, cited

in Allen, *Social Passion*, 308. Melissa Turkstra notes that labour leaders drew on Christian ethical teaching to "target the unequal distribution of wealth." Turkstra, "Constructing a Labour Gospel: Labour and Religion in Early 20th Century Ontario," *Labour / Le travail* 57 (spring 2006): 103–5.

170 Christie and Gauvreau, *A Full-Orbed Christianity*, 214–15.

171 Irvine mentioned the "amassing" of wealth: *The Farmers in Politics* (Toronto: McClelland and Stewart, 1920), 22–3, 35, 37, 196. The word "inequality" popped up only twice; "distribution of wealth" not at all.

172 Ibid., 22, 24.

173 Ibid., 53.

174 Valuable contributions include S.D. Chrostowska and James D. Ingram, eds., *Political Uses of Utopia: New Marxist, Anarchist and Radical Democratic Perspectives* (New York: Columbia University Press, 2016); Barbara Goodwin and Keith Taylor, *The Politics of Utopia: A Study in Theory and Practice* (London: Hutchison, 1982); and Lyman Tower Sargent, *Utopianism: A Very Short Introduction* (Oxford: Oxford University Press, 2010).

175 Fredric Jameson, "The Politics of Utopia," *New Left Review* 25 (Jan.–Feb. 2004), 43. Jameson is using encryptment in Derrida's sense, to indicate the crypt's ability to isolate or shelter from penetration.

176 Canada, *House of Commons Debates*, 17th Parliament, 6th Session, vol. 2, 2183–4 (28 March 1935); also vol. 4, 3823 (20 June 1935). In 1935 Woodsworth wrote a pamphlet on *The Distribution of Personal Income*, cited in Mills, *Fool for Christ*, 155. On the evolution of Woodsworth's economic thought see Mills, *Fool for Christ*, 149–87, and "Cooperation and Community in the Thought of J.S. Woodsworth," *Labour / Le travail* 14 (fall 1984): 103–20.

177 Partridge, *War on Poverty*, 23.

178 State assistance in the great project of social salvation was not unimportant, of course. But the focus tended to be on remedial reforms, such as factory legislation, criminal-law enforcement, liquor control, sabbath observance, and laws against prostitution and gambling. Taxation attracted some attention, especially during the First World War. On Presbyterians and legislation see, for instance, Brian J. Fraser, *The Social Uplifters: Presbyterian Progressives and the Social Gospel in Canada 1875–1915* (Waterloo, ON: Wilfrid Laurier University Press, 1988), 137–47. Relevant here is Gauvreau's conclusion that the affinities of most Canadian clergymen lay not with the radical social gospel of Rauschenbusch and Bland, but with a millennialist and prophetic

evangelicalism, which was unable to engage with the new social sciences, despite the connections to sociology and social work. Gauvreau, *Evangelical Century*, 116–17.

179 A few instances: *Report on a Limited Survey of Educational, Social and Industrial Life* (London, ON: Presbyterian Committee on Religious Education, 1913); Social Service Council, *The Community Survey: A Basis for Social Action* (Toronto: Social Service Council, 1919); Rev. L. Norman Tucker, *Council for Social Service, Church of England in Canada: A Memorandum* (Council for Social Service, 1919). See also Christie and Gauvreau, *A Full-Orbed Christianity*, 209.

180 Since 1901 the Canadian census (unlike the U.S. census) had asked all employees to report their annual earnings. Although the results did not include incomes of non-employees, and hence more affluent people, even these limited results were available in tabular form and demonstrated extreme disparities. To the best of my knowledge, nobody at the time pressed the government to ask employers and the self-employed to report annual incomes.

181 Christie and Gauvreau, *A Full-Orbed Christianity*, 141.

182 Ibid., 196.

183 Ibid., 189.

184 Rev. F.R. Beattie, *An Examination of the Utilitarian Theory of Morals* (Brantford, Ont.: J. & J. Sutherland, 1885), 220–1. See also the critique of utilitarianism in George Paxton Young, *The Ethics of Freedom* (Toronto: University Press, 1911), 12–13.

185 Murray, *The Industrial Kingdom of God*, 137–8.

CHAPTER SIX

1 Studies of economic thought in Canada include: Ian M. Drummond and William Kaplan, *Political Economy at the University of Toronto: A History of the Department, 1888–1982* (Toronto: Faculty of Arts and Science, University of Toronto, 1983); Barry Ferguson, *Remaking Liberalism: The Intellectual Legacy of Adam Shortt, O.D. Skelton, W.C. Clark, and W.A. Mackintosh, 1890–1925* (Montreal and Kingston: McGill-Queen's University Press, 1993); Craufurd D.W. Goodwin, *Canadian Economic Thought: The Political Economy of a Developing Nation 1814–1914* (Durham, NC: Duke University Press, 1961); Robin Neill, *A History of Canadian Economic Thought* (London: Routledge, 1991); S.E.D. Shortt, *The Search for an Ideal: Six Canadian Intellectuals and Their Convictions in an Age of Transition 1890–1930* (Toronto: University of Toronto Press,

1976); and Shirley Spafford, *No Ordinary Academics: Economics and Political Science at the University of Saskatchewan, 1910–1960* (Toronto: University of Toronto Press, 2000). There are also several biographies and specialized studies of individual economists.

2 The literature is voluminous. Recent introductions include Jeremy Dunham, Iain Hamilton Grant, and Sean Watson, *Idealism: The History of a Philosophy* (Montreal and Kingston: McGill-Queen's University Press, 2011); W.J. Mander, *British Idealism: A History* (Oxford: Oxford University Press, 2011); and W.J. Mander and Stamatoula Panakagou, eds., *British Idealism and the Concept of the Self* (London: Palgrave Macmillan, 2016). On the "afterlife": Admir Skodo, *The Afterlife of Idealism: The Impact of New Idealism on British Historical and Political Thought, 1945–1980* (Cham, Switzerland: Palgrave Macmillan, 2016); and Colin Tyler, *Common Good Politics: British Idealism and Social Justice in the Contemporary World* (Cham, Switzerland: Palgrave Macmillan, 2016). We hear even a case for the relevance of T.H. Green in the world of information technology: Alistair S. Duff, "Cyber-Green: Idealism in the Information Age," *Journal of Information, Communication and Ethics in Society* 13, no. 2 (2015): 146–64.

3 Leslie Armour and Elizabeth Trott, *The Faces of Reason: An Essay on Philosophy and Culture in English Canada 1850–1950* (Waterloo, ON: Wilfrid Laurier University Press, 1983); A.B. McKillop, *A Disciplined Intelligence: Critical Inquiry and Canadian Thought in the Victorian Era* (Montreal and Kingston: McGill-Queen's University Press, 1979); S.E.D. Shortt, *The Search for an Ideal: Six Canadian Intellectuals and Their Convictions in an Age of Transition, 1890–1930* (Toronto: University of Toronto Press, 1976); Charles Nicholas Terpstra, "A Victorian Frame of Mind: The Thought of John Clark Murray" (MA thesis, McMaster University, 1983).

4 Thomas Hill Green, *Prolegomena to Ethics*, ed. A.C. Bradley (Oxford: Clarendon Press, 1883), 38.

5 T.H. Green, *Prolegomena to Ethics* (1883), 72. On Green and consciousness: T.L.S. Sprigge, "T.H. Green and the Eternal Consciousness," in Sprigge, *The God of Metaphysics* (Oxford: Clarendon Press, 2006), chap. 5, 223–69.

6 McKillop, *Disciplined Intelligence*, 182.

7 John Watson, "Edward Caird," *Philosophical Review* 18 (Jan. 1909): 108; cited in ibid., 184.

8 John Watson, "The Idealism of Edward Caird. I," *Philosophical Review* 18 (March 1909): 157; cited in ibid., 185. Watson did not adopt the

pragmatism of William James and his followers; see for instance, his critique of the "humanism" of F.C.S. Schiller in his article "Humanism," *Queen's Quarterly* 13 (Oct. 1905): 106–26.

9 José Harris, "Political Thought and the Welfare State 1870–1940: An Intellectual Framework for British Social Policy," *Past & Present* 135 (May 1992): 123. See also José Harris, *Private Lives, Public Spirit 1870–1914* (London: Penguin Books, 1994), 182, 226–30.

10 John Clark Murray, unpaginated "Prefatory Note," in Murray, *The Industrial Kingdom of God* (first pub. 1887), ed. Leslie Armour and Elizabeth Trott (Ottawa: University of Ottawa Press, 1981).

11 Ibid., 13.

12 Ibid., 17.

13 Ibid., 25, 31, 32, 35.

14 Ibid., 29.

15 Ibid., 115.

16 John Clark Murray, "Philosophy and Industrial Life," *Monist* 4 (Jan. 1893): 544.

17 Murray, *Industrial Kingdom*, 76.

18 Ibid., 35.

19 Ibid., 35–6.

20 Ibid., 47.

21 Ibid., 64.

22 Ibid., 46.

23 Murray, "Philosophy and Industrial Life," 543–4.

24 Terpstra, "A Victorian Frame of Mind," 141–3. See also Terpstra, "A Tale of Two Cities: John Clark Murray's Search for the Industrial Kingdom of God," *Journal of Canadian Studies* 27, no. 3 (1992–93): 5–27.

25 Murray, *Industrial Kingdom*, 41.

26 J. Clark Murray, *"The Merchant of Venice" as an Exponent of Industrial Ethics* (Montreal: N.p., 1899), reprinted from *International Journal of Ethics* (April 1899). Murray argued that Shylock was not a Jewish stereotype but a model of amoral accumulation and selfish competition. Portia represented a higher morality, but Murray's argument was that a higher morality did not always work in the real world. Portia's decisive intervention occurred in a court of law, where she applied Shylock's own "lower morality" and the law to secure justice. Murray also wrote a novel in which he explored the ethics of social morality and wealth as a sacred trust: *He That Had Received the Five Talents* (London: T.F. Unwin, 1904).

27 The inequality problem did receive brief mention in the context of other subjects. In 1907 the Canadian economist W.W. Swanson argued that

wealth need not "excite apprehension" because the voluntary benevolence of the very rich was benefitting society as a whole, and because "actual statistics [he cited none] show that the rich are growing relatively fewer." W.W. Swanson, "Some Reflections on the Capitalist Organization of Society," *Queen's University Journal* 35, no. 5 (Dec. 1907): 203.

28 Gustavus Myers, *A History of Canadian Wealth* (first pub. 1914) (Toronto: James Lorimer and Company, 1975), xxxi. As Stanley Ryerson noted in his 1975 Introduction, Myers said little about the struggles of workers and the wage–labour relationship (xxi). There were occasional articles about combines laws: E.R. Peacock, "Trusts, Combines and Monopolies," *Queen's Quarterly* 6, no. 1 (July 1898): 1–35. Peacock argued that "combination is inevitable, and as it involves great changes, suffering is also inevitable, but because all progress involves suffering we should not seek to prevent progress" (26). Peacock was a student of Adam Shortt. The leading Canadian expert on combines, J.E. Le Rossignol, focused his studies on the United States.

29 Neill, *History of Canadian Economic Thought*, 119.

30 Inequality was an important issue for American social gospellers, but there would be no Canadian counterparts to Richard Ely.

31 A relevant example is the Tory idealism of James Cappon, Scots-born professor of English at Queen's. Although he wrote occasionally about social questions and worried about the disruptive effects of industrialization, he saw the future in terms of improved ethical and educational standards and literary culture as the distinguishing feature of civilized nations. S.E.D. Shortt, "James Cappon," in S.E.D. Shortt, *The Search for an Ideal: Six Canadian Intellectuals and Their Convictions in an Age of Transition, 1890–1930* (Toronto: University of Toronto Press, 1976), 70–4. As principal editor of *Queen's Quarterly* for many years, Cappon could have solicited articles on inequality and distributive justice but did not. See also the tory idealism of Maurice Hutton, English-born professor of classics at Toronto; see Shortt, *The Search for an Ideal*, 77–93. Another idealist was William Caldwell, professor of moral philosophy at McGill from 1903, author of *Pragmatism and Idealism* (London: A. and C. Black, 1913). John Watson wrote a critical review of this book: "Pragmatism and Idealism," *Queen's Quarterly* 21 (April 1914): 465–72.

32 George John Blewett, *The Christian View of the World* (Toronto: William Briggs, 1912), 307.

33 Ibid., 341. In his discussion of Aquinas, Blewett wrote: "Multiplicity and variety, diversity and inequality in created things, are necessary, that by this manifoldness a perfect copy of the divine perfection might be found."

Blewett, *The Study of Nature and the Vision of God: With Other Essays in Philosophy* (Toronto: William Briggs, 1907), 340.

34 These words did not appear in James Ten Broeke, *A Constructive Basis for Theology* (London: Macmillan, 1914), or his *The Moral Life and Religion: A Study of Moral and Religious Personality* (New York: Macmillan, 1922). See Leslie Armour and Elizabeth Trott, "Reason, Religion, and the Idea of Nature: George Blewett and James Ten Broeke," in Leslie Armour and Elizabeth Trott, *The Faces of Reason: An Essay on Philosophy and Culture in English Canada 1850–1950* (Waterloo, ON: Wilfrid Laurier University Press, 1983), 321–60. The long-serving Ten Broeke influenced a generation of students at McMaster; Harold Innis was a student and a member of Ten Broeke's Philosophy Club.

35 Elizabeth Trott, "Blewett, George John," in *Dictionary of Canadian Biography*, vol. 14 (University of Toronto / Université Laval, 2003–), 2020, http://www.biographi.ca/en/bio/blewett_george_john_14E.html, accessed 28 May 2020.

36 John Rae, *The Sociological Theory of Capital*, ed. C.W. Mixter (New York: Macmillan, 1905), 233 (a reprint of Rae's *New Principles of Political Economy* [1834]).

37 Ibid., 464.

38 O.F. Hamouda, C. Lee, and D. Mair, eds., *The Economics of John Rae* (London: Routledge, 1998). On Veblen see Roger Mason, "John Rae and Conspicuous Consumption," in ibid., 96–107.

39 Pierre Rosanvallon, *The Society of Equals*, trans. Arthur Goldhammer (Cambridge, MA: Harvard University Press, 2013), 135.

40 The protectionist Isaac Buchanan spoke of "social economy" and assailed Ricardo's defence of "unequal distribution." Distribution, and laws that made "the rich richer," were recurring themes: Isaac Buchanan, *The Relations of the Industry of Canada with the Mother Country and the United States*, ed. Henry J. Morgan (Montreal: John Lovell, 1864), 96–7, 98–9, 112, 129, 242. John MacLean summarized the egalitarian argument of free traders in order to refute it: MacLean, *Protection and Free Trade* (Montreal: John Lovell, 1868), 71. J. Beaufort Hurlbert commented on the ambiguities of "inequality" and "equality" when applied to trade: Hurlbert, *Protection and Free Trade with Special Reference to Canada and Newly Settled Countries* (Ottawa: A.S. Woodburn, 1882), 115, 121. See also Hurlbert, *Field and Factory … or, How to Establish and Develop Native Industries* (Montreal: John Lovell, 1870).

41 On system in Enlightenment political economy see David Wootton, *Power, Pleasure and Profit: Insatiable Appetites from Machiavelli to Madison*

(Cambridge, MA: Harvard University Press, 2018), 189–91. The word "system" appeared 105 times in Isaac Buchanan, *Relations of the Industry of Canada.*

42 W.J.A. Donald of McMaster University in Toronto wrote *The Canadian Iron and Steel Industry* (Boston: Houghton Mifflin, 1915), one of the rare studies of a Canadian manufacturing industry in this period. He focused on tariffs, conditions of growth, and company histories and said little about labour and labour–management relations. J.A. Estey of Dalhousie University wrote *Revolutionary Syndicalism: An Exposition and a Criticism* (London: P.S. King, 1913). He concentrated on Europe, and the only reference to the Industrial Workers of the World was in the introduction by J. Lovell Price.

43 John Davidson, *The Bargain Theory of Wages* (New York: G.P. Putnam, 1898), 119–20.

44 Ibid., 119.

45 Ibid., 119, 126.

46 Ibid., 169.

47 Ibid., 262.

48 Goodwin, *Canadian Economic Thought*, 180.

49 W.J. Ashley, *What Is Political Science? An Inaugural Lecture* (Toronto: Rowsell and Hutchison, 1888), 15–16.

50 "For years," Ashley wrote in 1893, "there has been a keen controversy going on upon the subject of Distribution; and economists, even economists of the first rank, seem as far from agreement as ever." W.J. Ashley, *On the Study of Economic History: An Introductory Lecture Delivered before Harvard University* (Boston: N.p., 1893), 12; reprinted from the *Quarterly Journal of Economics* 7, no. 2 (Jan. 1893).

51 Neill, *History of Canadian Economic Thought*, 110–11.

52 These included James Bonar, W.C. Clark, R.H. Coats, D.A. MacGibbon, W.A. Mackintosh, and O.D. Skelton, Many others, including Harold Innis, James Mavor, Adam Shortt, and W.W. Swanson, served on royal commissions or boards in the public service. See Barry Ferguson, *Remaking Liberalism* (1993); Hugh Grant, *W.A. Mackintosh: The Life of a Canadian Economist* (Montreal and Kingston: McGill-Queen's University Press, 2015); Norman Hillmer, *O.D. Skelton: A Portrait of Canadian Ambition* (Toronto: University of Toronto Press, 2015); Douglas Owram, *The Government Generation: Intellectuals and the State in Canada, 1900–1945* (Toronto: University of Toronto Press, 1986); and Robert A. Wardhaugh, *Behind the Scenes: The Life and Work of William Clifford Clark* (Toronto: University of Toronto Press, 2010).

53 C.S. Peirce, "How to Make Our Ideas Clear," *Popular Science Monthly* 12 (1878): 293.

54 For instance: James Mavor, *Wage Statistics and Wage Theories* (Edinburgh: William Brown, 1888); *The Political Situation and Labour Problems* (Glasgow: J.B. Douglas, 1892); and *The Radical Programme* (Glasgow: J.B. Douglas, 1892 or 1893). On his early reformist politics see S.E.D. Shortt, "James Mavor," in Shortt, *The Search for an Ideal: Six Canadian Intellectuals and Their Convictions in an Age of Transition 1890–1930* (Toronto: University of Toronto Press, 1976), 120–2; E. Lisa Panayotidis, "Mavor, James," in *Dictionary of Canadian Biography*, vol. 15 (University of Toronto / Université Laval, 2003–), http://www. biographi.ca/en/bio/mavor_james_15E.html, accessed 28 May 2020.

55 James Mavor, *Applied Economics* (New York: Alexander Hamilton Institute, 1914), 315–16. Mavor recorded his retreat from idealism and Fabianism in his 1923 memoirs. There he said that, apart from revolutionary socialism, which had failed, there had been enough "experiments in collectivism" to assess their effect. And his assessment? "Once individual initiative is destroyed in a nation there is little hope of its renaissance." Mavor, *My Windows on the Street of the World*, vol. 1 (London: J.M. Dent, 1923), 247–8.

56 Shortt, *Search for an Ideal*, 134.

57 Frank Underhill, "The Conception of a National Interest," *Canadian Journal of Economics and Political Science* 1, no. 3 (Aug. 1935): 404.

58 On Shortt's youth see S.E.D. Shortt, "Adam Shortt," in S.E.D. Shortt, *The Search for an Ideal: Six Canadian Intellectuals and Their Convictions in an Age of Transition 1890–1930* (Toronto: University of Toronto Press, 1976), 95–6; Ferguson, *Remaking Liberalism*, 13–14; and W.A. Mackintosh, "Adam Shortt," *Canadian Journal of Economics and Political Science* 4, no. 2 (May 1938): 164–5.

59 Adam Shortt, "Legislation and Morality," *Queen's Quarterly* 8 (April 1901): 354.

60 Ferguson, *Remaking Liberalism*, 60.

61 Adam Shortt, "The Influence of Daily Occupations on the Life of the People," Alma Mater Society, *Sunday Afternoon Addresses*, 3rd series (1893), 59, 65–6; cited in Ferguson, *Remaking Liberalism*, 46.

62 Adam Shortt, *Early Economic Effects of the European War upon Canada* (New York: Oxford University Press, 1918), 5.

63 Ibid., 14, 16.

64 Adam Shortt, *The Evolution of the Relation between Capital and Labor* (Kingston: n.p., 1889), 145. Shortt's 1897 critique of cooperatives

included a rejection of joint management systems: "Co-operation," *Queen's Quarterly* 5, no. 2 (Oct. 1897): 132.

65 American economists appear to have anticipated the Canadian trend. According to Rodgers, talk of appropriating the language of socialism began to vanish from American economic discourse in the late 1880s: Daniel T. Rodgers, *Atlantic Crossings: Social Politics in a Progressive Age* (Cambridge, Mass.: Belknap Press, 1998), 106.

66 J.A. Estey, *Revolutionary Syndicalism: An Exposition and a Criticism* (London: P.S. King, 1913). Estey focused on France. He saw revolutionary syndicalism giving way to moderation and reformism. Estey's first degree was from Acadia University; he completed his doctorate at Wisconsin in 1911. An earlier critique was John Hay, "A General View of Socialistic Schemes," *Queen's Quarterly* 3, no. 4 (April 1896): 283–95.

67 Adam Shortt, "Recent Phases of Socialism," *Queen's Quarterly* 5, no. 1 (July 1897): 12, 14, 20.

68 Le Rossignol spent most of his career in the United States. His Leipzig doctoral dissertation was a study of the English philosopher and theologian Samuel Clarke (1675–1729).

69 James Edward Le Rossignol, *Orthodox Socialism: A Criticism* (New York: Thomas Crowell, 1907), 138–40. See also Le Rossignol, "The March of Socialism," *University Magazine* 11, no. 3 (Oct. 1912): 429–45.

70 Le Rossignol was well aware of the contemporary criticisms of trusts and monopolies; he saw few costs from their effect on prices and little influence on competition. He thought inequality inevitable and recent increases in inequality a necessary cost of efficiency and growth. "The weak must fall by the way and the strong must push on to greater things. Only in this way can the best interests of mankind be served." James Edward Le Rossignol, *Monopolies Past and Present: An Introductory Study* (New York: Thomas Crowell, 1901), 175; on wealth distribution see also 136–7.

71 O.D. Skelton, *Socialism: A Critical Analysis* (New York: Houghton Mifflin, 1911), 18.

72 Ibid., 19–21.

73 Ibid., 201.

74 Ibid., 203–4.

75 Ibid., 202.

76 Ibid., 202–3.

77 Ibid., 309; Ian McKay, *Reasoning Otherwise: Leftists and the People's Enlightenment in Canada, 1890–1920* (Toronto: Between the Lines, 2008), 129–30.

78 Skelton, *Socialism*, 309.

79 Ibid., 310.

80 Skelton, *General Economic History of the Dominion 1867–1912* (Toronto: Publishers' Association of Canada, 1913), 100.

81 Ibid., 270.

82 Skelton's father was at various times a grocer, a teacher, treasurer for the Cornwall Paper Manufacturing Company, and a salesperson for the Hoover Vacuum Company. Hillmer, *Skelton*, 16–17.

83 Ibid., 19.

84 Skelton, *Socialism*, 55–6, 60–1.

85 Barry Ferguson summarizes Skelton's position as follows: inequality was often based on "differences in enterprise, in industry, in thrift" – any attempt to level such inequality risked "paralyzing industry." Ferguson, *Remaking Liberalism*, 106.

86 E.A. Heaman, *Tax, Order and Good Government; A New Political History of Canada, 1897–1917* (Montreal and Kingston: McGill-Queen's University Press, 397–8, 401, 430.

87 Skelton, *Federal Finance* (Kingston: Jackson Press, 1915), 21; reprint of "Federal Finance," *Queen's Quarterly* 23 (July 1915): 60–93.

88 These terms did not appear in his pamphlet *Federal Finance* (1915); see also "Are We to Have a Federal Income Tax?," *Monetary Times*, 22 Oct. 1915, 5–7.

89 Hillmer, *Skelton*, 12–13.

90 Ibid., 31. On Skelton's mix of pragmatism, eclecticism, and liberalism see also Terry Crowley, *Marriage of Minds: Isabel and Oscar Skelton Reinventing Canada* (Toronto: University of Toronto Press, 2003), 4.

91 Alexander John Watson, *Marginal Man: The Dark Vision of Harold Innis* (Toronto: University of Toronto Press, 2006).

92 John Bonnett, *Emergence and Empire: Innis, Complexity, and the Trajectory of History* (Montreal and Kingston: McGill-Queen's University Press, 2013), 267–79.

93 Michael Gauvreau, "Baptist Religion and the Social Science of Harold Innis," *Canadian Historical Review* 76, no. 2 (June 1995): 161–204; Watson, *Marginal Man*, 62–3.

94 Watson, *Marginal Man*, 188.

95 Harold Innis, *Political Economy and the Modern State* (Toronto: Ryerson Press, 1946), 126–7. On Innis's view of pubic activism, see also Liora Salter and Cheryl Dahl, "The Public Role of the Intellectual," in Charles R. Acland and William J. Buxton, eds., *Harold Innis in the New Century:*

Reflections and Refractions (Montreal and Kingston: McGill-Queen's University Press, 1999), 114–34.

96　Key examples are in Hugh Grant and David A. Wolfe, eds., *Staples and Beyond: Selected Writings of Mel Watkins* (Montreal and Kingston: McGill-Queen's University Press, 2006). For a critical perspective on the staples approach as "pragmatic empiricism" see Robert Sweeney, "The Staples as the Significant Past: A Case Study in Historical Theory and Method," in Terry Goldie, Carmen Lambert, and Rowland Lorimer, eds., *Canada: Theoretical Discourse* (Montreal: Association for Canadian Studies, 1994), 327–50.

97　Gauvreau, "Baptist Religion," 126–7.

98　"Distribution of wealth" appeared once, in the title of a book by the French economist Turgot, cited in one of Innis's footnotes. Also relevant is Richard Noble's argument that Innis held a conservative, Whig-like conception of freedom: liberties should be distributed equally only in so far as they helped balance and stabilize a political system. Richard Noble, "Innis's Conception of Freedom," in Charles R. Acland and William J. Buxton, eds., *Harold Innis in the New Century: Reflections and Refractions* (Montreal and Kingston: McGill-Queen's University Press, 1999), 31–45.

99　On the north, William J. Buxton, ed., *Harold Innis and the North: Appraisals and Contestations* (Montreal and Kingston: McGill-Queen's University Press, 2013).

100　Watson, *Marginal Man*, 12–13.

101　H.A. Innis, "The Returned Soldier" (MA thesis, McMaster University, 1918), 6–7, quoted in Gauvreau, "Baptist Religion," 176.

102　Gauvreau, "Baptist Religion," 187.

103　Ibid.,186.

104　Most of the early writings are cited in George F. Henderson, *W.L. Mackenzie King: A Bibliography and Research Guide* (Toronto: University of Toronto Press, 1998).

105　W.L. Mackenzie King, *Industry and Humanity: A Study in the Principles underlying Industrial Reconstruction* (Toronto: Thomas Allen, 1918), 60, 88–9.

106　In *Industry and Humanity*, King cited J.S. Mill, Arnold Toynbee, and William Cunningham, but offered no references to recent works in political economy or to the seminal works on industrial relations. He did not cite John R. Commons's *Labor and Administration* (1913). There was one footnote reference to Robert F. Hoxie, *Scientific Management and Labor*

(1915), but nothing on his *Trade Unionism in the United States* (1917).
King mentioned Sidney Webb, *The Restoration of Trade Union Conditions*
(1916), but not Sidney and Beatrice Webb's seminal *Industrial Democracy*
(1897).

107 King, *Industry and Humanity*, 342–3.

108 Reg Whitaker, "The Liberal Corporatist Ideas of Mackenzie King,"
Labour / Le travail 2 (1977): 146; see also Eric Tucker, "Industry and
Humanity Revisited: Everything Old Is New Again," *McGill Law Journal*
36, no. 4 (1991): 481–500.

109 King, *Industry and Humanity*, 81. King used profit-sharing and its growth
to support his optimism (see 280–1, 292–303, and 366–7), but mentioned
it only rarely as a way to solve the problem of inequality. John Davidson
was sceptical about it: Davidson, *Bargain Theory*, 83, 89, 150, 166, 173,
282–7, 304–6. For a more hopeful view on its being "better distribution":
"Profit Sharing a Success," *Canadian Manufacturer and Industrial World*
53, no. 6 (21 Sept. 1906): 33–4.

110 King, *Industry and Humanity*, 142–3, 209ff.

111 Ibid., xx.

112 There is a brief biography of MacIver by John M. Jordan in *American
National Biography Online*, and a useful survey of his work by George
Kateb in the *New York Review of Books*, 25 March 1965.

113 R.M. MacIver, *Labor in the Changing World* (Toronto: J.M. Dent, 1919),
126.

114 Ibid., 90–1.

115 R.M. MacIver, *The Elements of Social Science* (London: Methuen, 1921),
89.

116 Ibid., 125.

117 Ibid., 187–8.

118 Ibid., 203, 205–7.

119 Ibid., 104, 113, 206; MacIver, *Elements of Social Science*, 89. In his
memoirs Vincent Bladen noted: "MacIver's *Labour in a Changing World*
[*sic*] rather shocked Toronto businessmen, and his advocacy of birth
control led to some annoyance." Vincent Bladen, *Bladen on Bladen:
Memoirs of a Political Economist* (Toronto: Scarborough College, 1978),
32.

120 MacIver, *Labor*, 104–5.

121 All of these words appeared on the first page of the Preface to MacIver's
Labor in the Changing World, v.

122 R.M. MacIver, *Community: A Sociological Study* (London: Macmillan, 1917). MacIver offered his capacious, multifaceted definition of economics as a discipline (48–9). He rejected "the forecast of Marx that wealth would become the possession and power of an ever-richer and every-smaller minority" (354). He saw a current general tendency for land to pass from a few large landowners to a "vast number" of small proprietors. He then stated his own concern for "the industrial conditions" that led to expropriation and immiseration. "So long as great numbers are, through no fault of theirs, destitute and expropriated, they cannot attain any socialization. They cannot root themselves in community" (354–5).

123 Ibid., ix.

124 MacIver, *Elements of Social Science*, 76–7.

125 Ibid., 142.

126 John Neville Keynes, *The Scope and Method of Political Economy* (first pub. 1890) (London: Macmillan, 1897), 42–5.

127 MacIver, *Community*, 48–9.

128 Ibid., 51.

129 R.M. MacIver, *The Modern State* (London: Humphrey Milford, 1926), 304.

130 Ibid., 316.

131 Stephen Leacock, *How to Write* (New York: Dodd, Mead, 1943), 106, cited in Gerald Lynch, *Stephen Leacock: Humour and Humanity* (Montreal and Kingston: McGill-Queen's University Press, 1988), 51.

132 Leacock, *Charles Dickens: His Life and Work* (Garden City, NY: Doubleday, 1934), 110–11; cited in Lynch, *Leacock*, 52.

133 Leacock, *Last Leaves* (New York: Dodd, Mead, 1945), 106.

134 Stephen Leacock, *The Unsolved Riddle of Social Justice* (New York: John Lane, 1920), 66. J.B. Clark wrote: "When natural economic law has its way a working man gets the amount of wealth that he creates … Working man, working instrument, productive agent of any sort, would get under natural law what he or it is worth to society … 'To every man his product, his whole product, and nothing but his product,' is not merely the ethical standard of wages; it is the standard that society tends to realize … if there were nothing to vitiate the action of a true competitive law." John Bates Clark, "The Law of Wages and Interest," *Annals of the American Academy of Political and Social Science* 1 (July 1890): 44; cited in John F. Henry, *John Bates Clark: The Making of a Neoclassical Economist* (Basingstoke, England: Macmillan, 1995), 55.

135 Goodwin, *Canadian Economic Thought*, 191–3.

136 As Carl Berger points out, for Leacock economics was a moral domain of inquiry, not a set of techniques. Carl Berger, "The Other Mr Leacock," *Canadian Literature* 55 (winter 1973): 23–40. See also Leacock, *Hellements of Hickonomics* (New York: Dodd, Meade, 1936).

137 Leacock, *Unsolved Riddle*, 78–9, 84.

138 Ibid., 66.

139 Ibid., 14.

140 Ibid., 25.

141 Leacock had known Thorstein Veblen at Chicago. Leacock spoke of Veblen's main idea as being "that human industry is not carried on to satisfy human needs but in order to make money." As Myron J. Frankman has pointed out, this does not quite capture the main elements of Veblen's economics. Myron J. Frankman, "Stephen Leacock, Economist: An Owl among the Parrots," in David Staines, ed., *Stephen Leacock: A Reappraisal* (Ottawa: Ottawa University Press, 1986), 53. Nevertheless, Leacock had absorbed Veblen's teachings on the social instincts of emulation and predation, and on the quest for social status by those who could benefit from predatory capture of goods and services. He had also taken in Veblen's historical-social rejection of neoclassical economics and its teachings on wage determination.

142 Thomas Carlyle, *Past and Present*, 2nd ed. (London, 1845), 1; Lynch, *Leacock*, 14.

143 Leacock's scholarly writings prior to 1920 included *Elements of Political Science* (Boston: Houghton Mifflin, 1906) and *Baldwin, Lafontaine, Hincks: Responsible Government* (Toronto: Morang, 1907). A series of twenty-five articles of his on "Practical Political Economy" appeared in *Saturday Night* magazine between 12 November 1910 and 29 April 1911.

144 This paragraph summarizes the argument in Leacock, *Elements of Political Science* (first pub. 1906) (Boston: Houghton Mifflin, 1921), 74–6. His position was not unlike Richard Ely's: freedom would be increased by "laws which limit the power of the strong to oppress and which open the gates of opportunity." Ely, *Outlines of Economics*, 3rd ed. (New York: Macmillan, 1916), 27–8.

145 Leacock, *Elements* (1921 ed.), 360–9. Leacock's critique of laissez-faire began in his Chicago doctoral dissertation: Leacock, *My Recollection of Chicago and the Doctrine of Laissez Faire*, intro. and ed. Carl Spadoni (Toronto: University of Toronto Press, 1998).

146 Lynch, *Leacock*, 4. In rejecting socialism, Leacock focused on the American socialist Edward Bellamy, author of *Looking Backward 2000–1887* (1889) and *Equality* (1898). In *Unsolved Riddle*, Leacock

commented that Bellamy's utopian "dream" demanded rebuttal precisely because it was so appealing to a wide audience – "the most attractive and the most consistent outline of a socialist state that has, within the knowledge of the present writer, ever been put forward" (101–2). Modern socialism, "the direct outcome of the age of machine production," was dangerous precisely because its indictment of the weaknesses and injustices of the present system "is very largely right" (89, 96, 101–2). One cannot read *Unsolved Riddle* without repeatedly encountering the Anglican's deep sense of human fallibility and selfishness. Socialism "won't work" because it assumed a community of angels and ignored "a general selfishness or self-seeking as the principal motive of the individual in the economic sphere" (40). See also Frank Watt, "Critic or Entertainer: Stephen Leacock and the Growth of Materialism," *Canadian Literature* 5 (summer 1960): 33–42.

147 Leacock, *Unsolved Riddle*, 124–5.
148 Ibid., 128–52.
149 Ibid., 152.
150 Ibid., 138.
151 Leacock, *Humour: Its Theory and Technique* (London: John Lane, 1935), 118–19: cited in Lynch, *Leacock*, 46–7.
152 Leacock, *Arcadian Adventures with the Idle Rich* (New York: John Lane, 1914), 11.
153 Ibid., 183.

CHAPTER SEVEN

1 "*Et nous aboutissons à la situation paradoxale d'un monde réduit à la misère au milieu de l'abondance.*" Esdras Minville, "Libéralisme? Communisme? Corporatisme?" *Actualité économique* 12, no. 2 (Nov. 1936): 155–6.
2 Fernand Dumont, "Les années 30: La première Révolution tranquille," in Fernand Dumont, Jean Hamelin, and Jean-Paul Montminy, eds., *Idéologies au Canada française 1930–1939* (Quebec: Les Presses de l'Université Laval, 1978), 2.
3 Édouard Montpetit, *Propos sur la montagne* (Montreal: Éditions de l'Arbre, 1946), 159–60. Montpetit was quoting Charles Perin, the nineteenth-century political economist at Louvain, a pivotal figure in the early development of Catholic social teaching.
4 Jonathan Fournier, "Les économists canadiens-français pendant l'entre-deux-guerres: entre la science et l'engagement," *Revue d'histoire de*

l'Amérique francaise 58, no 3 (2005): 389–414. The influences were French and Belgian. If there was any affinity to Anglo-American political economy, it was with the American institutionalists such as John R. Commons. Keynesian ideas took longer to find support in Quebec than in English Canada. Gilles Dostaler et Frédéric Hanin, "Keynes et le keynesianisme au Canada et au Québec," *Sociologie et sociétiés* 37, no. 2 (2005): 153–81. See also Jonathan Fournier, "Le développement des sciences économiques en milieu universitaire au Québec francophone de 1939 à 1975" (PhD dissertation, Université du Québec à Montréal, 2004).

5 Montpetit, *Propos sur la montagne*, 161.

6 F.-A. Angers, "Neo-libéralisme et science économique," *Actualité économique* 15, no 1 (April 1939): 369.

7 The critique of economic liberalism and of the abuses of capitalism appeared among many of the diverse representatives of social Catholicism in Quebec. The focus here is on political economists, especially those associated with L'École des hautes études commerciales (HEC) and the journal *L'Actualité économique*. The Catholic youth movements did not ignore the subject of "just distribution," and Louise Bienvenue suggests that even after 1945 the "liberal humanism" orientation was concerned with the distribution of wealth. Louise Bienvenue, *Quand la jeunesse entre en scène: L'Action catholique avant la Révolution tranquille* (Montreal: Boréal, 2003), 166. During the 1930s the movement focused on the problems of youth and the national question. See, for instance, the "Manifeste de la jeune génération" at faculty.màrianopolis.edu, translated in Ramsay Cook and Michael Behiels, *The Essential Laurendeau* (Toronto: Copp Clark, 1976), 34–6.

8 *Evangelii gaudium* (2013) by Pope Francis contains clear echoes of earlier social Catholicism. Francis rejects "the invisible hand of the market" and argues that a simple welfare-state economics is inadequate in addressing "the structural causes of inequality."

9 Minville, "Libéralisme? Communisme? Corporatisme?," 155–6.

10 Quoted in "Position catholique en face des problèmes économiques et sociaux d'aujourd'hui," *Actualité économique* 15, no 1 (April 1939): 374.

11 Jonathan Fournier has reminded me that the virulent anti-communism in Quebec in the 1930s is relevant to the reluctance about state intervention, which some people thought opened the door to communism (personal communication, 21 Aug. 2019).

12 Distributism was also deeply indebted to the papal encyclicals. So far I have found no references in *L'Actualité économique*. Arthur Penty's *Distributism: A Manifesto* was published in 1937. U.S. Catholic teaching

on social questions appears to have had little influence in Quebec; even John A. Ryan's classic *Distributive Justice: The Right and Wrong of Our Present Distribution of Wealth* (New York: Macmillan, 1916) went unnoticed. The Antigonish movement flourished in the Maritimes; despite its debt to papal encyclicals, it did not make the problem of inequality a prominent theme. Moses Coady came close when arguing that cooperation was an instrument "by which the people could have piped down to themselves some of the wealth that flowed so generously in other directions." Moses Coady, *Masters of Their Own Destiny; The Story of the Antigonish Movement of Adult Education through Economic Cooperation* (first pub. 1939) (Antigonish, NS: Formac Publishing, 1980), 122.

13 Leo XIII, *Rerum novarum* (15 May 1891) at http://w2.vatican.va/content/leo-xiii/en/encyclicals/documents/hf_l-xiii_enc_15051891_rerum-novarum.html.

14 Leo XIII, *Rerum novarum*.

15 *Quadragesimo anno*, quoted in Eugene L'Heureux, "La dictature économique dans la province de Québec," *L'Action nationale*, 1 (Jan.–June 1933): 67–8; and quoted in Eugene L'Heureux, *Libéralisme économique et Action catholique* (Quebec: Action catholique, 1934), 32. Georges-Henri Levesque quoted another section of *Quadragesimo anno*: "D'un côté, une minorité de riches jouissant à peu près de toutes les commodités qu'offrent en si grande abondance les inventions modernes; de l'autre, une multitude immense de travailleurs réduits à une angoissante misère et s'efforçant en vain d'en sortir." Georges-Henri Levesque, "Socialisme canadien," *L'Action nationale*, 2 (Sept.–Dec. 1933): 99.

16 J.-E. Grégoire, "Lettre-Preface," in Eugène L'Heureux, *Libéralisme économique et Action catholique* (Quebec: Des ateliers de l'Action catholique, 1934), 5.

17 Lettre pastorale et mandement ... à l'occasion du malaise économique des temps presents, June 1932, https://archive.org/.../mandementslettre14glis/mandem, accessed 3 November 2016.

18 "À propos de la répartition de la richesse," *Le Canada* (Montreal), 23 Nov. 1934. The newspaper reprinted Leman's speech at HEC when he received an honorary doctorate. Leman was attempting to refute a common refrain within the school. He reiterated his case for an emphasis on economic growth rather than redistribution in "Évolution ou revolution économique?" *Actualité économique* 14, no 1 (April 1938): 105–7.

19 *Le programme de restauration sociale* (Nov. 1933), in Yvan Lamonde and Claude Corbo, *Le Rouge et le Bleu: Une anthologie de la pensée politique*

au Québec de la Conquête à la Révolution tranquille (Montreal: Les Presses de l'Université de Montréal, 1999), 400.

20 The Manifesto is at http://bilan.usherbrooke.ca/bilan/pages/documents/23. html, accessed 21 November 2016. On L'Action libérale nationale see Patricia Dirks, *The Failure of l'Action libérale nationale* (Montreal and Kingston: McGill-Queen's University Press, 1991).

21 Minville, "Le capitalisme et ses abus," in *Pour la restauration sociale au Canada* (Montreal: L'École Sociale Populaire, 1933), 7–8.

22 Minville, "Le lendeman de l'élection," *L'Actualité économique* 11, no. 7 (Oct. 1935): 459.

23 In 1907 the province created Montreal-based HEC as a corporation to offer technical and economic training so as to open doors for French Canadians to commerce and industry. Montpetit taught at the school 1910–39. Minville was its director 1938–62. In 1925 a group at the school founded the journal *L'Actualité économique*, with Minville as the principal editor. Robert Rumilly, *Histoire de l'École des Hautes Études Commerciales de Montréal 1907–1967* (Montreal: Beauchemin, 1966), 30–1, 89.

24 "*Nous assistons à une crise de structure, à une modification en profondeur de l'organisme économique.*" Minville, "Le lendemain de l'éléction," 456.

25 Minville, "Le capitalisme et ses abus," 5.

26 Ibid., 6. Quebec's "ideological effervescence" in the 1930s "can probably best be understood as a crisis of liberalism": Paul-André Linteau, René Durocher, Jean-Claude Robert, and Francois Ricard, *Quebec since 1930* (Toronto: James Lorimer, 1991), 71.

27 Gregory Baum comments on Minville's "somewhat puzzling" insistence that there was nothing intrinsically wrong with capitalism, in the same paper in which Minville offered his "devastating critique of capitalism." Baum speculates that the author "added the conclusion to satisfy the demands of orthodoxy." Gregory Baum, *Catholics and Canadian Socialism: Political Thought in the Thirties and Forties* (Toronto: James Lorimer, 1980), 177–8. I do not see Minville's endorsement of capitalism as an afterthought. There would have been no inconsistency in his mind between his critique of economic liberalism and his acceptance of the individualism underlying the spirit of capitalism. He was certainly aware of the long-standing Catholic critiques of Adam Smith and liberal political economy. He could have cited many sources for the Catholic distinction between the individualism that led to abuses in capitalism and the individualism that drove economic activity while serving social justice. The Belgian economist Charles Perin (1815–1905), for instance, had argued

that the root of the social problem was an *excess* of individualism, when people were encouraged to act *solely* with a view to self-interest. For Perin, individualism and freedom, properly understood, were constrained by justice and charity. Antonio Almodovar and Pedro Teixera, "The Ascent and Decline of Catholic Economic Thought, 1830–1950s," *History of Political Economy* 40, no. 5 (2008): 71. See also Stefano Solari, "The Corporative Third Way in Social Catholicism (1830 to 1918)," *European Journal of the History of Economic Thought* 17, no. 1 (Feb. 2010): 97. Minville neatly summarized his accommodation with liberalism: "*La liberté est nécessaire, mais il ne faut pas la confondre avec la licence*" ("Le capitalisme et ses abus," 17). Liberty and individualism were compatible with Catholic principles of justice and charity.

28 Minville, "Le Capitalisme et ses abus," 6–7.

29 Minville, "La juste répartition des richesses," in *L'Ordre sociale chrétien* (Montreal: L'École Sociale Populaire, 1932), 72. Gregory Baum states that there is nothing in Catholic social teaching corresponding to a Marxist concept of alienation (workers estranged from their human substance). Baum, *Catholics and Canadian Socialism*, 79. While this is undoubtedly so, social Catholicism is strongly aware of spiritual alienation. An obvious problem arose for Minville: if workers were so deeply estranged from their humanity, how could apparently modest reforms, such as a family wage, participation in management, and owning some company shares, fix that? Minville's answer becomes convincing only if one accepts the totality of his reform program.

30 Minville, "La juste répartition," 71. See also the references to "l'esclavage de la production" and "l'esclavage de la misère" by the French writer Daniel-Rops in an interview with André Laurendeau: "Le chrétien et le monde moderne," *L'Action nationale* 8, no 2 (Oct. 1936): 114.

31 Minville, "Le capitalisme et ses abus," 9.

32 Although it was the Depression of the 1930s that put the distribution of wealth and income into the forefront of Minville's thought, his economic nationalism of the 1920s rehearsed what he said about inequality in the 1930s. His earlier writings revealed a keen awareness of the distribution of power and wealth. See especially Minville's "Agir pour vivre!," *Actualité economique* 3, no. 8 (Nov. 1927): 146–61. He was calling for an economic plan "according to which industries would arise from the soil, for the greatest advantage of the entire population this time, and not only for a handful of foreign entrepreneurs as is the case at the present time." Minville, "Industrie et commerce," *L'Action française* (Oct. 1927), 212–13, quoted in Jean-Claude Dupuis, "La pensée économique de *L'Action*

française (1917–1928)," *Revue d'histoire de l'Amérique française* 47, no. 2 (1993): 211.

33 Minville, "Le capitalisme et ses abus," 10.

34 Minville, "Agir pour vivre," cited in François-Albert Angers, ed., *Esdras Minville: Syndicalisme, legislation ouvrière et régime social au Québec avant 1940* (Montreal: Les Presses H.E.C., 1986), 87.

35 Minville, "Le capitalisme et ses abus," 11–12.

36 Ibid., 12.

37 Emmanuel Mounier, a leading figure in the Catholic personalist movement in France, saw "indirect usury" as endemic in modern capitalism. See the interview with him: "La fecondité de l'argent, mécanisme contre nature," *L'Action nationale* 9 (Jan.–June 1937): 31–3.

38 Minville, "Le capitalisme et ses abus," 12. Louis Chagnon also condemned present-day usury and defined it as follows: "le prélèvement d'intérèts et de commissions exagérées dans les operations de credit, ou encore des profits excessifs camouflés et dissimulés par des manoeuvres financières." Louis Chagnon, "Directives sociales catholiques," in *Pour la restauration sociale au Canada* (Montreal: L'École Sociale Populaire, 1933), 44.

39 Rural restoration was no mere conservative dream of return to an agricultural and parochial past. It meant increasing French Canadians' economic base and purchasing power and expanding their small businesses. "*Ce n'était pas la rêverie bucolique mais calcul financier*": Dupuis, "La pensée économique," 203. On Minville's belief that cooperativism was a flexible form of organization well adapted to Quebec's needs and to the problem of distribution see Ruth Paradis, "La pensée cooperative de Esdras Minville de 1924 à 1943," *L'Action nationale* 69, no 7 (March 1980): 518–26.

40 Letter of Esdras Minville to Alexis Bujold, 1927, cited in Dominique Foisy-Geoffroy, *Esdras Minville: Nationalisme économique et catholicisme social au Québec durant l'entre-deux-guerres* (Sillery: Septentrion, 2004), 145.

41 Minville therefore did not share the admiration of many Quebec intellectuals for Portuguese corporatism: Clinton Archibald, *Un Québec corporatiste? Corporatisme et néo-corporatisme ... Le Québec de 1930 à nos jours* (Gatineau, QC: Les éditions Asticou, 1983), 28–9, 95,

42 Others who wrote about corporatism agreed. "Le régime corporative" was "une réforme de structure économique" that would result in "un meilleur équilibre de la production" and "une répartition plus équitable du produit." Alexandre Marc, "Le corporatisme français prepare-t-il sa révolution kopernicienne?" *Actualité économique* 14, no. 1 (April 1938): 313.

43 Minville, "Libéralisme? Communisme? Corporatisme?," 163. .

44 Corporatism was not a secular conception; it was deeply indebted to papal encyclicals and their formulation of the church's social doctrine, whereby the "*corps social*" represented the "*Corps mystique du Christ*." Archibald, *Un Québec corporatiste?*, 57–61, 85. Because it was a way to mobilize the nation against foreign-owned business and to advance petit-bourgeois control of the economy, it has been interpreted as anticipating the Quiet Revolution: ibid., 111.

45 Minville, *Comment établir l'Organisation corporative au Canada* (Montreal: L'École Sociale Populaire, 1936), 14.

46 Ibid., 11.

47 Ibid., 21.

48 Clinton Archibald has suggested that the social corporatism defended by the journal *L'Action nationale* had an affinity with Mackenzie King's vision of social peace in *Industry and Humanity* (1919). Archibald, *Un Québec corporatiste?*, 91.

49 Minville, "Libéralisme? Communisme? Corporatisme?," 165.

50 Minville, *Comment établir*, 23.

51 Foisy-Geoffroy, *Minville*, 134–8.

52 Minville, *Comment établir*, 13. This sentence was also in "L'organization corporative sur le plan national canadien-français," *L'Action nationale* 8 (Sept. 1936): 30.

53 Minville, *Comment établir*, 16.

54 Pierre Trépanier sees Minville as an intellectual father of the Quiet Revolution: Trépanier, "Esdras Minville et le traditionalisme canadien-français," *Les Cahiers de dix* 50 (1995): 273. Not everyone would agree: Jonathan Fournier points out that its major initiatives (nationalization, state intervention, deconfessionalization) were remote from Minville's ideas (personal communication, 21 Aug. 2019).

55 Minville, "La juste répartition," 62.

56 Ibid., 62.

57 Ibid., 78.

58 Kees van Kersbergen, *Social Capitalism: A Study of Christian Democracy and the Welfare State* (New York: Routledge, 1995), 225.

59 Minville did study labour legislation, of course, and wrote a report for the Royal Commission on Dominion–Provincial Relations. Minville, *La législation ouvrière et le régime sociale dans la province de Québec* (Ottawa, 1939).

60 *Quadragesimo anno* discussed the social and public aspects of ownership, distinguishing the right of property from its use.

61 On the elitism of Édouard Montpetit see Peter Southam, "La pensée sociale d'Édouard Montpetit," in Fernand Dumont, Jean Hamelin, and Jean-Paul Montminy, eds., *Idéologies au Canada française 1930–1939* (Quebec: Les Presses de l'Université Laval, 1978), 320, 334. Southam comments that for Montpetit an educated elite was the necessary replacement or substitute for a *dirigiste* state.

62 André J. Bélanger, *The Ethics of Catholicism and the Consecration of the Intellectual* (Montreal: McGill-Queen's University Press, 1997), 22.

63 Ibid., 22–3.

64 Foisy-Geoffroy, *Minville*, 94–6. Minville's hierarchical vision appeared to contrast with assumptions among the Catholic youth movements Michael Gauvreau explores, whose members defined society along more "democratic" and horizontal axes and adopted a limited, functional notion of hierarchy that based status on level of engagement and service. Michael Gauvreau, *The Catholic Origins of Quebec's Quiet Revolution, 1931–1970* (Montreal and Kingston: McGill-Queen's University Press, 2005), 22. Yet those movements seemed to accept social inequality as the will of God and to deem it necessary to facilitate harmony between employers and workers. See Lucie Piché, *Femmes et changement sociale au Québec: L'apport de la Jeunesse ouvrière catholique feminine 1931–1966* (Quebec: Les Presses de l'Université Laval, 2003), 135–6.

65 Minville, "Schéma d'une politique de sécurité économique et sociale pour la province de Québec," *Actualité économique* 20, no 2 (Dec. 1944): 127.

66 "Programme de restauration sociale," *L'Action nationale* 2 (Sept.–Dec. 1933): 210.

67 Foisy-Geoffroy, *Minville*, 121.

68 Minville, "Les allocations familiales en Italie," *Actualité économique* 13, no 1 (April 1937): 282–7.

69 Minville, "Schéma d'une politique de securité," 133. François-Albert Angers savagely attacked family allowances in "Les allocations familiales fédérales de 1944," *Actualité économique* 21, no 3 (June 1945): 228–62. Though granting that a more equitable distribution of "*richesses*" was a healthy goal, he thought that the plan would be self-defeating; it would lead to "demoralization of the masses" and reduce workers' productive effort and total output.

70 Minville, "Schéma," 128.

71 Ibid., 129–30.

72 Ibid., 129.

73 Ibid., 129.

74 François-Albert Angers, *La securité sociale et les problèmes constitutionelles*, vol. 1, 203, cited in John Grube, *Bâtisseur de pays: La pensée de François-Albert Angers* (Montreal: Éditions de L'Action Nationale, 1981), 62.

75 Grube, *Bâtisseur de pays*, 62.

76 Southam, "La pensée sociale," 340.

77 Dominique Marshall, *The Social Origins of the Welfare State: Quebec Families, Compulsory Education, and Family Allowances, 1940–1955* (Waterloo, ON: Wilfrid Laurier University Press, 2006), 14–15, 27–8, 78, 174.

78 On ideological pluralism within the Catholic church in Quebec in this period see Michael Gauvreau, "From Rechristianization to Contestation: Catholic Values and Quebec Society, 1931–1970," *Church History* 69, no. 4 (Dec. 2000): 803–33.

79 Pierre Trépanier, "Victor Barbeau, anarchiste du droite," *Les Cahiers des dix*, 59 (2005), 55–87.

80 Victor Barbeau, *Pour nous grandir: Essai d'explication des misères de notre temps* (Montreal: Devoir, 1937), 23.

81 Ibid., 227.

82 Ibid., 216.

83 Ibid., 221.

84 Ibid., 208–9.

85 Ibid., 230.

86 Ibid., 227.

87 Ibid., 53–4.

88 One of the few references to a *"plus équitable répartition de la richesse"* appeared in Carolus Fortier, "Préparons notre plan," *Actualité économique* 20, no. 5 (Oct. 1944): 469. But he saw the distribution problem as entirely national – English Canadians' *"prodigieuse richesse"* as it related to *"le problème de notre survivance"* (465, 468). In 1948 the French economist Victor Rouquet la Garrigue argued against a centrally planned *"économie de répartition"* in "Les besoins dans une économie planifiée," *Actualité économique* 24, no. 3 (Oct. 1948): 422–38.

89 Jonathan Fournier, "Le développement." The 1940s, according to Fournier, saw mixed approaches. *"L'on passé d'une époque dominée par la morale à une époque positiviste"* (3–4), with the latter dominant by the 1960s.

90 Francois-Albert Angers, "La répartition des moyens financiers," *Actualité économique* 21, no. 2 (Dec. 1945): 184–6.

91 Angers, "L'impôt sur la revenue et la guerre," *Actualité économique* 22, no. 1 (April 1946): 164–74.

92 Ibid., 173.

93 Angers, "Organisation corporative et démocratie," *Actualité économique* 15, no 2 (nov. 1939): 156–7. Angers's conservative reading of papal encyclicals and his emphasis on non-state solutions was increasingly evident after the war. In his review of sixty years of Catholic social doctrine, he wrote: "*Une solution qui prétend régler à la fois le problème de l'injustice de la répartition et celui du chômage par le plein emploi et la sécurité sociale n'est pas une solution parce qu'elle assure la justice aux dépens de la libre initiative et de l'exercice personnel des responsabilités.*" Angers, "Soixante ans de doctrine sociale catholique," *Actualité économique* 27, no. 2 (July 1951): 249.

94 A positive response from the labour movement appeared in "Une grande date dans la pensée sociale catholique de cette province," *Bulletin des relations industrielles* 5, no. 7 (April 1950): 61–3.

95 Suzanne Clavette, *La condition ouvrière au regard de la doctrine sociale de l'Église* (Quebec: Les presses de l'université Laval, 2007), 81.

96 Ibid., 82.

97 Ibid., 53.

98 *L'Actualité économique* had only one article on inequality or income distribution in the 1950s, none in the 1960s, and four in the 1970s, including Jacques Henry's remarkable and innovative piece, "L'éfficacité, l'égalité, l'équité et la repartition personelle, des revenus," *Actualité économique* 53, no. 2 (April 1977): 154–92. It had two articles on the subject in the 1980s, three in the 1990s, and nine between 2000 and 2009.

99 Pierre Harvey, "La répartition des revenus aux États Unis," *Actualité économique* 30, no 2 (July 1954): 337–47. The Lorenz curve reappeared in Bernard Bonin, "Observations sur l'emploi de la courbe de Lorenz," *Actualité économique* 36, no. 1 (April 1960): 150–3. By this time the problem was technical and statistical: Claude Tricot, "Précisions sur la courbe de Lorenz," *Actualité économique* 37, no. 4 (Jan. 1962): 734–9. The word "répartition" referred increasingly to the distribution of national income among economic sectors, and the debate over mathematical modelling and economics as a positivist science took priority: François-Albert Angers, "Revenu national et théorie de la répartition," *Actualité économique* 38, no. 1 (April 1962): 81–92.

100 Gauvreau, "From Rechristianization to Contestation," 818.

101 Quoted in Baum, *Catholics and Canadian Socialism*, 86.

102 Lamonde, *La modernité au Québec; Tome 1, La crise de l'homme et de l'esprit (1929–1939)* (Quebec: FIDES, 2011), 198.

103 "Le peril communiste," *L'Action nationale* 4 (Sept.–Dec. 1934): 89–90.
On the era's intense anti-communism see Christine Elie, "The City and the
Reds: Leftism, the Civic Politics of Order, and a Contested Modernity in
Montreal, 1929–1947" (PhD dissertation, Queen's University, 2015).

104 Montpetit, *Pour une doctrine* (Montréal: Librairie d'action canadienne,
1931), 123, quoted in Southam, "La pensée sociale," 339.

105 "Programme de restauration sociale," 210.

106 Clavette, *Condition ouvrière*, 49.

107 Cf. van Kersbergen, *Social Capitalism*, 201.

108 Yvan Lamonde discusses Catholic corporatism as an antidote to CCF
socialism: Lamonde, *La modernité au Québec*, tome I, 85–90.

109 Scott's letter of 21 October 1939 and Angers's reply of 27 October are
printed in François-Albert Angers, "Une nouvelle de portée historique,"
L'Action nationale 60, no. 8 (April 1971): 623–40. In *Bâtisseur de pays*
(214–17), John Grube emphasizes the nationalist, anti-federalist,
anti-centralizing case behind Angers's condemnation of the "colonial
spirit" of Anglo-Canadians.

CHAPTER EIGHT

1 Among idealist philosophers, J.M.E. McTaggart died in 1925, F.H. Bradley
in 1924, and Bernard Bosanquet in 1923. In Britain analytic philosophy is
associated with Bertrand Russell (1872–1970), G.E. Moore (1873–1958),
Alfred North Whitehead (1861–1947), and others. "More, perhaps, than
anywhere else, idealism flourished with reasonable continuity in Canada,"
report Leslie Armour and Elizabeth Trott, *The Faces of Reason: An Essay
on Philosophy and Culture in English Canada 1850–1950* (Waterloo, ON:
Wilfrid Laurier University Press, 1983), 411.

2 A clear statement of the trend is H.W. Wright, "A Plea for Eclecticism,"
Faculty of Arts, Queen's University, Philosophical Essays Presented to John
Watson (Kingston, ON: Queen's University, 1922), 254–74.

3 Years ago S.E.D. Shortt stated: "The fundamental battle of the period had
been decided: the idealists were defeated and the empiricists, secure as
victors, slipped into relative complacency." S.E.D. Shortt, *The Search for
an Ideal: Six Canadian Intellectuals and Their Convictions in an Age of
Transition, 1890–1930* (Toronto: University of Toronto Press, 1976), 147.
I extend the time period and attempt to see later thinkers transform and
redirect idealism rather than merely rejecting it.

4 One example: Armour and Trott point out that defenders of Social Credit

in the 1930s held to an empiricist position on money while accusing orthodox economists of a Platonic idealist superstition. Armour and Trott, Faces of Reason, 454.

5 There is a substantial Canadian literature. Illuminating the intellectual origins of social welfare in Canada are Raymond B. Blake, *From Rights to Needs: A History of Family Allowances in Canada, 1929–1992* (Vancouver: UBC Press, 2009); Nancy Christie, *Engendering the State: Family, Work and Welfare in Canada* (Toronto: University of Toronto Press, 2000); Nancy Christie and Michael Gauvreau, *A Full-Orbed Christianity: The Protestant Churches and Social Welfare in Canada, 1900–1940* (Montreal and Kingston: McGill-Queen's University Press, 1996); Dominique Marshall, *The Social Origins of the Welfare State: Quebec Families, Compulsory Education, and Family Allowances, 1940–1955* (Waterloo, ON: Wilfrid Laurier University Press, 2006); Marlene Shore, *The Science of Social Redemption: McGill, the Chicago School, and the Origins of Social Research in Canada* (Toronto: University of Toronto Press, 1987); James Struthers, *The Limits of Affluence: Welfare in Ontario, 1920–1970* (Toronto: University of Toronto Press, 1994); and Shirley Tillotson, *Contributing Citizens: Modern Charitable Fundraising and the Making of the Welfare State, 1920–66* (Vancouver: UBC Press, 2008).

6 Gregory Vlastos, "Ethical Foundations," in R.B.Y. Scott and Gregory Vlastos, eds., *Towards the Christian Revolution* (Chicago: Willett, Clark, 1936), 61, 66.

7 Henry Wilkes Wright, *The Moral Standards of Democracy* (New York: D. Appleton, 1925), 262. Wright was professor of philosophy at the University of Manitoba.

8 W.C. Keirstead, "The Golden Rule in Business," *Journal of Religion* 3, no. 2 (March 1923): 152. Keirstead was a philosopher and social scientist at the University of New Brunswick. See Daniel C. Goodwin, "The Origins and Development of Wilfred Currier Keirstead's Social and Religious Thought," *Acadiensis* 37, no. 2 (summer / autumn 2008): 18–38.

9 W.C. Keirstead, "Ideals in Dictatorships and Democracies," *Dalhousie Review* 19, no.1 (1939): 41.

10 Ibid., 47.

11 This line of argument was advanced in Anthony Giddens, *Modernity and Self-Identity: Self and Society in the Late Modern Age* (Cambridge: Polity Press, 1991).

12 Keirstead, "Ideals," 44. See also Rupert Lodge, "The Self in Modern Thought," *University of Toronto Quarterly* 5, no. 4 (July 1936): 585.

13 John Line, "The Philosophical Background," in R.B.Y. Scott and Gregory
Vlastos, eds., *Towards the Christian Revolution* (Chicago: Willett, Clark,
1936), 16. Line was professor of the history and philosophy of religion at
Victoria College, University of Toronto.

14 Keirstead, "Ideals," 44.

15 Vlastos, "The Ethical Foundations," 65. Vlastos, an eminent authority on
Plato, was professor of philosophy at Queen's University. He moved to
Cornell in 1948. For his understanding of the self realizing itself within
the interactive relationships of community see P. Travis Kroeker, *Christian
Ethics and Political Economy in North America: A Critical Analysis*
(Montreal and Kingston: McGill-Queen's University Press, 1995), 76–7.

16 Lodge, "The Self in Modern Thought," 604.

17 Line, "Philosophical Background," 23.

18 Vlastos, "Ethical Foundations," 73.

19 There was an overlap between philosophy and theology. H. Martyn Estall
taught philosophy at McMaster University; John Line was a professor at
Victoria College, Toronto; and Gregory Vlastos was professor of philosophy at Queen's. In the 1930s they belonged to the Fellowship for a
Christian Social Order (FCSO), which advanced Christian socialism in
Canada. It struggled to reconcile a transcendent idealism with Christian
social action; to steer a course between emphasis on sin and individual
redemption on the one hand, and secular social action on the other. For all
its internal divisions and debates, its activities fell within the transition
from idealism to pragmatism, as part of the effort to reduce inequality. Its
1935 constitution did not mention inequality but spoke of the need for
"some guarantee of economic security" and freedom from "cramping concern over getting a living." Roger Charles Hutchinson, "The Fellowship
for a Christian Social Order: A Social Ethical Analysis of a Christian
Socialist Movement" (doctor of theology dissertation, Victoria University,
Toronto, 1975), 207.
   For all its commitment to a classless society and the downfall of capitalism, the FCSO's members moved in the direction of social democracy and
its reformist measures, supporting unemployment insurance, rights for
organized labour, "minimum supply," civil rights, and opposition to racial
discrimination (ibid., 104, 118, 144, 175, 210). Except in the contributions of Eugene Forsey to the FCSO, the problem of vertical income and
wealth distribution received only occasional mention. See also P. Travis
Kroeker, "Christian Realism: Reinhold Niebuhr and the Fellowship for a
Christian Social Order," in P. Travis Kroeker, *Christian Ethics and Political*

Economy in North America: A Critical Analysis (Montreal and Kingston: McGill-Queen's University Press, 1995), chap. 3, 45–90.

20 Keirstead, "The Leadership of the Ministry in Industrial and Social Life," *Journal of Religion* 2, no. 1 (Jan. 1922): 44, 54, 55.

21 Lodge, "The Self in Modern Thought," 592.

22 For instance, Rupert C. Lodge, *Philosophy of Education* (New York: Harper & Brothers, 1937, 1947); John Macdonald, *Mind, School, and Civilization* (Chicago: University of Chicago Press, 1952).

23 Line, "Philosophical Background," 24. The search to understand fascism could also further interest in psychology, since popular seduction by fascism could be seen as a psychic disorder: J. King Gordon, "The Political Task," in R.B.Y. Scott and Gregory Vlastos, eds., *Towards the Christian Revolution* (Chicago: Willett, Clark, 1936), 154.

24 Line, "Philosophical Background," 15.

25 Wright, Moral Standards of Democracy, 264.

26 Line, "Philosophical Background," 8–9, 10.

27 Ibid., 12–13.

28 J.W. Pickersgill, "The Decay of Liberalism," *Canadian Forum* (April 1935), 251–3. See also the emphasis on equality in Gregory Vlastos, *Christian Faith and Democracy* (New York: Association Press, 1939), 22, 24, 39. The prominent American journalist Dorothy Thompson, whose articles appeared in the Globe, argued the egalitarian case for a radical reduction of pay gaps between workers, managers, and owners. Since "all creative functions in society are of equal value," the mechanic was not inferior to the executive, she said. *Globe and Mail*, 7 May 1941.

29 Rupert Lodge was aware of Pareto. The first chapter of his book on philosophy and business was about him, but not Pareto optimality; he was discussing, and rejecting, the writer's views on philosophy, science, and truth. Rupert C. Lodge, *Philosophy of Business* (Chicago: University of Chicago Press, 1945), 1–20.

30 Line, "Philosophical Background," 6.

31 Wright, Moral Standards, 262.

32 Havelock, "The New Society," in R.B.Y. Scott and Gregory Vlastos, eds., *Towards the Christian Revolution* (Chicago: Willett, Clark, 1936), 236, 238. On Eric Havelock on inequality and community see Richard Allen, *Beyond the Noise of Solemn Assemblies: The Protestant Ethic and the Quest for Social Justice in Canada* (Montreal and Kingston: McGill-Queen's University Press, 2018), 238–9.

33 J. King Gordon, "The Political Task" in R.B.Y. Scott and Gregory Vlastos, eds., *Towards the Christian Revolution* (Chicago: Willett, Clark, 1936), 152.

34 Keirstead, "Ideals in Dictatorships," 41–2.

35 John Macdonald, *The Expanding Community: A Political Philosophy for Today* (Toronto: J.M. Dent, 1944), 23, 25, 113.

36 A remarkable example of the pragmatist's reduction of inequality appeared in Lodge's *Philosophy of Business* (1945), which attempts a rapprochement between philosophy and business. Lodge was preoccupied with the differences among idealism, realism, and pragmatism; with fascism and communism; and with popular psychology. He said almost nothing about distributive justice. His discussion of distribution (ibid., 282–304) was about marketing and market distribution, not vertical distributions of income and wealth. He referred to the "bifurcation" of present-day societies into "the overprivileged" and "the underprivileged"; he pointed to the gulf between "the idle rich" and "the working classes." His solutions were a pragmatist recipe: "a complete re-education of the citizens"; "equality of opportunity": "the methods and results of co-operative social experimentation"; and expertise and efficiency. Ibid., 394–6, 401.

37 A similar shift was occurring in economics in the United States. Bateman and Banzhaf argue that in the late nineteenth and early twentieth centuries economists, including John Bates Clark, tried to retain utilitarian economics within a larger ethical frame. During the interwar period, they argue, the ethical frame eroded, leading to "a stripped-down and straight-up utilitarianism that would underpin the dominance of modern neoclassicism after the Great Depression." Bradley Bateman and H. Spencer Banzhaf, eds., *Keeping Faith, Losing Faith: Religious Belief and Political Economy* (Durham, NC, and London: Duke University Press, 2008), 10.

38 A dramatic passage from democratic socialism to conservatism was visible in the economist Gilbert Jackson, who edited the *Canadian Forum* in the early 1920s. See Don Nerbas, "Managing Democracy, Defending Capitalism: Gilbert E. Jackson, the Canadian Committee on Industrial Reconstruction, and the Changing Form of Elite Politics in Canada," *Histoire sociale / Social History* 46, no. 91 (May 2013): 173–204.

39 Freeman, the son of a Baptist minister, had studied at McMaster, Chicago, and Oxford. In the 1920s he was "Professor of Economics" (not political economy) at the University of Western Ontario. "Ralph Evans Freeman Is Rhodes Scholar," *Toronto World*, 10 Dec. 1915. Duncan Alexander MacGibbon, professor of economics at the University of Alberta in the 1920s, was yet another product of the University of Chicago.

40 Ralph Evans Freeman, *Economics for Canadians* (Toronto: Sir Isaac Pitman and Sons, 1928), 189, 191.

41 Ibid., 234, 237.

42 Ibid., 238.

43 Ibid., 237.

44 Ibid., 239–40. Canadian economists were aware of the complex relations among income, savings, and investment, but offered little on the subject. For example, Canadian-born economist Clyde E. Dankert wrestled with the relationship between inequality and economic growth. After rejecting inequality, "over-saving," and underconsumption as causes of the Depression, and after worrying that higher taxes might "discourage individual effort," he accepted that reducing inequality through higher inheritance and income taxes might not impede growth. Dankert had neither theory nor sufficient evidence to guide him out of uncertainty. C.E. Dankert, "Economic Inequality," *Canadian Forum* (Nov. 1932), 54–6.

45 Freeman, *Economics*, 267–9.

46 Duncan Alexander MacGibbon, *An Introduction to Economics for Canadian Readers* (Toronto: Macmillan, 1924); later editions came out in 1929 and 1935.

47 MacGibbon's five pages on socialism and the Soviet economic system (ibid., 1935 ed., 68–72) were remarkably dispassionate. He noted coolly that the economic system in Russia appeared to be evolving, had moved far from its original ideal of "the co-operative commonwealth," and represented "complete control of economic life by the state." It was almost as though refuting it was not necessary in the presence of the scientific validity of market economics. Ibid., 72.

48 Ibid., 151.

49 Ibid., 152.

50 Ibid., 158.

51 Ibid., 133.

52 Ibid., 68.

53 Ibid., 163.

54 Ibid.

55 Ibid. In an echo of Progressive-era economics, MacGibbon asserted that the "unfair competition" of "capitalistic monopolies" yielded rewards unrelated to "efficiency in production" (ibid., 184). Monopoly interfered with supply and demand, and anti-trust legislation had not destroyed it in the United States. And "monopoly profits" were clearly not consistent with fairness.

56 Ibid., 197.

57 Ibid., 18.

58 Ibid., 236.

59 V.W. Bladen, *An Introduction to Political Economy*, 3rd ed. (Toronto: University of Toronto Press, 1956), 10, 23.

60 Ibid., 23.

61 Paul A. Samuelson, *Economics: An Introductory Analysis* (New York: McGraw-Hill, 1948), 604.

62 Samuelson, *Economics*, 5th ed. (1961), 115–31.

63 Piketty, *Capital in the Twenty-first Century*, trans. Arthur Goldhammer (Cambridge, MA: Harvard University Press, 2014), 11. Kuznets was the American expert on national income who hypothesized in the 1950s that historically inequality took the shape of an inverted U, with inequality declining in more advanced capitalist economies. His hypothesis now seems optimistic at best.

64 F.H. Knight, "Unemployment: And Mr Keynes's Revolution in Economic Theory," *Canadian Journal of Economics and Political Science* 3, no. 1 (Feb. 1937): 100–23.

65 R. Clay Sproules, "A Historical Analysis of Lottery Terms," *Canadian Journal of Economics and Political Science* 20, no. 3 (Aug. 1954): 347–56. The problem of distribution of wealth and income was known, but with reference to studies of other countries: A.E. Grauer's review of four American books, including two by Harold G. Moulton, in *Canadian Journal of Economics and Political Science* 2, no. 2 (May 1936): 246–9; M.C. Urquhart, review of Tibor Barna, *Redistribution of Incomes through Public Finance in 1937* (Oxford: Clarendon Press, 1945) (the book was about Britain), in *Canadian Journal of Economics and Political Science* 13, no. 2 (May 1947): 312–14.

66 Frank Milligan, *Eugene A. Forsey: An Intellectual Biography* (Calgary: University of Calgary Press, 2004), especially chaps. 2 and 3, 33–68. Forsey's affinities in the mid-1930s were visible in the sources he cited in "The Economic Problem" and "A New Economic Order," in R.B.Y. Scott and Gregory Vlastos, eds., *Towards the Christian Revolution* (Chicago: Willett, Clark, 1936), 98–162. These included the British Labour politician and popularizer of Marx John Strachey; the American cooperative leader J.P. Warbasse; the Scottish philosopher John Macmurray; and Sydney and Beatrice Webb, Harold Laski, and R.H. Tawney.

67 Milligan, *Forsey*, 103. Much of Forsey's analysis in the 1940s focused on changes in wages and salaries among occupational groups and the impact of the Depression: Forsey, "Distribution of Income in Ontario," *Canadian Forum* (March 1942), 374–6; Harriet Roberts Forsey, "Distribution of Income in the Maritimes," *Canadian Forum* (Feb. 1942), 332–3.

68 Forsey, "The Economic Problem," 99.

69 Ibid., 101; Milligan, *Forsey*, 92. What did Forsey mean by idealism? He seemed to be associating it with naïve and complacent optimism. He connected it to "cheerful conclusions" that dissociated ideas from "material realities." Forsey, "Economic Problem," 119. In maintaining his Christian socialism, Forsey attempted to separate the roles of economist and citizen. The economist was a technical expert who set aside questions of ethics, and whether a specific social goal was desirable. As a citizen, however, the economist had a duty to use his knowledge for ethical and social ends. Milligan, *Forsey*, 102–3.

70 Among many others, Adrian Johnston, *A New German Idealism: Hegel, Žižek and Dialectical Materialism* (New York: Columbia University Press, 2018); Slavoj Žižek, *Less than Nothing: Hegel and the Shadow of Dialectical Materialism* (New York: Verso, 2012).

71 Forsey, "Economic Problem," 103–16.

72 Forsey, "A New Economic Order," 135–6.

73 Ibid., 139.

74 Ibid., 139–40.

75 Forsey believed that change would come through the pressure of the mass of the population, including organized labour, especially when the extent of inequality became more widely known. Milligan, *Forsey*, 108–9.

76 Ibid., 84. Forsey was experiencing Christian fellowship in an intense, personal way: he had become a member of the Society of Friends (Quakers).

77 J. King Gordon was the son of Charles William Gordon, Presbyterian minister and novelist (Ralph Connor); King Gordon was a United Church minister, studied at Oxford, and was influenced by Tawney. Frank R. Scott was the son of an Anglican priest; he studied at Oxford and was influenced by Tawney. Frank Underhill's rigorous Presbyterian upbringing was a seminal influence, although he questioned it; his tutor at Oxford was A.D. Lindsay. Graham Spry was a Rhodes scholar at Oxford. R. Douglas Francis, *Frank H. Underhill: Intellectual Provocateur* (Toronto: University of Toronto Press, 1986), 7. On religion and the League for Social Reconstruction see Michiel Horn, *The League for Social Reconstruction: Intellectual Origins of the Democratic Left in Canada, 1930–1942* (Toronto: University of Toronto Press, 1980), 89–90.

78 James Naylor, *The Fate of Labour Socialism: The Co-operative Commonwealth Federation and the Dream of a Working-Class Future* (Toronto: University of Toronto Press, 2016), 119–20.

79 Research Committee of the League for Social Reconstruction, *Social Planning for Canada* (first pub. 1935) (Toronto: University of Toronto Press, 1975), 37.

80 Ibid., 38.

81 Ibid., unpaginated Preface, 45.

82 Ibid., 15, 16.

83 So also were many of the CCF politicians. For instance, Grant MacNeil's patient display of data on housing and income distributions in House of Commons Debates, 10 Feb. 1938.

84 League for Social Reconstruction, *Social Planning*, 16–17.

85 Unravelling the complex relationship of Social Credit to inequality and distributions of income could take up an entire chapter. William Aberhart (premier of Alberta 1935–43) spoke of "poverty in the midst of plenty"; he argued that a few "big shots" controlled Alberta's wealth; he proposed redistributing income from a small number of creditors to a much larger group of debtors and low-income earners; Social Credit sought a distribution (not unconditional) of a social dividend; and Aberhart argued at one point for a maximum limit on incomes. William Aberhart, *Social Credit Manual* (Calgary: the Author, 1935), 5; C.B. Macpherson, *Democracy in Alberta: Social Credit and the Party System*, 2nd ed. (Toronto: University of Toronto Press, 1962), 159; Clark Banack, *God's Province: Evangelical Christianity, Political Thought, and Conservatism in Alberta* (Montreal and Kingston: McGill-Queen's University Press, 2016), 124; Alvin Finkel, *The Social Credit Phenomenon in Alberta* (Toronto: University of Toronto Press, 1989), 34.

Social Credit's apparent interest in income inequality and distributive remedy was severely qualified. The words "inequality," "inequalities," and "redistribution" did not appear in Aberhart's *Manual* (1935): "distribution" showed up once. Aberhart said that Social Credit did not plan any "confiscation scheme by which we take the wealth of the rich or well-to-do to give to the poor." The social dividend was to help provide "bare necessities" and nothing more (Aberhart, *Manual*, p. 5, no. 7). Social Credit economics was about under-consumption and -production; redistributing credit and restoring consumption would stimulate production. Such analysis did not equate with reducing inequality. Returning to citizens a portion of their "cultural heritage" was not the same as redistributing income or wealth. The Social Credit position followed in part from the rejection of collectivist action through the state. Aberhart associated "control of the many by the few" with "state socialism": Aberhart, *Post-War Reconstruction: A Second Series of Broadcasts* (Edmonton: Today and Tomorrow, 1943), 39–41, cited in David Laycock, *Populism and Democratic Thought in the Canadian Prairies* (Toronto: University of Toronto Press, 1990), 208–9.

Aberhart was first attracted to social credit by Maurice Colbourne's *Unemployment or War* (New York: Coward-McCann, 1928), which rejected the idea of inequality. Even if a more equitable distribution of wealth were practicable, he said, it "would result in an increased scarcity for everyone." "The world suffers not from unequal distribution but from a chronic shortage of total supply: that is, Scarcity" (9–10). The views of Aberhart and successor Ernest Manning on poverty, the state, and individual responsibility related closely to their pre-millennial, dispensational theology, which was very different from what most social gospellers believed – or so Clark Banack argues in *God's Province*, especially 128–33.

For later Social Credit governments under Manning (premier 1943–68), the oil boom, starting in the late 1940s, seemed to confirm that the real problem had been arrested growth and scarcity. Manning's government, claimed Ed Shaffer in 1984, could have used its revenues "to lessen income inequalities" but did not do so "because such a redistribution would undermine the incentives of the market system." It decided to spend on social services "in such a way as to minimize the redistributional effects." Ed Shaffer, "The Political Economy of Oil in Alberta," in David Leadbeater, ed., *Essays on the Political Economy of Alberta* (Toronto: New Hogtown Press, 1984), 182. An early leftist critique of Social Credit views on distribution was Jean Burton, "The Ten-minus-Nine Economics," *Canadian Forum* (Feb. 1929), 155–60.

86 *League for Social Reconstruction Manifesto* (first pub. 1932), in Research Committee of the League for Social Reconstruction, *Democracy Needs Socialism* (Toronto: Thomas Nelson, 1938), 153.

87 "Redistribute" also appeared twice, and in one instance seemed to refer to family allowances as a way to redistribute existing total wage bills. "Redistribution" surfaced once in ibid., 113: "The progressive redistribution of wealth will also injure the fortunes of the rich." The context was a discussion of the "parasitic groups" that would lose under socialism.

88 League for Social Reconstruction, *Social Planning*, 6–7.

89 Ibid., 5.

90 Ibid., 37.

91 League for Social Reconstruction, *Democracy Needs Socialism*, 61.

92 I examined every article containing the word "equality" in all issues of the *Globe / Globe and Mail* between 1910 and 1949. Its frequency peaked in 1944, at 270 times.

93 Pierre Rosanvallon, *Society of Equals* (Cambridge, Mass.: Harvard University Press, 2013), 185–6.

94 David Tough, "'The rich should give to such an extent that it will hurt': Conscription of Wealth and Political Modernism in the Parliamentary Debate on the Income War Tax," *Canadian Historical Review* 93, no. 3 (Sept. 2012): 382–407. David Tough, *The Terrific Engine: Income Taxation and the Modernization of the Canadian Political Imaginary* (Vancouver: UBC Press, 2019).

95 E.A. Heaman has shown that tax revolts long preceded the First World War and that debates over income tax really concerned "fairness": E.A. Heaman, *Tax, Order and Good Government: A New Political History of Canada, 1867–1917* (Montreal and Kingston: McGill-Queen's University Press, 2017), especially chap. 9, pp. 377–458. For the complex iterations of fairness and equity see also Shirley Tillotson, *Give and Take: The Citizen-Taxpayer and the Rise of Canadian Democracy* (Vancouver: UBC Press, 2017), and note the many references to fairness in her index.

96 Financial journalist Wellington Jeffers used these words in the *Globe and Mail*, 4 June 1945.

97 Ibid., 19 May 1942. J.G. Taggart, the federal food administrator, made the same point: ibid., 13 Feb. 1942. "I am getting tired of that expression 'equality of sacrifice', said Thorson" (minister of war services).

98 Ibid., 13 Sept. 1939.

99 Ibid., describing the 20 per cent income surtax J.L. Ilsley announced in his new budget.

100 Ibid., 2 Sept. 1943. On Ilsley's speech to the Trades and Labor Congress see Tillotson, *Give and Take*, 195–7.

101 *Globe and Mail*, 26 May 1942.

102 Ibid., 2 Sept. 1943.

103 Ibid., 10 and 11 Dec. 1943.

104 Politicians absorbed the rhetoric. "Equality of opportunity" was a Conservative Party principle (*Globe and Mail*, 11 Dec. 1942, 27 Nov. 1943).

105 Christine White of Winnipeg made this argument at the convention of the Canadian Congress of Labour: *Globe and Mail*, 15 Sept. 1943.

106 Ibid., 10 July, 8 Nov. 1943, 11 Feb. 1944.

107 Ibid., 2 April 1945.

108 Ibid., 11 Feb. 1942.

109 Ibid., 25 and 27 May 1940.

110 Ibid., 10 July 1942.

111 Ibid., 4 Feb. 1944.

112 Ibid., 4 Oct. 1945.

113 Ibid., 1 Dec. 1945, 20 Sept 1946. Efficiency and fairness of taxes within "social liberalism," and taxpayers' role in the debates over tax equity, are themes in Shirley Tillotson, "Warfare, Welfare, and the Mass Income Tax Payer," in Tillotson, *Give and Take*, chap. 7, pp. 174–209.

114 *Globe and Mail*, 11 June 1946.

115 Ibid., 11 April, 26 July, 27 Nov. 1945; 27 May 1946.

116 Ibid., 6 April 1940.

117 Ibid., 3 July 1946. Inequalities in municipal tax assessments became an issue in the civic elections: ibid., 1 Jan. 1942.

118 On equal pay for equal work see, for instance, ibid., 27 Jan., 2 Feb. 1945. On the campaign for "equality of status and reward" and "equality of status and opportunity": ibid., 4 July, 30 May 1944. The status of women in marriage could even come under judicial review and disagreement: see, for instance, the case before the Ontario Court of Appeal reported in ibid., 1 Oct. 1946.

119 The National War Labour Board endorsed "equal pay for equal work for men and women on the basis of efficiency" – a basis that allowed wide variations, of course. Ibid., 16 March 1944.

120 Ibid., 20 July 1942.

121 Unequal urban and rural schools caused increasing concern. "Inequality of opportunity" was extensive, it was noted, when school districts depended on local rates; low-income districts had poorer schools. Thus in provincial funding of teachers' salaries, equality of outcome required unequal grants – larger to poor districts, smaller to wealthy ones. Ibid., 4 Jan. 1943.

122 Ibid., 17 Oct. 1947.

123 Ibid., 22 June 1944, 3 Aug. 1945, 25 June 1948. John Bracken, leader of the federal Progressive Conservative Party, was able to link equality, abundance, and security from want without invoking Corinthians: ibid., 13 Dec. 1943.

124 A classic statement is Ronald Dworkin, *Sovereign Virtue: The Theory and Practice of Equality* (Cambridge, Mass.: Harvard University Press, 2000). There is a substantial literature on what is often called "luck egalitarianism."

125 *Globe and Mail*, 6 Oct. 1942.

126 Ibid., 2 March 1943.

127 Ibid., 10 Oct. 1942. In 1928 the classicist Maurice Hutton argued that equality was "unequalled" in Canada by 1880, and fifty years later Canada had "much more equality than exists elsewhere." Ibid., 6 April 1940.

128 W.J. Gartley in ibid., 12 May 1945. The obsession with equality, and
     reduction of inequality, as antidotes to communism appeared constantly in
     the *Globe*, especially in the late 1940s. The Universal Declaration of
     Human Rights, adopted by the United Nations General Assembly in 1948,
     supported the anti-communist agenda.

129 J.W. Pickersgill and D.F. Forster, eds., *The Mackenzie King Record*, vol. 2
     (Toronto: University of Toronto Press, 1968), 34, cited in Blake, *From
     Rights to Needs*, 91. King's linking of family allowances to equality
     appeared in his speeches outside Parliament in 1944 and 1945. For
     instance, *Globe and Mail*, 12 June 1945.

130 Blake, *From Rights to Needs*, 93.

131 On the meaning of redistribution see also Introduction above, n 40.

132 *Globe and Mail*, 17 May, 14 April 1945. One of the more savage critiques
     of social welfare as redistribution was François-Albert Angers, "French
     Canada and Social Security," *Canadian Journal of Economics and Political
     Science* 10, no. 3 (Aug. 1944): 355–64.

133 Andrew Armitage, *Social Welfare in Canada Revisited* (first pub. 1975),
     3rd ed. (Don Mills, ON: Oxford University Press Canada, 1996), 47.
     Despite the data deficiencies at the time, it was argued that the
     redistributive effect of family allowances and old-age pensions was
     negligible: Monteath Douglas, "Welfare and Redistribution," *Canadian
     Journal of Economics and Political Science* 19, no. 3 (Aug. 1953): 321.
     The more comprehensive social welfare of the 1960s did not have substan-
     tial redistributive effects: W. Irwin Gillespie, "On the Redistribution of
     Income in Canada," *Canadian Tax Journal* 24, no. 4 (1976): 417–50.
     Between 1976 and 2011 the tax and transfer system did redistribute
     wealth measurably, but the effects were complex and varied by time per-
     iod. Often they were offsetting the increase in inequality in pre-tax
     incomes: Andrew Heisz and Brian Murphy, "The Role of Taxes and
     Transfers in Reducing Income Inequality," in David A. Green, W. Craig
     Riddell, and France St-Hilaire, eds., *Income Inequality: The Canadian
     Story* (Montreal: Institute for Research on Public Policy, 2016), 435–73.

134 Canadian economists were aware of the vast data deficiencies. Other juris-
     dictions were trying to measure the redistributive effects of taxation: e.g.,
     see, for Britain, Tibor Barna, *Redistribution of Incomes through Public
     Finance in 1937* (Oxford: Clarendon Press, 1945). M.C. Urquhart
     reviewed this book in *Canadian Journal of Economics and Political
     Science* 13, no. 2 (May 1947): 312–14. Nevertheless, even by 1975 data
     problems prevented conclusive analysis of the redistributive effect of

welfare, as Harold L. Wilensky argued in *The Welfare State and Equality: Structural and Ideological Roots of Public Expenditure* (Berkeley: University of California Press, 1975).

135 The English sociologist T.H. Marshall lectured on the welfare state in 1949 and offered a sweeping justification, linking welfare to the reduction of inequality. The welfare state, he said, "assumed the guise of social action modifying the whole pattern of social inequality. It is no longer content to raise the floor-level in the basement of the social edifice, leaving the superstructure as it was. It has begun to remodel the whole building." T.H. Marshall, "Citizenship and Social Class," in Marshall, *Citizenship and Social Class and Other Essays* (Cambridge, 1950), 31–2, cited in Samuel Moyn, *Not Enough: Human Rights in an Unequal World* (Cambridge, MA: Harvard University Press, 2018), 42. William A. Robson of University College London suggested that the goal of the welfare state had been to "level down" as well as to "level up": William A. Robson, *The Welfare State* (London: Oxford University Press, 1957), cited in Moyn, *Not Enough*, 50.

136 Quoted in Monteath Douglas, "Welfare and Redistribution," *Canadian Journal of Economics and Political Science* 19, no. 3 (Aug. 1953): 320. St Laurent was addressing a meeting of the Canadian Conference on Social Work in Quebec City on 15 June 1952. The thesis that social security and progressive taxation, working together, were redistributive did surface, but rarely. One example was an article on pensions and medical bills by Warren Baldwin in the *Globe and Mail*, 15 Jan. 1948.

137 Keith G. Banting, "Dis-embedding Liberalism? The New Social Policy Paradigm in Canada," in David A. Green and Jonathan R. Kesselman, eds., *Dimensions of Inequality in Canada* (Vancouver: UBC Press, 2006), 431. A specific way of denying redistribution came from Tom Kent, a top adviser to Liberal Prime Minister Lester Pearson in the 1960s. Kent said that both critics and supporters of social security "think of redistribution as meaning, chiefly, taxing the rich to help the poor." While it did help provide social security, "it cannot and will not play the sole part, or even the main part." Only the very poor would pay less in taxes than they receive in transfers. The "redistribution" in social security affected "people of whom most are paying, most of the time, a good deal in taxation" – namely "people in different circumstances within the middle income groups." Tom Kent, *Social Policy for Canada: Towards a Philosophy of Social Security* (Ottawa: Policy Press, 1962), 16–17.

138 Leonard C. Marsh, *Canadians In and Out of Work: A Survey of Economic Classes and Their Relation to the Labour Market* (Toronto: Oxford

University Press, 1940). Marsh's understanding of class was Fabian and Weberian. He conflated class with occupational stratum: "professional classes," "commercial class," "clerical class," "skilled workers," and so on (13–27). Chapter 8 (165–99) covered "The Distribution of Income" – a "complement to the proportions of the occupational structure" (165). This chapter used the data to endorse minimal living standards or "level of decency" (176n1) and to identify which groups are likely to meet such standards. The analysis was comprehensive, including comparisons of male and female earnings and distinguishing between head-of-household earnings and total family earnings. Tables gave the percentage of employees at various income levels, but not of all income going to those at each level. The words "inequality" and "inequalities" did not appear.

A residual awareness of the problem of inequality surfaced in the final chapter on "policy implications," but "it was easier in the England of Disraeli's day to see it as divided between 'the two nations' of the rich and the poor" (448). "The progressive removal of the grosser inequalities and resentments can be achieved through a wide range of social legislation" (448). There was no plan for social-security legislation, but cautious support for unemployment insurance (340, 443) and old-age pensions (172, 343). The policy emphasis was on equality of opportunity, vocational training, and removal of "inequalities of educational opportunity" (429). There was mention of "progressive public finance," but redistribution involved only funding of welfare: taxation "secures revenue from those best able to pay and implements a re-distribution in the form of welfare services" (443). See also Richard C. Helmes-Hayes, "A Neglected Classic: Leonard Marsh's Canadians In and Out of Work," *Canadian Review of Sociology* 30, no. 1 (Feb. 1993): 83–109.

139 Leonard Marsh, *Report on Social Security for Canada*, new ed. with Introduction by Alan Moscovitch (Montreal and Kingston: McGill-Queen's University Press, 2017), 15–16.

140 Ibid., 203.

141 Harry M. Cassidy, *Social Security and Reconstruction in Canada* (Toronto: Ryerson Press, 1943), 2–5.

142 Ibid., 5–6.

143 Ibid., 141.

CHAPTER NINE

1 Pierre Rosanvallon, *The Society of Equals*, trans. Arthur Goldhammer (Cambridge, MA: Harvard University Press, 2013).

2 Ian McKay, "The Liberal Order Framework: A Prospectus for a Reconnaissance of Canadian History," *Canadian Historical Review* 81, no. 4 (Dec. 2000), 617–45; Michael Ducharme and Jean-François Constant, "Introduction: A Project of Rule Called Canada," in Ducharme and Constant, *Liberalism and Hegemony: Debating the Canadian Liberal Revolution* (Toronto: University of Toronto Press, 2009), 9.

3 On the problem of definition: Alan Ryan, *The Making of Modern Liberalism* (Princeton, NJ: Princeton University Press, 2012), 21–42.

4 For a valuable introduction see Lars Osberg, "Outcomes and Opportunities," in Osberg, *The Age of Increasing Inequality: The Astonishing Rise of Canada's 1%* (Toronto: James Lorimer, 2018), chap. 7, 148–65. There is a substantial literature on equality of opportunity; a recent discussion of the subject and its relationship to equality of outcomes and "fair inequality" is Lars Osberg, "Could Equality of Opportunity among Commoners Suffice?," keynote address, conference on Inequality of Opportunity, University of Queensland and Griffith University, Brisbane, 26–27 June 2019.

5 Of course equal opportunity for access to education is a highly desirable goal. Improving access is unlikely by itself, however, to much alter overall income and wealth distributions; furthermore, equality of opportunity is inseparable from equality of condition or outcome. On these points see Osberg, *Age of Increasing Inequality*, 162–5.

6 Margaret E. McCallum, "Keeping Women in Their Place: The Minimum Wage in Canada, 1910–25," *Labour / Le travail* 17 (spring 1986): 29–56; Bob Russell, "A Fair or a Minimum Wage? Women Workers, the State, and the Origins of Wage Regulation in Western Canada," *Labour / Le travail* 28 (fall 1991): 59–88. The Women's Labour League "created task forces and accumulated data to demonstrate that ill health, prostitution, and malnutrition were rooted in economic inequality": Patricia Roome, "Amelia Turner and Calgary Labour Women, 1919–1935," in Linda Kealey and Joan Sangster, eds., *Beyond the Vote: Canadian Women and Politics* (Toronto: University of Toronto Press, 1989), 97.

7 Joan Sangster, *One Hundred Years of Struggle: The History of Women and the Vote in Canada* (Vancouver: UBC Press, 2018), 3, 57.

8 Carol Lee Bacchi, *Liberation Deferred? The Ideas of English-Canadian Suffragists, 1877–1918* (Toronto: University of Toronto Press, 1983).

9 "The W.C.T.U. of Canada stands for more than the abolition of the drink traffic," said the president of the Women's Christian Temperance Union, Sarah Rowell Wright, in 1914. She went on to outline a society of common good based on Christian socialist principles of justice, equity, and

fairness. *Social Service Congress, Ottawa, 1914: Report of Addresses and Proceedings* (Toronto: Social Service Council, 1914), 324–5.

10 *Western Woman's Weekly*, 28 Dec. 1918, quoted in Veronica Strong-Boag, *The Last Suffragist Standing: The Life and Times of Laura Marshall Jamieson* (Vancouver: UBC Press, 2018), 70–1. An expansile egalitarianism continued to embrace the inequality problem among social democrats, as Laura Jamieson indicated. "Fair distribution of the national income" meant a more equitable dispersal of "purchasing power" through economic planning. Jamieson also emphasized mobility through education and equal opportunity. Laura E. Jamieson, *Women Dry Those Tears* (Vancouver: CCF Women's Council, 1945), 8, 16, 29, 32.

11 Oliver Schreiner, *Woman and Labour* (Toronto: Henry Froude, 1911), 98, 119.

12 A few examples: *The Daily News* [New Westminster], 27 June 1911; *Prince Rupert Optimist*, 10 April 1911; *Farmer's Advocate and Home Magazine*, 24 May, 15 Feb., 18 Feb. 1917; *Canadian Thresherman and Farmer* 19, no. 6 (June 1914): 67; *Canadian Magazine* 39, no. 5 (Sept. 1912); *Grain Growers' Guide*, 10 July 1912, 20 Aug. 1913; *Canadian Churchman*, 10 Sept. 1914; Sarah Rowell Wright (WCTU president), in *Social Service Congress, Ottawa, 1914: Report of Addresses and Proceedings* (Toronto: Social Service Council, 1914), 324; A.L. McCrimmon, *The Woman Movement* (Philadelphia: Griffith and Rowland, 1915), 172 (McCrimmon was chancellor of McMaster University). The socialist Percy Chew, summarizing Schreiner's arguments, proclaimed her book "probably the most important contribution to the literature of Sociology in the last quarter of a century." *Western Clarion*, 27 April 1912.

13 Jean Blewett, *The Canadian Woman and Her Work* (Toronto: Canadian Suffrage Association, 1912), 2; cited in Sangster, *One Hundred Years*, 107. The more radical Helena Gutteridge combined the labour theory of value with demands for state control of the distribution of wealth: Irene Howard, *The Struggle for Social Justice in British Columbia: Helena Gutteridge, the Unknown Reformer* (Vancouver: UBC Press, 1992), 118, 131.

14 Margaret M. Dickson, "A Radical Platform," *Grain Growers' Guide*, 16 Feb. 1916, reprinted in Barbara E. Kelcey and Angela E. Davis, eds., *A Great Movement Underway: Women and the Grain Growers' Guide, 1908–1928* (Winnipeg: Manitoba Record Society, 1997), 146–7.

15 Dickson, in Barbara E. Kelcey and Angela E. Davis, eds., *A Great Movement Underway: Women and the Grain Growers' Guide, 1908–1928*

(Winnipeg: Manitoba Record Society, 1997), 146–7. The harsh reality of material inequality was a theme in the fiction of immigrant and working-class women: Sangster, *One Hundred Years*, 166–7.

16 From one of Denison's columns in the *Toronto World*, quoted in Sangster, *One Hundred Years*, 148. See also Michele Lacombe, "'Songs of the Open Road': Bon Echo, Urban Utopians and the Cult of Nature," *Journal of Canadian Studies* 33, no. 2 (summer 1998): 155.

17 Charlotte Perkins Gilman, *Human Work* (New York: McClure, Phillips, 1904), 292; see also Gilman, *Women and Economics* (Boston: Small, Maynard and Co., 1900), 104.

18 *Sunset of Bon Echo* 1, no. 2 (April / May 1916): 32–3; see also Bacchi, *Liberation Deferred*, 44. Bacchi notes the ambiguity among suffragists over individual liberty (46–7).

19 Peter Campbell refers to Rose Henderson's "broad-based critique of hierarchies of power": Peter Campbell, *Rose Henderson: A Woman for the People* (Montreal and Kingston: McGill-Queen's University Press, 2010), 118. Henderson linked "the unequal distribution of wealth" to class distinctions, poverty, and "unequal opportunity" in her *Kids What I Knows* (Montreal: W.H. Eaton, n.d. [1906?]), unpaginated "Foreword."

20 International Monetary Fund, *Pursuing Women's Economic Empowerment* (2018), at www.imf.org/en/Publications/Policy-Papers/Issues/2018/05/31/pp053118pursuing-womens-economic-emplowerment; Christian Gonzalez et al., *Catalyst for Change: Empowering Women and Tackling Income Inequality* (IMF, Oct. 2015), at www.imf.org/external/pubs/ft/sdn/2015/sdn1520.pdf. The pattern is not simple, however: for Canada in the 1980s and 1990s Fortin and Schirle found that the contribution of women's economic progress to overall family welfare was "uneven": Nicole M. Fortin and Tammy Schirle, "Gender Dimensions of Changes in Earnings Inequality in Canada," in David A. Green and Jonathan R. Kesselman, eds., *Dimensions of Inequality in Canada* (Vancouver: UBC Press, 2006), 340.

21 Siep Stuurman, *The Invention of Humanity: Equality and Cultural Difference in World History* (Cambridge, Mass.: Harvard University Press, 2017), 487, 489.

22 Ibid., 491–2.

23 Samuel Moyn, *Not Enough: Human Rights in an Unequal World* (Cambridge, MA: Harvard University Press, 2018), 57–67.

24 Andrew Lui, *Why Canada Cares: Human Rights and Foreign Policy in Theory and Practice* (Montreal and Kingston: McGill-Queen's University Press, 2012), 3–5.

25 Lars Cornelisson, "'How Can the People Be Restricted?': The Mont Pelerin Society and the Problem of Democracy, 1947–48," *History of European Ideas* 43, no. 5 (2017): 507–24. The United Nations was, at best, highly suspect among neoliberals because of its perceived regulatory and redistributive policies: Dieter Plehwe, "Introduction," in Philip Mirowski and Dieter Plehwe, eds., *The Road from Mont Pelerin: The Making of the Neoliberal Thought Collective* (Cambridge, MA: Harvard University Press, 2009), 32–3.

26 Dieter Plehwe, "The Origins of the Neoliberal Economic Development Discourse," in Philip Mirowski and Dieter Plehwe, eds., *The Road from Mont Pelerin: The Making of the Neoliberal Thought Collective* (Cambridge, MA: Harvard University Press, 2009), 253.

27 Dominique Clément, *Equality Deferred: Sex Discrimination and British Columbia's Human Rights State, 1953–84* (Vancouver: UBC Press, 2014), 212–13.

28 Moyn, *Not Enough*, 213.

29 For references to the "classless society" see, for instance: Michele Landsberg's article on domestic servants, *Globe and Mail*, 24 Jan. 1963; "The Indolent Canadian," ibid.,4 Oct. 1961; "Canadians, Old and New," ibid., 27 Oct. 1962; "London This Week," ibid., 3 Sept. 1958; "Ordinary Mortal," ibid., 5 Oct. 1953; "Spotlight on the Royal Family," ibid., 1 Oct. 1957; "Class War Is Communism," ibid., 29 Nov. 1951; "Bluebloods of Canada," ibid., 21 Oct. 1958; "The Future of Canada," ibid., 19 Feb. 1957. One of those writers noting but questioning the myth was Christina McCall Newman, "Canada's Class System," *Maclean's* 75 no. 3 (17 Nov. 1962). Walter Gordon's reference to Canada as "virtually a classless society" was in the *Globe and Mail*, 19 Feb. 1957.

30 Benjamin Isitt, *Militant Minority: British Columbia Workers and the Rise of a New Left, 1948–1972* (Toronto: University of Toronto Press, 2011), 154.

31 Quoted in Rick Helmes-Hayes, *Measuring the Mosaic: An Intellectual Biography of John Porter* (Toronto: University of Toronto Press, 2010), 30.

32 Ibid., 394–5, quoting Porter, *The Measure of Canadian Society: Education, Equality and Opportunity* (Ottawa: Carleton University Press, 1987), 2.

33 CBC interview with Porter, 26 June 1972, cited in Helmes-Hayes, *Measuring the Mosaic*, 398.

34 "Privilege" or "privilege" (occasionally qualified as "social privilege" or "class privilege") appeared three times on the first page of the Preface of *The Vertical Mosaic* (Toronto: University of Toronto Press, 1965), and on 17, 46, 183, 188, 195, 341, 370, 371, 393, 395, 420, and 444.

35 One predecessor was Leonard C. Marsh, *Canadians In and Out of Work: A Survey of Economic Classes and Their Relation to the Labour Market* (Toronto: Oxford University Press, 1940).

36 Porter, *Vertical Mosaic*, 132.

37 Ibid., 372.

38 Ibid., 167. The problem with class was "not only that values of distributive justice are contradicted by the existence of class differences, but that a great deal of social potential and human ability necessary for a society's development and survival is wasted." Ibid., 372. Porter's conception of class was Weberian, and he often conflated it and inequality in the term "class inequality."

39 Ibid., 307.

40 Ibid., xii.

41 Ibid., 558.

42 Michael Ornstein, "Three Decades of Elite Research in Canada: John Porter's Unfulfilled Legacy," in Rick Helmes-Hayes and James Curtis, eds., *The Vertical Mosaic Revisited* (Toronto: University of Toronto Press, 1998), 148. In later years Porter moved further towards social democracy, and he endorsed the distributive ethics of John Rawls.

43 Peter Laslett, "Introduction," in Peter Laslett, ed., *Philosophy, Politics and Society: A Collection* (Oxford University Press, 1956), vii, ix. Cf. Kieran Egan, *The Educated Mind* (University of Chicago Press, 1997), 115–16.

44 Edmund Neill, "The Impact of Positivism: Academic Political Thought in Britain, c. 1945–1970," *History of European Ideas* 39, no. 1 (2013): 51–78.

45 D.C. MacGregor et al., *National Income: A Study Prepared for the Royal Commission on Dominion–Provincial Relations* (Ottawa: King's Printer, 1939), Appendix 4. The earliest estimates of national income were the work of R.H. Coats, the first Dominion statistician, and DBS publications started in the early 1920s. The Bureau did not produce a comprehensive study until 1934, and in the 1930s the Bank of Nova Scotia was generating its own estimates. There was also Major A.R. Lawrence, *The Canadian Income: Its Source, Distribution and Expenditure ... 1930–1931* (Toronto: Might Directories Limited, 1933). A brief history of the early estimates is in Paul Studenski, "National Income Accounts" (pp.78–84), in J.B. Brebner et al., "On Some Appendices to the Rowell-Sirois Report," *Canadian Journal of Economics and Political Science* 7, no. 1 (Feb. 1941): 69–91. See also David A. Worton, *The Dominion Bureau of Statistics: A History of Canada's Central Statistical Office and Its Antecedents, 1841–1972* (Montreal and Kingston: McGill-Queen's University Press,

1998), 112–13, 192–8, 206–9; Simon Goldberg, "The Development of National Accounts in Canada," *Canadian Journal of Economics and Political Science* 15, no. 1 (Feb. 1949): 34–52.

DBS heard complaints from within and outside the Bureau about the delay with national income accounts. In May 1941 John Deutsch and Robert Bryce stated that currently "there is no provision for the prepara-tion of satisfactory estimates of national income." They were upset that the Department of National Revenue had not transferred basic informa-tion to DBS. Estimates of "distribution of income by income groups could not be attempted." Memorandum on National Income Statistics, May 1941, by J. Deutsch and R. Bryce, Library and Archives Canada (LAC), RG 19, vol. 445, 111-1R.

46 Paul Studenski, "National Income Accounts," 82.
47 Shirley Tillotson discusses the arrival of the "mass income tax payer" in the Second World War in *Give and Take: The Citizen-Taxpayer and the Rise of Canadian Democracy* (Vancouver, UBC Press, 2017), chap. 7, 174–209.
48 Lawrence M. Read, *National Accounts Income and Expenditure* (Ottawa: Dominion Bureau of Statistics, 1946).
49 From some of the tables in ibid. one might have estimated the percentage of all incomes that went to the lowest-income "class," as well as the percentage of all persons in that group. Table IIIA (ibid., 37) gave the number of taxpayers at each of seventeen income levels. DBS annual reports also indicated the number and percentage of people at each of several income levels, as well as the total taxes they paid. The Bureau might have used these data to show the percentage of total wage and salary incomes accruing to each income "class" but did not. For example, *Incomes Assessed for Income War Tax in Canada 1938* (Ottawa, 1939), 5, gave a chart showing the number and percentage of taxpayers at each of eighteen income levels, but not the percentage shares of total incomes for each cohort. Some labour activists did the arithmetic, and their table appeared in "How the National Income Is Distributed," *Labour News*, 13 May 1946.
50 DBS did not ignore poverty and unemployment, but its comprehensive survey data were slow to appear. It started surveys of family income and expenditures, focusing on urban wage-earner families, in 1937–38. Dominion Bureau of Statistics, *Family Income and Expenditure in Canada 1937–1938* (Ottawa: King's Printer, 1941). It tried earlier to estimate family expenditure, in 1932 surveying 344 civil servants about that and income; not surprisingly, many low-income families spent more than they

earned. Dominion Bureau of Statistics, *Family Budgetary Expenditures Reported by 53 Dominion Civil Service Employees* (Ottawa: Minister of Trade and Commerce, 1932).

51 The percentage share of the top fifth fell from 48.5 in 1930–31 to 39.9 in 1951. Simon A. Golberg and Jenny R. Podoluk, "Income Size Distribution Statistics in Canada – A Survey and Some Analysis," in Milton Gilbert and Richard Stone, eds., *Income and Wealth Series VI** (London: Bowes and Bowes, 1957), Table II*, 159. The paper is also available at the Review of Income and Wealth website: http://www.roiw.org/1957.asp <30 May 2020>. The 1941–51 reduction in inequality among wage earners had been noted in an undated memo to Dominion Statistician Herbert Marshall in the early 1950s: "Changes in Earnings in Canada, 1941–1951," LAC, RG 31, vol. 1490, page 6, "Memos to Mr Marshall 1951–1961."

52 Goldberg and Podoluk, "Income Size Distribution Statistics," 157, 158. Their caution probably reflected the data's fragility; they knew that "the highest income groups understated earnings to a greater degree than did the lower income groups" (176 n 1). They had no means of estimating the extent of understatement.

53 Simon Kuznets, "Economic Growth and Income Inequality," *American Economic Review* 45, no. 1 (March 1955): 1-28, and *Shares of Upper Income Groups in Income and Savings* (Cambridge, Mass.: National Bureau of Economic Research, 1953), especially 24–8. See the discussion of Kuznets in Thomas Piketty, *Capital in the Twenty-first Century*, trans. Arthur Goldhammer (Cambridge, MA: Harvard University Press, 2014), 11–15. The Kuznets curve had already prompted much discussion, as well as alternative perspectives. See, for instance, Roberto Patricio Korzeniewicz and Timothy Patrick Moran, "Theorizing the Relationship between Inequality and Economic Growth," *Theory and Society* 34 (2005): 277–316.

54 Goldberg and Podoluk, "Income Size Distribution Statistics," 195.

55 Internal communications in DBS during the war revealed awareness of growing demand for income data. In May 1941, for instance, John Deutsch and Robert Bryce wrote: "The division of national income among areas and among social classes, its origin among the various industries and trades, its disposition in the various forms of consumption and capital formation, all these are more important even than the total itself." Deutsch and Bryce, Memorandum on National Income Statistics, May 1941, LAC, RG 19, vol. 445, 111-1R. In the postwar years the statisticians also understood that a fully accurate consumer price index needed to take into account expenditure

patterns by size of family income; weighting the index properly required knowledge of distributions of those sizes. In his public speeches Dominion Statistician Herbert Marshall frequently referred to the value of a "quantitative picture of distribution trends" for businesses in Canada: for instance, "Relations of the D.B.S. with the Canadian Business Community," Marshall speeches, 1954, LAC, RG 31, vol. 1421.

56 The vertical income distributions may not have had high priority even for Podoluk and Goldberg. When the latter surveyed DBS activities, he did not even mention income-size distributions: S.A. Goldberg, "Recent Developments in the Dominion Bureau of Statistics," *Canadian Journal of Economics and Political Science*, 21, no. 1 (Feb. 1955): 52–63.

57 Goldberg and Podoluk concentrated on data problems. They were aware that the censuses reported only wage and salary earnings, not investment returns. They understood that upper-level income earners tended to underestimate their annual earnings for the census. Another issue: housewives supplied much of the census information and knew probably more about after-tax earnings than gross pre-tax earnings. Goldberg and Podoluk were very conscious of the limits of income-tax data, including underreporting and tax avoidance.

58 A relevant argument appears in Stephen J. Kuntz, "Abstracted Empiricism in Social Epidemiology" (2008) at https://www.ep.liu.se/ej/hygiea/v7/i1/a2/hygiea08v7i1a2.pdf.

59 George Grant was apparently not aware of the DBS publications when he summarized U.S. income distributions in 1961, and he said: "Unambiguous statistics for this comparison are not available in Canada." Grant, "An Ethic of Community," in Michael Oliver, ed., *Social Purpose for Canada* (Toronto: University of Toronto Press, 1961), 10n4.

60 Harry G. Johnson, "The Political Economy of Opulence," *Canadian Journal of Economics and Political Science* 26, no. 4 (Nov. 1960): 552–64; John Kenneth Galbraith, *The Affluent Society* (Boston: Houghton Mifflin, 1958). Galbraith's book prompted a debate over whether increased affluence was leading to diminishing concern for inequality; see H. Ian Macdonald, "The American Economy of Abundance," *Canadian Journal of Economics and Political Science* 25, no. 3 (Aug. 1959): 352–7.

61 Michael Harrington, *The Other America: Poverty in the United States* (New York: Macmillan, 1962).

62 David Tough, "'At Last! The Government's War on Poverty Explained': The Special Planning Secretariat, the Welfare State, and the Rhetoric of Poverty in the 1960s," *Journal of the Canadian Historical Association* 25, no. 1 (2014): 181.

63 J.R. Podoluk, Research Development Division, to S.A. Goldberg, Assistant
    Dominion Statistician, 9 Dec. 1959, LAC, RG 31, vol. 1449, file 4000-C;
    S.A. Goldberg, memo of 17 Dec. 1959 to Walter B. Duffett, ibid., re
    meeting of Research Committee, Canadian Welfare Council.

64 Garson Hunter and Dionne Miazdych, "Current Issues surrounding
    Poverty and Welfare Programming in Canada," in Raymond B. Blake and
    Jeffrey A. Keshen, eds., *Social Fabric or Patchwork Quilt: The
    Development of Social Policy in Canada* (Peterborough, ON: Broadview
    Press, 2006), 408–9.

65 DBS surveys showed that the average family spent 50 per cent of its
    income on essentials of food, clothing, and shelter. The Bureau, somewhat
    arbitrarily, added 20 per cent to create the low-income cut-off (LICO) –
    the level of income at which a family was spending 70 per cent or more of
    its income on those basics. The measure was a compromise because the
    statisticians would have preferred a focus on family budgets: taking into
    account family size, age, composition, place of residence, and prices in that
    place, what minimum income would meet basic needs? Lack of data
    prevented this approach; as Podoluk noted, no minimum standard budgets
    had been constructed. She was also aware of the complex, value-laden
    judgments in all measures of poverty. The concept of "need," for instance,
    changed as real incomes rose (either within a population or intergenera-
    tionally) and as economic, technological, and cultural changes turned
    previously scarce goods into deemed necessities. Jenny R. Podoluk,
    Incomes of Canadians (Ottawa: Dominion Bureau of Statistics, 1968),
    185.

66 In *Incomes of Canadians* Podoluk wrote that Canada had "no official
    criterion of poverty"; she used a "low-income definition rather than a
    poverty definition" (14).

67 Jenny R. Podoluk joined DBS in 1948 and retired in 1981. She had a
    bachelor's degree from Toronto and an MA in economics from Chicago.
    There is an obituary in the *Globe and Mail*, 12 March 2003.

68 Podoluk, *Incomes of Canadians*. The reference to "objective criteria" is on
    p. 13. The quotation from Brady, which I have paraphrased, is on p. 179.
    The study included data on incomes by source and type; incomes by
    gender and age; "human capital" and private returns to education; family
    income and contributions of non-head earners; regional income distribu-
    tions; changes in real incomes 1901–61; and the effect of taxes and
    transfer payments on personal incomes.

69 Ibid., 267.

70 Ibid., 270–1.

71 Ibid., 284, 287.

72 In 1961 transfers accounted for 62.4 per cent of incomes of families earning under $1,000 a year and 50.2 per cent for those with $1,000–$1,999 – substantial increases since 1951. Ibid., 251.

73 Podoluk played a minor role in the Canadian war on poverty; she testified, for instance, before parliamentarians in 1969; Proceedings of the Senate Special Committee on Poverty, 24 April 1969, Senate Committees, 28th Parliament, 1st Session, vol. 1, 65, 67, 68. The LICO remained her major contribution to the study of poverty. The *Globe and Mail*'s only reference to Podoluk's *Incomes of Canadians* (1968) was by George Bain, "Down among the Quintiles," 22 Feb. 1969. It focused on the number of earners in a family, family size, and poverty in the Atlantic provinces. There was a brief reference to Podoluk in Scott Young's article on middle-class incomes, *Globe and Mail*, 4 April 1975, and in an article on the Maritimes in the issue of 25 April 1969. John Gilbert, MP, quoted Podoluk's book in *House of Commons Debates*, 8 Dec. 1969, 1705. A keyword search of newspapers in Peel's Prairie Provinces yielded no results for the author after 1967. There were two references to *Incomes of Canadians* in the *Canadian Journal of Political Science* between 1968 and 1980. Erroll Black cited her view that studies of low incomes and inequality in Canada were "sadly lacking": Black, "One Too Many Reports on Poverty in Canada," *Canadian Journal of Political Science* 5, no. 3 (Sept. 1972): 439. In 1980 Ornstein, Stevenson, and Williams cited her observation that income distributions had changed little since the war. Michael D. Ornstein, H. Michael Stevenson, and A. Paul Williams, "Region, Class and Political Culture in Canada," *Canadian Journal of Political Science* 13, no. 2 (July 1980): 239.

74 Podoluk, *Incomes of Canadians*, 14.

75 One of many available examples is Ontario Federation of Labour Research Department, *Poverty in the Midst of Plenty* (Toronto: Ontario Federation of Labour, 1964). It began with a reference to inequality: "A painful paradox of our times is the fact that the numbers of the poor are constantly growing in an age of plenty" (ibid., 4). But the report set aside societal-level inequality and class: the new sociology of poverty sought to locate population sub-groups vulnerable to low incomes (these include the unemployed, "Indians," people with little education, people in specific locations). The welfare state had not solved the problem of poverty: welfare schemes were designed, at best, "to sustain life only," and welfare propaganda obscured the "invisible poor, the unseen, the unheard" (ibid., 20, 43).

76 Antonia Maioni, "New Century, New Risks: The Marsh Report and the Post-war Welfare State in Canada," *Policy Options* (Aug. 2004) at https://policyoptions.irpp.org/fr/magazines/social-policy-in-the-21st-century/new-century-new-risks-the-marsh-report-and-the-post-war-welfare-state-in-canada/.

77 In his typology of welfare states, Gosta Esping-Andersen puts Canada among the liberal examples, which provide a social safety net for the poor but do not replace individualism and market relations with social rights, in contrast to systems in continental Europe and Scandinavia. Gosta Esping-Andersen, *The Three Worlds of Welfare Capitalism* (Princeton, NJ: Princeton University Press, 1990). See also Keith Banting and John Myles, "Introduction," in Banting and Myles, eds., *Inequality and the Fading of Redistributive Politics* (Vancouver: UBC Press, 2013), 4–6.

78 T.H. Marshall, *Citizenship and Social Class; and Other Essays* (Cambridge: Cambridge University Press, 1950).

79 T.H. Marshall, *Citizenship and Social Class* (London: Pluto Press, 1992), 8, cited in Ben Revi, "T.H. Marshall and His Critics: Reappraising 'Social Citizenship' in the Twenty-first Century," *Citizenship Studies* 18, no. 3–4 (2014): 455. See also Dann Hoxsey, "Debating the Ghost of Marshall: A Critique of Citizenship," *Citizenship Studies* 15 (2011): 915–32. There is a substantial literature on social rights: see, for instance, Toomas Kotkas and Kenneth Veitch, eds., *Social Rights in the Welfare State: Origins and Transformations* (Abingdon, England: Routledge, 2017).

80 Marshall, *Citizenship and Social Class* (1992), 47.

81 Gurvitch's *Sociology of Law* (1942) was listed in "books received" in *Canadian Journal of Economics and Political Science* 8, no. 2 (May 1942): 316–17. I find no reference to his Bill of Social Rights in the journal. The concept of social rights received some support from the United Nations Declaration of Universal Human Rights (1948): "Everyone has the right to a standard of living adequate to the health and well-being of himself and of his family."

82 A few examples must suffice. The LSR's *Social Planning for Canada* (1935), for all its iterations of inequality, had no references to Pareto, Pigou, or John Ryan; Hugh Dalton appeared in one footnote; there was a passing reference to Hobson on underconsumption and on interest rates. Research Committee of the League for Social Reconstruction, *Social Planning for Canada* (first pub. 1935) (Toronto: University of Toronto Press, 1975). In Scott and Vlastos's *Towards the Christian Revolution* (1936) T.H. Green made one appearance, Tawney got brief mention, but Dalton, Hobson, Pigou, and Ryan were absent: R.B.Y. Scott and Gregory

Vlastos, eds., *Towards the Christian Revolution* (Chicago: Willett, Clark, 1936). Ryan's work was available in Canada, and a search of the online Canadiana corpus for 1920–40 turns up several mentions: *Charlottetown Herald*, 1 Sept. 1920; *The Dawn of Tomorrow* (London, Ont.), 28 Nov. 1925; and references in the *Catholic Record*.

83 David Lewis and Frank Scott, *Make This Your Canada: A Review of C.C.F. History and Policy* (Toronto: Central Canada Publishing, 1943), 32, 155.

84 Ibid., 2–3.

85 James Naylor, *The Fate of Labour Socialism: The Co-operative Commonwealth Federation and the Dream of a Working-Class Future* (Toronto: University of Toronto Press, 2016), 311–13. Naylor notes that M.J. Coldwell declared Britain's hugely influential Beveridge Report (William Beveridge, *Social Insurance and Allied Services* [1942]) inadequate as a strategy; he also comments (313–14) on the cautious and defensive tone of Coldwell's *Left Turn, Canada* (New York: Duell, Sloan, and Pearce, 1945).

86 Lewis and Scott, *Make This Your Canada*, 97.

87 Winnipeg Declaration of Principles (1956), at Socialist History Project, at https://www.socialisthistory.ca/Docs/CCF/Winnipeg.htm, accessed 30 May 2020.

88 The New Party, Draft Program (National Committee for the New Party, 1961), 7 and 9, at https://www.poltext.org/sites/poltext.org/files/plateformesV2/Canada/CAN_PL_1962_NDP.pdf, accessed 31 May 2020. The more explicitly socialist "Waffle Manifesto" of 1969 mentioned inequality only once, in a reference to regions, and redistribution once, vis-à-vis power.

89 Murray Cooke, "The CCF / NDP and the Populisms of the Left and the Right," in Roberta Lexier, Stephanie Bangarth, and Jon Weier, eds., *Party of Conscience: The CCF, the NDP, and Social Democracy in Canada* (Toronto: Between the Lines, 2018), 166–7. At the same time the democratic-socialist understanding of capitalist ownership and control, argues Christo Availis, led David Lewis and Ed Broadbent "beyond a better distribution of capitalism's spoils." Christo Availis, "Tommy Douglas, David Lewis, Ed Broadbent and Democratc Socialism in the New Democratic Party, 1968–1984," in Roberta Lexier, Stephanie Bangarth, and Jon Weier, eds., *Party of Conscience: The CCF, the NDP, and Social Democracy in Canada* (Toronto: Between the Lines, 2018), 105. The NDP's lack of a doctrine of social rights for the welfare state may have complicated its conflicted and inadequate response to Pierre Trudeau's

Charter of Rights (1982), which left out social and economic rights. Neither organized labour nor the NDP articulated a coherent position on labour and social rights as human rights: see Christo Aivalis, *The Constant Liberal: Pierre Trudeau, Organized Labour, and the Canadian Social Democratic Left* (Vancouver: UBC Press, 2018), 164–70.

90 Berton's "profile of the Canadian poor" drew on sources from the Canadian Welfare Council, the Ontario Federation of Labour, and the Toronto Family Service Association. See Berton, *The Smug Minority* (Toronto: McClelland and Stewart, 1968), 93–112.

91 It is not clear how Berton came upon the idea of a guaranteed annual income or wage. He may have read about it in works by Robert Theobald, whom he quoted (*Smug Minority*, 108). Robert Theobald, *The Guaranteed Income: Next Step in Economic Evolution?* (Garden City, NY: Doubleday, 1966). The idea of basic income had a history in Canada, and Social Credit in Alberta supported it in the 1930s. Berton apparently intended it to be universal. He may not have noticed that the combination of guaranteed income and negative income tax left intact the "less eligibility" principle. Some conservative economists, including Milton Friedman, supported the guaranteed income. It had the obvious advantage for employers that the state would compensate them for the low wages they paid.

   Poverty in Canada: The Report of the Senate Special Committee on Poverty (1971) recommended a guaranteed income and negative income tax. Ian Adams, William Cameron, Brian Hill, and Peter Penz, *The Real Poverty Report* (Edmonton: M.G. Hurtig, 1971), 191–2, criticized guaranteed incomes set at too low a level, such as the one Milton Friedman suggested; these would "do more to perpetuate poverty than to eliminate it." It quoted Trevor Lloyd: "If the guaranteed income is applied at any level that ensures a decent standard of living it involves a large redistribution of income in an egalitarian direction." Trevor Lloyd, "State Capitalism and Socialism: The Problem of Government Handouts," in Laurier Lapierre et al, eds., *Essays on the Left* (Toronto: McClelland and Stewart, 1971), 171–2.

92 Berton, *Smug Minority*, 114–15. Median household income in Canada in 1967 was $7,200 per year. The first low-income cut-offs were published in 1969; the cut-off for a family of two in a city of 500,000 people or more was $3,769.

93 Berton cited T.B. Macaulay, Max Weber, J.K. Galbraith, Marshall McLuhan, the sociologist John Seeley, Bertrand Russell, the philosopher Sebastian de Grazia, the labour expert Einar Hardin, Michael Harrington,

Robert Theobald, John Morgan (School of Social Work, University of Toronto), John Porter, education professor W.G. Fleming, economist Theodore W. Schultz, economist Gordon W. Bertram, economist R.A. Jenness, and sociologist Wilson A. Head.

94 A.B. McKillop, *Pierre Berton: A Biography* (Toronto: McClelland and Stewart, 2008), 472–9.

95 On "poor-bashing" in the 1950s and 1960s see Jean Swanson, *Poor-Bashing: The Politics of Exclusion* (Toronto: Between the Lines, 2001), 53–7. On the backlash to the welfare state: Aivalis, *The Constant Liberal*, 76–8; Sid Gilbert, "Poverty, Policy, and Politics: The Evolution of a Guaranteed Annual Income Experiment in Canada," in John Harp and John R. Hofley, eds., *Structured Inequality in Canada* (Scarborough, ON: Prentice-Hall, 1980), 446–7. On Trudeau's government and the backlash against social security: Aivalis, *Constant Liberal*, 76–7.

96 Tillotson *Give and Take*, 278–85.

97 Myrna Kostash, *Long Way from Home: The Story of the Sixties Generation in Canada* (Toronto: J. Lorimer, 1980), 6, 7, 262; Bryan D. Palmer, *Canada's 1960s: The Ironies of Identity in a Rebellious Era* (Toronto: University of Toronto Press, 2009), 258–9.

98 Palmer, *Canada's 1960s*, 388–92.

99 William Robert Langford, "'Helping People Help Themselves': Democracy, Development, and the Global Politics of Poverty in Canada, 1964–1979" (PhD dissertation, Queen's University, 2017), 334, 385. See also Sean Mills, *The Empire Within: Postcolonial Thought and Political Activism in Sixties Montreal* (Montreal: McGill-Queen's University Press, 2010).

100 Langford, "Helping People," especially 385–96.

101 Alvin Finkel, *Social Policy and Practice in Canada* (Waterloo, ON: Wilfrid Laurier University Press, 2006), 272.

102 The Liberal government of Pierre Trudeau outlined its income-security policy in *Income Security and Social Services* (Ottawa: Queen's Printer, 1969). The document stated: "It is highly unlikely that an equitable distri-bution of income across Canada will be achieved ... unless Parliament has the power to support the incomes of the poor" (66), quoted in Rodney S. Haddow, *Poverty Reform in Canada, 1958–1978: State and Class Influences on Policy Making* (Montreal and Kingston: McGill-Queen's University Press, 1993), 97, 174–5. Trudeau and his ministers were following a path outlined earlier in the 1960s. Tom Kent also argued for a "collectivist framework," a transcending of nineteenth-century economic liberalism, and a "much more equal society." The principles led Kent directly to his "philosophy of social security," which was, he said, "an

equalitarian philosophy." Kenneth C. Dewar, "Liberalism, Social
Democracy, and Tom Kent," *Journal of Canadian Studies* 53, no. 1
(winter 2019): 183–4.

103 Finkel, *Social Policy*, 274.

104 C.W. Gonick, "Poverty and Capitalism," in Bryan Finnigan and Cy
Gonick, eds., *Making It: The Canadian Dream* (Toronto: McClelland and
Stewart, 1972), 288–307. Podoluk's table also appeared in Gonick,
"Poverty and Capitalism," *Canadian Dimension* 6, no. 5 (Oct.–Nov.
1969): 33. Howard Buchbinder saw guaranteed income and "just society"
models as "misdirection perpetrated by those who would study poverty
rather than the inequitable distribution of wealth and the kinds of exploit-
ation which maintain and perpetuate poverty." Buchbinder, "Guaranteed
Annual Income: The Answer to Poverty for All but the Poor," *Canadian
Dimension* 7, no. 4 (Oct.–Nov. 1970): 27–32.

105 Rosanvallon, *Society of Equals*, 255–6.

106 Wallace Clement, "Power, Ethnicity, and Class: Reflections Thirty Years
after *The Vertical Mosaic*," in Rick Helmes-Hayes and James Curtis, eds.,
The Vertical Mosaic Revisited (Toronto: University of Toronto Press,
1998), 39.

107 R.H. Tawney also pointed to the necessary connection between equality of
condition and equality of opportunity in his famous book: Tawney,
Equality (first pub. 1931), 4th ed. (London: George Allen, 1952), 102–16.
"In the absence of measures which prevent the exploitation of groups in a
weak economic position by those in a strong, and make the external condition of health and civilization a common possession, the phrase equality
of opportunity is obviously a jest ... It is the impertinent courtesy of an
invitation offered to unwelcome guests, in the certainty that circumstances
will prevent them from accepting it" (115).

108 Anthony Crosland, *The Future of Socialism* (London: Jonathan Cape,
1956), 229, 233. The American philosopher Charles Frankel offered a
critical but pro-egalitarian analysis: Frankel, "Equality of Opportunity,"
Ethics 81, no. 3 (1971): 191–211. In 1961 George Grant asked: "Do we
not have to move forward to a richer conception of economic equality
than equality of opportunity?" Grant, "An Ethic of Community," in
Michael Oliver, ed., *Social Purpose for Canada* (Toronto: University of
Toronto Press, 1961), 20. Gad Horowitz referred to the liberal conflation
of equality with equality of opportunity in "Conservatism, Liberalism, and
Socialism in Canada: An Interpretation," *Canadian Journal of Economics
and Political Science* 32, no. 2 (May 1966): 144. For a pithy dismissal of

equality of opportunity see Ed Broadbent, *The Liberal Rip-off:*
Trudeauism vs. The Politics of Equality (Toronto: New Press, 1970), 28.

109 Crosland, *Future of Socialism*, 230, 232–3.

110 Ibid., 236. Luck egalitarianism is the form of distributive justice,
associated with Ronald Dworkin and others, that emphasizes chosen
circumstances, or outcomes that result from conscious choice, rather than
outcomes determined by unchosen circumstances or brute luck.

111 "Statement by the Prime Minister on the Just Society" [September 1968],
Trudeau fonds, LAC, cited by Aivalis, *The Constant Liberal*, 69–70.
Ramsay Cook drafted the original "just society" address. The Liberal government's speech from the throne in October 1976 announced three goals
"that all Canadians share": "national unity, equality of opportunity, and
the enhancement of individual rights." The document declared that inflation was a "destructive force" that obstructed "the fight against poverty
and inequality." The emphasis was also on reducing the size of government
and stimulating economic growth: *Globe and Mail*, 13 Oct. 1976. The
liberal-egalitarian formulation of the inequality problem appeared succinctly in "An Appeal for Realism" (*"Pour une politique fonctionelle"*),
signed by Trudeau and six others in 1964: "An Appeal for Realism,"
Canadian Forum (May 1964), 29–31. This text conflated the "inequitable
distribution of wealth and income" with regional disparities; its solutions
included "mobility" as a condition for "the achievement of maximum
yield from human capital." On Trudeau's position on inequality in 1964
see Aivalis, *The Constant Liberal*, 59–62.

112 *Canadian Transport*, 15 May 1969, cited in Aivalis, *The Constant Liberal*, 71.

113 The fate of the Royal Commission on Taxation, appointed in 1962 and
chaired by Kenneth Carter, offered one priceless lesson on the effects of
the neoliberal surge at both policy and wider ideological levels. The Carter
Commission sought a balance between equity or "fairness" and efficiency
in the tax system. Its "social objectives" included "the equitable distribution of output" so that those who "have little economic power" and
"particularly heavy responsibilities or obligations" were "able to maintain
a decent standard of living." *Report of the Royal Commission on Taxation*
Vol. 2 (Ottawa, 1966), 10. Carter recommended some redistributive
reforms and a tax on capital gains. The Trudeau government retreated
from most of the recommendations following loud protests from business,
although it instituted a partial capital-gains tax. By the late 1980s, if not
before, the redistributive function of the tax system had been weakened.
Neil Brooks argues that the reforms of the late 1980s "disable[d] the tax

system as an effective policy instrument for the redistribution of income." Neil Brooks, "The Changing Structure of the Canadian Tax System: Accommodating the Rich," *Osgoode Hall Law Journal* 31, no. 1 (spring 1993): 137–93. On the Carter Commission: Kim Brooks, ed., *The Quest for Tax Reform Continues: The Royal Commission on Taxation Fifty Years Later* (Toronto: Carswell, 2013); Tillotson, *Give and Take*, 286–8. A popular study is Linda McQuaig, *Behind Closed Doors: How the Rich Won Control of Canada's Tax System* (Toronto: Penguin, 1987).

114 Ian McKay, "A Half-Century of Possessive Individualism: C.B. Macpherson and the Twenty-first-Century Prospects of Liberalism," *Journal of the Canadian Historical Association* 25, no. 1 (2014): 307–40; Frank Cunningham, *The Political Thought of C.B. Macpherson: Contemporary Applications* (New York: Palgrave Macmillan, 2018). Phillip Hansen, *Reconsidering C.B. Macpherson: From Possessive Individualism to Democratic Theory and Beyond* (Toronto: University of Toronto Press, 2015). My debt to Ian McKay will be clear in what follows. I cannot aspire to the lucidity of his analysis; I attempt to draw out the relevance of Macpherson's thought to the problem of inequality.

115 McKay notes the *longue-durée* perspective: "A Half-Century of Possessive Indivdualism," 322–3. On Macpherson and Marxism there has been much controversy. Key sources include Victor Svacek, "The Elusive Marxism of C.B. Macpherson," *Canadian Journal of Political Science* 9, no. 3 (Sept. 1976): 395–422; C.B. Macpherson, "Humanist Democracy and Elusive Marxism: A Response to Minogue and Svacek," *Canadian Journal of Political Science* 9, no. 3 (1976): 423; B.N. Ray, *C.B. Macpherson and Liberalism* (New Delhi: Kanishka Publishers, 1999); Robert Meynell, *Canadian Idealism and the Philosophy of Freedom: C.B. Macpherson, George Grant, and Charles Taylor* (Montreal and Kingston: McGill-Queen's University Press, 2011), 61–84; Hansen, *Reconsidering C.B. Macpherson*, 125–86.

116 C.B. Macpherson, *The Real World of Democracy* (Toronto: Canadian Broadcasting Corporation, 1965), 47.

117 C.B. Macpherson, "Revisionist Liberalism," in Macpherson, *Democratic Theory: Essays in Retrieval* (first pub. 1973) (Toronto: Oxford University Press, 2012), 86.

118 Macpherson, *Democratic Theory*, 12, and *Real World of Democracy*, 48. Macpherson rooted his argument here in his concept of "transfer of powers." What was transferred "from the non-owner to the owner of the means of labour" was "the non-owner's ability to labour, i.e., his ability to use his own capacities productively." The owner of capital has purchased

the labour power and "the actual work"; because he owns the work therefore he owns the product and "the value added by the work." However apparent the debt to Marx, the terms exploitation and surplus labour were absent. Macpherson, *Democratic Theory*, 64–5.

119 Here I summarize Macpherson's arguments in response to John W. Chapman and John Rawls, in Macpherson, "Revisionist Liberalism," 80–94.

120 Macpherson, *Democratic Theory*, 94.

121 Macpherson, "A Political Theory of Property," in Macpherson, *Democratic Theory: Essays in Retrieval* (first pub. 1973) (Toronto: Oxford University Press, 2012), 212.

122 C.B. Macpherson, "Property as Means or End," in Anthony Parel and Thomas Flanagan, eds., *Theories of Property: Aristotle to the Present* (Waterloo, ON: Wilfrid Laurier University Press, 1979), 5.

123 I am relying especially on Macpherson, "A Political Theory of Property," 120–40.

124 The universal basis of the right to property lay in the principle that a person's labour was peculiarly his own: every person possessed property, if only the property of "his" own labour. Mill and Green's mistake, according to Macpherson, was "their failure to recognize that the individual property right on which they insisted meant a denial to most men of equitable access to the means of life and the means of labour" (Macpherson, *Democratic Theory*, 120).

125 Macpherson, *Real World of Democracy*, 51.

126 Macpherson, *The Life and Times of Liberal Democracy* (first pub. 1977) (Don Mills, ON: Oxford University Press, 2012), especially 98–115, and *Democratic Theory*, 138.

127 Macpherson, *Democratic Theory*, 139.

128 Macpherson, *Life and Times*, 102.

129 Macpherson, *Democratic Theory*, 138–40.

130 McKay, "A Half-Century of Possessive Individualism," 328. The capability approach is an alternative to "equality of opportunity" that begins with the normative principle affirming freedom to achieve well-being and "a person's capability to achieve functionings that he or she has reason to value." Amartya Sen, *Inequality Re-examined* (first pub. 1992) (Cambridge, MA: Harvard University Press, 1995), 4–5, 7–10.

131 How to support such a provocative generalization? Perhaps with a lament about disciplinary and intellectual silos that were so entrenched in the 1970s and 1980s (and perhaps also today). Is it possible to imagine a session at the annual conference of either the Canadian Economics

Association or the Canadian Historical Association, with papers by three
people – an economist specializing in income distributions; a philosopher,
expert on John Rawls and distributive justice; and a feminist historian of
the politics of gender? But see note 4 above and the reflections on
feminism and equality at the beginning of this chapter.

132 Edward Broadbent, "But Who Will Listen to This Fabian Song?," *Globe
and Mail*, 27 Oct. 1973. Broadbent was reviewing J.K. Galbraith's recent
book, *Economics and the Public Purpose*, without endorsing the author's
Fabian incrementalism. C.B. Macpherson was the supervisor of
Broadbent's 1966 doctoral dissertation.

CONCLUSION

1 Karl Polanyi, *The Great Transformation: The Political and Economic
Origins of Our Time* (New York: Farrar and Rinehart, 1944).

2 John Clark Murray, *The Industrial Kingdom of God* (written 1887), ed.
Leslie Armour and Elizabeth Trott (Ottawa: University of Ottawa Press,
1981), 13.

3 On Canada see Introduction, n 7, above.

4 Richard Wilkinson and Kate Pickett, *The Spirit Level: Why Greater
Inequality Makes Societies Stronger* (New York: Bloomsbury Press, 2009).

5 Harry G. Frankfurt, "Equality as a Moral Ideal," *Ethics* 98, no. 1 (Oct.
1987): 21–43; *On Inequality* (Princeton, NJ: Princeton University Press,
2015).

6 There is no claim to Canadian exceptionalism here. There was, however, a
distinctive path towards the welfare state, which arrived relatively late and
with a narrow theoretical foundation.

7 Anthony Atkinson, interviewed by *Prospect Magazine* (9 April 2015),
cited in Carsten Jensen and Kees van Kersbergen, *The Politics of
Inequality* (London: Palgrave Macmillan, 2017), 12.

8 Mariana Mazzuccato, *The Value of Everything: Making and Taking in the
Global Economy* (New York: Public Affairs, 2018), 6–8.

9 Ibid., 202.

10 John Rae, *The Sociological Theory of Capital* (orig. *New Principles of
Political Economy*, 1834), ed. Charles W. Mixter (New York: Macmillan,
1905), xi and 245–76 (his chapter "Of the Nature and Effects of
Luxury").

11 Adam Smith also had a strong sense of waste, which included unproductive spending by the wealthy on frivolous luxuries. Mazzuccatto, *The Value
of Everything*, 38.

12 T.H. Green, *Lectures on the Principles of Political Obligation* (first pub. 1895) (Kitchener, ON: Batoche Books, 1999), 22.

13 Ibid., 175.

14 John Watson, *An Outline of Philosophy* (Glasgow: James Maclehose, 1908), 270. On hedonisms: John Watson, *Hedonistic Theories from Aristippus to Spencer* (Glasgow: James Maclehose, 1895).

15 Murray, *The Industrial Kingdom*, 117–18.

16 Ibid., 68–9.

17 Gavin Kennedy says that the metaphor was virtually unknown in the century after Smith's death in 1790, and Paul Samuelson's economics textbook *Economics: An Introductory Analysis*, first published in 1948, popularized it. Gavin Kennedy, "The Myth of the Invisible Hand – A View from the Trenches," at https://papers.ssrn.com/sol3/papers.cfm?abstract_id=2143277, accessed 2 July 2019; Kennedy, "Adam Smith and the Invisible Hand," *Economic Journal Watch* 6, no. 2 (May 2009): 239–63. See also Gavin Kennedy, *Adam Smith: A Moral Philosopher and His Political Economy* (Basingstoke, England: Palgrave Macmillan, 2008).

18 The neoliberal appropriation of the "invisible hand" metaphor is a selective and abridged reading of Smith's *Wealth of Nations* that ignores Smith's ethics and his *Theory of Moral Sentiments*. See, among other titles, Jerry Evensky, "Ethics and the Invisible Hand," *Journal of Economic Perspectives* 7, no. 2 (spring 1993): 197–205; Kennedy, *Adam Smith*; Mazzucato, *The Value of Everything*, 36; and Maria Pia Paganelli, "The Adam Smith Problem in Reverse: Self-Interest in *The Wealth of Nations* and *The Theory of Moral Sentiments*," *History of Political Economy* 40, no. 2 (2008): 365–82.

19 Robert M. MacIver, *Community: A Sociological Study* (London: Macmillan, 1917), 356 (see also 338).

20 Ibid., 40.

21 Phillips Thompson, *The Politics of Labor* (New York: Belford, Clarke and Co., 1887), 55.

22 Samuel Fleischacker, *A Short History of Distributive Justice* (Cambridge, MA: Harvard University Press, 2004), 126.

23 Enjolras [Phillips Thompson], *Palladium of Labor*, 24 April 1886.

24 This sociological insight antedated the social-gospel era in Canada. It appeared very clearly in 1887 in Murray, *The Industrial Kingdom*, 40–2.

25 John E. Roemer, "Ideology, Social Ethos, and the Financial Crisis," *Journal of Ethics* 16, no. 3 (2012): 273–303. There is also evidence for inequality's "discouragement effect" leading to lower work effort: Hyejin Ku and Timothy C. Salmon, "The Incentive Effects of Inequality: An Experimental

Investigation," *Southern Economic Journal* 79, no. 1 (2012): 46–70. A substantial literature deals with the relationship between inequality and economic growth. Executive compensation and its rise relative to workers' average wages in the United States, Canada, and other countries have generated a great deal of writing. Many economists have pointed out the absence of correlation between changes in executive compensation and performance or firm productivity. Cultural and other factors may play a role: executives in Germany and Japan earn far less than their U.S. and British counterparts, despite comparable productivity levels. The relationship between cash transfers (and expanded credit) and productivity appears to be different at the lowest income levels; hence the rise of the micro-credit movement in developing countries. See, for instance, Nobel Peace laureate Muhammad Yunnus, *A World of Three Zeros: The New Economics of Zero Poverty, Zero Unemployment, and Zero Net Carbon Emissions* (New York: Public Affairs, 2017).

26 Short summaries of the critique appear in Jonathan Aldred, *The Skeptical Economist: Revealing the Ethics inside Economics* (Abingdon, England: Earthscan, 2009), 26–36; Domènec Melé and César González Cantón, "The Homo Economicus Model," in IESE Business Collection, *Human Foundations of Management* (London: Palgrave Macmillan, 2014); and Dante A. Urbana and Alberto Ruiz-Villaverde, "A Critical Review of Homo Economicus from Five Approaches," *American Journal of Economics and Sociology* 78, no. 1 (2019), 63–93. A popular version is Peter Fleming, *The Death of Homo Economicus: Work, Debt, and the Myth of Endless Accumulation* (London: Pluto Press, 2017).

27 Murray, *The Industrial Kingdom*, 21–2.

28 O.D. Skelton, *Socialism: A Critical Analysis* (New York: Houghton Mifflin, 1911), 58.

29 Frankfurt, *On Inequality*, 7–8.

30 Ibid., 6.

31 Thompson, *The Politics of Labor*, 55–9.

32 Shoshana Zuboff, *The Age of Surveillance Capitalism: The Fight for a Human Future at the New Frontier of Power* (New York: Public Affairs, 2019).

33 Thomas Piketty, *Capital in the Twenty-first Century*, trans. Arthur Goldhammer (Cambridge, MA: Harvard University Press, 2014), especially 195–6. In 2100 the entire planet, Piketty said, could look like Europe at the turn of the twentieth century in its extremes of inequality and capital intensity – but "just one possibility among others" (196).

34 Piketty, "Éléments pour un socialism participative au XXIe siècle," in *Capital et idéologie* (Paris: Éditions du Seuil, 2019), chap. 17, 1111–90. Among the author's solutions: workers' seats on company boards, capping the largest shareholders' voting power, steeply graduated wealth taxes, individualized carbon taxes, and a substantial lump sum of capital for all citizens at age twenty-five. The right-wing media in France have of course freaked out.

35 Piketty, *Capital in the Twenty-first Century*, 479–83, 493–514, 515.

36 Anthony B. Atkinson, *Inequality: What Can Be Done?* (Cambridge, MA: Harvard University Press, 2015), 237–9 (his list of proposals). Also well known are the diagnoses and proposals of Nobel Economics laureate Joseph Stiglitz: Joseph E. Stiglitz, *The Price of Inequality* (New York: W.W. Norton, 2012), and *The Great Divide: Unequal Societies and What We Can Do about Them* (New York: W.W. Norton, 2015). Proposed remedies for Canada include those of Lars Osberg in *The Age of Increasing Inequality: The Astonishing Rise of Canada's 1%* (Toronto: James Lorimer, 2018), 183–208.

37 Atkinson, *Inequality*, 305.

38 Walter Scheidel, *The Great Leveler: Violence and the History of Inequality from the Stone Age to the Twenty-first Century* (Princeton, NJ: Princeton University Press, 2017), 442. The increasing frequency of epidemics in the twenty-first century is well documented. Their impact on income and wealth distributions is already the subject of debate.

39 As the "yellow vest" protests in France in 2019 remind us, it is easier to mobilize against specific material grievances such as a gasoline tax than against a structural problem such as inequality.

40 Scheidel, *The Great Leveler*, 442.

41 Robert J. Gordon, *The Rise and Fall of American Growth: The U.S. Standard of Living since the Civil War* (Princeton, NJ: Princeton University Press, 2016).

42 T. Jackson, "The Post-Growth Challenge: Secular Stagnation, Inequality and the Limits to Growth," CUSP Working Paper 12 (Guildford: University of Surrey, 2018), at www.cusp.ac.uk/publications.

43 Piketty considers climate change briefly: *Capital in the Twenty-first Century*, 567–9. Recent discussions began with Nicholas H. Stern, *The Economics of Climate Change: The Stern Review* (New York: Cambridge University Press, 2007).

44 Murray, *The Industrial Kingdom*, 13.

45 Lane Kenworthy, *Jobs with Equality* (Oxford: Oxford University Press, 2008), 22 (Table 2.1); Jensen and van Kersbergen, *The Politics of Inequality*, 12–17.

46 John Rawls, *A Theory of Justice* (Cambridge, Mass.: Harvard University Press, 1971); Robert Nozick, *Anarchy, State and Utopia* (New York: Basic Books, 1974). A very useful survey of works in egalitarian political philosophy from Rawls to 2006 is Colin M. MacLeod and Avigail Eisenberg, "Normative Dimensions of Inequality," in David A. Green and Jonathan R. Kesselman, eds., *Dimensions of Inequality in Canada* (Vancouver: UBC Press, 2006), 33–64. See also Colin MacLeod, *Justice and Equality* (Calgary: University of Calgary Press, 2012).

47 A provocative attempt to relate radical egalitarian ideas to political action is Erik Olin Wright, *Envisioning Real Utopias* (London: Verso, 2010). Also essential is Pierre Rosanvallon, *The Society of Equals* (Cambridge, Mass.: Harvard University Press, 2013). David Harvey makes the case in *The Enigma of Capital and the Crises of Capitalism* (Oxford: Oxford University Press, 2010).

48 It means also analyzing the difference in income distributions among nations with capitalist economies as well as why some have significantly lower inequality. A discussion of alternatives would require another book, but socialist alternatives are experiencing a revival, at both scholarly and popular levels: for instance, Axel Honneth, *The Idea of Socialism: Towards a Renewal* (Cambridge: Polity Press, 2017); and Bhaskar Sunkara, *The Socialist Manifesto: The Case for Radical Politics in an Era of Extreme Inequality* (New York: Basic Books, 2019). The micro-credit movement presents itself as an alternative to failed capitalism and to inequality: for instance, Yunnus, *A World of Three Zeros*. The contentious idea of universal basic income is winning new attention: for instance, Rutger Bregman, *Utopia for Realists: How We Can Build the Ideal World* (New York: Little, Brown and Company, 2017); for Canada see Robin Brodway, Katherine Cuff, and Kourtney Koebel, *Designing a Basic Income Guarantee for Canada*, Queen's University Economics Department Working Paper No. 1371 (2016), at http://qed.econ.queensu.ca/working_papers/papers/qed_wp_1371.pdf.

49 In 2019, protests against specific injustices occurred in a range of countries: Albania, Brazil, Chile, Ecuador, France, Haiti, Hong Kong, India, Iraq, Lebanon, Peru, Russia, Serbia, Spain, Ukraine, the United Kingdom, and Venezuela. While particular local events or changes were triggers, many of the protests reflected and expressed anger at the associated evils

of economic inequality and political corruption. At the time of writing, anti-racism protests are transnational and enduring.

50 According to Alan Patten, in Kant reciprocity referred to the thesis that morality and freedom were reciprocal concepts: Alan Patten, "The Reciprocity Thesis in Kant and Hegel," in Patten, *Hegel's Idea of Freedom* (New York: Oxford University Press, 1999), chap. 3, 82–103.

51 T.H. Green, *The Prolegomena to Ethics*, 3rd ed., ed. A.C. Bradley (Oxford: Clarendon Press, 1890), 308; cited in Avital Simhony, "T.H. Green: The Common Good Society," *History of Political Thought* 14, no. 2 (summer 1993), 229.

52 J. Clark Murray, *A Handbook of Psychology* (London: Alexander Gardner, 1888), 242. Reciprocity is connected to the human capacity for sympathy and the apprehension of a "community of interest" between self and others: John Watson, *Hedonistic Theories from Aristippus to Spencer* (Glasgow: James Maclehose, 1895), 169. See also George Paxton Young, *Miscellaneous Discourses and Expositions of Scripture* (Edinburgh: Johnstone and Hunter, 1854), 246–7. A near equivalent to reciprocity was Blewett's concept of a "community of nature" between individuals: George John Blewett, *The Study of Nature and the Vision of God* (Toronto: William Briggs, 1907), 177, and *The Christian View of the World* (Toronto: William Briggs, 1912), 113.

53 MacIver, *Community*, 241.

54 G.A. Cohen, *Why Not Socialism?* (Princeton, NJ: Princeton University Press, 2009), 39. Pierre Rosanvallon discusses homo reciprocans and "reciprocity as equality of involvement" as alternatives to homo economicus and "rational choice theory" in *The Society of Equals*, 269–76. A summary of the literature on reciprocity and homo reciprocans appears in Samuel Bowles and Herbert Gintis, "Reciprocity, Self-Interest, and the Welfare State," *Nordic Journal of Political Economy* 26 (2000): 33–53.

55 For instance, Ronald L. Trosper, *Resilience, Reciprocity and Ecological Knowledge: Northwest Coast Sustainability* (London: Routledge, 2009), definitions on 13 and 15; Ingrid Sub Cuc and Mark Camp, "Philanthropy as Reciprocity," *Cultural Survival Quarterly Magazine* (Dec. 2014), unpaginated.

56 Recent explorations of the reciprocity concept include Patrici Calvo, *The Cordial Economy: Ethics, Recognition, and Reciprocity* (Cham, Switzerland: Springer, 2018); and Antti Kujala and Mirkka Danielsbacka, *Reciprocity in Human Societies from Ancient Times to the Modern Welfare State* (Cham, Switzerland: Palgrave Macmillan, 2019).

57 This sentence draws on a sociological literature on the relationship between prosocial behaviour, egalitarianism, and income level. For instance: Ana Guinote, Ioanna Cotzia, Sanpreet Sandhu, and Pramila Siwa, "Social Status Modulates Prosocial Behavior and Egalitarianism in Preschool Children and Adults," *Proceedings of the National Academy of Sciences* 112, no. 3 (20 Jan. 2015): 731–6; Ade Kearns et al., "All in It Together? Social Cohesion in a Divided Society: Attitudes to Income Inequality and Redistribution in a Residential Context," *Journal of Social Policy* 43, no. 3 (July 2014): 453–77; Hansung Kim and Yushin Lee, "Socioeconomic Status, Perceived Inequality of Opportunity, and Attitudes toward Redistribution," *Social Science Journal* 55, no. 3 (Sept. 2018): 300–12; and Antony S.R. Manstead, "The Psychology of Social Class: How Socioeconomic Status Impacts Thought, Feeling, and Behaviour," *British Journal of Social Psychology* 57, no. 2 (April 2018): 267–91.

58 Lars Osberg and Timothy Smeeding, "'Fair' Inequality? Attitudes toward Pay Differentials: The United States in Comparative Perspective," *American Sociological Review* 71, no. 3 (2006): 450–73.

59 In Canada the Broadbent Institute has conducted a series of polls. See, for instance, "Wealth Inequality Poll" (17 Dec. 2014), at https://www.broadbentinstitute.ca/wealth_inequality_poll_finds_canadians_want_a_much_more_level_society.

60 "Equalization" involved egalitarian principles, however weakly specified. The purpose of federal tax-equalization payments, beginning in the 1950s, was to redistribute fiscal capacity between "have" and "have-not" provinces. The system helps explain the difference between overall income inequality in Canada and the United States. Less obvious perhaps: the presence of egalitarian principles, and debate over equal rights, in the growth and stabilization of trade unions in mid-century Canada. The Rand principle (1946), for instance, was key to union security: it compelled workers to pay union dues in the presence of a collective agreement. It emerged from the 1945 United Auto Workers (UAW) strike at the Ford plant in Windsor, Ontario. Negotiations between union representatives George Burt and Pat Conroy and Mr Justice Ivan Rand explored how to operationalize four principles of justice in what Rand called "a democratic economy": relating equal benefits to equal representation; rejecting the inegalitarian "getting something for nothing"; the principle that "no one should be above the law"; and Rand's principle that "responsibilities are correlative of rights." For a summary see William Kaplan, *Canadian Maverick: The Life and Times of Ivan C. Rand* (Toronto: University of Toronto Press, 2009), 196–208.

61 Irene Bloemraad, Will Kymlicka, Michele Lamont, and Leanne S. Son Hing, "Membership without Citizenship? Deservingness and Redistribution as Grounds for Equality," *Daedalus* 148, no. 3 (summer 2019): 75–9.

62 Ibid., 85.

63 As Lars Osberg says: "We should face squarely the fact that equalizing opportunity to be at the top necessarily implies equalizing chances to be at the bottom." Osberg, *Age of Increasing Inequality*, 165.

64 Siep Stuurman, *The Invention of Humanity: Equality and Cultural Difference in World History* (Cambridge, MA: Harvard University Press, 2017), 6.

65 W. Frank Hatheway, *Poorhouse and Palace: A Plea for a Better Distribution of Wealth* (Saint John, NB: N.p., 1900), 39.

66 Shirley Tillotson discusses the federal government's efforts to encourage discussions of war finance and taxation, and its appeal to collective responsibility and common good. Of course a large part of the motive was to secure tax compliance. Shirley Tillotson, *Give and Take: The Citizen-Taxpayer and the Rise of Canadian Democracy* (Vancouver: UBC Press, 2017), 188–209. She points out that taxation often was a burden for those with low incomes (240–50).

67 Emmanuel Saez and Gabriel Zucman, *The Triumph of Injustice: How the Rich Evade Taxes and How to Make Them Pay* (New York: W.W. Norton, 2019); Gabriel Zucman, *The Hidden Wealth of Nations; The Scourge of Tax Havens* (Chicago: University of Chicago Press, 2015). There is a growing literature on Canada; one recent survey that includes Canada is David Kerzner and David W. Chodikoff, *International Tax Evasion in the Global Information Age* (Toronto: Irwin Law Inc., 2016).

Index